# Child Health Encyclopedia

# Emergency
# Telephone
# Numbers

*DOCTOR*

_____

*POISON CENTER*

_____

*HOSPITAL*

_____

*DRUGGIST*

_____

*FIRE DEPARTMENT*

_____

*POLICE*

_____

*TAXI*

_____

# Emergencies

## The Boston Children's Medical Center
## Publications for Parents

*CHILD HEALTH ENCYCLOPEDIA*
The Boston Children's Medical Center
and Richard I. Feinbloom, M.D.

*A CHILD'S EYE VIEW OF THE WORLD*
Marc Simont
and Members of the Staff of The
Boston Children's Medical Center

*PREGNANCY, BIRTH & the NEWBORN BABY*
*A Complete Guide for Parents and Parents-to-be*
Members of the Staff of The
Boston Children's Medical Center

*NO MORE DIAPERS!*
Joae Graham Brooks, M.D.,
and Members of the Staff of The
Boston Children's Medical Center

*BELTS ON, BUTTONS DOWN*
*What Every Mother Should Know about Car Safety*
Edward D. Fales, Jr., and Members of the Staff
of The Boston Children's Medical Center

*KEEPING YOUR FAMILY HEALTHY OVERSEAS*
James P. Carter, M.D., M.S., Dr. P. H.
Eleanora de Antonio West, M.A.,
and Members of the Staff of The
Boston Children's Medical Center

*THE EMERGING PERSONALITY*
*Infancy Through Adolescence*
George E. Gardner, M.D., Ph.D.,
and Members of the Staff of The
Boston Children's Medical Center

*WHAT TO DO WHEN "THERE'S NOTHING TO DO"*
Members of the Staff of The
Boston Children's Medical Center
and Elizabeth M. Gregg

*CURIOUS GEORGE GOES TO THE HOSPITAL*
Margret and H. A. Rey
in collaboration with Members of the Staff of The
Boston Children's Medical Center

*ACCIDENT HANDBOOK*
*A New Approach to Family Safety*
(A pamphlet; also available in
Spanish and in a purse book edition)
Members of the Staff of The
Boston Children's Medical Center

*HOW TO PREVENT CHILDHOOD POISONING*
(A pamphlet)
Members of the Staff of The
Boston Children's Medical Center

*THE BOSTON CHILDREN'S MEDICAL CENTER*
*and RICHARD I. FEINBLOOM, M.D.*

# Child Health Encyclo-pedia

## THE COMPLETE GUIDE FOR PARENTS

*A Merloyd Lawrence Book*
A DELTA SPECIAL/SEYMOUR LAWRENCE

A DELTA SPECIAL

Published by
Dell Publishing Co., Inc.
1 Dag Hammarskjold Plaza
New York, New York 10017

Copyright © 1975 by The Children's Hospital Medical Center
and Richard I. Feinbloom, M.D.

"Car Safety Restraints for Children"
copyright © 1977, 1978 by Consumers Union of United States, Inc.
Used by permission.

All rights reserved. No part of this book may
be reproduced in any form or by any means without the prior
written permission of Delacorte Press/Seymour Lawrence, New York,
New York 10017, excepting brief quotes used in
connection with reviews written specifically for inclusion in a magazine or newspaper.

Reprinted by arrangement with Delacorte Press/Seymour Lawrence
Delta ® TM 755118, Dell Publishing Co., Inc.

ISBN: 0-385-28148-X

Manufactured in the United States of America
9 8 7 6 5 4 3

BOARD OF EDITORS

*Joanne B. Bluestone*
*Patricia Nelson*
*Jennifer Wilcox*
*Philip C. Ward*

Grateful acknowledgment is made to
Harriet H. Gibney, formerly Director of
Health Education at The Boston
Children's Medical Center, who first
thought of the idea for this book.

# Contributors

RICHARD I. FEINBLOOM, M.D.
Assistant Professor of Pediatrics, Harvard Medical School; Director, Family
Health Care Program, Harvard Medical School; Associate in Medicine, Children's
Hospital Medical Center. *Quality in Pediatric Care; The Regular Checkup; Diet
of Infants and Children; If Your Child Goes to the Hospital; Poisoning; Bicycle
and Minibike Safety; Dental Care*, and all other articles not bearing another
contributor's name.

ANTHONY BASHIR, Ph.D.,
Speech Pathologist, Children's Hospital Medical Center. *Hearing and Speech.*

T. BERRY BRAZELTON, M.D.,
Senior Associate in Medicine, Chief of Division of Child Development,
Children's Hospital Medical Center; Associate Professor of Pediatrics, Harvard
Medical School. *Complaints with an Emotional Element.*

CARL G. COHEN, D.M.D.,
Assistant in Pedodontics, Children's Hospital Medical Center; Clinical Instructor
in Pediatric Dentistry, Harvard School of Dental Medicine. *Dental Care.*

MARY E. COLLINS,
Nutritionist, Peter Bent Brigham Hospital. *Diet of Infants and Children.*

ALLEN C. CROCKER, M.D.,
Senior Associate in Medicine and Director of Developmental Evaluation Clinic,
Children's Hospital Medical Center; Associate Professor of Pediatrics, Harvard
Medical School. *Developmental Disabilities.*

MARIE M. CULLINANE, R.N., M.S.
Director of Nursing, Developmental Evaluation Clinic, Children's Hospital
Medical Center; Adjunct Assistant Professor of Maternal-Child Nursing, Boston
College. *Developmental Disabilities.*

MARGARET GOLICK, Ph.D.,
Senior Psychologist, McGill-Montreal Children's Hospital Learning Center.
*Learning Disabilities.*

ROSANNE HOWARD,
Nutritionist, Children's Hospital Medical Center. *Diet of Infants and Children.*

**ELLENORA LENIHAN, R.N.,**
Head Public Health Nurse, Child and Family Health Division, Children's
Hospital Medical Center and Family Health Care Program, Harvard Medical
School. *Caring for the Sick Child at Home.*

**CONNIE LOTZ-TEXTOR,**
Nutritionist, Peter Bent Brigham Hospital. *Diet of Infants and Children.*

**LEONARD C. MARCUS, V.M.D., M.D.,**
Consultant in Infectious Diseases, Children's Hospital Medical Center; Assistant
Director of Health Services, State Laboratory Institute; Visiting Assistant
Professor, Department of Microbiology and Molecular Genetics, Harvard Medical
School; Assistant Clinical Professor of Pathology and Assistant Clinical Professor
of Pediatrics, Tufts University School of Medicine. *Pets and Children.*

**PATRICIA NELSON, M.P.H.,**
formerly Director, Department of Health Education, Children's Hospital Medical
Center. *Quality in Pediatric Care; If Your Child Goes to the Hospital.*

**ANNEMARIE SHELNESS,**
Executive Director, Physicians for Automotive Safety. *Car Safety.*

**SYLVIA TOPP, M.S.,**
Audiologist, Children's Hospital Medical Center. *Hearing and Speech.*

**ALFRED YANKAUER, M.D.,**
Consultant in Maternal and Child Health, Children's Hospital Medical Center;
Senior Lecturer in Health Services, Harvard Medical School. *Health Care Delivery:
The Broad Picture.*

# Consultants

In addition to reviewing the sections of this book within their special fields, many of the following consultants supplied important new material which was incorporated into the articles.

JOEL J. ALPERT, M.D., Consultant in Family and Child Health, Children's Hospital Medical Center; Chairman, Department of Pediatrics, Boston University Medical School. *Vomiting.*

KENNETH A. ARNDT, M.D., Associate Chief of Dermatology, Children's Hospital Medical Center. *Various Skin Disorders.*

IRVING W. BAILIT, M.D., Associate in Allergy, Children's Hospital Medical Center. *Allergy.*

WILLIAM BERENBERG, M.D., Senior Associate in Medicine and Chief of Cerebral Palsy in Division of Services to Handicapped Children, Children's Hospital Medical Center. *Cerebral Palsy.*

REYNOLD JOHN BUONO, M.A., Milton Academy. *Bicycle and Minibike Safety.*

ANITA CAVALLO, M.D., Former Fellow in Endocrinology, Children's Hospital Medical Center; Allegheny County Health Department, Pittsburgh, Pa. *Hormones.*

DOROTHY CLEVELAND, M.S., Associate Professor of Health Dynamics, Boston University. *Exercise and Physical Fitness.*

JONATHAN COHEN, M.D., Consultant in Orthopedic Surgery and Pathology, Children's Hospital Medical Center, and Joseph P. Kennedy Memorial Hospital. *Muscular Dystrophy.*

ARNOLD H. COLODNY, M.D., Associate in Surgery and Acting Chief of Division of Urology, Children's Hospital Medical Center. *Urinary Tract Infections and Defects.*

THOMAS E. CONE, JR., M.D., Senior Associate in Medicine and Senior Associate in Clinical Genetics, Children's Hospital Medical Center. *Genetics.*

JOHN F. CRIGLER, M.D., Senior Associate in Medicine and Chief of Endrocrinology Division, Children's Hospital Medical Center. *Height Problems; Hormones.*

BRUCE R. DITZION, M.D., Assistant in Medicine in Family and Child Health Division, Children's Hospital Medical Center. *Venereal Disease.*

*SIDNEY FARBER, M.D.*, (deceased) Formerly Pathologist-in-Chief, Director, Children's Cancer Research Foundation, Children's Hospital Medical Center. *Leukemia.*

*FRANCIS X. FELLERS, M.D.*, Senior Associate in Medicine, Children's Hospital Medical Center. *Nephritis.*

*ROBERT M. FILLER, M.D.*, Chief of Clinical Surgery, Children's Hospital Medical Center. *Appendicitis.*

*JOSEPH N. FISHER, M.D.*, Associate in Medicine, Associate in Endocrinology and Consulting Physician in Division of Adolescent Medicine, Children's Hospital Medical Center. *Hormones.*

*IRWIN M. FREEDBERG, M.D.*, Chief of Dermatology Division, Children's Hospital Medical Center. *Various Skin Disorders.*

*EMIL FREI, III, M.D.*, Senior Associate in Hematology and Oncology, Children's Hospital Medical Center. *Hodgkin's Disease.*

*DONALD FYLER, M.D.*, Senior Associate in Medicine, Associate Chief of Cardiology and Director of Cardiac Catheterization Laboratories, Children's Hospital Medical Center. *Heart Murmurs.*

*KENNETH H. GABBAY, M.D.*, Associate in Endocrinology, Children's Hospital Medical Center. *Diabetes.*

*PIERCE GARDNER, M.D.*, Associate in Medicine, Associate in Infectious Diseases, Children's Hospital Medical Center. *Coccidioidomycosis.*

*GENEROSO GASCON, M.D.*, Assistant in Neurology and Consulting Physician in Division of Adolescent Medicine, Children's Hospital Medical Center. *Learning Disabilities.*

*JOHN GRAEF, M.D.*, Associate in Medicine, Children's Hospital Medical Center. *Lead Poisoning.*

*RICHARD J. GRAND, M.D.*, Associate in Medicine, Associate in Clinical Nutrition and Consulting Physician in Division of Adolescent Medicine, Children's Hospital Medical Center. *Colitis, Ulcerative.*

*JOHN E. HALL, M.D.*, Chief of Clinical Services in Orthopedic Surgery, Children's Hospital Medical Center. *Aches and Pains; Orthopedic Concerns; Spinal Defects.*

*GERALD HASS, M.D.*, Clinical Instructor of Pediatrics, Harvard Medical School; Clinical Associate Professor of Pediatrics, Boston University School of Medicine. *Diet of Infants and Children.*

*BURTON F. JAFFE, M.D.*, Senior Associate in Otolaryngology, Children's Hospital Medical Center. *Earache.*

*NORMAN JAFFE, M.D.*, Associate in Medicine, Senior Associate in Hematology and Oncology, Children's Hospital Medical Center. *Hodgkin's Disease; Leukemia, Neuroblastoma; Wilms' Tumor.*

*RUTH JOHNSTONE, M.P.H.*, Massachusetts Lung Association. *Smoking.*

ELLEN KANG, M.D., Assistant in Clinical Genetics, Children's Hospital Medical Center. *PKU (Phenylketonuria)*.

ROBERT B. KELLER, M.D., Assistant Professor of Orthopedic Surgery, University of Massachusetts Medical School. *Aches and Pains*.

HOWARD S. KING, M.D., Assistant in Medicine, Children's Hospital Medical Center. *Quality in Pediatric Care*.

ALAN LEVITON, M.D., Assistant in Neurology, Children's Hospital Medical Center. *Headache*.

DAVID C. LEWIS, M.D., Assistant Clinical Professor of Medicine, Harvard Medical School; Chief of Medicine, Washingtonian Center for Addictions. *Drug Problem*.

CESARE T. LOMBROSO, M.D., Senior Associate in Neurology and Chief of Division of Neurophysiology and Seizure Unit, Children's Hospital Medical Center. *Febrile Seizures; Seizure Disorders*.

FREDERICK H. LOVEJOY, M.D., Associate in Medicine and Associate in Clinical Pharmacology, Children's Hospital Medical Center. *Anaphylactoid Purpura; Poisoning*.

DONALD MCCOLLUM, M.D., Senior Associate in Surgery, Department of Plastic Surgery, Children's Hospital Medical Center. *Cleft Lip and Cleft Palate*.

FREDERICK MANDELL, M.D., Associate in Medicine and Associate in Cerebral Palsy in Division of Services to Handicapped Children, Children's Hospital Medical Center. *Handicapped Child; Sudden Infant Death Syndrome*.

ROBERT MASLAND, JR., M.D., Senior Associate in Medicine and Chief, Division of Adolescent Medicine, Children's Hospital Medical Center. *Adolescence*.

JEAN MAYER, PH.D., President, Tufts University. *Diet of Infants and Children*.

HARRY L. MUELLER, M.D., Consulting Allergist in Division of Allergy, Children's Hospital Medical Center. *Allergy; Asthma; Bites, Insect; Hay Fever*.

CONSTANCE C. MURRAY, PH.D., Director, Lexington Teacher Training Program. *Learning Disabilities*.

JOSEPH E. MURRAY, M.D., Senior Associate in Surgery and Chief of Division of Plastic Surgery, Children's Hospital Medical Center. *Cleft of the Lip and Cleft of the Palate*.

ALEXANDER NADAS, M.D., Senior Associate in Medicine, Chief of the Department of Cardiology, Children's Hospital Medical Center. *Heart Murmurs*.

DAVID G. NATHAN, M.D., Senior Associate in Medicine and Chief of Hematology and Oncology Division, Children's Hospital Medical Center. *Anemia*.

HERBERT L. NEEDLEMAN, M.D., Associate in Psychiatry, Children's Hospital Medical Center. *Lead Poisoning*.

PATRICIA NELSON, M.P.H., Assistant Professor, Boston University Medical School. *Traveling Abroad*.

ELI H. NEWBERGER, M.D., Associate in Medicine and Associate in the Division of Child Development, Children's Hospital Medical Center. *Child Abuse.*

BARBARA O'NEILL, M.P.H., Massachusetts Lung Association. *Smoking.*

MICHAEL N. OXMAN, M.D., Assistant in Infectious Diseases, Research Associate in Virus Research Unit, Children's Hospital Medical Center. *Immunization.*

ROBERT A. PETERSEN, M.D., Senior Associate in Ophthalmology, Children's Hospital Medical Center. *Conjunctivitis.*

RICHARD M. ROBB, M.D., Ophthalmologist-in-Chief, Children's Hospital Medical Center. *Vision Problems.*

JOHN S. ROBEY, M.D., Senior Associate in Medicine in Family and Child Health Division, Children's Hospital Medical Center. *Constipation.*

FRED S. ROSEN, M.D., Senior Associate in Medicine and Chief of Immunology Division, Children's Hospital Medical Center. *Infections.*

ROBERT D. ROSENBERG, M.D., Assistant Professor of Medicine, Harvard Medical School; Associate Physician, Beth Israel Hospital. *Bleeding Disorders.*

EVELYN SARSON, Director, Action For Children's Television. *Television and Children.*

SAMUEL R. SCHUSTER, M.D., Senior Associate in Surgery, Children's Hospital Medical Center. *Diaphragmatic Hernia.*

JOHN SHILLITO, JR., M.D., Senior Associate in Neurosurgery, Children's Hospital Medical Center. *Head Injuries.*

HARRY SHWACHMAN, M.D., Senior Associate in Medicine and Chief of Clinical Nutrition Division, Children's Hospital Medical Center. *Celiac Disease; Cystic Fibrosis.*

DAVID H. SMITH, M.D., Senior Associate in Medicine and Chief of Division of Infectious Diseases, Children's Hospital Medical Center. *Coccidioidomycosis.*

DENISE J. STREIDER, M.D., Research Associate in Cardiology and Director of Pulmonary Laboratory, Children's Hospital Medical Center. *Emphysema.*

LEONARD T. SWANSON, D.M.D., Dentist-in-Chief, Children's Hospital Medical Center. *Dental Care.*

LLOYD D. TARLIN, M.D., Assistant in Medicine, Children's Hospital Medical Center. *Fever.*

MELVIN L. THORNTON, M.D., Clinical Professor of Pediatrics, University of Texas School of Medicine at San Antonio; Chairman of American Medical Association Committee on Medical Aspects of Sports. *Exercise and Physical Fitness.*

STANLEY WALZER, M.D., Senior Associate in Psychiatry and Senior Associate in Clinical Genetics, Children's Hospital Medical Center. *Genetics.*

KENNETH J. WELCH, M.D., Associate in Surgery, Children's Hospital Medical Center. *Chest, Pigeon and Funnel.*

*MARY ELLEN WOHL, M.D.*, Associate in Medicine and Research Associate in Cardiology, Children's Hospital Medical Center. *Emphysema.*

*ALFRED YANKAUER, M.D.*, Consultant in Maternal and Child Health, Children's Hospital Medical Center; Senior Lecturer in Health Services, Harvard Medical School. *Quality in Pediatric Care.*

# Contents

# PART 2: Safety

# PART 3: Childhood Diseases and Conditions

NOTE:

All conditions referred to in the text in

*boldface italic type*

are described in separate articles in Part 3.

# Child
# Health
# Encyclopedia

# PREFACE
## by
## CHARLES A. JANEWAY, M.D.

This companion volume to *Pregnancy, Birth & the Newborn Baby* is truly an encyclopedia of child health and the diseases affecting children. It should prove a gold mine of information and sound advice for the conscientious and literate parents who want to educate themselves about their responsibilities for the health of their children and would like a ready reference book to consult in time of illness or after a visit to the physician. Although presented in clear, non-technical language, the coverage is so broad and the discussions of many problems are so sufficiently detailed and thorough as to make this a valuable reference book even for the pediatrician or family physician caring for children.

While the editor, Dr. Feinbloom, stresses in his Introduction that the emphasis is upon physical rather than psychological health, one is impressed that, in discussing diseases and conditions with predominantly physical manifestations, he has skillfully put his finger on many of the parental attitudes and responses that we believe to be critically important to the development of emotional stability and socially desirable adaptive behavior in children. There are not only sound discussions of such concrete subjects as anemia, appendicitis, pneumonia, immunizations, and tonsils and adenoids, but also excellent sections on those aspects of child health that are intimately related to contemporary society, such as adolescence, developmental disabilities, drug problems, learning disabilities, smoking, television and children, and weight problems.

This book is aimed at parents, recognizing that they are in the front lines of the health-care system for children. Once upon a time in this country, when several generations lived under one roof, members of the older generation, particularly the grandmother, were tremendously helpful to young parents bringing up and caring for their first child. In this day of small houses, mobility, and small families, young parents are usually living alone, and, although they may be well educated, they have had little experience with either sick or healthy young children. This book aims to provide them with authoritative information, readily available at all times, to help them use their physician or medical facilities more effectively when needed and to answer many of the inevitable questions that arise whenever a child becomes ill or after a visit to a busy physician's office. Moreover, the first two parts provide basic education for parents on the major elements of health care and on the all-important subject of safety.

It is our firm hope that this book will not only relieve the natural anxieties of many parents, but also will promote better health for their children, and thus diminish the extent to which institutions like ours will need to provide in-hospital care for those who are sick, for every child in a hospital bed represents a failure of some sort—of a parent for not calling or utilizing a physician in time, or of a physician for not recognizing the early signs of serious disease, or of society for not providing adequate food, housing, or medical care, or of medical science for lacking the knowledge of how to prevent the development of the child's disease. We believe in parents, in their motivation to provide a healthy life for their children, and in their capacity to learn to do so. This volume bears witness to our faith in them.

*Charles A. Janeway, M.D.*
*Physician-in-Chief, 1946–1974*
*The Children's Hospital Medical Center*

## PREFACE
### by
### JULIUS B. RICHMOND, M.D.

**D**uring the twentieth century we have taken great strides in the United States to improve the health of children and their families. Our infant mortality is about one-seventh (approximately 20 infants under one year per 1000 live births) what it was at the turn of the century; many of the nutritional and infectious diseases that were common have been virtually eliminated through improvement in living conditions, the abolition of child labor, the development of preventive knowledge and practice, and the great advances in the treatment of many diseases.

These advances have not been achieved by the health professionals alone. The interest in improving the social and economic conditions under which families live has been a continuing interest of citizens in our country even though we have not achieved enough—especially for families rearing their children in environments of poverty. The health professions have had strong allies in parents, who have gradually become better educated and persistent in seeking better health for their children. As a consequence it has been feasible for parents to take over many child-health practices that previously were the province of the physician. For example, a literate, well-educated parent today can arrive at a diet for the child that is as adequate as that prescribed by the physician two decades ago. Educated parents now know much about the need for preventive services, such as immunization, periodic examinations, and preventive dental care, and the need for early detection of various illnesses in order that treatment can be early and most effective.

As parents have become better informed and as our methods of prevention have improved, there has been a significant conservation of time for our health professionals. Were this not so, we would be suffering from greater shortages of physicians, dentists, nurses, and other health professionals than those that exist now. But the importance of more educated parents does not lie only in saving time for professionals. In the long run it results in better health and health care for their children.

Therein lies the importance of this book. Those who are privileged to have been educated to care for the health of children have taken on one of the most important responsibilities a society can confer. This implies a contract with parents and the broader society to share our knowledge in order that we may all participate in rearing a healthier generation of adults. This book is one step—a major one—toward the fulfillment of this contract. It is written with the conviction that our provision of health services is not enough. In communicating their collective knowledge concerning child health, the authors have taken an important step in helping to assure that each child will come closer to attaining his or her greatest potentialities.

*Julius B. Richmond, M.D.*
*formerly Psychiatrist-in-Chief*
*The Children's Hospital Medical Center*

# *INTRODUCTION*

This book on child health was written for parents because parents are the providers of most of the health care given to children. The doctor's contact with the child is an unusual event, while mothers, fathers, day-care workers, grandparents, and sitters are "on call" 24 hours a day. The parent, whether he or she knows it, is the key member of the health-care team. Our encyclopedia on child health is designed to strengthen this role.

This book is about child health more in the physical than the psychological sense. While separating mind and body represents an artificial division of the child, limitations of space and a superabundance of material led to the decision to exclude discussions of important topics in child rearing and development. In no way should this emphasis be interpreted as a value judgment on the relative importance of physical as opposed to psychological issues. Since so much has been written on the latter during recent years, we felt it worthwhile to concentrate on updating publicly available information on the former.

The book deals with child health from infancy to the physical changes and common problems of adolescence. It is a sequel to a previous book in our Publications for Parents series, *Pregnancy, Birth & the Newborn Baby* (New York: Delacorte Press/Seymour Lawrence, 1972).

The essay and safety sections (Parts 1 and 2) are for general reading and provide background information applicable to most, if not all, children. The section on First Aid is designed for quick reference. The individual discussions of signs and symptoms in Part 3: "Childhood Diseases and Conditions" are intended to be used as the need for information arises.

We have attempted to provide the basic scientific theory underlying the various topics, on the premise that parents' care would therefore be improved. For example, since infections are so common in children, it seemed important to discuss viruses, cultures, immunity, contagiousness, and so forth, as well as chicken pox and sore throats.

In general, the length of a topic is proportionate to the number of children it affects. Although this book is called an encyclopedia, rare and obscure problems that might be of great interest to specialists at a university medical center but to few parents are not discussed.

The editor thanks the various contributors and reviewers. I have always been inspired by the pursuit of excellence, the constant search for new answers, and the deep commitment to the well-being of children that characterize the remarkable staff of The Children's Hospital Medical Center. Acknowledgment is due to my colleagues at the Family Health Care Program, a teaching program in family medicine at the Harvard Medical School and Children's Hospital directed by the editor (at times, it seemed, in his spare moments when he was not working on this book), for demonstrating the importance of preventive medicine applied to the family.

The Health Education Department of The Children's Hospital Medical Center has provided the day-to-day support for getting the job done. Special thanks go to its Director, Patricia Nelson, and to Jennifer Wilcox, Assistant to the Director, who worked most closely on editing the manuscripts. Credit is due Dr. Leonard Cronkhite, President of The Children's Hospital Medical Center, Joanne B. Bluestone, Patient Care Administrator, and Charles A. Janeway, M.D., formerly Physician-in-Chief, for their roles in conceiving and supporting the project and for having had the vision to establish a Health Education Department. Finally, I express my gratitude to the many children and families who have shared their concerns with me, to Dr. Joel Alpert, currently Chairman of the Department of Pediatrics at Boston University, my former chief, and to my own family for their forbearance.

This is a book about the health of the fortunate minority of children who live in families that are generally well off. As I worked on it, I often thought of the other children, the majority of children in the world, including many in this country, for whom this book has little bearing. They are the children of miserable poverty who have no childhood. They are children victimized by the insane priorities of the world we live in. They are the maimed, homeless, orphaned children of Indochina and elsewhere whose health and childhood are destroyed by mindless acts of commission. Ultimately, the health of the world's children depends on whether their parents will beat their swords into plowshares and learn war no more.

*Richard I. Feinbloom, M.D.*
*Director, Family Health*
*Care Program*
*Harvard Medical School*

# 1

# Health Care for Children

# 1
# Quality in Pediatric Care

In this era of rapid change in medical care, when many alternatives are under discussion, it is important to discuss what is meant by quality of care for children. What should parents look for in a source of health care?

It is difficult to make generalizations about quality which can apply to all families and doctors in this large and varied country. In a practical sense, anything we say will inevitably be used to judge available sources of care. By our ideal standards, existing care programs, including our own, may be found inadequate. It may be that what we propose is too costly and impractical, that other concerns like defense, housing, and space exploration, which compete with health care for available public and private resources, are of greater importance.

Nevertheless, it is important for us as physicians interested in the well-being of children to say what we think is important.

We believe that all children in the United States have the right to expect what is called "comprehensive health care." By comprehensive care we mean care that includes both curative (treatment) and preventive services, preferably by a single group of health professionals who are continuously available and come to know the particular child and his or her family. Let us look more closely at this definition of comprehensive care.

This book deals mainly with what to do if and when a particular symptom arises. In this sense it deals with curative medicine—how to treat. An even more important objective is the prevention of disease altogether. *Immunization,* automobile seat belts (see Part 2, Chapter 12: "Car Safety"), and fluorides for teeth (see *dental care*) are examples of preventive measures. From this perspective, becoming sick or injured or needing hospitalization represent failures of health care. However, although we will always need improved methods of treatment, we should not let our triumphs in therapy detract from the importance of prevention.

Every medical contact has preventive and curative aspects. In a regular health examination we might review the parents' management of a recent cold, give pointers on how to give medicine to young children, talk about the use of home remedies or over-the-counter medicines, discuss the parents' decision to call or not to call for help, as the case may be, and talk about risk factors for the child during his next stage of development, such as accidental poisoning (suggesting that ipecac syrup be kept in the home, and so forth). During a home visit for an illness, we go over the findings of our examination. We try to describe our assessment of the patient's health in understandable terms in order that the parents learn how to recognize and communicate to the doctor important facts about their child's condition. We check the family's medicine chest in regard to accident prevention. We ask to see the child's room to get a better feel for his environment, and so on. Illness and health are intimately interwoven.

One important advantage of comprehensive care is that we receive more input from families than we would if care were fragmented: for example, illness handled in one place—the emergency room—and regular health maintenance in another—the well-child clinic. The result is that we and our families get to know each other better. We have set it up that way. How well we know and trust each other is a basic concern. We will discuss this point in greater detail later.

We believe that every American should have the right to a doctor to whom he can relate. However, we recognize and respect the fact that not everyone wants a single doctor-patient relationship. For example, some people prefer the anonymity of receiving their regular medical services in the emergency rooms of hospitals. These services are being greatly improved so that there is not the great disparity in quality of service that once existed between the private medical setting and institutional ambulatory care. From the doctor's point of view, the one-to-one relationship makes practice easier, more effective, and more satisfying. Most doctors feel that they can give better advice on the telephone when they know the patient on the other end of the line.

While there is clearly a need for expanding the roles of nurses and other health professionals, the numbers and kinds of professionals involved in the front-line care of families should be part of a well-thought-out plan with the family being the major focus. We want to avoid an assembly-line approach, efficient but impersonal, and try to keep the numbers of health workers involved with any particular family small so that they can communicate easily among themselves.

Parents should understand that the doctor assumes responsibility for the child's care. If the problem is one for which the doctor needs consultation, he will arrange it with a consultant he knows and with whom he can communicate. If hospitalization is needed, he arranges this, and he will play an important coordinating role for the child in the hospital regardless of how many specialists are also involved.

Comprehensive care also involves 24-hour-a-day coverage. The doctor or nurse or a specifically designated stand-in should be reachable by phone at any time. Substitutes should have ready access to the child's medical record, and parents should know that their call will receive attention. The doctor or nurse going off call tries to brief his substitute on outstanding problems. Obviously, parents themselves will have to fill in the details just as they will have to brief even their own busy doctor about their child's problem. It is impossible for doctors or nurses, however well intentioned, to keep all the details about every patient in mind.

The family doctor should be notified when hospitalization is being planned. Of course, an emergency condition can make this impossible. In turn, a hospital substitute physician should communicate his observations to the child's regular doctor. Complete coverage can be more nearly obtained if health professionals do not fail to communicate with one another in regard to each patient.

A very important ingredient in the quality of care is that health workers and parents get to know each other and develop a sense of mutual trust. Again, this kind of relationship is not for everyone, but the choice should be open. Doctors strongly favor personalizing care. Many patients and parents are searching for a personalized care in which the doctor and nurse are genuinely interested in them as individuals, are available and eager to hear them out completely. If more time is needed, there should be no hesitation in scheduling more time. Simple solutions, automatically prescribed, like "He will outgrow it," or "Take this pill," "Ignore it," may suffice in many cases, but it is also important to look beyond the symptoms to the cause. (See Chapter 4: "Complaints with an Emotional Element.") Nurses and doctors, we believe, should be able to help families in this search.

Ideally, doctors and nurses hope to strike a balance between various kinds of testing and a personal approach to the patient as person. Many tests are helpful for spotting serious problems, but an attentive ear can be just as useful in ferreting out a smoldering psychological problem which seriously affects the general health of the patient. Tests are not magic, and yet the American fascination with gadgetry often produces a false security about the use of modern technology. Even false diagnoses and treatments have occurred where there has been inadequate patient contact and understanding. Above all, time is needed. Overworked schedules and high costs often make good quality care impossible. The status quo, however, is not irreparable. New approaches to financing and organizing health care are under development. In the long run, a philosophy of prevention that allows (and pays for) patient and parent education will save time and expense.

When viewed as a part of all health services, the comprehensive, first-line, first-contact type of care is designated as *primary medical care*. Most of the health problems that people have are of this type. If a technically complex problem is involved (for example, an unusual *heart murmur*), consultation is achieved with what is called *secondary* or *consultative care*. If the problem is very unusual and requires elaborate investigation and treatment (for example, heart surgery), *tertiary* or *third-level care* is required. As one shifts from primary to secondary and tertiary levels of care, the number of children involved decreases. At the primary-care level of prevention and early diagnosis, all children are involved.

At the primary-care level, health advice from the doctor and other members of the care team merges with public campaigns to educate citizens about health. Information about nutrition, immunization, accident prevention, and seasonal hazards is included with advice about illness. Parents are more disposed to heed such advice from the family doctor than a message on the radio or television.

Most of the deficiencies in health services in the United States are in primary care. In general, we are splendidly set up for secondary and tertiary levels of care but are laggards in applying our impressive medical knowledge to all of the people. Much Federal funding has been spent on secondary and tertiary care programs, but this is not as true of primary care. Even in the shadows of our greatest medical centers, good primary health care has usually been imperfect. Here we find some of our worst health morbidity and mortality statistics. Health planners and the public need to understand clearly the importance of primary health care.

Medical specialization has received overemphasis in response to the explosion of medical knowledge. Experts in all parts of the body have been developed. Too often the *person* with the complaint has been forgotten. Patients themselves must choose from a smorgasbord of specialists, each of whom disclaims responsibility for anything but his own increasingly narrow area of concern. The greater the number of specialists, the more complicated becomes comprehensive communication and, in the end, comprehensive care. For example, the obstetrician who has developed a relationship with the pregnant mother-to-be is usually not able to pass on his insights to the pediatrician or family doctor who takes on the care of the newborn. The mother with a headache goes to specialists who investigate her brain, sinuses, neck, eyes, and so forth. What is missing is a specialist for the patient himself, whose problem is often emotionally based and whose need, as likely as not, falls between the cracks separating the disciplines. The story about the patient in one of our large, sophisticated teaching hospitals who had to call the information desk to find out about her condition may be a slight exaggeration, but also contains a grain of truth.

Not only is the care of the single patient fragmented, but also the care of a family is often divided among specialists who do not communicate well with each other. Many families have 3 or 4 doctors, and sometimes more. While an individual's complaints often have family causes, all too often in today's split-up care system the several pieces of the jigsaw puzzle are not put back together. The 2-year-old having sleeping problems, the mother with a vaginal irritation, and the father with an ulcer may all represent an underlying marital conflict. Too often the total family picture is unrecognized and the treatment compromised because each doctor focuses on the problems of only one family member.

Group practice is in many ways the wave of the medical-care future. But merely bringing specialists together under one roof is itself no guarantee that comprehensive care of families will occur; there is urgent need that it be built into the financing mechanism of our medical-care system.

Another aspect of the problem of overspecialization in medical education is a shortage of family physicians, pediatricians, internists, or obstetricians. Therefore, those who are doing this job become even busier and their care tends to become less personal. This style of life is not attractive to younger doctors, and they often avoid the kind of practice that provides so few colleagues with whom they can share their responsibilities. Families, even in the suburbs, come to rely more and more on emergency rooms as their doctors.

All of these weaknesses in health services are compounded by our rapidly changing American way of life which has been aptly described as a "pursuit of loneliness." Families are increasingly isolated, far from the helping hands of relatives, whether in the suburbs or in the inner city. Seemingly never anywhere long enough to develop close human relationships, the American family itself is a barrier to high-quality health care.

The growing impersonality of health services has not caused the problems of the family, but neither has it helped. In many cases it has reinforced the patient's isolation. The plight of the family can be relieved only by broad changes in our society, of which medicine has a small but important part to play.

Many people are concerned that vital services are not planned to care for the most urgent needs of the family. Psychological needs of people are especially neglected, and reaction to this neglect is setting in. For example, some churches are assigning new families in the community to established groups of 4 or 5 other families for help in adjustment to a new setting and ongoing support. There are efforts to recapture the supportive elements of the extended family of the past in which 3 generations lived under one roof. People are experimenting with encounter groups, communes, and new life-styles. Day-care services are being extended as funds become available. Medical schools are revising their curricula to deal with community needs, and schools are educating more family practitioners.

Spurred on largely by lay groups, a clear shift in attitudes toward health and illness is occurring. An example is the prepared childbirth movement in which enlightened women and men are demanding alternatives to drugs and anesthesia in order to humanize what has become an overly technological medical practice. The pendulum in obstetrical care is swinging away from heavy use of pain medication and anesthesia and toward self-understanding, mastery, and psychological growth. Doctors are slowly but surely accepting the importance of less medication and more education as part of the comprehensive medical-care package which patients want. Better understanding of life processes can make a happier, healthier patient. Books such as this one and the health-education programs offered by schools and hospitals can prepare the doctor and patient for a more meaningful dialogue.

The same process of group support is occurring in the management of death and dying, menopause, breast-feeding, and so forth. The mystique of medicine is being stripped away, and people are being taught to understand normal life processes in relation to technology. For most people, accurate information and psychological preparation can decrease dependence on doctors, drugs, and hospitals. The implications are great, both for human fulfillment and for medical economy. Medical costs can be cut as people rely less on hospital care and medication as the solution to their problems. Preventive medicine makes sense and also saves secondary and tertiary health care dollars in the long run. Consumers will be demanding more education in regard to planning child care, understanding medical procedures, and judging the quality of nurseries, day-care centers, and schools.

Within medical schools, family medicine training is gaining hold. Universities are developing so-called "teaching office practices" to complement teaching hospitals and are using community settings for medical education. In these new teaching practices, physician trainees and other health workers are made responsible for the health and illness care of families over a period of time. They are thus exposed to the common, everyday, but no less complex, issues faced by most families. Many of these experiences have deep psychological implications, and the trainees are challenged to become adept in managing behavioral disorders in children, drug addiction, marital conflict, learning disorders, sexual inadequacy, problems of aging—all areas that medicine has traditionally neglected in favor of its fascination with disease.

Our work with parents at The Children's Hospital Medical Center is based on the conviction that "the patient of tomorrow" and "the parent of tomorrow" are integral members of the health-care team whose knowledge, attitudes, and behavior regarding issues of health and illness are of prime importance. Keeping the family healthy means making available both accurate health information and someone with whom the patient may discuss concerns as they arise. As our knowledge about disease grows, new information systems using the computer and modern means of communication will be developed to keep both doctor and patient or parent up to date. It is likely that both will have access to the same sources of constantly updated knowledge.

The public will increasingly try to understand issues of quality care and see that newly developing arrangements for health care take them into account. Ultimately, a system of care requires caring professionals, which in turn requires a caring society. The public's need for personalized primary care must be translated into funding priorities which help medical schools and medical institutions to provide quality care with a personal approach. Examination of new health proposals to make certain they ensure good, complete, comprehensive care will be a responsibility for everyone. Otherwise, we run the decided risk of perpetuating the same fragmentation which presently exists.

*Richard I. Feinbloom, M.D.*
*Patricia Nelson, M.P.H.*

# 2

# The Regular
# Checkup

The ideal regular checkup can be described as preventive medicine in action. It is the time when the child, family, and health team compare notes and check out difficulties that might impede the healthy development of the child patient. Most pediatricians in hospitals such as The Children's Hospital Medical Center have certain standards which are considered ideal, and it is well to be reminded of these guidelines even though many circumstances prevent the attainment of perfection.

One of the first concerns is the atmosphere or setting in which the regular checkup takes place. The sterile, clinical atmosphere of the doctor's examination room is not the ideal environment for seeing the child in his or her best mood. It is not surprising that the doctor has to examine a tense child. The situation can be compared to viewing an animal in a zoo rather than in the jungle. One can understand why some old-time children's doctors used to like to do regular checkups in the child's home. In order to obtain good results, the child needs to be in a relaxed atmosphere for his examination. While talking with parent and child, the doctor can directly observe the child's development, including speech, hearing, vision, and coordination. What better way to find out how he is progressing and what kind of a child he is? However, even under the best of circumstances, a child's behavior in the office may not be typical. Parents need to be reassured that their child's unruly behavior will not result in the doctor's negative judgment. Doctors try to understand the fears which children bring with them to the examining room.

When there are no physical complaints, the doctor may go no further than an observation and history. Or he may do a selective physical examination of, for example, the ears, teeth, and throat. Many parents still feel that the laying on of hands by the physician is what the checkup is all about. Yet the examination of a child without symptoms who has had several careful examinations in the first year will probably reveal no new abnormalities. The medical focus may turn to behavior, and parental questions. Some of the checkups might not even involve the child at all, just the parents. At other times the doctor may do an examination to reassure the child that he is normal and well. The doctor can encourage the insecure child by telling him that his eyes are strong, that he won't lose his tonsils, or that he is a good climber as he mounts the examining table. The exam can give the child opportunities to demonstrate competence as he follows instructions, for example, during a test of vision. By letting him try the examining instruments, the doctor can minimize their mystery and reduce anxiety. The doctor can become a friend to the child.

Doctors and nurses like to know how the child spends his time, something about his likes and dislikes, and what are the problems and successes the parents have experienced in dealing with their child. Does he have eating, sleeping, playing problems? The doctor likes to hear about the child in the parents' own words. Obviously, the questions asked vary with the age of the child, but the principle is always the same—to inventory or sample from the child's life in order to form a picture of his style, character, and interaction with others. New impressions from each conference are integrated with other previous contacts in the office, home, newborn nursery, or on the telephone. A total picture of the patient begins to unravel over succeeding visits.

It is essential that parents have an unhurried opportunity to air their concerns. Before jumping in with advice, the doctor should try to understand why parents have particular questions. The question must be understood in order to give a meaningful answer. If not enough time is available during the regular appointment, another appointment should be made. Often the doctor or nurse has to cut corners, but parents should ask for time when they need it. Sometimes the busy physician may not realize that the parents' questions are not being fully answered. It is important for parents to point this out tactfully.

When behavior is a concern, it is sometimes helpful for one of the health team (doctor, nurse, social worker) to visit the child in his home or at school in order to form a more accurate picture of him in his usual environment. Closer communication with teachers is an important part of good health care. Some cities are training the classroom teacher to be able to spot and understand the management of difficult health problems. Problem areas related to the parents' attitudes and their own experiences in being reared should be brought out into the open. It is easy for a child to develop a feeding problem when the mother herself has a weight problem. This is a good example of how a parent's own experience can color her views. (See *weight problems.*) The mother should be encouraged to review her childhood experiences regarding food. It is very important, if not essential, that the doctor find the time to do this if the child's difficulty is to be remedied. While fathers are not seen too often, they should be encouraged to bring the child in for some visits, especially when a major difficulty is under discussion. Both parents' viewpoints must be considered. Marriage counseling may be needed.

The medical team is concerned about its direct relationship with the child. The doctor must try to keep in mind that from a small child's point of view he looms large and powerful; the nurse in white might also look scary. Certain routine office procedures such as immunization injections are painful or unpleasant. Although these are necessary, they do undermine the doctor's relationship with young children. If children are afraid of the doctor because he gives them shots, he loses rapport. The child should be helped to understand why immunizations are given. One gimmick some doctors use is to give the child a plastic syringe (without the needles) so that he or she can play out his or her feelings and fantasies on dolls at home. Similarly, they try to counteract the unpleasantness of throat cultures by bringing children into the laboratory to show them how germs are grown on culture media in the incubator. A child should be told when a procedure will be painful; no one should sneak up on him. Sometimes watching the injection can reduce fear and pain. Children should be encouraged to verbalize their angry feelings about these painful procedures, right away or later, in the friendly home environment.

During the checkup, certain tests are routinely employed to detect problems. These are known as screening tests. Screening tests are determined according to age and risk for the disorder being looked for. Some screening tests are used for all children. A vision check, evaluation of the child's development, urine culture for girls, PKU test for newborns, and blood pressure readings are examples. When a special risk is established because of family history, selective screening is done. For example, in certain families with a history of heart attacks in very young adults (not older ones), the child's blood should be screened for a fat pattern which could indicate an inherited disorder predisposing him to heart attacks at a young age. If such a finding is present, the doctor would initiate a preventive dietary program. The *tuberculosis* skin test, the blood hemoglobin to detect *anemia,* and the test for lead in blood (see *lead poisoning*) are other specific tests which can be used for children with unusual risks.

Sometimes problems are identified and require immediate treatment; at other times the nature of the problem is unclear, and observation and reexamination are called for. Doctors and nurses always have to deal with uncertainty. They are not gods; they are far from knowing all of the answers. If parents seem hesitant, the doctor will gladly arrange for another professional opinion. His willingness to propose such a consultation is, in itself, usually reassuring. Parents are encouraged to express their feelings honestly on this point, and to understand that their doctor will not view this request as a personal affront or expression of a lack of confidence. On the other hand, the doctor dislikes parents' securing another opinion without involving him in the decision. The consultant should have sufficient background information to render an effective opinion. Honesty both ways is needed.

Immunizations play a large part in preventive care, so much so that many parents equate well-child care with shots and feel there is little point in continuing checkups once the shots have been completed. Many doctors also have organized a preventive-care program around physical examinations and shots, supporting the parents' bias that this is all that is involved. Ideas about the checkup are changing to include a more complete look at the child's life. For this approach to become more prevalent, changes in the attitudes of both professionals and public must take place. Parents must be willing to ask for and pay for this type of checkup.

Looking ahead to the next stage in growth and development is a
very important part of the visit. In what is called anticipatory guidance, the doctor will try to anticipate issues that will arise in the
months ahead and act as a sounding board for parents to test out their
thoughts. Examples are toilet training, **dental care**, common feeding
issues in the toddler (see Chapter 3: "Diet of Infants and Children"),
prevention of accidental poisonings and automobile accidents (see
Part 2, Chapter 8: "Accident Prevention," Chapter 10: "Poisoning,"
and Chapter 12: "Car Safety"), preparation for school, and the normal "magical" thinking in preschool children. Some other topics are
the quality of television viewing (see **television and children**), and the
needs of children for stimulation. In discussing these topics, either
directly with each parent, or in groups of parents (in which such
discussions are ideal), the doctor should talk to the parent about specific health hazards.

Ideally, to provide continuity, the same people—a doctor and one or
two nurses—should be involved in the care program for a particular
child. As discussed in Chapter 1: "Quality in Pediatric Care," nurses
are playing an increasingly important role in child care. Sometimes
social workers are helpful with families having particular problems
with child care. The emphasis should be on limiting the number of
professionals so that families and health professionals can get to know
each other well. Trust and rapport can then develop.

There is no absolute rule about how often to have a checkup. Each
family's needs are different. In many child-care settings, visits are
scheduled on a routine basis. In general it is advisable that babies be
seen 3 or 4 times during the first year, twice in the second and third
years, and yearly thereafter. First children usually require more attention. If more visits are needed, they are scheduled. When special
concerns are raised that cannot be handled in the allotted time, every
effort should be made to schedule additional time. Sometimes, to complete the immunization schedule, the child is invited back just for an
injection or dose of polio vaccine and nothing else.

There are clearly limits to health care, even at its best. Most support
and help for families must come from nonmedical sources. Even
though the medical team often finds itself playing the role which
grandmothers once served, they are strong advocates of the kinds of
changes needed to improve the support of families in present-day
society—better day care, new communal arrangements to restore some
of the strengths of the extended family of the past, reduction of isolation and loneliness, design in communities and apartment complexes

that takes into account the needs of children and families. Parents can learn a great deal from the strengths and successes of other families faced with similar problems.

Parents also need to know how they are doing as parents. Child care can be a very difficult job. Most mothers and fathers try hard to do the right thing and yet often have doubts that they have made the mark. Doctors and nurses should tell parents that they are doing well when that is the case. Everyone needs encouragement and praise. Parents are hardly an exception.

When the doctor first meets a family, he should ask them what their expectations are for care and what their previous experiences with physicians have been like. The parents should know how the doctor may be reached, who covers when he is away, fees, and so forth. More and more doctors and nurses have "call hours," time set aside, usually in the morning, when they sit at the phone to receive calls. Be sure you get this information clearly explained. In the first visit a doctor might ask parents how they feel about hearing his observations on their family situation. How would they feel if he should point out to them problems that they may be too involved with to see themselves? Do they want their doctor to help with the solution of such problems? For example, if marital conflict develops and divorce becomes a consideration, would they value and understand his willingness to stand up for the rights of the child who is all too often caught in the middle? Do they value the doctor as an advocate? It is important that parents realize that the doctor's wide experience is valuable to them and their child in an advisory capacity as well as in his commonly known medical role. An honest dialogue between parents and the doctor will help set the stage for optimum health care.

*Richard I. Feinbloom, M.D.*

# 3

## Diet of Infants and Children

The diet of infants is now receiving some long overdue attention. Among poor children, even in the United States, there are reports of malnutrition. Among the more well-to-do, interest in faulty nutrition stems from two related major public-health concerns: coronary artery disease (narrowing of the blood vessels of the heart due to deposits of fat, also called *atherosclerosis*) and obesity. These are more likely to be of immediate concern to the average reader of this book, although we strongly hope that you would see malnutrition at home and abroad as your problem, too. Until recently, most concern with these two health hazards has focused on adults, since it is the older members of our society who actually suffer most. Now, however, there is mounting evidence that in some individuals these disorders may begin far earlier in life, perhaps in infancy.

## Infant feeding and atherosclerosis

There is strong suspicion that the average American diet, particularly its heavy use of animal fats, contributes significantly to the development of atherosclerosis in susceptible individuals and probably the entire population. It is understandable, then, that renewed interest is being directed toward the diet of infants and children. (See below for general discussion of fats in the diet.) Our understanding of this problem is quite limited at present.

Until more information is available, we do not recommend any fundamental change in feeding practices regarding the type of fat in the milk of infants. Specifically, we caution against elimination of fat by using skim or half-skim milk unless there is a special reason. Babies very much need the essential fats milk contains. There are more appropriate ways to reduce calories, to be discussed later.

Some babies and children deserve special attention—those whose close adult relatives have had heart attacks at an early age (below 45 or so) and/or have other signs of excess fat, such as fat deposits in tendons or skin associated with excess blood fat. These children should be checked for a blood-fat excess. If this fat pattern is present, a change in diet and other measures can reduce blood fat and may help prevent early heart disease. The value of checking all children for this and related disorders of fat is under study.

## Infant feeding and obesity

Babies of today are undoubtedly larger and heavier as a group than those of thirty or forty years ago. It seems reasonable to suspect a connection between this development and our national problem of obesity. Next time you are at the beach take a look at our overweight population undisguised by street clothes. Thirty percent of American adults are obese and one-third of these were obese children. (See *weight problems.*)

An interesting experiment recently conducted on rats suggests how obesity in infants may set up a lifelong pattern. Infant rats in this experiment were fed average diets and then compared with other rats overfed to the point of obesity. When the rats were killed and their fat analyzed, it was found that the ones overfed in infancy had more, and larger, cells that store fat. Rats made obese as adults, on the other hand, increased only the size, not the number, of fat cells. The number of fat cells present at the end of infancy in these rats persisted throughout life, regardless of diet. Thus, the rats made obese by overfeeding as infants had more fat cells as adults. It appears that appetite may be related to the number of fat cells. If the number of fat cells increases, appetite may permanently increase. This increase in fat cells may be the way the food thermostat ("appestat") is raised by overfeeding in infancy. If the same situation applies to humans, as accumulating evidence suggests, it may help explain why infants and children who become obese because of too many calories in their diet tend to remain so, why dieting to lose weight is often difficult, and why a premium should be placed upon preventing obesity in infants, if possible.

Another factor is that babies seem to be less responsive to the caloric density or richness of food than are normal (nonobese) adults. Thus, it is possible to increase the caloric richness of food without their rejecting it, while overfeeding in quantity alone will cause them to vomit. As a group, young babies are more vulnerable to caloric overfeeding leading to obesity than older children or adults who can regulate themselves better. Attention to calories is therefore important.

Why some babies are fat and others are thin is an intriguing question to which a satisfactory answer is not yet available. Heredity, about which nothing can be done, is undoubtedly of major importance. Paradoxically, thin babies may consume more calories than obese ones under normal circumstances. The apparent explanation is that thin infants are very active and "burn up" energy, while chubby ones tend to be quieter, converting more of their calorie intake to fat. The number of calories which a baby is offered unquestionably plays a part, but probably more so for some infants than others. Variation in number of calories taken depends on the richness, calorically speaking, of the diet and the emphasis placed on food by parents. For some babies, it seems likely that chubbiness has resulted from "overfeeding" and/or excessive richness of the foods given. On the other hand, some infants adamantly refuse any more food than they actually need despite coaxing. Nothing will put more weight on these babies. Why some babies are more susceptible to the influence of feeding practices has remained a mystery. It is an important question that deserves research.

While there are no clear rules yet, we are rethinking the old idea that a "fat baby is a healthy one" and are looking much more into obesity and feeding patterns of infants and children as the precursors of obesity in adults. Much additional research is needed on this topic. For example, we have no way of predicting which baby's obesity will be "outgrown" and which sets in motion a lifelong pattern. Which babies should be put on a diet and which left alone? What can now be said is that there is a general problem with obesity and that a general avoidance of excess calories is a wise preventive measure. Careful plotting of a baby's length and weight is the best index of a normal growth pattern and identifies the infant needing special attention. Parents should not become overly concerned with this issue, as most babies do fine when left to their own devices. Sensible measures would include delaying the introduction of solid foods, especially of high-calorie solid foods (see below), and being careful to stop feeding infants when they give us the clue that they have had enough. We should view hunger and eating as the child's responsibility, not ours, from the very first days of his or her life. The infant and child should eat to satisfy hunger, not our preconceived idea of how much he should eat. Children should not eat "for Mama," but for themselves. We try to separate eating from other issues, such as love and discipline. Food should not be a reward or a penalty for desired or undesired behavior.

Many parents whose children are feeding problems had feeding problems themselves with their own mothers and fathers when they were children. While these parents probably cannot ever change the way they feel, they can learn to modify their behavior with their babies so that the cycle can be broken. It is essential that these feeding experiences of parents be brought out for discussion so that parents can become more objective about their children. (See Chapter 4: "Complaints with an Emotional Element.")

At The Children's Hospital Medical Center we are paying much more attention (in early health supervision visits) to each parent's own diet and exercise experiences, both as adults and as children. In fact, we like to explore these issues before a baby is born. If a parent is overweight or has had chronic problems with his or her weight, we consider the children, including the newborn, to be at special risk. We provide all families with general information about nutrition for both children and adults, the kinds of foods to use and avoid, and a philosophy of feeding and exercise. (See *exercise and physical fitness.*) Holding down calories is particularly emphasized for the special risk family. An ounce of prevention is worth a pound of cure.

## Breast- and bottle-feeding

Because this book is a sequel to our *Pregnancy, Birth & the Newborn Baby,* it deals with the baby *after* the first several months of life, beginning at the point when the decision about starting the baby on solid foods is to be made. The topics of breast- and bottle-feeding and weaning are thoroughly discussed in this first volume, and the reader is referred to it for guidance.

## Juice

We usually begin juice around 1 to 2 months. Many baby juices have added sugar and are expensive. You can use the same juices that you serve to the rest of the family—fresh, frozen, or unsweetened canned juices. Try to select only those containing vitamin C. Check labels for contents. Initially, dilute juices to ensure baby's toleration (1 ounce of juice to 2 ounces of water) and then use them full strength. You may find it convenient to give juice between feedings on a hot day. Once the baby is taking 2 ounces of juice containing vitamin C and is getting adequate vitamin D from milk, you can discontinue supplementary vitamins (see below).

## Solid foods

There are a number of considerations entering into the decision of when to begin solid foods. One part of the decision is the infant's readiness and ability to accept the spoon. This varies with age and rapidity of physical development. Some infants reject spoon feedings at one age while accepting them one month later. There is no risk in waiting.

A nutritional consideration which has entered into the recommendations for early introduction of solids, particularly in the past, is the infant's need for a source of iron. Without dietary iron by 4 to 6 months, infants will tend to become anemic (see *anemia*). Neither unfortified commercial milk formula nor cows' milk contains sufficient iron for the baby's needs, whereas human milk from an adequately nourished mother does, according to recent studies. Another source must be found for the non-breast-fed infant. Traditionally, this source has been iron contained in fortified cereals, meats, and eggs, and the introduction of solids, particularly cereals, by 3 months of age was advocated on these grounds. The trend nowadays is to add iron to infants' formula from birth through one year, so that starting the baby on solid foods in order to meet iron needs is a less compelling necessity.

Another factor which often enters into the decision about beginning solids is the parents' belief that milk alone does not satisfy the baby, as evidenced by too-short intervals between feedings and inability to sleep through the night. Parents give solids in the hope that feedings will be stretched out and sleeping through the night will occur earlier. (In our tense society of families with only one or two adults, preserving the adults' sleep is understandably at a premium.) Despite the strong convictions of many parents, in studies of this issue, no connection has been observed between the age at which solid foods are introduced and the daily number of feedings or age of consistently sleeping through. In short, the studies say that, if a baby seems hungry, giving him more milk (formula or breast) is just as effective as giving him solids. The average age of sleeping through is 3 to 4 months regardless, and depends, as does *number* of feedings, primarily on the size of the infant. Solids, according to the studies, don't "hold" an infant's hunger any longer than milk does.

It appears from the above that there is no strong scientific argument for introducing solids at one time rather than another. Such is the case. No one should feel, according to the evidence at hand, that they must begin at 1 week, 2 months, or 5 months. Everyone agrees that by the time teeth are in, babies should have begun to take table foods. Exactly when to begin is less critical.

There is another point to consider. As we have said before, we are concerned about obesity in infants (see **weight problems**), and solids introduced early in life might play a role, at least for some babies. Accordingly, because there is no evidence of special benefit in beginning early, we tend to be conservative and suggest, in general, starting after 3 months, depending on the "readiness" of the infant to take from the spoon. We see no advantage in giving solids from the bottle and advise waiting until the baby is able to manage spoon feedings.

It is important to understand the relative caloric values of foods.

Breast milk and infant formulas have some 67 calories per 100 grams. Commercially available infant foods have considerably greater concentrations of calories than the milk formulas, with some vegetables and fruits being the exception. Cereals, eggs, meats, and desserts are all highly concentrated contributors of calories, as well as being unpredictable and expensive sources of essential nutrients.

Dr. Nathan Smith, a nutritionist at the University of Washington, has emphasized that obesity control, which should be individualized to the needs of each baby, can be implemented by limiting the use and delaying the introduction of high-calorie foods. Breast-feeding or use of iron-fortified infant formulas with their known nutritional content permit calorie control in the early months. For the obese infant, using a low-caloric formula is also helpful (see below). The mixed dinners, mixed breakfasts, wet pack cereals, and desserts should have no significant place in a well-supervised program of infant nutrition. Dr. Smith concludes that they should have no place at all in the diet of the large, obesity-prone infant with one or two obesity-prone parents.

Infants vary in their readiness to accept solids. Some may take to them readily at 2½ months. Others at the same age are disinterested or even strongly opposed, spitting out everything put in their mouths. If your baby is a member of the latter group (a perfectly normal one, by the way), simply postpone the solids for a week or two.

When you do begin on solids, don't be discouraged if at first every spoonful of food comes out on the baby's chin as fast as you put it into his mouth. This is caused by the thrusting movement of the baby's tongue, used to extract milk from the nipple. The behavior does not indicate stubbornness or lack of appetite. Simply scrape the food off and reinsert; his ability to take in and swallow solids will improve as he gains better voluntary control.

Our usual suggestion for starting solids with the average baby is to offer cereal at the 10 A.M. and 6 P.M. feedings, somewhere between 3 and 4 months. It is all right to begin later if iron intake is adequate. You might start with a few small spoons of rice cereal heavily diluted with formula or, if you are breast-feeding, with either your own milk or ordinary whole milk. Gradually, you will strengthen the mix and increase the volume, working up to 7 tablespoons (roughly one-half cup) per day, which is enough to satisfy a baby's iron needs. If the baby continues to take rice cereal well, you can add oatmeal and barley and then the others. Sugar or other sweeteners are best avoided. A baby who has not had sweetened food will never miss it.

Fruits and vegetables are usually introduced at about 4 or 5 months. Common starters are applesauce or banana, but nothing in these two is inherently preferable. If he seems to be fussy or has loose stools with a particular fruit or vegetable, then temporarily discontinue it.

Meats are usually introduced at about 5 months and eggs by 5 to 6 months.

The above plan for introducing solids is an easily remembered point of departure. The order of introduction of these foods can be changed. For example, you might have begun with fruits and vegetables and worked on to introduce cereals and meats a month or two later. Similarly, you can skip around among the food groups, moving, for example, from cereals to vegetables and back to cereals again.

## Switching to regular milk

When to begin homogenized milk is a subject of interest because of the question of the fat it contains. Research in the next few years should provide some answers. By 5 months, you can change to homogenized milk (although, of course, from the nutritional point of view, you could continue to use evaporated milk or commercial formula, or, better yet, nurse) and stop sterilizing.

If your infant is obese, we recommend using either a modified evaporated milk formula or one of the newer, low-calorie, iron-fortified formulas especially designed for the 5- to 12-month-old instead of homogenized milk, which is higher in calories. The one that is commercially available now has 16 calories per ounce. (Regular milk has 20 calories per ounce, as does formula and breast milk.) It and others that will soon be available have a somewhat higher protein content, with vegetable fats substituted for animal fats. A similar reduction in calories can be achieved with a less expensive evaporated milk formula prepared as follows: one 13-ounce can of evaporated milk, one measuring cup of powdered skim milk, and three 13-ounce cans of water. We have already cautioned against the use of skimmed milk alone for such infants.

At about 5 to 6 months, you may find it possible gradually to reduce the milk intake of the baby to about 4 bottles of 6 to 8 ounces of milk per day, at approximately 7 A.M. to 8 A.M., 11 A.M. to noon, 4 P.M. to 6

P.M., and 8 P.M. to 10 P.M. Each family, however, will work out the best schedule for itself, depending upon when the parents get up in the morning and so forth. Between this time and the time when the child is one, the milk intake will be gradually reduced to 2 or 3 8-ounce glasses daily at the same time other foods are being increased in his diet. Most children will have been weaned sometimes during this period, although there is now an encouraging trend to continue breast-feeding into the second year.

## Selecting commercially prepared baby foods

*Cereal:* Use instant, dry baby cereals (iron enriched). The cereals sold in jars are lower in nutritional value. Your best buy is in the large box, rather than the one-ounce boxes.

*Fruit:* Use plain baby fruits without added sugar, if you can find them. The "fruit desserts" and puddings are high in calories, but low in nutritional value.

*Vegetable:* Use plain baby vegetables. The vegetables in cream sauce or with added carbohydrate (sugar and starches), such as baby cream corn, are high in calories with little nutritional value. Sugar is added primarily to improve taste for the mother. Babies can take it or leave it. Hopefully, manufacturers will cease this practice.

*Meat:* Buy plain baby meats. Remember that a 3½-ounce jar of meat provides 16.7 grams of protein, while a 4½-ounce jar mixed dinner provides 3.3 grams of protein and a 4½-ounce jar high meat dinner provides 8.3 grams of protein. You can see the better buy is plain meat. Read labels when purchasing food. The food item listed first is always the highest in content, and the one lower on the list is lower in content. (For example, some children's cereals have sugar as their first listed and, hence, major ingredient.) Vegetables and meat dinners will have more vegetables and less meat, and therefore little protein. New labeling methods which are to be tested soon (see below) should make choices easier for the buyer.

## Home-prepared versus commercial baby foods

Both options are available, and we have no very strong opinion one way or the other, assuming that sanitary procedures are followed in home cooking to prevent infection of the baby and cost is not a factor. Unless you are freezing the food, the safest policy is to prepare the foods for each meal and not to save them beyond the meal. You can blenderize canned or fresh vegetables. If you use canned vegetables, include the liquid in the can in mixing. Put the blenderized mixture into small jars or plastic bags and freeze. Use promptly after thawing and do not store or refreeze once-frozen food. If you do cook foods on your own, there is no need to salt to taste or to sweeten the food. Certainly, if calories are an issue, the lower-calorie, home-cooked foods, without the added sugar or starch (necessary for maintenance of consistency) used in most commercial baby foods, have an edge at present. There is greater predictability of the vitamin content of manufactured baby foods because of the close control possible in their preparation. However, fresh vegetables and fruits are fine if the produce used is truly fresh (not always possible to ensure), and cooking measures minimize destruction of vitamins (see below). The cost of wisely purchased fresh or canned vegetables can be significantly lower than commercial baby foods.

Several books with good recipes for parents interested in making their own foods are *Feeding Your Baby the Safe and Healthy Way*, by Ruth Pearlman (New York: Random House, 1971); *Making Your Own Baby Food*, by Mary and John Turner (New York: Workman Publishing Company, 1972); and *The First Babyfood Cookbook*, by Melinda Morris (New York: Grosset and Dunlap, 1972). These books tend to be opposed to processed foods as a matter of principle.

One deficiency in the marketing of commercial foods is inadequate information on contents. Shortly you will be seeing a new Food and Drug Administration experimental project called nutrition labeling. A variety of labels will be tested with the eventual goal of finding the most useful one. All of the labels will give calories for a measured serving and list the carbohydrates, protein, and fats either by grams or by percentages. Labels also may tell you whether the fats are saturated or polyunsaturated and what the recommended daily amount of each food component is.

## Taste and texture in a baby's diet

In feeding small infants, you should remember that the physical characteristics of the food, such as consistency, are clearly important. However, acceptance of various food items by infants may depend more on parental attitudes than on the infant himself. Manufacturers of strained foods for infants have long recognized that the taste and odor of the products must be acceptable to parents as well as to infants. It was for this reason that salt and sugar have been added to infant foods. If a product is unattractive in smell, taste, or appearance to a parent, he or she is likely to interpret the infant's response to it as unfavorable. Needless to say, this standard is one we should consciously try to reject.

By 6 to 7 months a child usually shows readiness to chew solids (distinguished from thickened feedings). At this time we introduce foods which can easily be grasped in the hands, like soft banana, soft peeled pear, strips of beef, asparagus spears, mushrooms, carrots, mealy apples, waxed beans, strips of chicken or turkey, cheese (Cheddar is soft and yet not too crumbly), Zwieback, hardboiled eggs, salmon (no bones), tuna fish, liverwurst, and ground beef. By the time your child is 8 to 9 months old, he should be able to take so-called family foods without recourse to a large number of infant foods. We are not convinced of the need for junior foods (pureed foods of coarser texture than infant foods). This customary step in feeding can easily be eliminated.

## Calories

By the age of 12 months the average child should be consuming a varied diet probably in the vicinity of 1000 calories per day. For each year of growth thereafter you can add 100 calories. Thus the average 2-year-old child needs about 1100 calories; a 5-year-old child, 1400 calories; and a 10-year-old should receive somewhere in the vicinity of 1900 calories. In *adolescence*, adequate provision must be made for the period of growth. Teen-age girls may require 2400 to 2700 calories per day and boys possibly up to 3100 to 3600 calories per day. These averages are just that; obviously the size and activity of the child will influence caloric needs.

## Fats in the diet

As we said at the beginning of this chapter, the heavy use of animal fats in the American diet is coming under increasing criticism as contributing to atherosclerosis. The recommendations which follow in regard to fat in the diet, while primarily for children with high blood fat levels, should probably extend to the entire population. Although the evidence is incomplete, many experts now favor such a change in diet, which is not without major economic consequences. Even though it is possible to alter the kinds of fat in animals through changing their diets, increasing pressure from the world food situation is likely to be of overriding importance in lessening the enormous consumption of meat and dairy products in this country.

In children with high blood fat levels which predispose to heart and blood vessel disease, the usual recommendation is to alter the pattern of intake. At present, these children are identified through association with an older family member with a similar problem or because of the presence of deposits of fat in the skin or tendons. Whether the low-cholesterol diet proves effective remains to be seen.

*Cholesterol* is a fatty substance manufactured by the body and present in many foods of animal origin. Most medical authorities agree that you can reduce elevated amounts of body cholesterol by controlling the amount and kind of fat you eat (for example by using unsaturated fats instead of saturated fats as discussed below).

Fat is made up of *fatty acids*. These fatty acids can be classified into three types—*saturated* fatty acids, *monounsaturated* fatty acids, and *polyunsaturated* fatty acids. The word *saturation* refers to chemical composition and means that the fat is holding as much hydrogen as it can. Saturated fatty acids tend to raise blood cholesterol levels; polyunsaturated fatty acids on the other hand tend to lower blood cholesterol levels; and monounsaturated fatty acids neither raise nor lower blood cholesterol levels. The following fats are grouped according to their degree of saturation:

| SATURATED FAT | MONOUNSATURATED FAT | POLYUNSATURATED FAT |
|---|---|---|
| Animal fat | Peanut oil | Safflower oil |
| Lard | Olive oil | Corn oil |
| Butter fat | | Soybean oil |
| Coconut oil | | Cottonseed oil |

Fats consisting predominantly of saturated fatty acids are solid at room temperature, while those with a high proportion of unsaturated acids are usually liquid. In the manufacture of vegetable shortenings and margarines, hydrogen is added and, therefore, makes these oils more saturated, which keeps them somewhat solid at room temperature. In general, even after hydrogen is added, the various oils retain their rank order in raising or lowering cholesterol. If you are trying to lower an elevated blood cholesterol level, avoid all animals fats and, when choosing a margarine, look for one made from an oil with a higher content of polyunsaturates. Margarines made from safflower or corn oil would be first choices because they are highest in polyunsaturates. If your purpose is to have lower cholesterol, use safflower or corn oil rather than peanut or olive oil. While these latter two don't raise the cholesterol level, they won't help lower it either. Peanut butter can be bought nonhydrogenated, that is, relatively more unsaturated. It is generally known as natural peanut butter. However, you will have to read the label carefully, as most peanut butter contains hydrogenated peanut oil.

For a diet lower in cholesterol and higher in unsaturated fats:

| INCLUDE OR ENCOURAGE | EXCLUDE OR MINIMIZE |
|---|---|
| Skim milk (and skim milk yogurt) | Whole milk, cream (sweet and sour) |
| Cottage, Swiss, farmer, and mozzarella cheese | All other cheeses |
| Margarines and oils of corn and safflower | Butter, ordinary margarines, lard, hydrogenated shortening |
| Vegetables (green/yellow) | Avocado |
| Breads and cereals | Cake and cookies with animal or hydrogenated shortening or with chocolate |
| Fruits | Coconut |
| Chicken and turkey (no skin) | Duck and goose |

| | |
|---|---|
| Beef (eye of round, top and bottom round, lean ground round, lean rump tenderloin) | Beef with fat distributed throughout which cannot be removed, that is, choice or prime |
| Lamb and veal | |
| Pork (lean loin) | Bacon, salt pork, spareribs |
| Fresh ham (lean, well trimmed) | Frankfurters, ham, luncheon meats |
| Fish | Fish deep-fried in saturated fat |

In general, the use of skim milk, lean meats with more emphasis on chicken and fish in meal planning, and the use of corn or safflower oils and margarines in baking and cooking will make the diet lower in saturates and higher in unsaturates. These measures will also help to control calories. However, it must be remembered that one teaspoon of margarine has the same amount of calories as one teaspoon of butter, and therefore margarine should not be used indiscriminately. Fat, whether saturated or unsaturated, is the most concentrated source of calories and can therefore contribute many unwanted pounds. It is good hygiene to watch both the *type* and *amount of fat* when planning family meals.

*Cooking tips to reduce fat in diet (to reduce calories for weight control and/or to lower elevated blood fats):*

1. Use a rack when broiling, roasting, or baking so that the fat can drain off. If possible, do not baste, since basting returns some of the fat to the food. (To keep meat moist, pour tomato juice or bouillon over it.)

2. When you make stews, boiled meat, soup stock, or other dishes in which fat cooks out into the liquid, do your cooking a day ahead of time. After the food has been refrigerated, the hardened fat can be removed easily from the top.

3. Make gravy for the meat or poultry after the fat has hardened and has been removed from the liquid. In cream sauces and cream soups, make with skim milk.

4. When a recipe calls for browning meat before combining it with other ingredients, try browning it under the broiler instead of frying in a pan.

## Salt

Our American diet is very high in salt, beginning even with baby foods in which salt is added mainly to make them palatable to mothers. There is no nutritional need for added salt and there is growing concern that it *may* be harmful, for example in contributing to high blood pressure, particularly in families with this tendency. Accordingly, many baby food manufacturers are reducing the salt added to their products. It seems worthwhile to accustom babies and children, particularly those with family histories of hypertension, to a diet lower in salt than is presently the practice.

## How much milk?

By one year when your child is eating a mixed diet of meat, fish, or poultry, enriched breads and cereals, fruits and vegetables, he will get 25 percent of his recommended daily dietary allowance (RDA) for calcium from these foods. The other 75 percent must come from high calcium dairy foods. Therefore, there is a need to incorporate some dairy products in your child's daily diet. If he doesn't like milk, don't force him. From the chart below you will see that far less milk is needed (1 pint per day at 1 year) than many people think. While it is a perfect food for infants, the need for milk becomes less critical as other nutrients are introduced into the diet. Intolerance to milk— manifested by diarrhea, bloating, and abdominal pain—will affect some children, increasing in frequency as children grow older. For a discussion of the inherited loss of capacity to digest milk sugar, see chronic nonspecific diarrhea under *diarrhea.* Continue to offer a small glass with each meal, but don't be upset if he doesn't drink it. Make cereals, soups, and desserts with milk, and vegetables, potatoes, and meat with creamed sauces. Serve cheese and crackers, cottage cheese mixed with jelly or fruit, ice cream, puddings, frozen yogurts, and frappes for nourishing desserts or snacks. The following guideline is based on the assumption that your child is eating a mixed diet.

| AGE/YEARS | AMOUNT OF MILK/DAY |
|-----------|---------------------|
| 1–2 | 16 oz. (½ qt. or 1 pt. or 2 cups) |
| 2–3 | 18 oz. |
| 3–4 | 18 oz. |

| 4–6 | 18 oz. |
| 6–8 | 20 oz. |
| 8–10 | 24 oz. |
| 10–18 | 26–30 oz. |

**DAIRY PRODUCTS EQUIVALENT TO ½ CUP MILK (4 OZ.)**

2 tbs. nonfat dry milk solids
½ oz. cheese (a standard cheese slice weighs 1 oz. or 30 gm.)
½ cup pudding
½ cup yogurt
½ cup custard
½ cup cottage cheese
½ cup ice cream (calories and lower protein content make this a less desirable alternative)

Obviously, any combination of the dairy products will do. For example, 8 ounces of milk and one cup of ice cream will fulfill the milk requirements for an 18-month-old child.

If the child will not eat or drink the amount of milk or number of dairy products suggested in the diet or if you live where they are hard to get, try offering some of the following foods. However, these foods are only fair sources of calcium and do not completely take the place of dairy products. Discuss the issue with your doctor or nurse.

*Fish, poultry:* Turkey, clams, scallops, flounder, haddock, canned salmon.

*Breads, cereals:* Bread enriched with nonfat dry milk solids; enriched or "quick" cream of wheat or cereals made with milk.

*Vegetables:* Red kidney beans, broccoli, chard and other green leafy vegetables, okra, onions, parsnips, spinach, dried peas, or beans of any type.

*Fruits:* All dried fruits; fresh fruit, especially rhubarb, pineapple, loganberries, raspberries, blackberries, strawberries.

*Miscellaneous:* Eggs, almonds, medium dark molasses, maple syrup.

## Food as a source of pleasure and satisfaction

Feeding is the initial means of establishing human bonds. Food and love become synonymous as a child is held in a mother's comforting and secure arms. Food and eating contribute to cultural and emotional life as well as to psychological needs. Through food the infant forms a basic concept of the world in which he lives, the people in it, and their relationships with him. Since the feelings of being loved and feedings are closely intertwined, appetite is strongly influenced by emotions and attitudes as well as physical hunger. Therefore, the first aim is to keep eating enjoyable. When eating becomes an arena of conflict, symptoms such as overeating (see *weight problems*) are likely to develop.

## How much to eat

*Anorexia* or lack of appetite is one of the most common complaints about child feeding. Frequently, the origin of indifferent appetite displayed by a child is traced to the food habits started in infancy. The conscientious parent may overlook normal variations in appetite, being too zealous about fulfilling the prescribed home schedule and amount of feeding. Rebellion against food can begin because of a rigid rather than flexible feeding schedule. So be flexible and in tune with your child. Ours is to offer; his is to take or leave. A healthy child's appetite nicely matches his food needs. When sucking comes to a full stop, he has had enough. When his mouth fails to open wide for another spoonful, that means enough. Let's not argue. Arguing and cajoling him to take more is a mistaken kindness as well as an easy way to annoy your child. Let him have as much as he wants of nutritionally balanced meals. A parent's anger, so easily aroused by the child who refuses food, has no place in feeding. If you can't contain your anger, be sure to bring this up with your doctor or nurse.

## Developmental aspects of feeding patterns

Feeding is a learned experience that begins for better or worse with the first nursing or when the first bottle is fed to the newborn. Among the many things an infant has to learn about food are not to suck solids, to chew and swallow—all new manipulative skills which we take for granted. He will do best if you let him progress at a speed natural to him.

The following chart gives a *guide* for self-feeding; it is not a rigid plan. The time to teach a child to do things is when he shows he wants to learn. Some children express this readiness earlier or later than others. If he is pushed too early, he will be frightened by failure. If he is held back when he is ready, he may lose interest in learning later. When he is able to sit alone without support, able to grasp a spoon and complete hand-to-mouth motion, he is ready to begin to self-feed.

Because feeding is a learned experience, *you* can teach your child. BE CONSISTENT. BE RELAXED. BE FLEXIBLE. TRY TO BE EMOTIONALLY DETACHED. It is important to *teach* your child good food habits during infancy and childhood, as they form the basis of his food habits throughout life.

## SELF-FEEDING: AVERAGE AGE LEVELS

| | |
|---|---|
| 6–9 months | Holds, sucks, and bites finger foods |
| 9 months–1 year | Holds own bottle (or may have given up bottle by now); enjoys finger foods; eats most table foods; drinks from cup with help; will hold and lick spoon after it is dipped into food |
| 15 months | Begins to use spoon, turns it before it reaches mouth; **may** no longer need bottle; may hold cup; likely to tilt cup rather than head, spilling contents |
| 1½ years | Eats with spoon, often spilling; turns spoon in mouth; requires assistance; holds glass with both hands; size of glass is important |
| 2 years | Puts spoon in mouth correctly, occasionally spilling; holds glass with one hand; distinguishes between food and inedible materials; plays with food |
| 2–3 years | Feeds self entirely, with occasional spilling; uses fork; pours from pitcher; can obtain drink of water from faucet by self |
| 3–4 years | Can serve self at table |
| 5–6 years | Uses table knife for spreading; generally independent at meals |

**Years 1–3
(toddler)**

35

*Diet of
Infants
and
Children*

Feeding problems are likely to begin around 1½ years when a child's growth rate slows and his appetite lessens. At this time, the child is developing an increasing sense of "I," of being a person distinct and apart from Mother, rather than just an extension of her. His increased mobility leads to an increased sense of independence and further leads him to balk at many requests for the sheer assertive joy of refusal. He is discovering himself and trying to express his likes and dislikes. He should be allowed to have these likes and dislikes as long as his menu is not too impractical. After all, he has a different nose and set of taste buds than you do and therefore will respond to food differently. If you accept his verdict in a matter-of-fact way, he will not get the idea that refusing food is a way to gain attention.

Swings in taste are also quite common during the toddler period and feeding pitfalls abound. A child may want just one food every day for lunch and then suddenly refuse to eat it at all for a spell. Giving in to these quirks will not spoil him. It is at this point, out of concern for their child's well-being and fear of his not eating enough, that mothers are motivated to buy glamorous snack foods, sugared cereals, drinks, flavorings, and vitamins advertised to children on television (see *television and children*). Once begun, the pattern is set, perhaps for life. We caution parents to resist these pressures. Don't allow your children to bribe you into faulty nutritional patterns.

Vitamin supplements should not be used. Vitamin needs are 2000 units of A, 50 milligrams of C, and 400 units of D. (For B vitamins well represented in usual diet, see later in this chapter.) These are contained in the properly selected diet. The iron need, supplied from diet, is 10 milligrams daily. Fluoride (see *dental care*) should be continued. Mineral supplements are not necessary, and so-called *tonics* and *appetite stimulants* (including vitamins for this purpose) are worthless.

When it comes to this age group, assume a casual air—what we call friendly indifference. As you become less demanding, he will become more reasonable. This, of course, does not mean that there should be no rules. A child needs the security of a few rules. He needs to know what to expect from you. You must be consistent. If he plays with food, remove it without threats. Do not use food as a means of reward and punishment; this may lead to obesity in later life. It is at this time that desserts often become a bribe to clean the plate. If a child is full, that is, cannot finish appropriate-sized portions, then it is better to end the meal right there. Don't insist on a clean plate, but do give small portions. Portion size is important. A child cannot eat as much as an adult and large servings discourage him. A baby eats one-third to one-half as much as an adult; a 3-year-old eats one-half as much or a little more; and a 6-year-old, two-thirds the amount of an adult. Always keep the portion in proportion to your child's age. Give your child time to enjoy his meal. He does not have your sense of time. If he loses interest in his meal or dawdles, after about 15 minutes quietly but firmly remove his food. It is probably best not to make cleaning the plate a requirement for dessert. Again, assume that air of friendly indifference.

As you read this section, you may become aware of how much our own deeply held attitudes about food influence how we deal with our children. Try to discuss this with your doctor or nurse. Talking about attitudes toward food permits parents to be more objective and to see food and eating from the child's point of view.

As your child continues to grow, both the type of food and the amount he needs will change, as will his response to food and the feeding situation. The opposite chart can serve as a guide to a well-balanced diet for toddlers. The same food can be increased proportionately for older children.

## Years 3–6 (preschool)

The preschool child continues growth in spurts. Accordingly, his appetite is variable. The family meals become an important time for socialization and helping to form an identity. A child of this age is very much influenced by Mother and Father as he learns a widening variety of food habits and forms new social relationships. He will usually prefer simple foods over mixed dishes and enjoys using his fingers. Vegetables are usually less well liked. However, crisp raw vegetables are more acceptable than cooked vegetables. Bright food colors encourage a preschool appetite. Children at this age also enjoy tender, easy-to-chew meat with "no strings." Daily vitamin needs are 2500 units of A, 50 milligrams of C, 400 units of D. Added vitamins are not necessary. Needs can be satisfied by the diet alone. Fluoride (see

# GUIDELINES FOR A BALANCED DIET:
## AGES 1 to 3

37

*Diet of*
*Infants*
*and*
*Children*

| Food | Approximate quantity needed daily | Average size of a serving 12–24 mo. | 24–36 mo. |
|---|---|---|---|
| Milk to drink and in or on foods | 2–3 measuring cups needed daily | ½–1 cup | ½–1 cup |
| Eggs | 1 | 1 | 1 |
| Lean meat with fat trimmed, poultry, fish, cheese | 2 servings | 1 tbs. (noon & night) | 2–3 tbs. (noon & night) |
| Potatoes, white or sweet, or potato substitute, rice, noodles, spaghetti | 1 serving | 2 tbs. | 4 tbs. |
| Other cooked vegetables (mostly green leafy or deep yellow ones) | 1–2 servings | 2 tbs. | 4 tbs. |
| Raw vegetables (carrot, cabbage, tomato, lettuce, etc.) | 1 serving | Small portion such as ¼ of small carrot | |
| Fruit for vitamin C (citrus fruits, tomatoes, berries) | 1 serving (1 medium orange or ⅓ cup citrus fruit juice or 1 cup tomato juice) | ⅓–½ cup | ⅓–½ cup |
| Other fruits (apples, apricots, bananas, pears, peaches, prunes, etc.) | 1 serving | ¼ cup | ⅓ cup |
| Bread, whole grain | 3 servings | ½ slice to 1 slice | 1 slice |
| Cereal, whole grain or restored | 1 serving | 2 tbs. cooked, ⅓ cup ready to eat | 3 tbs. cooked, ½ cup ready to eat |

Nourishing desserts: ⅓ cup of pudding, ice cream, custard, may be given occasionally as a dessert.

_dental care_) should be continued. The daily iron requirement which should be met in the diet is 10 milligrams.

While obesity is a problem in this age group (see _weight problems_), there is mounting evidence that as a result of inactivity (see _television and children_ and _exercise and physical fitness_), many children are actually reducing their calorie intake to the point that their diet provides insufficient iron, leading to iron deficiency _anemia._

## _Years 6–12_
## _(school age)_

During the school-age period resources are being stored for growth needs in _adolescence._ Growth rates vary widely. Increments in weight sometimes outdistance those in height, and children during this stage frequently take on a round appearance. If weight far outdistances height, intervention with diet and activity is necessary to prevent overweight from becoming obesity. Girls generally grow faster than boys. Remember that you have no control over your child's rate of growth. You cannot hurry it. You can only help it by providing proper food for growth. There is a gradual decline of food requirement per unit of body weight until the period just prior to adolescence.

Growing interest in other activities may compete with mealtime, and midafternoon snacking is common. An attempt should be made to curtail continuous snacking by establishing a set midafternoon, after-school snack, again to prevent overeating and overweight. This should be a nutritious snack, such as a meat, cheese, or peanut butter sandwich and milk. Milk puddings, ice cream, fruit, and yogurt should be used for nourishing desserts instead of cookies, candy, cake, or pie. Brushing of teeth should be required after meals.

Daily vitamin needs are 4000 units of A, 60 milligrams of C, and 400 of D. (These should be in the foods eaten, and added vitamins should not be necessary.) Daily iron needs which should be met from diet are 12 milligrams for 6- to 9-year-olds and 15 milligrams for 10- to 12-year-olds. Fluoride should be continued.

Keep in mind that less eating is occurring at home. The family meal is fast disappearing from the American scene. Forty percent of the dollar spent for food today in the United States is for food out of the home. Nutrition planning must take this trend into account. All the more reason that children, as well as adults, should understand nutrition so that they can choose foods properly on their own.

## *Years 12–18*
## *(adolescence)*

During this period, the final growth spurt of childhood occurs, and caloric needs increase with metabolic demands of growth and energy expenditure to between 2000 and 3600 calories per day. There is evidence that the large caloric needs and vigorous activity of boys usually lead them to an adequate appetite and intake. However, boys in low-income families may receive inadequate calories. Girls have more of a problem, as physiological sex differences associated with fat deposits, coupled with lack of activity, may lead them to gain excessive weight. The adolescent girl needs 20 milligrams of iron a day in contrast to the boy who needs only 15 milligrams. Iron-poor diets and iron losses with menstruation make iron deficiency a common problem among teen-age girls. Because of limited activity, many girls eat so little that their diets contain inadequate iron and they become anemic (see *anemia*). If they were more active, they could eat more without gaining weight, and in this way obtain sufficient iron to prevent anemia. Thus, one way of preventing iron deficiency anemia is through physical activity. Encourage high iron foods (see discussion of iron-rich foods later in this chapter) and more exercise. If snacking is inevitable, teach the child to pick nutritious snacks. For example, pizza made with plenty of cheese is almost a balanced meal, while the average doughnut contains mainly empty calories. On the other hand, the child who comes home from school for an afternoon snack to a larder of fruit, peanut butter, whole wheat bread, dried fruit, nuts, seeds, yogurt, fresh juice, or raw vegetables is better off than with either of the other snacks. We hope that more parents will understand the rich supply of vitamins, minerals, and energy that can be had in these foods as opposed to soft drinks, potato chips, candy, ice cream, cookies, and package prepared drinks. Any signs of fatigue, tiredness, or shortness of breath should be checked by your family physician. Added vitamins should not be needed. Daily needs are 5000 units of A, 80 milligrams of C, and 400 units of D. Fluoride should be continued until all permanent teeth are in, usually at age 12 to 14. (See *dental care.*)

It is during these years that decreased exercise begins to be more of a problem (it is a general problem of our society) and needs careful attention (see *exercise and physical fitness*). Many teen-agers continue to eat robustly even after growth has ceased, with obesity the result (see *weight problems*). (See also *adolescence.*)

## Food additives

There is much public interest in additives. These are substances added to foods to change texture, taste, appearance, nutritive qualities, or preservability. The use of these substances is watched by the United States government for safety and we rely on this surveillance, which hopefully will become tighter in the years ahead, to guarantee the healthfulness of the foods we eat and feed our children. We advocate testing and justification for additives before they are used, not afterward. We oppose the addition of salt and sugar to infant foods to make them more palatable to mothers or for any other reason. (Most manufacturers of baby food are eliminating salt, sugar, and some other additives from their product lines.)

## Organic and health foods

There is a growing movement to use organic foods. These are crops grown without pesticides or artificial fertilizers. Health foods are relatively less processed than their commercial cousins.

Retail stores with organic foods are spreading across the land. These foods are generally more expensive than usual varieties. We have no objection to their use as long as the basic nutritional guidelines outlined here are followed.

The organic and health food trend also involves an implied blanket criticism of processed foods and a rejection of technology in food production. While we would not go this far, we see the positive message of the health food movement to be an increased awareness of nutrition, which, from our point of view, can and should be applied to all food selection and preparation, organic or otherwise.

## Vegetarian diets

Diets of fruits, vegetables, and whole grains are nutritious if milk is added to meet vitamin $B_{12}$ needs, and iron supplements or eggs are taken by menstruating females to cover iron losses. A good guide to planning vegetarian meals with adequate protein is *Diet for a Small Planet*, by Frances Moore Lappé (New York: Ballantine Books, 1971).

## Vitamins

Vitamins are organic chemicals which our bodies must have if we are to remain healthy. Deficiencies of the various vitamins are associated with certain specific disorders, such as scurvy and rickets. Most people are aware that every child from birth on requires vitamins in his diet, but not everyone realizes that in the consumption of vitamins it is possible to overdo a good thing, although even in our overvitaminized society we rarely see any toxic effects of overdosage.

The most important vitamins are A, D, and C, which are discussed below, and the B group. The B vitamins are well represented in the foods (including human and cows' milk) given to babies and children in the United States and are not discussed except for vitamin $B_{12}$, which is missing in a strict vegetarian diet. Vitamin $B_{12}$ is found in fish, eggs, milk, and cheese and is important in the manufacture of red blood cells and in maintaining the integrity of the nervous system. While there are generally no problems with the B group of vitamins, the child's diet may, however, be short of A, D, or C, and parents should have a little information about them. There are other vitamins besides those we have mentioned, but they are widely enough distributed in the diet so that no conscious decision about them is necessary. An example is folic acid, another vitamin important in the production of red blood cells, which is found in liver, green vegetables, nuts, cereals, and cheese (see *anemia*). We will confine our discussion to the three we cite as important, plus a comment on vitamin E.

## Vitamin deficiency

Vitamin A is important to vision. A deficiency of A causes *night blindness* and other disorders of the eye. There is no scientific basis for its use by teen-agers in treating acne. Vitamin D is essential to normal growth of bone. The bone condition known as *rickets*, not seen as often nowadays as it once was, results from a deficiency of vitamin D. Vitamin C, whose chemical name is *ascorbic acid*, is essential to the healthy development of the small blood vessels and other body structures. Easy bruising, bleeding gums, and hemorrhages around the bones are symptoms of deficiency of vitamin C. The medical name for this condition is *scurvy*. Some studies have suggested that vitamin C, taken in large doses far above those needed as a vitamin, may shorten and decrease the intensity of cold symptoms. However, the answer is not yet in, for recent critical review has cast doubt on these findings.

Many symptoms beyond those noted in the previous paragraph are commonly attributed to vitamin deficiencies. Among them are poor appetite, stunted growth, whining, and frequent colds (see *infections* and *resistance and frequent colds*). It is true that these symptoms are often seen among severely malnourished children, but the deprivations of these children go beyond vitamin deficiencies. In our affluent society, we do not see any direct relationship between these symptoms and lack of vitamins. Though parents often pour vitamins into children exhibiting these symptoms, the children rarely respond. The parents are right to be concerned about the problems, but they should look in another direction for solutions. As a general comment, it can be stated that we Americans, under the pressures of our high-powered advertising, grossly overuse vitamin preparations.

Because they occur in various plants and animals, vitamins can be harvested from natural sources. They can also be manufactured in the laboratory. These manufactured vitamins have the same effect in the body as the naturally occurring ones and often are identical. Vitamins are added and/or occur naturally in the foods we eat, including margarine, butter, milk, juices, fruit drinks, cereals, breads, and so forth, so that it is next to impossible for the child who is eating a well-balanced diet to avoid getting enough.

If for any reason the diet is inadequate in vitamins, they can be given in the form of drops or tablets, and many commercial preparations for the infant are available. The usual practice with infants whose diets are deficient (breast-fed infants and some formula-fed infants—check the label on the formula to see which vitamins are present) is to begin giving vitamins a few days after the baby is home from the hospital. He takes his prescribed amount once a day from a medicine dropper. You will discover that he is quick to learn how to suck on the dropper and that he seems to enjoy it. The supplementary vitamins can be stopped as soon as the diet contains adequate amounts.

## Food sources
## of vitamins

Vitamin A is found in milk, butter, cheese, egg yolk, animal fats, and the yellow vegetables (carrots, squash, and sweet potatoes). Fish liver oils (cod, halibut, and tuna) contain large quantities. Human milk contains vitamin A, usually in adequate quantities if the mother herself has a normal diet. Cows' milk varies with the season, depending on the available forage, but in general contains adequate amounts for infants. Many margarines are fortified with vitamin A.

Vitamin C appears in almost all fresh fruits and vegetables, but especially in citrus fruits, tomatoes, berries, and leafy green vegetables. Overcooking tends to destroy the vitamin, but modern canning and freezing methods are preservative. Vitamin C is often added to fruit drinks.

Here are some tips on handling vegetables and fruits to preserve vitamin C (and, for that matter, B):

1. Wash vegetables quickly, and only when necessary. Don't soak them. For example, there's no need to wash peas in pods at all, or other vegetables before storage.

2. Refrigerate vegetables as soon as possible, preferably in a plastic bag; place them in vegetable crisper.

3. Peel vegetables only when necessary, to avoid removing vitamins which are stored next to the skin.

4. Don't cut or tear leafy vegetables or other vitamin C vegetables such as broccoli and cauliflower before time to use. This initiates an enzyme action that immediately starts reducing the vitamin C content.

5. Time cooking of vegetables so that they can be served immediately. Don't let them sit around in a pot.

6. Serve vegetables raw. Even young children can grow to like them this way.

7. Choose cooking methods that use as little water as possible to avoid drawing off B vitamins and vitamin C in the cooking water. Some excellent practical tips for the cook were contained in the June 1972 issue of *Redbook* magazine in an article by Ruth Fairchild Pomeroy.

Baking is an excellent way to prepare many vegetables. Stir-frying or crisp-cooking thin-sliced vegetables in a small amount of oil in a *wok* or skillet will preserve nutrients. Braising also is a good method. Put vegetables, with a small amount of butter or oil and a very little water or consommé, in a skillet with a tight-fitting cover. Allow them to simmer until just done and serve the juices as a sauce. Steam vegetables by putting them on a rack over boiling water. This keeps the liquid completely away from the vegetables. Reheating vegetables results in more than half the nutrient loss. It's better to use leftover vegetables in salads or sandwich fillings.

Canned vegetables do sustain some vitamin and mineral loss because of solubility. However, if you pour the can liquid into a pan and cook it down to a small amount before adding the vegetables and serve it as a sauce over the vegetables, you will have retrieved a good number of the vitamins.

There is relatively little nutrient loss in the freezing of vegetables. However, frozen vegetables should never be defrosted before cooking. When a choice of methods is given on the package directions, choose the one that uses the least liquid. The only hitch in these recommendations is that the fruits and vegetables should be fresh picked to start with, something not always easy to determine.

Cows' milk is an unreliable source of vitamin C and supplementation is required. Human milk contains adequate amounts if the mother receives 60 milligrams daily in her diet.

Vitamin D is found in fish oils and (in lesser quantities) in eggs. It is manufactured from chemicals naturally occurring in human and animal skin under the action of sunlight. Hence, during the summer months average exposure to sun stimulates sufficient production to meet our needs. Vitamin D is passed poorly into human or cows' milk, and, therefore, as a general practice in this country it is added both to cows' milk and to commercially prepared formulas as well as many margarines.

Vitamin E has received much publicity in recent years. Most of the claims about it, such as the claim that it promotes long life, are without foundation. Its exact function is not completely clear.

The richest dietary sources of Vitamin E are vegetable oils (corn, soybean, peanut), with cereal products and eggs next in order. By contrast, animal fats and meats, fruits, and vegetables are relatively poor sources.

It is passed well in breast milk, meeting the infant's needs. If the older child eats a well-balanced diet, he should get the estimated daily requirements of between 10 and 30 units (5 units for infants). No supplements should be required. However, knowledge about vitamin E is not complete at present, and there may be changes in the recommendations in the years ahead.

## Iodine

This chemical is needed for healthy thyroid gland functioning (see **hormones**). Good sources are iodized salt and seafood. A recent problem is the addition of more, usually noniodized, salt to processed foods for adults and children. Less iodized salt from the shaker is used. The result is the reappearance of thyroid goiter in some parts of the country where iodides are naturally low in the drinking water.

## Fluoride

Fluoride is needed daily to prevent tooth decay until the permanent teeth are in during adolescence. The daily requirement for children between 6 months and 3 years is 0.5 mg, and 1.0 mg for those over 3. The requirement for those less than 6 months old has not been worked out yet. The fluoride can come from the water, if the municipal water is naturally fluoridated or has had fluorides added and if the child drinks the water. Many children we know in this era of soft drinks (see *television and children*) fail to realize that water is still the best and cheapest thirst quencher. If the water is deficient in fluoride, supplements are needed. Fluoridated water used in preparing evaporated milk formulas will supply the baby's fluoride needs. For babies on premixed commercial formulas, it has been shown that the water used in their preparation usually contains fluoride. Breast-fed babies also need fluoride because fluoride passes poorly into breast milk. Check with your doctor or nurse. (See *dental care.*)

## *Iron*

Cow's milk and unfortified formulas are deficient in iron. Recent studies show that breast milk, from an adequately nourished mother, contains sufficient iron to meet baby's needs at least through the first 15 months, without iron from any other source. An additional supply of iron is made possible at birth by late clamping of the umbilical cord, allowing added iron-rich red blood cells to reach the baby's body. For the baby who is not nursed and especially one whose cord was clamped early, iron should be added to the diet by no later than 4 months and preferably from birth. As a baby grows, he outgrows the supply of iron he was born with, and in the absence of iron intake, because of growth alone will become iron deficient (see *anemia*). A reasonable precaution to ensure iron intake is the fortification of infant milks with iron or the addition of iron drops to the non-breast-fed baby's diet until he is eating sufficient quantities of iron-rich foods to meet his daily needs. Accordingly, more and more commercial formulas contain added iron. There is a growing trend to use these formulas through the first year. The infant on non-iron-fortified evaporated or whole milk formulas should receive iron drops daily. Check with your doctor or nurse for the dose. (Remember that iron tablets or drops taken in excess are extremely dangerous. See Part 2, Chapter 8: "Accident Prevention" and Chapter 10: "Poisoning.")

When it is clear that in the non-breast-fed infant other dietary sources (cereals, meats, eggs) are being taken in sufficient quantities, the iron-fortified formulas or supplemental iron drops may be discontinued. Check with your doctor or nurse.

The major sources of iron in infant foods are listed as follows:

| FOOD | AMOUNT | IRON | QUALITY AS SOURCE OF IRON |
|------|--------|------|---------------------------|
| Vegetables | 7 tbs. | 0.6 mg. | Poor |
| Fruit | 7 tbs. | 0.5 mg. | Poor |
| Cereal, baby, enriched | ½ cup | 14.0 mg. | Excellent |
| Meat | 7 tbs. | 1.7 mg. | Good |
| Liver (beef) | 7 tbs. | 4.39 mg. | Excellent |
| Mixed dinners | 7 tbs. | 0.6 mg. | Poor |
| High meat dinners | 7 tbs. | 0.83 mg. | Poor |
| Regular meats | 7 tbs. | 1.0 mg. | Good |
| Egg yolk | 7 tbs. | 3.0 mg. | Good |
| Fruit desserts | 7 tbs. | 0.4 mg. | Poor |

We have mentioned the difficulties preschool children and teen-age girls in particular have in obtaining enough iron on the limited calories many take in. Also at risk in our society for iron deficiency anemia is the low-income pregnant woman. Beyond the period of infancy good sources of iron are:

1. Lean red meats, especially liver, other organ meats, and eggs.

2. Whole grain breads and cereals such as whole wheat, rye, pumpernickel, enriched cereals, raisin bran, bran flakes, whole wheat crackers, and nourishing oatmeal-raisin cookies. Presently under discussion is a proposed Federal regulation that would require that flour be fortified with iron.

3. Dried fruits, raisins, prunes, apricots.

4. Dark-green vegetables.

5. Dried beans and peas.

Nutrition is a complex subject. Economic and public policy factors are of major importance. Public interest is high, and many theories and fads come into vogue and, just as quickly, fade away. This discussion will dissatisfy some as being too radical, and others as being too conservative. However, we have tried to sift through incomplete and sometimes conflicting information in order to present you with the best possible advice for the establishment of healthful nutrition patterns from the very beginning of your child's life.

*Richard I. Feinbloom, M.D., with the assistance of
Rosanne Howard, Mary Ellen Collins, and
Connie Lotz-Textor*

# 4
# Complaints with an Emotional Element

The connection between the mind (psyche) and the body (soma) is not completely understood, but we do know that tension in children can set the stage for psychosomatic disease later on. Childhood tension and anxiety not only shape the child's later personality, they can produce specific organ diseases. High blood pressure and coronary disease have been linked with some certainty to an ambitious, hard-driving, and stressful style of life. As another example of mind-body linkage, there is recent evidence to suggest that a susceptibility to infection may be closely associated with tension. In a preschool in Cambridge, Massachusetts, the teachers reported that they could predict which fathers were writing theses and which mothers were taking exams by the number of infections that the children suffered. Even more obvious is the incidence of acute respiratory infections in small children just as their parents are about to go away on a trip, or make a move to another city. This may simply be a matter of lowered resistance which results from tension in a household.

More serious are the organic complaints commonly associated with stress, such as asthma, eczema, stomach ulcers, and colitis. In an individual with one of these diseases, a particular part of the body (respiratory system, skin, stomach, or large intestine) is vulnerable to stress. Pressure from the environment of any sort causes these organs to react with symptoms and a spiraling circle of psychosomatic disease may result.

If we knew more about the way psychological problems become expressed as bodily symptoms, perhaps we could better advise parents and help them to prevent these patterns from developing in their children. This is not to say that we could prevent stress. Growing up is bound to be a stressful process, and every child is burdened with a set of conflicts which must be handled. The best we can do is understand the inevitability of stress in a growing child, and look for ways in which to help him or her cope with it which will warp neither his personality nor his body.

The parents' ability to shape a child's behavior is limited by individual differences in his endowment, and these differences are present at birth. At birth, we see one infant who overreacts to every noise or stimulus—starting visibly, crying out, changing color, spitting up, and having a bowel movement—all as part of a reaction to a single stimulus. Another infant will react to the same stimulus by lying quietly in his crib, his eyes widening, face alerting, color paling, and bodily activity reduced to a minimum, as he seems to conserve all his energy in order to pay attention to the stimulus. These are both normal reactions, at different ends of a spectrum. The involvement of the infant's whole body is apparent in each of these reactions. Even at this stage of development, it is obvious that his attention and psychological mechanisms are intimately tied to his physiological reactions. As he gets older, the physiological reactions in his body may appear less connected to his personality. This lack of connection is more apparent than real, for there are well-defined *psychophysiological* (mind-body) differences in reactivity among individuals of all ages. A stressful environment will reinforce certain physiological patterns as the infant tries to handle his stress. The mechanisms which he uses will differ markedly from those that another infant may use. For instance, one infant may resort to crying—insistently and for long periods—as a way of shutting out the tension of an overwrought mother. Another may begin to withdraw into more and more sleep. Both mechanisms can be used as ways of coping with stress which might otherwise overload the baby's system. So this reaction may become the pattern which each child falls back on whenever he is under stress. As he grows, he may outgrow this pattern or it may survive in the kind of bodily reaction he has to pressure from the outside—the first kind of person reacting with anger, flushing, and other symptoms of violent reaction all on the surface, whereas the second person may become quieter, more withdrawn, pale, and suffering internally but showing little of it to the outside world. These two infants are bound to grow up as very different kinds of people. Although the second type may be an easier one for others to live with, the first person may suffer less.

Although parents cannot change these individual differences, they can control their own reactions to their child's behavior. Often an eager or anxious parent will focus his attention on and overemphasize a normal developmental pattern. Parental anxiety can center around a routine behavioral event, such as thumb-sucking, in itself of no import, and reinforce it until it is a problem. All babies suck their thumbs as they grow, and will give up sucking in time as their interest in other pleasures increases. But, a parent who is concerned with this sucking may try to stop it. In his or her effort to stop the thumb-sucking, he or she increases the baby's frustration. He or she creates tension for the infant whose only way of relieving tension may be to suck his thumb. So the parents' efforts end up reinforcing the very symptom they are trying to relieve, and the child begins to use the physical act to elicit a predictable parental response, to express a feeling, or to let off tension.

As another example, spitting up milk after feedings is common in infants. Since it is objectionable to parents, it is hard for them to see that it could become pleasurable for an infant. However, it can become a way of handling tension, frustration, and even appears to be satisfying for certain infants whose environments are not providing other, more satisfying experiences. Spitting up milk and chewing on it is called *rumination*. Rumination is a rare but dramatic symptom which turns up in the last half of the first year in infants who are failing to thrive. As they lie in bed between meals, they make themselves regurgitate their food, chew on it as a cow does on her cud, then swallow the milk curds again and again. This behavior has been associated with social deprivation in children and was first recognized in babies who were not getting enough stimulation from their environments.

Now we have become aware of a new group of ruminators who are not deprived of stimulation from their environment but suffer from inappropriate stimulation. The kind of stimulation they are receiving is unacceptable to them as individuals. An infant recently at Children's Hospital ruminated whenever we overstimulated her—whenever there was too much noise or confusion, or after a tense, hurried nurse had fed her. As she began to spit up, those caring for her rushed to distract her, to stimulate her so that she wouldn't lose her meal. Although these efforts staved off her symptom for the moment, she waited until she was alone, then proceeded to disgorge her entire meal—as if she'd waited to discharge all of the extra internal stress caused by the over-reaction to her. As we reconstructed the evolution of this symptom with her mother, we found that she had begun to spit up as a new baby, just as many infants do, but her spitting continued through her first 9 months of life. The family was under a great deal of stress at the time, and this baby's normal spitting up became upsetting to the mother. She overreacted to it, feeling that the baby was abnormal and might die unless she corrected this tendency to spit up. With her physician's help, she ruled out every possible cause, frantically chang-ing formulas, holding her propped after feedings, having her intestinal tract X-rayed, and so forth. After each new episode of spitting, she overreacted, and soon the baby was set in a pattern of spitting up more and more. At first, this may have been the result of overstimulation. As it became a regular pattern, it also became the baby's reaction to any stress around her. Eventually we were able to clarify the evolution of this symptom pattern, and saw it as a secondary reaction to stress. We reduced the stimulation and the anxiety around each feeding, substi-tuting an affectionate nurse to sit near her and sing quietly to her. The baby responded within a week! She not only stopped ruminating after feedings, but began to gain weight. We shared our insight into this with the mother, helped her with her own anxiety about the infant, and reunited her with her infant in unstressed feeding situations under supervision in the hospital. Now that this symptom no longer alarms the mother, she and her baby are thriving with each other. (For fur-ther discussion of feeding problems and emotional factors, see *weight problems*.)

Parents are likely to focus on a normal developmental aberration and reinforce it as a pattern at any age. They are likely to do so for unconscious reasons, and may not be aware of their role in reinforcing it until it is already a habit. Even at this point it is not too late to relieve tension for the child, and to break the vicious circle. The experience of alleviating a disturbing symptom can then become a learning experience from which the child and his parents can gather strength.

Each age has its natural stresses and it would be beyond the scope of this chapter to discuss each one. But, there are certain age-determined physical or psychological symptoms that crop up regularly. By recognizing them as normal, transitory signs of development, parents can avoid setting them up as problem areas.

### First year

Colic and crying—normally 2 to 3 hours a day in the first 3 months.
Spitting up after feedings.
Thumb- or finger-sucking.
Infrequent bowel movements in a breast-fed baby.
*Constipation*—hard bowel movements which can be softened by changes in diet.
Waking at night just prior to developmental spurts.
Feeding refusals associated with wanting to feed self at 8 months or so.

### Second year

Feeding aberrations—refusing one food after another, eating only one meal a day.
Temper tantrums and breath-holding spells.
Withholding stools and problems around toilet training—usually from too early and too much pressure to conform.

### Fourth to sixth year

*Headaches* or sick stomachs in boys just before school.
Bellyaches in girls (see *abdominal pain*).
Tics, masturbation, lying, stealing, fears, and nightmares, especially in boys as they develop aggressive feelings which they can't handle during the day.

### Latency period

Overreaction to illness, to injury.
Using illness to substitute for school phobia.
Constipation.
Occasional bed-wetting during illness or hospitalization.
Headaches due to tension.

Lack of appetite.

Overeating.

Delayed appearance of menstruation (see *adolescence*).

Concern about body image, associated with early or delayed development.

Many of the symptoms named above are likely to be expressed somewhere along the way and could become of concern to the child as he develops. If parents add their own overreaction, they are redoubling anxiety in the child about his own symptom. He might be able to handle his concern, but not both his and his parents'. If parents block communication by, for example, being overly strict or punitive, the child may settle on the physical complaint as a safe way of getting attention or otherwise dealing with the adult.

As the child expresses his concern about a symptom, there is a fine line between the possibility of the parents' overlooking a possibly serious disorder or neglecting the child's genuine needs or, on the other hand, taking it too seriously and emphasizing its value in his mind. When he has a pain, it must be taken seriously enough for the parents to make sure it isn't serious. They then can reassure the child, both by their attitude and by their having checked it out, that he needn't be overconcerned either. If it is ignored, the child may need to redouble his efforts or subconsciously change to a subtler form of bid for the parents' attention.

When symptoms are occurring frequently, and are obvious bids for parental attention, they should become a red flag, indicating that there are other underlying problems. I am personally wary of using Band-Aids, aspirin, or harmless pills to alleviate such symptoms. I think they too easily become crutches for both parents and child and really don't help them face up to the problem. If the child needs a symptom to express his conflicts, he needs a parent's solid attention to his worries. Giving a child an aspirin for a headache which is caused by the tension of facing school is dodging the underlying issue. If the mother allows him to lie down or to stay home from school, she adds reinforcement to his problem. Since his real problem is that of dealing with his anxiety about leaving home and handling the adjustment to schoolwork, to teachers, to peers, a parent who wants to help must look beyond the headache. If she dodges her opportunity to examine the underlying anxiety about separating from her, about facing responsibility, she is contributing to his problem in growing up, and she is tightening the attachment bonds which are difficult enough for him to loosen. If she could talk to him about the reasons for his anxiety over separation and school, she might expect the headaches to decrease. Not talking to him directly is as bad as ignoring a symptom in the hope that it will go away. Physicians, too, dodge their responsibility to help parents and children by such advice as, "He'll grow out of it." Parents can usually look behind the symptom to reasons for anxiety, and then interpret them to the child. This will not only bring the underlying worries to a level of consciousness where both can deal with them, but it will also demonstrate to the child that his parents care, understand, and want to help.

Although direct questioning is not likely to uncover the real reasons for a child's anxiety or distress, when a mother hits upon the right area as she talks with him, it is obvious. Children let you know by a facial sign or a visible change in attitude when a sore spot is touched upon. They may relax and smile, or they may turn away or change the subject. For example, fear of going to school may be expressed directly in words or as a physical complaint like belly pain in the morning. Commonly, it is a combination of anxiety about growing up, coupled with fears about what might happen while he is away at school. A mother or father can approach these feelings and encourage a child to talk by saying such things as: "I think you are worried about going to school. Maybe you are upset by your teacher, and maybe by the other children. But I really think you just hate to leave home and me. It is hard to grow up, but you are getting bigger and I must help you become a big, independent boy"; or, "Maybe you are worried about what will happen to me while you are gone. Nothing will happen. It is really up to me to take care of myself—not up to you. Perhaps the reason you worry about me is that you sometimes wish something would happen to me. All children get angry with their parents and wish that something bad would happen. But wishing at times like that won't make it come true, and you don't need to be afraid of your wishes. Maybe this is why you won't go to school sometimes." If the child listens, but changes the subject afterward, the mother can suspect that she has hit the nail on the head. And such an understanding interpretation for a child may help him understand himself. The two techniques, attentive listening and helping him to understand his reasons for a symptom, are effective in many, many instances—especially in normally developing children. They are extensions of good open communication between parent and child, and are important as such.

Another typical complaint with emotional implications is the "stomachache," that is, a pain in the belly. Many little girls in the 4- to 6-year-old age range have these. Whether they know that their mothers have bellyaches, too, or whether they associate the belly with memories of seeing their mother pregnant, the importance of the belly for women seems firmly fixed in little girls' minds. Unconsciously, it may become a way of identifying with older females. At any rate, many little girls in this age group go through a period of having bellyaches. As soon as they complain, the symptom is one which makes most mothers prick up their ears, and they are taken seriously. There must be many other bids for attention that go unnoticed because they don't strike such a sympathetic chord in the parent. Soon, the bellyache may become fixed as a means of complaint or relieving tension, and the severity and frequency are likely to increase. At this point, the parent must first be certain that there is no real pathology present. Then, she can treat the reason for her child's bellyaches. She has three choices— to ignore the complaint and hope it will disappear; to offer pills (for example, aspirin); or to pay appropriate attention to the symptom and treat the bid for attention. There are three ways a parent can check for serious physical causes: (1) checking on bowel movements for constipation, mucus, or blood which might reflect gastrointestinal problems; (2) having a urinalysis done to rule out kidney problems; and (3) gently but firmly palpating the belly for localized pain at the time of the bellyache. (See *abdominal pain.*) If all of these are normal, a mother can feel pretty confident that there is no organic disease. Attention, devoid of anxiety, can avert psychosomatic pathology in many children. Implicit in attention is understanding, as well as assurance that pain need not be frightening. As we all know, pain is largely made up of fear, and if a child can understand that pain need not be feared, he can accept it, as adults can. A pill for each pain becomes a crutch which is nowhere as effective as this kind of understanding. It may be easier at the time, and may even be effective *at the time*, but we have become aware from our adolescents that we have set the stage for "pill-popping" by our tendencies as parents to use pills instead of parenting.

In addition to recognizing fears and tension behind complaints without physiological causes, parents should also be aware that any illness can be reinforced by anxiety. For example, croup (see *croup and laryngitis*) is an acute difficulty in breathing and is a common complication of *colds* in small children. It always comes on suddenly, usually in the middle of the night. The child is acutely hoarse and breathes in with a loud, croaking noise. As a result of this trouble in breathing, he becomes frightened. Since the difficulty is located in the larynx (or voice box) and is due to a swelling of the tissues which then interfere with the size of his airway, there is less air coming into his lungs. As he panics, his need for oxygen increases, he begins to breathe more shallowly and rapidly. The tension brings about a spasm of the larynx which acts to cut down the size of the airway further. Steam is a specific antidote which both relaxes the spasm and reduces the tissue swelling, so it quickly facilitates the passage of air by the partially obstructed airway. If parents can respond to the child's anxiety with reassurance, calming and comforting him, and sitting with him in a room cloudy with steam, 95 percent of croup can be alleviated quickly and at home. If, on the other hand, their anxiety adds to the baby's own, the spasm of his larynx will increase with his fear, and emergency hospitalization may become necessary. Unfortunately, hospital experience may frighten him further, and as a last resort, surgery may become necessary to relieve the obstructed airway. So it is urgent that a parent try to protect her child from serious complications by dealing with her own anxiety, rather than transmitting it to the child.

"Inherited" psychosomatic disorders are even more likely to arouse anxiety in parents. If a parent has had a problem with a particular disease or symptom, it is very likely that he or she will reinforce it if it occurs in his or her child. For example, a child with his first attack of *asthma* is likely to be frightened by his inability to breathe properly. If the father (who has allergies, has had asthma, and knows how frightening it is) becomes excited, overreacts, and transmits his own anxiety, the child's problems are magnified. The physical component of an *allergy* is inheritable, and we are not in any way denying this inherited tendency. But the organic (physical) disorder may quickly be aggravated by overattention. In some cases, anxiety interferes with a parent's capacity to use simple, effective remedies. We have seen many allergic parents who, in denying their anxiety about asthma, can't hear us when we suggest that ridding a house of a cat or of feather pillows might help cut down the allergens in the household for the child. They wait too long before they give medication to break up a frightening cycle for the child—wait because they keep hoping the wheezing will disappear. As a child's tension builds up, it is expressed in more labored breathing, and there becomes less and less likelihood of his being able to break the cycle easily. Over a period of time, such a disease becomes a way of expressing all anxiety. We see a 3- or 4-year-old child wheezing actively as he watches his mother's anxious face. When the parent leaves the room, and a more objective nurse or physician takes over, the child's anxiety and wheezing subside. This is not a magical form of medical intervention, nor even a difficult one to understand. At the point where the disease or symptom is fixed as the child's way of working out tensions, and simple forms of treatment do not suffice, we would urge the parents to seek professional help.

While not the major thrust of this chapter, the same issues arise in any chronic illness such as *cystic fibrosis,* ulcerative colitis (see *colitis, ulcerative*), *cerebral palsy, leukemia,* hyperactivity syndrome, or mental retardation (see *developmental disabilities*). The severity of symptoms in any handicapping condition is affected by the child's feelings, and these symptoms in turn have an effect on his feelings. How to deal compassionately with the real discomforts and limitations and at the same time foster independence and normal development are problems for every parent. Parents need support through such trying experiences.

In summary, symptoms such as those outlined above are not "faked" by the child, nor does it help to think of them as weakness on the child's part. Trying to shame or punish him to give them up is likely to work the wrong way—to reinforce them—for such symptoms usually arise as a way of coping with tension from other sources, tension which often is not obvious to the parent. Many of the tensions are based on normal stresses of growing up. If parents' concern centers attention or anxiety on the symptom, it becomes set as a "habit" pattern used instead of words to express feelings. Such habits cannot be given up by the child at will.

As we said earlier, a parent's first responsibility is to check out the symptom, to make sure there is no serious physiological cause. Then, the parent's role is to evaluate and understand the reasons behind the symptom. If the child is functioning well in other areas of his life, and there appears to be no real reason for concern about his development in general, the best rule may be to wait and see whether he won't give up the symptom as he masters the next stage of development. If, on the other hand, he seems locked in the habit, and it is one which is serious enough to interfere with his present or future adjustment, there are at least three courses open to parents. The first is to try to let up on the other pressures in his life, to help him in other areas of adjustment, to encourage him and support him, to give him a better image of his strengths. The second is to attempt to look beyond the symptom to the conflicts behind it. This is harder, and there are many reasons why parents cannot always understand a child. For example, they may be blinded to his conflicts for their own reasons, since his conflicts touch on their problems, too, and they may find it particularly hard to admit that he has any problems at all. One of the commonest sources of problems in a child is tension between parents. As soon as they admit to a difficulty in the child, they begin to blame each other for it. Of course, this increases the family tension and adds to the child's problem. One of the most difficult things to do at a time like this is to face it squarely and work together to solve it. We have spoken of some of the ways in which a parent can put into words his or her understanding of the reasons behind the child's conflict, uncovering them for the child, and thereby helping him both to understand himself and to feel understood by his parents.

When these efforts are not enough, or when the child may need to keep his parents out and cannot respond to their efforts, the third course open to parents is to seek outside help. Help can be in the form of an understanding teacher, friend, physician, or guidance counselor.

A physician who is interested in the total child and his problems can be of invaluable help both in prevention and cure. Obtaining this kind of help is not always easy in this age of superspecialization, but it is surely worth seeking a physician who can work with the whole family. A pediatrician or family doctor may be such a person. The first step in incorporating a doctor's help is that of establishing an open, confident, working relationship with him. Bare your concerns and fears, and seek his advice in putting them into perspective. As the child grows, see that he, too, develops a positive, trusting relationship with the doctor. He can act as an objective third party and confidant for the child. He can make observations, see beneath the symptom to the reasons behind it, and even interpret his insights directly to the child. If there is a trusting relationship built up, all of this will mean a great deal to the sick child. If he can have a direct relationship with the physician, not through his parents, this relationship may be even more effective in breaking the vicious circles of psychosomatic symptoms and disease. It is always impressive to see the real relief with which a small child greets the doctor who comes to "fix him," while his anxious parents stand by. A 6-year-old looked at his doctor one day, as he stopped wheezing after a shot of adrenalin, and said, "If you'd been here sooner, I'd never have been wheezing." This kind of trust is worth a great deal of pediatric time and effort.

A physician who knows the family can be of real help to parents at such a time. Unfortunately many practitioners do not feel adequate to the task of giving advice, and hide behind "being too busy," or reassuring parents "that he'll grow out of it," when they know better. We

would urge concerned parents to ask the doctor for a special consultation time, to ask for his counsel as a concerned, understanding person.
If this help is not enough toward remedying the problem, ask him for a
consultation with a therapist who knows children's problems. If you
are in a medical center, ask for a psychiatric or psychological evaluation. On the strength of this, the child's problems may be uncovered so
that you, yourself, can help him with them. If not, seek psychiatric
help. The sooner this can be done, the less his problems have a chance
to become ingrained, and the more amenable they are to treatment.
Everyone in the family will profit, and after the initial difficulties of
facing up to treatment are overcome, the rewards begin to be apparent
to the child and those around him.

A psychiatric center with expertise in child guidance may not be
easily available, although they are more and more widespread each
year. Their waiting lists are long, and it may not be easy to find the
help you seek. As a citizen this situation should concern you. As a
wealthy nation we should be able to do better at prices every family
can afford. If you are in need of advice or guidance, ask your family
doctor or pediatrician to refer you to the nearest center. You must then
apply in person. You will be accepted by a screening person, most
often a social service worker. She will then help you obtain the needed
evaluation and therapy.

The psychiatrically trained social worker will see both parents to
gather information and to continue to work with you as the child's
evaluation and therapy continue. The information and advice about
the child will come to you within the context of your work with her. In
this kind of teamwork, it is advisable to have separate counselors for
the parents and child. Then, the child can feel his therapist is his own
and not allied with you against him. These individual relationships
may seem frustrating and burdensome when you want to talk directly
to the therapist, but we have found in most cases over the years that
children need to feel the freedom of having an individual to work with
who is all their own.

In a child guidance center, the child is evaluated by two trained
specialists. First, a clinical psychologist evaluates him in test situations
(such as Stanford Binet for an IQ, Thematic Apperception Tests for
freer kinds of associations, personality tests such as the Rorschach)
and comes away with a set of standard evaluations which help assess
the child's way of functioning in his world. The child psychiatrist will
then see him in several play-therapy sessions to evaluate his capacity
for relating to other people and to understand his problems within the

context of his total personality. The psychiatrist will collect all of the evaluation data and make a judgment for the team about the depth of the child's problems and, if psychiatric help is indicated, what kind of therapy is indicated and available. At the end of the diagnostic session, he should be ready to talk with the parents.

There are several variations on the theme of evaluation as we have described it. Sometimes one person will combine the different roles mentioned. The kind or kinds of psychotherapy recommended may vary. For some children one-to-one play sessions will be used. For others more active approaches in groups involving physical skills, confidence building, self-defence, and so forth—are employed. One noteworthy program in the Boston area is The Academy of Physical and Social Development, Newton Center, Mass. 02159.

One always wonders about the quality of a guidance center and a therapist. Seeking guidance, trusting oneself and one's child to someone else are such difficult steps that the inner resistance to them makes objective judgment very difficult. It is hard enough to accept the need for help, and you are bound to have a healthy kind of resistance which clouds your judgment of the effectiveness of a therapeutic team. Coupled with a parent's or parents' resistance is that of the child. It is hard for a child to understand what a psychiatrist does, and why he needs to see one. He should certainly be prepared for it ahead of time, with an explanation that includes relief for whatever troubles he is aware of. But usually he won't see the need for relief, and if he does, will not understand that a "mind" doctor can offer it. You as parents must help him, and, while he is in therapy, your own conviction that this course is necessary must shore up his ambivalence and resistance.

How do you judge a good therapeutic situation? The reputation of a therapeutic institution or individual therapist is always available, most often via members of the medical community, or from other parents. Some physicians are doubtful about the effectiveness of psychiatric therapy themselves, and their evaluation will be clouded by this, but you can ascertain the medical reputation of the therapeutic team if you persist and check around. Other parents who have sought and found help can be of supportive and informative value to you. Then, as your diagnostic evaluations progress, you can begin to evaluate them from the kinds of questions, perceptions you receive, and the relationships which are made with you as a family. When a therapeutic team sees your problems in much the same way that you do, when they assess the child as you have, and then offer insight into dimensions of the problem which have not yet occurred to you, but which seem to fit, you may be fairly certain that their efforts will be beneficial. If, on the other hand, their assessment is too quick, too superficial, and their solutions too pat and easy, you might be on your guard. Psychiatric therapy is not easy nor is it superficial if it is going to help. Pay attention to your own reactions. You should have a sense of trusting the therapist. You should understand what is happening. Your questions and concerns should be treated with dignity and respect. You should begin to see results in the child, but you will have to be patient. By the time parents are willing to seek guidance, they are aware that their problems are not superficial, not easily solved. If it is worth the seeking, it is worth the waiting lists, the anguish of uncovering old conflicts, or of turning over your child and his problems to another, and worth investing your trust and patience to achieve the goal of a healthy child for the future.

*T. Berry Brazelton, M.D.*

# 5

## Caring for the Sick Child at Home

In these days of high medical costs and a shortage of doctors, more responsibility for judging the need for expert care and for carrying out medical instructions may well be required of parents. The mystique that traditionally surrounded medical knowledge is gradually disappearing. Parents are asking to be told what symptoms mean, what the treatment or medicines are expected to accomplish, and what side effects or complications they may expect. Sometimes parents have felt left out of the decisions that were being made about their child's care and treatment because of their own lack of knowledge about medical techniques. At other times, parents become so dependent upon the doctor's opinion and advice that they are unable to exercise any initiative of their own. Times are changing; parents are becoming much more sophisticated about diseases and medical techniques. Many parents want and should be able to use their own common sense in handling minor illnesses, and can do so with a few guides.

These pages are intended to help parents to cope with the general problems of common, everyday illnesses of children in their own homes. Naturally, parents are anxious and uncertain when taking care of a sick child for the first time. That is to be expected. However, confidence increases as they learn to master techniques and judge medical situations. This confidence should result from advice and guidance received from experts, rather than from an equally inexperienced friend. These suggestions are intended to help parents evaluate illness within their families and learn how to cope with it both before and after they call the doctor.

Many parents are acquainted with the rare illnesses of children around which fund-raising drives are organized for research and treatment. Yet even the onset of a common physical illness in their child at home is often a harrowing experience, especially to the new parent. Minor illnesses, especially *infections,* are part of growing up. No child is totally immune by nature and no parent is capable of preventing all infections. Actually, children need to develop immunity over the years through the process of being exposed to common germs. Very seldom is a child deliberately exposed to an illness. Most of the time, the person from whom an infection is "caught" did not yet show symptoms of illness when he was actually transmitting germs. Therefore, parents should not feel guilty about baby's first cold. Rather they should concentrate on helping the baby get well and learning from the experience.

## Attitudes toward illness

When caring for a sick child, it is wise to be as matter-of-fact about your actions as you can so that you won't communicate your own fears and uncertainties. Don't look for a magic pill to pop into a child's mouth to make it all go away. Most of the "magic" is in your own calm attitude, in the giving of yourself, and the comfort you bring your child when you ease his or her symptoms. Children who are used to taking a pill for everything unpleasant may look for a pill to change life's unpleasantness in later years.

Approach the temperature taking, fever control, or giving of medicine as you would an ordinary event, like dressing a child for play or getting him off to school. Try not to bribe, coax, or cajole. Children can quickly turn anxiety on the part of a parent into the promise of a new bike or doll outfit. The things you do for him may be different from when he is well. He should be told that they may be unpleasant but are being done to make him well. Expect his cooperation and give him an extra hug to show your love as well as your appreciation that he lived up to your expectations. But don't let him turn his cooperation into a sword that he holds over your head until you give in to a special whim. If brother's Peanuts game was forbidden before he became ill, then it should remain so during his illness, unless brother wishes to let him play with it. If sister's watercolors are her special prized possession, help him respect her pride in ownership. Don't let him have everything he wants just because he is sick. He may feel awful, but he'll feel even worse if he is constantly having to think up little things to ask for to make him happy.

Acute illnesses don't often turn into chronic, long-term illnesses, but they may. If this does happen, the initial attitudes parents assume can be long lasting. If parents can maintain the same discipline with love that they had before the acute illness, they and the sick child can face chronic illness far better if it should arise. The whiny, indulged child is in no position to help with his rehabilitation and is a most unhappy child.

If your attitude is one of too much indulgence, the child feels that his illness must be serious because his parents are not exercising the same discipline that they did prior to his sickness. Think of it. If you as an adult were suddenly allowed to have everything you wanted, you would feel that it was because you were not going to be around for very long—that nothing mattered because you were going to die.

However, parents must also realize that children (and adults, too) regress when they are ill. The toilet-trained toddler will often start wetting. The child who can brush his own teeth may want help or want it done for him. He may want you to stay and play with him when he has never asked for it before. Try to understand that when he is well, he'll return to his normal routine. So give him extra love and attention, give him as much of yourself as you can while he is ill. Take his backsliding in stride. The line between indulgence and tolerance of regression is a fine one, which parents must find for themselves.

## Mobilizing
## for illness

When a child is ill, many small tasks are added to the daily routine. A great deal of time goes into caring for the sick child, even throughout the night. These pages will point out the quickest and simplest ways to deal with the child's care. Parents should give thought at the start of an illness to the following:

1. Cut out unnecessary household tasks. The time saved is better spent reading, talking, or playing games with the child.

2. Share as many household chores as possible with other members of the family. Fathers are able to read a story; a sister or brother may amuse the sick child or assist with bed making, dishes, and so forth. If everybody helps during the daytime, Mother's and Dad's night shift won't be so burdensome.

3. The mother should plan to get some rest during the daytime. (Even a short nap while the child sleeps can be a lifesaver.)

4. Ask neighbors and friends to help with shopping, baby-sitting, and so forth. Don't wait until Mother is exhausted before asking for help. Friends usually are pleased to be able to be of assistance and parents can reciprocate when their turn comes.

## General signs
## of illness

You are not likely to miss the signs of an acute illness. Usually these symptoms develop rather quickly, and even though your child is an infant and cannot complain about what "feels bad," you will be able to recognize that he is off key. The early signs generally grow more specific within a few hours or they may disappear altogether. Stay calm and sort out the clues your child is giving you.

*General appearance:* He may just not look right to you. His face may be flushed, hot, and dry. He may be sweating profusely. He may just look pale or his skin may be cold. He may become unusually quiet or just look unhappy.

*Personality or behavior changes:* The child may become fussy, whiny, and cranky at times when he's usually happy. He may begin to complain about not feeling well. He may be drowsy or sleepy when it's not his usual nap- or bedtime.

*Loss of appetite:* Even infants' appetites vary as do adults', so a baby who is not sick may refuse food for a meal or two. However, his usual desire for nourishment should return after a couple of poorly taken feedings. If it doesn't, this often signals some underlying discomfort of illness.

If your child exhibits any of these vague symptoms, check to be sure he is lightly clothed and dry. Let him rest quietly in his room or on the sofa. He may well take a nap. Give him liquids in small quantities, such as drinks of fruit juice. If his skin feels hot or his cheeks are flushed, take his temperature. If he has a temperature elevation of 100.5° to 101.5° you may want to remove most of his clothing to allow the heat to leave his body. An ordinary sponge bath may make him more comfortable. Check his temperature again in an hour to see which way it is going, and start fever control (see below) if it is climbing toward a dangerous level. If these symptoms persist for more than a few hours, the chances are that more specific signs of acute illness will soon show themselves. Cuddle the child a little to let him know you understand that he doesn't feel well, but let him know also by your calm carrying out of these comfort measures that you are able to help. Many times the child experiences a few hours of feeling unwell, but then his body defenses come to the fore and he feels better later on in the day.

## Caring for the sick child: the most common questions

When children become ill, parents have many questions. They want to know whether to keep him in bed or let him go out and play, whether to take him to the grocery store and so forth. We'll take these questions one at a time and discuss them. There are no pat answers, because situations may differ within individual families and with each child within these families. However, these guidelines should help parents make informed decisions.

*Question:* Should I keep my child in bed during an illness?

*Answer:* During short-term acute illnesses a child usually paces himself pretty well. If he has a fever or pain, he is likely to want to stay in bed or on a sofa or lounge chair. He should be near enough to his mother (or father) to call or signal for help, and also to save the parent from constantly running up and down steps to watch and care for him. If he is more content playing quietly on the floor, avoid the hassle and let him do so. Parents know their children and usually choose the best place for them. Unless the doctor says he must stay in bed, the sick child can go to the bathroom rather than use a bedpan or a urinal. If he feels up to it, he may join the family at mealtime. He has already shared his germs with the rest of the family before his illness became symptomatic, so there is no need to ostracize him. Only in very specific instances must his dishes and so forth be kept separate, but rarely (see **chicken pox**) is he more of a hazard to the family at the table than he is anywhere else in the house.

If he says he wants to stay in bed, let him do so. He probably prefers the quiet of his room and feels ill enough to want to be away from the confusion of the family mainstream. He'll probably get more rest. On the other hand, if staying in bed feels strange to the child and means constant demands for extra attention, a parent should feel no guilt about relocating the sick child in a convenient place where he can be more easily cared for. If he is running a fever, he'll probably be more comfortable if he is wearing pajamas or clothes that can be changed frequently when they become sweaty. As he begins to recover, it is wise to dress him in his usual playclothes. Then he doesn't need covers over him when he's dressed, and this saves on laundry.

If he feels up to it, he may safely play anywhere in the house. Don't believe the old wives' tale that drafts and cool air will necessarily expose the child to further illness. We have no proof either way. But if you are worried about the temperature in the room, dress him as you would want to be dressed in the same environment.

*Question:* How shall I occupy my child's time when he is sick?

*Answer:* Ingenuity and imagination are needed to keep a child occupied, especially if he is alone during the day, and has no brothers or sisters with whom to play checkers or other games. Cover the lounge chair or divan with a large piece of plastic (a tablecloth works perfectly). Draw up a table so that there is a place to put his playthings and food. Put a wastebasket nearby and a box of tissues to wipe up spills or noses. Leave a small glass of fluid with him which can be sipped as needed. Decide with the child what TV shows he can watch and be prepared to monitor television viewing. Don't expect the picture tube to fulfill his needs for companionship and play while he's ill. Let him clip pictures out of magazines and paste them onto paper—

paper towels or opened out paper sacks make good book pages if nothing else is available. Paper dolls, crayons, clay, finger paints, and countless other playthings can provide quiet occupations for children. Improvised equipment can range from pieces of straw or old thread spools strung on twine to trains made of round cereal boxes pasted to flat boxes with button wheels. Covering the gamut of activity would take a whole chapter of this book. So use your imagination. The time spent in preparing makeshift toys for the child can reap tremendous rewards in the sharing of the finished product and the happiness of a busy sick child. (See The Boston Children's Medical Center publication *What to Do When "There's Nothing to Do"* [New York: Dell, 1972] for more ideas.)

*Question:* May I let my child go outdoors when he's sick?

*Answer:* Although there are many superstitions about keeping a child indoors, we see no reason why on a warm day he can't be outside for brief periods in quiet activities if he feels up to it, assuming he can be kept away from others, even if he has a mild fever.

*Question:* Is it harmful to take my child to the doctor when he is sick with fever or pain?

*Answer:* Even when winter winds blow, most parents have no objection to taking their children out to the doctor's office or clinic when his fever is 102°, or less. But when the temperature is 103° or more, they have real doubts. They want to have a medical opinion about the child's condition, but they have been told that if the child is exposed to draft, he will develop pneumonia or some other dread disease. This is far from the truth.

If a child's fever is in the range of 104° to 106°, or if he's in pain, he may need the additional facilities available in a medical center or doctor's office; for example, a blood test or an X-ray and which are not available at home. After reading the section below on fever control, you will realize that the major goal is to prevent the fever from climbing higher. It is highly unlikely that pneumonia or other complications will result if the following instructions are carried out: (1) call your doctor and arrange to meet him in a medical center or his office; (2) wrap your child in his nightclothes, plus one outside covering—his bathrobe or a warm blanket will do; (3) do *not* run down and turn the heater on in the car. If you yourself are uncomfortable, put on extra clothing yourself. Turning on the heater can raise the temperature in the car to over 90°. You can be sure that this will raise your child's already high fever further into the dangerous zone. Let the car remain cool; you may be surprised to find that when you reach the doctor's office the child will be two or three degrees cooler than when you left home. Some doctors do not agree that fever, even in the danger zone, needs to be treated, but they all agree that putting the child into an overheated environment (like a car with the heater blasting) will cause more harm than good. If the doctor does come to your home to see your sick child, it is more often done because of a situation such as a sick parent or lack of facilities to transport the patient than because of the severity of the child's illness. In many communities the police or private ambulances will transport the child.

*Question:* What should I feed my child when he is sick?

*Answer:* If your child is *vomiting* and has pain in his stomach (his belly), or has *diarrhea,* he should not be given any solid food. He should stick to a clear liquid diet. With any illness, he will rarely have his usual appetite. If your child does not have vomiting or diarrhea, try to choose foods which will be nutritious and supply his body with extra energy.

*Solid foods*

Most children enjoy chicken, eggs, boiled or baked potato, cereal, soup, toast, vegetable, hamburg, jellied salad, bananas, or other fresh or canned fruit. For desserts they can be tempted with applesauce, gelatin dessert, pudding, custard, ice cream, or sherbet. Add a colorful touch with an orange section or cherry on top. Peanut butter sandwiches or marshmallow with grated carrots and raisins may be your child's sole choice of solid food for several days. Try to balance this with other nutritious foods or liquids, but do not be upset if you can't. Natural appetite will return when the child recovers.

Give small amounts of food at a time. It is better to give two tablespoons, leaving him surprised and asking for more, than to kill his appetite with an excessive amount of food. Give in-between snacks of fruit or liquid even if he is eating fairly well. These extras will give extra energy, prevent constipation, and help control fever.

*Fluids*

Children with *infections* accompanied by fever are not likely to want solid foods. However, they do need lots of fluid in order to replace moisture lost when they perspire. Offer the child something to drink every half hour while he is awake. Leave a small glass of fluid and remind him to take a small sip frequently. As with solid foods, prepare small amounts of a given drink and give it in a small juice glass. Let him choose from whatever liquids you may have at home. The following are good sources of fluid:

Water
Fruit juices
Milk
Floats
Milk shakes
Ice cream
Sherbet
Parfaits
Eggnog

Weak tea
Tonic or pop with the fizz removed
   (Add a few tablespoons of warm water or a teaspoon of
   sugar to remove the carbonation.)
Gelatin desserts
Soup

If you have a blender, check your blender recipes for intriguing drinks.

Sometimes a few tricks are needed to entice a child to drink as much as he needs. (1) Give him liquids from a demitasse or long-handled spoon. (2) Vary the drinks. (3) Let him suck on cracked ice chips. (4) Let him use a small shot glass or one with a picture of a cartoon character. (5) Try a straw for sipping. (6) Offer lollipops—they make him thirsty. (7) Make popsicles on toothpicks (in the ice tray) with fruit juices, sweetened fruit-flavored drinks, or gelatin water. (8) Try fresh or canned fruits such as oranges, watermelon, peaches, pears, applesauce, and many others; they contain a lot of liquid. (9) Give him a small, plain, salted cracker occasionally. The salt also makes him thirsty. (10) If your child has recently been weaned from the bottle, you may find that you will have to give it back, especially if he has completely stopped taking any fluids for a period of 6 to 8 hours. Remember, children tend to regress in development during illness and you can help him to give the bottle up again when he is well.

Remember to brush a sick child's teeth several times a day or have him rinse his mouth between meals when he is having a lot of fruit liquids. If he is too sick to brush or rinse, wet all the surfaces of his teeth with a soft washcloth or cotton-tipped swab several times a day.

*Question:* What is fever and what causes it?

*Answer:* Normally, the temperature of the body ranges from 97° to 100.5°. Temperatures above this range are called "fever," and temperatures below 97° are called "subnormal." Fever is one of the most common symptoms of illness in children, and, as well as being a symptom, the fever itself can cause problems. However, some children who have serious illnesses do not have fever at all.

Changes in body temperature occur for several reasons: activity, time of day, age, infection, temperature of the environment, and individual variations. Let's discuss each of these in detail.

## Activity

Strenuous exercise in play or work pushes the temperature toward the upper normal range. More food is burned up by the body to produce the energy needed for the increased activity, thus producing heat.

## Time of day

The body is usually cooler in the mornings, presumably because of the decrease in activity during sleep. The temperature rises later in the afternoon when the body is at peak activity.

## Age

The temperature center in the brain is not completely developed in infants and small children. Their temperatures can shoot up into the dangerous range much faster than those of older children and adults. This is why it is important to check the feverish baby's temperature more frequently. Remember—temperature is only one indicator of illness. If your child seems ill, even if he does not have a fever, you may want to call the doctor anyway.

## Infection

Fever can be a response of the body to *infection.* The degree of fever the child exhibits does not necessarily indicate the seriousness of an illness. A fever of 104° may be alarming, yet some children have this amount of fever with a minor ailment. Some children run higher fevers than others.

*Temperature of the Environment*

Children especially, but adults also, respond to the temperature of the room or outdoor air. We all recognize this fact by putting on extra clothing in cold weather and wearing light apparel when it is hot. However, when a child has a fever, he and his skin are giving off heat. Bundling him up only keeps the heat around his body and makes him even hotter.

*Individual variations*

Certain individuals seem to have consistently lower normal temperatures. This is an individual variation and is of no real significance.

*Question:* How do I know if my child has a fever?

*Answer:* It is a good idea to check the forehead and take the temperature of any child who doesn't feel well, is shivering, looks or acts sick, or has a specific complaint such as a sore throat. The child who has a fever is usually warm to the touch, although you will sometimes find an elevated body temperature in a child whose skin feels cool. A thermometer reading of above 100.5° in a child who is quiet (not overheated from physical activity) and dressed normally (not bundled up) indicates the presence of fever no matter where the temperature was taken.

*Question:* How do I take a temperature?

*Answer:* A temperature can be recorded in three ways—by rectum, by axilla (armpit), or by mouth (orally). Rectum or armpit temperatures should be taken on babies and children up to 6 or 7 years of age. Armpit temperatures should be taken when children have diarrhea. We also prefer this technique in infants to avoid injury to the rectum. The rectal thermometer can irritate the inside of the rectum and stimulate another bowel movement. The oral thermometer is the same one used for armpit temperature—the one with the thin longer shaft holding the mercury. It is marked "oral." The rectal thermometer has a stubby mercury bulb on the end and is marked "rectal." Both thermometers work the same way and give the same readings. The only reason for the different shape of the bulb on the rectal thermometer is that it allows easier insertion into the rectum.

If you are taking a temperature for the first time, you need some guidelines. Always hold it at the top, the opposite end from the bulb. Roll the thermometer between your fingers until you find the place where there is a wide silver ribbon of mercury. Usually thermometers are marked by a series of long and short lines. Between each long line there are 4 short ones. The even numbers between 94 and 106 are printed on the glass next to the long lines. Each short line represents two-tenths of one degree. There is often a red line at the 98.6 point, which is the middle of the normal temperature range previously discussed.

The column of mercury should be at or below the 95° mark before using the thermometer. Dry your hands and give yourself plenty of room to move around and stand over a bed or soft furniture as you prepare to "shake down" the mercury column. Hold the thermometer firmly at the top and shake it with a wrist-snapping motion. As you take the temperature, the mercury column will rise with the temperature of the child's body. If you have trouble with shaking down or using the thermometer, ask the nurse in the doctor's office or clinic or the visiting nurse to help you.

## *Rectal temperature*

Never leave a child alone with a rectal thermometer in place, whatever his age.

1. Shake down the rectal thermometer.

2. Grease the bulbed end with petroleum jelly taken from the jar on a piece of tissue.

3. Lay a small child across your lap face down. He's more secure this way, and you can hold him better. An older child can lie on his side on a bed with his knees slightly bent to relax his buttocks.

4. Gently put the thermometer bulb about one inch into the rectum.

5. Hold the thermometer between the index and middle fingers with the palm down so you can grasp the buttocks and hold them together with the thumb, ring, and small fingers. In this way, you can control the thermometer so that it won't come out or injure the rectum if the

child moves. If the child is especially active, hold his hips tightly against your legs with your other hand.

6. Keep the thermometer in place for 3 whole minutes if you possibly can.

7. Wipe off the petroleum jelly with the same tissue that you used to lubricate the thermometer.

8. Write down the reading. Don't hesitate to have someone else check if you are not sure of it. Reading a thermometer takes practice.

## Temperature by armpit

1. Shake down the oral thermometer.

2. Wipe one armpit dry.

3. Place the bulb end of the thermometer under the dry armpit.

4. Hold the child's elbow close to his side and place his hand on the opposite shoulder to keep the thermometer in place. If you hold the child in your arms or on your lap, you may feed him or read to him during the time you are taking the temperature.

5. Keep his arm in this position for at least 5 minutes before removing the thermometer.

6. Write down the reading.

## Oral temperature

Be sure the child is mentally and emotionally able to cooperate with an oral temperature-taking, regardless of his actual age in years. He should be able to hold the thermometer firmly between his lips without biting on the glass, thus cutting his mouth or swallowing the glass. Also, to avoid false readings, be sure he has not had a hot or cold liquid to drink within the last fifteen minutes.

1. Shake down the oral thermometer.

2. Place the mercury end under the child's tongue slightly to one side.

3. Have the child close his lips firmly to exclude air. Be sure he does not hold the thermometer with his teeth. If he wishes to hold the end of the thermometer with his fingers to keep it in place, let him do so.

4. Never leave a child alone with a thermometer in his mouth.

5. An accurate reading takes three minutes. If you find that the child's nose is so stuffy that he is opening his mouth to breathe, you will not be getting an accurate reading. In this event take his temperature by armpit or rectum.

6. Record the reading.

## Reading the thermometer

The point on the thermometer where the wide silver column of mercury ends is the temperature reading. Watch the decimals. Be sure that you know the difference between readings of one hundred point five (100.5) and one hundred and five (105.0). Jot the number down on a piece of paper. Although there are slight variations in temperature readings through the different temperature-taking methods, they are really insignificant. Normal temperature is within the 97° to 100.5° range.

## Cleaning the thermometer

1. Wash the thermometer with cold water and soap. (Hot water will crack the glass or break the thermometer.) If the thermometer is cracked, discard it. The glass will cut the child.

2. Rinse the thermometer with cold water.

3. Dry and wipe it with rubbing alcohol.

4. Shake down the thermometer and replace it in its case.

*Question:* What do I do if my child has a fever?

## Fever Control

Fever can be moderated in three ways: radiational cooling to allow excess heat to leave the body; medication; and sponge baths to increase the circulation to the skin and allow the heat to be absorbed by the cool water surrounding the child.

### Radiational cooling

If your child's temperature is between 100.5° and 103°, you can start fever control by removing some clothing so that excess heat may leave the body and disperse in the cooler air surrounding it. Night clothing or underwear should be adequate. If he has on the newer synthetic fabrics, change him into cotton clothing, which allows perspiration to be absorbed more readily, cooling him faster. If the temperature is over 103°, underpants or diapers and a short-sleeved shirt should be adequate in a comfortable room.

### Medication

Aspirin and acetaminophen are medications which reduce fever. As customarily packaged, each aspirin tablet contains 5 grains or 325 milligrams of the medicine. (Flavored children's aspirin comes in smaller doses but is not recommended because it can lead to a confusion between medication and candy.) The 5-grain tablet can be broken into halves or quarters to obtain the proper dosage for children. The rule of thumb for the dose of either drug, given every 4 hours, is 1 grain per year of life. Thus, the dose from age 4 to 6 months is ½ grain; from 6 months to 1½ years of age, 1 grain; from 1½ years to 3 years, 2 grains; from 3 to 5 years, 3 grains; from 5 to 10 years, 5 grains (or one adult aspirin); and for over 10 years, the usual adult dose of two 5-grain tablets. The larger the child, the more he needs, so you must increase the dose as the child grows. The proper dose for a 1-year-old is inadequate for a 4-year-old. If the prescribed dose does not work, do not be tempted to increase it on your own.

Because it is dispensed as a liquid, acetaminophen is perhaps easier to give to a baby or a young child. However, it is generally more expensive than ordinary aspirin. Aspirin tablets can be crushed and given straight, or with jelly or fruit. Remember that aspirin and acetaminophen taken in excess are among the most common causes of poisoning in children. (See Part 2, Chapter 8: "Accident Prevention" and Chapter 10: "Poisoning.")

If the child vomits a dose of aspirin or acetaminophen within 45 minutes, it can be repeated. If he vomits again, you can use an aspirin rectal suppository. Check with your doctor. These suppositories usually contain 5 grains of aspirin, but can be cut in halves or quarters to obtain the prescribed dose. (See the discussion of suppositories later in this chapter.)

*Sponge bath*

If your child's fever stays at or above 104° for over half an hour despite fever-reducing medicine and light clothing, a more vigorous measure—the tepid-water sponge bath—is called for.

It is important to realize that a child with this degree of fever feels something like a hiker in Death Valley. The shock of being put in icy water or rubbed with cold alcohol would make him shiver (which produces heat through rapid muscle action) and his teeth chatter. His temperature might actually climb. He would become upset and fight and struggle against the treatment. For these reasons we advise against cold-water baths or alcohol rubs in preference to a more gradual change of temperature.

Use your bathtub, Bathinette, or large basin or tub. Run hot and cold water into it until it feels comfortable to your own elbow. It will still feel cool to your child. The water should be deep enough to reach just higher than the child's waist. Leave the cold-water tap on so that a trickle of cold water keeps running into the tub. Throw two washcloths into the water along with a few floatable toys. With one dripping washcloth, sponge the entire body from face to toes. Use a brisk stroke, much like that which you would use with a whisk broom to remove lint from clothing. Your aim is to bring the blood to the surface so that the water can take out the heat from the blood vessels. When the first washcloth becomes warm, put it back into the tub and use the second one. To make the rubbing most effective, spend more time around the face, neck, the crooks of the elbows and knees, and the stomach, where the greatest concentration of blood vessels is. If the child starts to shiver, warm the water temperature a little. Try to keep him in the tub and keep up the rubbing for 20 minutes.

Then take the child out of the tub and pat him dry. Do not rub. Moisture left on the skin will evaporate and cool him down even further. Put his short-sleeved shirt and underpants or diaper back on, and take his temperature one-half hour after the bath has been completed.

Occasionally the temperature will be no less than when you began. If this is the case, another 20 minutes of bathing is necessary. Usually, the temperature starts to drop 1 or 2 degrees after the first bath. If this does not happen, you may have to keep the child in, more than out of, the tub for several hours. When a high fever appears at night, as it so often does, get set for a long siege. Many families we know have been up all night. By morning, the fever is often down, only to zoom up again the next evening. It is rare to have to spend more than two such nights, however.

*Question:* How do I know whether to call the doctor or nurse for fever?

*Answer:* Whether and when to call the doctor or nurse for fever depends on a number of considerations, including the age of the child, associated symptoms like *earache,* your experience in managing illnesses, and your doctor's own policy. We ask parents to call without fail for fever in an infant under 6 months, for fever over 103° in a child from 6 months to 2 years, and when the following symptoms are present in a child of any age, with or without fever: unusual drowsiness and loss of mental alertness (see *drowsiness, delirium, and lethargy*); labored breathing (fever alone causes breathing to be faster but not labored) (see *breathing, noisy*); or if the child looks dreadfully sick. If you are frightened by the child's appearance, you should call at any time of day or night. Also, call for temperature over 104° which you can't reduce after 4 to 6 hours of fever-control measures. If there is just fever less than 103° present with no other symptoms except general signs of illness, like decreased activity and appetite, we feel that you can generally wait for 48 to 72 hours before calling, particularly with the older child who can reliably report symptoms. If the fever persists beyond 3 days, the doctor should know about it, regardless of its cause. The younger the child, the more the doctor is likely to want to investigate the possible presence of an unsuspected ear or throat infection. (See *earache* and *throat, sore.*) When in doubt, call.

Remember, once again, that the height of the fever isn't necessarily related to the severity of the illness. Many if not most children with a temperature of 104° or even 105° have infections which are basically nondangerous. You might say that their bodies are overreacting. Children who do have serious infections usually show other symptoms such as those mentioned above.

*Question:* Why treat fever?

*Answer:* There are two reasons. Firstly, the cooling that results from the reduction of fever seems to make children feel better. Secondly, keeping the fever down can prevent the convulsions that are associated with very high fevers (usually over 104°) in some children. The tendency to have so-called *febrile seizures* is inherited. The main age of risk in susceptible children is between 1 and 3 years. After this time, they generally tolerate fever without this reaction. Following a convulsion associated with fever, the doctor must decide whether the convulsion was a simple febrile one which the child will outgrow or whether it resulted from a true epileptic condition (see *seizure disorders*) in which fever acted as a trigger. The medical treatment for each condition differs. Vigorous measures to reduce any fever are called for with the child who is in the age group of maximum risk and who has previously had a convulsion with fever. Medication, usually phenobarbital, may have to be taken daily to prevent recurrent convulsions.

There is no way of knowing whether a child is prone to febrile convulsions until he has had one. Therefore, we try to control the temperatures of all young children. Once a child is out of the age group in which febrile convulsions occur, the only ground for treating fever in a child is for comfort, which may be more important for some children than others.

Despite much research, it is not yet clear how fever functions in the body's defenses against infection. One would assume that after so many years of evolution and natural selection the febrile response, which is so characteristic of man and other mammals, must play some useful role in the body's battle against invading germs. It may someday be shown through research that we should not try to eliminate this response, at least not completely. It might be that we pay more attention to fever than it deserves.

How vigorously and long to treat fever depends on the individual situation. The height of the temperature, the age of the child, and whether or not he has previously had a convulsion with fever are all important factors. The 2-year-old with a temperature of 104° who convulsed with a previous febrile illness is one extreme. In such a case, you would want to keep on top of the situation, following carefully all fever-control steps—checking the temperature every hour, keeping him coolly dressed, giving aspirin or acetaminophen punctually every 4 hours day and night until the temperature is normal for 24 hours, and sponging as necessary. The other extreme is the school-age child who has a mildly elevated temperature, perhaps of 101.5°. In this case, you might give him medication only if he complains of being uncomfortably hot, and, after the first temperature-taking, you can usually rely on feeling his forehead to verify the fever.

*Question:* How do I get my child to take medicine?

*Answer:* Before discussing the specific techniques of getting medicine into a child, it seems wise to discuss the topic of medicine in general. Medicines are substances which are used to treat illnesses. They are intended to be given in specific doses, based on the severity of the illness and the age and weight of the patient. Medicines should be labeled with the name of the child, the name of the drug, and the instructions for giving it. In many states this is law. If it is not a law, parents should put this information on the bottle. When buying medicine, the parents should insist on safety caps which are difficult for children to open. (See Part 2, Chapter 8: "Accident Prevention" and Chapter 10: "Poisoning.")

Before giving medicine to a child, read the label to be certain that you have the right medicine and the right dose. Jot down the hour that the medicine is due and set the alarm clock for the time of the next dose. When you have prepared the medicine, approach the child with the attitude that he will take it without fussing. Tell him that the medicine is being given to make him well, something you both want. Perhaps you can tell the child a story or divert him in some other way. The job may be finished before the child knows what's going on. Be sure he is sitting on your lap or on a chair so that you can control him better and so that he will not choke. Never give him medicine when he is lying flat.

In spite of your wiles the 2-year-old will probably resist. Do not bribe him. If you do, you will have to bribe him for every other dose he requires. Be firm but not harsh or threatening. Spanking or loss of a privilege means nothing to him at the moment. You cannot continue punishment and tears and struggles with each dose of medicine. Sometimes it is wise to wrap a blanket around his arms and put the medicine in his mouth a little at a time. If he spits it out, pour it back into his mouth. Have a glass of his favorite beverage nearby to wash down the medicine. This method may seem barbaric and you may feel bad to have to use force, but most children do not require this approach more than once or twice. Once they are convinced that taking the medicine is felt to be necessary and that parents are insisting on it out of love and concern, they quite often open their mouths and swallow it, especially if a favorite "chaser" is in evidence. (Remember that no matter how much a child may resist taking medicine when sick, that same child when well may seek out the same medicines you keep in the house if they are not stored in a safe place.)

Most medicines are given the same number of hours apart in order to keep a certain level of the drug circulating in the blood. This is why a full dose should be repeated if the child spits out more than a little bit. If he vomits the whole amount within a half hour, repeat the dose. If he continues to vomit a medicine, especially if the vomiting does not merely result from his struggle against taking it, call the doctor. This may be a medicine your child's body cannot tolerate. Another drug may have to be substituted.

## To give a pill
## or tablet

Many children will surprise you by being willing to chew and swallow a pill. However, most youngsters under 5 will need to have them crushed. Capsules should not be crushed or opened, since the medicine contained in them is meant to dissolve in the stomach, not in the mouth.

1. Place the pill in the bowl of a spoon and grind it into a fine powder with the bottom of another spoon. Take time to be sure it is really crushed well; otherwise the child may refuse the medicine or pick pieces of the pill out of his mouth and get less than the required dose. If the tablet is hard to crush, place it in the bowl of a spoon with a few drops of water for an hour before you plan to use it. It will dissolve by itself.

2. Mix the crushed or dissolved tablet into a teaspoonful or less of applesauce, honey, jelly, chocolate syrup, or whatever your child prefers.

3. Follow it by a drink of water or another liquid.

Swallowing whole pills and capsules is a skill which some children find difficult to master. Have the child place the pill or capsule at the back of the tongue and concentrate on swallowing the half glass or more of liquid he takes with it. Moistening the capsule first makes it easier to swallow. As we said above, capsules should not be opened or chewed.

## To give a liquid medicine

It is a good idea to put half a dose into one spoon and the second half into another In this way, there is less chance of spilling on its way into the child's mouth, and if he pushes it away, you will know how much was lost. Mix the liquid with a heavy syrup like chocolate or honey if necessary. However, drinking the medicine down straight followed by a glass of a favorite beverage usually works best. Some cautions to be observed: (1) Don't add the liquid to a beverage; it will probably sink to the bottom or stick to the glass and the child won't get the whole dose. (2) Don't put medicine into the baby's bottle or formula. The same separation mentioned above will occur. The child may not drink the whole bottle and will lose part of the dose. (3) Don't hold the child's nose to force him to swallow. He may breathe the liquid into his lungs. Older children can hold their own noses and thereby avoid some of the unpleasant taste. If they are old enough to do this for themselves, they are old enough to swallow and breathe at the same time. Some manufacturers are now making small plastic cups with markings for 1 and 2 teaspoons and 1 tablespoon. These seem easy to use and are recommended.

## To give nose drops

Medicated nose drops are usually given to shrink the swollen *mucosa* (the membrane lining the nasal passages) at the back of the nose, thus allowing air to pass more easily. Saltwater nose drops (1 level teaspoon salt per quart of tap water) are used to dilute the mucous secretions in infants, which can then be sucked out with a nasal aspirator (see *colds*). You can give an infant nose drops by laying him on his side across your lap with his head hanging slightly over your thigh. Place the required number of drops in the lower nostril and keep his head in the hanging position for a minute or two. Turn the baby on his other side and place the drops in his other nostril. The best time for giving an infant nose drops is a half hour before feeding. This will clear the nose so that he can suck and swallow better.

Once a child reaches a few months of age, he will not stay still long enough for you to use the above technique. Children seem to develop all sorts of extra arms and legs for you to contend with when something unpleasant like putting in nose drops is concerned. Perhaps it is because they feel they won't be able to breathe if liquid is added to their already stuffed-up nostrils. If another person is present, he or she can hold the child's head and arms. If you are alone, the easiest way to put nose drops in is to sit the child on your lap facing you with his legs straddling your hips. Bend him backward so that you can hold his head firmly between your knees. Hold both his hands over his head with one of yours and with the same hand turn his head to one side, chin up. Your other hand is free to rest your fingers on the child's cheek and squeeze the required number of drops into the lower nostril. This allows the drops to run into the nose and nasal passages. Resting your fingers on his cheek helps prevent damage to the nose if he moves suddenly—your hand will move with his face. Keep the child in this position for a minute or two before you switch to the other side.

There are several precautions to take when giving nose drops: (1) Use a plastic dropper, preferably a soft plastic one. Many dropper bottles contain a glass or hard plastic dropper. The latter are fine for measuring the drops. However, your druggist can supply you with a very soft plastic dropper to use in giving the drops. (2) Be sure to check with your doctor on the correct strength nose drops to buy. Some common preparations come in three strengths. (3) Be sure to count the number of drops you put into the nostril. Two or three are usually sufficient and more than this will run into the child's throat, making him choke and sputter. (4) Medicated nose drops can be irritating to the lining of the nose and produce what we call a rebound effect. They will cause the body to make excess mucosa and result in more nasal stuffiness. Stop using nose drops after 3 or 4 days. In another 24 hours you can resume if needed. (5) Use the dropper that comes with the bottle to measure the required number of drops onto a spoon. Use the soft plastic dropper to give the drops. In this way you are not placing the germs from the child's nose back into the original bottle. You may be able to use the same bottle for 2 or 3 colds in various members of the family.

## *To give nasal spray*

Nasal sprays are prescribed by some physicians to be used instead of nose drops. The purpose of the spray is the same as that of the nose drops, and the droplets are intended to reach the same area of the nose—the back of the nose toward the openings leading to the ears and the sinuses.

Each child should have his own bottle of nasal spray so that infection won't be spread from child to child. The tip of the spray nozzle is placed into one nostril without completely blocking the opening. With the child's head bent slightly forward, squeeze the spray bottle quickly 2 or 3 times. The child should sniff briskly while the spray is being squeezed into his nostril. The second nostril is then treated in the same way. Try to discourage the child from blowing his nose immediately so that the medication can remain in contact with the mucous membranes long enough to be absorbed. (See *colds; sinusitis.*)

## *To give suppositories (medications by rectum)*

Rectal medications are given when a child is vomiting and cannot take medicine by mouth. Most suppositories are bullet-shaped, tapered at one end. The medicine has been mixed with a meltable glycerin base and should be kept in the refrigerator until ready for use. Check the dose on the suppository wrapper to make sure it is correct for your child. Usually twice the recommended oral dose of aspirin is given by rectum, since the absorption is less complete than in the stomach. The suppository should be at room temperature when inserted. If it is necessary, suppositories may be divided by cutting them lengthwise with a knife heated by being run under hot water. (Do not use any lubricant other than water; it will interfere with absorption of the medicine.) Push the suppository, smaller, tapered end first, as high in the rectum as your finger will go. If resistance to insertion is encountered, inserting the blunt end may be more successful. Hold the buttocks together for 5 to 10 minutes. If the suppository is pushed out or a bowel movement occurs within a half hour, insert another.

## *Medical supplies to keep in the home*

Oral and rectal thermometers
Aspirin
Vaporizer, cold steam
Phenylephrine nose drops (¼%)
Nasal aspirator
Ipecac syrup
Canned or frozen
 fruit drinks or juice
Blender
Adhesive and other bandages, including
 an elastic bandage

Unscented soap to wash cuts and
 scrapes
Ice bag (a hot-water bottle with a
 wide mouth will serve for hot and
 cold)
Antiseptic (isopropyl alcohol 70%)
Possibly an antihistamine
(See also Part 2, Chapter 9: "First
 Aid.")

Keeping the facts discussed in this chapter in mind, you are in a good position to become a working member of the health-care team in caring for a sick child. To round out your understanding, check the encyclopedic entries for specific symptoms, such as *cough, diarrhea,* or *vomiting,* as the occasion arises.

*Ellenora Lenihan, R.N.*

# 6
## If Your Child Goes to the Hospital

The prospect of taking a child to the hospital for the first time is not an easy one for parents. Many questions loom large, and the uncertainty of the immediate future can cause a great deal of apprehension in the family. Parents who understand what is being done to their child and why are more able to offer support and relieve his or her anxiety. The doctor and hospital are concerned that parents' questions be answered carefully.

The first thing to consider is how your child feels about going to the hospital. It is very common for a child to be apprehensive about leaving the security of his home, especially the security of his parents. His main concerns and fears at this time depend upon his age. Sometimes he is afraid of being abandoned in a strange place. If he is between 3 and 10 years, he may already be conditioned by TV stories, books, and tales of friends to fear the hospital. He can experience real anxiety about what is going to happen to him, fearing the unknown and the possibility of pain. Strange as it may seem, the child may also fantasize that he has been put into the hospital as a punishment. Although the child will rarely verbalize this feeling, it is well for the parent to assure the child that he is missed at home. Some children will never accept the idea that their parents chose to put them into the hospital. For this reason, the onus of the decision should reside with the doctor "because he knows what is best."

The last thirty years have seen a change in our understanding of how hospitalization affects young children and how we can make the experience less frightening for them. In the old days, regardless of a child's age, it was deemed important that visits by parents be strictly limited to an hour or so per day at most. Because of concern about this approach to hospitalization, a number of studies have been done since World War II. These have shown that young children predictably become frightened, extremely unhappy, and depressed when separated from their parents in hospitals. The hospitalization reaction resulted in decreased activity. At one time, a morose, passive acceptance of painful procedures was interpreted as a normal adjustment to hospitalization, an understandable reaction. Because the depressed child is in a sense more compliant, this kind of adjustment was used as an argument for keeping parents away from children as much as possible. The appearance of parents on the scene seemed to make the child agitated and less cooperative. We now know that after returning home, these seemingly cooperative children suffered from problems such as regression of behavior, tantrums, nightmares, and difficulty in getting along with others. Moreover, actual physical recovery from illness appears to be delayed. Our observation is that, in children who react too passively to the hospital experience, infections do not respond to treatment as quickly and recuperation following surgery is retarded. We therefore urge parents to acquaint themselves with some of the new ideas regarding the hospitalization of children and establish an attitude of friendly inquiry about any questions they may have.

Our concern with the harmful effects of hospitalization centers mainly on children up to the age of 6. Children over 6 are usually sufficiently mature to make a constructive and healthy adaptation to the hospital environment. The toddler or the preschool child often finds the stress of hospitalization more than he can cope with, regardless of how well his parents prepare him for separation or how sympathetically he is treated by the hospital personnel. We have assumed in the past that the infant is too young to react to separation, but we are no longer as sure of this. Infants are much more aware of their surroundings than was once thought. The case against separation can be made even with infants, if for no other reason than the needs of their parents. Of course some 5-year-olds are able to handle separation from parents extremely well. As in other aspects of child care, it is important to take into account the specific needs of an individual child.

We recommend that parents stay with infants and young preschool children through their hospitalization, whether it be elective (scheduled) or emergency. In many communities, there is at least one hospital where rooming-in of the parents is permitted. Discuss this with the doctor and see if he can arrange that the elective procedure be done at such a hospital. Let older children stay with friends or relatives if need be. A new Boston group called Children in Hospitals (31 Wilshire Park, Needham, Mass. 02192) has organized to assist parents in coping with hospitalization problems. Their stated policy is to support, educate, and encourage parents to stay with children who must undergo medical treatment. As a second-best alternative to a mother or father staying with a young child during hospitalization, we advocate very liberal visiting hours so that the child may be visited during most of the waking part of the day. But there is no need to make hard-and-fast rules. Some children are remarkably able to be away from their parents even at 3½ and 4. If this is the case, there is no reason why you must stay. What you do should depend upon your own child's response. Also, be sure to discuss with the nurses and doctors what your role will be. While in general the presence of parents makes care of the child easier, you should avoid getting in the way of the hospital staff and making its job harder in special situations, such as a very ill child requiring constant complicated care. Encourage the nurses to tell you if you are interfering. Ask them for specific roles in the hospital— if you are not taking care of your own, how about reading to another child?

We also urge parents to try to prepare a child for hospitalization and partial separation, even when his state of intellectual and language development are such that he cannot fully comprehend what the parents are talking about. A try at preparation is worthwhile because whatever the child may pick up from the parents' tone of voice or a familiar word may become symbolic and helpful. Furthermore, in preparing a child the parent is challenged to work out his or her own feelings, which in the long run may be the most important factor in reassuring the child.

The older child, between the ages of 4 and 6, definitely needs preparation for the hospital experience. Discuss the hospitalization with him several days before admission. There is little point in bringing up the topic weeks in advance, for this will only cause him needless worry. The child should be told frankly and matter-of-factly in words he can understand that he needs to go into the hospital and why this is necessary. He should be given as complete a verbal description as possible of what it will be like in the hospital and told where his mother and father will be. If you cannot stay with him constantly, he should be informed of this ahead of time in a matter-of-fact way. If he is going to have a painful or uncomfortable procedure, it is best that he know about it. For example, it is perfectly appropriate to tell a child that his throat will be sore after tonsillectomy just as it is when he has a sore throat. If anesthesia is to be employed, this should be described as honestly as possible. Find out yourself what kind of anesthesia will be used. If, for example, gas is to be used, you can tell the child that he will have a mask over his face and will smell a sweet gas which will make him fall asleep. If a medicine is to be given before the anesthetic, find out which kind and tell the child he will be taking something either by mouth or by injection or by a tube inserted in his rectum which will make him feel drowsy. Assure him that when he wakes up his operation will be over.

Tell him why he needs the operation. For example, in the case of a tonsillectomy, you can tell him that by removing his tonsils he will not be as sick as he was previously (see **tonsils and adenoids**). To the extent possible, try to inform him about the parts of his anatomy that will be worked on. Few children have ever seen tonsils or know where they are located. A good drawing of the tonsils in the mouth can be very helpful. If a young child is having an operation on an **undescended testis,** point out to him as completely as possible exactly what will be done (and specifically what will *not* be done, such as cutting off his penis). Ask your doctor for photographs or drawings in simplified form of the anatomical part. Try to get a book which describes the hospitalization of a child. Fred Rogers (of *Mr. Rogers' Neighborhood*) and his colleagues have produced three video cassettes, "Going to the Hospital," "Having an Operation" and "Having a Cast Changed," each featuring Mr. Rogers himself. These are available at many hospitals. For more information contact Family Communications Inc., 4803 Fifth Avenue, Pittsburgh, Pa. 15213. Ask your doctor about sound movies available which portray a hospital in a pleasant documentary fashion. PTAs might encourage schools to include a unit on "going to the hospital" as part of the curriculum. Some hospitals encourage visits by the child to the hospital prior to the time of his admission. During these visits, the child sees where children stay, gets to meet doctors and nurses, and talks to other children.

Equally as important as informing the child about what he should expect is giving him the chance to express his own feelings and concerns. Do not assume that what you tell the child will be interpreted by him in the way you intend. Young children are normally prone to distort information. Just as many 4-year-olds imagine that there are monsters and tigers in their bedroom at night, so they may imagine that their tonsils are really not located in their throats at all but somewhere else in their body, perhaps in their abdomens. Their concept of tonsillectomy may be of an enormous cut into the belly with resulting disfigurement and perhaps even death. Don't assume that the child understands you, even if he nods his head obediently. Give him ample opportunity to voice his own concerns and questions about what will happen. You may be amazed at some of the thoughts he expresses. When he gives you his own ideas about what is going to happen, you will have a chance to correct his misunderstandings. You may not be able to correct them completely because of the strength of his powers of distortion.

One good technique in communicating with a child is to turn his questions around. If he asks why he has to go to the hospital, ask him why *he* thinks he must be hospitalized. Try to resist answering him until he lets you know what he really thinks and feels and what underlies his question. Another way of getting at some of his hidden feelings is to have him draw out and describe a hospital scene on a piece of paper. Yet another approach is to have him pretend with dolls and tell a story about a boy or girl who goes to the hospital. Make sure to have a nurse doll, mother doll, doctor doll, and so forth. However you do it, be sure to let the child express his own concerns. Don't merely give him a lecture.

The critically important and long-neglected skills of communication with a child are something that can be learned. They are important, of course, whether or not your child has a problem. One way to develop these skills is through a Parent Effectiveness Training (P.E.T.) course. These are given in most parts of the country. For more information, contact P.E.T. Information, 531 Stevens, Solana Beach, Calif. 92075.

Hospitalization may be recommended by your doctor for a number of different reasons. First, there is the genuine emergency—the sick child who needs hospital services to save his life. Examples are the child with a serious infection like *meningitis* or the child with *appendicitis.* Secondly, hospitalization is sometimes recommended mainly in anticipation of a possible serious complication of an illness. One example is the child with *croup* who is brought into the hospital so that if the obstruction of his upper airways should suddenly progress, interfering with respiration, help will be right at hand. Another example is the child with a moderately severe concussion (see *head injuries*) who needs closer observation than would be possible at home and whose condition may require prompt intervention.

Some hospitalizations are planned ahead and scheduled. Elective surgical procedures like tonsillectomy, the correction of strabismus (see *cross-eyes*), and orchiopexy (surgical correction of an *undescended testis*) are good examples.

Other hospitalizations are for diagnostic purposes; for example, the child with chronic *diarrhea* who needs evaluation. Another example is the child whose symptom might have a psychological component, like chronic *headache* or *abdominal pain.* In such cases, the hospitalization is designed to gain information not only about the affected body part, but also about the child's personality, style of behavior, and interaction with his parents.

If at all possible, it is a good idea to avoid elective hospitalization for surgery like tonsillectomy during times of family stress. When a death or a separation in the family has occurred, children are prone to blame themselves. If hospitalization for surgery is arranged at these times of normal self-blame, the child in his own fantasy world may look upon the operation as a form of punishment for his having caused a divorce or death in the family. (He may even see it as punishment for everyday misbehavior, such as picking on his younger sister.) If hospitalization must occur at these times, be sure to allow the child to express such guilty thoughts so that you can try to correct them. Better yet, try to postpone the hospitalization if you can until a time when the family has settled down to a more normal routine. As a general rule, we always suggest postponing elective procedures if at all possible until children are older. They are then better equipped emotionally and intellectually to handle the stress of hospitalization and surgery. The decision to hospitalize the child for an elective procedure should take into account the child's developmental stage as well as the state of his health. The psychological issue is one that you should discuss with your doctor when plans are being made.

Another good idea is to encourage a relationship between the child and the health professional who will be with him in the hospital. This individual may be a nurse or perhaps the doctor himself. It is worthwhile for the child to talk to this person before hospitalization about what will happen. In the hospital this individual will be a familiar face to the child and very reassuring. In more and more hospitals the personnel are paying attention to the emotional needs of children. Thus the anesthetist may meet with the child on the evening before surgery to introduce himself, to show the mask and let the child practice with it, and to answer any questions of both parent and child.

If you are to be helpful to your child, it is important that you yourself understand what is happening. If there is a parent group in the hospital, try to join it, or at least find out, through your doctor or at the library, or in this book, the nature of your child's problem and what must be done. For instance, learn where tonsils are and why they have to be taken out and what kind of anesthesia and premedication are going to be used. Inform yourself. If you are very frightened about some aspect of hospitalization, you will be of little value to your child. Just as you encourage your child to talk to you about his fears, be sure to bring up your own with the physician or nurse. Some parents themselves feel very guilty about hospitalization and blame themselves for such things as not having had the child checked earlier. Usually these reasons have nothing at all to do with the need for hospitalization. However, if a parent feels guilty, try as he may, he is not going to be very helpful to his child. Just as we encourage parents to look for guilty feelings in their children, so they should look for them in themselves and not be ashamed to express them to the doctor, nurse, or to each other.

*Richard I. Feinbloom, M.D.*
*Patricia Nelson, M.P.H.*

# 7
# Health-Care Delivery: The Broad Picture

**M**an has always had to cope with disease. In every human society there are some specialists (medicine men, priests, or physicians) who are expected to treat and cure human ills. Yet modern medicine as we know it is scarcely more than a hundred years old. Even a hundred years ago parents rarely consulted a physician when a child was ill. Physicians were for adults. Hospitals were primarily institutions for the sick poor rather than the sick, and almost all babies were born at home. Pediatrics today is one of the major pillars of medical education, but a century ago it was virtually ignored by medical schools. It is hard to realize that so much of what we take for granted today was unknown just a few years ago, but this should serve to remind us of the rapid pace of change and alert us to the likelihood of even greater and faster change in the future.

Other sections of this encyclopedia focus on changes in the picture of childhood disease and its prevention, diagnosis, and treatment. This section will focus upon changes in the *health-care delivery system*—the methods that society relies upon to bring together the providers and consumers of health care. This system is part of what is sometimes called the *health industry*—the social and economic structure within which scientific knowledge is applied to combat disease and to promote the healthy growth and development of children.

Although the mass media still continue to report new advances in medicine with a sense of admiration and awe, severe criticism has been directed toward the health-care delivery system and its leading characters: doctors, hospitals, and drug companies. The "system" is referred to as "fragmented" and as a "nonsystem." Phrases such as "health-care crisis" and "health manpower shortage" are common parlance. The infant mortality rate, which is a measure of the risk of death during the first year of life, is almost twice as high for a black baby as a white baby born in the United States, and the United States infant mortality rate ranks fifteenth among the countries of the world. These and other statistics are sometimes cited as evidence of the "sickness" of the American health-care system.

Although there may be some room for argument about the interpretation of these statistics, there is little doubt about the validity of complaints which the mass media report: medical care is expensive and the costs seem to rise steadily every year at a faster rate than the cost of living; a great many parents can't find a doctor when their child needs one; and, if they do find one, he often does not have enough time to spend with the case.

For the poor, these are complaints of long standing. However, for a significant portion of the large American middle class, they are new. In the past, middle-class parents of children with special problems, such as mental retardation or cystic fibrosis, have expressed their concerns and succeeded, to some extent, in influencing government policy. At last, the complaints of the poor as well are becoming more widely recognized. Furthermore, there is increasing acceptance of the principle that all children have a right to grow and develop in health, and that access to high-quality medical services is a necessary component of that right. Thus the plight of children whose parents are unable to afford to purchase high-quality care has become a concern of society at large.

Although the health needs of children with special problems have certainly not been met by our society—conditions in most public institutions for the retarded are still shameful, for example—the complaints which are most often heard today concern what is termed "primary care." As discussed in Chapter 1: "Quality in Pediatric Care," primary or front-line health-care services for children include parental counseling and support during child rearing, counseling of the adolescent, immunization, screening for specific defects of vision, hearing, and the like, regular checkups, and care of the vast majority of episodic illnesses and minor accidents to which we are all heir. Most encounters with physicians and other health workers are for these reasons rather than for esoteric or complex diseases. For the most part, primary care is delivered on an ambulatory (office or clinic) basis and does not require hospitalization. Dental and eye care, although necessary enough to be considered part of primary care, are special subjects in their own right and will not be covered in the discussion which follows (See *dental care* and *vision problems.*)

When we perceive ourselves or our children to be sick, we seek a remedy or cure. Sociologically, there is wide variation in the way illness affects individuals and cultural groups. In the United States, illness strikes most often at either end of the life-span and least often among the adult working population. Medicare was introduced into the American health system as a response to the health needs of the elderly. No comparable program—covering the total population rather than merely the population segment defined as indigent (lacking adequate means of support) by bureaucratic standards—has been introduced to meet the needs of children. Hence, complaints about primary health care for children are commonly heard.

Primary child-health care, as defined, is not a major component of health-care costs. Hospital costs are by far the largest contributor. The reasons for rising hospital costs can be traced, in part, to technological and scientific advances which are more expensive to apply and, in part, to the need to pay hospital workers, underpaid and exploited for many years, a decent wage. Other reasons, however, relate to inefficient operation of hospitals, a more complex issue. To some extent these inefficiencies are a reflection of the shortage and unequal distribution of primary child-health caretakers to which attention will now be directed.

Although physicians are usually the focus of discussion about health manpower, they are a small minority of those who work in the "health industry." At the turn of the century, physicians outnumbered all other kinds of health workers put together; today, for every active physician there are at least 13 other workers. This change is a reflection of the growth and importance of hospitals. Most non-physician health workers are hospital-based, whereas most physicians are office-based.

Nevertheless, it is logical to start this discussion with physicians, since their activities and their distribution provide the keys to an understanding of current problems. In spite of recent efforts to promote neighborhood centers and similar projects—a development that will be discussed a little later on—most American children, probably over 80 percent of them, receive their primary health care from physicians in office-based private practice. In 1947 when the American Academy of Pediatrics carried out a national child health survey, more than two-thirds of the physicians in office-based practice were general practitioners or family physicians. By 1969, this figure had been reduced to 28 percent. Furthermore, general practitioners on the average were 10 to 15 years older than pediatricians. In 1970 there were about 3000 fewer general practitioners in office-based practice than in 1968, but only about 600 more pediatricians. Even if it is assumed that a pediatrician, because he sees only children, can care for 4 times as many children as a general practitioner, it is clear that the net result of the trend toward specialization in medical practice is fewer physicians to give primary care to children.

This trend toward specialization with the resultant disappearance of general practitioners or family doctors was recognized more than 20 years ago. Numerous attempts have been made to reverse it. In 1970, a "specialty" Board of Family Practice was established and in 1971, Federal legislation to support training of "family practitioners" was enacted. It is still too soon to know whether these latest efforts will meet with greater success than earlier ones.

The United States is unique among the countries of the world in that *both* pediatricians (specialists) and family physicians (generalists) are responsible for the primary health care of children. In other countries *either* family physicians deliver such care—the case in England, Scandinavia, and Western Europe—*or* pediatricians do so, as in the Eastern European countries where the "generalist" physician restricts his services to adults. It is probably fair to say that no clear consensus has been reached in the United States concerning the type of physician, generalist or specialist, that should be responsible for the primary health care of children.

In the United States, both the type and the distribution of primary-care physicians are strongly influenced by community size. In rural areas—where about 20 percent of the population lived in 1970—61 percent of the physicians in office-based practice were general practitioners and only 2.4 percent were pediatricians. In metropolitan areas of over 1 million population—where 39 percent of the population lived —21 percent of the physicians in office-based practice were general practitioners and over 6 percent were pediatricians. Assuming again that 1 pediatrician is equivalent to 4 general practitioners, there were almost twice as many primary caretakers available to serve children in our two largest metropolitan areas as in our rural areas.

Metropolitan areas, however, are large aggregates which include the deteriorating slums of a city as well as its affluent suburbs. Slums and ghetto areas are as short of primary caretakers as the areas of rural poverty. A reflection of this shortage is the extraordinary rise in visits to hospital emergency services. This has not occurred because of any increase in true emergencies, but because there is nowhere else for parents to turn when their child is ill.

To some extent both the trend toward specialization and the unequal distribution of primary caretakers in the United States is a reflection of the solo practitioner, small-business enterpreneur mechanism upon which we rely for the delivery of primary health care. By force of circumstance the entrepreneur must earn his own way through the fee which he charges. Thus, he will tend to select a field or market which yields a high fee, such as surgery, rather than a low fee, such as general practice or pediatrics. He is also forced to locate in a geographic area where there is a clientele that can afford to pay for services.

In recent years a number of new government-sponsored programs have been launched in response to criticisms of the health-care system. Most of the programs are small. The laws establishing them are separate, and the programs are largely uncoordinated with each other. Neighborhood health centers, based in poverty areas, were first established through the Office of Economic Opportunity (now dismantled) but now are funded by other agencies in the Department of Health, Education, and Welfare. Still another agency in the same department supports centers for maternity and infant care and centers for children and youth. Through the National Health Service Corps the U.S. Public Health Service is setting doctors up in practice in medically underserved communities, both rural and urban. All of these different projects have in common the establishment of primary health-care delivery points in pockets of poverty, where there are few, if any, physicians and where the population cannot afford to pay for health care. They are dependent upon the annual appropriation of funds by Congress and the annual release of funds by the President's budget office. This makes for an unsatisfactory and insecure situation. These various projects have certainly helped bring physicians into some poverty pockets, providing free care, and combining preventive and curative services. However, they neither meet the needs of everyone in such pockets nor the needs of the poor and lower middle classes who live elsewhere.

The largest single government medical program providing care to children is known as Medicaid. Basically, it is an extension of welfare medical care. Families are screened by a means test, and, if income is below a given level, the caretaker of their choice, private physician or clinic, may bill the government for his services. The scope of services is limited (not always covering preventive services), and the costs are borne by both state and Federal governments on a matching basis. Poorer states are at a disadvantage. Furthermore, the costs of this program were much greater than originally anticipated so that the means test has become more stringent over time. The administration of the program has been cumbersome both to physicians and government, since reimbursement is based on a record of each service charge, requiring much paper work, and is difficult to audit or control.

Both Medicaid and "project" programs serve to create a separate system of care for the poor, rather than a single system of care for all children. A social stigma is attached to a means test and to indigence, which many families seek to avoid even though their children are in need of health-care services.

A number of bills have been introduced into Congress which would effect even greater changes in the health-care delivery system. These range from a complete system of government health insurance which would include primary health care to less radical changes in the current American system, such as expansion of the voluntary and private health insurance schemes which do not usually cover primary health care at present. Another type of potential legislation would provide funds to finance primary health care for children in day-care centers.

Although the eventual outcome of these bills is unknown, there is no question but that government will assume more responsibility for both defraying and controlling the costs of health care than it has in the past and that physicians will be less free to practice as individual entrepreneurs who respond only to market forces and their own consciences. The American Academy of Pediatrics, the professional organization that speaks for the American pediatrician, and, in its own words, "for the attainment by all children of their full potential for physical, emotional, and social health," has recognized and supported these trends. The following statements are selected from among many goals which it has advocated in a report titled *Lengthening Shadows:*

1. The creation of a National Advisory Council on Children, responsible to the President and a Deputy Assistant Secretary for Children and Youth in the Office of the Secretary of the Department of Health, Education, and Welfare.

2. The expansion and added support of the special health projects which serve children in poverty areas until these are replaced by more effective, continuous family-centered programs.

3. The development of a national health insurance program that will ensure comprehensive coverage of all children. Any program for the general population should give priority to children, and encourage parental responsibility and continuance of physician-patient relationship. (As an example of comprehensive coverage, we have reproduced the *Guidelines for Your Family's Health Insurance* of the American Academy of Pediatrics, at the end of this chapter.)

4. The inclusion of consumers in health planning for the future. This is a helpful step toward the development and execution of a national health policy, but only a few individuals can serve as members of community, state, or national planning groups. Every patient, as a citizen, has the obligation to keep himself informed and to inform his legislative representatives concerning pending legislation that will affect the health of his family. (See end of article for sources of information regarding health legislation.)

The most controversial aspect of new legislation, of course, is the extent to which the taxpayers and consumers will support the health-care system as a whole, including the education and services of physicians, nurses, and other health workers who deliver health care. In our opinion, both education and services should be fully supported by a government program that builds upon educational and service institutions responsible and accountable to the people they serve. New legislation should enable the currently fragmented government programs and the inequitable coverage of private practice settings to be converted in an orderly manner into community-based systems of comprehensive care.

These systems would not distinguish between the poor and the rich, and no one would be forced to pay for being sick. The funding of the systems should not be dependent upon annual appropriations by

Congress, but should be subject to careful periodic review and evaluation. Special efforts to serve families who reside in poverty pockets and rural areas will continue to be needed, but these should be integral parts of the same system and the same national program that serves all the citizens of the country, rather than the isolated, temporal efforts they are now.

In addition to these measures designed to improve the health-care system, 3 other trends that will affect the future deserve special mention. During the past 20 to 30 years, there has been a significant growth in group practice arrangements. The greatest such growth has occurred in specialty groups, consisting of 2 or more specialist physicians (such as 2 pediatricians) who share space, equipment, and office personnel, and can spell each other. This makes for greater efficiency than solo practice. However, there has also been a significant growth of multispecialty groups, usually composed of 5 or more physicians of different types who together can provide primary care to a family (for example, an obstetrician, pediatrician, and internist). The larger groups of this nature are often able to contract with a family or an employer to provide prepaid health insurance benefits which include primary (ambulatory) care as well as hospital care. The term "health maintenance organization" (HMO) has been applied to these groups, and all of the pending Federal legislation includes some measures to promote more such groups. The best-known organization of this type is the Kaiser-Permanente Foundation on the West Coast.

Clearly, it is possible for family physicians (general practitioners) to function as part of a group, and many HMOs already include general practitioners. The trend toward various types of group practice and the prepayment of primary health care will probably accelerate, regardless of what kind of a physician delivers primary health care to the nation's children.

Another recent trend which one can safely predict will continue and accelerate is the training and use of health workers other than the physician to deliver primary health care to children under his supervision. Federal legislation in 1971 both encouraged and helped to fund such training programs. In the field of child-health care the nurse (rather than a physician's assistant) has been the primary figure involved. Although the use of nurses in what is termed an "expanded role" seems new to the United States, nurses have been relied upon to furnish most of the child-health supervision offered to children in Western Europe, Australia, and New Zealand for many years. Furthermore, public-health nurses attached to health departments or visit-

101

*Health-
Care
Delivery:
The Broad
Picture*

ing nurse associations have provided much counseling and parent education, although they have not carried out physical assessments or made medical management decisions.

Starting with a training program in Denver in 1966, many other programs have developed to prepare graduate nurses as "pediatric nurse practitioners" or "pediatric nurse associates." The American Nurses' Association and the American Academy of Pediatrics have issued guidelines for such training and defined the role of these nurses in primary care. There were at least 350 such nurses at work at the end of 1971, and numerous studies of their effectiveness and acceptance by parents had been published in the medical literature. In addition to functioning as a health counselor and educator with special skills in the areas of child rearing and child growth and development, pediatric nurse practitioners are prepared to take medical histories and perform medical examinations. They can carry a large part of the routine health supervision of children, referring cases to the pediatrician only when they find complex problems. In addition, they are able to handle most of the day-to-day concerns of parents either by telephone or by an office visit with the pediatrician at hand for backup if his judgment seems needed. They can also manage much of the continuing care of children with special problems such as allergies. Functioning in this way, the nurse practitioner allows the pediatrician to increase his primary caretaking case load by at least 50 percent. The nurse's particular skills often enable her to establish a very special relationship to parents.

It is clear that this trend toward collaborative caretaking, if continued at the same pace, can have a significant impact upon the overall shortage of primary child-health caretakers. However, it cannot affect the distribution of caretakers very much, since this is more closely related to how health is financed than to who is paid to deliver it.

Another development which can be expected to influence child-health services is increasing sophistication in the use of computers and communication media and advances in communication theory. Much of medicine is based upon careful history taking, an interchange between physician and patient. By translating this interchange into the language of computers, it may be possible to automate a great deal of it. If the computers are programmed carefully enough, they may even be able to make certain kinds of decisions and give out advice. Closed-circuit television allows this interchange to occur at a distance. Television can also bring a physician face-to-face with a patient at a distance. The camera can be focused down for careful inspection, and a stethoscope can transmit breath and heart sounds to an observer many miles away. These methods and instruments are still in very early stages of development and use, but once a better understanding of their limitations and their usefulness is achieved, they will probably have important effects upon the delivery of child-health care.

Another trend that may affect the delivery of health care to children in years ahead is the growth of day-care centers and health services associated with them. Although Head Start is the earliest and best known of such programs, Federal legislation was introduced in 1971 and 1972 to expand preschool group care and education greatly and to attach health services to these programs.

For many years health services of a screening nature (tests for vision and hearing, and medical examinations) have been carried out within the school system. It is logical to apply screening tests to a group because the tests can be done efficiently and do not require a medical presence, since they are neither diagnostic nor therapeutic. However, the value of school medical examinations has been questioned, especially in the case of children who are already receiving adequate primary care and regular checkups from an established source. Furthermore, schools are not in a position to provide care themselves and must refer parents to a source of treatment which may or may not be available to all parents in a community.

The ideal situation for children in preschool or school groups would be one which would take advantage of the group situation to carry out screening tests. Other health problems could be handled by regular communication among the school, parent, and primary-care source. However, for such a system to function for the benefit of all children, the financial barriers and manpower problems which now block access of many children to a regular source of primary care would have to be overcome.

In this chapter we have tried to summarize briefly how the health-care delivery system is responding to the pressures upon it and the complaints about it. The responses are multiple and too slow, but they are taking place Some of the future developments, such as the use of computers, growth of prepayment group practice services for primary care, closer collaboration between doctors and nurses in the delivery of primary care, and an increasing proportion of its cost being borne by government, are fairly clear. Other developments, such as whether or not pediatricians and general practitioners will both continue to deliver primary care and whether or not we will have one system of care for all, or separate systems for the poor and the less fortunate, are less easy to predict.

If there is any lesson to be learned from this journey, it is that the United States badly needs a national health-care policy. If it were possible to start from a clean slate with the simple statement that every child is entitled to the best health care the nation can provide, it would not be too hard to spell out what is needed to provide it. Unfortunately the slate is full of false entries and erasures, and all the forces which want to write on it are human and fallible.

*Alfred Yankauer, M.D.*

*103*

*Health-
Care
Delivery:
The Broad
Picture*

## WHERE TO WRITE FOR INFORMATION ABOUT LEGISLATION AFFECTING CHILD HEALTH AND WELFARE

### General Health Legislation

1. Your Congressman.
2. Congressmen sponsoring a specific bill.
3. Committee for National Health Insurance, Suite 432, 821 15th Street, NW, Washington, D.C. 20005.
4. American Hospital Association, 840 North Lake Shore Drive, Chicago, Ill. 60611.
5. American Medical Association, 535 North Dearborn Street, Chicago, Ill. 60610.
6. American Public Health Association, 1015 18th Street N.W., Washington, D.C. 20036.
7. Physicians Forum, 510 Madison Avenue, New York, N.Y. 10022.

### Child Health and Welfare Legislation

1. American Academy of Pediatrics, 1801 Hinman Avenue, Evanston, Ill. 60204.
2. Child Welfare League of America, 44 East 23rd Street, New York, N.Y. 10010.
3. Citizens Committee for Children of New York, 112 East 19th Street, New York, N.Y. 10003.
4. Day Care and Child Development Council, 1401 K Street N.W., Washington, D.C. 20005.

104

*Health
Care
for
Children*

GUIDELINES FOR YOUR FAMILY'S HEALTH INSURANCE*

The American Academy of Pediatrics, an organization representing nearly 12,000 board-certified pediatricians, has developed the following guidelines to help you select a good health insurance program for your family from the great variety of policies available, or to aid you in improving your present policy.

A. FEATURES THAT ARE ESSENTIAL TO ANY SOUND HEALTH INSURANCE POLICY

1. All members of a family should be covered equally, including each child from birth.

2. Provision should be made to cover all major medical and surgical expenses.

3. Provision should be made for protection from catastrophic health expenses.

4. Provision should be made for converting and continuing a health insurance policy when the subscriber terminates his employment.

5. Exclusions should be clearly identified and completely understood.

6. The health insurance policy or the insurance agent should explain the meaning of coinsurance, corridors, or deductibles if they are a facet of your policy. The total out-of-pocket expenditure that the policy owner could incur should be clearly stated.

B. PRIORITIES

Comprehensive health insurance coverage will change with changes in medical technology, but the following are benefits that should be covered in a comprehensive medical insurance policy.

1. *First Priorities:*

a. Medical care to include health supervision and preventive care supervised by a physician wherever performed.

b. Surgical care wherever performed, and the diagnosis of injury, illness, or disease. Plastic or reconstructive surgery where necessary to restore function or the emotional well-being of an individual.

c. Pregnancy should be all or partially included. All complications of pregnancy must be covered, including the care of the unborn child.

d. Care of the newborn infant from *birth*. (Many policies exclude infants for two weeks to thirty days.)

---

*Reprinted with the permission of the American Academy of Pediatrics.

105

Health-
Care
Delivery:
The Broad
Picture

e. Laboratory and pathological services requested by a physician and performed in an approved laboratory.

f. X-ray services wherever performed.

g. Radiation therapy wherever performed.

h. Anesthesia services.

i. Consultations wherever performed.

j. Concurrent care (services rendered to a patient by more than one physician).

k. Inhalation and physical therapy under the direction of a physician.

l. Drugs while in a hospital, and other drug costs beyond an annual deductible.

m. Emergency psychiatric care.

n. Emergency ambulance service.

o. Extended care services ordered by a physician.

p. Prosthetic appliances, braces.

2. *Second Priorities:*

a. Psychiatric services.

b. Podiatry.

c. Rental or purchases of medical equipment.

d. Psychological testing.

3. *Third Priorities:*

a. Cosmetic surgery (elective).

b. Transplantations (nonexperimental).

c. Eyeglasses.

d. Social services, if beneficial, and overall medical care of the patient.

## C. KNOW YOUR INSURANCE POLICY

The type of policy that usually contains most of the provisions called for in these guidelines is termed comprehensive major medical health insurance. These policies pay a percentage of all charges in a calendar year after a deductible is met. As in automobile insurance, the cost of the policy is reduced as the deductible is increased. The deductible should consider the family's *total* yearly medical expense, and not individual expenses or separate illness costs. Preventive medicine should be encouraged and, if not covered by the policy, included as part of the policy's deductible.

It is important to remember that a portion of every dollar paid into health insurance is required for administrative expenses. Because of these administrative expenses, money which you expend directly for health care buys more care than the same amount of money funneled through an insurance firm.

Coinsurance usually applies after the deductible is paid. When coinsurance is in effect, the insurance company is responsible for a percentage of the total expense, while the subscriber is responsible for the remaining cost.

Basic hospital-surgical policies are usually inadequate protection. Insurance programs that pay all medical expenses are very expensive and encourage overutilization. One is advised to utilize these guidelines to purchase a health insurance program that offers the greatest amount of protection at the least possible cost.

Health insurance is purchased through your private insurance agent, union, employee representative, or group insurance through your place of work. It is advisable for everyone to study his health insurance policy individually. There are many private insurance companies that are offering excellent policies with good benefits, while others offer substandard programs. It is up to you, the individual purchaser, to study your own policy to evaluate its effectiveness and determine how you can get the most return for your money so as to provide adequate protection for your family's medical expenses.

*Committee on Third Party Payment Plans
Council on Pediatric Practice*

# 2

## Safety

# 8
# Accident Prevention

Accidents should be a major concern of every parent. More children die and are injured from accidents than from the next 5 most frequent causes of childhood death combined. For children ages 1 to 4 years, 37 percent of all deaths are caused by accidents. Of these, 34 percent die in motor vehicles; 19 percent die in fires or of burns; 16 percent die by drowning; 6 percent die in falls; and 6 percent die from poisons. For children 5 to 14 years of age, 46 percent of all deaths are due to accidents. Of these, 47 percent die in motor vehicle accidents; 21 percent die by drowning; and 11 percent die in fire or of burns. For babies under 1 year who were born healthy, accidental death is 1 of the 2 major causes of death. These figures emphasize the importance of accident prevention.

What causes accidents to children? To try to answer this complex question, a research team of doctors, psychologists, and social workers made a detailed study of preschool children admitted to The Children's Hospital Medical Center for treatment of accidental injury. In addition to investigating the immediate facts surrounding the accident, the research team looked into the child's family, his or her relationship with his parents and brothers and sisters, his physical environment, and his daily routine. The research findings show that while some accidents just "happen" and seem unavoidable, simple everyday events and troubles in family life often set the stage for many others.

Most accidents seem to be triggered by a chain of events, not by a single event. Most children are exposed regularly to dangerous situations, but it is not this exposure alone that precipitates accidents. Certain seemingly ordinary conditions or problems—minor family illness, a parent who is overly tired, a child who is very hungry—set the stage for the majority of accidents. Small troubles and irritations pile up until a mother (or father or grandparent or baby-sitter) is so tired or worried that she hasn't the energy to take the usual precautions. An aspirin bottle is left within a child's reach; a sewing kit is left on a coffee table; a boiling teakettle is left on the front burner of a stove. There are hazards of some sort in every home, but it is not these "ordinary" hazards alone that are responsible for most accidents to children. In many cases, we also find that a period of prolonged or unusual stress—a chain of events that places an extra strain on family members—has relaxed their precautions and thus increased the possibility of an accident.

Based on The Children's Hospital Medical Center study, the conditions below are those that most often precipitate accidents to children. Be aware of these conditions; avoid them whenever possible. If they cannot be avoided, take special precautions. Any one of the factors might not, by itself, cause an accident; but 2 or 3 together greatly increase the chances.

## Accidents occur more often:

When a child is hungry or tired.
When a mother is ill, about to menstruate, or pregnant.
When there is no safe place to play.

When a child is considered "hyperactive" by his parents (see *learning disabilities*).

When the relationship between parents is tense.

When a child's surroundings change, often at moving or vacation time.

When other family members are ill or the center of the mother's attention.

When the family is rushed.

When parents overestimate the ability of a child to protect himself at each stage of the child's development.

When a child is in the care of an unfamiliar person or a brother or sister too young to be responsible.

If an accident occurs, don't underestimate the injury. In The Children's Hospital accident study, less than 50 percent of the parents said that they were aware of the extent of their child's injury—*regardless of its severity*. Of course, try to stay calm if your child has an accident, but don't ignore or underestimate it either.

Think before you act. For example, grabbing up a child who has suffered a *fracture* or who has internal injuries may do more harm than good. See Chapter 9: "First Aid." If you have any questions about what to do, don't do anything until you have telephoned your doctor or the emergency ward of the nearest hospital for advice.

Try not to panic if your child is injured. Children are ever alert to adult reactions, and if you panic, your child may panic, too. An injured child needs a calm, reassuring manner to help him overcome his natural fear.

## Rules for accident prevention

*Be aware of potential dangers* as you work in and around the house. Look for "ordinary" little things that could lead to trouble. Imagine what you might get into if you were a child.

*Teach your child all the simple safety rules* and encourage schools to emphasize safety education in the classrooms. Swimming lessons and traffic safety deserve special emphasis.

*Slow down and take extra precautions* if the pressure of everyday problems and troubles begins to take its toll. In particular, simplify your daily chores if you or other family members are ill, worried, or otherwise upset emotionally. (See Chapter 5: "Caring for the Sick Child at Home.")

*Protect your child*, but don't so overprotect him that he is unaware of dangers. Remember, all children must gradually be taught to protect themselves. When to let the child do things on his own, like crossing a street, is always a difficult decision. Use the occasion of an accident to discuss the hazards of car, pedestrian, skating, swimming safety, and so forth.

*Don't take chances with guns!* Firearm accidents have shown the greatest increase of all types of home accidents in recent years. The figures show that in America there are now two guns for every family, a third of them handguns. Teach your child about gun dangers, and remember the possible influence of gunplay to which he has been exposed on television. He cannot be expected to realize that a gun is not a toy, so protect him and others in the family by keeping guns locked away at all times. Gun control legislation is an urgent national necessity.

*Don't be overly trusting of preschool children.* A child's memory is short, and he may forget words or not fully understand their meaning. Even discipline may be quickly forgotten by a very young child. Many accidents occur because parents genuinely believe they have "taught" preschool children about dangers.

*Try to understand your child's needs* at each stage of his growth and development. If you can, anticipate what he'll be able to do next.

## Safety checklist
## for parents

Do you store all drugs and chemicals (insecticides, bleaches, detergents, and so forth) away from food and where children can't reach them?

Do you put all medicines—particularly flavored aspirin—safely away after using them? Does each medicine bottle have a child-proof safety cap?

Do you double-check labels on medicines before you give or take them? Do you turn on the lights when giving your child medicine at night?

Do you keep substances in their original containers and never store poisons—such as kerosene and cleaning fluids—in pop bottles?

Are all glasses used by children unbreakable?

Do you turn pot handles toward the back of the stove? If possible, do you remove the burner knobs when the stove is not in use?

Do you keep your baby and his toys off the kitchen floor when the kitchen is being used? Is the high chair or playpen at least 2 feet away from your working counters in the kitchen?

Do you keep the fireplace screen in place?

Do you make a special point of asking for flame-resistant clothing, including nightwear?

Are electric cords of movable appliances (fry pan, toaster, and so forth) out of reach so that they can't be tripped on and so the baby can't chew the cord?

Are all of your baby's toys free of splinters and too big for him to swallow?

Are you sensitive to water hazards in the bathtub, backyard, swimming pools, and at lakes or skating ponds?

Do you stay with your preschool child when he is in the bathtub? Do you plan to have him learn to swim as soon as possible?

Do you keep knives, pointed scissors, needles, pins, tacks, matches, table lighters, and nuts out of the reach of preschool children?

Do you keep guns away from children, and do you store ammunition separately from any gun in the house?

Are furniture and lamps heavy enough so that they can't be pulled over easily?

Are hot radiators and pipes covered or insulated?

Are all unused electric outlets fitted with dummy plugs? Are all electrical cords in good condition—neither frayed nor damaged?

Do you keep electrical devices (radios, electric light pulls, and so forth) away from the bathtub?

Are attic and basement free of oily cloths?

Is there a gate at the head and the foot of the stairs to keep babies or toddlers from falling down or climbing up?

Are all stairs well lit and fitted with firm handrails and treads? Are all stair and porch railings secure?

Are all upper-story windows properly screened or barred to prevent your child from falling out?

Are clotheslines strung out of children's reach?

Do you slow down and take extra precautions in the 4 to 7 P.M. hours when everyone is tired and hungry?

Are swimming pools in the neighborhood adequately fenced?

Do you make sure your son or daughter understands why certain safety rules must be observed while riding in or driving a car?

Do you check that your child knows water safety rules and something about the hazards of drowning? Even on frozen ponds?

Does your child abide by pedestrian and bicycle safety rules? (See "Bicycle and Minibike Safety," in Part 2.)

Have you stressed the danger of fire from cigarettes—in the woods and at home?

Have you checked your house and porch for peeling lead-containing paint and plaster? (See *lead poisoning.*)

If you answered "No" to any of these questions, make changes. Your house and neighborhood may have other hazards you can remove. Think about these, too.

See Chapter 9: "First Aid."

See also *bites, insect; bites, snake; bruise; burns; choking and swallowing foreign objects; cuts, scratches, abrasions, and scrapes; drug reactions, allergic; ear, foreign object in the; eye, injuries and foreign objects in the; fracture; head injuries; lead poisoning; nose, injuries and foreign objects in the; pets and children* (animal bites and rabies); *puncture wounds; shock; splinters;* and *sprains.*

# 9

## First
## Aid

In this section we briefly summarize the major points in first
aid. For more complete information, we strongly recommend
that every parent obtain and study the current version of the book,
*First Aid*, published by the American National Red Cross (New York:
Doubleday and Company, Inc.) and take an approved first-aid course.

## *Artificial respiration*

To be used when breathing has stopped. Continue artificial respiration until seen by a physician or until normal breathing resumes.

Mouth-to-nose or mouth-to-mouth rescue breathing is the method of choice.

*Rescue breathing technique* (best learned by taking a first-aid course): Clear the throat—wipe out any fluid, vomitus, mucus, or foreign body with fingers. Place victim on his or her back. Tilt the head straight back—extend the neck as far as possible, so that chin is pointing upward, which will automatically keep the tongue out of the airway. Place one hand under the neck and lift. Place the heel of the other hand on the forehead and rotate or tilt head backward. If the head is not tilted, the tongue may block the throat. If additional clearance is needed later, it may be necessary to push or pull the jaw upward into a jutting-out position. Pinch the victim's nostrils shut with the thumb and index finger of the hand that is pressing on the forehead. This maneuver prevents leakage of air when the lungs are inflated through the mouth. Open your mouth widely and take a deep breath. Apply your mouth tightly around the child's mouth and blow into his mouth. If the airway is clear, only moderate resistance to blowing will be felt. Watch the chest to see when it rises. When the chest is expanded, stop blowing. Release your mouth and listen for exhalation. Watch the chest to see that it falls. Repeat the cycle.

The desired rate of respiration is approximately 40 per minute for infants, 30 per minute for toddlers through age 10, 20 per minute for early teens, and 12 per minute for adults. The pressure required to inflate the lungs of an infant is not great. Merely blow the air contained in the mouth (with outpouched cheeks), using your cheeks, not your chest muscles, to expel the air.

In many cases when breathing has stopped, the heart has also stopped beating and it will be necessary to support the circulation through pressure on the chest to squeeze blood through the heart. This technique is called closed cardiac massage. It is very difficult to describe with words and is best learned through a first-aid course.

## Bites or stings

*Insect:* Remove stinger *at base* if present. Do not squeeze stinger as it is removed. Apply cold compresses. Consult physician promptly if there is *any* reaction other than at the site of the bite. See *bites, insect.* (All references in *boldface italic* type refer to Part 3 of this book.)

*Animal:* Wash with clean water and soap. Hold under running water for two or three minutes if not bleeding profusely. Apply sterile dressing. Consult physician. If possible, catch or retain the animal and maintain alive for observation regarding rabies. Notify police or health officer. See ***bites, animal.***

*Snake:* See ***bites, snake.***

## Bleeding

See below under cuts.

## Bruises

Rest injured part. Apply cold compresses for half an hour (no ice next to skin). If skin is broken, treat as a cut. For heavy or extensive bruises, consult physician.

## Burns and Scalds

If burn is not extensive or deep (with tissue destruction), pain can be relieved by cold packs (clean cloths wrung out in cold water) or by submerging the burned hand or foot in cold water.

If burn is caused by chemicals, wash burned area thoroughly with water. Remove clothes if chemical is on them. Consult physician. Take chemical container to physician or hospital.

If a burn is extensive, keep patient in flat position. Remove clothing from burned area, but if it sticks to the burn, leave in place. Cover with clean cloth. Keep patient warm. Take patient to hospital or to a physician at once. *Do not* use ointments, greases, powder, and so forth. See electric burns below and ***burns.***

## *Choking*

If the choking child can breathe adequately, take him or her to the nearest hospital emergency room or other medical facility. If the child cannot cough, speak, or breathe, or points to his or her neck, give four sharp blows to the upper back between the shoulder blades to shake loose the foreign object. If this does not work, perform the Heimlich maneuver immediately. This is a recent advance in emergency treatment of choking on a foreign object, developed by Henry J. Heimlich, M.D., of Cincinnati.

With the victim standing, wrap your arms around his waist. Make a fist with one hand and grasp the fist with the other hand. Place the thumb side of your fist into the abdomen with a quick upward thrust and repeat four times if necessary. The maneuver can be performed with the victim sitting if you include the chair back in your wrap. Press quickly into the abdomen with your fist or heel of hand as described. The pressure on the abdomen is transmitted to the lungs and the expelled air forces the obstructing object out of the airway. Do not punch, compress lung, or squeeze.

If the bolus of food is not expelled, hold the child upside down or positioned across your knee or arm with head lower than chest, giving four sharp upward blows to the back between the shoulder blades. If this is still not effective, keep repeating these steps, Heimlich maneuver and then sharp blows, until they are effective or the victim loses consciousness.

In cases of choking, if you can see and grasp the offending object, do so, but only if you can avoid pushing it further in. Because of this risk, when in any doubt the Heimlich maneuver should always be tried first. If these maneuvers fail, rush the child to the nearest emergency facility. A *tracheotomy* (specifically, a *cricothyreotomy*, cutting directly into the windpipe) will be done if necessary.

The Heimlich technique is worth knowing about for adults as well. It is the emergency treatment of choice (following unsuccessful blows to the back) for choking on a piece of meat, a very common offender which can be fatal if not removed. See **choking and swallowing foreign objects.**

## *Convulsions*

Prevent child from hurting himself. Give artificial respiration, if indicated. Do *not* place blunt object between the teeth. Do *not* restrain him or pour any liquid into his mouth. Do *not* place a child in a tub of water. If the convulsion is caused by fever, sponge body with cool water and apply cold cloths to head. Lay child on side with hips elevated. If repeated convulsions occur, call for medical help immediately or take the child to a hospital. In any case, contact your physician.

## *Cuts with major bleeding*

Apply dressing. Press firmly to stop bleeding. If pressure alone is insufficient to stop bleeding, which is rarely the case, apply pressure to artery supplying the extremity.

For an open arm wound including the hand, apply pressure to the brachial artery, forcing it against the arm bone. The pressure point is located on the inside of the arm about midway between the armpit and the elbow. The artery can be felt to pulsate in this area. To apply pressure on the artery, grasp the middle of upper arm with your thumb on the outside of the arm and your other fingers on the inside, using the inside surface of your fingers, not their tips. Press your fingers toward your thumb to create an inward force.

For the control of severe blooding from a leg wound, apply pressure on the femoral artery by forcing it against the pelvic bone. The pressure point is located on the front, center part of the crease in the groin area, where the artery crosses the pelvic bone on its way to the leg. Place the child flat on his back, if possible, and place the heel of your hand directly over the pressure point. Then lean forward over your straightened arm to apply the small amount of pressure needed to close the artery. If bleeding is not stopped, it may be necessary to press directly over the artery with the flat surfaces of the fingertips and apply additional pressure over the fingertips with the heel of the other hand.

The use of a tourniquet is rarely necessary. It is dangerous and reserved for use only when other measures have failed (direct pressure and pressure on arteries) and when life is threatened.

When a dressing has been applied to control bleeding, whether bleeding has been severe or not, precautions must be taken. Do not remove or disturb the cloth pad or attempt to cleanse the wound. The next step should be left to the doctor. Immobilize the injured area. When possible, adjust the victim's lying position so that the affected limb can be elevated.

See discussion of *shock* for how to recognize and deal with this effect of excessive blood loss.

## Cuts without major bleeding

To cleanse the wound, wash your hands thoroughly with soap and water. Use ordinary hand soap or mild detergent. Wash in and around the wound to remove foreign matter. Flush with clean water, preferably running tap water. Blot dry with a sterile gauze pad or a clean cloth. Apply a dry sterile bandage or clean dressing and secure it firmly in place. Consult a physician promptly if evidence of infection appears. Your doctor may advise additional home remedies for small wounds. See *cuts, scratches, abrasions, and scrapes.*

## Drowning

See artificial respiration above.

## Electric burns

Pull child away from source of current with wooden object such as a chair, or other nonconductive material. *Do not use bare hands.* Electric burns with shock may interfere with breathing and require artificial respiration (see above). See *burns.*

## Eyes

For chemicals in the eye, see *burns.* For all other injuries, see *eye, injuries and foreign objects in the.*

## Fainting and unconsciousness

Keep in flat position. Loosen clothing around neck. Summon physician. Keep patient warm. Keep mouth clear. Give nothing to swallow.

## Fractures

Any deformity of injured part usually means a fracture. Do not move person if fracture of neck or back is suspected. Summon physician at once. If person with a fractured limb must be moved, immobilize the limb with adequate splints. See discussion of *fractures.*

## Head injuries

*Do not* move unless additional danger would occur to injured person. Consult physician immediately. See *head injuries.*

## Nosebleeds

See discussion of *nosebleeds.*

## Puncture wounds

Stop bleeding. Consult physician immediately.

*Splinters:* Wash with clean water and soap. Remove with tweezers or forceps, sterilized over a flame or in boiling water. Wash again. If large or deep, consult physician.

See *puncture wounds.*

## Scrapes

Use wet gauze or cotton to sponge off gently with clean water and soap.

## Seizures

See convulsions (above) and *seizure disorders.*

## Shock

See discussion in Part 3.

## Sprains

Elevate injured part. Apply cold compresses for half an hour. If swelling is unusual, do not use injured part until seen by physician.

## *Basic first-aid supplies*

Roll of thin, clean plastic wrapping (the kind ordinarily used to cover food).

Plastic-covered gauze squares (various sizes).

Sterile gauze squares ($2'' \times 2''$ and $4'' \times 4''$ individually wrapped).

Roll of gauze bandage ($2''$ wide).

Roll of adhesive tape.

Adhesive bandages (various sizes).

Splints.

Ipecac syrup (to induce vomiting).

Much of the above first-aid advice was taken from the pamphlet *Your Child and Household Safety*, with the kind permission of the American Academy of Pediatrics and the author, Jay M. Arena, M.D.

# 10
# Poisoning

Poisoning is one of the leading causes of death, disability, and hospitalization in children. It is a topic about which every parent should be informed.

## *What is poisonous?*

A poison is any substance that can cause internal damage to the body if taken in sufficient quantity. Aspirin in excess is by far the most common poison and was once responsible for as many as 100,000 childhood poisonings in the United States each year. (Safety caps on aspirin bottles have reduced this toll.) Children are also commonly poisoned by other medicines, bleach, detergents, cleaning agents, furniture polish, kerosene, and disinfectants.

Different poisons have different effects on the body. For example, kerosene can cause coma, convulsions, and inflammation of the lungs, sometimes called "chemical pneumonia." Aspirin can cause breathing difficulty, coma, and widespread internal bleeding. The effects of any poison vary with the amount taken and the size of the child. Many relatively harmless poisons cause only mild abdominal pain and _diarrhea._

Common household products which are either not, or very mildly, toxic and do not generally require any treatment are:

Ball-point inks
Bar soap
Battery (small dry cell)
Bubble bath soap
Candles
Chalk
Clay (modeling)
Crayons with A.P., C.P., or C.S.
   130-46 designation
Dehumidifying packets
Detergents (anionic): Tide, Cheer,
   Ajax, Top Job, Comet, Windex,
   Mr. Clean, Lestoil, Joy, Spic and
   Span, among others, cause mild
   vomiting
Eye makeup
Fishbowl additives

Hand lotion and cream
Ink (blue, black, red)
Lipstick
Mercury (from broken thermometer)
Newspaper
Pencils (lead and coloring)
Putty and Silly Putty
Sachets
Shampoo
Shaving cream
Shoe polish (with rare exceptions)
Striking surface materials of
   matchboxes
Sweetening agents (saccharin,
   cyclamate)
Toothpaste

Common household items which can cause poisoning if taken in large amounts (check with poison center) and which should be removed from the child's stomach by induced vomiting are:

After-shave lotion
Alcohol, wood (methyl)
Birth control pills
Bleach (give milk first)
Body conditioners
Boric acid
Camphor
Carbon tetrachloride
Colognes
Deodorants

Detergents (cationic)—Phisohex, Di-
   aperene, among others, cause nau-
   sea, vomiting, convulsions, coma
Fabric softeners
Fingernail polish and remover
Fluoride
Hair dyes
Hair permanent neutralizer
Hair sprays
Hair tonic

Hydrogen peroxide
Indelible markers
Ink (green and purple)
Iron tablets
Matches (more than twenty wooden
    matches or two books of paper
    matches)

Mothballs, flakes or cakes
Oil of wintergreen (methyl salicylate)
Perfumes
Suntan preparations
Toilet water
Vitamins (especially A and D)
Wick deodorizer

Many common plants, including houseplants, and fungi are poisonous. Among them are:

Azalea
Buttercup
Daffodil
Holly berries
Ivy, English
Laurel

Lily of the valley
Mistletoe
Mushrooms (wild)
Philodendron
Rhododendron
Yew

If your child has swallowed some leaves or berries, try to identify the plant, and call your nearest poison control center. If in doubt, induce vomiting. An excellent resource for schools or outdoor education groups is the film *Poisonous Plants*, distributed by Macmillan and Co., 34 MacQuesten Parkway South, Mount Vernon, N.Y. 10550.

The poisonous substances listed below contain a strong base such as lye (L) or strong acid (A) or petroleum (P). Lye and acid burn the mouth, esophagus (food tube), and stomach going in or coming out, and petroleum products can be aspirated into the lungs. Vomiting should *not* be induced with lye-containing products or strong acids. For petroleum-containing products, vomiting is recommended only if the ingestion is large and only under the advice of a doctor or poison control center. See first-aid treatment for poisoning later in this chapter.

Ammonia (L)
Battery acid (A)
Brush cleaner (L or P)
Charcoal lighter (P)
Corn and wart remover (A)
Dishwasher granules (L)
Disinfectants such as Lysol (A)
Drain cleaner (A)
Furniture polish (P)
Gasoline (P)
Grease remover (L or P)
Gun cleaner (P)

Kerosene (P)
Lighter fluid (P)
Metal cleaner (P)
Oven cleaner (L or A)
Paint thinner (P)
Toilet bowl cleaner (L or A)
Turpentine (P)
Typewriter cleaner (P)
Washing soda (L)
Wax for floor or furniture (P)
Wood preservatives (P)

# *Preventing poisoning*

If you have preschool children, be sure to store all potential poisons out of reach. Put your medicines in a locked cabinet or box after using them. Many children are poisoned when they find medicines around the house. There are 5 major places to check: (1) under the sink or on kitchen shelves; (2) bedroom night tables and dressers; (3) bathroom; (4) basement, back porch, or garage, where substances are often stored out of their original containers (in pop bottles, and so forth); (5) women's purses. Young children love to explore purses and a purse very often contains medicines: headache remedies, "nerve pills," vitamins, nitroglycerin, and contraceptives. One survey of women showed that approximately 40 percent occasionally or always carried medications in their purses.

Remember that preschool children love to put everything in their mouths. (Mouthing is part of their normal growth and a way of learning about things.) Toddlers will eat or drink anything and are ingenious in searching out objects which you "couldn't believe he or she could get into." They have been known to drink a whole tin of kerosene without minding the taste. Don't rely on their judgment.

Be aware of the dangers of flavored children's aspirin. A bottle of 50 can kill a child. Unlike other poisons, such as ammonia or floor polishes, "candy" aspirin tastes good, and a child not only will eat it if it is lying around but will search it out on high shelves or in the medicine chest. When urging a feverish child to take aspirin, don't tell him that it is "just like candy." Say it is "medicine."

Ask for child-proof safety caps for all medicines. (These are being increasingly used for other household products as well.) Check the label of each medicine before use. Be particularly careful at night when dim lights and drowsiness may make you less likely to read the label correctly. Be sure each bottle of medicine is properly labeled with its contents.

Be particularly careful when you are moving or going on vacation. Medicines and other poisons are likely to be out of their normal places.

Whenever possible, keep the most dangerous products listed above out of the home entirely. If substances such as drain cleaner, disinfectants, rat poison, carbon tetrachloride (cleaning fluid), paint thinner, charcoal lighter, and insecticides must be used, lock them up where children cannot possibly reach them.

# First-aid treatment for poisoning

In order to save time, you should always have the telephone numbers of the poison center, doctor, hospital, and taxi company readily at hand.

In all cases except poisonous bites, the principle of first aid is to get the poison OUT or OFF, or to DILUTE it. ALWAYS CALL A PHYSICIAN, HOSPITAL, POISON CONTROL CENTER, or RESCUE UNIT PROMPTLY. The following are basic first-aid measures for various types of poisoning:

1.  SWALLOWED POISONS. THIS IS AN EMERGENCY—ANY NONFOOD SUBSTANCE IS A POTENTIAL POISON.

    A.  Get container. Read list of ingredients. If container is not available, ask child what he has taken.

    B.  Call physician, hospital, poison control center, or rescue unit promptly.

    C.  Dilute poison by giving water, one or two glassfuls. (Except for petroleum distillates; see [F.] below.)

    D.  If child is unconscious, having fits, or groggy, do not make him vomit, but take him directly to the hospital.

    E.  If swallowed poison was a strong corrosive (lye, strong acid, drain cleaner, and so forth), do not make him vomit. For acid (A) products give milk of magnesia, or antacid and glass of milk. For alkali (L) products give fruit juices, diluted vinegar (1 part vinegar to 4 parts water), and milk. In all these cases, take patient to hospital.

    F.  If swallowed poison contains kerosene, gasoline, or other petroleum distillates, do not make him vomit. Do not give anything to drink. (For turpentine, vomiting is generally recommended. Call poison center.) Take patient to hospital.

    G.  If, as is true of pills, the substance does not have a lye or petroleum base or contain a strong acid, or if you are instructed to make your child vomit, use one of the following methods:

    DIRECTIONS FOR MAKING A PATIENT VOMIT
    • Give one tablespoonful (one-half ounce) of syrup of ipecac for a child one year of age or older, plus at least one cup of water.

Encourage the child to move around. If no vomiting occurs in 20 minutes, this dose may be repeated *once only*. Ipecac syrup can be purchased without prescription and should be in the medicine chest of all homes with small children.

• If no ipecac syrup is available, give child a glass of water. Then try to induce vomiting by tickling back of throat with a spoon handle or other blunt object.

• Do not waste time waiting for vomiting, but transport patient promptly to a medical facility.

H. Transport child directly to nearest medical facility. *Bring package or container with intact label.*

2. FUMES OR GASES. For example, fuel gases, auto exhaust, smoke from fires or fumes from poisonous chemicals.

A. Get victim into fresh clean air.

B. Loosen clothing.

C. If victim is not breathing, start artificial respiration promptly. *Do not stop* until patient is breathing well, or help arrives.

D. Have *someone else* call a physician, hospital, poison control center, or rescue unit.

E. Transport to a medical facility promptly.

3. EYE. For a discussion of chemicals in the eye, see **burns.**

4. SKIN. Acids, lye, other caustics, pesticides, and so forth.

A. Wash off skin immediately with a large amount of water; use soap if available.

B. Remove any contaminated clothing.

C. Call physician, hospital, poison control center, or rescue unit, and transport victim to a medical facility if necessary.

See also **lead poisoning.**

*Richard I. Feinbloom, M.D.*

Much of the advice in this section on First-Aid Treatment for Poisoning was taken from the pamphlet *Your Child and Household Safety,* with the kind permission of the American Academy of Pediatrics and the author, Jay M. Arena, M.D.

# 11
# Bicycle and Minibike Safety

## Bicycles

Bicycle use has skyrocketed in the United States during recent years and, as would be expected, the number of accidents associated with bicycles is also on the rise. One million injuries are estimated to occur annually, including 20,000 fractures, 60,000 concussions, and a minimum of 850 deaths from collisions with vehicles or pedestrians alone (data from 1972 *Accident Facts*, compiled by the National Safety Council). Many of these problems are related to the mingling of bicycle and motor vehicle traffic. One answer to the problem should certainly be the separation of the two types of vehicle traffic. This would mean the establishment of bicycle paths in urban areas.

Bicycle accidents among children have been studied and several recommendations about bicycle use and construction and also rules of the road can be made. There are now Federal guidelines for the manufacturers of bicycles, including a required road test. Parents should make sure any bicycle they buy meets these standards.

### Bicycle use and construction

1. Riding double should be strongly discouraged because the bike is not easily controlled with a second rider. Direct injuries by catching the feet between the spokes are common. This possibility exists whether the second rider is sitting on the crossbar, in front of, or behind the driver, or, as in the case of young children, on a special seat over the rear wheel. Child carriers should have built-in protection for keeping the child's foot out of spokes.

*Consumer Reports* (July 1975) makes the following recommendations for add-on bike seats for children: "If you have an infant or a small toddler, the front-mounted *Sears 48525* is the one to choose. But it does present size limitations. A larger child will be more comfortable —and easier to transport—in a rear-mounted seat. Among the top-rated rear mounts, the *AMF AC45* or the *Sears 48523* are the best models in every way. The *Troxel 4, Troxel Deluxe 6*, and *Wards 82656* are nearly as good. The rest of the rear-mounted seats have a safety or a handling disadvantage or both."

2. Night riding should be discouraged whenever possible. Reflectors are needed on the sides as well as the fronts and backs of bicycles to improve recognizability under dim lighting conditions. A large headlight should be used. Pedals with built-in reflectors are available on all new bicycles and are now required by Federal law. Some riders achieve increased visibility by attaching a red bicycle light to one ankle, thus creating a moving warning light as they pedal. An armband reflector is also recommended. Both ankle and arm lights should, of course, be worn on the side next to cars. Bright-colored clothes are preferable to dark ones, which are less visible. The orange vests used by hunters or by road crew workers can be put over outer garments by the evening or night biker. Even better are reflectorized materials.

3. The bike should fit the child. The advice of a reputable bike shop should be sought in fitting a bike. The seat should be no higher than the rider's hips so that the feet can just touch the ground without

having to lean the bike. There is an understandable temptation to use hand-me-down bicycles in families to avoid the need for purchasing new ones. When selecting a conventional bicycle, make sure you pick one with a suitable frame size. Frame size is measured from the pedal crank axis to the top of the frame seat tube. Usually, a frame measuring nine or ten inches less than the rider's inseam (crotch to floor, in stocking feet) would give a good fit. The inseam formula is especially useful in selecting an open-frame bicycle. For a conventional closed-frame bicycle, you might be able to judge fit simply by having the rider straddle the bicycle; the rider should be able to stand without having the crossbar touch the crotch.

4. The handlebars should be tight to prevent loss of control. One study at the University of Vermont under the direction of Dr. Julian Waller found that it was quite easy for handlebars and forks to loosen and get out of alignment during the normal, average use of the bicycle. This loosening can be expected to occur much more often if the bike is used for "wheelies," that is, riding momentarily on the rear wheel only, a popular maneuver. (The loosening of the handlebars would be made much more difficult if the bicycles were constructed so that the surfaces at which the bars and fork are held together were flattened instead of being perfectly round, a change manufacturers should seriously consider.)

5. Bike should be supplied with a bugle horn to warn pedestrians. (Battery-run horns wear out, often not to be replaced.)

6. High-rise bicycles, also known as "banana bikes" or "choppers," are somewhat controversial. They have been claimed to be (a) orthopedically unsound because of increased strain on the back; (b) unsafe; and (c) mechanically inefficient. Consumers Union, in its tests of high-rise bicycles (see the January 1975 issue of *Consumer Reports*) noted no inherent mechanical inefficiencies and found the bikes to be no more unsafe than any conventional model. In fact, Consumers Union's engineers considered the high-rise bicycle to be safer for a child to ride in one respect: It enhances the rider's control of the bike because of the size advantage of the child over the machine. Another advantage of these bikes noted by Consumers Union was that they are not easily outgrown because of their extended seat-height adjustment. For example, a bike bought for a child of eight could be used for some four years simply by raising the seat periodically.

7. An older child should be taught how his bike is constructed and how to make minor repairs. This will encourage better care for the bike and a sense of control while riding.

There are a number of riding rules of the road which should be known to all bike riders. Many of those which we enumerate here are derived from the State of Illinois pamphlet, *Bicycle Rules of the Road* (reprinted with the kind permission of the Secretary of State of the State of Illinois). Parents should teach these to their children and observe the rules themselves. Basically cyclists should follow the same rules as cars.

## Rules of the road

1. Be aware at all times of what cars may do, and whether the driver can see you. Watch for opening of doors on the street side of parked cars into the cyclist's path. Many motorists are not used to bicycles and will unintentionally cut off a bike in making a right-hand turn. Cyclists have to be aware of these blind spots of motorists and should always be in the position to stop. They should check behind them before sudden stops. Cars can't stop as quickly as bicycles.

2. *Turns.* At busy intersections it may be safer to make a left turn by crossing the street or road, waiting for the light to change, and then proceeding across rather than trying to make a left turn directly from one road to the other. Never turn around on hills or curves. Don't make a U-turn without first looking carefully to see if it is safe. On some streets U-turns are not allowed. Know the various traffic signs.

3. Signal well ahead of all turns and stops.

4. Never cross the center line to pass without first making certain there is plenty of room to do so safely. Never move into the left-hand lane to pass when there is a yellow stripe on your side of the center line. Never pass at intersections or railroad crossings.

5. If several people are biking, they should stay in single file, riding with the traffic, and to the right edge of the road. Never weave back and forth from one lane to another. This is a traffic law violation and it is also very dangerous. When it is necessary to change lanes, always give a turn signal.

6. Keep hands on handlebars.

7. Stay on the seat. Don't sit on the fenders or any other part of the bike. Control of the bike will be impaired.

8. Hitching rides by holding onto cars or trucks is very dangerous.

9. *Braking*. Test brakes before starting out. If there is a coaster brake on the bike, put the pedals in a level position for stop when coming to an intersection. Hand brakes must be used properly for them to be safe and effective. Both front and rear brakes should be functioning. It is unsafe when one set is out of order. Try to put equal pressure on the control lever so that the two wheels will brake evenly. Use the front brake with caution; avoid using it altogether under poor traction conditions. When riding on gravel or wet pavement, it is even more dangerous to make a turn, so begin braking sooner, but more gently. Wet weather may interfere with brake action. Test the brakes and adjust speed accordingly.

10. Overloading a bike with large or heavy packages will make it hard to handle in traffic and may cause a spill. Watch for dogs; they like to chase bikes and will snap at feet or tires.

11. If bicycle paths are available, use them. If your city does not provide them, work with other cyclists to get them established.

## Minibikes

The minibike is defined by the United States Department of Transportation as "a two-wheeled vehicle with wheel rims of less than 10 inches diameter . . . or with hub to hub wheel base of less than 40 inches . . . or an engine rated at less than 45 cubic centimeters . . . or a seat height of less than 25 inches from the ground."

An estimated 2 million minibikes are in use in the United States, two-thirds of them driven by children between the ages of 10 and 14 years. The number sold continues to rise at a remarkable rate. The Bureau of Product Safety has estimated that during 1973 there were 75,000 minibike injuries.

Most injuries and fatalities on minibikes occur in collisions with motor vehicles on the highways and streets, according to information published by the Department of Transportation. Among the major reasons for accidents are:

1. Aside from those models designed for use on public highways, most minibikes are not intended for road use and do not belong in traffic.

Minibikes have a low profile and small size, making their young riders hard to spot in traffic. They are often unseen by motorists in time to avoid a collision. And minibikes, unless they are equipped for public roads, do not carry lights.

2. Some minibikes, such as those without front and rear suspensions and front brakes, are notorious for their poor handling characteristics.

In view of these dangers, the American Academy of Pediatrics has urged parents to "hold firm in their refusal to allow their children the inescapable risk-taking involved in owning and/or operating a mini-bike." In a statement on minibike safety, the academy's Joint Committee on Physical Fitness, Recreation, and Sports Medicine said: "The trend toward allowing underage children to operate minibikes should be deplored and condemned. This would be indicated on general principles even if the minibike were a quasi-safe vehicle, which it most emphatically is not." In its conclusion, the committee recommended "that state legislatures outlaw the operation of any motor vehicle by a person who does not have a full operator's license for which he has qualified by an approved driver training program. We call on the manufacturers of minibikes to cease and desist from the exploitation of children implicit in the promotion of minibikes to parents of children below the age of driver's licensure."

Our first advice to parents, therefore, in regard to minibikes, is not to buy them for their children. If your child does ride a minibike, the following rules should be observed:

*The do's and don't's of minibike use:*

*Do* as a parent, be sure that your minibiker uses an off-road area in which to ride.

*Do* make sure that experienced instruction is available. Parents can form or join minibike clubs, organizations that teach proper highway safety standards.

*Do* require that the child wear a safety helmet and sturdy shoes and clothing.

*Do* find out from your insurance company what additional coverage is necessary to protect fully the minibike rider and yourself from liability.

*Do not* allow your child under any conditions to use the minibike on highways, streets, or sidewalks.

*Do not* allow your child to lend the minibike to an inexperienced friend.

*Do not* assume that a vacant, off-road area is necessarily a legal area for riding. Many owners of property have closed their lands to cyclists and minibike riders. Inquire beforehand.

*Do not* scrimp on a good safety helmet or sturdy, protective clothing. Even the most experienced riders will fall on occasion. The right equipment will decrease the risk for your young rider.

*Do not* assume that your homeowner's or automobile insurance policy will necessarily adequately protect you or your minibike rider. You will usually need additional protection.

Having said this, we should again emphasize how we feel about mini-bikes. Basically, we see them as a dangerous risk and an extravagance. We must prefer nonpolluting vehicles like bicycles which offer exercise and develop physical fitness at the same time that they provide a means of transportation.

See *exercise and physical fitness.*

Recommended reading: Eugene A. Sloane, *Complete Book of Bicycling* (New York: Trident Press, 1970).

*Richard I. Feinbloom, M.D.*

# 12
## Car
## Safety

**P**arents need to be reminded that automobile accidents are *the leading* cause of death in children. More than 1000 children under the age of 5, and 1700 between 5 and 15 are killed in automobiles every year. Many more are injured, some of whom remain permanently disabled, physically and/or mentally. Better-designed cars and roads and better drivers are part of the answer. In addition, simple parental action can reduce the severity of injuries and prevent death. The lowering of speed limits to conserve fuel has also helped lower the accident rate.

At present, protection of youngsters in cars is the exception rather than the rule. Using the cargo area of station wagons for young passengers is an accepted practice. Children are allowed to kneel on the front seat, faces pressed against the windshield, or to romp around the vehicle at will. Sometimes arms and even heads can be seen protruding from fast-moving cars. Playpens are considered a convenient means of transporting infants or toddlers. At best, small children are placed in special kiddy seats that keep them confined and may prevent them from losing their balance on curves or in sudden stops. Car pools are a time-honored institution, with mothers taking turns driving each other's children; the larger the number of youngsters accommodated in one vehicle, the less likely they are to be properly restrained. The possibility of an accident is one that the majority of the motoring public is unwilling to face.

Medical science has virtually wiped out many once-dreaded childhood diseases. Today's "epidemic" is one of man's own making. No "shots" are available to protect children from the dangers of the highway; the responsibility for their protection rests with their parents.

Innumerable studies have shown safety belts to be the single most effective safety device presently available. Yet recent statistics indicated that a large percentage of people do not use this precaution. Use of lap and shoulder belts, combined with the protection built into late-model cars, makes the majority of accidents survivable. Yet most parents, who otherwise conscientiously safeguard their children's health, fail to recognize the need for taking precautions in automobiles.

Seat-belt campaigns have consistently ignored the special needs of infants and small children. Lack of information, combined with the difficulty of procuring effective devices, is partly responsible for public apathy.

The protection of small children presents special problems. Because of structural differences between adults and young children, lap belts must not be used until the child is at least 4 years old and weighs 40 pounds or more. Weight rather than age is the determining factor. The pelvic structure of small children is insufficiently developed to protect internal organs from the forces that press the belt into the child's abdomen in a crash. In addition, small children's heads are larger and therefore heavier in proportion to their bodies than those of adults; the pressure exerted by the seat belt on the child's body becomes proportionately greater. Injuries to the spine and neck can also occur. Small children must therefore use devices capable of distributing collision forces over a large body area. Devices that meet this requirement are available.

Starting on page 568, "Car Safety Restraints for Children" has been reprinted from the June 1977 issue of *Consumer Reports* to provide readers with product information about these devices.

Studies conducted at the University of Michigan Highway Safety Research Institute have provided the following basic guidelines for buying a safety device:

1. For the infant, a device which positions him or her in the rearward-facing position is best.

2. For the child able to sit up unaided, three types of devices are satisfactory:

 a. The *shield*, which distributes collision forces evenly over the child's body. This is preferred by safety experts.

 b. The *conventional car seat;* a five-point harness restrains the child; some seats require anchoring at the top.

 c. The *safety harness;* child may be seated on booster cushion.

(Some devices combine the design features of 1, 2a, and 2b.)

Simulated crash tests carried out at the Highway Safety Research Institute have shown all devices listed here to give effective protection in frontal crashes. Side protection varies, and its rating is given for each device. (Side crashes are less frequent than head-on crashes.)

*Bobby-Mac* (Collier Keyworth)—for babies from birth to 35 pounds; obtainable from department and juvenile specialty stores. The device is used in the rearward-facing position for the infant. Once the child can sit up without support, the seat is used facing forward, with a shield attached to distribute collision forces. The shield may be purchased separately and used with the earlier model, increasing its protective value. A harness must be used in combination with the shield. The device is easy to install. Protection in side collisions is good in the rearward-facing position for the infant, but poor for the older child.

*Infant Love Seat* (General Motors)—for infants only; obtainable from the parts department of all General Motors, Chrysler, and American Motors dealers, as well as some department and juvenile specialty stores. This deep, tub-like container offers good protection in side impact also; it is designed to be installed facing backward. On a sloping car seat the device may be positioned horizontally by placing a rolled-up blanket between the front of the carrier and the car seat. This will allow the baby to ride more comfortably in a slightly reclining position. Do not tip the carrier more than just indicated; the semi-upright position of the infant is a valuable safety factor.

*Infantseat Harness* (Questor)—from the time baby can sit up to 50 pounds; obtainable from department and juvenile specialty stores. Easy to use, side protection is fair.

*Kant-Wet Care Seat* (Questor), Models 784 and 884 *only*; other seats made by this company are not recommended. May be used from the time the baby sits up without support to 45 pounds. Obtainable from department and juvenile specialty stores. Side protection is fair. Must be secured at the top.

*Love Seat* (General Motors)—for children able to sit up to 40 pounds; obtainable from the parts department of all General Motors and American Motors dealers, as well as some department and juvenile specialty stores. Protection in side impacts is excellent. Seat must be secured at the top.

*Motor Toter* (Century Products)—from the time the baby can sit up to 40 pounds; obtainable from department and juvenile specialty stores. Other devices made by the same company are not recommended. Excellent side protection. Requires securing at the top.

*Peterson 74 and 75 only* (Peterson Baby Products); other models made by the same company are not recommended. Usable from birth to 40 pounds; obtainable from department and juvenile specialty stores. The device is adaptable for use in the rearward-facing position for the infant; once the child is able to sit up, the seat is used facing forward with a shield attached. Once this is outgrown, a harness is used. The device is very convenient, with excellent side protection.

*Tot-Guard* (Ford Motor Co.)—from 20 pounds until outgrown, as long as the head is supported by the car seat back or a head restraint. Available from all Ford dealers. The device consists of a seat cushion and a plastic shield that forms a tunnel over the child's body. The vehicle lap belt is used to anchor the shield, no harness is necessary. The device is very easy to use—most children can slip in and out of it without the belt having to be released first. A large, firm pillow should be wedged between the child and the car door. The child may sleep with the head resting on the shield, but should not be allowed to droop over the sides. Side protection is poor.

*Important facts to remember*

1. In car crashes, passengers are hurled with tremendous force in the direction of the impact until they are stopped by an interior part of the vehicle or are ejected through the windshield, a window, or door. Restraints keep passengers safely contained inside the vehicle. Fear of

becoming "trapped" in the event of fire or immersion is unjustified. Restraints prevent or lessen injury, and help rather than hinder escape.

2. Some parents believe that they can prevent a child who is sitting beside them from being flung forward by extending their arm in moments of danger. This may be feasible when braking, but is impossible in a crash. It is far safer to keep both hands on the steering wheel and concentrate on the road ahead. The knowledge that children are securely restrained can itself be instrumental in avoiding accidents.

3. Although the most secure place for a small child may ordinarily be his mother's arms, this is not so in an automobile. In a collision, the child may be crushed between the adult and the vehicle interior. Even if the adult is wearing a combination lap and shoulder belt him- or herself the child would be wrenched from his or her arms by collision forces.

4. A seat belt must *never* be used to restrain both an adult and a child on her lap; in a mishap, the weight of the adult would press the belt into the child's abdomen—with grave consequences. *Even on the first car ride, the drive home from the hospital, the infant should be transported in an effective safety device.*

5. Most parents think of children's car seats simply as positioning devices, giving no thought to how the child would be protected in an accident. The commonly used car seats on department. store shelves are now required to meet government safety specifications. While these seats (if used correctly) no doubt give better protection than in the past, crash testing has found them to be inadequate. (See the August 1972 and February 1974 issues of *Consumer Reports.*) The Federal standard will soon be upgraded to meet more stringent safety requirements.

6. Harnesses that are secured by merely looping a strap around the back of the car seat are useless, because the seat back does not provide safe anchorage in the event of a crash. In addition, narrow straps can cut into the child's soft body tissue, *causing* injuries instead of preventing them.

7. *The best of devices cannot perform their function unless installed and used according to the manufacturer's instructions.* This point cannot be stressed sufficiently. Harnesses must not only be fastened but carefully adjusted to fit the wearer. Child seats must be pushed firmly against the back of the car seat. The vehicle lap belt must always be

used to secure a seating device. The belt should be pulled as tightly as possible. If additional anchorage straps are provided, these must also be used. Failure to follow manufacturer's instructions may render a device virtually useless.

8. The back seat is safer than the front; the center of the vehicle is safer than the sides. However, accident *avoidance* is a factor that must also be considered. A driver who has to turn around frequently to check on the child in the back seat may get into an accident situation. Car seats and seat backs must lock in position if they are to accommodate a child restrained by a safety device. If seating devices or harness are installed in the rear seat, they should be in the center, away from doors or sides.

9. Children over 4 years of age should be placed on a firm cushion and strapped in with a standard lap belt while sitting upright against the back of the seat. The cushion serves to position the belt at the correct angle across the child's hips (45 degrees). *The belt must not be permitted to ride up across the child's abdomen.* The cushion may be omitted as soon as the child is tall enough. Diagonal belts are not suitable for persons below a certain height because the belts would position dangerously across the wearer's neck or face in a collision (consult your car manual). Never strap two children into one belt.

10. Devices should be used until outgrown, but the child's head should never extend above the top of the seat.

11. A hazard exists when bicycles, lawn mowers, luggage, skis, or any hard, heavy, or sharp objects are carried unsecured inside the vehicle. Check also for potentially dangerous toys your children may be playing with while the car is in motion.

12. All doors should be locked. Engaging the safety latch helps prevent doors from springing open in a crash. Windows should never be lowered more than necessary for ventilation. Under certain conditions, an open tailgate window can admit dangerous carbon monoxide fumes from the vehicle's exhaust into the inside of the car.

13. Convertibles and other vehicles with soft tops expose passengers to serious injury in roll-over accidents. Sedans with a center post for additional support are believed to afford the best protection.

This article contains all available information at the time this book went to press. However, additional devices will come on the market as public demand for effective crash protection for children increases.

The standards for child safety restraints are constantly in flux and parents must make every effort to inform themselves as to the latest research and devices available.

An informative, illustrated pamphlet entitled *Don't Risk Your Child's Life!* is obtainable from Physicians for Automotive Safety, 50 Union Avenue, Irvington, N.J. 07111. It is printed in small quantities to make revisions possible as soon as new information becomes available. Requests for the pamphlet should be marked BCH and must be accompanied by a *stamped, self-addressed envelope and $.25 for each copy requested.*

If you are interested in supporting efforts for safer school busing, camp transportation, and public information on child auto safety in general, including car pools and school buses, write to Action for Child Transportation Safety, 400 Central Park West, #2R, New York, N.Y. 10025. ACTS is a recently formed citizens' organization founded by three young mothers who were concerned about the safety of their own children and felt strongly enough about the problem to want to help other parents. Mention this article in your letter. Another similar group is Mothers for School Bus Safety, Ossining, N.Y. 10562.

A major program to reach new parents is the In Hospital Program of Physicians for Automotive Safety. The kit they have prepared includes a short film, pamphlets, and teachers' lesson plans. For more information send a self-addressed envelope to Physicians for Automotive Safety (address above).

Information in this chapter about restraints has been derived from, or checked against, *Don't Risk Your Child's Life!*, published by Physicians for Automotive Safety.

*Annemarie Shelness*

# 3

---

# Childhood Diseases & Conditions

*Abdominal pain* is a very common complaint in children. It may be only one of several complaints or symptoms during a given illness. It is commonly associated with nausea, *vomiting*, and *diarrhea.* At other times the abdominal pain may be the most striking part of the child's complaint or, for that matter, his or her only complaint.

In general the more abdominal pain interferes with a child's normal routine, and the steadier (more constant) the pain is, the more reason for concern. If he continues to walk, run, play, eat, and sleep much as usual, you can rest assured that the pain is not of a serious nature. On the other hand, if the child wants to remain seated or to lie down and resents being asked to move, refuses to eat, or awakens from sleep because of pain, take his complaints more seriously. Press around his belly to see if there is a tender area. If he winces in pain, the cause of the bellyache is more apt to be serious (for example, *appendicitis*), and the doctor should be notified. Even mild steady pain persisting more than 4 hours should be reported. If a bellyache begins in the middle of the night, the same rules apply. Don't wait until morning for fear of inconveniencing either yourself or your doctor. If he is *incapacitated* with pain, obviously call for help.

Sometimes the pain will come in cramps. Crampy pain is characteristic of infections of the stomach and intestine (*gastroenteritis*). In crampy belly pain, the child will complain of pain which lasts usually no more than a minute. He will then be completely free of symptoms for several minutes or more until another cramp occurs. Often crampy pain will occur in association with *diarrhea* and *vomiting.* If the cramps are severe, that is, cause the child to stop his regular activity and cry or complain during the cramp itself, and if this pattern repeats itself over a period of 1 hour, get in touch with your doctor. In a very young child or infant, intermittent pain of this type, especially if associated with vomiting and marked quietness between cramps, suggests *intussusception.* If the cramps are mild and cause less trouble to the child, but go on for as long as 4 hours, let your doctor know.

The same rules apply to children too young or upset to tell you what is bothering them. In such children, the site of the pain must be interpreted by the child's behavior. A young child with abdominal pain may point to or clutch his belly.

In general, avoid giving medicines like aspirin or paregoric to relieve the pain. These medicines are not all that effective in relieving pain and may conceal a problem deserving of medical attention. It is perfectly safe and often helpful for you to apply a hot-water bottle to the child's belly and have him lie down until you see exactly which way things are going. These simple measures are about as far as we suggest that you go in attempting to relieve the discomfort.

There is still a common belief (with some basis in truth) that belly pain can be caused by *constipation.* In general, we urge parents always to check with their physician before giving laxatives or enemas and never to give them without a physician's advice. We would underline this warning when it comes to the child who is having belly pain. If, in fact, the child does have an early case of appendicitis, the use of a laxative or enema could do real harm and for that reason should be avoided.

Abdominal pain may occur in association with urinary frequency and burning, suggesting *urinary tract infections.* It is also common in sore throats (see *throat, sore*), particularly strep throats. The source of the pain appears to be swollen lymph nodes in the abdomen which are responding to the infection (see *infections*). *Pneumonia* is also often associated with abdominal pain.

Food is often incriminated as a cause of abdominal pain—"something he ate." This association is often a hard one to prove. True food poisoning involves the poisons (toxins) produced by bacteria which have multiplied in food, usually unrefrigerated spreads, mayonnaise, or custards. These toxins commonly cause vomiting and diarrhea as well as abdominal cramps. Intestinal infections, which may cause abdominal pain, can be contracted by contaminated food or water (see *typhoid fever* and the discussion of salmonella infections in *pets and children*).

In recent years one food, namely milk or milk products, has been identified as a relatively common cause of recurrent diarrhea, abdominal pain, and bloating. The symptoms occur because of inability to digest the milk sugar lactose. This problem is discussed in the section on chronic nonspecific diarrhea, under *diarrhea.*

Parents often ask about worms as a cause of belly pain. The *pinworm* is the most common worm in children in this country. We are not convinced that it causes symptoms other than itching around the rectum.

Children can develop ulcers of the stomach or intestine which produce a recurring pain localized in the mid-upper portion of the abdomen. It is not a common cause of abdominal pain.

Sometimes abdominal pain recurs in a child over days, weeks, or even months. Common associated symptoms are *headache,* paleness, and tiredness. Sometimes there is a family background of headache, particularly of the migraine variety. Such children need careful medical evaluaction. Sometimes a specific cause can be found and treated. (See *colitis, ulcerative.*) At other times the doctor's examination will show no abnormalities and it is hard to pin a specific diagnosis on the problem. The child may be suspected of faking his symptoms. However, further investigation into the child's life situation often shows that he is using the symptom of abdominal pain to express troubled feelings.

See Part 1, Chapter 4: "Complaints with an Emotional Element."

*Abortion, therapeutic:* see *genetics.*

*Abrasions:* see *cuts, scratches, abrasions, and scrapes.*

*Abscess* is the medical term for a collection of *pus* in the body tissue, regardless of location. Pus is the creamy mixture of bacteria (germs), germ-fighting white corpuscles (leukocytes), and destroyed tissue that is formed in one type of local bodily response to *infection.* The effect of this response is to confine the infection to a comparatively small region, preventing its spread to other parts of the body. The human body is usually able to combat mild infection without additional help, but specific measures will sometimes hasten recovery. Sometimes abscesses are so severe that medical help is necessary.

One familiar example of the small abscess is the *whitehead* or *pimple*. This common blemish is less than one-quarter inch in diamter and has a raised white central portion—often with a black plug at the center—and a surrounding rim of reddened skin. Whiteheads often occur at the bases of strands of hair. Germs enter the skin opening through which the hair grows.

We don't really know what causes the whiteheads. Even children who keep very clean may develop them. Small ones (less than one-quarter inch in diameter) usually heal without treatment. You can keep large ones from enlarging further into boils and speed up the healing if you apply warm, moist compresses to cause them to open and drain. It is *not* a good idea to squeeze them. Let them drain by themselves, with assistance from the warm compresses. If whiteheads continue to recur after old ones have healed, consult your doctor. See *acne.*

A *boil* is an abscess more than one-quarter inch in diameter. It is a painful swelling, with a white center surrounded by a rim of reddened skin. Boils need not be considered emergencies, but in general it is wise to consult your doctor. The appearance of the boil will determine the treatment, which can involve moist, warm compresses, antibiotics, or surgical opening of the abscess.

A *carbuncle* is a cluster of boils connected by channels beneath the skin. This affliction, which is not common, is extremely painful. It may result from neglect or failure to treat properly the boil from which the cluster developed, or may develop in some people especially predisposed to such infections. (See *diabetes.*) Call your doctor promptly.

A pimple on the margin of an eyelid, but not within the lid itself, is called a *sty.* (A pimple inside the lid is a *chalazion.*) Warm, wet towels or cotton compresses cause them to open and drain, and heal more rapidly than if they are left alone. If 2 days of warm applications fail to bring improvement, get in touch with your doctor. Consult your doctor promptly if the eyelid itself should swell, or if the white part of the eye becomes red or pussy.

Apart from the pain, which is likely to be considerable, a pimple in the ear canal is similar to a pimple anywhere else and calls for similar treatment. Hot wet applications will relieve pain and hasten healing. Cotton pledgets dipped in hot water are inserted in the canal. If one day of treatment brings no improvement or if pain increases, consult your doctor.

A *wound abscess* is a collection of pus in a cut of the skin and can usually be prevented if cuts are properly and promptly cared for. If you see pus and an area of redness in a wound, apply moist, hot compresses and seek medical attention. If the redness is spreading rapidly, get in touch with the doctor immediately.

*Stitch abscesses* occur around the small punctures where **sutures** (surgical stitches) pierce the skin. They appear 2 or 3 days after suturing as reddened swellings which later discharge pus. Proper care of wounds after suturing reduces the danger of this complication. Stitches left in place beyond the time necessary for healing of a laceration are more likely to become infected. If abscesses develop, consult your doctor at the earliest convenient time. Usually the stitches will have to be removed.

*Impetigo* is a superficial skin infection of a special kind. You will recognize it as a golden-yellow scabbed lesion, often less than one-half inch in diameter, at times leaking pus, but lacking the surrounding rim of reddened skin characteristic of most abscesses. Impetigo gives the appearance of being "stuck on" the skin rather than growing out of it. There is a tendency for the sores of impetigo to occur in groups, often affecting several areas of the skin. It is first noticed on exposed areas of the body. While more common under unsanitary and very warm conditions, children receiving even the best of care may develop impetigo.

Impetigo is a contagious skin infection, and a child may spread it from one part of his or her body to another by scratching. While it is not a serious problem, impetigo demands a vigorous course of treatment. After the lesions are softened with a soak or compress gently rub away the crust and the underlying pus. This procedure is essential because the lesions will not heal until the pus escapes, no matter what else you may do. Once the crusts are off, cover the lesions with an antibiotic ointment, an over-the-counter product which can be purchased in many places without a prescription. Continue the ointment until new uninfected scabs form. Most children with impetigo will also need to take antibiotics by mouth. (Check with your doctor.) Try to discourage scratching and trim fingernails to minimize the transfer of infection. Make sure that the child has his own clean towel and washcloth.

Abscess of the tooth has been recognized through the ages as one of the more disagreeable crosses man has to bear. This abscess occurs in the gum at the base of a carious tooth (one with a cavity in it). In more advanced stages, the swelling may spread to the cheek, lip, and jaw. This infection is preventable if proper **dental care** is maintained. A tooth abscess calls for prompt dental attention.

Abscesses of the lymph glands of the neck make their presence known by pain, swelling, and redness, and signify the spread of germs from infections of the throat and tonsils. Abscessed glands must be distinguished from the common swelling of the neck glands seen with many **colds** and sore throats (see **glands, swollen**). In the former case, the glands rarely exceed an inch in diameter and are never reddened or especially painful, though they may be tender to the touch. They are more easily felt than seen. In contrast, abscessed glands can be easily seen, are red and painful, and their diameter exceeds an inch. They call for prompt medical attention.


*Aches and pains.* Children experience many transient aches and pains in their limbs, bones, and joints whose explanation is not clear but probably involve the combined effects of rapid growth and vigorous use. For example, painful heels are common in children from 8 to 10 and during *adolescence.* It is not a serious condition and represents excess strain upon a growing area. Relief of the pain can usually be achieved by raising the heel about one-half inch. Occasionally, walking casts are needed. Another example is the pain in the calf of the leg resulting from muscle fatigue which often awakens the child from sleep. Aches and pains such as these are commonly called "growing pains," not a very precise term.

Medical attention may be needed to sort out these common wear-and-tear problems from diseases causing similar symptoms. Guidelines for seeking medical attention or taking a wait-and-see attitude are contained in the individual discussions.

See *arm, favoring of; hip pain; joint pain; knee pain;* and *neck pain.*


**Acne** is such a common problem that it may be considered almost a normal part of *adolescence.* It is a source of concern in our society largely because of its cosmetic implications. Except in unusual cases, acne leaves no permanent damage to the skin and disappears when adolescence is completed.

Acne is seen most commonly on the skin of the face, neck, and chest. Sometimes it also appears on the upper back and shoulders. The characteristic sign is the *blackhead* or *comedo,* with the skin surrounding the central blackened area often slightly raised and reddened. Sometimes the central area is white, and hence called a *whitehead.* The blackhead is a plugging of the opening of a hair follicle. This plug consists of a mixture of *sebum,* the normal secretion of the *sebaceous glands* (microscopic glands connected to the shaft containing the root of the body hair), and of *keratin,* the normally present outermost layer of the skin. The sebum produced by these glands serves to lubricate the hair and gives it its oily sheen.

The basic reason for the formation of the plug of the sebum and keratin obstructing the opening of the hair shaft is not well understood. There is strong evidence that the hormonal changes of adolescence play an important role. Once the plug has formed, its exposure to air results in the dark coloration commonly recognized as a blackhead. Despite the resemblance of the blackhead to ordinary dirty skin, the blackhead is not dirt and should not be regarded as such. A popular misconception is that acne results from lack of cleanliness and is therefore in some way preventable by proper hygiene. This viewpoint is true to the extent that cleanliness helps control acne and lack of cleanliness may make acne worse. But lack of cleanliness does not *cause* the condition. In fact we do not understand exactly why it is that comedones are produced during this single phase of a person's life. These comedones produce an irritation of the surrounding skin, making it swollen and reddened. Often they become secondarily infected with normally present skin bacteria, making acne hard to distinguish from ordinary pimples. (See *abscess.*)

The management of acne is a subject you should discuss with your doctor. Although most acne disappears eventually and leaves no scar, more severe cases can permanently disfigure the skin. We suggest taking acne seriously, however trivial it may appear. Early treatment usually can prevent the more serious complications. Your adolescent's annual checkup affords an excellent opportunity to discuss acne. Acne is one of a number of common problems of adolescence in which a discussion with your doctor can be very profitable.

There is no known cure for acne in the sense that there is a cure for pneumonia or appendicitis, but acne can be controlled. Nor is there any known way of preventing this common problem in the sense that measles can be prevented by immunization or accidents can be prevented by "accident proofing" your home. Efforts are directed toward healing the skin and at removing any aggravating factors which may be playing a part. These measures usually suffice to tide the child over the period of adolescence after which acne undergoes a normal disappearance.

The basic aim of local or topical treatment of acne is to remove the comedo or plug which produces the undesirable inflammatory changes of the surrounding skin. The comedo can be removed by ointments applied to the skin which dissolve the plug or by mechanical means with a so-called "comedo extractor." Your doctor can advise you on an ointment or lotion for your child and, if indicated, on the type of comedo extractor to purchase. Many of the extractors available in the drugstore are not satisfactory. You must be given instructions by your nurse or doctor about the use of the extractor. We urge patients not to squeeze blackheads with their fingers. Such squeezing serves only to increase inflammation and to make the acne worse. Your doctor can discuss the proper technique for extracting comedones mechanically.

The role of diet in acne is now considered to be much less important. If a case can be made for any food aggravating acne, that food is chocolate. Occasionally, your doctor may recommend the elimination of additional foods on a trial basis to see if the acne is benefited.

Some adolescents have the almost unconscious habit of scratching their skin or of rubbing and picking their face. They might also rest their face on their hand while reading or studying. If possible, these habits should be discouraged, as they tend to make acne worse.

Adolescents with more pronounced cases of acne almost always have some *seborrheic dermatitis* (dandruff of the scalp). Treatment of this condition is an important aspect of the topical treatment of the acne itself. Acne tends to be more pronounced in the areas in which the hair comes in contact with the skin adjacent to the scalp. For this reason it is suggested that hair be worn away from the skin adjacent to the scalp.

While natural sunlight appears to be beneficial to acne, ultraviolet lamps have not produced impressive results and may be harmful if not used under professional supervision.

Ordinary powder base or cake type makeup does not seem to have any bad effects on acne, but greasy cosmetics can aggravate the condition. In general, we suggest putting a minimal amount of makeup on the skin if it is necessary that it be used at all. Particular care should be taken to wash off the makeup before going to bed. It will help to apply a drying lotion after removing makeup.

There is no question that acne, as are so many other conditions, is related to the physical and emotional well-being of the adolescent. Tension, irregular sleeping habits, inadequate exercise, and inappropriate diet are all factors that can aggravate acne. Your doctor, especially if he has established a relationship with your child over the years, is particularly useful in assessing these factors and in suggesting ways of dealing with them. Parents are encouraged to look upon acne in the context of normal adolescence and not to view it as a special problem in itself. The exception to this, as we said above, is very severe cases which require careful treatment by the physician, often including the use of antibiotics.

See Part 1, Chapter 4: "Complaints with an Emotional Element," and *adolescence.*

**Adenoids:** see *tonsils and adenoids.*

**Adolescence** has its beginning by about 10 years of age in girls and 12 years in boys and ends with the assumption of adult responsibilities usually somewhere in the mid-twenties. It is a complex time of life. This discussion focuses on the physical changes and common physical problems associated with it.

The word *puberty* refers to the *menarche* (onset of menstruation) in girls and a less clear point of sexual maturation in boys which occurs on the average some 2 years later than the menarche. *Pubescence* is the 2- to 3-year period preceding puberty during which, under the influence of the sex hormones (testosterone in the male and estrogen in the female, see *hormones*), secondary sexual changes appear, such as breast development and the growth of pubic hair.

There is wide variation in the time of onset and the rate of maturation in adolescence. We do not fully understand the factors that affect these differences. Clearly hereditary, nutritional, and socioeconomic influences play a part. Along with the trend toward increased height and weight in both adults and children which has occurred over the past 100 years and more, there has been a corresponding tendency for the menarche to appear earlier. In the United States the average age of a girl's menarche is now one year earlier (just under 13 years) than it was 50 years ago.

Prior to pubescence there is a reaccumulation of body fat, at about 8 years in girls and 10 years in boys. This body fat tends to remain in girls but is only temporary in boys. About one year later, the growth spurt of puberty begins along with the first signs of sexual maturation.

In the boy, the earliest sex changes are an increase in the size of the testes and scrotum, and later of the penis. During this time about one-third of all boys have a noticeable, uncomfortable swelling of one or both breasts. This breast enlargement causes many youngsters to be anxious. They feel that something is wrong with them inside—that they may be becoming a girl rather than remaining a male. The swelling may last for several months. Nothing need be done about it. No medication or surgery is indicated. The most important thing is to reassure the boy that everything is all right and to find out what his anxieties are concerning the change.

About the time of early increase in size of the testes and penis, a sparse growth of frizzy pubic hair begins. It gradually becomes darker during the next year and in 2 or 3 years becomes curly and more extensive, achieving the usual adult distribution. About 2 years after pubic hair begins to grow, hair in the *axillae* (under armpits) appears along with facial hair. The growth of axillary hair is accompanied by the characteristic odor of perspiration from the armpits. The boy's voice gradually lowers, beginning in early pubescence. Nocturnal emissions occur for the first time about a year and a half following the first signs of sexual development. It is not clear when spermatozoa are competent for reproduction. It seems likely that the spermatozoa produced during the first 2 or 3 years, until the age of 15 or 16, may not be fertile.

In girls, the sexual maturation of pubescence begins on the average 2 years earlier than in boys. One of the first physical signs is the growth in width of the pelvis. This growth accelerates during the year prior to the menarche, the period of overall greatest growth. The first clear sign of pubescence is the development of the breasts, followed shortly by the appearance of pubic hair. Along with early breast development, the secretions from the vagina change from alkaline to acid. In some girls pubic hair appears for as much as a year prior to the development of the breasts. In rare situations, development of breasts or pubic hair may precede true pubescence by a number of years. Development of the breasts alone earlier in childhood is known as *premature thelarche*, and early development of pubic hair is known as *premature pubarche*. Needless to say, children with earlier than normal sexual development should be examined medically. Often, nothing more need be done, although on occasion some cause for the premature development is uncovered.

Menarche occurs about 2 years after the first changes in the breasts. It is usually preceded for several months by a regularly recurring, clear vaginal discharge. For the first year, irregularity of menstruation is quite common. Many of the earliest menstrual periods are not accompanied by ovulation.

## DELAYED MENARCHE

Delayed menarche is the failure for the menses to occur by the age of 16 years. Girls who have not had their first period by 16 should be evaluated medically.

## DYSFUNCTIONAL (IRREGULAR, PROTRACTED, OR EXCESSIVE) UTERINE BLEEDING

Dysfunctional uterine bleeding is a very common problem during the first several years following menarche. It is caused by imbalanced secretion of the **hormones** normally controlling menstrual function and by variability in the responsiveness of the ovaries and uterus, the target organs of these hormones. Most dysfunctional menstrual cycles occur without ovulation, the discharge of the egg from the ovary. The control of menstruation involves the coordinated action of the *hypothalamus* (that part of the brain that controls the secretions of the pituitary gland), the pituitary gland itself, and the ovaries and uterus. This system takes from as little as a few months to as long as several years to achieve fine integration. Ovulation occurs in only about 2 percent of women during the first 6 months and in only about 18 percent by the end of the first year. Nonovulatory cycles can be considered normal for the first 1 to 3 years after menarche. This period is known as the time of *relative fertility*.

Dysfunctional bleeding is self-limited for most adolescents, going away on its own as the individual matures. However, medical evaluation is in order. Occasionally a contributing factor like hypothyroidism (see *hormones*), obesity, or psychosomatic problems may be found. There is also the possibility of cancer in the special circumstances discussed below. Usually, no contributory causes are identified and time alone straightens things out. If the bleeding is of sufficient severity to lower the **blood count,** more vigorous treatment may be required.

Normally, as the egg ripens in the ovary before ovulation, estrogen hormone is secreted from the ripening egg into the bloodstream, bringing about the initial vascular changes in the endometrium (inner lining of uterus). Ovulation occurs and is followed with the secretion by the ovary of progesterone, another hormone, which brings about further changes in the endometrium. Withdrawal of the progesterone secretion brings on menstruation. In a nonovulatory cycle, progesterone is not secreted and the only effects on the uterus are from estrogen, leading to irregular, prolonged bleeding. Treatment consists of cycling with birth control pills for several months followed by the use of a potent progesterone hormone tablet given during the last 5 to 7 days of the cycle.

### PRE-CANCER OF THE VAGINA AND CERVIX

Recently it has been discovered that pre-cancerous changes of the vagina and cervix are more common, although still very rare, among girls whose mothers took stilbestrol or other synthetic estrogens during pregnancy, usually given to prevent miscarriages. Such girls should be under close medical surveillance from pubescence onward whether or not they have symptoms, the most common of which are vaginal bleeding and discharge.

### DYSMENORRHEA (PAINFUL MENSTRUATION)

The crampy abdominal pain and back and leg pain associated with the menstrual period are extremely common complaints during early adolescence. These symptoms do not usually appear during the first few cycles, which are likely to be nonovulatory. They usually occur with ovulatory cycles toward the end of the first year following menarche. Needless to say, these symptoms are sensitive to emotional factors, and anxieties can accentuate the common experience of discomfort. Medical examination is called for. An exploration of the adolescent's own feelings about the many changes in her body is the foundation for treatment. If the discomfort is marked, hormones, either estrogen or progesterones, are occasionally used to suppress ovulation for several months. Birth control pills are often used for this purpose. For milder discomfort, aspirin or some other mild analgesic will suffice.

Painful menstruation is less a problem today than it was a generation or two ago, largely because of a greater openness toward sex in general.

Nonetheless, surveys have shown that about one-third of all adolescent girls experience significant discomfort and that at least 10 percent find menstruation so uncomfortable that they miss school several times per year. In many cases the most important factor is the girl's reaction to what might almost be described as normal discomfort.

Needless to say both boys and girls who have reached the age of puberty should have access to complete information about sex and reproduction, including contraception. Parents should inform themselves, and answer questions as they arise. If they feel uncomfortable while discussing these matters, they should find out whether their teen-agers are receiving reliable information at school, or whether a professional known to the family, such as the family physician, would be willing to discuss the facts with the individual boy or girl in private. There are also many sound and informative books on the subject. If they are made available to the teen-ager, not thrust upon him, he will no doubt turn to them when puzzled or curious.

*For further reading*

FOR YOUNG ADOLESCENTS ( 12–15 )

Johnson, Eric W. *Love and Sex in Plain Language*. Philadelphia: Lippincott, 1970.
Pomeroy, Wardell. *Boys and Sex*. New York: Dell Publishing, 1971.
———. *Girls and Sex*. New York: Dell Publishing, 1973.

FOR PARENTS

Child Study Association of America. *What to Tell Your Child About Sex*. New York: Pocket Books, 1974.

FOR OLDER ADOLESCENTS

Bohannan, Paul. *Love, Sex, and Being Human*. New York: Doubleday, 1969.
Student Committee on Human Sexuality, Yale University. *The Student Guide to Sex on Campus*. New York: New American Library, 1970.

There are a number of other issues concerning adolescence which are discussed elsewhere.

See *acne; drug problems; smoking; venereal disease; weight problems;* and Part 1, Chapter 3: "Diet of Infants and Children," Part 2, Chapter 11: "Bicycle and Minibike Safety," and Chapter 12: "Car Safety."

*Air sickness:* see *motion sickness.*

*Akinetic spell:* see *seizure disorders.*

*Allergy.* An allergic reaction is a special type of inflammatory response in various parts of the body to a foreign substance in the environment which most people tolerate without problems. Many people sneeze when opening an old and dusty book. An allergic person sneezes from dust that is barely noticeable to the average person. Allergic reactions may take several forms, depending upon which part of the body is affected. The parts of the body most likely to show allergic responses are the lungs, nose, eyes, skin, middle ear, and the stomach and intestines. Depending on the site, allergic reactions can result in *asthma, hay fever, conjunctivitis, eczema, hives, sinusitis,* and any combination of *abdominal pain,* nausea, *vomiting,* or *diarrhea.* Of course these symptoms can have other nonallergic causes as well. Substances that provoke an allergic reaction are known as *allergens.* In hay fever sufferers, for instance, the pollen of the ragweed plant is an allergen.

Allergic reactions have some similarities to the normal helpful responses of the body against foreign materials. The ability of the body to ward off the numerous microorganisms (viruses, bacteria, and so forth) with which it comes into daily contact is absolutely essential for our survival. Otherwise we would fall prey to every bug that came along. Elsewhere we have discussed the way in which the body can contend with these living invaders through the manufacture of antibodies (see *infection*). Small wars between the body and these microbes are going on all the time, usually so silently that we are not even aware of them.

There are many kinds of common foreign substances in our environment to which most people *don't* react. Grass pollen is an example. Allergic people differ from nonallergic individuals in that their bodies do not discriminate between these common particles and other more threatening substances. An individual who is allergic to grass produces antibodies to grass pollen, which serve no useful purpose. These antibodies are distributed throughout the body but cause symptoms only where and when they come in contact with their allergen.

Allergic symptoms arise from the interaction of an allergen with an antibody made by the allergic individual. The meeting of allergen and antibody sets in process a local reaction that releases various substances, which causes the dilation (opening up) of small blood vessels, the leaking of fluid through these vessels into the surrounding tissues, resulting in swelling, spasm of the smooth muscles in air passages, and an outpouring of mucous secretions. The particular resulting symptoms depend upon where the antibody and allergen meet. For example, if the reaction occurs only in the lungs, as with some inhaled particles, affecting the small air passageways (bronchi and bronchioles), the characteristic wheezing symptoms (labored breathing with a whistle-like quality) of asthma appear. If the gastrointestinal tract is involved (foods), symptoms are tingling of lips and tongue, itching of throat, nausea, vomiting, abdominal cramps, and diarrhea. Spread of an allergen, either eaten or injected, throughout the body of a sensitive individual can lead to itching, redness of the skin, hives, asthma, swelling of the voice box, and, in the extreme, collapse and death. Unlike other sorts of antibody reactions, allergy works to the harm of the individual rather than to his benefit. Genetic factors (see *genetics*) play an important role. The characteristics of an individual's antibody responses are probably determined just as much by genes as are skin color and body shape. We do not know which genes are responsible or how to change them. But we do know that when allergy has been a problem in both the father's and mother's families, their children are likely to be affected.

When we say that a person is *allergic*, we do not mean that he or she is actually experiencing symptoms all of the time. What we mean is that he has a tendency to react (produce antibodies to allergens) which can become apparent under certain circumstances. The particular symptoms he experiences (and whether he has them at all) vary with age and the kinds and quantities of substances to which he is exposed. Predicting the course of an untreated allergic problem is difficult. A common pattern is eczema as a baby, asthma as a young child, and hay fever as an older child or adult. The substance that triggers the allergic reaction may differ from one stage in life to the next, as does the part of the body that shows the response. Allergy is a kind of theme that weaves its way through the life of the allergic individual, showing up at various times and in various ways. The allergic individual is allergic for life.

Individuals who are allergic to one substance are more likely to be allergic to other similar substances. While it is possible for just about any substance known to stimulate an allergic reaction, certain ones are good sensitizers and frequent troublemakers. House dust is a common offender. The question of which component of house dust is the culprit is now under investigation. Since a child spends three-quarters of his time at home and much of this in his bedroom, house dust assumes a role of great importance. The allergens of the outdoors—pollens of trees, grasses, weeds, and spores of molds—are also important. Allergic symptoms that occur at certain specific times of the year cast suspicion on these. The child who has a runny, sneezy nose and itchy, bloodshot eyes during the early spring months is more than likely sensitive to the tree pollens, while the child who develops such symptoms late in the summer and early in the fall is probably reacting to the pollen of ragweed. Another common offender is mold outdoors on vegetation or in damp basements. Animal products are well-known allergens. Examples are the hair or fur of household pets, the feathers of ducks and geese used in pillows and mattresses, and the venom of stinging insects such as bees, wasps, yellow jackets, and hornets (see *bites, insect*). Foods can bring on allergic symptoms. Among the chief offenders are nuts, chocolate, and shellfish. Cows' milk and wheat are common allergens for infants.

Infections play a role in allergic symptoms. It is not completely clear whether the person has an allergic reaction to the infection itself or, as is more likely the case, the infection increases sensitivity to other allergens. It may be that the allergic person is more susceptible to infections and that the infection worsens the allergic symptoms in a kind of vicious circle. How allergy and infections relate to each other is not yet precisely understood. In addition to environmental allergens, certain other factors tend to heighten the reaction of the allergic individual. High on the list are emotions. Tension, anxiety, fatigue, and exhaustion all make the allergic individual more sensitive. To understand why a person has an allergic problem, we must take a comprehensive look both at the individual and his environment. Consideration of one or the other affords only a partial explanation. The allergic individual is in a state of precarious equilibrium with his surroundings and the balance may be weighted toward or away from the development of symptoms, depending upon circumstances.

Consider the case of Johnny, a 4-year-old boy with a family background full of allergy. Both parents had asthma when they were children and now, although these attacks have largely disappeared, continue to sneeze during the ragweed season. As an infant, Johnny had mild eczema, which was helped by switching from cows' milk to soybean formula. He also developed hives whenever he ate oranges. Now 4 years old, he has begun to have mild wheezing attacks beginning in the early spring months. Johnny is clearly a child with a genetic tendency to allergic symptoms. By having had eczema as a baby, he has already demonstrated his abnormal reactivity. With his background, asthma could have almost been predicted. During the first few springs of his life, he had contact with numerous grass and tree pollens and began to manufacture antibodies against them. With each succeeding spring, the amount of antibody in his system increased until now it has reached a point where, upon exposure to grass and tree pollen, his sensitized bronchial air passages, coated with these antibodies, go into spasm and pour out mucus, the characteristics of an asthmatic attack. Whether or not he has an attack on any given day depends in part on how heavy the pollen is in the air. If he has a cold, his reactivity is much greater to the same quantity of pollen, and he is even more prone to attack. If he is particularly fatigued or has just been through an emotional upset, his reactivity will be increased and an attack may occur with no rise in pollen level. The different allergens in his environment have a cumulative effect. Should his mother miss a day of thoroughly cleaning his room, he is more likely to wheeze, even when little pollen is in the air. Recently he has begun to sneeze when playing with the family cat.

In looking at a boy like Johnny, we can see that pollen is only part of the problem. The asthmatic attack results from the cumulative effects of the genetic and environmental factors in his life. Helping Johnny depends on dealing with not one but all of these factors, up to the point where the cure can become more troublesome than the illness itself. Some of the contributing factors are more easily dealt with than others. The pollens in the air are difficult to control. Short of taking a long sea voyage it is difficult to avoid them. A bedroom air conditioner or electronic air cleaner may help. Dust in the house, the family pet, emotional upsets, and fatigue can be modified or eliminated. With our present knowledge, we can't change Johnny's genetic makeup, but his tolerance to pollen can be increased by medications and by the injection technique known as *hyposensitization* if necessary. Thus, the treatment of Johnny is directed toward lowering his sensitivity by eliminating or reducing some of the contributing factors and, if this is not sufficient, building up his tolerance to the pollen. In this sense we do not cure Johnny of his problem, we control it. Keeping him free of symptoms depends on day-in-and-day-out measures to reduce his reactivity. The care of children with severe allergies involves much more than treating symptoms with medicines when they occur. The major objective is prevention, which means a regular program of care. This program is divided into three parts: medication, hyposensitization, and the avoidance of allergens. These will be discussed at length below.

When should a parent be concerned about allergies? We suggest contacting your doctor when a child has persistent (longer than two weeks) nasal discharge, sneezing, rubbing of the eyes, or coughing (see *cough*). Other symptoms deserving medical attention are *hives,* especially recurrent attacks, *eczema,* and wheezing.

In assessing a child with a suspected allergic disorder, the doctor will first take a history of the symptoms, their severity, and the circumstances under which they occur. When appropriate he will ask for more detailed information about the home environment, the general behavior of the child, and his relationship with parents and friends. He will ask about similar allergic problems in other members of the family.

How to treat an allergic disorder is an important decision. It is made in different ways by parents and doctors. The questions to be asked are: how much is this condition interfering with the child's life, and what is the best course to follow? Just how far to go in diagnosing and in treating the symptoms depends on their severity. For mild spring *hay fever,* medication alone might be tried. But if it persists for more than two years, no matter how mild, the patient should have more specific treatment: elimination of the cause or injections. Year-round hay fever (perennial rhinitis) should be treated with environmental control measures in the home, particularly in the child's room. (See below.) For *asthma* not responsive to simple measures like drugs and environmental control, hyposensitization should be considered with attention to emotional factors if they are of importance. Exclusion of a pet may be important. The rule is to upset the child's routine as little as possible, to do just as much as is needed to control the symptoms, and yet not to make the child miserable in the process. Otherwise the treatment might be worse than the disease.

Let's take a look at the kinds of treatment used for allergic problems. Any one or a number of these approaches to treatment may be used. Each child is a special case and will require individual treatment.

First, there is a group of very useful drugs. Commonly used are *antihistamines, decongestants,* and *bronchodilators. Antihistamines* "block" or neutralize some of the chemicals liberated in reactions between allergen and antibody, which cause the changes in blood vessels, smooth muscle, and mucous glands. Symptoms are thus reduced. The dose or quantity taken is important. A gradual increase in dose may be necessary to achieve the desired effect. The antihistamines, some more than others, usually have a sedative effect, although some patients do not experience this. Drowsiness may limit the amount that can be given. Antihistamines also may cause loss of appetite, nausea, constipation, or diarrhea in some patients. Different antihistamines may have to be tried to find the one that provides the most relief with the least undesirable effects. Antihistamines can combat itching, probably by sedating the patient to the point where the itch is less bothersome. While applying antihistamines directly onto the skin in ointment form can ease itching, there is a high likelihood of making the patient allergic to the antihistamine itself. Therefore, topical or local use of antihistamines is not recommended. Antihistamines are particularly useful with hay fever and with hives. They are less useful with asthma and eczema. Antihistamines are used widely in over-the-counter medicines, but it is unwise to use these without guidance from a physician.

*Decongestants* are medicines that cause constriction (tightening) of blood vessels. Dilation or opening up of blood vessels is an important element of the allergic response. One decongestant is phenylephrine (Neo-Synephrine), often used as nose drops or spray. It "shrinks" nasal mucous membranes by causing the smooth muscles in the walls of the blood vessels to contract or tighten. Decongestants may be added to prescribed and over-the-counter drugs to be taken by mouth. The same caution applies as with other over-the-counter drugs.

*Bronchodilators* are drugs that relax the muscles of the bronchioles, the small air tubes in the lungs. (See *asthma.*) These muscles are thrown into spasm during an asthmatic attack. This narrows the air passages, and wheezing and obstruction to air flow results. Bronchodilators relax the spasm by inhibiting the allergic reaction between allergen and antibody and by acting directly on the muscle. There are a number of bronchodilators in common use. Some are given by injection, like *epinephrine*. (A common name for epinephrine is adrenaline.) Others are inhaled, like *isoproterenol* (Isuprel). Still others are given by mouth. Some, like aminophylline, can be taken orally or can be given intravenously or by rectal suppository. This flexibility is desirable. For example, a child in acute distress with asthma needs quick relief and is too ill to take medicines by mouth. Epinephrine is fast acting and easily given by injection, the perfect drug for such a situation. For mild wheezing, oral medicines are preferable. Their effect is sustained over several hours and can easily be repeated if necessary. *Glucocorticoids* (cortisone-like **hormones**) are also used in the treatment of allergic diseases which do not respond to simpler drugs and measures.

The next kind of treatment for allergic problems is to reduce the child's exposure to allergens. For the child with continuous year-round allergic nasal symptoms and for the asthmatic child, *environmental control measures* may be necessary. The following methods are used at The Children's Hospital Medical Center. Depending upon the severity of the child's symptoms, some or all of these might be recommended. Again, individual attention is the rule.

An allergen-free bedroom is essential, since a child spends about half of his life in this room. The room should contain only one bed, if possible. If not, the other bed must be treated in the same way as the child's. Dressing and undressing must be done outside the room. The room is for sleeping and study only. The door of the room should be kept closed at all times. Do not keep toys or books that will accumulate dust in the room. Eliminate all stuffed toys.

For initial cleaning purposes, all the furniture, rugs, curtains, and drapes must be taken from the room and the clothes closets emptied. Wash walls, ceilings, woodwork, floors, closets, bed and bed springs. Make up the bed with freshly washed bedding. Use smooth, not fuzzy, washable blankets, washable bedspreads, cotton sheets and pillowcases. Eliminate all feather, down, or fiber-stuffed pillows, mattress pads, and quilted bedspreads. Use foam or latex pillows. No upholstered furniture should be in the room. Plain light cotton or synthetic fiber curtains washed once a week may be used at the windows, or window shades on rollers. No drapes should be used. Only cotton throw rugs washed weekly should be on the floor. Keep a minimum of clean clothing in the closet. Avoid use of closet for storage purposes.

The room must be cleaned daily. The bedspring and walls should be cleaned weekly. Use a damp mop and damp cloth for cleaning. Do not use a vacuum cleaner in the child's room, as this spreads tiny dust particles. Vacuum the rest of the house only when the child is not present. Allergex or Dust Seal may be used to treat blankets and furniture according to the directions that accompany the product.

An air conditioner can be helpful, since it will filter pollens and some dust particles, and will control humidity. An electronic precipitating air cleaner is more effective in filtering out the tiny dust particles, but it has no effect on temperature or humidity, both of which can be troublesome factors in hot weather. Avoid use of insect and other sprays in the child's room, as this may irritate his condition.

Seal all hot air furnace pipes and ducts leading into the bedroom. If this makes the room too cold, place a triple-density, fiber-glass filter over the hot air register, or use a small electric heater in the room. If you use a heater, do not leave it alone in the room with a small child. Make sure that the filter will not become a fire hazard or cut down too much on the efficiency of your heater. Clean this filter twice a week when the child is not present. Make sure that there is an air filter in the furnace, and clean or replace this every two weeks, if possible, and at least monthly.

Plastic polyurethane or latex foam mattresses are desirable and should be firm for posture and comfort. They are best used on a plain wooden platform but may be used over a box spring having an allergy-proof cover or with open springs. Cover all other mattresses and box springs in the bedroom with dustproof, airtight covers and seal the zippers with masking tape. There are two kinds of dust-free encasings available. Plastic bags with zippers that enclose the mattress (not just a plastic sheet) are available from many local stores. Some parents say they are cold in the winter, hot in the summer, and tear easily, but they are inexpensive. Allergen-proof encasings are more suitable in that they last much longer, may be washed, and are more comfortable. They are more expensive. They may be ordered by mail from either Allergy-Free Products for the Home, 226 Livingston Street, Brooklyn, N.Y. 11201, or Allergen-Proof Encasings, Inc., 4046 East Superior Avenue, Cleveland, Ohio 44103, or from your own supplier.

It is also very important to eliminate sources of trouble throughout the rest of the home. Forced hot-air heating systems should be avoided if possible. So should felt rug pads (because of their animal hair content) and overstuffed furniture and pillows with any fiber or feather content. Mattress pads, puffs, comforters, heavy rugs, drapes, chenille spreads, and stuffed toys should be avoided.

When refurnishing, buy foam furniture and foam rubber pads. Avoid wall-to-wall carpeting. When reupholstering furniture, use leather or washable plastic for the entire piece, including the bottom, or place allergy-proof material underneath upholstery fabric (including the bottom) and use smooth, closely woven Allergex-treated fabric. When a slipcover is used, it should be washable. The very best allergen-free chairs and sofas are wooden with removable latex foam backs and seat cushions, covered with smooth, washable upholstery covers.

It is best not to keep furry and feathered pets, but if such pets are kept, they should not be allowed in the house at any time. A family with a history of allergy, or with a child who has shown allergic symptoms, would be wise to test the reactions to animals of all members of the family *before* acquiring a pet. This will save much grief, especially the child's, as well as suffering on the part of the animal.

It is important to eliminate mold or mildew. Mold is found more profusely in damp, musty places, usually cellars and bedrooms where vaporizers have been used extensively. Molds can occur anywhere in the home and are not always visible to the naked eye. When mold is present or suspected, spray every six months with Captan or Orthocide, prepared by adding 8 tablespoons of the powder to 1 gallon water for use in cellars and basements, 4 tablespoons of powder to a gallon of water for bedrooms and other living areas. Mold growth can be stopped on walls and floors when Captan is added to paint in proportion of 1 tablespoon per gallon of paint. Spraying must be done with pressure-spraying equipment. The room must be filled with a fine mist spray of the mixture and, following this, the room must be closed for 2 to 4 hours until the mist settles and dries. Neither Captan nor Orthocide is toxic to human beings or animals, but they may be slightly irritating to the lungs if inhaled deeply during the spraying process. This powder is inexpensive and may be obtained at a gardeners' or farmers' supply store.

House plants should be kept at a minimum, sprayed every few weeks with Captan, and should never be kept in the child's room.

When foods, pets, or drugs are implicated in causing allergic symptoms avoidance is the best treatment. If a child is sensitive to shellfish, eggs, milk, fresh fruits, fish or nuts, these should be avoided. Food allergies are more common in younger children. The most reliable way to test for them is to eliminate them from the diet and see whether the symptoms (usually vomiting, diarrhea, or hives) improve. The only treatment is avoidance of the food in question. While allergy to food may cause some *colic* with crying in infants, most colic is not due to intolerance of foods. Like teething, food almost automatically becomes suspect in explaining all of the ills of babies.

One of the most common drug-caused allergies in the past was reaction to tetanus antitoxin prepared from horse serum. Human antitoxin is now available and carries none of the risk of the equine form. (See *immunization.*) Moreover, proper immunization against *tetanus* makes the use of any antitoxin almost completely avoidable. For a discussion of drugs causing allergic problems, see *drug reactions, allergic.*

An exception to this advice of simple avoidance is the individual sensitive to bee, wasp, hornet, or yellow-jacket stings who should always be hyposensitized to them. (See *bites, insect.*) Since this can be a life-endangering sensitivity, avoidance and emergency medications cannot be depended upon or may not be available at the time. Injection treatment is protective in almost all instances.

The basic idea in hyposensitization is to produce a special antibody capable of binding to the allergen and thereby blocking the allergen antibody reaction that produces symptoms. It is resorted to only when simpler measures are inadequate, for prolonged respiratory allergic symptoms, and always for allergy to bees, wasps, hornets, and yellow jackets. For injection treatment to be successful, it is necessary to determine the causative allergens as precisely as possible. Again, an accurate, detailed, medical history is most important. For example, if sneezing, itching, and runny nose occur in late August and September, ragweed is probably the cause, but molds could be as well. Skin testing can be helpful in confirming the exact allergen involved. The antibodies in the skin of the allergic individual react to the diluted solution of the causative allergen dabbed onto a shallow skin scratch or injected into the skin, producing a hivelike reaction at the site of the test. The doctor is thus able to confirm his tentative diagnosis made from the history. Those allergens that are causing symptoms should yield a positive test, while those to which no allergy exists should give a negative test. However, skin tests are not 100 percent reliable. Sometimes people who are sensitive to certain allergens will have a negative skin test to them. Also, sometimes a person will have a positive skin test to an allergen which is not causing any clinical problem. Although not perfect, the skin test is useful. With a careful history of the child's symptoms and aided by the information gained by skin testing, the doctor will be able to make a tentative list of allergens and form a judgment about the need for any of the various kinds of treatment that have been discussed.

Once the allergens are identified, if injection treatment is to be given, a solution of allergens is made up in various concentrations and strengths. The amount and concentration given by injection is increased, usually weekly, until a protective dose is reached. Then a maintenance dose of the extract is continued, given less frequently than weekly. The idea is to give only as much of the allergen as the patient can tolerate at a given time without causing a large local reaction. Injecting any more might cause symptoms, nonserious but annoying local swelling and redness of the injection site, and if the allergen spreads through the body and reacts with antibody elsewhere, wheezing, hives, itching, and even more serious symptoms. Severe reactions from the allergic injection may be dangerous to the child and observation for 15 to 20 minutes following any injection is recommended to make sure that no serious reaction has occurred or that, if a reaction does occur, it can be treated promptly.

Injection treatment (or hyposensitization) is most helpful for asthma and rhinitis caused by airborne allergens such as pollen and molds. Occasionally it is used for unavoidable animal danders. It is not useful for food allergies or drug sensitivities. The latter type of allergies should be controlled by avoiding the allergens.

In caring for the allergic problems, your doctor may want the advice of an allergist, a specialist in allergy. Many family doctors and pediatricians have had special experience with allergic disorders. If injection treatment is recommended, the allergist or your own physician can carry out this procedure. The collaboration of your doctor and the specialist consultant is an effective approach to care. Your own doctor knows your child and family well and can advise how best to go about treatment for your child.

See Part 1, Chapter 4: "Complaints with an Emotional Element"; *asthma; eczema; hay fever;* and *hives.*

*Amniocentesis:* see *genetics.*

*Amoebic dysentery:* see *diarrhea.*

*Anal fissure:* see *blood in the stools.*

*Anaphylactoid purpura,* also known as *Henoch-Schoenlein purpura,* despite its exotic-sounding name, is not rare in children, particularly in boys between 2 and 8 years of age. The most common finding is a rash, usually consisting of large *hives* with central bruised areas which are hemorrhages deep in the skin. The colors of the central areas undergo the same changes seen in a black eye. Initially blue, they gradually change to green and yellow before disappearing completely. The bruised areas may be the last signs to disappear even after the child is well again. In addition, pinhead-size red spots, which are little skin hemorrhages called *petechiae,* are seen. The rash is most commonly on the legs, thighs, and lower abdomen, but may be scattered over the skin. The skin over the back of the hands, tops of the feet, and scalp is often swollen. Arthritis or joint inflammation of the knees and ankles and sometimes of the hips, wrists, and elbows is very common. Many children complain of belly pain (see *abdominal pain*), often colicky with *vomiting.* This results from inflammation of the intestine. At times the pain is so severe that a surgical problem like *appendicitis* comes to mind. Occasionally, abdominal pain precedes the other symptoms and can really fool the physician. A small number of children with abdominal pain develop an *intussusception,* a telescoping of a segment of intestine into itself which requires specific treatment. Many children with abdominal pain pass small quantities of blood in their stools. (See *blood in the stools.*) The most worrisome complication is the development of kidney inflammation or *nephritis.* Occasionally, the nephritis associated with anaphylactoid purpura persists. There is a very wide range of severity of the disorder. Some children have nothing more than a few spots and *fever,* while others require hospitalization with severe abdominal pain and kidney inflammation. In a given child it is hard to predict just what the course will be. Fortunately most children with anaphylactoid purpura recover completely.

Anaphylactoid purpura runs its course on the average in 1 to 3 weeks. At present there is no medicine that will speed up healing. Steroid *hormones* such as cortisone have been found to relieve abdominal pain and perhaps to decrease the risk of intussusception. If nephritis develops, the care is similar to that described under acute glomerulonephritis. (See *nephritis.*) For infection, antibiotics are prescribed.

It is characteristic of anaphylactoid purpura to involve many different parts of the body rather than just one. While the cause is unknown, we have the impression that the inflamed small blood vessels throughout the body seen in this illness are undergoing a kind of allergic reaction. If this is so, we do not know what the allergic trigger is, although attacks often seem to follow an upper respiratory infection. There is no known way of preventing the condition.

*Anemia* means having less than normal numbers of red blood cells in the body's circulation, no matter what the cause. In contrast to the clear-cut symptoms of other disorders, the symptoms of anemia are vague and overlap with those of other disorders. Frequent complaints are paleness, listlessness, breathlessness, and loss of appetite. While a symptom like listlessness can result from anemia, it can also have other causes, including psychological or emotional ones. Anemia is not a diagnosis to make on yourself or your child. If you suspect it because of symptoms you experience or see in your child, consult your physician or nurse. Don't treat it yourself. In the infant, the symptoms of anemia are similar to those of the adult—paleness, fussiness, and picky eating.

### BLOOD

To understand anemia, it is necessary to know something about blood. Blood is a liquid consisting of a fluid part called the *plasma* in which the *red* and *white blood cells* and *platelets* (small blood cells which play an important role in blood clotting) are suspended, much as chopped onions are suspended in onion soup.

The job of red blood cells is to carry oxygen from inhaled air in the lungs to all the body parts for energy production and to return carbon dioxide from these body parts to the lungs for elimination in the exhaled breath. Red blood cells are manufactured in the *bone marrow*, a specialized tissue in the hollow of bones. Samples of bone marrow show red blood cells in various stages of maturation. Mature red blood cells enter the bloodstream to do their job of gas (oxygen and carbon dioxide) transport. The average life-span of a red blood cell is 120 days. During this time, the cell travels an estimated distance of 100 miles through the blood vessels. Aged or damaged cells are removed by special "scavenger" cells located mainly in the spleen and liver. Here the old red cells are smashed up into their constituent parts. Some protein and most iron from these "junked" cells are salvaged and used by the body anew. Other parts of the disassembled cells are eliminated and passed from the body.

Both production of new red blood cells and elimination of old ones proceed continuously. Under normal circumstances, production and elimination balance each other evenly and the number of red blood cells in the circulation is constant. In a state of good health, the ability of the body to produce red blood cells exceeds the actual production. Much as the heart can increase its output during exercise, high fever, or excitement, so can bone marrow respond up to a point to demands for more blood cells occasioned by excessive loss.

Red blood cells are living, disc-shaped cells. They have nutritional requirements and need oxygen for their own respiration. Red blood cells contain a red pigment called *hemoglobin*. This chemical pigment gives blood its characteristic red color and is the part of the red blood cell that actually holds oxygen and carbon dioxide within the cell as it shuttles between the lungs and various body parts. Hemoglobin is a remarkably complex chemical molecule which includes protein and iron. There are several kinds of normal hemoglobin and a number of abnormal ones, of which sickle-cell hemoglobin, to be discussed later, is a notable example. Hemoglobin is produced in the maturing red blood cells during their development in the bone marrow. It is removed from aged cells or ones prematurely destroyed.

The red blood cell also contains special chemicals known as *enzymes*, which control and regulate the chemical reactions necessary for the cell's housekeeping functions. To survive, the red cell must maintain its special disc configuration, resisting the natural tendency to become ball-shaped, must keep its hemoglobin in proper condition to transport oxygen and carbon dioxide, and must maintain a proper concentration of salt within its boundaries. All of these activities depend on proper quantities of critical enzymes. Deficiencies of enzymes impair the ability of the cell to keep its house in order, making the cell more vulnerable to premature aging and removal from the circulation.

The correct assembly of the red blood cells in the bone marrow depends upon the availability of certain essential building blocks in the diet. Red blood cells can be stunted if the right ingredients are not available during production. While red blood cell production requires many different building blocks, the most important are proteins, iron, vitamin $B_{12}$ and folic acid. (See Part 1, Chapter 3: "Diet of Infants and Children.") If any of these essential nutrients are lacking, the quantity and quality of red blood cells produced will be affected. For example, if inadequate iron is available, fewer cells will be produced; those which are produced will be smaller than normal and will contain less hemoglobin than normal. Deficiencies of the other essential building blocks produce different characteristic changes in the red blood cells. Just as a car's performance is impaired in different ways by a defective axle or a defective steering wheel, so deficiencies of each of the essential nutrients for red blood cells produce their own brands of anemias. Certain diseases of the stomach and intestines may impair the absorption of vitamin $B_{12}$ and folic acid even when they are present in the diet in adequate quantities. The vitamins fail to pass from the food in the intestinal tract into the body. The effect on red blood cell formation is the same in either case. (See, for instance, *celiac disease.*)

Iron is an essential metal which is jealously guarded by the body. Relatively little is gained or lost each day. Iron from aged red blood cells undergoing destruction is salvaged and returned to the body stores for recycling in the production of new hemoglobin. A small amount is lost each day in the stools and urine. Adult females lose an additional quantity in the menstrual blood flow, and thus the amount of iron needed in the female diet is slightly more than that needed by males. The daily loss of iron also increases during pregnancy, as iron is transferred from mother to fetus. During pregnancy, exclusive reliance on a well-balanced diet will not guarantee adequate iron intake. Accordingly, the recommendation is that pregnant mothers receive supplemental iron.

The newborn has stores of iron acquired from his or her mother prior to birth, especially if his umbilical cord was clamped late, after it stopped pulsating, allowing an extra transfusion of iron-rich red blood cells. As the baby grows, he literally outgrows this iron endowment. It now appears that breast-fed infants obtain enough iron in mother's milk, at least for the first years of life and probably longer. Milk from the cow is deficient in iron, and if the infant is fed cow's milk formula alone for more than 6 months, he will surely become anemic. Certainly by the time he is 4 to 6 months old and probably long before, the formula-fed infant needs dietary iron if he is not to become anemic. Most babies in this country are given iron-fortified cereals by 3 months along with other solids, and more and more are being given formulas enriched with iron or iron supplements.

The body removes just as much iron as it needs from food and no more. The excess iron is passed through the intestines into the stools. While some dietary iron is essential, too much iron is dangerous. Taking a whole bottle of iron pills can poison a small child. (See Part 2, Chapter 10: "Poisoning.")

Up to a certain point, loss of iron by chronic bleeding can be compensated for by absorption of additional iron from the diet. Beyond that point, a net loss of iron occurs; iron stores in the body are called upon to meet the famine and gradually become depleted. The inadequate quantity of iron available for the production of hemoglobin then causes anemia.

Hemoglobin is just one place where iron is used in the body. Iron is also found in enzymes occurring in the intestine and other organs and is necessary for their normal functioning. Anemia, as such, is probably a late sign of iron deficiency. It is possible that children can have symptoms of listlessness and poor performance from iron deficiency even before they show anemia. All the more reason to prevent iron deficiency through good nutrition.

## TYPES OF ANEMIA

After the red blood cells are assembled, they enter the circulation to live out their average 120 days before death and removal. If their life-span is shortened, the marrow may not be able to keep pace and anemia can result. Various abnormalities of red cells in hemoglobin, cell shape, or enzyme content interfere with their survival.

An example of abnormal hemoglobin is *sickle-cell hemoglobin*. If sickle hemoglobin is exposed to low concentrations of oxygen, the hemoglobin realigns and causes the cell to become sickle-shaped. The sickled cell is removed from circulation as an "abnormal" cell. Anemia results. About 10 percent of American blacks carry the trait for sickle-cell anemia but are not anemic or symptomatic themselves except under extraordinary situations. The offspring of two parents with the trait have a 25 percent chance of having the disease of sickle-cell anemia. (See **genetics.**) Sickle-cell anemia is a serious disorder manifested by anemia and its related problems, and intermittent and often severe attacks of pain. Such patients usually die of the disease in early life, and few live a normal life-span. (See **handicapped child.**)

Many Americans whose ancestors came from the Mediterranean countries have yet a different kind of hereditary hemoglobin problem called *thalassemia*. The mild form (trait or carrier) of this anemia is called *thalassemia minor* and rarely causes symptoms. Individuals with thalassemia minor are not anemic, but the proportion of red blood cells and hemoglobin in their blood is often on the low side. While they live normal lives, their blood counts are abnormal and can be confused with those of iron deficiency anemia. They are often identified in a study of relatives of a patient with *thalassemia major* (also known as *Cooley's anemia* and *Mediterranean anemia*), which is the more severe form of this disease and may occur in the offspring of parents both of whom have thalassemia minor. There is no cure for thalassemia major. Patients usually need frequent blood transfusions to survive. Gradually the transfused blood leads to a buildup of iron in the patient's body, which deposits in kidneys, heart, and other tissues. Eventually what amounts to iron poisoning results. Individuals with thalassemia minor should know about it so that they can alert health personnel who care for them and can become informed of the risks of producing an affected child. (See *genetics.*)

The distribution of such abnormal hemoglobin came about over many thousands of years of evolution in different eras and settings in which these pigments played a protective role in human survival. It seems quite clear that sickle-cell hemoglobin protects against infection with severe malaria, although we really don't know why. Thus, blacks with sickle-cell hemoglobin are more likely to survive malaria and consequently more likely to marry and reproduce than those with normal hemoglobin. Natural selection favored the propagation of sickle-cell hemoglobin in the black population in the malaria-infested regions of the world. In the malaria-free United States this hemoglobin serves no useful purpose and blacks with normal hemoglobin have a distinct advantage for survival. Individuals with the thalassemia trait also may have been more likely to survive malarial infection.

A common example of an enzyme-related cause of anemia is *G6PD* (*glucose-6-phosphate dehydrogenase* deficiency). It is found in about 10 percent of American black males and 2 percent of American black females. The deficiency is also common among Orientals. This deficiency of G6PD causes the red blood cell to be destroyed on exposure to certain medicines like aspirin or sulfa. A mild anemia can result.

Just as anemia can result from a lack of essential nutritional building blocks or from defective construction leading to early removal of red blood cells, so can blood be lost from the body by bleeding (hemorrhaging). Bleeding may be severe and acute as in the case of a deep cut or it may be chronic and slow, even unnoticed, as from a tumor of the intesitne, which is more likely to occur in adults than children.

Anemia may result from impaired production of blood cells. Underproduction can be caused by insufficient building blocks like iron and vitamins (see above). Blood formation can be suppressed by certain medications or some other disease like *leukemia* which interferes with red blood cell production or by poisonous metals like lead (see *lead poisoning*). Chronic liver or kidney failure can "turn off" the marrow.

The development of anemia depends on a tip in the normal balance between production and destruction of red blood cells. Within a certain range, the marrow can compensate for increased destruction or loss. Thus, assuming an adequate supply of nutrients, a mild increase in blood destruction or blood loss can be corrected by a step-up in red blood cell production and anemia does not result. In this situation, the accelerated destruction and production can be identified only by special blood tests.

## DIAGNOSIS

The diagnosis of anemia depends on the symptoms, findings on physical examination, and selected laboratory studies. The diagnosis should be made by a doctor, not by the patient alone trying different tonics. The symptoms have already been outlined. (If anemia is not proven it is very important to look for other causes of these symptoms, including psychological ones.) Important in diagnosis is an assessment of the diet with respect to iron, vitamin $B_{12}$, and folic acid, a review of all medications being taken by the patient, a history of bleeding, including the quantity of blood flow in the menstrual periods, and information about the occurrence of anemia in other family members.

The basic laboratory studies are discussed under *blood count.*

## TREATMENT

Depending on its cause, treatment of anemia may include changes in diet, injections of iron or vitamins, blood transfusions, and, when possible, correction of factors leading to blood loss or suppression of blood production. Since causes are so varied, no attempt will be made here to discuss treatment in any great detail. In general, anemia resulting from nutritional deficiency (iron, vitamin $B_{12}$, folic acid, and protein) can be corrected. The anemia resulting from the destruction of blood in G6PD deficiency can be prevented. No cure exists at present for the anemia of abnormal hemoglobins as in sickle-cell anemia or thalassemia. However, patients so affected can be helped by prompt treatment of *infections,* prevention of dehydration, and, when necessary, by transfusions of blood to correct immediately their red blood cell deficiency. Much research effort has been and will be directed at these disorders and progress is expected.

What are the ways to prevent anemia? We can summarize this with some simple rules:

1. Adopt a diet that contains adequate quantities of iron, vitamin $B_{12}$ and folic acid. Encourage your school to teach children about proper nutrition.

2. Be sure that non-breast-fed infants receive added iron from birth on.

3. Follow the advice of your doctor or nurse for taking additional iron during pregnancy.

4. If you are black or of Mediterranean ancestry, find out if you or your teen-age children carry the trait for sickle-cell or thalassemia and obtain genetic counseling so that you can make an informed decision about having children in full knowledge of the risks of producing an affected infant and of the possibility of a preventive abortion. If you have the thalassemia trait (which might have been discovered because of a low normal blood count), be sure to tell doctors and nurses so that you will not be mistaken for having the iron deficiency anemia with which the trait is frequently confused.

See *jaundice; genetics;* and *blood count.*


**Animal bites:** see *bites, animal.*


**Appendicitis,** or inflammation of the appendix, is on everybody's mind when a child complains of stomach pain (see *abdominal pain*). Yet, of all the children who have such pain, only a very small percentage turn out to have appendicitis. It is a rare condition. Still, it is one we like to detect early, because prompt treatment is very important. The guidelines of when to call the doctor, which we discuss in the section on abdominal pain, are designed in part to catch early cases of appendicitis. If you follow them, the chances are that appendicitis will not be overlooked in your child.

The emphasis upon early diagnosis is easily explained. If inflammation and infection are confined to the appendix, the surgeon's job is quite simple: remove the appendix, a relatively simple operation followed by quick recovery. However, if the infection has spread beyond the appendix, that is, if rupture or abscess has occurred, the problem becomes much more complicated. The pus from the appendix spreads through the abdominal cavity, causing *peritonitis,* or inflammation of the *peritoneum,* the thin, glistening membrane that lines the inside of the abdomen and covers the abdominal organs. Today, with antibiotics and intravenous fluids, it is possible to bring more patients through this complication which was often fatal in the past. Even so, the length, discomfort, and cost of hospitalization are significantly increased.

If the appendix is inflamed and bulging with pus, increased intestinal activity will make rupture more likely. For this reason we advise strongly against giving laxatives to children with abdominal pain unless the doctor says it is all right.

Doctors have a healthy respect for appendicitis. It is a tricky disorder. Many times its early diagnosis is unclear. For every child operated on there is at least another who is observed in the hospital and discharged without treatment. During the period of observation the child is given, at most, sips of clear fluids to drink so that, if surgery is necessary, he or she will have an empty stomach, a requirement for general anesthesia. This consideration of possible surgery is one reason we advise that children with abdominal pain not be given solid foods without the doctor's approval.

Using the most exacting criteria for operation, we are likely to be wrong 10 to 25 percent of the time—that is, we operate on a child with what seemed to be appendicitis only to find a normal appendix. We are willing to accept this batting average. Far, far better to overoperate than to miss a diagnosis, so serious is rupture or abscess of the appendix. Even with the best of intentions, appendicitis progresses to rupture with great rapidity in a small number of children. Sometimes a particularly stoic, uncomplaining child may put off informing his parents of his discomfort, thus delaying early recognition. It is important to know your child.

The appendix is a long, wormlike pouch several inches long, which is attached to the *cecum*, the baglike part of the large intestine which is joined directly to the small intestine. It is usually located in the right lower side of the abdomen. The appendix is of no obvious benefit to present-day man and is a vestige of human evolution. Why it becomes obstructed so that inflammation and infection develops is not clear. It is likely that virus infections (see infections) of the intestine, which cause swelling of the inner lining, play a role, by blocking the junction between the appendix and the cecum. One bit of evidence is that appendicitis is more common during the summer months, when intestinal virus infections (see *gastroenteritis*) are more common.

See Part 1, Chapter 6: "If Your Child Goes to the Hospital."


*Appetite, poor:* see Part 1, Chapter 3: "Diet of Infants and Children."


*Arm, favoring of.* In general, it is best to check with your doctor if your child stops using an arm and resists your moving it, particularly in the child too young to give a verbal accounting of his or her symptoms. In the older child, the cause is more likely to be obvious, allowing you to make a simple decision about whether or not to seek help.

A common cause in toddlers is a partially dislocated elbow, an injury that results from a sudden forceful pull of the hand or arm, by grasping the child's hand to prevent his falling, or picking him up by the hands alone. The child cries with pain and stops using the injured arm. There is no obvious bruise or break. Characteristically, the arm is held close to the chest with the palm facing to the rear. The treatment consists of manipulating the lower arm around so that the palm faces forward while applying pressure at the elbow. The recovery is usually dramatic and recurrence infrequent although not unheard of. Sometimes the child will continue to favor the arm for several hours after the dislocation has been corrected.

Often the doctor will find no obvious explanation for favoring of the arm, and it will be written off as due to some minor injury which will heal on its own. Sometimes the cause is more serious, requiring specific treatment. More serious causes include fractured collarbone (see *fracture*), *osteomyelitis* (infection of the bone), and *sickle-cell anemia*.

See also *joint pain* and *sprains*.

**Arthritis, rheumatoid.** Rheumatoid arthritis is an uncommon disorder in children, of unknown cause and variable duration (sometimes lasting years) and intensity, ranging from barely noticeable to severely crippling. Common symptoms include stiffness and pain in the joints (see *joint pain*), joint swelling and inflammation, *fever*, and *rash.* The latter symptoms may precede or occur without joint findings. While any joint can be involved, those commonly affected are the knuckles, wrists, ankles, and spine, particularly the neck. (See *neck pain.*)

Treatment is directed toward reducing inflammation and preserving use of the joints through physical therapy and exercise. Aspirin in large doses is commonly used to relieve pain and reduce inflammation. For more severe cases, hydrocortisone-like hormones (see *hormones*) may be needed.

See *handicapped child.*

**Artificial respiration:** see Part 2, Chapter 9: "First Aid."

**Asthma** is a respiratory problem whose chief feature is labored or difficult breathing, often accompanied by a characteristic wheezing or whistling sound. During asthmatic attacks, children usually seem to have more difficulty exhaling than inhaling. The whistling or wheezing sound of asthma is loudest when breathing air out.

Asthma in a child can be a frightening experience. If this is your child's first asthma attack, contact your doctor right away. If he can't be reached and your child is having real trouble breathing, take him or her to a hospital emergency room or clinic. If your child is breathing hard but is reasonably comfortable, there is less cause for immediate action but, of course, contact your doctor anyway.

Here are some suggestions while you wait for the doctor.

First, stay calm yourself. If you have never seen an asthmatic attack before, the first episode is likely to be frightening both to you and to your child. Be reassured that most attacks subside on their own with or without treatment, although medical treatment hastens the recovery. Put your child to bed and keep him quiet. Sometimes children prefer to sit halfway up, and if your child seems more comfortable in this position, prop him up with several pillows. Give him something to do to get his mind off the trouble he is having with breathing. Read him a book or turn on the television or radio. Try to be as reassuring as possible. This will be difficult if you yourself are upset, but for your child's sake stay as calm as you can.

Encourage your child to take as much fluid as possible, of any variety. He is likely to be somewhat nauseous during an asthma attack and may want only a little bit of fluid at a time. Don't try to force him into taking more but offer him any kind of fluid that he wants, even in small sips, every few minutes.

If you have cough medicine available, particularly of the expectorant type, which you know does *not* contain any antihistamine, you can give it to your child safely. It is generally best not to give cough medicine containing antihistamines to a child having an asthmatic attack because it dries the secretions of the chest, making their removal more difficult. If in doubt, the best policy is not to give him the medicine.

If some obvious environmental factor seems to have triggered the attack, such as the frying of fish, or recent painting of the child's room, or introduction of a pet into the family, remove the child from this possible irritant. If in addition to the asthma attack your child seems to have an ordinary cold, take those measures discussed under **colds.** Moistening the air with a vaporizer may help other types of respiratory difficulties but rarely helps asthma, and in some cases may make it worse, since most asthmatics are worse in damp, humid weather.

The symptoms of asthma are caused by changes in the respiratory system, the system of passageways that carries air from the mouth into the lungs. The respiratory system is shaped very much like an upside-down tree with trunk and branches. The major air passageway which communicates with the throat is the *trachea.* Within the chest near the heart, the trachea divides into two major branches called the *bronchi,* which enter the lungs and promptly undergo further subdivision into smaller bronchi and *bronchioles.* The smallest branches of the bronchial tree communicate directly with the microscopic air spaces in the lungs.

The tubes of the respiratory system are elastic and contract and expand with respiration. We ordinarily do not think of muscle being present in the body except in obvious visible places. But many of the inner organs contain muscle, which accounts for their ability to change in size. The bronchial tree contains muscle which contracts and relaxes to change the size of the passageways. Just as the muscles of the arms and legs are under the voluntary control of nerves which find their origin ultimately in the spinal cord and brain, so the muscles of the body organs, also known as smooth muscles, are under the control of a different system of nerves called the *autonomic nervous system*, which functions involuntarily, without conscious attention. This nerve connection of the smooth muscles in the bronchial tree with the central nervous system (brain and spinal cord) means that the emotions experienced in the brain can influence the tone of muscles in the bronchi. As we will later discuss, emotional factors play an important role in asthma.

The entire respiratory tree is lined on its inner surface with the thin membrane known as the *mucosa*. Within this mucosa are microscopic glands which secrete mucus through tiny holes to keep this inner lining moist and lubricated. Small microscopic filaments project from the mucosa into the passageway and move in a rhythmic, wavelike fashion away from the lungs and toward the trachea. These filaments propel small particles of dirt from the lungs into the larger air passageways, from which they are either coughed and swallowed or carried by the flow of air out of the body. Thus the bronchial tree has the important ability to cleanse itself of foreign materials.

In asthma, the small air passageways are the ones which are chiefly affected. The muscles in these passages go into spasm, narrowing the width of the tubes, and thus making the passage of air in and out of the lungs more difficult. In addition to muscle spasm there is an outpouring of mucus into the small air passages, further obstructing the flow of air. Finally, the mucosa becomes inflamed and swollen, thus narrowing the air passageway even further, much as an accumulation of rust on the inner surface of a pipe would partially obstruct the flow of water through the pipe. All of these changes, the spasm, the swelling, and the outpouring of mucus, occur together, affecting to a greater or lesser degree almost all of the small air passages. The resistance to the flow of air, particularly during expiration, or breathing out, is significantly increased, and the child must work harder to move air in and out of his lungs. Thus the whistling sound. All of the muscular movements of respiration, which ordinarily pass unnoticed, become exaggerated and readily visible. Between asthmatic attacks, the child's small air passageways and his breathing return to normal, and nothing about his breathing distinguishes him from the nonasthmatic.

Asthma is considered to be an allergic disease. (See **allergy.**) Allergic reactions tend to localize in a particular part of the body. In asthma the site of reaction is the small air passageways, and it is here that the reaction between antibodies and allergens, the foreign substances, takes place. In asthma, we find that the most common foreign substances stimulating the allergic reaction are airborne materials such as pollen, molds, house dust, animal hair or feathers (from pets or from the stuffing of pillows and mattresses), and the particles that account for odors (odors are produced by vapors of the substance smelled). Air pollution is an aggravating factor.

Many asthmatic individuals also respond with wheezing to respiratory infections. (See **infections.**) The condition is sometimes called asthmatic **bronchitis.** The relationship between infections and allergic symptoms appears to occur in several ways. One is that protein substances contained in bacteria act as allergens, much as dust and pollens do. Or it may be that an infection in some way alters the tolerance of the asthmatic to other allergens such as dust, animal dander, and pollen. With a lowered tolerance, the same dose of allergen that usually causes no trouble may now lead to an asthmatic attack.

To confuse the picture somewhat, infections may affect the small bronchial passages in nonasthmatics, causing breathing problems just like those of asthma. Such an infection is called *bronchiolitis* (inflammation of the bronchioles). It is mainly a problem of infancy. (See **bronchitis.**) Foods may also cause asthmatic attacks, although this is less common. Asthmatic individuals are often sensitive to fatigue, sudden temperature changes, and emotional stress. As with other allergic symptoms, asthma cannot be attributed to any one cause. Rather, asthmatic symptoms result from the interaction of many factors, seasonal and environmental. The asthmatic individual may be thought of as being in a state of balance that can be upset by any one of a combination of developments. For example, he may be exposed to an unusually heavy concentration of an airborne material to which he is sensitive, thus provoking an attack. Or a relatively normal concentration of airborne substances, in conjunction with an emotional upset or respiratory infection, may be sufficient to provoke symptoms. The care of the asthmatic must take into account all of the factors operating and not merely the last straw that tipped the balance.

A major limitation in treatment is our inability at present to determine the basic constitutional difference between allergic and nonallergic people and to change this. Thus we cannot speak in terms of curing asthma. We must for the present treat the specific allergies as they develop by removing the cause, or by lessening the patient's sensitivity to the cause with immunizing injections, or by using drugs to relieve the symptoms resulting from the specific cause. Cleaning up the air we breathe will no doubt be beneficial to asthmatics as well as to all others.

Fortunately, even with this limitation we are able to do much to help the asthmatic. Individual attacks can be treated effectively, and measures can be employed to make recurrent attacks less likely. Some children may have only one or two attacks. In others, the tendency to asthmatic attacks may persist for life. Sensitivities change with the passage of time, and an allergic person of any age may lose an allergy or gain a new one. The site of reaction may shift from chest to nose to skin, for example. A child whose allergy goes untreated is more likely to continue to have trouble or get worse than to improve spontaneously. It is impossible to predict which pattern a child's allergic condition will follow.

Your doctor will advise you on medicines which you can use to help the child having an attack of asthma. (For a full discussion, see *allergy*.) These medicines interrupt the allergic reaction and also directly relax the spasm of the muscles of the small airways (the so-called bronchodilators perform this function), reduce the swelling of the surface lining of the passageways, and cut down on the excessive secretions of the mucous glands. The medicines can be taken by mouth or given rectally in the form of suppositories. Aerosols containing bronchodilators are useful in selected situations but should be used only under the doctor's direction. Some medications such as epinephrine are given by injection, and are usually administered by a physician or nurse rather than by the parent.

A drug known as *disodium cryoglycate* (trade name: Aarane/Intal), which has recently become available, shows great promise for helping asthmatics to prevent attacks. This drug is packaged in capsules. These are inserted into an inhalator and the fine powder is inhaled by the patient. This drug is effective primarily in individuals who have clear-cut allergies to inhaled substances such as pollens. No side reactions have been reported and disodium cryoglycate can be taken along with other medications used to treat asthma without interference.

Occasionally children with asthmatic attacks need additional treatment available only within the hospital. Sometimes they require intravenous fluids, especially if they are nauseous and unable to take adequate amounts of fluid at home. Children with marked difficulty in breathing may require oxygen. Most asthmatic attacks, however, can be cared for successfully at home or at the doctor's office.

Preventing attacks is a major goal in caring for the asthmatic child. Your physican must make a careful assessment of your child and will try to identify which, if any, airborne particles might be playing a role. (See *allergy*.) He will also want to know something about what kind of child the asthmatic is, how he gets along with his peers and relatives, how he handles stresses. He may perform skin tests to aid in the identification of materials to which a child might be sensitive.

Based upon your physician's assessment of the child, specific recommendations can be made. In general these consist of suggestions about control of the child's environment—steps to reduce sharply the amount of dust present in the home and the child's bedroom and the removal of animals and animal products, such as feather or hair stuffing in pillows, cushions, and mattresses. Steps can also be taken to control the ventilation of the child's room in order to decrease the household and pollen dust present. (See *allergy.*) The child may be maintained on medication on a chronic basis. *Aminophylline* is a current favorite and it is becoming increasingly popular to adjust the dose according to the blood level as measured in the laboratory. When indicated, the physician may attempt to hyposensitize the child to certain allergens. The purpose of these injections is to build up the child's tolerance to allergens causing his symptoms, thus decreasing the capacity of those materials to stimulate an asthmatic response. (See *allergy.*) The physician may also suggest certain breathing exercises, to keep the child from tiring so easily during an asthmatic attack. A booklet entitled *Breathing Exercises for Asthmatic Children* can be obtained for $1.00 from the American Academy of Pediatrics, P.O. Box 1034, Evanston, Ill. 60204.

We have already mentioned that emotional factors are of great importance to asthmatic children. (See Part 1, Chapter 4: "Complaints with an Emotional Element.") Asthma can profoundly affect the relationship between parent and child. Similarly, difficulties in the parent-child relationship may have an effect on the frequency and severity of asthmatic attacks. For example, we know that asthmatic attacks can be triggered by angry feelings in a child. Some angry feelings are an everyday experience for most children, often precipitated by parental discipline. If a child is angry and the anger leads to an attack, parents may have second thoughts about being too firm. This leniency may not be truly in the best interest of the child. The parent is clearly caught on the horns of a dilemma and must try to strike a balance between being too firm and too lenient. (See *handicapped child.*)

Asthma can lead to certain complications. We have mentioned how asthmatic children are prone to wheeze when they have respiratory infections, such as the ordinary common cold. Once symptoms begin, the setup for a complicating infection of the bronchial tree or lungs exists. The normal cleansing mechanism is interfered with and there is a tendency for secretions to accumulate and stagnate in the distal parts of the bronchial tree, providing a fertile field for the multiplication of microorganisms. Should infection be present, your doctor will probably prescribe an antibiotic. Another similar but less frequent complication of asthma is the complete sealing-off of one of the smaller air passageways, with the resulting collapse of that portion of the lung it supplies. This condition is known as *atelectasis* (see *lung rupture and collapse*) and is often associated with the acute attack of asthma. It usually clears on its own. Tearing of a part of the lung may allow air to escape into the chest cavity (see *pneumothorax*).

For a condition like asthma, once again we emphasize the importance of establishing a close working relationship with a pediatrician or family physician. (See Part 1, Chapter 1: "Quality in Pediatric Care.") If a clinic is the source of the care, we suggest choosing one where the same health professionals will continue to supervise the care of your child over a period of time. There are some physicians who specialize in problems of allergy. These doctors are known as allergists, and their expert understanding is often sought by your own doctor for help in caring for your child's difficulty. We suggest that you do not go directly to a specialist but ask to be referred by your own physician. The specialist and family doctor or pediatrician usually function best when they work as a team.

See *allergy; emphysema.*

*Astigmatism:* see *vision problems.*

*Atelectasis:* see *lung rupture and collapse.*

*Athlete's foot* is usually signaled by the development of itching between the toes and by unpleasant odors emanating from the feet. The part of the foot most usually involved is the skin between the toes. The affected skin appears reddened, scaly, cracked, and soggy.

Athlete's foot is unusual in childhood but is not at all uncommon during *adolescence,* particularly in boys. Surveys of the feet of young men show that mild degrees of inflammation between the toes are present in over half. Athlete's foot is generally thought to be a fungus infection of the skin. Common belief is that these fungi are picked up in public places such as swimming pools, showers, and gymnasiums. Studies have failed to isolate fungi from these places, so this popular belief is probably incorrect. Furthermore, many young adolescent males have athlete's foot who do not frequent such public places.

Probably the most important factor in the development of athlete's foot is the civilized habit of wearing shoes. Shoes cause sweating and irritation of the feet, particularly in the crevices of the toes. Athlete's foot is not seen in primitive tribes where individuals go barefoot. The fungi seem to be normally present on the feet in a high percentage of adolescents in shoe-wearing societies. The common germs, heat, and sweating associated with shoe wearing combine to produce the changes between the toes which we have come to call athlete's foot. Why some people are more susceptible than others is unclear. Athlete's foot is not contagious in the sense that one person can pass it on to another. Although many grown men have this condition, it is very unusual for their wives to develop the problem.

Very mild cases of itching and redness and scaling between the toes can be managed without consulting a doctor. The most important thing is to keep the area between the toes dry. Toes should be dried very carefully after bathing or after removing shoes. It is best to do this with a washcloth, applying enough friction to remove the soggy skin and the scales. It is important to air the feet. Open footwear, such as sandals or "ventilated" shoes, are preferable, especially in warm weather. Avoid wearing rubber-soled footwear such as sneakers, or shoes of nonporous leather like cordovans. They cause increased heat and sweating. It is helpful to dust the toes with absorbent baby powder on getting up in the morning and also at other times. If sweating is excessive, socks should be changed more than once daily. There is no need to wear socks which are white or to boil the socks after use. If the athlete's foot is a source of considerable discomfort, it is best to rest, staying off the feet as much as possible. The less the feet are used, the quicker the healing will occur. Obviously, if the condition has reached this point, a doctor should be consulted. If the simple measures described above do not serve to relieve the problem or if the condition is pretty severe to start with, consult a doctor. In addition to the measures described above, he will probably prescribe some medication to promote healing.

A person with a tendency to flare-ups of athlete's foot should probably use these measures as a matter of course, whether his feet are infected or not. Careful drying of the skin, use of powder, and cool footwear during seasons of the year when flare-ups are more likely can help prevent the condition.

*Autism:* see *developmental disabilities.*

*Back problems:* see *spinal defects.*

*"Battered child":* see *child abuse.*

*Bee stings:* see *bites, insect.*

***Biliary atresia.*** In biliary atresia, a congenital condition, the major bile ducts which carry bile from the liver to the intestine are missing. Statistically, this condition is rare.

Bile, a thin yellow fluid, is a vehicle for the excretion of a number of body products, including *bilirubin*, the major component in the breakdown of aged red blood cells (see *jaundice*). Bile also contains chemical compounds that are important in the digestion of fats. Microscopic channels carry the bile from the liver cells in which it is produced to larger tubes in the liver that, like streams joining a river, come together to form the *common bile duct*. This duct connects the liver with the *duodenum*, the uppermost section of the intestine. There is one major branch, the *cystic duct*, which leads to the *gallbladder*, the storage place for bile.

Obstruction of bile flow, from whatever cause, can bring on progressive damage and scarring of the liver with consequent impairment of function. When the outflow of bile is blocked, all the substances normally excreted in the bile back up into the bloodstream. Since bilirubin is one of these substances, jaundice is therefore an important symptom of biliary obstruction (although this condition will be rare among all the possible causes of jaundice in the newborn). The insufficiency of bile in the intestine results in incomplete digestion of fatty foods. Chronic *diarrhea* and the signs of poor nutrition will be the symptoms. If unrelieved, complete obstruction of bile flow causes so much liver damage that death results.

The flow of bile can be impaired by congenitally deficient or absent bile ducts external to the liver, that is, between the liver and the duodenum. Sometimes this blockage is accompanied by deficient or absent bile ducts within the liver as well. Defects in the external bile system may be correctable by surgery. Even in the complete absence of an external collecting system it is now possible to hook up the intestine directly to the base of the liver where the internal bile ducts come together if these ducts are present. The presence or absence of these internal ducts is determined by biopsy (removing a small specimen of liver for examination under the microscope) at the time of surgery. This corrective operation is moderately successful but not completely so. If the ducts are absent, the defect is not correctable at present.

Although the symptoms are similar, congenital biliary atresia must be distinguished from **hepatitis** (inflammation of the liver). The two conditions are difficult to tell apart, but it is important to diagnose biliary atresia as early as possible. The sooner a repairable biliary atresia can be corrected, the less liver damage will result. The diagnosis of hepatitis is made by inspecting the liver and bile ducts at surgery and by a liver *biopsy*. There is no medical treatment yet available but healing is the rule.

**Birth defects, severe.** When a baby is born with severe abnormalities or deformities, a decision must often be made almost immediately about whether to perform surgery or other measures to save the baby's life. Severe **hydrocephalus,** advanced enough at the time of birth to have caused brain damage; **Down's syndrome** with associated abnormalities; myelomeningocele (see **spinal defects**); and other multiple congenital defects which can mean a lifetime of dependency and minimal brain function are among the conditions which raise such a decision. A decade or two ago babies born with these conditions did not survive. Now, new advances in medical knowledge and technology make it possible to save their lives. There is a growing trend, however, and with it a growing controversy, to involve parents in the decision, and to withhold treatment if they so desire.

Since these issues, and their ethical dilemmas, are going to be faced more and more, we feel that all prospective parents should be aware of them and think about what their views and feelings might be if confronted with such a situation.

"It is no longer mere physical life which is at stake, but the quality of life. There are times when preserving life would go against our deepest convictions about its meaning and sanctity; there are other times when making a decision about the quality of life would seem to be an attack on the sanctity of life itself, an assumption of power we tremble to accept. In other words, contemporary medicine has propelled to center stage the sanctity of life in a new guise: the quality of life. It asks us to view life *also* in terms of its quality, to admit that there comes a time when living is no longer *human* life—and to take the consequences of this admission." (Richard A. McCormick, S.J., in *The Teaching of Medical Ethics*, Hastings-on-Hudson, N.Y.: a Hastings Center Publication, 1973.)

**Birthmarks.** Very many, perhaps most, babies are born with a birthmark or *nevus*. One type is *hemangioma*, a cluster or growth of small blood vessels on or under the skin. Another is the common *mole*.

The commonest hemangioma is the *salmon patch*, a cluster of small red spots on the nape of the neck, across the bridge of the nose, or on the upper eyelid. It used to be said that the marks on the neck were left by the stork's beak. The salmon patch never requires treatment and disappears so gradually over the first year of life that the parents may not even notice its going.

The *strawberry mark* is another very common hemangioma, occurring in as many as 10 percent of all babies, more frequently among females. Bright red, this mark looks as if a strawberry had been cut in half and stuck to the baby's skin. Most often it appears on the face or neck.

Characteristically, it may be so small at birth as to be hard to find, but it enlarges rapidly, attaining peak size by 6 months. Almost without exception, this rapid growth signifies that the strawberry in time will wither away. A change of color to dark red and the appearance of small islands of gray in the red herald this *involution* (lessening in size) of the strawberry mark. At age 3, one-third of all strawberry marks have disappeared, at age 4, 60 percent, and by age 6, 70 percent. Altogether, 90 percent disappear on their own. The rare mark that grows at an excessive rate or is on a site subject to repeated bruising may call for earlier intervention. For a few, surgery and/or X-ray treatment may be in order.

A minority of strawberry marks extend deep down in the skin. The visible portion may be only a small part of the total hemangioma. Some hemangiomas are completely submerged, recognizable only by the resulting lump or by the suggestion of a large blue mass under the skin. By and large, all these submerged hemangiomas follow the same pattern of growth and involution that is characteristic of the visible ones. The conservative approach to treatment is always in order.

A third hemangioma of relatively common occurrence is the *port wine stain*. These stains are areas of skin that appear to be normal except for the red coloring. The most common variety is a patch shaped like a diamond on the forehead, extending to the bridge of the nose. When the infant cries, the diamond flushes, and even in adults the coloring of the patch gives a clue to the emotions. The port wine stain, which may also occur elsewhere on the head or body, is especially prominent on blondes. There is no treatment for this lesion. It usually fades in time, but sometimes will remain at least faintly visible. Cosmetics will render the mark less conspicuous.

Yet a fourth hemangioma is the *Mongolian spot*, a common bluish stain of the lower back and buttocks. This hemangioma presents no problems. It is entirely benign and is usually found only in infants, totally disappearing by the time the child reaches school age.

Moles are very common on the skin of children and adults. These are dark brown, flesh-colored, or black spots or lumps, usually the size of a freckle or slightly larger. Some are flat, barely raised over the skin surface; others are raised like warts, and some even have a suggestion of a stalk. With few exceptions, they cause no harm, but may be objectionable cosmetically and therefore candidates for removal. Rapid enlargement, ulceration (development of a sore), fragmentation of color or texture, and development of a halo or ring of color around the mole are reasons for consulting your doctor, who may then suggest removing it surgically.

***Bites, animal.*** Animal bites, especially dog bites, can cause very serious injury and may be disfiguring. Any animal bite brings with it the danger of infection, due to the many bacteria carried in the animal's mouth. Bite wounds also carry the danger of ***tetanus.***

If an animal should bite your child, notify a physician promptly. First aid includes thorough washing of the wound with warm water and soap and application of an antiseptic. The doctor will determine whether a tetanus booster is needed. Any redness, swelling, pus, or increasing pain that develops later should be brought immediately to a doctor's attention. This is especially important if it is accompanied by fever, loss of appetite, pain in joints distant to the bite, or unusual irritability or fatigue, for these may all be signs of infection developing in spite of the first aid and doctor's treatment.

Because of the danger of rabies, the animal who bit the child should be captured and observed. If it is a pet, the owner should be found and notified.

See discussion of rabies under ***pets and children;*** also ***tetanus.***

***Bites, insect.*** Insect bites are very common in childhood. Mosquitoes, fleas, spiders, bees, hornets, wasps, and flies are the most common offenders. The local skin reaction is similar for all types of insect bites. There is usually some swelling, redness, burning, and itching. Stings are likely to be especially large and swollen. Young children often react more intensely than adults, who have developed some immunity over the years to insect substances. Swelling is likely to be more marked in parts of the body where the skin is loose or has many blood vessels, as in the skin on the face or around the eye. Occasionally a mere mosquito bite will result in enough swelling to close the eye almost completely. Scratching is common because of the itching. Bites may become secondarily infected (see ***abscess***) by scratching.

The prevention of bites is the best treatment. Screens, mosquito nets, and long-sleeved shirts and trousers are helpful. Commercially available insect repellants are useful if used correctly. In general, however, repellents are effective for only 45 minutes to 2 hours after application to skin. They must be reapplied if longer protection is necessary. After being applied to fabrics, however, they are effective for several days. Precautions against stirring up hornets' nests or beehives need hardly be mentioned. Particular care should be exercised in the use of outdoor privies or toilets. Dangerous spiders (including the black widow) find these sites very attractive for egg laying. Often spiders are found lurking beneath or around toilet seats. The poor lighting in these places makes it even harder to spot and avoid these creatures.

Unfortunately, no medicine exists that will cure a bite. Treatment is directed toward the relief of the discomfort and the prevention of secondary infection. Beyond such measures, there is no way of hastening recovery. Cold compresses or ice cubes applied to bites often reduce swelling and itching. Calamine lotion and anti-itch creams are of little value beyond a few moments' relief. Antihistamines taken by mouth may have some benefit in reducing the itching and the swelling. Their usefulness is probably overrated, however. They may work to a large extent by quieting the victim down, that is, making him or her sleepy and less active so that the itch is less bothersome. It is doubtful that they do much of anything to the bite itself. Try to discourage your child from scratching bites by explaining the reasons for not scratching. Keep his nails well trimmed. During the first few hours after the child has been bitten, when the itching is most intense, engage your child in activities that will distract his attention. As with other skin irritations, sweating will increase the itch and discomfort. Keeping the child cool and quiet will decrease sweating and cut down on the itching. This is easier said than done with an active child in warm weather.

Usually the swelling and redness reach a peak after 1 or 2 hours. They will rarely worsen after that time unless a complication has set in. Children have a much greater amount of swelling and redness than adults. Particularly alarming, as we said before, is the amount of swelling and redness often seen when a bite is near the eye. Take the same measures here that you would take for bites anywhere else. Be sure to look at the eye itself. As long as there is no redness in the whites of the eye or yellowish discharge (for which you should contact the doctor), you can feel secure that the bite is affecting only the surrounding skin and not the eye itself. Skin swelling represents no danger to the eye.

If after 1 to 2 hours following a bite or bites you notice that the amount of redness and swelling are increasing rather than decreasing and particularly if the child develops *fever*, contact your doctor and discuss the problem with him. If at any time after the first day or two you notice any discharge coming from a bite, handle the situation as you would any other skin infection (see *abscess*). One other point is worth making. If mosquitoes or other insects are much of a problem in your area, be sure to contact your local health department and inform it of the situation. Mosquito control programs can be quite effective. Cooperation by the public assists the health department in carrying out its programs.

While insect bites are usually no more than annoying, there are certain special situations which may be dangerous, even life-threatening. Some children (and adults) may have generalized allergic reactions to the sting of hornets, bees, yellow jackets, or wasps (see *allergy*). These stinging bugs are all members of the same family. The characteristic of an allergic reaction is a bodily response somewhere other than at the site of the bite itself. Marked swelling and redness around the bite does not alone constitute an allergic reaction. Symptoms you might see are general body itch, flushed appearance of the skin (other than at the site of the bite), scattered hives or any rash elsewhere on the body, and a complaint of feeling warmth or heat all over the skin. Later, the child may complain or act as though he is having weakness, dizziness, nausea, abdominal cramps, and difficulty in breathing. If you see any of these symptoms developing in your child, however long after the bite (sometimes even hours later), be sure to let your doctor know *right away*. If the bite is on the arm or leg, place a tourniquet (belt or tie, for example) above the bite to limit spread of the venom. You should be able to slip your index finger under the band when it is in place. Keep the affected part down, below the level of the heart, and apply to the site ice held in a plastic bag or towel, or cold cloth. In the case of a bee sting, remove the stinger and venom sac. If your doctor can't be reached promptly, move your child immediately to his office (if he is expected) or preferably to the nearest hospital emergency room. Try to have someone call ahead to let them know that you are coming, saying that you are concerned about an allergic reaction from an insect bite. Do not wait for the doctor to call back if you suspect this condition. Time is important. There is often little time between the appearance of mild symptoms such as *hives* or generalized body itching and serious incapacity. If *shock* occurs, signified by cold, blanched, clammy-wet skin, apprehension, and lethargy, lay the child down with legs elevated. The place for a child with a suspected allergic reaction is in the doctor's office or in the hospital emergency room. Waste no time in getting him there.

If your doctor feels that your child indeed has had an allergic reaction to an insect bite, he will want to take certain precautions to prevent recurrences. The danger with allergic bite reactions, even with mild ones, is that the next episode will be more severe. In the extreme case, allergic reactions can be life threatening. It is possible to hyposensitize children to the venom of insects to which they are allergic by injecting progressively increasing quantities of insect extract over many months (see *allergy* on hyposensitization). In fact, once the diagnosis of insect bite allergy is made, hyposensitization is a must. Sensitivity to the venom of one of the entire family of stinging insects usually signifies sensitivity to all. Because of this cross reactivity, hyposensitization is directed against all four insects and not just to the one that caused the difficulty. In addition to this preventive program, sensitive individuals must scrupulously avoid the insects in question. When boating or camping, they should carry an emergency treatment kit with medicines to combat an allergic response should a bite occur.

The toxins of certain insects, notably black widow spiders, brown recluse spiders, and scorpions, may have general effects on the child similar to the allergic response to the four stinging insects mentioned above. Symptoms resulting from a black widow spider bite are pain and swelling at the site plus the systemic (general) reactions of profuse sweating, nausea, painful cramps of the abdominal muscles, and difficulty in breathing and speaking. The brown recluse spider causes a severe local reaction which forms an open sore from one to two weeks later. Systemic reactions include chills, fever, joint pains, nausea, and vomiting. Scorpions, which inject venom through their tails, cause severe pain at the injection site plus the systemic effects of nausea, vomiting, abdominal pain, shock, and, possibly, convulsions and coma.

Treatment of the systemic reactions to these insects is similar to that described above for wasps, bees, hornets, and yellow jackets. However, this is not an allergic reaction and does not call for the hyposensitization treatment.

Ticks are common biting insects which adhere tenaciously to the scalp and skin. A tick may be removed by covering it with heavy oil (mineral, salad, or machine) to plug its breathing pores. If it does not disengage in a half hour, carefully remove it with tweezers, being careful to remove all parts. Then, thoroughly and gently scrub the area with soap and water. Should a feverish illness later develop, be sure to inform your doctor about the bite so that he can consider the possibility of *Rocky Mountain spotted fever.*

For a discussion of flea and tick bites, see *pets and children.*


*Bites, snake.* There are two major classes of poisonous snakes in America, the pit vipers and the coral snake, a member of the cobra family.

Copperheads, rattlesnakes, and cottonmouth moccasins belong to the family of snakes known as pit vipers. These snakes have a pit between the eyes and nostril and each side of the head, two well-developed fangs, and elliptical-shaped pupils.

The coral snake is a variety of cobra found along the coast and low-lands of the Southeastern United States. It is a small snake with tubular fangs having teeth behind them. It is characterized by red, black, and yellow rings about the body with the red and yellow adjoining. These snakes always have a black nose.

The signs and symptoms of pit viper bites are extreme pain at the site of the bite, rapid swelling, and general discoloration of the skin. One or more puncture wounds are created by the fangs. General body symptoms from the absorption of the poison are weakness, rapid pulse, nausea and vomiting, shortness of breath, dimness of vision, and shock. The signs and symptoms of coral snake bites are slight burning pain and mild swelling of the site of the wound, blurring vision, drooping eyelids, blurring speech, drowsiness, increased saliva, and sweating. More

advanced symptoms are nausea and vomiting, shock, respiratory problems, paralysis, convulsions, and coma.

The objectives of first aid are to reduce the circulation of blood to and
from the bite area, to delay absorption of the poisonous venom, to
prevent aggravating the local wound, and to maintain respiration.

Immobilize the bitten area in a lowered position, below the child's
heart if possible. If the bite is on an arm or leg, apply a constricting
band about 2 to 4 inches above the bite between the wound and the
heart. The band should not be tight. If properly adjusted, there should
be some oozing from the wound, and you should be able to slip an index
finger under the band when in place. Then get a sharp knife, the blade
in a snake bite kit if one is available. Otherwise sterilize a knife blade
with a flame. Make a cut through the skin at each fang mark and over
the site where the venom appears to be deposited. Snakes strike downward, and the deposit point for the venom is lower than the fang marks.
Be careful to make the cut through the skin following the direction of
the arm or leg; that is, don't make crosscut incisions. The cuts must not
be deeper than the skin because of the danger of severing muscles and
nerves. Be particularly careful in making incisions in the hands, wrist, or
foot because of the closeness of nerves, muscles, and blood vessels to the
skin surface in these locations. The cuts should not be more than one-
half inch long. Then apply suction with the suction cup in the snake bite
kit if one is available. Otherwise use your mouth. Snake venom is not a
stomach poison but nevertheless should not be swallowed. Rinse it from
your mouth. Continue the suction for one-half hour to 60 minutes. If
swelling extends up to the constricting band, apply another band a few
inches above the first but leave the first band in place. Wash the wound
thoroughly with water and soap, and blot dry. Apply a sterile or clean
dressing and bandage securely. You may place a cold wet cloth or ice
wrapped in cloth over the wound to slow absorption but don't pack the
wound in ice. Don't give alcohol in any form. Treat the child for *shock* if
it develops and give artificial respiration if needed. Move the child as
quickly as possible to the nearest medical facilities for professional attention.

*Bleeding disorders.* A bleeding disorder is one in which there is evidence of
prolonged, excessive, or unexpected bleeding out of proportion to that
which would be predicted under the circumstances. The socket of an
extracted tooth may begin to bleed 4 to 6 hours later. A joint may swell
with blood following a minor fall. Gums may bleed following brushing
of the teeth. Bruises may easily form on the skin following minimal
bumps. A sutured cut on the skin will bleed some hours later, or may
bleed excessively at the time of injury.

Children who show symptoms of excessive bleeding should be evaluated for a bleeding disorder. At the very least, parents should call to the doctor's attention such symptoms prior to the child's undergoing an operation so that evaluation of risk from bleeding can be made prior to the procedure.

The bleeding disorders fall into 3 major types. In the first there is an abnormality in the quantity and/or quality of one of the several blood proteins responsible for the formation of a blood clot. These protein abnormalities (sometimes called protein factor abnormalities) are known as the hemophilias. In the second, there is some abnormality in the platelets, the specialized blood cells that stop bleeding from damaged blood vessels (the first line of defense) and help initiate the formation of a blood clot. Platelets may be reduced as a result of a reaction to drugs or infection. More often, the cause is unknown and the reduction of platelets is called *idiopathic thrombocytopenic purpura*, which is the medical terminology for a condition of unknown origin characterized by easy bruising due to a deficiency of platelets. The third type, known as *Von Willebrandt's disease*, involves both a platelet abnormality and protein (specifically, a protein which is only indirectly involved in blood clotting) abnormality.

The hemophilias are characterized by delayed bleeding after trauma; that is, the bleeding stops initially but resumes or begins sometime later. The platelet abnormalities are characterized by prolonged and excessive bleeding directly following the episode of trauma. The individual with Von Willebrandt's disease has both the immediate and delayed problems of bleeding. There is a wide variation in the severity of each of these disorders which, depending on the efficacy of treatment, can range from no practical consequence to severe crippling. Even within an individual, the severity of symptoms waxes and wanes.

There has been major progress in the treatment of bleeding problems. In the case of hemophilia and Von Willebrandt's disease, the defective and/or reduced blood clotting protein can be replaced by, depending on the specific disorder, transfusion with normal plasma (which contains the protein in question) or injection of concentrates of the protein to restore the blood to an acceptable clotting level. Nowadays with many of the hemophilias, it is possible for patients to keep a supply of the protein concentrate at home and give it to themselves (or have their parents administer it) as needed. The prophylactic (preventive) use of the concentrates on a regular basis is being studied. When a platelet deficiency causes severe symptoms, platelets obtained from donors (by removal from whole blood) can be transfused to restore the effective platelet level in the patient's blood to normal or near normal levels. Idiopathic thrombocytopenic purpura is commonly treated with a short course of hydrocortisone-like hormones (see *hormones*). The condition usually improves on its own.

One problem in about 10 percent of patients with hemophilia is the development of antibodies to the transfused or injected replacement protein, inactivating it and, in effect, nullifying the treatment. The production by the patient of antibodies to the protein which he so desperately needs is a major unanswered problem in the management of hemophilia. A similar problem with antibodies to transfused platelets may be solved by more precise tissue typing of platelets to determine immunologic compatibility.

Patients and the parents of patients with bleeding disorders should be aware of the ability of certain common drugs such as aspirin, Phenergan (an antihistamine which is widely used in cough medicines), glyceryl guaicolate (a common expectorant in cough medicines), and tranquilizers to aggravate a bleeding tendency. It appears that these drugs work to interfere with platelet function in people with bleeding disorders as well as normal individuals. The inhibiting effect on clotting is of course much more pronounced in the individual with a clotting disorder. Sometimes a bleeding disorder becomes manifest after the use of such drugs, and therefore review of the use of drugs is part of the evaluation of the patient with a bleeding problem. In some situations, simply eliminating the use of the drug will prevent recurrence of the bleeding disorder.

The majority of the hemophilias are inherited as a sex-linked recessive gene carried on the mother's X chromosome with one-half of male offspring affected, and one-half of female offspring carriers. Hemophilia can occasionally arise by mutation, that is, by spontaneous genetic change in an individual unrelated to his heredity. A minority of the hemophilias are transmitted by a recessive non-sex-linked gene also called an autosome, and require for their expression the pairing of recessive genes, one from the father and one from the mother. Male and female offspring are equally affected. On the average, one-fourth of the children have the disease, one-fourth are normal, and one-half are carriers. Von Willebrandt's disease is transmitted as a dominant non-sex-linked gene which can be passed to males and females alike. In this situation, the parent also is affected, although the severity of the disease may differ between parent and child. Idiopathic thrombocytopenic purpura does not appear to be inherited.

The female carrier of hemophilia can now be identified by studies of her blood clotting process. Even though she has no symptoms, clotting abnormalities can be detected. Females who are relatives of hemophiliacs or who produce hemophiliac children should be studied. Knowing that one is a carrier is important in deciding whether or not to have children. Studies are under way to determine whether affected hemophiliac fetuses can be identified prenatally (by amniocentesis), permitting a decision to be made about therapeutic abortion.

For further information, contact The National Hemophilia Foundation, 25 West 39th Street, New York, N.Y. 10018.

For a discussion of sex-linked recessive genes, mutation, autosome, carriers, and amniocentesis, see *genetics.*

*Bleeding, severe:* see Part 2, Chapter 9: "First Aid."

*Blindness:* see *developmental disabilities* and *vision problems.*

**Blisters.** In the ordinary blister a patch of the outermost layer of the skin *(epidermis)* has separated from the under layer *(dermis.)* Friction, from a rubbing shoe, for example, or a burn or chemical action (see *burns*), usually causes this separation. The separated skin, deprived of nourishment, dies, but remains intact for several days if not disturbed. Meanwhile, the bloodstream reabsorbs the fluid in the blister and, beneath the blister, the dermis regenerates a new outer layer of skin. After the blister collapses, the dead skin sloughs off.

Infection is the principal complication of blisters and dictates our treatment of them. If the blister is very large, or likely to be bumped or broken because of its location, puncture it with a sterile needle at its base to drain off the fluid. A small blister, left alone, will ordinarily heal in a few days. Treatment should be confined to keeping the site clean as a protection against bacterial invasion.

Since the blister is the best protection for the wound, you should try to preserve it, whether intact or broken, until the skin beneath it is regenerated. Clean the area by soaking it in soapy water. A sterile Vaseline gauze over the blister will help to keep out dirt and protect the detached skin. The Vaseline prevents sticking and makes removal of the gauze easier. After 3 or 4 days, when the blister has collapsed, soak the area in soap and water and rub gently to remove the dead skin.

If at any time pus appears in the blistered area, or if redness and swelling spread out into the unblistered surrounding skin, you should get in touch with the doctor at once. Infection has probably set in.

**Blood count.** The blood count is a laboratory test performed on a drop of blood which measures the number and characteristics of the red blood cells, white blood cells, and platelets. (The function of each of these cells is discussed elsewhere under *anemia, bleeding disorders,* and *infec-*

*tions,* respectively.) The measurements of these cells are then compared with standards for the normal individual.

The blood count is done in several parts, including the hematocrit, the hemoglobin, and the blood smear. The *hematocrit* measures the proportion of red cells in a unit of blood. This test is done by placing a very thin capillary tube filled with blood in a centrifuge (a machine that spins its contents at a very rapid speed for the purpose of separating substances of differing densities) with the top of the tube toward the center and the bottom toward the outside. When the tube is spun, the blood is separated into the cells and the plasma. The proportion of the centrifuged column of blood occupied by the red blood cells is known as the hematocrit. The *hemoglobin test* measures the quantity of hemoglobin (the red chemical contained in the red blood cell which binds oxygen and carbon dioxide) in a unit volume of blood. Another measurement of red blood cells now being performed more commonly since the advent of electronic counters is the determination of the size of an average red cell, also known as the *mean corpuscular volume.*

The *blood smear* measures a number of things including the number of white cells per cubic centimeter of blood and the differential white count (the proportion of the various kinds of white cells present). A drop of blood is placed on a glass slide and spread thin. The smear is stained with a special dye which colors the red blood cells, white blood cells, and platelets, making them more visible. One hundred white blood cells are counted and classified according to cell type. The shape, size, and intensity of coloration of the red blood cells and the number of platelets can also be determined.

Depending on the condition under investigation, the doctor or nurse may order a complete or partial blood count. For example, when anemia is under consideration, interest focues on the red blood cells. In cases of **infection,** the characteristics of the white count provide evidence about the underlying microorganism (germ). The platelet count is of importance in determining the cause of **bleeding disorders.**

**Blood in the stools.** Although even the idea of seeing blood in the bowel movements of your child may alarm you, this symptom is not all that unusual nor is it always serious. In general, the condition is harmless and easily managed. We adults think immediately of the danger signals of cancer, but the cancer that might cause this particular symptom in children is so rare that for all practical purposes you can put the possibility out of mind.

The most common cause of blood in the stools is *anal fissure.* This condition is seen most often in very young children. The bleeding occurs from a little tear just inside the anal opening. The passage of an unusually large or hard stool almost always causes the tear. Children who are constipated are more likely to have such tears and hence to show bleeding in their stools. (See *constipation.*) The blood that a parent sees under these circumstances is always bright red and on the surface of the stool, never mixed in with the fecal material. The toilet paper used by trained youngsters after the bowel movement probably will show similar streaks of bright red blood. Often the child will cry or complain of pain at the time of the passage of a large or very hard stool.

Usually, children with this problem are otherwise entirely well. If they are frequently constipated, they may have some lower abdominal cramps at the time of moving the bowels. These children are not sick in the sense of having *fever, diarrhea,* sharp *abdominal pain,* nausea, or *vomiting,* but their problem is likely to recur as long as they continue to pass hard or large stools. There is no cause for alarm. Inspect the child's anus. Often you will be able to see the little tear which is causing the trouble. The occurrence of this bleeding should alert you to the fact that your child is probably having unusually hard or large stools and that something should be done to improve the situation. We suggest that you discuss this problem with your doctor at the earliest convenient time, during his regular office hours. There is nothing dangerous about this condition, and really nothing that can be done right away to correct it. Treatment is directed at the establishment of a more normal bowel pattern.

In contrast to this common and harmless bleeding from anal fissure, other types of rectal bleeding are deserving of more concern and prompt attention. These types of bleeding are not hard to recognize, being quite different from the type seen with anal fissure. The amount of blood is likely to be greater. Often the blood, rather than being bright red, is dark red. Blood may be mixed in with the stool, not merely streaked on the surface. The stools are more likely to be loose. Often, threads of mucus are passed as well. The child is likely to show signs and symptoms other than bloody stools. Fever, malaise, marked abdominal pain, vomiting, loss of appetite, and decreased activity are common. You can see from this description that rectal bleeding from more serious causes is quite different and not likely to be confused with bleeding from anal fissure. Our suggestion for procedure here is clear-cut. Get in touch with your doctor as soon as you can.

One further word is in order. Occasionally, blood in the stools occurs without any other symptoms at all. That is to say, the bleeding is the only symptom noticed. In this situation, call your doctor as soon as you can. Most often the bleeding is recognizable as such; the color of the stools suggests only one thing, blood. At times, however, the blood will show in the stools as black instead of red. This means that the blood came from some part of the stomach or intestines and underwent color change in its passage to the rectum. Pitch-black stools have the same significance as bloody stools. If you see them, get in touch with your doctor promptly.

See also *colitis, ulcerative* and *constipation*.

**Bloodstream infection.** In the course of many infections, the blood is often invaded by microorganisms. In many viral infections (such as *measles*), virus is carried in the blood throughout the body as part of the natural course of the illness. Bacteria can also travel from a point of entry like the skin, nose, throat, intestine, or genital tract through the blood to distant parts, causing conditions such as *meningitis* or urinary tract infection (set *urinary tract infections and defects*). If the bacteria begin to multiply in the blood and do not merely pass through it, we call the resulting infection a bloodstream infection or *sepsis* (sometimes known as "blood poisoning").

Bacterial sepsis usually, but not always, causes children to be profoundly sick with high *fever* and marked change in activity. This is one reason why the doctor will ask you to call if fever occurs with a skin infection (see *cuts, scratches, abrasions, and scrapes.*) Rashes occur with sepsis, especially ones with an element of hemorrhage or bleeding. Small, pinpoint-size skin hemorrhages are known as *petechiae* and are tip-offs to sepsis, although they can also occur in rashes caused by viruses. (See in particular the discussion on Coxsackie and echo viruses under *rash.*) If untreated, sepsis can lead to *shock* and even death.

The diagnosis of sepsis is confirmed by blood culture (see discussion of cultures under *infections*). When it is strongly suspected, cultures are taken and the child is taken to the hospital where intravenous antibiotic treatment is begun. Sometimes sepsis is revealed as the explanation for *fevers of unknown origin. Typhoid fever* is one bacterial infection which commonly involves bloodstream infection, as is *Rocky Mountain spotted fever.*

See *infections*.

**Blue baby:** see *heart disease, congenital.*

**Boat sickness:** see *motion sickness.*

**Boil:** see *abscess.*

*Bowlegs:* see *orthopedic concerns.*

*Brain damage:* see *cerebral palsy; developmental disabilities;* and *learning disabilities.*

*Brain tumors* are rare in children. There are different types, some of which are cancerous and others which are benign. Many can be cured through surgery and radiation therapy (X-ray treatment to destroy cancer cells), while others are fatal. In the case of noncurable tumors, symptoms can usually be relieved for variable periods of time. Common symptoms are change in personality, loss of coordination, muscle weakness in specific parts of the body, difficulties with vision, seizures (see *seizure disorders*), and *headache.* None of these symptoms is specific to brain tumors and careful medical assessment is required to sort out the possible causes.

*Breast development:* see *adolescence.*

*Breathing, noisy.* Any obstruction of the upper airway (nose, throat, larynx, trachea) can cause noisy breathing (*stridor*), a fairly common symptom in infants. Resistance to the passage of air sets up vibrations which cause noise, and severe obstruction can cause real difficulty in breathing. Severe stridor can be recognized shortly after birth, but the milder forms may go undetected until after the baby has been taken home from the hospital.

The breathing of many infants is audible. Their nasal passages are proportionally smaller in diameter than those of adults and the passage of air to and fro tends to cause a whistling sound. The relatively narrow nasal passages are often further obstructed by normal accumulations of mucus in a baby who doesn't know about nose blowing. This snorting type of breathing is always of greater concern to the parents than to the infant, who couldn't care less. Gradual disappearance, so slow that you will forget all about it, is the rule by the first birthday.

Because of the short distance—mere inches—between the infant's nose and throat and chest, it is common for noises originating in nose and throat to be transmitted to the chest, giving the illusion that the chest is the site of difficulty. In *colds* it is this illusion in large part (plus the accompanying *cough*) which leads us to label the cold as a "chest cold," when in fact the disorder may be confined exclusively to the nose and throat.

The most common cause of stridor in infants is *laryngomalacia* (literally, soft larynx). The cartilages comprising the voice box are normally firm and relatively inflexible, but in this condition they are (for reasons unknown) overly pliable. They collapse in breathing, and as air passes the narrowed passage, vibrations are set up which can be heard and felt as they are transmitted to the child's chest. Babies with laryngomalacia tend to improve as they grow older, as the cartilages firm up. By about the age of 2, the stridor of laryngomalacia cases will disappear, leaving so gradually that one scarcely notices its passing.

Children with congenitally underdeveloped jawbones may have an associated displacement of the tongue resulting in partial obstruction of the airway and, with it, stridor. The breathing difficulty will be relieved when the jawbones have grown enough for the tongue to assume a more normal position.

In *choanal atresia*, a bony overgrowth blocks the rearmost part of one or both nasal passages. If both sides are affected, the child cannot breathe through his or her nose at all, and at feeding time he or she will be in a great deal of difficulty. The definitive therapy is surgical removal of the bony obstruction.

Abnormal vocal cords can cause stridor. Instead of being separate, the two cords may be partially fused. Or there may be benign growths (*papillomas*) on the ends of the cords. Children with these defects have recognizably weak and peculiar-sounding cries. Neurological disease may paralyze the cords. There also can be abnormal growths in the trachea. A common form is *subglottic* (meaning below the voice box) *hemangioma*, which is a nonmalignant tumor of blood vessels. Abnormally positioned blood vessels or an enlarged thyroid can compress the trachea and also cause stridor.

Croup (see *croup and laryngitis*) is the most common cause of stridor in older children. Enlarged **tonsils and adenoids** can obstruct the flow of air through the nose and throat, causing noisy breathing and mouth breathing. A foreign body stuck in the airway can cause noisy, labored breathing. (See **choking and swallowing foreign objects.**)

All cases of stridor should be brought to a doctor's attention. Treatment of stridor varies with the cause. For many cases the passage of time is enough. For others surgery will be in order. In the most severe obstructions, tracheostomy (surgical opening through the neck into the trachea [windpipe]) may be found necessary to bypass the obstruction and allow respiration to continue until the child is old enough for definitive surgery.

See also **asthma; bronchitis; emphysema;** and **lung rupture and collapse.**

*Broken bones:* see *fracture,* and Part 2, Chapter 9: "First Aid."

*Bronchiolitis:* see *bronchitis.*

*Bronchitis* means inflammation of the *bronchii* (see discussion of the structure of the respiratory system under *asthma* ). It is usually an extension of *colds* or upper respiratory infection and has many of the same symptoms as *pneumonia: cough, fever,* and labored breathing. *Asthmatic bronchitis* is a somewhat imprecise term for the wheezing and cough which occur in allergic children who have symptoms particularly in response to infection. *Bronchiolitis* is a viral inflammation of the smallest air passageways *(bronchioles),* usually occurring in infants. Its symptoms and signs are fever, cough, and labored breathing. The more severe cases require hospitalization.

The term "chest cold" is very vague and should probably be discarded. With any cold, the cough seems to come from the chest and the muscles of the chest ache because of the coughing even when the infection is actually in the nose and throat and not in the chest. Ointments applied to the chest have no scientific basis.

Bronchitis, upper respiratory infection, laryngitis (see *croup and laryngitis* ), and pneumonia may coexist in any given illness. An infection often involves several parts of the respiratory tree to varying degrees.

See *allergy; asthma; colds;* and *pneumonia.*

*Bruise.* A bruise ("black and blue" mark) is the visible effect of bleeding from broken blood vessels into the surrounding skin, resulting from trauma with a blunt object or surface. It may occur without broken skin or may be associated with *cuts, scratches, abrasions, and scrapes.* Initially the color is blue. As the blood is broken down and the constituent parts reabsorbed, the color changes to green and yellow. Usually 2 weeks are required for all traces of the bruise to disappear.

There is little to do for a bruise other than to wait for it to disappear. Use of cold packs after an injury for about one-half hour may decrease blood flow into the injured area, and thereby minimize bruising.

Determining what constitutes abnormally easy bruising such as occurs in certain *bleeding disorders* is difficult. If you suspect that a child bruises too easily or excessively (out of proportion to what would be expected from the trauma), seek a medical opinion.

*Burns.* Extensive burns, deep burns, electrical burns, or burns involving the eyes, face, or fingers, should receive a doctor's prompt attention. For "First Aid," see Part 2, Chapter 9.

Small burns (less than the size of a silver dollar), in which only reddening or blistering of the skin is present, can for the most part be managed at home. The burn should be gently washed with soap and water. Pain may be relieved by applying cold packs or, if a hand is burned, by dipping it in cold water. The pain usually subsides in one-half to three-quarters of an hour. The old-fashioned remedy of applying butter or grease should be avoided. Not only does butter not help healing, it may cause the burn to become infected. Anesthetic sprays purchasable without a prescription relieve pain, but can sensitize (that is, cause future allergic reactions) the patient and, for this reason, are not recommended. A bandage is not necessary unless the burn is in an area subject to being bumped or rubbed. If this is the case, use a gauze impregnated with sterile Vaseline to prevent sticking. The skin of *blisters* forms a good protection and prevents infection. The blister can be broken antiseptically if it is large, but the collapsed blister should be left alone. Usually blisters collapse of their own accord after several days.

If at the end of 6 days the burn does not appear to be healing, contact your physician. If at any time during the 6-day period the burn becomes more painful, begins to discharge pus, if the extremity or area affected becomes red or swollen, or if the youngster develops an elevated temperature, contact your doctor promptly. The younger the child, the more inclined we are to suggest that he or she be examined by a physician, even for small burns. Even small burns in infants may become troublesome and probably should be cared for by a physician from the beginning. As we said above, if burns are extensive, or involve the eyes, face, or fingers, they should be examined by a physician, regardless of how minor they may seem.

The way in which burns heal depends on the depth of the skin affected. If the skin is only partially destroyed, as is the case with most scalds from hot liquids, new skin can be expected to form in 1 to 3 weeks. The new skin may be darker and may not resume normal color for months. If complete destruction has occurred, as is common with burns from flames or contact with hot metal or electrical current, a scar will form. The latter kind of burn is characterized initially by a charred or "cooked" appearance of the skin and should receive prompt medical attention. Complete burns of the full thickness of skin require grafting of skin to avoid disfiguring scar formation.

Electrical burns present special problems. If electrical current at the outlet is controlled by a wall switch, turn it off. If not, pull the child away from the outlet or appliance with a nonconductive material (such as a board or *wooden* chair). *Do not use bare hands.* Then, if the child is not breathing, apply mouth-to-mouth resuscitation (see Part 2, Chapter 9: "First Aid"). Always consult a doctor for electrical burns. They can be terribly severe, permanently deforming the face, mouth, or hands. Two types of extension cords—those with pronged plugs at both ends, and those with a pronged plug on one end and a bulb socket on the other—are extremely hazardous. Remove them from the home. If you have small children, put safety caps (available at hardware stores) on all *unused* outlets and discard frayed cords. (See Part 2, Chapter 8: "Accident Prevention.")

Chemical burns call for prompt treatment and some special procedures. If the chemical is on the child's clothes, remove them immediately. Instructions for treating burns are often printed on the chemical's container. If instructions are available, follow them. If not, wash away the chemical with large amounts of clean water. When the chemical is completely washed away, treat the burn as a fire burn.

Chemical burns of the eye require instant treatment. If a faucet is nearby, hold the child's head beneath it. Turn on cool water at medium pressure. Rinse the eye for at least 15 minutes, directing the water away from the unaffected eye. If the victim is lying down, turn his head to the side, hold his eyelids open, and pour clean water from the inner corner of the eye outward. After all chemical particles are washed away, or removed by lifting off gently with a sterile gauze or clean handkerchief, cover the eye with a sterile compress (avoid loose, absorbent cotton) and take the child to a doctor or hospital. Caution against rubbing the eye.

See Part 2, Chapter 8: "Accident Prevention" and sunburn.

*Cancer:* see **brain tumors; Hodgkin's disease; leukemia; neuroblastoma; tumors; Wilms' tumor.**

*Cancer, vagina and cervix:* see **adolescence.**

**Canker sores** *(aphthous stomatitis)* are painful recurrent ulcers or erosions of the mouth which appear on the lips, gums, inner cheeks, tongue, palate, and throat. They appear as small, shallow depressions in the *mucosa* (lining of the mouth), with sharp borders covered by a gray membrane and surrounded by an intense red halo. Tingling or burning sometimes precedes them by 24 hours. During the first 2 to 3 days, canker sores are extremely painful and can interfere with eating or speaking. Most lesions heal without scarring within two weeks.

If the pain is mild, it is best to grin and bear it. Dyclone (dyclonine hydrochloride solution), Xylocaine (lidocaine), either solution or viscous, or elixir of Benadryl (diphenhydramine hydrochloride) applied to the ulcers will act rapidly and numb the pain for up to one hour. If these solutions are used over too large an area, a disturbing "cut in mouth" feeling and loss of taste will result, symptoms which are usually worse than the sores for which the medication was given.

The cause of canker sores is not known but stress appears to be a predisposing factor. They are to be distinguished from *fever blisters.*

*Carbuncle:* see *abscess.*

*Car sickness:* see *motion sickness.*

*Cat scratch fever:* see *pets and children.*

*Cavities:* see *dental care.*

*Celiac disease* is an intestinal disorder of young children, and sometimes of adults, characterized by bulky, greasy, foul-smelling, diarrheal stools, and, for the child, potbelly, arrest of growth, and weight loss. The digestive upset reflects an inability of the child to tolerate *gluten,* the protein of wheat or rye flour. In this disease, the protein causes an inflammation of the walls of the small intestine which, in turn, interferes with normal digestion. The partially digested food, particularly fat, passes out in the stools, depriving the body of essential nutrients. This overall picture is an example of the *malabsorption syndrome* for which there are a number of causes, *cystic fibrosis,* for example. Celiac disease must be distinguished from the much more common chronic, non-specific *diarrhea* which is of no harm to a child.

Diagnosis is usually made by means of an intestinal biopsy, easily performed by a special capsule which the patient swallows. The child with celiac disease improves rapidly when gluten is removed from the diet. This step is mandatory. In fact, this improvement positively establishes the diagnosis. A gluten-free diet must be taken for life. Celiac disease is less common today than it once was, for reasons which are not clear.

*Cerebral palsy* is a persisting impairment of movement and posture which appears in the early years of life and is caused by a nonprogressive disorder of the brain present during its development. The quality of the impairment may change, for example from flaccid (floppy) to spastic (tense) weakness. In general, there is no cure for the underlying disorder of the brain so that cerebral palsy is a lifelong problem.

There is great variation in severity, ranging from barely noticeable weakness and spasticity (increased muscle tension) of an arm and leg to profound crippling. Affected children often have other disabilities. In one study, visual disorders (other than refractive problems) were found in 16 percent (see *vision problems*), speech defects in 49 percent (see *hearing and speech*), general intellectual impairment in 35 percent. Specific learning disabilities (see *learning disabilities*) are also common. The diagnosis of cerebral palsy is often made in late infancy or the toddler stage before higher brain functions, such as reading, are present and can be tested. Accordingly, prediction of performance in these other areas is difficult and a wait and see attitude regarding associated problems must be adopted. Each problem should be met and dealt with when and if it appears.

The known causes of cerebral palsy are many and include any diseases that can damage the brain. Excessive *jaundice* in the newborn period used to be a leading cause. With the advent of effective treatment and preventive methods for jaundice, it is now relatively rare. As a group, premature babies have a higher incidence of cerebral palsy. Because of modern intensive-care techniques, more preemies are surviving, and these babies who would have died in the past are more likely to have cerebral palsy (an example of how progress in one area can lead to problems in another). Two other important causes of cerebral palsy are *meningitis* in the newborn period, and injuries to the brain, nowadays commonly related to automobile accidents (see Part 2, Chapter 12: "Car Safety"). There is a strong suspicion and mounting evidence that impaired blood flow to the brain during labor and delivery, leading to brain damage, may be an important factor in the many cases of cerebral palsy for which at present no other explanation can be found. Research efforts are being directed to test this theory.

Children with cerebral palsy and their families profit from individualized comprehensive health care in which their total needs are identified and met. The principles of this care are discussed in *handicapped child, developmental disabilities* (including mental retardation), and Part 1, Chapter 1: "Quality in Pediatric Care."

For parents needing specific information, we recommend the following: Nancy R. Finnie, *Handling the Young Cerebral Palsied Child at Home* (New York: E. P. Dutton & Co., 1970), and Mildred Shriner, *Cerebral Palsied Children Learn to Help Themselves: Growing Up,*

Parent Series Number 7 (Copyright 1961, The National Society for Crippled Children and Adults, Inc., 2023 West Ogden Avenue, Chicago, Ill. 60612). For additional information, contact the United Cerebral Palsy Associations, Inc., 339 East 44th Street, New York, N.Y. 10016.

*Chemical burns:* see *burns,* and Part 2, Chapter 9: "First Aid."

*Chest pain* is a common symptom in children. A blow to the chest is a common cause. Marked pain and bruising raises the question of a rib *fracture.* Pain in the chest often accompanies *colds.* In this situation the pain comes from aching chest muscles called upon in coughing to do more than their usual work. The aching chest plus the cough is the basis of the notion of a "chest cold," when in reality the cause of the cough is more likely an irritation of the upper airway (throat, larynx, and so forth). Liniments applied to the chest, while they may help to soothe aching muscles, have no effect on the infection itself. The labored breathing associated with *asthma* and *pneumonia* can understandably lead to painful chest muscles. Inflammation of the *pleura* (lining of the lung and inner chest wall) which may occur with pneumonia also gives rise to chest pain. The pleura may also be the cause of the chest pain occurring in atelectasis (see *lung rupture and collapse*). Treatment of these lung problems is, of course, directed to the underlying problem. *Influenza* is usually accompanied by generalized muscle aching which can include the muscles of the chest. A particular virus infection with one member of the Coxsackie group of viruses can cause chest pain which, because of its severity, has been named "devil's grippe" (see *rash*). While chest pain in adults commonly stems from heart problems, this cause is so extremely rare in children that you can put it out of your mind.

*Chest, pigeon and funnel.* There are two types of changes that affect the breastbone *(sternum).* Either the breastbone and the front (anterior) chest are pushed outward, causing the condition known as *pigeon chest (pectus carinatum),* or they are pushed inward, causing *funnel chest (pectus excavatum).*

Temporary inward deformity may result from blockage of the upper airway due to congenital narrowing of soft cartilages (see *breathing, noisy*) and later with enlarged *tonsils and adenoids.* Surgery of the chest wall is not required.

True *funnel chest,* which is always present at birth or evident within months of birth, may result in progressive deformity. Heredity plays a role in this condition. Corrective surgery is never indicated before age 2, but should be undertaken shortly thereafter in moderate to severe cases as defined by X-ray measurements. Results are excellent in preschool children. If uncorrected, bony deformity and asymmetry add to the complexity of repair, and a normal, balanced chest is difficult to achieve. In addition to the cosmetic problem, funnel chest can cause heart and lung problems in late adolescence and later on in life. Patients who are not to be operated on must be followed closely by an expert in the field since the chests may cave in rapidly and asymmetrically at adolescence.

*Pigeon chest* is a much less common condition. In infancy, it is usually associated with congenital heart disease (see *heart disease, congenital*). It is seldom seen as an isolated defect before age 6 and then often in association with *asthma.* Most cases first occur at adolescence when the anterior chest wall suddenly projects as much as 4 to 8 inches. A lung problem known as progressive *emphysema* can occur in severe cases because the chest is rigid and locked in the position of full inspiration (breathing in). Surgical correction is completely effective in permanently restoring normal chest contour.

Surgical correction of funnel chest and pigeon chest is not cosmetic surgery, although the psychological benefit is great in the correction of both conditions.

**Chicken pox** is one of the "routine" diseases of childhood. Few children escape it. Although to date no vaccine is available to prevent chicken pox, its days are numbered in this area of vaccine research. Chicken pox is also one of the most contagious diseases. Exposure to someone who has it will almost invariably result in the exposed child coming down with the disorder. Chicken pox is caused by a virus. (See *infections* for a discussion of virus.)

About 24 hours before the rash erupts, the child may act mildly ill and have a low-grade temperature. The rash characteristically first appears on the trunk (chest, abdomen, and back) as clusters of red, raised spots. Within several hours, a delicate fluid-filled blister develops in each spot. Within 24 hours, the blisters collapse, and scab over. New crops erupt over a 3- to 4-day period, spreading to face and scalp and tending to spare the arms and legs. The mouth, throat, and *conjunctiva* (white of eyes) are sometimes affected. At any given time the child is likely to have old crusted spots and some fresh new red ones, as well as some which are still in the blister stage. The scabs may last for 1 or 2 weeks before detaching. Fine scars may remain for several months following the detachment of scabs. In black children the scars are light and more noticeable because of the contrasting darkness of the surrounding normal skin. These white spots may persist for as long as several years.

There are all degrees of severity in chicken pox. At one extreme, the child may have only one or two spots, detectable only after a deliberate search. Other children may be literally covered with the pox, with little uninvolved skin remaining. Most cases fall somewhere in between and offer no mystery to the observant parent. Our impression is that children exposed to a family member with chicken pox are prone to develop more severe cases, presumably because of more prolonged exposure to the initial case and a heavier dose of virus. This is not invariably true and seems to depend upon individual characteristics of the child's own response to infection.

Most children have a low-grade temperature—about 101°. Children with more extensive involvement of the skin may have temperatures up to 103° or 104°. Aspirin may be given for temperatures in this range to help lower the *fever*. (See Part 1, Chapter 5: "Caring for the Sick Child at Home" for dosage.) The child's major complaint is itching, and finding relief sometimes becomes a problem. The older child should be encouraged not to scratch the lesions lest they become infected. His or her nails should be trimmed. With this skin condition, as with many other itchy ones, keeping the child as quiet and cool as possible minimizes heat production and sweating, which is a potent stimulus to itching and scratching. The child need not stay in bed but should be allowed quiet activity and kept in a cool environment. If the weather is nice and there is a yard or play area adjacent to the home, it is perfectly all right for the child to be in a shady spot out of doors. Whether it is important to keep him away from other children to prevent the spread of the chicken-pox virus is debatable, since the disease is much milder in children than adults and immunity is lifelong. While it is practically impossible to isolate the child from other members of his immediate household, prolonged exposure of susceptible children should be avoided, as the severity of the disease seems related to exposure. Colloidal oatmeal baths (these oatmeal preparations can be purchased without a prescription from the druggist) and calamine lotion are helpful in relieving itching, as are some medications that can be taken by mouth. In general, with restriction of activity and maintenance of a cool environment and use of calamine lotion, we find drugs unnecessary. In fact, bathing with chicken pox is all right. Cleansing of the skin may relieve some of the itching and prevent infection. There are no special rules about diet. As is true in most illnesses, appetite with chicken pox is likely to be off, and we suggest concentrating on simple foods which the child enjoys.

On the sixth day after the rash began to erupt, if all the lesions have scabbed, the child is usually not contagious and may return to school and contact with others. However, the child should feel better and behave normally before resuming full activity.

The interval between exposure to chicken pox and the development of symptoms is on the average 14 to 16 days. This time lag is called the incubation period. (See *infections.*) During this time the virus is beginning to take hold in the child's body but is not yet causing symptoms. The child is not contagious during the incubation period.

The child is contagious for about 24 hours prior to appearance of the rash, during which time he is showing mild general signs of illness. This is called the *prodromal period.* Others may be exposed without knowing it. Contagiousness lasts, as mentioned, until all spots have firmly scabbed. If a child has not yet come down with chicken pox 2½ to 3 weeks following exposure to someone who clearly had the disease, you can rest assured that he is unlikely to do so from that particular exposure. While unusual, the possibility exists, however, that he did indeed develop chicken pox, but so mild a case as to go undetected.

Newborns are protected for several months from chicken pox, assuming that they received protective antibodies from their mother prior to delivery. These antibodies diminish and are practically gone in 10 to 12 months. By their first birthdays, almost all children are susceptible to chicken pox. Once infection has occurred, the child develops antibodies which make him almost 100 percent immune to reinfection by this virus.

After chicken pox runs its course, the virus itself goes into hiding, so to speak, remaining perhaps for life (probably in the roots of certain nerves near the junction of nerve and spinal cord). Occasionally infection flares up once again as the condition known as *herpes zoster* (commonly called "shingles"), which develops only in adults and children who have had chicken pox in the past. The rash of herpes zoster is identical in appearance to that of chicken pox and is caused by the same virus. It occurs on any part of the body and is preceded by a period of intense itching and burning of the area in which the rash is scheduled to erupt. The evolution of the rash is similar to the pattern in chicken pox, with early red, raised spots that go on to form teardrop blisters, which then break and scab over. The eruption usually clears in 7 to 14 days, but in unusual cases the blisters continue to appear for more than one week, and healing may not occur for several weeks. Second attacks of shingles are rare. Although, unlike chicken pox, it is not a highly contagious condition, susceptible people can pick up the virus of chicken pox from persons ill with shingles and develop full-blown chicken pox after the usual incubation period. As is the case with chicken pox, there is no specific treatment for shingles. The same measures useful in chicken pox can be applied to this disorder.

**Child abuse.** "I was so mad I could have killed him!" How many of us have said words like these about our children at one time or another? While few of us act on such impulses, the number of American parents who actually inflict physical injury on their children each year runs into the thousands. Hard as it is to believe, hundreds of children die from inflicted injury. We are only now beginning to get some appreciation of the extent of this parental behavior. Although most of the reported cases of child abuse have come from large city hospitals and poor families, there is little doubt that this disorder occurs in all strata of society. It is probably as common proportionately in the suburbs as in the core city.

We define child abuse as any situation in which a child is not safe in his or her home environment, either because of injury inflicted directly by his or her caretakers or because of hazardous conditions resulting from inadequate protection. When we suspect child abuse, we almost always admit the child to the hospital for safekeeping. Many times the child's injury, for example a fracture or burn, dictates treatment in the hospital. All states now require physicians (in some cases nurses, teachers, and social workers as well) to file a report with the state authority responsible, which then investigates the situation. The primary purpose of an enlightened agency's inquiry is to determine whether of not the child is safe in his own home, not to point an accusatory finger at anyone. Often it is only much later that the truth comes out, if it ever does. The major concern is not "Who did it?" but whether or not the child is safe in his environment. If child abuse is deemed to be present, the state agency will continue to supervise the care of the child in the home. Infrequently, when the agency feels that the child's life is in danger should he remain in the home, it will seek custody in the courts to remove the child from his home, either temporarily or permanently. The main emphasis these days is on helping the parents to control their own behavior. For example, one group of mothers in Los Angeles is dealing with their impulses to harm their children through a group called Mothers Anonymous, much like Alcoholics Anonymous for the alcoholic. They meet regularly and they are available to each other by phone when tensions mount. Some parents require psychiatric help, either individually or in groups.

One of the most encouraging developments in managing child abuse is growing public awareness of the problem. In the city of Denver, Colorado, where much research into child abuse has been done, this disorder is well known to the public. Spot announcements on television spread the message widely. Parents are so well alerted to child abuse that many come to the medical center for help when they feel themselves losing control, before they have actually injured their children. This is ideal prevention. We would urge any parent to do the same. Call your doctor before the fact, not after. Do not be ashamed to admit angry feelings. Parents who abuse or want to abuse their children have very mixed feelings of love and hate toward them. It is their loving sides to which we appeal.

Child abuse in one sense is a measure of the quality of life around us. Poverty, unwanted pregnancies, lack of family planning services, shortage of mental health facilities, underfinancing of many state agencies, sanctioning of the use of force in child rearing such as spanking, condoning violence on a national level both at home and abroad, isolation, and loneliness all contribute to the problem. Eventual control of child abuse will depend upon our dealing with these pressing social issues. For instance, one researcher feels that we must eliminate the use of any physical force in discipline, that is, no more whipping or strappings at home or in school. Child abuse can be seen as an exaggeration of this method of child rearing, he maintains. As long as physical punishment is generally accepted, it creates attitudes which lead overwrought and disturbed parents to abuse their children.

In 1974 the Child Abuse Prevention and Treatment Act (P.L. 93-247) was signed into law. The Act established for the first time within the federal government a National Center on Child Abuse and Neglect. This Center can be reached c/o Office of Child Development, P.O Box 1182, Washington, D.C. 20013.


*Choanal atresia:* see *breathing, noisy.*


*Choking* is a sudden, involuntary closing off of the upper airway at the level of the voice box (larynx). The closing of the airway results from a combination of mechanical blockage and a reflexive tightening of muscles of the larynx to prevent aspiration of the irritating material into the lung. Choking may be viewed as a defense against impairment of the air system. The reflex works day and night, asleep or awake. It is often accompanied, and triggered by, *cough,* which serves to forceably expel any foreign material, and by *vomiting.* The child gasps for breath, is frightened, and may lose his or her voice for a brief period. Impaired breathing during choking may give rise to *cyanosis,* the bluish discoloration of the skin resulting from impaired oxygenation of blood. Unrelieved choking can, of course, lead to death.

There are many causes of choking as there are materials that can block or irritate the airway. Among these are mucus from the nose dripping down the throat (see *colds* and *sinusitis*), inflammation of the throat from a virus, leading to cough and reflexive choking (see *croup and laryngitis* and *whooping cough*), stomach contents regurgitated in vomiting, aspiration of a foreign body, including food and drink (see

212

---

*Choking
and
swallowing
foreign
objects*

*choking and swallowing foreign objects*), and the gagging resulting from medical care procedures, such as depressing the tongue with a tongue blade or taking a throat culture.

Emergency care is discussed under *choking* in the section "First Aid," Part 2, Chapter 9.

***Choking and swallowing foreign objects.*** Emergency care is discussed under *choking* in "First Aid," Part 2, Chapter 9. The discussion below is about the problems which ensue once the foreign object has gotten past the windpipe and has lodged further down.

Objects that lodge in smaller air passages may cause **cough** and wheezing which should alert you to seek help. Sometimes these symptoms may come on days after the aspiration. X-rays may reveal **pneumonia,** *atelectasis* (see **lung rupture and collapse**), or **emphysema,** each of which requires specific treatment.

If your child has choked on an object and then suddenly gets better, but the object has not appeared, suspect that it may have become lodged somewhere in the air passages or *esophagus* (food tube). He may or may not have symptoms of difficulty in swallowing, pain in his neck, wheezing, drooling, or trouble breathing. If he can swallow water and then bread without discomfort, then his swallowing passage is probably not blocked. If he has no cough or wheeze, then his air passage is probably open. However, if any of the above symptoms develop, or if his original choking episode was severe, seek prompt medical attention.

Smooth swallowed objects such as coins, beads, or marbles will cause little difficulty once they pass into the stomach. They almost always will pass through the intestinal tract and will appear in the stools within 2 to 3 days. Check the stools until the object has passed. Pull tabs from aluminum cans (common litter objects) are a recent addition to the list of objects especially prone to lodge in the esophagus. They are also hard to see on X-ray.

Checking the stools will involve the unpleasant task of breaking them up to be sure the object is not concealed within them. If you don't find anything within 3 to 5 days, your physician should be notified. During the period of observation, there need be no concern unless the child develops symptoms, which is rare. Symptoms to look for are **abdominal pain, vomiting,** or the passage of bloody stools (see **blood in the stools**). If none of these is present, you can safely wait for the object to pass.

On the other hand, swallowing sharp, irregular, or jagged objects such as pins and pieces of glass is cause for immediate concern. Contact your physician promptly should your child swallow any of these. Be particularly alert for difficulty in swallowing, as evidenced by drooling. This symptom means that the object may have lodged itself in the back of the throat or in the esophagus. This requires prompt medical attention.

If your child seems particularly prone to putting things into his mouth or has had previous experiences of swallowing objects, it is a good idea to discuss this kind of behavior with your doctor.

See Part 2, Chapter 8: "Accident Prevention" and Chapter 10: "Poisoning."

*213*

---

*Cleft of
the lip
and
cleft of
the palate*

*Chorea:* see *rheumatic fever.*

*Chronic, nonspecific diarrhea:* see *diarrhea.*

*Cleft of the lip and cleft of the palate* (roof of the mouth) are two often related birth defects. While not common in the United States, these defects appear frequently enough for most people to have seen them or at least to know of them.

Cleft lip, also known as harelip, almost always involves the upper lip and varies from a small notch confined to the lip alone to a sizable gap extending from the edge of the lip up to the nose. Cleft palate can affect both the hard palate, which is the bony roof of the mouth behind the upper teeth, and the soft palate, the soft rearmost part of the roof of the mouth which includes the movable flap (*uvula*) easily seen hanging down into the throat. Cleft palate can vary from a small slit in the uvula, also called a bifid (two-part) uvula to a half-inch gap involving the uvula and extending across the hard palate, even including the upper gums. When the gum is involved, the teeth may be absent or misplaced. In the extreme, the nasal passage is in direct communication with the mouth, which leads to obvious problems in feeding.

Almost 2 percent of Caucasian American children have a bifid uvula. Sometimes in association with a bifid uvula there is a small cleft of the rearmost part of the hard palate. It is not visible on inspection but can be felt with the examining finger. It is called a submucous cleft.

The soft palate is composed mainly of muscle and moves as one talks or swallows. It acts as a valve between the upper and lower parts of the throat. The soft palate keeps food and air from entering the nose in the act of swallowing or talking. The sealing action of the soft palate makes it possible to whistle, gargle, blow up balloons, and utter a number of sounds including those for the letters *t, b, d, p, h, v,* and *f.* A cleft involving the soft palate or a uvula which prevents it from making contact with the back of the throat can impair this sealing action and lead to problems of feeding, with food regurgitating from the throat into the nose, and, later, of speech. Children with clefts of the hard palate, including submucous clefts and those with bifid uvulas, are also very susceptible to ear infections and hearing loss (see *earache* and *hearing and speech*). For the child with cleft lip there is also the obvious problem of appearance.

The treatment of cleft lip and a cleft of the hard palate is surgical repair. The lip is usually repaired in the first 6 weeks of life. Repair of the hard palate is a more individual matter, but in most cases is accomplished by the time the child is 1½ or 2 years old. The surgery may have to be done in several stages. A complete cleft of the uvula, bifid uvula, and submucous cleft require individual assessment and are generally treated only if they cause symptoms. Speech therapy may have to be continued into the school years.

Until the cleft lip or palate can be repaired, feeding of an infant has to be done with a "cleft-lip feeder," which is a sort of syringe with a long tube, somewhat like the gadget used to baste roasting meats. After surgery, the infant's hands must be immobilized to prevent him or her from reaching into his mouth and damaging the repair.

About one-third of children with cleft lip or cleft palate will have one or more relatives with the same defects. The hereditary influence seems stronger for cleft lip, but prediction on the evidence of a known family tree is not yet very precise. On the other hand, there is no evidence suggesting that these defects arise from anything mothers do in pregnancy or may have done prior to pregnancy.

See *hearing and speech.*

**Cleft palate:** see *cleft of the lip and cleft of the palate.*

**Club foot:** see *orthopedic concerns.*

**Coccidioidomycosis** (also known as *San Joaquin Valley fever*) is a disease well known to the inhabitants of California's San Joaquin Valley, scattered regions in Southern California, central and southern Arizona, and southwest Texas, where the fungus that causes the disease is prevalent. People living in the northeastern part of the United States are less likely to have heard of it. The fungus *Coccidioides immitis* is a common inhabitant of soil and thrives in the lining of rodent burrows. The fungi are accidentally picked up by breathing dust from such soil. Recently a group of archeology students, sifting through dirt in Chico, California, were infected en masse by coccidioides, interrupting the dig.

In most cases, fungi lodge in the lungs, where they set up an infection (see *infections*). Usually the infection is so mild as to produce little in the way of symptoms. The body confines the invaders and kills them off. In a smaller number of people, particularly those who receive a heavy dose of the fungus, as with the archeology students, symptoms of *pneu-monia* develop. These include *cough, fever,* chest pain, *headache,* mus-cle aches, shortness of breath, chills, skin rash, malaise, sweating at night, weight loss, and stiff neck. While coccidioides can cause a severe and debilitating illness, recovery is almost always complete if the infec-tion is limited to the lung. In very rare cases, the fungi spread from the lungs throughout the body. Dark-skinned people seem particularly prone to such spread. With spread the infection carries a very high fatality rate. In this unusual, life-threatening, disseminated coccidi-oidomycosis, a special antibiotic called Amphotericin B is of some value.

As is true of *tuberculosis* and *histoplasmosis,* a kind of allergy to the fungus of coccidioidomycosis develops several weeks following infec-tion. Injection of killed and, therefore, harmless coccidioidomycosis fungi into the skin of a previously infected individual may lead to redness and swelling at the injection site. Thus the skin test can identify infected individuals. A positive skin test does not tell whether the infec-tion is active or controlled, only that the patient has had contact with the fungi at some time. The skin test may be positive even in individuals who have had subclinical or asymptomatic infections. The skin test is used when a person has symptoms which might be due to coccidioido-mycosis to help distinguish this condition from similar diseases like tuberculosis and histoplasmosis.

*Colds.* The very commonness of the common cold almost forces one to go into some depth and detail when discussing this universal annoyance. Doctors think of colds as one form of upper respiratory infection (see *infections*). By either name, they afflict us through all the ages of man, but their misery is most apparent in young children. Few parents have trouble recognizing the symptoms.

### SYMPTOMS AND CAUSES

A cold is a virus infection of the nasal passages, sinuses, and throat. Nasal discharge (runny nose) is the major symptom. A child with a cold often has difficulty breathing through his or her nose and may experi-ence considerable discomfort thereby. Sneezing is common with colds, and coughing is usual. This *cough* comes from irritation of the throat, caused by the infecting viruses and the drainage of nasal secretions from the back of the nasal passageways. Everyone has had firsthand experi-ence with the nagging "tickle" in the throat which can't be cleared regardless of how much one tries. *Fever* often occurs, particularly in younger children. The temperature usually stays below 102° but may go higher, especially if the victim is under 3. While a temperature over 102°

may occur with uncomplicated colds, that degree of fever suggests a bacterial complication, such as ear (see *earache*) or sinus infections (see *sinusitis*). Children with colds frequently have very mild inflammations of the eye, which result from infection by the same germs that are causing the other symptoms. The eyes may look watery, be slightly pink, and contain small amounts of a whitish-yellow discharge. The older child may complain of sore throat (see *throat, sore*). The child with a cold, like the victims of other childhood ailments, is inclined to be cranky and may lose interest in food. He may pass fewer stools than normally; the stools passed may be looser or firmer than usual for him. Occasionally, actual *diarrhea* will accompany a cold.

Hoarseness is commonly present. It represents an inflammation of the voice box or larynx. The vocal cords do not work properly. The technical name of the condition is *laryngitis*. Coughing aggravates it. Except for relieving the cough, there is no specific treatment for laryngitis caused by the cold virus. (See *croup and laryngitis*.)

The average preschool child has from 5 to 8 colds a year. The years between 3 and 6 are the ones of peak incidence—that is, statistically, you can expect your child to have more colds in those years than in the first 3. If you are tempted to think your child unusually susceptible to colds, check his total for the year against these figures before you arrive at a conclusion. Under normal conditions, the children who have the greatest number of contacts with other children or adults outside the family are the ones who have the most colds. A preschooler whose older brothers or sisters attend school is a likely candidate for more than his fair share. The older ones may bring very minor symptoms home from school but may then pass on the germs to the younger sibling, who may develop a full-blown cold. Children going to school—nursery or regular—for the first time are likely to have more colds, simply because they are being exposed for the first time to more children with colds. (See *resistance and frequent colds*.)

The blame for causing colds cannot be pinned on a single organism. To date, scientists have identified at least 80 different types of viruses capable of producing the symptoms of the common cold. There are probably many more not yet identified. We know that if we get certain infections, *measles* and *chicken pox* among them, we can look forward to becoming almost completely immune to a second attack. This is not so with colds. Whereas there is only a single virus that can cause chicken pox, for example, there are very many that can cause colds. Recovery from an attack by one cold-producing virus will offer little protection (if any) against attack by another cold virus of a different type. Furthermore, for reasons not yet understood, the body's response to infection by some cold-producing viruses gives only short-lived immunity.

Winter, as most everyone knows, is the season for colds. Experiments have shown that lowered environmental temperature in itself has no bearing. However, the weather drives people indoors. This increased crowding in confined spaces increases the risk of exposure to infected persons. Dampness or chilling of the body appears to be a minor influence, and the unnatural dryness of the air in heated houses and apartments may be important. Thus, there does seem to be some limited validity to the popular lore about colds, at least insofar as it concerns the conditions under which we are most likely to catch them.

Colds are highly contagious. One hearty sneeze can project literally millions of infected particles into the air, any one of them capable of setting up infection in the nose of the unfortunate person who inhales it. To develop a cold, one must have contact with a virus capable of producing the cold. The greater the chances of contact, the greater the risk of contagion. The youngster at home has uncountable contacts with the viruses his older siblings bring from school. Some cold-causing viruses appear to be transmissible by a transfer of mucus containing the virus from the fingers of one child to another or through an intermediary inanimate object. Handwashing, though often a nuisance, would appear to be a useful preventive measure.

The so-called *acute*, or early, *stage* of a cold rarely lasts more than 3 or 4 days. The nasal discharge is loose and watery; the nose, as we say, runs. Mild fever is likely to occur. The child is listless; his appetite is off. Usually he coughs. During this stage, the virus is multiplying and growing in the mucous membranes of the nose and throat. The cold virus can be passed on to others during this stage.

After 3 or 4 days, the body's natural resistance begins to overcome the virus, and the acute phase comes to an end. But even though the invading virus is coming under control, some symptoms of the cold linger on, perhaps for as long as a week and a half. This aftermath is the so-called *late stage*. This continuation of symptoms has a twofold explanation. First, it takes time for the swollen, inflamed mucous membranes to return to normal. Still irritated, they continue to produce the mucus that accounts for the runny nose. Second, the temporary damage inflicted on the membranes by the virus often allows a secondary overgrowth of the bacterial germs normally present. This overgrowth may sometimes produce a secondary infection which adds its effect to the original viral infection and prolongs the symptoms. In the late stage of a cold (after the first 3 or 4 days), the loose, runny nasal discharge gives way to a thick yellow one. The fever departs. The child becomes more active, and his appetite perks up. The cough, however, usually persists, becoming worse at night, often much worse. The duration of contagiousness into the late stage is unknown.

To date, we have effective drug treatment for only a very few viral infections, and there is no cure for the common cold. All doctors can offer are recommendations for managing the symptoms of colds. These measures are intended to relieve the discomfort and hasten the recovery of the victim and, equally important, to prevent the spread of infection through the community. The only other option open to us is to sit back and let the cold run its course. We know of no medicine capable of "knocking" a cold out of a child's system. In particular, the antibiotics (penicillin, sulfa, the mycins, and so forth) have not been proved useful in the treatment of uncomplicated colds. For all the great advances in medicine over the last generation or so, there has been little improvement in the treatment of the common cold. After the first few encounters with colds, a parent has usually gained enough experience to manage a child's colds without calling the doctor. There are simple measures to keep in mind. First, to the extent that it is practical, you will be benefiting both the community and your child if you can keep him away from other children and adults (except for family members) for the first 3 or 4 days of his cold, when he is probably most contagious. This will mean, of course, keeping him home from his school or camp. We suggest also that you do not invite other children or adults into the house during this period. Preventing contact with other family members is almost impossible and not worth the bother. Face masks are, in general, useless in preventing the spread of organisms. We are suggesting only that you try to avoid unnecessary contacts. In addition to protecting others from your child's infection, you will be defending him from further infection at a time when he himself is particularly vulnerable. He can be up and around while he has the cold, but it is advisable to discourage vigorous activity. In nice weather he can play quietly outdoors as long as he stays away from other people. There is no point in trying to keep a child with a cold in bed. It will not speed his recovery and will only make him unhappy. On the other hand, encourage him to rest from time to time.

The loss of appetite characteristic of colds should be accepted. Do not be concerned if your child shows little interest in eating. (See Part 1, Chapter 5: "Caring for the Sick Child at Home" for discussion of diet for the ill child.) In any event, his appetite will return in a few days.

Rarely, if ever, is there occasion to worry about the bowel movements of your child when he has a cold. As already mentioned, he may have less frequent stools, or looser ones, than normally. There is no occasion to give laxatives or an enema with colds. If the stools should become truly diarrheal, manage the situation as you would in other cases of diarrhea.

The mild inflammation of the eyes common with colds requires no special treatment. Just wipe away any collected mucus, using a cotton pledget moistened with water.

Your child will be much more comfortable if the obstruction of his nasal passages can be relieved. A humidifier in his room will be most effective. Nose drops sometimes help, but be sure to check with your doctor before you use them. Various types of drops can be obtained at the drugstore without prescription. Saline (saltwater) drops can be made up at home. Your doctor will have an opinion about which one to use and for how long. With babies too young to blow their noses, it may be helpful to use an infant nasal aspirator. The aspirator (purchasable without prescription) is a rubber bulb with a plastic tip. Compress the bulb with your hand. Insert the nozzle, continuing pressure on the bulb. Then release slowly. The suction so produced will draw the mucus into the nozzle. If the mucus is very thick and sticky, you can loosen it by putting 2 or 3 drops of saline (salt) solution (1 level teaspoon salt per quart of tap water) into each nostril. (Remove the nozzle after use and wash with soap and water.) Babies have particular difficulty with colds at feedings because their mouths are occupied and thus unable to assist the blocked nose in breathing. Aspirating mucus from the nose just before feedings is often helpful. Never insert cotton-tipped swabs into the nostrils to clear them. Instead, catch the discharge outside the nostril onto a tissue or a swab and roll it around, pulling the secretion out of the nose.

Many young children, especially infants, can be helped to sleep better by placing a pillow under the mattress at the head of the bed to keep them in a slightly sitting position or by propping the baby on his side for part of his sleeping.

Lubricate the inside of the child's nose every evening with petroleum jelly. Simply take the cover of the jar and place the petroleum jelly in it. Older children can dip their little finger into the jar and just run it along the inside of their noses. The mother can do this for the smaller child who cannot do it for himself.

Teach the child to blow his nose at an early age. Gentle exhaling through both nostrils into a paper tissue will prevent his sniffing the mucus into the tubes leading to his ears. He should also learn to dispose of the tissue immediately into a waste container and wash his hands, thus cutting down the spread of his cold. He should also cover his mouth with a tissue when he coughs, again followed by handwashing. Have him blow his nose prior to sleeping to cut down on nighttime cough.

Cough medicines, some with decongestants, are probably useful to some extent for relieving the symptoms but they will not cure *cough.* They do nothing for the infection itself. It is a good idea to discuss cough medicines with your doctor (perhaps at a routine checkup) and ask him to recommend one to keep on hand (*out of reach*). But remember, cough medicines do not cure the cough, they only make it more bearable. Not until the infection has been brought under control completely, both the early and late stages, can you expect to hear the last of the coughing. In general, we use cough medicines only if clearly necessary. If the child is not particularly bothered, let him be. Here is another excellent opportunity to build good health attitudes.

The coughing associated with a cold always involves using the muscles of the chest cage. These muscles are likely to become tired and achy. An older child might even complain that his chest hurts while coughing. Both the aching and the vigorous movements of the chest might lead you to believe that the infection has settled in the chest. This belief is strengthened if the child also makes a rattling noise when breathing. In infants, noises from the nose and throat are easily transmitted to the chest, giving the illusion that the sounds originate in the lungs (see also *asthma; breathing, noisy; bronchitis*). Many people use the expression "chest cold" to describe this group of symptoms and their belief that the infection has gone into the lungs. In reality, we find that true lung infection (*pneumonia*) is quite unusual with colds, even though many children give the impression of such a complication. We do not advise applying liniment or ointment to the chests of such children. Such treatment makes little rational sense although it may ease some aches. Later in this section we will discuss which symptoms really suggest pneumonia and other complications and should prompt you to contact your physician or nurse.

Probably because of the enormous publicity they have received, the subject of antibiotics keeps cropping up in connection with colds. "Why not use one anyway, just in case?" patients ask. As already stated, there is no place for antibiotics in the management of simple, uncomplicated colds. The days of giving the patient a shot of penicillin "just in case" are over. We caution parents most earnestly against ever giving children antibiotics without a doctor's permission. It is often tempting to parents to use antibiotics left over from previous illness. This practice is reckless and dangerous. When you have finished the course of treatment prescribed by your doctor, get rid of the leftover antibiotics. (See discussion of the harmful side effects of antibiotics in the section on *infections.*)

For fever with a cold, give aspirin (see Part 1, Chapter 5: "Caring for the Sick Child at Home" for dosage), and for a full 24 hours after the disappearance of all the symptoms, continue the measures you have been using in the acute stage of the cold.

Children's colds almost always seem worse at night. In the daytime the child swallows the secretions from his irritated nose without much difficulty, but in his sleep the secretions accumulate in the throat, causing him to gag or cough. Strange as it seems, coughing is a good thing in one sense, for it guards against aspirating mucus into the lungs. The spells of coughing may on occasion progress to retching, even **vomiting.** If you have the doctor's permission, you may find it helpful to give a larger dose of cough medicine at bedtime in the hope of tiding your young sufferer over the trying hours. A humidifier (vaporizer) will help (preferably one using cold steam), as will a pillow and blowing the nose before bed. A certain amount of nighttime disturbance, however, seems inevitable with colds. You yourself are tired then and understandably less able to cope with the stresses of illness. Besides, it is part of the human reaction to darkness that the symptoms you have borne with commendable calmness in daylight should seem louder or more severe in the quiet of the night.

Since the most infective phase of a cold is probably the first 3 or 4 days, barring complications, it is reasonable at the end of this period for your child to go back to school or camp and take up his normal rounds. Though less likely to be infectious, he will continue to exhibit late-stage symptoms. The nasal discharge, now thick and sticky, may last as long as a week or two. Breathing through the nose will be hampered. Coughing, especially at night, will persist, now due almost entirely to the draining of secretions into the throat. Cough medicines will lose a good bit of their soothing effect, but the vaporizer will still bring relief.

The persistence of late-stage symptoms and the frequency of infection in the preschool years may lead you to believe that the youngster is never wholly free of colds. ("His nose is always running.") Don't worry. This feeling is a normal condition of parenthood. The fact that you have it is by no means proof that yours is a sickly child or one prone to infection. (See **resistance and frequent colds.**) If your child is having his first cold and if you have never had the experience of living through the colds of other children, it is probably a good idea for you to have a talk with the doctor, at the earliest convenient time. He can comfort, encourage, and educate you, even if he can't cure the cold. As you gain experience, you will become more confident of your ability to handle the uncomplicated cold without the doctor's help.

There are, of course, occasions when it is not only appropriate but wise to call your doctor about a cold. If the acute symptoms, as we have outlined them, persist beyond 3 or 4 days, your doctor will expect to hear from you. The management of an **earache** accompanying a cold, a not infrequent complication, is the same as for any earache. You need not regard earache as an emergency, but you should seek medical attention within 12 hours. If the child complains of sore throat (see **throat, sore**) get in touch with the doctor at the earliest convenient time within the next 24 hours. A child too young to complain may also have inflammation of the throat with a cold. You can ignore this possibility as a reason for checking with the doctor because throat infections with colds in preschool children do not have the same significance that they do in older children.

Irritability and crankiness, as already mentioned, are common in the acute phase of a cold, but if your child seems to you to be lethargic, irritable, or drowsy to an unusual degree, you should call the doctor promptly. (See *drowsiness, delirium,* and *lethargy.*) Persistent complaints of *headache* or pain in the cheekbones suggesting sinusitis are also signals for prompt medical attention. If the child's spells of coughing seem to be longer than the interims of not coughing, call your doctor at the earliest convenient time. If the cough isn't gone in 10 days, call. Difficult or labored breathing also calls for prompt medical attention, particularly if it comes between bouts of coughing. (See *cough, croup, and laryngitis.*) (Fever alone causes *faster* breathing but not labored breathing.) Fever over 102°, or fever lasting for several days is also a reason to call (see discussion of fever in Part 1, Chapter 5: "Caring for the Sick Child at Home").

### PREVENTION

Parents of young children have a special interest in the prevention of colds. Unfortunately, as we have stated, there is to date no effective vaccination. Recent research suggesting vitamin C, taken in large doses far above those needed as a vitamin, may shorten and decrease the intensity of cold symptoms has not been well confirmed. We can only recommend measures that have been in the public domain for many, many years. You can modify the excessive dryness of your home in winter by installing a humidifier in the heating system or placing pans of water on the radiators. Holding the temperature of your home under 70° is probably good for the health of your family. The special problem of resistance and frequent colds is discussed elsewhere in this book as is the important question of *allergy.* If you are really concerned over the seeming frequency of your child's colds or if you feel you have cause to suspect unusual susceptibility to these infections, you will want to have a talk with the doctor.

At the present time, possibly the one most effective measure to prevent colds is isolation of persons with colds until they have emerged from the most infective stage, usually in 3 or 4 days. At best this measure is of limited value because children become contagious even before they develop symptoms. The child with an acute cold at school or at day camp is following the habits of his parents, who rarely stay out of work or stop shopping for a mere cold. The net effect, of course, is undoubtedly an increase in the total number of days lost to this miserable malady, a price we seem to be willing to pay. Bring up this question whenever you can at PTA meetings or at gatherings of mothers of your child's nursery school. If you can agree on a policy and stick to it, everyone—including the parents opposed—will benefit in the long run.

See *cough; infections; pneumonia; resistance and frequent colds; throat, sore;* and Part 1, Chapter 5: "Caring for the Sick Child at Home."

*Colitis, ulcerative. Ulcerative colitis* and *regional enteritis* are two probably closely related but relatively uncommon chronic, inflammatory disorders of the intestine. Both are characterized by **diarrhea, abdominal pain,** passage of **blood in the stools** (especially in ulcerative colitis), weight loss, and fatigue. Regional enteritis affects mainly the small intestine, while ulcerative colitis is an affliction primarily of the large intestine. A common pattern in regional enteritis is a prolonged period of loss of appetite, nausea, marked weight loss, unexplained fevers, and recurrent episodes of abdominal pain. Such symptoms may go on for as long as 2 to 3 years before the telltale signs of intestinal inflammation are detectable. Both disorders tend to persist over many years, being sometimes better and sometimes worse, and they may continue into adult life. They are highly variable in severity from one child to another. At one extreme is the child with just one attack, at the other is the child who may be incapacitated by his other illness. Most affected children fall somewhere in between. X-ray studies of the large and small intestine are essential parts of the diagnostic evaluation. Children with ulcerative colitis require frequent *proctoscopic examinations* (the insertion of an illuminated tube into the rectum for direct examination of its inner lining) to determine the extent of the inflammation.

Complications of these disorders may sometimes include liver inflammation, arthritis, interference with growth, delay of sexual development, abscess formation in the abdomen, and, in ulcerative colitis, the possible later development of cancer of the colon.

The causes of these disorders are not known at present. Emotional factors certainly compound the problem and bear careful attention. Treatment consists of the use of antibiotics when infection is contributing to the picture (see *infections*), steroid hormones (see *hormones*) to control inflammation fo the intestines, antidiarrheal medicines to decrease the cramping and diarrhea, iron and vitamins to combat *anemia* and vitamin deficiency respectively. When all else fails, surgery may be called for to remove the diseased sections of the intestines. Surgery for ulcerative colitis usually cures the disease permanently.

Children and families with these disorders need the ongoing support of a family pediatrician or family doctor working along with a consultant in children's gastrointestinal diseases, usually based at a large medical center. Because emotional factors play such an important part in this disorder (see Part 1, Chapter 4: "Complaints with an Emotional Element"), early contact with a psychiatrist, psychologist, or social worker is in order.

Those wishing additional information can contact the National Foundation for Ileitis and Colitis, Inc., 295 Madison Avenue, New York, N.Y. 10017.

*Concussion:* see *head injuries.*

*Congenital abnormalities:* see *genetics.*

*Congenital heart disease:* see *heart disease, congenital.*

*Conjunctivitis* is an inflammation of the *conjunctiva*, the membrane lining the inner eyelid and whites of the eyes. Its characteristics are redness, discharge, discomfort (itching and/or burning), and sensitivity to light. The conjunctiva can be inflamed as a result of exposure to chemicals, bacteria, or viruses (see *infections*), or allergens (see *allergy*). The response to these various irritants differs and, along with a history of exposure, helps to distinguish one form of conjunctivitis from another.

A common example of chemical conjunctivitis is seen in newborns who have received silver nitrate drops as a routine preventive measure against bacterial infection (see *venereal disease*). The infant's eyelids are swollen and there may be a mucousy discharge for 2 to 3 days. The redness and burning which follow the splashing of soapy water in the eye is another example. These kinds of conjunctivitis usually require no specific treatment other than flushing the eye with water without delay. Emergency treatment of chemicals splashed in the eye is discussed under *burns.*

The well-known *pinkeye* is an example of conjunctivitis caused by bacteria. Redness, discharge, and swelling of the lids is characteristic. Treatment consists of antibiotic drops and ointment. For most children, ointment is preferable to drops. With the child lying down, pull the lower lid gently and instill the ointment into the pocket formed by the lower lid and eyeball. To prevent spread of the condition to others, use disposable paper towels, discourage rubbing of the eyes, and insist on frequent hand washing. (Transfer is usually from hands to eyes or from hands to hands to eyes.) Sometimes antibiotics are given by mouth as well.

The common conjunctivitis of the newborn, which the silver nitrate drops discussed above are designed to prevent, is also bacterial. The bacteria in this case is the *gonococcus*, the cause of gonorrhea. Gonorrheal conjunctivitis is often a serious infection, stubborn to treat, and in the days before antibiotics was a major cause of blindness.

Viruses are common causes of conjunctivitis. The watery, slightly reddened eyes seen in many *colds* result from an attack on the conjunctiva by the cold viruses. One particular family of contagious viruses, the *adenoviruses*, are notorious for their propensity to cause conjunctivitis with or without an associated cold. Another virus known as *inclusion blennorrhea* is commonly contracted at swimming pools contaminated by urethral discharges. It is not to be confused with the mild irritation of the conjunctiva resulting from swimming in chlorinated pools. *Measles*, now uncommon, characteristically produces red, watery eyes which are so sensitive to light that dark glasses may be needed. In these viral inflammations, antibiotics are of no value and healing occurs with time. There are no permanent aftereffects.

One virus, herpes simplex (see *fever blisters*), is notoriously dangerous when it affects the cornea of the eye. The infection first consists of small blisters. These break, forming ulcers or sores. Herpes simplex is one viral illness for which treatment is available: idoxuridine or IDU.

Conjunctivitis can occur in allergic children on exposure to their allergens, for example, ragweed pollen. Treatment consists of avoidance of the allergen and application of cold compresses. Eye drops containing derivatives of hydrocortisone used over a short period can bring relief. Antihistamines taken by mouth may be helpful.

Except for mild conjunctivitis which occurs as part of the common cold, the swelling of the eyelids in the newborn following the installation of silver nitrate drops, and the mild irritation from swimming in chlorinated pools or exposure to smoke or smog, parents are best advised to seek medical opinion when they see a red eye. Not all red eyes are due to conjunctivitis, and a correct diagnosis is essential. Treatment will not always be prescribed, particularly if the doctor or nurse strongly suspects a viral cause. Sometimes a culture (see *infections*) will be taken to identify the causative germ, particularly if treatment, once begun, is unsuccessful.

**Constipation.** Although it is a basic principle of this book to point out and even to emphasize how much parents can do for the health of their children without direct medical assistance (or before obtaining medical assistance), we must depart from this principle on the issue of constipation. Only your physician is qualified to decide that your child needs treatment for constipation.

Too often in the past, well-meaning parents have given laxatives or enemas to "correct" patterns of bowel function which were, in fact, perfectly normal for their particular children. Our understanding of habits of elimination has changed. We recognize now that, in the patterns of their bowel movements, children are as variable as they are in height or weight or the ages at which they begin to talk. It is normal for some children to have 2 or 3 movements a day; other children may be no less normal when passing stools as infrequently as once every 5 to 7 days. The basic question is whether the pattern constitutes a problem for the particular child.

The child with a genuine bowel problem will exhibit a definite symptom other than the seeming infrequency of the movements. Pain on the passage of stools, inability to complete a movement though the urge is strong, **blood in the stools,** involuntary soiling of the clothes between movements—all these are symptoms to be brought to the doctor's attention. If you see any one of them, you have reason to suspect a bowel problem and should seek medical help. If, however, you have seen none of these symptoms, although your child is moving his or her bowels only once every 3 or 4 days, you can relax. The pattern may be quite normal for him. Of course, there is no reason for your own concern to go unheard. If the bowel habits of your child bother you, by all means have a talk with your doctor. But *wait for his advice* before taking any action.

Some reminders here about infants. While most infants have several bowel movements a day, some will skip 1, 2, or 3 days and occasionally more in their normal pattern. While most breast-fed babies tend to have loose stools, some are prone to infrequent bowel movements. Many babies grunt and some turn brick red for several minutes when passing stools. Though the first appearance of this behavior may be rather startling to new parents, the baby is not really in distress, nor is he necessarily "constipated." Your doctor or nurse will reassure you on this point.

From the foregoing you will see that we discourage giving laxatives or enemas or changing diet without the specific approval of your doctor. We cannot emphasize our attitude too strongly. As we have said, doctors see more problems arising from misuse of laxatives and enemas than they see children helped by those measures. In respect to supposed constipation, make it a rule to discuss before you act.

Some bowel problems have their beginnings in the period of toilet training. If you have a child who is not yet trained, we suggest that you read a reliable book on this subject, such as *No More Diapers!,* by Joae Graham Selzer, M.D., and members of the staff of The Boston Children's Medical Center (New York: Delacorte Press/Seymour Lawrence, 1971).

*Convulsion:* see *febrile seizures* and *seizure disorders.*

*Cough* is a symptom of irritation in the respiratory system. The irritation may be located anywhere from the throat to the lungs, including the *larynx* (voice box), *trachea* (windpipe), or *bronchi* (major air tubes leading to the lungs). Whenever possible, the cause of cough, such as the postnasal drip of *sinusitis,* should be identified and treated.

Coughs most often occur as part of the picture of the common cold. This kind of cough is discussed in the section on *colds,* as are persistent coughs which are worse at night, and postnasal drip. Coughs can also be related to *allergy* and can be an early sign of *asthma.* Coughs in and of themselves, although annoying, rarely harm the child. If in addition to cough there is any difficulty in breathing, you should contact your doctor. Such difficulty is signaled by fast, labored, or noisy breathing in which the child is obviously working harder than normal. Noisy breathing can take several forms. It may have a whooping sound (see *whooping cough*) or be harsh and high-pitched (see discussion of stridor in *breathing, noisy*), or sound like a bark, as in *croup.* In these three conditions the sound is loudest when the child breathes in rather than out. Or the noise may be wheezy or whistling in quality, loudest when the child breathes out, as in asthma. (See also *emphysema.*) Quick breathing alone can occur with *fever,* but in these instances it is rarely labored.

Severe or persistent cough should also prompt you to contact your doctor. Distinguishing between a severe and a mild cough is often difficult. As a rule of thumb, the cough that exhausts the child or interferes with his or her normal activity may be considered severe. Coughs that come on shortly after a choking spell—particularly if you have noticed a small toddler eating something or playing with an object near his mouth —suggest that he has aspirated (breathed in) some sort of a foreign body into an air passageway in the lung (see *choking and swallowing foreign objects*). This, of course, deserves investigation.

In general, coughing is useful in the sense that it helps dislodge and expel foreign matter such as mucus or pus. It also protects against aspirating drippings from the nose and throat into the lungs. This is particularly important at night when swallowing (the usual means of disposing of nasal drippings) is decreased by sleep.

At times, however, a cough may be so severe that it is exhausting and counterproductive. This is especially true when the cough is brought on by a constant tickle in the throat, unrelieved by even the most violent hacking. (That "something," which you wish you could reach in and extract, is an illusion created by an inflammation of the lower throat, larynx, or trachea, usually caused by a virus.)

Coughing, regardless of cause, may lead to aching chest muscles (because of the extra work they are called upon to perform). No doubt this achiness contributes to the idea of "chest cold," even though in most cases the source of the cough is not in the chest at all but in the upper airway (throat, larynx, trachea). Liniments, therefore, have absolutely no impact on the cough itself.

Cough medicines, at best, treat the symptom of cough but not its cause. They are sometimes useful but are probably overrated. In general, if the symptom is tolerable without medication, we tend not to prescribe any. In this overmedicated society of ours, encouraging children to do without drugs if they can builds a health habit which will stand them in good stead for the rest of their lives. Some cough medicines are *expectorants*, in other words they loosen mucus so that it can be coughed up. None has proven as effective as plain old water (hence the recommendation to "drink plenty of fluids"). Others act specificially to suppress the urge to cough. Codeine is the classic example of a cough suppressant. Still others exert an effect by directly soothing an irritated throat, like the old remedy of lemon and honey. Vaporizers, by liquefying sticky mucus, may also be helpful.

See *bronchitis; croup and laryngitis; pneumonia;* and *tonsils and adenoids.*

*Coxsackie virus:* see *rash.*

*Cramps:* see *abdominal pain* and *diarrhea.*

*Cramps, menstrual:* see *adolescence.*

*Creeping eruptions:* see *pets and children.*

*Crib death:* see *sudden infant death syndrome.*

*Crippled child:* see *developmental disabilities* and *handicapped child.*

*Cross-eyes* or *strabismus* is a surprisingly common symptom in children and affects between 1 and 2 percent of the population. Unlike many of the symptoms that we discuss in this book, cross-eyes is one for which there is no home treatment except under the direction of a physician. If you suspect this condition, be sure to let your doctor know about it. It is not an emergency. If the doctor confirms your impression, he will refer the child to an *ophthalmologist*, who is a physician with special training in the care of eyes. We underline this point about promptly seeking medical attention because not too many years ago people thought that cross-eyes (which also goes under the name of "lazy eye") was something which children would outgrow. Within the past several decades sufficient evidence has accumulated (some of it, frankly, tragic) to indicate that we cannot rely on the mere passage of time to remedy this condition.

Before discussing cross-eyes in greater detail, we should mention the very common condition among young infants which looks in every way like real cross-eyes but actually isn't. This condition is known by the medical name of *pseudo-strabismus* or *false cross-eyes* to distinguish it from the real thing. False strabismus is most noticeable when a baby looks all the way to the right or left. One eye will seem to roll in toward the bridge of the nose, giving the impression that the two eyes are not directed at the same object. The illusion is created by the absence of whiteness between the colored portion of the eye (iris) and the inner corner of the eye. In the adult when the eyes are turned completely to one side, some whiteness is still visible. In the infant there is relatively less whiteness to start with and there is a tendency for the iris to tuck right under the inner angle of the eye. This tendency is exaggerated if the child happens to have a flat, broad-bridged nose, a fold of skin running over the corner of the eye, a relatively narrow distance between the two pupils of the eyes, or a more oval shape to the outline of the lid margins, such as is seen in individuals of Oriental background. (In fact false cross-eyes is more common in Orientals.) False cross-eyes is of no significance and requires no treatment. It will become less apparent with the passage of time. The condition is very common, far more common than true cross-eyes. Despite its commonness and harmlessness, it is a condition that requires identification by the physician to distinguish it from the true condition which requires treatment. Don't try to distinguish the two conditions by yourself. Seek medical attention when you see crossing.

In true strabismus, when a child looks at an object, only one eye is actually doing the work of seeing. The other eye is directed elsewhere. In such a situation, you would expect that one eye would be seeing one thing and the other eye would be seeing something else altogether, resulting in double vision. Double vision is an extremely unpleasant sensation, one which a child could not tolerate for long. He or she combats this sensation by suppressing sight in the eye which is not being used to focus on the object of interest. The child drives the image received by the crossed eye out of his mind, thereby avoiding the unpleasantness of double vision. If you have ever used a microscope or looked through a telescope with one eye only, you will recall that by concentrating you are able to ignore, as it were, the things perceived by the eye not applied to the eyepiece of the instrument. This process of suppression is done automatically by the child to avoid double vision. Suppression permits comfortable, relatively normal vision but with only one eye.

If this were the only effect, the problem would be less serious. But difficulty arises in the eye which is not being used. Over a period of months, this eye gradually loses the capacity to see. Treatment must be instituted early. Unfortunately, there are many adults who have lost much of the vision in one of their eyes because this fact was not too well appreciated many years ago. Today, all parents should be aware that much vision can be lost over a period of months in an unused eye. It is this fact that underlies our sense of urgency about having children with cross-eyes seen promptly.

The mildest degrees of strabismus, just as serious a threat to vision, are often not recognized by the parents but can be detected by the physician or nurse during the routine checkup. Many communities have compulsory screening programs for children to detect not only crossing but other eye problems as well. It is possible to gain a fairly accurate impression of a child's visual acuity by the time he is between the ages of 3 and 4. Although eyes cannot be checked for acuity very easily or reliably before this age, it is possible to detect milder degrees of cross-eyes by tests that do not involve the child's ability to report what he is seeing.

Cross-eyes or strabismus is a symptom, not a disease. There are a number of contributing factors. It is the job of the physician to diagnose the factors contributing to strabismus in a particular case. Common factors are refractive errors (farsightedness, for instance) or imbalance of the muscles that move the eye in its socket. (See *vision problems.*) A rare cause of strabismus is *retinoblastoma,* or cancer of the retina. Strabismus resulting from refractive errors is more apt to become apparent after one year of age, when the child begins to pay more attention to the fine details of closeup objects. Strabismus resulting mainly from muscle imbalance is likely to show up even before the first birthday. In most, but not all situations, strabismus appears during the preschool years. The point to remember is that cross-eyes can occur from birth onward and that whenever it appears the same concern is in order. Similarly, cross-eyes may be more apparent at one time of the day than another. Tiredness may bring out the condition when it is just beginning. Also the degree of crossing may be greater in one direction than in another. Sometimes the crossing is more pronounced when looking at near objects than at ones far away, and vice versa.

Treatment has several objectives. First and foremost is the preservation of vision. Steps must be taken to force the child to use the eye in which vision has been suppressed. The most effective way to force this eye to work is to cover or patch the eye that has been doing all the seeing. If suppression has continued for a long time, months may be required before normal vision will return. If excessive delay has occurred before beginning treatment, the vision may never return completely and, in the most extreme cases, may not return at all. In addition to dealing with the urgent problem of preserving normal vision, the physician will direct his attention to realigning the eyes. For children with refractive errors, glasses and eye drops may be in order. For a few with muscle imbalance, special exercises may be useful if the child is old enough to cooperate. In many cases surgery is required. Sometimes more than one operation is necessary. In corrective surgery, the points of attachment of one or more muscles that control the movements of the eyeball are relocated to bring the eyes into more correct alignment.

Some cross-eyed children use one eye only; others use both eyes, but at different times, and are said to have alternating strabismus. These children are less likely to develop permanent impairment of vision, because each eye is being used regularly although not at all times. Even so, their strabismus should be corrected by surgery if for no other reason than the disagreeable effect which crossing of the eyes has on others and the feeling the child gets that he is funny looking.

See also *vision problems.*


**Croup and laryngitis.** *Laryngitis* is a self-limited illness which rarely lasts more than 48 hours. It is caused primarily by viruses similar to the ones that cause colds, and by some bacteria (see *infections*). Usually occurring as part of a virus cold, laryngitis signifies that the virus has moved down from the nose and throat to produce an inflammation of the voice box *(larynx)* and the windpipe *(trachea)* below it. Common symptoms are hoarseness, a tickle in the throat, and *cough.* The viruses that cause most cases of laryngitis do not respond to antibiotics. Accordingly, there is little to do to hasten the end of the infection, although much can be done to make the child more comfortable, including relieving the cough. Because the diameters of the larynx and trachea below it are smaller in young children, inflammation of the larynx can obstruct the passage of air, giving rise to the condition known as *croup*, which may be viewed as a severe form of laryngitis. The major symptoms of croup are labored breathing, sucking in of the chest, hoarseness, a hacking kind of cough, and an unmistakable barklike noise with each inspired breath. Croup often comes on at night.

If the breathing is very labored, both you and your child may be frightened. Don't panic. You will be able to help your child more if you can stay relaxed. And there are some definite steps you can take to ease matters.

First, take the child immediately into the bathroom. Close the door. Turn on the hot water of the sink, tub, or shower (best of all) to steam up the room. If hot water is not available, open up the windows to let in the cold air. These measures will almost always relieve the breathing in several minutes.

If someone else is available, have him call your doctor while you are taking the measures just described. In any event, don't leave the child alone.

If after 10 minutes of steam or cold air your child has not shown improvement in his or her breathing, make arrangements to take him or her promptly to the nearest emergency room. Stay in the steamed-up bathroom until you are ready to move. Don't be afraid about taking him out into the cold night air. Not only is this air not harmful to him, but it may actually ease his breathing difficulty. Don't wait for the doctor's return call if he has not answered promptly. Leave word with his home or answering service that you are going to the hospital and try to alert the hospital that you are coming, but move right along.

If the child's breathing does improve, you can remove him from the bathroom and take him with you while you call the doctor or wait for his return call. Use something to moisten the air, preferably a cold steam vaporizer. The child may be more comfortable in a semisitting position. If this is the case, prop him up from behind with pillows. Try to distract him so that he can relax. Television, radio, or a good story will help. Above all, stay calm yourself. Your child will quickly sense anxiety and is then likely to become more tense himself. If at any time his breathing worsens so that he becomes short of breath and frightened, take him back into the steam-filled bathroom.

Most children with croup do very well and can stay at home. If difficulty with breathing persists, it is sometimes necessary to have the child enter the hospital for more extensive treatment and, more importantly, for observation. The thing to remember is to contact your doctor, even if the croup is relatively mild.

If your child is able to stay at home, he should have a vaporizer in his room. If he has *fever,* you can give him aspirin according to the dosage schedule suggested in Part 1, Chapter 5: "Caring for the Sick Child at Home." He is likely to have little appetite while the croup lasts and may find taking fluids difficult. Offer him small quantities of fluids frequently. Any fluids that he wants are all right, although we prefer clear ones such as water, ginger ale, tea, fruit juice, or cola drinks. Because the coughing may lead to *vomiting,* it is best not to feed him solids.

*233*

Cuts,
scratches,
abrasions,
and
scrapes

In the very mildest attacks of croup, the labored breathing and barking noise may be apparent only when the child coughs or cries. The treatment is similar to that of *colds.* But discuss even these mild cases with your doctor, within twelve hours.

See *breathing, noisy; choking and swallowing foreign objects; emphysema; infections;* and *throat, sore.*

**Curvature of the spine:** see *spinal defects.*

**Cushing's syndrome:** see *hormones.*

**Cuts, scratches, abrasions, and scrapes.** If a *cut* or *scratch* has not already stopped bleeding by itself, simple direct pressure with a clean cloth (preferably a sterile gauze pad) will bring it to a halt in almost all cases. If bleeding fails to stop after 15 minutes of constant direct pressure, the cut should be seen by a physician. If bleeding has ceased, carefully inspect the cut. Notice if the skin edges are separated or together. If the edges are separated and the wound is "open," seek medical help within 4 hours of the accident. Healing of lacerations with separated skin edges can be hastened by suturing (stitching) or by using butterfly-shaped adhesive bandages to hold the edges together. Furthermore, the resulting scar will be smaller and less noticeable. The 4-hour rule is an important one to follow. If more than 4 hours pass after the accident, suturing becomes hazardous because of the likelihood of infection occurring around the sutures. (See *abscess.*)

If the skin edges are not separated, home treatment is appropriate. Wash the laceration with generous amounts of soapy water to clean out all of the particles of dirt which might be present. (Cleansing under a running faucet is very helpful.) If you are unable to remove these particles completely, it is best to contact your physician to discuss further treatment. Following cleaning, it is a good idea but not absolutely necessary to apply an antiseptic solution or ointment. The old remedy of Mercurochrome is no longer considered useful. Tincture of iodine, while still an effective treatment, has been improved upon by newer iodine compounds such as povidone-iodine. Antibiotic ointments are sometimes effective in preventing infection.

After cleaning, scratches can be left uncovered. However, if the wound is deeper than a scratch, cover it with a gauze pad. The "stickless" variety has an obvious advantage. Also less likely to stick to the cut is Vaseline gauze, which can be purchased at the drugstore without a prescription. The Vaseline gauze can be the first layer of the dressing. Cover it with a dry gauze and tape everything to the skin. Keep the cut and dressing dry. Cuts usually heal within 3 to 4 days. At the end of this time, the bandage can be removed.

Cuts should not be painful for more than 12 to 18 hours. If the pain continues for longer or if it grows worse, contact your physician. If the area around the cut becomes swollen or red, if a line of redness extends up the extremity from it, or if the cut begins to discharge pus, contact your physician promptly. The spread of infection through the skin increases the risk of a **bloodstream infection. Tetanus** is a consideration with certain types of wounds (see **immunization**).

The treatment of *abrasions* or *scrapes* is similar to that of cuts and scratches. Bleeding is not usually a problem with a scrape, but if it does not stop by itself, follow the advice given above for cuts. As with cuts, it is important to see a physician if you cannot remove all the particles of dirt by washing with soap and water. This is particularly important if the scrape happens to be on the face.

While abrasions, unlike lacerations, do not need to be stitched, it is important to see a physician if they do not heal within 3 or 4 days, or if redness or swelling develops in the area around the wound.

**Cystic fibrosis** is a chronic disease which affects the mucous-producing glands throughout the body but especially those in the pancreas and in the air tubes in the lungs. While a cure it not yet at hand, treatment has significantly improved the lot of affected children.

Cystic fibrosis is an inherited disease. There is nothing that mothers do or do not do during their pregnancies that determines it. Each parent of an affected child is a carrier of the cystic fibrosis gene. If the baby receives a double dose, that is, one gene from each parent, he or she will develop the disorder. There are no symptoms of the carrier state, nor are there tests to identify carriers. About 3 to 6 percent of the population are carriers of the gene, so that the incidence of cystic fibrosis is about 1 in 1000 to 2000 babies, making it quite common. Obviously, if cystic fibrosis has appeared in one child in the family, there is a greater-than-average chance that siblings also will be affected. (See **genetics**.)

The abnormal mucus produced in the air tubes is sticky and hard to clear. It plugs the small air tubes, causing cough, labored respirations, and fatigue as prominent symptoms. The blockage leads to *emphysema* (ballooning out of the lung segments), *atelectasis* (collapse of lung segments, see **lung rupture and collapse**), and predisposes to infection of the lungs (see **pneumonia**). Without treatment, the lung literally fills up with mucus and pus and breathing is interfered with. Permanent damage to the lung may result by scarring from lung abscesses and stretching and thickening of the large and small air passageways *(bronchiectasis)*.

The abnormal mucus in the pancreas blocks the ducts that connect that organ with the main tube leading to the small intestine and prevents the flow of the pancreatic juice which contains enzymes needed to digest fat, protein, and carbohydrate. The pancreas becomes lumpy and scars down to a small size. The changes in the pancreas were the first ones identified in this disorder and gave rise to the name cystic fibrosis of the pancreas or, for short, cystic fibrosis. The pancreas is eventually destroyed and digestion disturbed, resulting in the passage of incompletely digested food in the stools, which are foul smelling, fatty, and bulky, and in the weight loss, potbelly, and increased appetite associated with food deprivation. Without treatment the course may be progressively downhill.

In about 15 percent of newborns with cystic fibrosis, the intestinal contents have not been digested normally *in utero* because of the lack of pancreatic juice, and the sticky *meconium* (secretions accumulated in the intestines before birth) blocks the intestine at various points. This form of **intestinal obstruction** is known as *meconium ileus* and requires surgical treatment.

A small percentage of children with cystic fibrosis go on to have inflammation and scarring of the liver in various degrees of severity. Cystic fibrosis children are more prone to develop polyps (growths) in their nasal passageways and protrusion of the rectum, sometimes called *rectal prolapse*.

One feature of cystic fibrosis is an abnormally high concentration of salt (sodium chloride) in the sweat. The skin of cystic fibrosis babies often tastes salty. The measurement of salt in sweat is a common laboratory test done to establish the diagnosis of cystic fibrosis and helps distinguish this disorder from other causes of chronic respiratory difficulty, for example, **asthma,** and from malabsorption from other causes like **celiac disease.** This test is called the *sweat test*. Another laboratory study is analysis of the intestinal juices for pancreatic digestive enzymes. A sample of intestinal fluid is obtained by passing a thin tube down through the nose and esophagus into the small intestine.

There is as yet no cure for cystic fibrosis, although much research is under way. Treatment is directed at restoring lung and digestive function to as near normal as possible. The approach to the child's lung problem, both in the hospital and later in the home, involves: (1) sleeping in a tent filled with a very fine mist which can reach the smallest air passageways and liquefy the sticky mucus (this traditional practice is now being questioned by some doctors); (2) use of aerosol spray containing special medicines such as antibiotics; (3) physical therapy or chest pounding to shake lose the sticky plugs of mucus (like shaking a partially filled ketchup bottle), and postural drainage (positioning the patient so that gravity drains the clogged areas of the lungs), also handled under the advice of a physical therapist; and (4) antibiotics to treat infection when present. Meticulous long-term care like this by parents and the health team can help children lead reasonably comfortable lives well into adulthood, particularly if the disorder is detected early, before permanent damage has occurred. How long the lungs can be kept functioning remains to be seen, since modern therapy has been available only during the past ten years.

Treatment of the pancreatic juice deficiency consists of feeding, along with meals, digestive enzymes made from the pancreas of animals, in effect replacing what the body lacks. With some alteration in diet, particularly a restriction in fat, it is possible to improve digestion and to restore weight gain and normal appetite. An extra dose of vitamins soluble in water is given each day.

As with any other chronic disease there are important effects on behavior. Parents often need special help in dealing with the many child-care issues which arise. Children are encouraged to live as normally as possible with full activities. There are special pamphlets prepared by the National Cystic Fibrosis Research Foundation (3379 Peachtree Road, NE, Atlanta, Ga. 39326) for teachers, parents, and for older children. The foundation has organized parents' committees and special medical diagnostic treatment centers in every part of the country. The addresses can be secured by mail on request. The group has publicized the importance of cystic fibrosis as a very common disorder in children and has stimulated research into its causes and treatment.

See *handicapped child.*


**Cystitis:** see *urinary tract infections and defects.*


**Cytomegalovirus.** Infection with the cytomegaloviruses is little known by the public in comparison with other viral infections (like *measles* and *mumps*), yet, because of its role in causing birth defects, it is of major importance and will unquestionably receive far more attention in the years ahead.

The pattern of spread of these viruses is not completely understood despite their apparently wide distributions in humans. Cytomegaloviruses cause an illness in adults similar to infectious mononucleosis (see *mononucleosis, infectious*). As is true of many infectious diseases, the severity of the illness is highly variable, ranging from severe to subclinical (see *infections* for discussion of subclinical infections). Continued excretion of the virus in the patient's urine and saliva following the disappearance or even in the absence of clinical symptoms seems to be fairly common and increases the likelihood that the virus will spread to others.

It is a certainty that the virus can pass from the mother's blood across the placenta to infect the fetus in a way similar to *rubella* (*German measles*) virus. Infected infants show a wide spectrum of problems ranging from death to severe brain damage with stunted head growth to moderate degrees of deafness and mental or motor retardation to no symptoms at all in many cases. The infected infant, with or without symptoms, excretes virus for many months following birth and undoubtedly plays an important role in the spread of the virus. Studies have shown that cytomegaloviruses can be cultured from the cervices of between 4.5 and 28 percent of women during the third trimester of pregnancy. It is likely that the infant can also be infected during the birth process as he or she passes through the mother's cervical secretions that harbor the virus. At least 1 percent of all infants have been infected before or during birth, a figure of major magnitude.

The full implications of cytomegalovirus infections are not yet understood, but because of their effect on newborn infants they appear to be of major importance in terms of disease, disability, and financial cost, which includes not only medical care, but also special education and institutionalization for severely damaged infants. Cytomegalovirus infection must be listed among the causes of mental retardation.

See *developmental disabilities.*


*Dandruff:* see *seborrheic dermatitis.*


*Deafness:* see *hearing and speech problems.*


*Dehydration:* see *diarrhea* and *vomiting.*


*Delirium:* see *drowsiness, delirium, and lethargy.*


*Dental care.* The proper care of a child's teeth begins on the day he or she is born. Care revolves around diet, feeding practices, cleanliness, and dental supervision.

The value of *fluoride* in forming strong decay-resistant teeth is now beyond question. Children living in communities in which the water supply is fluoridated either by natural or by artificial means experience less than one-half the number of cavities of children living in communities whose water supplies lack fluoride. Dietary fluoride is important to teeth as long as growth is taking place. Growth and formation of teeth begin prior to birth and continue into the mid-teens. During this entire span of time (some fifteen or sixteen years), the diet should include adequate supplies of fluoride. Fluoride is important to the infant even prior to the eruption of teeth because the teeth are actually being formed within the gums before they emerge. When moving into a new community, find out whether or not the water is fluoridated. We urge parents to help to bring about the fluoridation of water in their own communities if this is not already the case. In communities where fluoride is absent from the water supply, parents should supplement the diet with fluoride tablets or drops, following a doctor's or dentist's advice.

The well-balanced *diet* which we have referred to elsewhere (see Part 1, Chapter 3: "Diet of Infants and Children") provides the proper nourishment in terms of protein and minerals for the development of healthy teeth. One widespread dietary habit must be regarded as a threat to the health of teeth. This habit, fostered by TV advertisements (see *television and children*), is the eating of highly refined carbohydrates such as are contained in candies, ice cream, sweetened cold cereals, chewing gum, soft drinks, cookies, and cake. If our only interest in life were the health of our teeth, we would strongly recommend outlawing all of these appealing foods. Obviously, we must choose some middle ground, and so we suggest limiting the use of these foods. The most effective way of limiting their use is to be cautious about introducing them into the child's diet in the first place. The child will miss them less if they are either not offered to him or offered in a limited way. It is much easier to establish good habits at the outset than to change unhealthy ones later on. Keep this fact in mind when deciding what kinds of snacks and desserts to give your child. This issue comes up early, by the time the child is 1. It makes good sense to stay away from or at least to limit sweets to once a day in snacks and desserts and to use alternatives like fruits and nuts and nonsweetened crackers. If possible, and the child is old enough, try to time the giving of sweets so that brushing can follow soon thereafter. For example, if one meal of the day is to be followed by a highly sweetened dessert, make it a meal after which you can easily brush the teeth. For a school-age child lunch would not be a good meal, whereas dinner might be. Also, choose those types of sweets that are eaten and rapidly swallowed as opposed to those that linger in the mouth, such as hard candies. Sugar-free chewing gums are now available.

As discussed elsewhere (see Part 1, Chapter 3: "Diet of Infants and Children"), we recommend weaning of non-breast-fed children from the bottle when the child is ready to handle a cup (somewhere toward the end of the first year). Weaning from the bottle when the child is ready is not only healthy psychologically but is also important for proper dental health. First, children who are not weaned are also likely to be put to bed with a bottle of milk. Milk taken from a bottle by a drowsy child tends to "sit" in the mouth and promotes the growth of mouth bacteria which produce the acids that help cause tooth decay. Ideally, a child should not go to bed with a bottle of any kind at any age. If, temporarily, a bottle seems necessary, we recommend that milk or juices be avoided and that water alone be used. Second, prolonged use of a nippled bottle can result in deformity to the teeth. We encourage the discontinuation of bottle feeding no later than 1½ years unless there is some special reason. If weaning is a real problem for your child or it seems next to impossible to put the child to bed without a bottle, discuss this issue with your doctor or nurse.

Closely related to bottle feeding and its effect on teeth are the questions of *pacifiers* and *thumb-sucking*. From the dental point of view alone, both prolonged use of pacifiers and extended thumb-sucking can lead to deformities of the teeth which may require correction. We are not suggesting that either thumb-sucking or use of pacifiers has no role to play in normal child development but want to point out that prolonged or excessive sucking has its definite drawbacks. Generally speaking, we encourage parents to try to discourage both practices in their children by no later than two years of age. Talk to your doctor or nurse about some of the newer kinds of pacifiers which may be less deforming to the teeth. Breast-feeding may make the use of a pacifier unnecessary.

*Cleanliness* of the teeth plays an important role in preventing tooth decay. Cleanliness is achieved by proper brushing, using an effective anticavity toothpaste. Toothpastes that contain stannous fluoride are more effective in preventing tooth decay. Despite some advertising claims to the contrary, only this kind of toothpaste has been proven to be of value in cavity prevention. Toothbrushing should begin just as soon as the child is able to do so or will allow the parent to do so. Most children are able to brush their teeth by no later than 2½ years and for some it is even earlier. Toothbrushing is fascinating for children, and, if exposed to older siblings or adults performing this ritual, many toddlers will want to imitate this activity just as they do any other. Take advantage of the natural imitativeness of the young child and provide him with a small brush, readily available in most drugstores. Electric toothbrushes are excellent for handicapped children and children with braces but are not necessary otherwise. In any case they are not designed for easy use by the young child. In the beginning, the objective is not to do a perfect job of brushing but to establish the habit of brushing. You can help with the brushing, but let the child do as much as he can by himself. You can "take turns" with the child who is having difficulty. Whereas for adults an up-and-down motion of brushing is usually suggested (down on the upper teeth and up on the lower teeth), with children such a technique is difficult to achieve and not that important. Brushing with a back-to-front (and vice versa) motion along the outside, inside, and top portions of the teeth is perfectly adequate. Brush a minimum of twice a day with at least one brushing following breakfast. Cereals are particularly sticky and hard to remove—all the more reason to avoid the sugared ones which provide a rich culture medium for mouth bacteria. The second most important time to brush the teeth is before going to sleep. Ideally, the teeth should be brushed after each meal as well as after each snack. Most children in school have no opportunity to brush after lunch. This issue is one to raise at PTA meetings. Second best to brushing after meals is "swishing and swallowing," that is, rinsing the mouth with water and then swallowing the water.

Unfortunately, brushing does not effectively reach the hard-to-get places between the teeth. For this reason we recommend use of dental floss as an adjunct to careful systematic brushing, ideally twice a day and at least before bed. The technique for this method of cleansing can be taught to school-age children by the dentist or hygienist. To be effective it does, however, require a high degree of motivation, for plaque builds up every day and, therefore, needs to be removed every day if the harmful action to teeth and gums is to be prevented. Without the parents' active participation and interested support, which includes using floss themselves, children will not floss their teeth, which, after all, is more time consuming and demanding than the usual cursory toothbrushing. It is not enough simply to ask, "Did you brush your teeth?" Parents should check for themselves and help give credence to the importance of a *sustained* effort. Your dentist's 6-month review is not enough, nor is the cleaning (or prophylaxis) he or the hygienist provides at your visit adequate if there is no follow-through at home. Every youngster will cut a corner now and then, and the ritual of oral hygiene is easily neglected, particularly at the end of a busy day.

By the time most children are between 2½ and 3 years of age, they already have all of their primary dentition (the so-called "baby teeth"). This is the time for the *first visit to the dentist*. Suggesting that children go to the dentist when they are as young as 2½ may strike parents as being unusually early. However, we know that teeth can begin to decay at a very early age, and if decay is to be caught in an early stage, 2½ is the right time to begin.

One of the reasons why some parents might choose to delay in taking their child for routine dental care until a later age is that they do not fully understand the importance of maintaining the primary teeth. A common mistaken notion is that the "baby teeth" are not really important, and, since they eventually fall out anyway, there is no point in bothering to repair cavities in them. If a cavity occurs, why not simply pull the tooth out? This kind of thinking is fallacious. In truth, the primary teeth are of great importance not only for speech and chewing, but also for paving the way for permanent teeth. If the primary teeth have been removed, or are diseased, the permanent teeth may erupt irregularly and in poor alignment unless special measures are taken. Correction of the permanent teeth is difficult, time consuming, and costly. It is far better to maintain the primary teeth.

Another reason why some parents find it hard to take their children to the dentist at an early age stems from their own negative feelings about dentists, often based on their own unpleasant experiences with dental care. In recent years, dentists have become concerned that the widespread negative attitude toward dentistry interferes with proper dental care. A great deal of thought has been given to making the early dental experiences more pleasant. Studies have shown that rather than naturally fearing the dentist, young children are capable of having very positive attitudes and of actually looking forward to dental examinations and treatment. Familiarize yourself with those dentists in your own community who are particularly interested in caring for children and who have adopted some of the more modern psychological techniques for dealing with children in their offices. Once you have convinced yourself that dental care does not have to be unpleasant, you will find it far easier to prepare your child for dental examinations and to transmit positive feelings to him. It is not enough for a parent to say that a child should not fear the dentist if the parent himself is afraid. Dental examinations can and should be approached positively. Discuss the visit prior to the fact. Talk about what will happen honestly and frankly. Acknowledge that there may be some discomfort with certain procedures but that the child's cooperation can keep this to a minimum. There are a number of good books for children that tell about visits to the dentist. Ask your dentist or librarian to recommend one.

It is highly desirable that the first contact with the dentist occur before dental symptoms arise. The first visit should be brief and more one of becoming acquainted than of having something done. Meeting the dentist, seeing his office, familiarizing himself with the chair and with the examining equipment may be quite enough for the child's first trip. If the child is cooperative, more may be done. Keep in mind that you are interested not only in dental treatment, but also in establishing positive attitudes which can permit faster acceptance of dental care.

*Regular checkups* should be scheduled twice a year *for life.* (For adults with good dental health, once per year may be enough.) Some children with special problems may need to be seen more frequently. At a regular checkup, the dentist will review the home care of the teeth and examine your child's teeth. Try to schedule the visit for a time when the child is most alert and cooperative. Mornings are usually best. Keeping the child out of nursery school for one morning is far better than taking him to the dentist's office for an initial contact at the end of an afternoon when he is sleepy, grouchy, or hungry. If your child appears to be having an off day, try to avoid taking him to the dentist at this time. Better to reschedule the appointment than to get off on the wrong foot. If your child tires in the dental office and the dentist finds him becoming uncooperative, it might be better to have him come back another time than to prolong an unpleasant experience. You can help by making it clear to the dentist that you are concerned about your child's attitudes toward dental care and that he should not hesitate to end a session when a child becomes tired or uncooperative. If you demonstrate that you are willing to go to the trouble of returning as frequently as necessary, the dentist's job in caring for your child's teeth and in instilling proper attitudes will be much easier.

*X-rays* are an important part of the examination. X-rays allow the detection of cavities in parts of the teeth that are not visible to direct examination alone, as well as other hidden conditions. In general, you can expect that one complete set of X-rays will be taken of the primary teeth (between 2½ and 6 years), one set during the period of so-called mixed dentition (when combinations of primary and permanent teeth are present from 6 to 12 years), and one set when all of the permanent teeth have erupted (sometime during mid-teens). More frequent X-ray examinations may be necessary for the detection of decay, but will usually be limited to bite-wing X-rays (X-rays of the back teeth).

Small *cavities* should be repaired as early as possible. Failure to do so may result in abscessed teeth and even possible loss of the tooth. More and more, with children, dentists are getting away from the use of local anesthetics to kill the pain of drilling. With a positive attitude toward dental care and with more effective drills, many cavities can be repaired without anesthesia and its unpleasant numbing sensation and painful needle prick. It is remarkable to see how well young children will tolerate drilling without anesthesia. Your dentist or the hygienist will also want to clean the child's teeth. Periodically the dentist will apply a gel containing fluoride to the teeth. The gel makes the surface of the teeth more resistant to decay. Topical fluoride is not a replacement for fluoride in the diet which strengthens the internal structure of the teeth. Both forms of fluoride treatment, along with brushing with a fluoride-containing toothpaste, are important in maintaining the strength of the teeth and in reducing cavities.

Your dentist should be viewed as an important health consultant. We have discussed a number of ways in which you can promote the health of your child's teeth. If any one of these issues are unclear to you, be sure to question your dentist about them. It is very important that you feel free to review what you have been doing at home in connection with promoting healthy teeth, just as you would review other areas of your child's life with your doctor or nurse.

The ultimate goal of the dental profession is to provide good oral health for all. It is clear that dentists cannot do this alone any more than the physician can render total medical care by himself. For this reason you will be seeing more assistants helping the dentist in the future. These auxiliaries themselves will carry out prescribed procedures for the patient so that the dentist's time can be spent on diagnostic and technical procedures that require his special skills. This is not entirely new, for the dental hygienist has been an important part of the team for many years.

Parents sometimes feel that their dentist is no longer interested in them, having relegated their child to the care of the hygienist. This, of course, is not true. The hygienist is highly trained for the services he or she is allowed to perform and is knowledgeable in the latest and most effective means of prevention of tooth decay and gum diseases. Thus, feel free to discuss your concerns with the hygienist as well.

The most common problem with eruption of the baby teeth is, of course, *teething*. All babies have discomfort with teething with no apparent lasting ill effects. Fretfulness, drooling, biting of fingers, crying (even screaming), finicky eating, and occasional disturbed sleep (parents and infant) are symptoms. It is not a condition about which too much can or, some would say, should be done. Babies seem to derive some comfort from biting. For this reason, teething rings, chilled carrot or celery slices, and teething biscuits have been tried. Whether the biting as such really helps or actually represents an attempt to get at and remove the source of pain is not clear. In a way it would seem that biting with a sore gum would be the last thing one would want to do, but babies cannot be interviewed on this point. For the most distressed babies we have found aspirin helpful as a mild antipain medication but have not been impressed with the value of rubbing medicines directly on the gums.

There is wide variation in the timing of the eruption of the primary (baby) teeth. It is not at all uncommon for some infants to have teeth at birth. On the other hand, for some children, teeth do not erupt until after their first birthday. Generally speaking, children who begin to teethe early complete their primary dentition early (by 24 months), whereas it is not unusual for a late teether (one who begins at 1 year) to complete his primary dentition by as late as 4 years of age. Early teethers tend to achieve their permanent dentition earlier than do late teethers.

The primary teeth are still being lost by the time a child is 11 or 12 years of age. Also, the permanent teeth are still erupting into early teen-age life. Sometimes there is a delay of as much as 6 months between the time of shedding of a primary tooth and its replacement by a permanent tooth, even though generally speaking one follows soon after the other. For a number of years the child will have both primary and permanent teeth at the same time, side by side. Very commonly the front lower permanent teeth (incisors) erupt behind the baby teeth before these have fallen out. We do nothing about this situation for several weeks, giving "nature" the chance to run its course. If the baby teeth are not shed, we extract them. Assuming there is adequate space, the permanent teeth will gradually be pressed forward by tongue action into normal position. Just prior to eruption of a tooth it is quite common for the overlying gum to be swollen, red, or tender. In a few cases, a cyst of blood forms which obstructs the eruption and may require treatment. Permanent teeth are normally yellow in comparison with the primary teeth. This yellowness is particularly noticeable when the very white primary teeth are still present for comparison. The yellowness of the permanent teeth does not mean there is anything wrong or that the teeth are not being kept clean. The color can vary from pale to quite dark and in either case is entirely normal. Once the primary teeth have been shed completely, the contrasts between yellow and white will disappear and the yellowness becomes less noticeable. Tetracycline antibiotics can permanently stain the forming teeth and should be avoided if possible in pregnancy and childhood.

Failure of the upper and lower teeth to come together properly (so-called *malocclusion*) can occur at any age and may involve primary as well as permanent teeth. Malocclusions are corrected both for cosmetic reasons and for good dental health. Uncorrected malocclusions during childhood, even if they are not cosmetically objectionable, can lead to some serious problems of the teeth during adult life. Proper dental care from birth onward can prevent many kinds of malocclusion. Other kinds of malocclusion, however, are frankly not preventable and are related to hereditary factors that affect the size of the bones of the face. Studies of the evolution of man indicate that there has been a general tendency for these bones to grow smaller, allowing less room for the teeth and result-ing in crowding, crooked eruption of teeth, and malocclusion. Some families are more likely to have difficulty than others. Even with what appear to be very similar problems, different children require different types of treatment. Determining when and how to correct the teeth requires expert judgment which takes into account the individual pat-tern of malocclusion and the dental and emotional development of the child. The correction of malocclusion, and other problems involving the spacing or position of the teeth, is done by a specialist known as an *orthodontist*.

*Injuries to the teeth* are common. In mild injuries, the tooth may be merely chipped or loosened. In more severe injuries, the tooth may be broken, driven back up into the gum, or knocked completely out of its socket. If a primary tooth has been completely dislodged, no treatment is necessary. Usually the teeth which are affected are the anterior (front of the mouth) ones. The loss of such a tooth represents no permanent problem for the child, but should be discussed with a dentist in case it affects the eruption of permanent teeth. (See below.) On the other hand, when a permanent tooth has been knocked from the mouth, immediate attention is in order. If not too much time has elapsed, there is a possibility of replanting the tooth in its socket. Wrap the tooth immediately in a wet cloth and take the tooth and child to your dentist or to a hospital emergency room if your dentist is not available. Generally, if more than an hour has passed before treatment has begun, successful reimplantation is unlikely. Any injuries to the teeth, however minor they may appear, should be seen by the dentist as soon as possible.

Injured teeth often become discolored. Discoloration is a sign of bleeding within the tooth and usually means that the tooth has died. Special treatment of dead primary teeth is not usually necessary unless other symptoms develop. If a tooth has been injured, the major worry is infection above or around the tooth. This infection will be signaled by swelling, pain, and tenderness of the gum at the base of the tooth. There is no justification for leaving an infected tooth in the mouth even if it is "just a baby tooth." This kind of infection needs treatment, just as infection occurring anywhere else in the body does. In the case of an infected primary tooth, there is even more reason for concern because of the additional danger of damaging the underlying permanent tooth.

*Toothaches* require prompt attention. Toothaches point to trouble in the tooth. Without treatment, this trouble will only get worse, not better. The simplest type of toothache is one in which a slight twinge of pain is felt on eating sweet or highly spiced food. However slight the pain, seek dental help promptly.

Should it ever be necessary to extract a primary tooth because of decay or injury, parents should recognize that, without special measures being taken, the other healthy teeth surrounding the removed tooth tend to crowd in on the space that has been left. More important, the permanent teeth will erupt in the same poorly aligned way and the malocclusion will persist and tend to grow worse. For this reason, dentists, often an orthodontist, nowadays bridge the space left by the removed tooth with an appliance called a space maintainer. This device prevents the normal teeth from crowding into the space and keeps them in normal alignment. Malocclusion is thereby prevented. This treatment is a bit different from what existed when many parents themselves were children and is important to know about. The extra cost of inserting a space maintainer is more than paid for when one considers the cost of straightening crooked teeth later on.

See Part 1, Chapter 3: "The Diet of Infants and Children."

*Carl G. Cohen, D.M.D.*
*Richard I. Feinbloom, M.D.*

*Dermatitis:* see *eczema* and *rash*.

## Developmental disabilities

### INTRODUCTION: HEALTHY DEVELOPMENT

Human development is a continuous process which begins before birth and proceeds through a series of stages which eventually lead to maturity. It is determined both by the basic constitutional makeup of the individual and by the effects of the environment and society in which he or she lives.

Studies of child development have provided much knowledge about the "growing-up" process and the factors that affect it. This knowledge can be used to promote positive, healthy development in normal children, and it also provides a basis for recognizing that in some children development may not be progressing at the typical rate or according to the usual pattern. In thinking about the developmental process, it is important to realize that the whole person is composed of many factors, all of which interact and affect each other. For the purpose of discussion only, these factors may be considered in separate categories: physical, cognitive, and affective.

*Physical growth* occurs in different parts of the body at varying rates from infancy to adulthood. Physical or biological growth is most commonly recorded as increase in body weight, length (or height), and head circumference. During infancy, growth is steady and rapid. By 1 year of age the birth weight has usually been tripled and the length increased by at least 9 inches. During the early childhood or preschool years, ages 2 to 5, gains are relatively steady. Steady, slow growth continues throughout the middle childhood or school years until a spurt of rapid growth occurs just prior to *adolescence*—usually about age 10 in girls and 12 in boys. Rapid growth continues then until full height is reached in late adolescence at about age 16 in girls and 17 or 18 in boys.

Head size is also recorded as an index of physical growth. The heads of babies are larger relative to total body size than they will be later. The major increase in the size of the skull will be achieved by early childhood. Growth of the head (skull) reflects to some degree brain growth, but brain size as such may not relate to the quality of its function. It is true in general that if the head size remains significantly small as general linear growth proceeds, there is cause for concern, since this suggests a deficiency in brain development. Small heads in the presence of poor body growth have less significance. Unusually rapid increases in head size, on the other hand, may indicate obstruction to fluid outflow inside the head (*hydrocephalus*) and, if progressive, require investigation.

*Cognitive development* refers to the increasing knowledge and intellectual skills that a person possesses and his capacity to use them in thinking through problems, making decisions, and forming judgments. The process involves taking information from the environment, organizing it, and building a structure of knowledge. It also involves perception, memory, imagination, and the ability to formulate ideas. Cognitive development is clearly dependent upon the maturing function of the brain and special senses (hearing, vision) and upon opportunities to acquire information and to learn. Cognitive development is founded in part upon the sensorimotor activities of early infancy. The actions of the very young infant are his natural, undeliberate response to stimulation of the senses (response to hunger, sound, light, touch, and so forth). This is called *sensorimotor behavior*. Later when activities are performed through understanding and control, the term *psychomotor* is used, implying interaction of mind (psyche) and body. The term *motor function* refers to the use of body parts to perform acts in a controlled and purposeful way (changing position, walking, using one's hands, and so forth).

The beginnings of language development are found in the first months of life. However, it is from about one and a half to two years of age that acquisition of language (or the symbolic use of sounds and words) becomes a very significant indicator of intellectual progress. The child of this age responds to the verbal stimulation of others, and begins himself to speak words with appropriate meaning. This developing ability enables him to respond to simple instructions and to communicate in words his feelings, desires, and wishes. (See *hearing and speech.*) During the preschool period, the child progresses in learning such things as his own identity and that of others, his place within the family, his relationship to others, what their expectations are, and what is or is not acceptable behavior within his social group (the continuing process of socialization). He also learns to perform such mental tasks as making comparisons and selections. Language gains are extensive during these years. In middle childhood (the school years), the child's capacity for thought and reasoning shows very significant growth. This is apparent particularly in relation to skills in academic areas, such as in reading and writing. Beyond childhood the skills which have already been acquired continue to be improved and refined. New knowledge continues to be gained thereafter, but the basic mental capabilities will probably not increase in any significant way after the childhood years.

The quality of personal and social adjustment achieved in later life is largely the product of the *affective* (or emotional) *development* that takes place during the early years. The capacities for giving and receiving, for loving and being loved, for having respect for oneself and for others are essential to social adjustment. The ability to accept failures and disappointments and to overcome adversities is also important to one's adaptation and social capacity, whatever the level of competence may be in other areas of achievement. Whether these characteristics of personality will fully develop depends to a great extent upon the quality of personal nurturance which the young child receives. "Nurturance" here means nourishment of the child's spirit with the warmth, love, stimulation, enjoyment, and the type of gratification that is received only through person-to-person communication. The ability to respond to situations in which one may learn is strongly influenced by one's state of emotional and personal adjustment. This interrelatedness between emotional factors and other aspects of development is most clearly demonstrated in situations where emotional nourishment (input, stimulation) is lacking. Children who are unwanted and unloved or those who for reasons of necessity (war, natural disaster) are cared for in depersonalized group settings often show developmental inadequacy which is due primarily to emotional deprivation (see Part 1, Chapter 4: "Complaints with an Emotional Element").

The child cannot grow on love alone, but without the happiness it brings, he may not achieve the richness of living that in the beginning was possible to him. This is particularly true for children with developmental handicaps.

### DELAYS IN DEVELOPMENT

Deviations from a normal developmental course can occur in conjunction with a general mental handicap. For instance, the development of a child with **Down's syndrome** (Mongoloidism) is slower and different in all aspects, including bodily growth and motor development, as well as cognitive development. Developmental delay can also be the result of a specific sensory handicap. Most notable of these disorders are deficits in vision, indicated by the infant's failure to focus and to follow with his eyes, and deficits in hearing, signaled by lack of response to sound and absence of vocalization and language development. A sharp contrast between general abilities and performance in specific areas such as these is just cause for concern and early examination.

In the case of overall retardation, a *pattern* of general slowness in attainment of developmental milestones makes itself apparent. Slight delay in limited areas of accomplishment should not be a cause for alarm. When it is seen that a pattern of delay has become established either in general development (such as slowness in major motor milestones and also an absence of babbling and of social response) or in one specific but broad area (such as slowness in motor achievements), an investigation of the child's developmental condition should be undertaken. The following summary of major developmental milestones gives a rough idea of what to expect with a healthy baby during the first 2 years. (For a fuller understanding one should read more extensively on the subject of growth and development throughout childhood and adolescence.)

*Major developmental milestones of the first 2 years*

*During the first 3 months* the baby begins to gain control over his motor activity. He develops the ability to hold his head erect and steady when he is held upright. He becomes interested in watching his hands as he holds them before his face, and he learns to bring his hand to his mouth at will. During this time he gains control of his eyes and can watch objects as they move up and down and from side to side. He reaches out for bright objects but misses them. He turns to see things that are out of his range of vision. He cries when hungry or uncomfortable. He learns to smile in response to his mother's smile. He begins to laugh and show pleasure in making sounds.

*From 3 to 6 months* the baby becomes able to sit briefly without support when placed in a favorable position. He learns to roll all the way over when lying on his stomach. He succeeds in reaching for objects and grasps them with his whole fist. When something is in his hand, he usually brings it to his mouth. He becomes increasingly more sociable, showing that he wants attention and that he enjoys having people with him. He smiles at others and coos and giggles when talked to. He cries out when displeased.

*From 6 to 9 months* he becomes able to pull himself to the sitting position and while sitting learns to move (hitch) himself forward and backward. While holding an object in his hand, he learns to bang with it. He also learns to grasp an object with one hand and to pass it from one hand to the other. He babbles increasingly during this period. Although continuing to become a more social person, he learns to distinguish strangers from familiar people and may become frightened when first approached by the former.

*From 9 to 12 months* the baby develops the ability to pull himself to a standing position and begins to walk with help. He may crawl or creep first, although not all children do. He continues to become more skillful in using his hands, learning to hold his own bottle and to feed himself with his fingers. He learns to grasp with his thumb and forefinger rather than with the whole fist. He can release or let go of objects at will (and may make a game of dropping things to be picked up). He begins to play simple gesture games such as pat-a-cake and peekaboo. He shows affection for his close people and reaches out to be picked up and held by them. From babbling he goes on to imitate sounds ("ma-ma," "da-da") and learns to say a word or two. He learns the sound of his own name and pays attention when it is said.

*From 12 to 15 months* the baby becomes a "toddler." He walks with help, feet widely apart. He learns to "cruise" or walk sideways, holding on to furniture. He becomes able to hold a cup using both hands. He learns to grasp a spoon and to dip it into a dish (but cannot get the food into the spoon yet). He drops and throws things and learns to place one object on top of another (2 blocks). In speech development he progresses to use "jargon," that is, vocalizing with expression as though carrying on a conversation in his own language. He learns to point and to name familiar objects.

*From 15 to 18 months* the toddler becomes able to walk by himself (still with feet widely apart) and learns to climb stairs one at a time. He travels about, exploring a great deal, "getting into everything" (especially drawers and cabinets). He becomes skilled in drinking from a cup without help and learns to fill a spoon, although he still has difficulty with placing it into his mouth (much spilling). He may indicate when his diaper is wet, showing that he is getting ready for toilet training. He continues to learn words and to talk increasingly. He can succeed in building a tower of 3 blocks. He becomes interested in playthings that move or fit into each other (nesting toys, stack toys) and push-and-pull toys.

*From 18 to 21 months* the toddler walks and runs with his feet placed less widely apart. He gains skill in climbing furniture as well as stairs. He makes progress in feeding himself with a spoon but still spills often. He enjoys active play by himself or watching others. He enjoys such playthings as building blocks, toy trucks and cars, carts and kiddy cars, and form board puzzles (pieces that can be lifted out of the form). He begins to show temper when things displease him, especially if desires are not granted quickly enough. He gains control of bowel movements and may make progress in toilet training. He has about 10 words in his vocabulary and is beginning to use 2 or 3 words together in phrases.

*By 2 years* the toddler has learned to run, walk, and jump. He can climb up and down stairs, holding on and placing both feet on each step. He becomes able to open doors by turning the knobs. He can feed himself completely and is learning to help undress himself. He has built a vocabulary of approximately 30 words and can speak in short sentences (3 or 4 words). His attention is gradually increasing and he can learn to follow simple instructions. He can enjoy hearing stories with pictures to look at, can scribble with a crayon, and learn to make a vertical line by imitating the motion. He is very energetic and enjoys physical activity. He is trying to master his situation and to become more independent.

When parents notice that their children are different in some respect, they react in many ways. Some subconsciously deny or fail to acknowledge what they see, hoping that there really is no cause for concern. Others may become unduly frightened or anxious about the child. Some anxiety and bewilderment are, of course, normal. Many people, however, have incorrect and distressing ideas about handicapped or mentally retarded children. Most parents, mothers especially, feel that they must somehow be to blame for any difficulties in their children. A few people still feel that there is something shameful about a weakness or an illness in a family member. Any of these feelings—fear, guilt, shame— may cause parents to delay in seeking help.

There are strong reasons why developmental disabilities should be diagnosed as soon as possible. In early childhood the developmental or learning value of each month is proportionately much greater than it is for the older person. The 2-month-old child, for example, has accumulated 50 percent of his total knowledge in the past month (a statement which no adult can make). The biologic process of brain maturation requires that efficient development of certain types of learning must be accomplished in the early years. It is therefore very important that a child with a disability receive help as soon as possible in order that he may use his developmental time as fully as possible. This may not mean a cure or removal of the cause of disability, although medical assistance may be important. It is more likely to consist of efforts to reduce the effects of the child's disability by working with the strengths and capabilities he does have. For a child with a sensory deficit, it is important that alternate pathways for communication and nurturance be used in order to reach him. Early help is also a way to prevent secondary effects arising from the disability, that is, adjustment difficulties that result from unfair expectations and needless encounters with frustration and failure. Diagnosis and understanding of the child's situation are the first steps toward planning a positive program of care and education for him.

## CAUSES OF DEVELOPMENTAL DISABILITY: DIAGNOSTIC TERMS

Almost as soon as one begins to wonder about the possibility of a child's development being delayed, one starts to speculate about the causes for this delay. Parents seek a "cause" or reason in order to put their own thoughts in order. Actually, however, many of the conditions in children that produce developmental retardation are not clear, or there may be a complex of possible causes without any certainty about which one is the most important. For example, in studies of late preschool and early-school-age children suspected of retardation, the cause of the handicap is found in less than half of the cases. And even some of the so-called "causes" of retardation which are offered are really just guesses about the timing of the events that must have taken place rather than true explanations for how they occurred.

Here is a list (presented chronologically) of the special circumstances that may interfere with a child's normal development:

1. *Hereditary factors* account for a very small percentage of developmental disabilities in such well-defined genetic disorders as **PKU** (*phenylketonuria*), **Tay-Sachs disease,** and galactosemia (see **genetics**) —all diseases in which biochemical abnormalities affect the brain. There appear to be cases in which parents with developmental disabilities (including mental retardation) produce offspring with similar handicaps. We infer that hereditary factors play a role in such cases, even though we have little understanding of the specific mechanisms.

2. *Spontaneous changes in the chromosomes or in individual genes* ("mutations") of the primitive cells that will form the baby are puzzling biological events which produce permanently altered individuals, often with serious handicaps. The most frequent example of this is the child with **Down's syndrome** (or, as it used to be called, "Mongoloidism"), in which studies show important abnormalities in the chromosomes, of unknown origin. In a small percentage of children with Down's syndrome, clinically indistinguishable from the others, the handicap is transmitted hereditarily ("translocation" Down's syndrome). There are a number of other less common chromosomal changes that produce other disabilities.

3. *Prenatal influences,* or effects on the very young embryo (particularly in the sixth to thirteenth weeks of pregnancy), seem to be an important and relatively frequent factor behind so-called "congenital anomalies," often including mental retardation. Babies with unusually small heads (microcephaly) or large heads (hydrocephalus), both of which lead to retardation, with congenital heart disease (see **heart disease, congenital**), with abnormal formation of the kidneys and other parts of the urinary tract (see **urinary tract infections and defects**), or with abnormalities of the hands and feet seem most often to derive their handicaps from influences on the body's development occurring very early in pregnancy. The association of retardation with subtle physical abnormalities known to stem from defects of early embryological development gives rise to speculation that the retardation also has its origins in defective brain formation occurring at the same time. Such abnor-

malities include relatively minor modification of the postion or structure of the ears, the external characteristics of the eyes, the shape of the nose, the size of the lower jaw, or even the patterns of the fingerprints or the skin markings in the palm. There has been much speculation about what might produce these modifications in body formation, but usually no reasonable cause can be assigned. Occasionally an infection of the mother (see *cytomegalovirus* infection, *German measles,* and toxoplasmosis in *pets and children*) seems to be correlated with the changes in the baby. Certain medications that the mother has taken are sometimes implicated (such as the "thalidomide babies" of a few years ago), but most of these prenatal influences have not been identified.

4. *Influences on the fetus in the last two-thirds of pregnancy,* after his structures are basically formed and he is increasing in size and maturity, may well be critical to brain development, but relatively few have been identified. It is usually felt that nutritional deficiencies in the mother's diet must be extreme to affect significantly the baby's development late in pregnancy. In multiple pregnancies (twins, triplets, and so forth), one of the babies may receive a less adequate blood supply, and trouble with the structure of the placenta may lie behind the production of some unusually small babies. The causes of prematurity, a leading factor in developmental disabilities, are poorly understood.

5. *Birth injuries,* or troubling effects proven or suspected to be caused by the actual delivery and first period of adaptation to life outside the uterus, can result from intervals of poor oxygen supply to the brain, and later from low blood sugar or excess bile pigments (bilirubin) in the blood (see *jaundice*). Babies who have been through these difficult circumstances may later show a handicap in the use of their muscles, have stiffness, or be troubled with coordination problems. There may be accompanying changes in the reflexes (so-called "spasticity"), or limited motion at the joints ("contractures"). (See *cerebral palsy.*) Premature babies are especially vulnerable to impairment from troubles occurring in the immediate newborn period, such as impaired oxygen supply to the brain because of breathing difficulties. Reduction in the incidence of premature delivery, by means of improved prenatal care for mothers, is one of the most promising approaches to the prevention of mental retardation.

6. *Childhood diseases* that cause interferences with development are less frequent in current times. Encephalitis or *meningitis* may leave some residual handicap, but early treatment and support will minimize this. *Head injuries,* poisoning, and other accidents (see Part 2, Chapters 8 and 10: "Accident Prevention" and "Poisoning") can produce special difficulties, but the number of children with mental retardation of this type of origin is not great. However, concern does exist over increasing accident rates. Chronic *lead poisoning,* as an environmental hazard in

circumstances of substandard housing, remains an important threat in certain population groups. Endocrine disorders (see **hormones**) such as thyroid deficiency are a rare cause of mental retardation in childhood.

7. _Social and emotional deprivation_ with undesirable effects on normal child development constitutes a large and important cause of developmental problems. Long overdue national recognition of the human cost of environmental deprivation has given rise to Head Start, "Sesame Street," and the day-care-center movement. It is often difficult, however, to know how much loss of nurturance and emotional support has resulted from the circumstances of broken families, disturbed parents, or a deprived and handicapped environment. In a setting of serious deprivation one often finds other issues as well: poor prenatal care, nutritional limitations, frequent infections, and so forth. Social and emotional deprivation can occur in adequate economic conditions as well. (See _child abuse._)

The words we use to label or describe children who have a developmental disability tell a lot about the cultural standards of our times; so often we are less considerate or precise than would be appropriate. The term "mental retardation" itself is a troubling one. By one standard definition it refers to subaverage general intellectual functioning that originated during the developmental period and is associated with an impairment in adaptive behavior. This acknowledges that the major point of reference is the issue of a handicap in intelligence, but this is frequently an unfairly restricted consideration, since other learning disorders, certain bodily handicaps, and emotional difficulties are commonly included in the child's total picture. The definition does acknowledge, however, that by occurring in the important period of development (childhood), broad social and personal effects will most likely occur as well. Many people feel that by referring to a child as "mentally retarded," or simply "retarded," one often sets up a constrained and prejudicial atmosphere that works against planning for his future or acknowledgment of his rights. The term "retardate" is particularly glib, suggesting a limited outlook for the child's potential progress or fulfillment. The use of the designations "special children" or "exceptional children" can be more fair (as in "special education"), but may also be rather patronizing. Current Federal program planning now often identifies such children as having "developmental disabilities," and although this term is somewhat awkward, it does have a more open implication. Certainly the old terms of "mental defectives" and "feeble-minded" are best eliminated altogether.

There are a number of classification schemes that have a certain legal or educational utility. The ratings of "borderline, mild, moderate, severe, and profound" mental retardation are supported by the American Association for Mental Deficiency, an important and active professional society. School systems commonly use "educable, trainable, and subspecial" groupings, but these categories tend to downplay the importance of social adaptability, physical handicap, or emotional disturbance that also affect school class placement.

Certain kinds of children are particularly difficult to classify and may really require a paragraph of description rather than a single term to present their special features. Their abnormal characteristics, however, usually derive from the same list of causes already presented. They may have especially notable "motor function" handicaps (awkwardness, poor coordination, trouble with movements in sequence, and so forth) and be labeled as "brain-damaged" (an imprecise term of limited usefulness), or they may show a particularly irrepressible behavior pattern said to be characteristic of "minimal cerebral dysfunction" (again, a singularly un-satisfactory "diagnosis"). One may find their increased motion and activity labeled as "overactivity" (a normal behavior variant), "hyperactivity" (a neurotic type of increased movement), or a "hyperkinetic disorder" (excessive distractibility, short attention span, and unresponsiveness to direction or discipline which usually has a true brain handicap behind it, and which will often respond to medications like the amphetamines). Or they may have specific types of functional difficulty such as "learning disorders," or "perceptual handicaps" (see *learning disabilities*). In the latter situations the child is troubled in his ability to integrate visual or auditory stimuli into his vocabulary or knowledge, and shows special difficulties in reading, thinking of the words he needs to use, or in the use of numbers. Finally, the child whose inability to relate socially in a normal fashion to those around him causes a special isolation or de-creased participation, is referred to as having "atypical" behavior, or, in the more extreme situation, as being "autistic." Children of this sort also have great problems with learning, and will with time have increasing degrees of so-called "educational retardation."

It can be seen that considerable confusion can occur from the use of various names or classifications for different types of handicaps, with seeming inconsistency or divergent implications in the hands of different workers. In the ultimate sense, the major responsibility of parents and professionals is to be certain that an accurate study is made of the functioning and needs of the child, without becoming preoccupied about the "labels" to be used.

## SEEKING HELP: EVALUATION STUDIES

The physician is usually the primary source of professional help for chil-dren during the infant and preschool years. A pediatrician or family doctor should prove both observant and responsive to expressions of concern about a child's progress. A responsible physician does not ignore or minimize parental worries about development. Once having recog-nized a significant delay or disorder he does not tell a parent simply that the child will "grow out of it." He might suggest that he himself observe the child more closely and frequently, in order to monitor the trends in development for an additional period of time, or else he might arrange for a more thorough developmental assessment elsewhere. For the young child this latter approach would include examination by a clinical psychologist and assessment of motor function by a physical therapist. If language development is a concern, testing of hearing by an audiologist and assessment by a speech pathologist experienced in working with young children would be included (see *hearing and speech*). If preliminary testing indicates, however, that the situation is complex and not easily defined, the multidisciplinary services of a child-development clinic may be needed for a comprehensive study and analysis of the child's developmental status.

For the child whose difficulties first appear in relation to school achievement, psychological evaluation is the primary mode of diagnostic study (see *learning disabilities*). This should focus on general educational skills and the possibility of specific learning disorders, and also provide for consideration of emotional and social adjustment. Here again if primary study indicates subtle diagnostic problems, then more sophisticated in-depth studies may be indicated. Such studies, if not locally available, may be obtained through a special child-development clinic. These clinics are usually located in major medical centers or within the framework of the state programs for mental retardation or developmental disabilities. Guidance in locating a diagnostic center may be obtainable from a physician, public health service, local child-guidance center, or through the Department of Education in one's particular community.

A child-development clinic is a facility in which the services of many different professionals are utilized for comprehensive study of the medical, psychological, and social aspects of a child's developmental status. The central or core disciplines of such a unit are usually pediatrics, psychology, nursing, and social service. In addition to specialists from these basic disciplines, the services of many other child-study professionals may be utilized according to the circumstance of each individual child. Depending on the medical center, patients with cerebral palsy are seen in such clinics or in specially organized clinics for them alone. The multidisciplinary approach should be the same.

The goal of the multidisciplinary study is to provide an accurate description of the child's strengths and weaknesses in all areas of development, plus an understanding of his social environment. These data then serve as a basis upon which the staff of the center can work with the parents and community agencies to plan, locate, and arrange the kind of program the child needs.

*The pediatrician* performs a physical examination and parent interview in order to identify the biomedical factors related to the developmental problem. This exam may include laboratory studies and X-rays and medical consultations. Pediatric care can be adapted to the special health requirements of handicapped children.

*The physical therapist* contributes evaluation of *motor function*, which includes muscle strength and control, flexibility, balance, and agility, as well as identification of the level of achievement in motor function. He or she can instruct parents in ways to stimulate motor development.

*The nurse* is concerned with the child's overall nurturance and care requirements, and helps parents to adapt care to meet the special needs of their child.

*The psychologist* employs a number of tests to identify the characteristics of the child's personality and intellectual functioning. From interpretation of test results he or she can guide parents in understanding the child's intellectual and emotional development as well as other aspects of the parent-child relationship. A psychologist is also able to assist in prescribing a suitable educational program.

*The social worker* investigates the relationships between the child and other family members, and the social factors that are important to the child's care and program planning. He or she can provide counseling when needed to assist the family in reaching positive and practical solutions to difficulties in such areas as payment for medical care, assistance in the home, and special educational needs.

*The audiologist* determines through special testing techniques the extent of a child's hearing deficit, if any, and the degree to which it interferes with his communication and education. He or she can provide help with amplification and assistance in securing appropriate programs for auditory training and language development.

*The speech pathologist* examines the means employed by the child to communicate his needs and ideas and identifies the factors responsible for any communication disorder. He or she can offer the necessary help in establishing programs of language stimulation or speech therapy as needed. (See *hearing and speech.*)

*The nutritionist* provides an assessment of the diet and development of feeding patterns. From this, he or she can provide guidance in diet and suggestions in regard to the feeding situation.

*The special educator* tests for specific learning disabilities, tries to match the child with the best educational program, and communicates with the teacher and parents about the child's educational needs.

*The ophthalmologist* examines the eyes for significant abnormalities of visual function and for identification of congenital abnormalities or acquired pathological changes. He or she can provide medical treatment and prevention or correction of altered vision. (See *vision problems.*)

*The psychiatrist* explores the emotional life and adjustment of the child and family with special attention to the stresses and problems common to handicapped children and their families. He or she can offer psychiatric therapy when it is needed by the parents and the child.

*The play therapist* observes the child's behavior in the unstructured setting of a play situation. He or she assesses the play skills, relationships, and spontaneous functioning that occur there, and offers guidance to parents in selecting play activities to promote the child's development.

*The pedodontist* examines the child's teeth, and contributes to the data on the biological characteristics of the child. He or she can provide for a program of specialized dental care and oral hygiene often required by handicapped children. (See *dental care.*)

*The occupational therapist* considers the child's capabilities and social adjustment, particularly in relation to play. Upon this basis he or she can design a program of creative activities that provide training in psychomotor skills and social interaction.

*The orthopedic surgeon* plays a central role in treating muscle and joint problems, in particular those of the child with cerebral palsy, working with the physical therapist.

*The vocational rehabilitation counselor* reviews the capabilities and interests of the older individual (adolescent or adult) and provides guidance in relation to vocational training and employment opportunities.

### SEEKING HELP: PROGRAM PLANNING

As mentioned, the primary goal of these evaluation studies is to provide an analytical description of the child. From that description both the strengths and weaknesses can be identified, and a program to enhance the child's growth and development can be planned. It may be too simple, however, to say that program development is merely a rational outgrowth of understanding the child's intellectual, physical, and emotional situation, since difficulties may come in practical matters. The special kinds of teachers or classrooms one might hope to find are often scarce, and counselors to help both child and parents are in short supply. When the child's condition is quite serious, his progress in training may be painfully slow, so that discouragement may place heavy internal pressures on the whole family group. In turn, there may be difficult behavioral reactions in the child himself, precipitated in part by the confusion around him, which only serve to intensify the problems.

The child with mental retardation or other specific handicaps has the right to receive support in all areas where handicaps have been identified. For most children this means using a group of special services, involving many of the same professional specialties that assisted in the evaluation studies. Conferences between the parents and the agencies, schools, clinics, and so forth, that are involved can produce a reasonable set of principles and aims, and should be followed by periodic reviews of the child's progress and the continuing appropriateness of the program. The parent should feel a responsibility to keep informed and to insist that the plan for the child be creative and kept current with changing circumstances. And the professionals involved should remain available for discussion and for consideration of fresh approaches.

In planning for the individual child, those handicaps that are correctable or treatable should of course have priority. A partial list would include:

*Hearing handicaps:* medical treatment, hearing aids if appropriate, auditory training, speech therapy, and so forth (see **hearing and speech**).

*Visual problems:* eyeglasses, surgical correction (see **vision problems**).

*Muscular or skeletal abnormalities:* orthopedic care and physical therapy.

*Nutritional deficiencies:* review and counseling (see Part 2, Chapter 3: "Diet of Infants and Children").

*Dental abnormalities:* acute and chronic care (see **dental care**).

*Other physical defects,* such as congenital heart disease (see **heart disease, congenital**), **hernia,** and defects in other organs and systems.

*Seizures:* special medications (see **seizure disorders**).

*Learning problems:* special educational programs (see **learning disabilities**).

*Hyperactivity:* medication and special educational programs (see **learning disabilities**).

There is a need in these treatment programs to establish coordination between the workers performing the specific therapy and those who are providing continuing education and personal guidance for the handicapped child; in such a setting one can then expect a minimum of confusion or apprehension in the child.

*Educational planning* is a specialized matter. Ideally, the evaluating psychologist discusses the case with the special educator from the appropriate school. Parents have a responsibility to learn whether the available programs are appropriate for their child. If, due to lack of space or personnel, children with mental handicaps are mixed with children whose handicap is limited to vision, hearing, or motor function, neither group will benefit. Public school systems have traditionally been charged with the establishment of many types of "special" programs: those for children with mental retardation primarily, those for emotionally disturbed children, classes for the hearing handicapped, for the visually handicapped, for children with serious physical difficulties, those for special learning disorders (perceptual handicaps), and home instruction for brief periods in certain circumstances. As could be anticipated, children with truly multiple problems are very difficult to fit into conventional special education facilities. At the present time, providing a sustained educational program for the mentally retarded child who also has deafness or a severe behavior disturbance, for example, is a very complicated matter.

Education for handicapped children must be conceived in the broadest sense. Design of an appropriate teaching program involves much more than academic classes; training in self-help skills, socialization, and vocational work all are important. Special preschools (nursery schools) can be of great value for the child with retardation; their programs should be reviewed for appropriateness by those who provided the diagnostic evaluation for the child. In many areas of the country, good-quality special day-care programs are also available, following the preschool, and continuing up as far as 21 years of age. For the older mentally handicapped persons, sheltered workshops, or youth programs run by clinical or educational centers, can be enormously valuable. The social experience of the handicapped child can be further extended in recreational programs, often sponsored by parents' groups (private, or from schools), which may include sports, outings, social events, and travel. If handled intelligently, and suited to his level of understanding, a sex education program can orient a handicapped young person; ideally, guidance personnel should follow through and offer continuing support. Parents would do well to think in advance of the long-term aspects of the life-plan for children with major handicaps, discussing it with personnel at the clinical centers, with parents' groups, and, at the appropriate age, with the siblings of the handicapped child. For the mentally handicapped, there now exist many alternatives to the former plan of state school residence in adult life, including more imaginative and higher-standard living schemes (small groups) and vocational plans.

So far we have considered primarily the practical or technical problems involved in building a program for the handicapped or retarded child. In the long run these matters must be seen in relation to a more central goal, that of the child's personal adaptation and achievement, the shaping of his entire life situation. Underlying all these efforts is the search for the basic happiness of both child and parent.

At first, to a parent still beset by surprise or disappointment at the results of the diagnostic studies, it may seem as if the road ahead has so many concerns that peace of mind is forever out of reach. A sense of bewilderment over the problem of understanding and meeting the true personal needs of one's special child is a common feeling. On reflection, however, one soon comes to realize that *the fundamental needs of the mentally retarded child are exactly the same as those of any other human being*. For happiness he needs the same warmth, support, understanding, opportunity for expression, and education that all of us require. It is true, of course, that some of these needs will have to be met in ways that fit the child's level of perception, but love is still love, and concern is still concern. Personal support for the handicapped child may have to be a little more generous and more constant than usual, since his ability to perceive or remember may be limited. Throughout our society there is a tendency to devalue the importance of the "person within." The special child's personal needs are even more likely to be neglected.

The personal goals one seeks for the handicapped or retarded child can be considered in two areas: *development of a good self-image and achievement of a sense of fulfillment*. A positive self-image in a child with mental retardation is more likely to develop if he feels a sense of understanding in those around him. This implies that his parents, siblings, teachers, and other involved people relate to him (in both offerings *and* demands) in a way which shows that they are indeed identifying with him. Such understanding and caring are central, and mean a thoughtful personal outreach instead of just provision of automatic services. The child grows up feeling valued, even if he senses simultaneously that he is quite different from other children. Recently, after urging from parents' groups, television networks have begun portraying handicapped children on children's programs, a step that should encourage understanding.

Insight about what is important to the child can be gained by allowing him adequate opportunities for self-expression in activity programs and in interpersonal contact. Toys should be selected according to interest, sports and crafts encouraged, family functions planned so that the child can participate, and appropriate responsibilities gradually transferred. From this encouragement of the child's interests and responsibility, the sense of fulfillment mentioned above will develop. Discipline and training become more natural in such a setting. Certain unfortunate secondary problems, such as obesity resulting from diminished motivation and activity, can be prevented or controlled in a busy and yet supportive family atmosphere. (See *weight problems.*) In a setting of love and acceptance the child's positive self-image will grow and provide lasting security.

It is important that the family maintain a continuing liaison with a facility for counseling and evaluation (such as a child-development clinic). From time to time specific advice will be needed regarding home training for motor development, growth in use of language, diet, toilet training, personal grooming, and so forth. At the same time, guidance regarding the needs of the normal brothers and sisters as they relate to the special child should be obtained. There will be real stresses on other children in the family which deserve acknowledgment and frequent attention.

The family that feels strong *identification* and a sense of *giving* is most likely to progress toward peaceful adaptation and acceptance of the situation. In an atmosphere of understanding, intelligent programming, and visible love, the parents themselves will have the best opportunity for finding their own fulfillment as well.

Many parents when confronted by the diagnosis of a handicapping condition in their child, especially mental retardation, feel the understandable need to obtain a second opinion at another competent facility. They have every right to do so. Eventually, however, it is in the best interest of the child to establish a relationship with one center and one group of workers in whom they have faith so that a continuity of understanding help may be provided over a period of years. To persist in traveling to many clinics and subjecting the child to unnecessarily repeated examinations is disruptive to development and becomes an emotionally and financially depleting process. Once they have consulted a child-development team such as those described above, parents are well advised to try to settle down and work in a positive way with the problems presented. Repeated attempts to find someone who will tell them that the diagnosis is not true will only exhaust their energies and delay the child's potential progress and adaptation.

Even before professional direction enters the scene, parents can effectively respond to the basic human needs of their special child. The need to know the warmth and pleasure of being touched and held, of being played with, talked to, and comforted by another human being is there from the beginning. Parents and others should not remain aloof from the "different" child but rather should reach out to him. Only in this way will they come to know his developing personality in a close and personal way. This means such things as getting down on the floor with the child and joining in at his level of activity, having fun together, making believe, and setting apart special times for sharing and growing together. To establish genuine contact and interaction with others is one of any child's most important achievements. The child who does not naturally appeal for or invite attention is often the one who needs it most. It is essential that the child develop a special loving and trusting relationship with the persons (usually parents) who are to provide his intimate care. These are the aspects of nurturance which are nonspecialized and should be begun in the earliest days.

It is also the parents' responsibility to make sure that the care and teaching of their child are developed and carried out on an individual basis. What is good for one child is not necessarily good for another. For example, physical activities that are stimulating for a child who has muscle weakness and tends to be rather inactive may be very poor for one who has spasticity of his muscles and is a tense, easily excitable child. Toilet training may be reasonable for a particular 2-year-old child while it may be a futile and even emotionally harmful effort for another whose bowel and bladder function have not sufficiently matured to make control possible. Parents should make sure that those who offer specific instruction in techniques know the individual child and his situation. At the same time it is important to obtain whatever help is necessary in teaching the child to play, to feed himself, to talk, and to learn other basic abilities. Such help can be sought from the variety of professionals described above, including child-development workers, physical therapists, nurses, and nursery-school teachers. They may work with parents on a regular basis, either in the home or in a clinic or school setting. They can recommend special techniques, equipment, and furniture which are suitable, as well as offer appropriate literature which has been prepared for parents' use. Here again, the materials and methods must be selected on the basis of the needs and capabilities of the particular child and family.

## CURRENT CHANGES IN PUBLIC ATTITUDES AND PROVISIONS IN PROGRAMS FOR HANDICAPPED CHILDREN

In recent years a heartening acceleration has taken place in thinking about the overall needs of children with mental retardation and other handicaps. This is expressed in professional attitudes, community planning, and Federal actions. One example would be the growing dissatisfaction (mentioned above) with simple, single-issue diagnostic terms, and the rigid and exclusive programs that result from them. Thus, instead of "the retarded child," one often now hears the terms "special child," "child in need," and "children with developmental disabilities" (as, for example, in Public Law 91–517, the Developmental Disabilities Act). The large influx of multiply handicapped children that resulted from the German measles epidemic of 1963–1964 has now forced the admission that there are significant numbers of children with combinations of major educational handicaps. New programming in this regard has stimulated the development of fresh curriculums for deaf children, particularly to allow for serious associated perceptual handicaps. And there is now finally a network of centers for the education of deaf-blind children (sponsored by Public Law 90–247), including those with general retardation as well.

Equally encouraging is the major shift that has occurred in recent years in the social attitude toward huge state residential facilities ("schools" or "hospitals") for long-term care of children with mental retardation and other handicaps. Such impersonal, custodial institutions are now widely deplored. Many special children of this sort are now being cared for at home, with backup by community-based day-care programs which have a strong educational component (and social service provisions as well). Within existing institutions, programs are being set up that emphasize small-group living. In Massachusetts, there are now 90 community clinical nurseries for handicapped children from 3 to 7 years of age, and 28 day-care programs for the 7-to-16-year age group. In October 1971, the Pennsylvania Association for Retarded Children won a vitally important court suit from the state attorney general, which conceded that there was an obligation to provide education for *all* retarded children between 6 and 21 years of age (and not just for the uncomplicated "educable" children, as had become the custom). It is expected that other states will gradually make similar concessions, although for many, extensive legal actions may be necessary.

Groups of involved parents meeting together have also been effective in bringing about the creation and reinforcement of needed programs and services. This can occur in the form of specialized local action groups of spontaneous origin, regional chapters of the established national organizations (National Association for Retarded Children, United Cerebral Palsy, and so forth), or membership of parents in local planning groups and citizen advisory panels and councils. Such groups can provide the necessary public voice, and ultimately the legislative action, to close the gap between services that are needed and those that are actually available. And for members they have offered valuable support, easing the bewilderment and sense of isolation so often felt by parents of handicapped children.

Many professionals and public officials have been appropriately jarred by the new activism, but agency leadership has often been slow to come. Much work remains to be done. Pressures need to be continued regarding the maintenance of high standards in the public programs, with joint professional and lay participation. Vocational training ("rehabilitation") is still often a hollow promise for handicapped young people, with realistic employment opportunities woefully sparse. Adequate social and residential facilities for adults with mental retardation and other handicaps are generally lacking, with a clear need existing for more community planning and assistance. And the whole area of the civil rights of handicapped citizens (marriage, property ownership, contracts, and so forth) remains broadly neglected and unclarified. It is to be hoped that as stronger services and fresh philosophies become more commonly available for families who have handicapped members, the unfinished business of providing fair treatment and fulfilling life-styles for "special" children and adults will become a reality.

See *cerebral palsy; Down's syndrome; genetics; handicapped child; hearing and speech; learning disabilities; orthopedic concerns; vision problems.*

*Marie M. Cullinane, R.N., M.S., and*
*Allen C. Crocker, M.D.*

*For further reading*

GENERAL

*Developmental Disabilities.* Booklet. Developmental Disabilities Act (P.L. 91–517). U.S. Department of Health, Education, and Welfare, Rehabilitation Services Administration, Washington, D.C. 20201.

*The Exceptional Parent.* Magazine for parents of children with any sort of handicap. Six issues per year. 20 Providence Street, Boston, Mass. 02117.

Frantzen, June. *Toys . . . The Tools of Children.* Booklet. Chicago: National Society for Crippled Children and Adults.

Suggestions for promoting the child's development through play.

Spock, Benjamin, M.D., and Lerrigo, Marion O. *Caring for Your Disabled Child.* New York: Macmillan paperback, 1966.

A guide for parents of physically or mentally handicapped children. Practical suggestions for planning education, vocational guidance, recreation, and social and sexual development.

BLIND CHILD

Lowenfeld, Berthold. *Our Blind Children: Growing and Learning with Them.* Springfield, Ill.: Charles C Thomas, 1971.

A guide for parents covering a blind child's development from birth through adolescence, including schooling and multiple-handicapped children. Extensive bibliography.

Ulrich, Sharon, with Wolf, Anna W. M. *Elizabeth.* Ann Arbor: University of Michigan Press, 1972.

First-person account of rearing a blind child. Introduction and commentary summarizing development of blind children by Selma Fraiberg and Edna Adelson.

DOWN'S SYNDROME

*Facts about Mongolism for Women over 35.* Pamphlet. Department of Health, Education, and Welfare.

Available without charge from National Institute for Child Health and Human Development, National Institutes of Health, Building 31, 2A-24, Bethesda, Md. 20014. May also be available through local office of the Association for Retarded Children.

Smith, David W., and Wilson, Ann Asper. *The Child with Down's Syndrome.* Philadelphia: W. B. Saunders Co., 1973.

## HEARING AND SPEECH HANDICAPPED CHILD

Lowell, Edgar L., and Stoner, Marguerite. *Play It by Ear!* Available from John Tracy Clinic, 806 West Adams Boulevard, Los Angeles, Calif. 90007. Auditory training games devised at the John Tracy Clinic to develop good listening habits.

Semple, Jean E. *The Hearing-Impaired Preschool Child.* Springfield, Ill.: Charles C Thomas, 1970.
Practical suggestions, with home lesson plans.

Van Riper, Charles. *Your Child's Speech Problems: A Guide for Parents.* New York: Harper and Row, 1961.
Shows how home and family can hinder or help in speech therapy.

*Volta Review.* Issued nine times a year by the Alexander Graham Bell Association, 1537 35th Street, NW, Washington, D.C. 20007.
Of interest to parents and professionals.

*When Your Child Is Deaf.* Massachusetts Parents Association for the Deaf and Hard of Hearing. P.O. Box 303, Boston, Mass. 02101.
(Similar material might be available from local parent groups.)

## RETARDED CHILD

Blodgett, Harriet E. *Mentally Retarded Children: What Parents and Others Should Know.* Minneapolis: University of Minnesota Press, 1971.
Guide for laymen about causes of retardation, testing, rearing of retarded children. Good material on school and on the welfare of the whole family.

Buckler, Beatrice. *Living with a Mentally Retarded Child: A Primer for Parents.* New York: Hawthorn Books, 1971.
Simple primer with useful appendices listing diagnostic centers and treatment facilities throughout the country.

Carlson, Bernice Wells, and Ginglend, David. *Play Activities for the Retarded Child.* Booklet. Nashville, Tenn.: Abingdon Press, 1961.
Guidance in selection of toys and play activities.

Dittman, Laura L. *The Mentally Retarded Child at Home, A Manual for Parents.* Booklet. Children's Bureau Publication, no. 374–1959. Superintendent of Documents, U.S. Government Printing Office, Washington, D.C. 20402. $1.10.
Suggestions for training the mentally retarded child in self-help skills (eating, dressing, toilet training, manners, etc.)

Doorly, Ruth K. *Our Jimmy*. Service Associates. Publishers of literature and materials in special education. Box 224, Westwood, Mass. 02090.

Written for brothers and sisters of retarded children with special emphasis on understanding and helping.

Kempton, Winifred, et al. *Love, Sex and Birth Control for the Mentally Retarded: A Guide for Parents*. Planned Parenthood Association of Southeastern Pennsylvania, 1402 Spruce Street, Philadelphia, Pa. 19102. 1971. $1.10.

Helpful and reassuring guide.

Roberts, Nancy, and Roberts, Bruce. *David*. Richmond, Va.: John Knox Press, 1968.

Parents' portrayal of the first four years in the life of their mentally handicapped son David.

*Selected Bibliography for Parents and Siblings of Mentally Retarded Individuals*. National Association for Retarded Children, 420 Lexington Avenue, New York, N.Y. 10017.

### ASSOCIATIONS

American Foundation for the Blind, 15 West 16th Street, New York, N.Y. 10011.

American Hearing Society, 817 14th Street, NW, Washington, D.C. 20005.

American Speech and Hearing Association, 1001 Connecticut Avenue, NW, Washington, D.C. 20036.

National Association for Retarded Children, 420 Lexington Avenue, New York, N.Y. 10017.

United Cerebral Palsy, 339 East 44th Street, New York, N.Y. 10016.

**Diabetes** is a disease occurring in all ages which affects some 3 million people in the United States. In about 4 percent of these the onset of the disease occurs in childhood. This type is known as *juvenile diabetes*. Its exact cause and prevention are not yet known. Many affected children have a family history of diabetes. Sometimes diabetes in an older family member develops after the onset in the child. It is generally thought that a hereditary contribution from both parents is necessary to produce an affected child.

Adults may experience either gradual or sudden onset of diabetes. Sometimes it is detected by finding sugar (glucose) in a routine urine examination. Symptoms are often precipitated by obesity, and, under these circumstances, weight control alone without insulin will control them. Diabetes is preventable in these adults in the sense that avoiding obesity will decrease the likelihood of symptoms developing in the first place. Juvenile diabetes differs from adult diabetes in that with children the symptoms almost always appear suddenly, often flagrantly so. If, as seems likely, newer treatments become available, it is also likely that testing children for very early presymptomatic diabetes will become standard. As it is now, when children are first diagnosed, they are usually already quite ill with diabetic *keto-acidosis* (see below). Unlike adults, children with diabetes are rarely obese and weight loss is not part of therapy. Almost without exception, diabetic children require treatment with insulin.

Normally, sugar moves smoothly from the blood into fat and muscle cells as needed for energy, and the level of sugar in the blood remains within a confined range. As the cells call for more sugar, *insulin*, a hormone made in the pancreas, is released to allow transport of sugar from blood to cells. As the cells' fuel needs are met, insulin output is reduced.

Sugar is stored in the liver and in muscles as a chemical compound called *glycogen*. When the blood sugar level falls as cell use increases, another hormone of the pancreas, *glucagon*, is produced. Glucagon acts on glycogen in the liver, converting it to glucose, which then enters the bloodstream. As the blood levels of sugar are restored, glucagon production is cut back.

The problem in diabetes is a lack of adequate insulin to permit passage of sugar into hungry cells. If sugar cannot get into the cells, more is passed into the bloodstream in an effort to overcome the blockage. The blood sugar level rises. The accumulation of sugar in the blood exceeds the kidney's threshold for conserving sugar and the sugar appears in the urine. The sugar passing into the urine draws along a great deal of water, resulting in frequent urination and excessive thirst. (One common symptom of diabetes is bed-wetting in an otherwise dry child.) The starvation of body cells deprived of sugar stimulates the breakdown of body fat into building blocks known as fatty acids which can be used for energy in the absence of sugar. This mobilization of fat leads to weight loss and increased appetite, both characteristic signs of diabetes. In the process of using the fatty acids, the blood becomes acid, leading to quickened deep breathing. The fatty acids are processed into *acetone* which appears in the urine along with the sugar. Without treatment the course of childhood diabetes is progressively downhill, with weight loss, dehydration, coma, and death.

This syndrome of untreated diabetes is known as diabetic keto-acidosis. When diabetic children are first diagnosed, they usually are suffering from this pattern of symptoms. Diabetics who are under treatment can experience these symptoms when their diabetes is out of control. Most newly detected juvenile diabetics are hospitalized for treatment of their first episode of keto-acidosis.

Treatment of diabetes consists of daily injections to increase blood insulin, a consistent diet without concentrated sugars but adequate to meet the child's needs for hunger and growth, appropriate exercise, and education of parents and child about how to live with this disorder. Pills to lower blood sugar have no place in treating juvenile diabetics. The family and the patient must become familiar with the testing of urine for sugar and acetone, the administration of insulin by hypodermic needle, and the adjustment of insulin dosage to keep the urine spillage of sugar and the blood sugar level within acceptable ranges. They learn how infection, exercise, and diet can change the insulin requirement. As the child grows older he or she must assume increasing responsibility for his own care. For some children attendance at a summer camp for diabetic children may aid in this maturation.

The parents' and older child's initial reaction to a diagnosis of diabetes is often one of disbelief, denial, and guilt. We frequently see signs of increased family stress evidenced by marital conflict. At The Children's Hospital Medical Center, the health care of the diabetic child and his family is the shared responsibility of the physician, nurse, and social service worker and, of course, the family itself. When needed, psychological and psychiatric consultation is arranged.

Just as there are symptoms associated with too high blood sugar reflecting insulin deficiency, excessive lowering of blood sugar by administered insulin produces symptoms of fussiness, headache, hunger, drowsiness and inattention, sweating, and coolness of the skin. The way in which hypoglycemia (low blood sugar) is expressed varies somewhat from one child to another. Each child follows his own pattern. At first, hypoglycemia leads to changes in the child's behavior. Severe and prolonged lowering of the blood sugar causes unconsciousness and coma. An injection of glucagon (see above) by the parents at home or an intravenous dose of sugar by the doctor should temporarily bring the blood sugar back to normal and allow the patient to wake up to take food. The immediate treatment for the early symptoms is simply to restore blood sugar by giving sugar-containing foods like orange juice or candy. These symptoms can also occur in nondiabetic children (see *hypoglycemia*).

The kind of hypoglycemia associated with administered insulin is known as an *insulin reaction* or *insulin shock*. Its occurrence in a diabetic child may be related to: (1) too much exercise; (2) too much insulin; (3) inadequate or missed meal; or (4) unknown factors, and may require an adjustment of insulin and diet.

In general, diabetics do not cope with **infections,** particularly bacterial infections, as well as do normal individuals. This difficulty is more apparent in adult diabetics. Infection also tends to throw the balance of diet and insulin out of control.

With rare exceptions, once children develop diabetes they have it permanently. The overall outlook for survival and for a comfortable life is problematic. The first generation of treated childhood diabetics is only now securely in the adult age group. Many adults with childhood onset of diabetes that has persisted for as long as 15 to 20 years have developed complications which include kidney disease, high blood pressure, arteriosclerosis, changes in the blood vessels of the retina, and cataracts in the lenses of the eyes.

Present-day research in diabetes is making important strides and it is hoped that a major breakthrough in prevention will occur in the near future. For more information, contact the American Diabetes Association, 600 Fifth Avenue, New York, N.Y. 10020 and Juvenile Diabetes Foundation, 23 East 26th Street, New York, N.Y. 10010.

*Diaper rash.* In our society the almost universal skin problem of babies is, of course, diaper rash. Many remedies are offered, but it is useful to remember that the less we apply to a baby's skin the better off he or she is likely to be. In primitive tropical societies where few clothes, if any, are worn by small children, diaper rash is said to be nonexistent. Indeed, the very name of the affliction would suggest this possibility, and the quickest cure for it, weather and other circumstances permitting, is to let the baby go naked, his bottom exposed at all times to the air.

Since the conventions and conditions of our society demand the diaper, the best we can do is to try to prevent and to ameliorate its rash. To that end, we admit the one exception to our objection to nonspecific ointments. We suggest zinc oxide ointment (purchasable without prescription) applied to the buttocks and anal region at diaper changes. This spreads a protective, chemically inert blanket between the baby's skin and his urine and stools. (Zinc oxide is the main ingredient of a number of commercial preparations for babies' bottoms.) The combination of 2 or 3 washings of the region every day and the application of the zinc oxide is about as far as the mother can go in defending against diaper rash. Even with the best of care, the baby can have diaper rash, and it will take at least 3 or 4 days to heal. The mother can take consolation in knowing that diaper rash happens to almost all babies and is not a reflection on the quality of her care. With a marked rash which does not respond to treatment, or perhaps as a first step, leave the diapers off altogether. Healing, as we have said, is then predictable.

The rough redness of the skin in diaper rash is easy to recognize and there may be scattered pimples. If the pimples becomes pustules (that is, show whiteheads) or if the rash becomes quite angry looking, you should call the doctor. A medicated cream may be needed.

Rubber pants, because they hold in heat and shut out air, undoubtedly aggravate rashes, but most mothers use them to save on laundry. It probably is wise to avoid using rubber pants in the first 3 or 4 weeks of life. If the infant's skin is particularly susceptible to rash, use such pants only when absolutely necessary. If you are washing your own diapers, be sure to rinse out the soap and softener thoroughly. An extra rinse cycle may be necessary.

How hard you work to prevent diaper rash can be individualized according to the baby's skin. Some infants require only the barest essentials of hygiene, while others require every trick in the book. Few infants escape with entirely rash-free skins.

See *rash.*

*Diaphragmatic hernia.* Occasionally, the *diaphragms,* which are the two thin sheets of muscle separating the chest cavity from the abdominal cavity, fail to form completely in embryological life, and a child is born with the quite rare congenital defect known as diaphragmatic hernia. An opening is left in the diaphragm through which the contents of the abdominal cavity (stomach, intestines, and so forth) can intrude into the chest (thoracic) cavity.

The abdominal contents pushing up into the thoracic cavity may thrust the heart and great blood vessels to one side and compress the lung. The understandable result will be severe difficulty in breathing. A second problem is the kinking of the intruding intestine with resulting obstruction and perhaps strangulation of a segment of the gastrointestinal tract. (See *intussusception* and *intestinal obstruction.*) In the most severe forms, diaphragmatic hernia becomes a medical (and surgical) emergency in the newborn nursery. Even in the best circumstances of early recognition and good surgical technique, many babies with severe diaphragmatic hernia die. In less severe cases there may be no symptom, and the hernia may not be detected for several years. Fortunately, diaphragmatic hernia is very rare.

*Diarrhea* is the medical term for liquid stools. The color of diarrheal stools may vary from light brown to green. Sometimes, the stools are mainly liquid or mushy but of normal yellow or brown color. Flecks of blood, mucus, or partially digested food may appear in the movement. This definition of diarrhea does not apply necessarily to the movements of young infants, whose stools may vary considerably in consistency and still not be abnormal. The size of a diarrheal stool can also vary considerably, from less to more than the amount of fecal material contained in a normal stool. In children with diapers, the diarrheal stool may run out around the edges of the diaper.

Diarrhea is a symptom with many causes. Sometimes loose stools are related to changes in the diet. Loose stools are quite often seen with the common cold (see *colds*). Milk intolerance due to lactose deficiency is being recognized increasingly as a cause of recurrent diarrhea and cramps. See discussion later in this section. Most diarrhea results from infections of the intestines, *gastroenteritis.* The inflamed and irritated intestine is less able to absorb food and liquids. It leaks fluid (mainly salt and water), is overactive, and tends to pass its contents through and out of the body more rapidly than normal. The following discussion applies mainly to this type of diarrhea. Less common, prolonged diarrheas requiring special study and treatment are taken up elsewhere (see *cystic fibrosis* and *celiac disease*). A less serious type which requires little or no treatment is *chronic nonspecific diarrhea,* discussed later in this chapter.

In the generally sanitary conditions of the United States, infections of the stomach and intestines with viruses or with agents presumed to be viruses are the cause of most diarrhea. Some viruses characteristically attack the stomach and intestines, while others may also cause colds and sore throats (see *throat, sore*) and their complications. In a given family, the same virus may cause a cold in a father and diarrhea and *vomiting,* with or without a cold, in a toddler.

Bacteria can also cause diarrhea. *Salmonella* and *Shigella* are among the more common types. These can be transmitted from humans and, in the case of Salmonella, from animals as well (see *pets and children*). Salmonella and Shigella infections cause diarrhea and *fever.* Sometimes the bacteria spread beyond the intestine to invade the blood and are carried elsewhere in the body (see *bloodstream infection*). An uncommon cause of diarrhea in this country, which is quite prevalent in the tropics, is infection with amoebae, producing *amoebic dysentery.*

At the present time, there is no drug proven effective against most viruses. Antibiotics not only do not help, but may make matters worse. Antibiotics are called for only in the small percentage of children who have diarrhea from bacterial or amoebic dysentery. When the doctor is suspicious about a bacterial infection, he may culture the stools.

Because there is no cure for viruses and hence for most cases of diarrhea, doctors concern themselves mainly with treating the effects of the diarrhea rather than the ailment itself, trying to maintain the child's general condition to give the natural recuperative mechanism a chance to work. Parents and doctors tend to have a somewhat different view of this problem. Parents are usually most concerned with the frequency and appearance of movements and want to give the child something to "bind" his or her bowels. Doctors, although no less eager to cure the diarrhea, are aware that in the vast majority of cases they can do little about the diarrhea directly, but can prevent and, when necessary, treat its harmful consequences.

Most diarrheal infections of children improve after 3 to 5 days, within the usual range expected of infections. The inflammation of the intestine may take a number of days more to settle down, and the intestine often continues to function improperly even after the infection itself has gone. This is somewhat like the aching of a bruised shoulder muscle, in which pain and stiffness endure long after the blow that caused it. Because of this delayed healing process, the diarrhea may go on another 5 to 7 days, making the total illness about 10 days.

Diarrhea itself is mainly a nuisance and a mess. It may cause some tenderness of the skin of the buttocks and sometimes a rash in this area (see **diaper rash**). Otherwise the loose stools as such do no harm. The harmful effects of diarrhea are almost entirely a result of excessive loss of water and salt from the body, which can sometimes be severe enough to bring about *dehydration*.

A dehydrated child is listless, inactive, and lethargic, and disinclined to drink anything. These symptoms, to be sure, are present to some extent in many illnesses, but we are talking here of extreme degrees. The child's mouth will be dry, and his eyes sunken. If he cries, he will produce less than the usual amount of tears. Urination will be infrequent. The child will lose weight. Severe dehydration can lead to **shock** and if untreated can be fatal. If you even suspect dehydration, you should call the doctor. Before a child becomes dehydrated there is a warning period when the loss of fluid is excessive in relation to the intake of fluid. This signal should alert you to seek medical help. Your doctor will be able to take the necessary steps to correct this condition.

Preventing dehydration, then, is a major purpose of the recommended treatment. It is important to keep this goal in mind. We urge parents to worry less about the appearance of the stools (about which little can be done) and more about the possible effects of the diarrhea on the child. Diarrhea in and of itself has never harmed a child, but excessive loss of fluids and salt has caused some children real difficulty.

The younger the child, the greater the threat of diarrhea harming him. Infants have a far greater turnover of water each day than do older children. They must drink more per pound of body weight to meet their needs, and their "reserve" during water deprivation or loss is much less. While the vast majority of infants and young children will encounter no problems during episodes of diarrhea and vomiting (a common associated symptom), an occasional child, even with the best of care, will slip over into a state of dehydration. Fortunately, these days, dehydration is manageable by giving the child what he needs—water and salt—by intravenous infusion, that is, directly into his bloodstream. For the child too ill to take fluids by mouth, or whose vomiting brings them back up again, intravenous feeding is the answer. Its availability should be a source of reassurance to parents, just as it is to physicians.

Medicines like kaolin-pectin mixtures are commonly used to "bind" the intestine and stop the diarrhea. For children over 6 these are all right, in general, but for younger children and babies, we suggest that you consult your doctor or nurse first. Binding medicines do just what the name implies. They tend to keep the stool within the intestine and to decrease the frequency of movements, but they do not prevent the production of liquid stools or shorten the course of the illness, both of which depend mainly on healing of the infection. The diarrhea, in a sense, continues, but is less conspicuous. In respect to the loss of body fluids and salt, which is the greatest concern, it makes no difference whether the diarrheal stool is contained within the intestine or passed to the outside. The drain of fluids and salt from the body itself continues. Thus it is possible for a child to become dehydrated even though the diarrheal stools are not being expelled.

The frequency of passage of diarrheal stools is actually an important indicator in judging whether or not dehydration is developing. Reducing the frequency of stools but not the total quantity may mask the severity of the diarrheal infection and lull parent and doctor into a false sense of security. We prefer not to give infants and toddlers binding medicines, even though more frequent movements may result. Keep in mind that the main goal is to try to prevent dehydration and to recognize it early if it develops.

If your child has diarrhea it may be helpful to keep a written record of the appearance of the stools and the times of passage. Note what kinds and amounts of fluid your child drinks, and the hours at which he takes them. Write down temperature readings. (See Part 1, Chapter 5: "Caring for the Sick Child at Home.") If you have a scale, weigh the child (if he is under 3 years) as soon as you can after the diarrhea has set in and enter the weight in your record. The doctor may want subsequent weighings. Weight change will be important to him when he assesses the child's state of hydration.

With these facts in hand, should you need to call your nurse or doctor, they will find it much easier to decide whether the child should be brought in for a check. Suppose that the diarrhea began at 4 A.M. and you talked with the doctor at 11 A.M. You can help by reporting, for instance, that your child passed loose green stools at 4 A.M., 6:30 A.M., and 10 A.M., had three ounces of water to drink at 4:30 A.M., and that his temperature was 102°.

Diet is very important. In setting the diet, the prime goal is to replenish the water and salt loss from the body in the frequent stools. Fluids come first, above all other foods. Indeed, even if a child ate no meat, vegetables, or other solid foods over the several days of an attack of diarrhea, he would not be harmed if his fluid intake kept up with the depletion of fluids and salt through his stools and urine.

We measure the amount of liquids in the diet according to the severity of the diarrhea. The more severe the diarrhea, the more liquid should be in the diet. When the child is having frequent loose stools, we recommend giving him liquids only. When the diarrhea begins to improve (or if it never was very severe), soft solids can be offered. When the diarrhea has abated completely, the child can return to his regular diet. As the stools become more solid, more solids can be added to the diet.

Simple clear fluids are recommended: sugar water, made with 2½ level *table*spoons sugar per quart of water with a *pinch* of salt added (not more than one-half *tea*spoon per quart of water—be sure not to make the dangerous mistake of reversing the sugar and salt measurements); tea with sugar; diluted and dissolved gelatin; flat ginger ale or root beer. The carbonated drinks (ginger ale or root beer) will be tolerated better if you stir them to remove the gas bubbles. Note that milk is excluded from this list. Whole milk is best avoided if diarrhea is present. Skimmed (fat-free) milk has a place, however, provided it is not boiled, lest you boil off the water and leave too concentrated a solution of salt behind. Also, do not boil water after salt has been added. If you must boil the water, do so prior to measuring it and adding salt. This caution against boiling is to prevent the liquid from becoming too concentrated. Water is lost in boiling but salt is not. Whereas some salt is helpful, extra amounts may be quite harmful.

A sick child will get along better if you give him fluids a little at a time—but frequently—than he will if you try to get him to drink a lot at once. Children with diarrhea are prone to vomit. While they can tolerate small amounts of fluid, too much at one time may exceed their capacity and cause them to vomit everything that has been taken. (See *vomiting*.)

General guidelines can be set for fluid intake at different age levels: for infants, 2 ounces every hour (12 ounces per 6-hour period); for preschool children, 4 ounces every hour (24 ounces per 6-hour period); for school-age children, 5 ounces every hour (30 ounces per 6-hour period).

If your child takes the amount appropriate to his age, or close to that amount, he is not likely to have difficulty. If he still seems thirsty, you can safely give him half again as much, but be careful not to "push" him to the point of vomiting. Offer your child the fluids once an hour when he is awake. There is no need to rouse him out of a sleep to keep to the schedule. Often a sick child will not take as much fluid as our guideline recommends. Our figures are the *upper* limits of the amounts he should have. We do not expect that every child will want to or be able to drink the exact recommended amount every hour on the hour. Try every hour but think in terms of amounts over 6-hour periods. Not every child will be able to replace all the fluids he has lost. Children can tolerate mild fluid deficiency.

Here are some general suggestions for the care of diarrhea in young children over 6 months:

If, in addition to frequent passage of loose stools, your child is vomiting or has a temperature over 102.5° for more than 4 hours or is uncharacteristically confused, listless, or lethargic, get in touch with your doctor as soon as you can. (See *drowsiness, delirium, and lethargy.*) Vomiting is a common beginning to virus infections of the stomach and intestines. The vomiting may last 6 to 18 hours, giving way to diarrhea later on.

If the stools contain blood, call the doctor.

If the fluid intake recommended falls below one-half of the suggested amount per 6 hours, let your doctor know.

If the temperature is under 102.5° and only a small degree of lethargy, drowsiness, and sickish behavior accompanies the diarrhea, and if there is no vomiting, we normally proceed according to the following general plan:

1. Unless stools follow rapidly one after another, you can almost always wait safely for 2 to 3 hours to call the doctor. Observe the child's condition carefully. After 2 or 3 hours you should have a clear picture of his condition.

2. If the diarrheal stools occur no more often than twice in 24 hours, keep up the regular diet, including milk. Call the doctor if the stools are still loose after 36 hours.

3. If the diarrheal stools are passed as often as once every 4 hours, switch your child to a soft diet and give him clear liquids in the amounts set in our guidelines. The soft diet consists of bland carbohydrates: rice, oatmeal, crackers, arrowroot cookies, gelatin, mashed banana, apple pulp, sherbet, and so forth. Stop whole milk and offer skimmed milk (unboiled). If no improvement is apparent under this regimen in 24 hours, call the doctor.

4. If the diarrhea is occurring once every 2 to 3 hours, stop regular foods, give clear liquids in the recommended amounts and soft solids. Stop milk (including skimmed milk) altogether. Call the doctor if your child continues to pass stools at the same frequency for 8 hours.

5. If the diarrhea is occurring as frequently as once an hour, stop regular food and give clear fluids only, in the recommended amounts. Stop all milk. If the bowel movements continue at the same rate for 4 hours, call the doctor.

6. If the stools are passed more often than once an hour for 2 to 3 hours, stop regular food, give clear liquids in the recommended amounts, stop all milk, and call the doctor.

7. If there is a change in the frequency of the bowel movements,

either up or down, adjust the diet accordingly and use the new conditions in determining how soon to call the doctor. For example, if after loose stools an hour apart, your child has no movement for 3 hours, you can change from clear fluids alone to solids plus clear fluids. Or, if loose stools have been appearing every 4 or 5 hours through the day and then begin coming every hour, you should drop the soft solids and give clear liquids alone. As the diarrhea improves (that is, fewer and more solid stools), move toward a more solid diet, adding whole milk, meat, vegetables, and fruits back in that order.

8. The virus or bacteria causing diarrhea are contagious. Finger-to-mouth spread can occur and careful handwashing by child and parent seems to be a simple and worthwhile precaution. Since virus is often shed into the air as well as the stools, these measures will not always prevent spread of viral infections. There is no need to keep the child in bed. He can play quietly about the house. Follow the usual suggestions about activity and dress for an ill child (see Part 1, Chapter 5: "Caring for the Sick Child at Home"). If the skin around the buttocks is irritated, wash with water and apply a mild ointment like Vaseline. When the crampiness and inconveniently frequent stools have ceased, fever is gone, and the child looks and acts well again, he may resume normal activities and resume contact with playmates.

9. Unless the doctor has specifically given his assent, it is best not to administer "binding" medicines to a child under 6. For the child over 6 it is all right to use the medicines, provided your observe the guidelines about calling the doctor.

10. The *abdominal pain* that usually accompanies diarrhea is the crampy, intermittent kind—that is, it comes and goes, rarely lasting more than 5 minutes. Often a cramp precedes a stool. Between the cramps, the child should be free of pain. Your doctor may prescribe a medicine for the cramps, particularly for the older child in whom the sedative side effects of antispasm drugs are less likely to confuse the diagnosis of this condition. If the pain should persist for more than half an hour or become severe enough to make your child cry or to immobilize him, call the doctor at once. Have the child rest and apply a heating pad or hot-water bottle to his abdomen. *Do not* give medicines —even aspirin—or enemas.

In the above guidelines, we have talked mainly of the frequency of passage of stools and have largely ignored the question of size, consistency, and color. Frequency of stools is the most important point to watch with respect to determining how severe or mild an attack is. If the volume passed is really excessive (more than 3 times the usual volume of a stool), more caution is in order and the doctor should be called earlier than suggested in the stated guidelines. Color of the stools is a less important consideration.

For a discussion of bacteria, virus, antibiotics, subclinical illness, and culture, see *infections*.

See also *blood in the stools, celiac disease.*

### CHRONIC NONSPECIFIC DIARRHEA OF CHILDHOOD

There are a number of children, usually between the ages of 1½ and 3½ years, who have many loose stools off and on, or continuously, for months to years. The movements often contain undigested vegetable fibers and mucus. Characteristically, most of the stools are passed during the morning hours. These children, despite their diarrhea, *do very well*; they grow and develop normally and have no signs of malnutrition. At most, their stools are a nuisance, and they may have irritated buttocks at times.

There is no known cause for this diarrhea. It appears that the families of these children are more prone to intestinal malfunction in general, intermittent *constipation* and/or diarrhea.

It is characteristic of this disorder that medicines that "bind" the stools and changes in diet have essentially no effect. There is no known treatment for chronic nonspecific diarrhea. Fortunately, the outlook is uniformly excellent. Stools of normal consistency usually reappear by about age 3½.

After we have made this diagnosis, we tell the parents to pay attention to the child, not to the stools. The loose stools may worsen or, if gone for a while, reappear with colds or teething. Above all, parents should be reassured that their child is normal and that the stools have no special significance. Patience is called for.

As we said above, inability to digest lactose, the common sugar in milk, has been identified as a frequent cause of recurrent diarrhea. The absorption of this sugar from the intestine depends upon the enzyme lactase in its lining. While all infants have adequate quantities of this enzyme (when milk is the basic food), older children and adults of certain ethnic groups, including blacks, Orientals, American Indians, Mexican Americans, Arabs, and Ashkenazic Jews, do not. All together it has been estimated that about 33 million people in the United States are lactose intolerant.

In these individuals, lactose can cause gas, indigestion, diarrhea, bloating and/or vague abdominal pain. The only treatment is limiting the intake of milk products to a tolerable level.

*Diphtheria* is a serious infection manifested by severe sore throat, fever, runny nose, and headache. Common and serious complications are temporary paralysis of muscles, heart failure, obstruction of the airway, and *pneumonia.* There is a high incidence of death in untreated or late treated cases.

The diphtheria bacteria produce a powerful chemical toxin (poison) which destroys surrounding tissues, thereby making it easier for the bacteria to spread and multiply. Toxin also enters the blood and is carried to distant body parts where it affects nerves and heart muscles, accounting for the weakness, paralysis, and heart failure which can occur. A thick coating composed of bacteria, white blood cells, and dead tissue adheres to the throat and may extend up into the nose or down into the voice box (larynx) or below to the airway (trachea), causing difficulty in breathing and loss of voice. Diphtheria may also infect the skin, so-called *cutaneous diphtheria.* Its effect on heart and nerves is similar regardless of the site of infection.

Cases vary in intensity from mild, with complete recovery, to severe, resulting in death. With modern treatment, most of the patients who are caught early enough recover completely. As with most other infectious diseases, there are individuals who develop subclinical infections too mild even to cause symptoms, and there are carriers, people who harbor the organisms for long periods of time without having trouble themselves but meanwhile spreading it to others. Immunity following recovery from diphtheria infection is not complete and reinfection can occur.

Treatment for clinical infections involves antibiotics to kill the multiplying bacteria and antibodies to the toxin (also called an antitoxin). In addition to these mainstays of treatment, good care is essential.

Diphtheria **immunization** is directed against the toxin, not the bacteria themselves. The toxin produced by diphtheria organisms grown in a test tube is altered in the laboratory so that it is no longer dangerous, but when injected can still stimulate antibodies to the true toxin. This modified toxin is known as a toxoid. Diphtheria toxoid is the D part of the DPT injection. Boosters of diphtheria toxoid are necessary to maintain immunity. These are usually given along with tetanus toxoid as the DT of the immunization schedule.

Diphtheria is a preventable disease. Outbreaks which, sad to say, still occur, even in the United States, are related to lack of immunization and to poverty with its associated crowding and poor sanitation.

For a discussion of subclinical infections, carriers, bacteria, antibiotics, and antibodies, see **infections.**

*Dislocated hip:* see **hip, congenital dislocation of.**

*Dislocation:* see **fracture.**

*Dizziness* is a common complaint of children. It rarely occurs alone. Accompanying symptoms like *earache, fever, headache, head injuries,* or *vomiting* will give you a clue to the cause and the course of action indicated. If dizziness is the only complaint, the child can be observed for 24 hours prior to seeking medical help. If it persists, then contact your doctor or nurse. If dizziness is associated with staggering or unsteadiness, lack of coordination, buzzing in the ears, or refusal to get out of bed, it should be reported promptly.

*Dog bites:* see *bites, animal.*

*Down's syndrome,* also known as *Mongolism,* is a common cause of mental retardation and is caused by a genetic abnormality of chromosomes whereby an extra chromosome is present in the cells of the body. (See *genetics.*) The term Mongolism (the old name for the disorder) refers to the superficial facial resemblance of affected individuals to Asians and reflects a certain racial bias of Caucasians in naming a disease after the appearance of over one-half of the world's population.

Down's syndrome occurs in about 3 births per 2000 and accounts for approximately 10 percent of the retardates in institutions. Physical as well as mental growth is retarded. The degree of retardation varies. Characteristic physical findings include a small head flattened in front and back, a lateral upward slope of the eyes, small ears, small jaw and mouth, protruding tongue, short flat nose, delayed eruption of teeth, and a short broad neck. A characteristic line in the palm of the hand is known as a *simian crease.* In the infant and young child *hypotonia* (looseness and laxity of muscles) and potbelly are prominent. The hands and feet tend to be flat, broad, and square. Heart defects are relatively common, and the occurrence of leukemia, for reasons not yet understood, is 10 to 20 times greater than in the general population.

In certain cases, Down's syndrome is associated with other birth defects or conditions which, if left untreated, would cause the newborn baby's death. Some parents, faced with this situation, have requested that treatment be withheld. The legal and ethical implications in these cases are currently the subject of considerable discussion.

There are 2 high-risk groups of families: (1) those in which the mother is nearing the end of her reproductive ability, particularly one over 40 in whose pregnancy there is an increased risk of a chromosomal abnormality known as *nondisjunction* and (2) families in which a parent is a carrier of the relatively rare form of hereditary Down's syndrome. Pregnancies in both groups should be monitored with an amniocentesis and chromosome analysis of fetal cells in the first trimester of pregnancy to determine whether the infant is affected. The potential carrier mother or father is identified either by having produced a child with Down's syndrome or by being a close relative of a parent who is a known carrier, identified through having produced an affected child. Both circumstances should prompt the prospective parents to have a chromosome analysis to determine whether or not they are carriers. See discussion of amniocentesis and therapeutic abortion under *genetics.*

There is no cure for Down's syndrome at this time. The question of institutionalization usually arises as the child reaches school age. Difficult problems also arise with adolescence, and again when the parents of a non-self-supporting retarded person living at home become sick or die. This issue is handled differently by different families. There is no clear answer about whether or when to institutionalize the child. Families must make this decision themselves, aided by the professionals working with them. Discussion with other affected families through parents' groups is both supportive and very informative. Parents who choose to care for the child at home will find that helpful programs, such as special preschool and school programs, homemaker servives, and summer camps, are becoming more available. Halfway arrangements are finding great popularity. Parents are now given a wider latitude of choice and need not think only in terms of home care versus institutionalization.

See *birth defects, severe; developmental disabilities; genetics.*

For information on local associations write to National Mongoloid Council, P.O. Box 140, Park Ridge, Ill. 60068 or the National Association for Retarded Children, 420 Lexington Avenue, New York, N.Y. 10017.

*Drowsiness, delirium, and lethargy.* Children whose mental alertness changes or becomes noticeably depressed should be brought to the attention of a physician or nurse. The child who is "out of contact," "not with it," who claims to see or hear imaginary sights or sounds, who is "high," hyperactive, and wild, or who lapses into a stuporous sleep needs assessment. In delirium, characteristically, the mental state of the child fluctuates, with alternating periods of normal and impaired alertness. Delirium does not mean mere sleepiness or fatigue which accompany many illnesses but a disordered state of thinking. The distinction is not easy to make. When any doubt exists it is always better to seek medical attention.

There are many causes for these disorders of alertness. When they are associated with *fever, infections* are high on the list. Any infection or fever can cause delirium, but some like *meningitis* are notorious. *Head injuries* can cause delirium. Accidental poisoning (See Part 2, Chapter 10: "Poisoning") with many different drugs and other chemicals is another common cause. Some drugs, even when taken as prescribed over several days or in doses too large for the needs of the specific individual, may lead to drowsiness and delirium. Antihistamines (see *allergy*), given plain or in combination with *cough* mixtures, and antinausea medications (see *vomiting*) are good examples. *Aminophylline,* a drug commonly used in treating *asthma,* is another. Plants can be toxic. All parts of the common Jimsonweed, also known as Jamestown weed, thorn apple, stinkweed, or Datura contain belladonna compounds which, when taken in any quantity, can lead to delirium, flushed skin, slowed pulse, high temperature, dryness of mouth, dilation of the pupils, and convulsions (see *seizure disorders*). A very common cause of delirium today is the psychoactive drugs both legal and illegal taken to produce a "high." Alcohol also falls into this latter group. (See *drug problem.*)

The point has often been made in first-aid manuals that people with altered states of consciousness should not be given anything by mouth. The purpose in this warning is to prevent choking on the solid or liquid. It is a good rule to follow.

The care of the delirious child depends on the cause. For example, antibiotics are given for meningitis, and fever control measures are taken for high temperatures. (See section on fever control in Part 1, Chapter 5: "Caring for the Sick Child at Home.") For the delirium itself there is usually no treatment. Delirium is only a symptom. In itself it does no direct harm.

*Drug problem.* Drugs have become a major issue throughout the United States. A recent study of tenth, eleventh, and twelfth graders in Monroe County (Rochester), New York, gives an indication of the magnitude of drug use. Eighty-five percent of these students used alcohol, making it the most commonly used drug; 27 percent had used marijuana; 8.6 percent, LSD; and 2.6 percent, heroin. A survey on Long Island, New York, showed similar findings and also indicated that students regarded cigarettes (see *smoking*) more dangerous to their health than marijuana. (Interestingly, even though 45 percent reported this attitude toward cigarettes, 43 percent said they were "very likely" or "likely" to use them in the future.)

We encourage parents to inform themselves and to take an interest *now* in treatment and prevention programs in their own communities, regardless of the age of their children or their use of drugs. Some basic facts about drugs, their symptoms, and their street names are listed at the end of this chapter. Both the type of illegal drugs used and the slang terms for them change constantly, so parents would do well to inform themselves as much as possible. There are many excellent books about drugs, including: *Drugs and Youth* by Robert Coles and Joseph Brenner (New York: Liveright, 1971); *Understanding Drug Use* by Peter Marin and Allen Cohen (New York: Harper & Row, 1971); and *Marihuana Reconsidered* by Lester Grinspoon (Cambridge, Mass.: Harvard University Press, 1971).

Rather than lumping drugs together, each one should be considered separately. Marijuana is a drug about which there is a great deal of controversy—legal, medical, and otherwise. Some consensus should develop in the next several years. At the time of this writing our attitude at The Children's Hospital Medical Center is that, if the hazards of marijuana are thoroughly investigated and publicized, it should be legalized. At the very least, penalties for its use should be reduced. In our way of thinking it falls more into the category of alcohol; that is, it is a question of how it is used rather than whether it is used. If marijuana disrupts the child's or teen-ager's life or if he or she is dependent on it to function, then help is needed. Certainly teen-agers should know the penalties for use of this drug. Until these are removed, we would not sanction its use. Depressants like secobarbital, and stimulants, such as amphetamines, used as intoxicants can be extremely dangerous and disruptive to a child's or teen-ager's life. LSD, mescaline, and other psychedelics are clearly dangerous drugs in terms of their direct, acute effects and the disturbed behavior that can be related to their use. Heroin and other opiates are strongly addictive; a habit can be formed after only a small number of doses.

In addition to becoming knowledgeable about drugs and community resources for treatment, and keeping the all-important lines of communication with children open, what can a parent do upon finding that his or her child is using drugs or alcohol? There is no simple answer to this question. Drug use is somewhat different from other topics discussed in this guide, like sore throat, headache, or painful urination. Perhaps the best advice is not to panic. In itself there is nothing necessarily terrible about using drugs. The end of the world is not in sight. The question to be asked and answered is what purposes do the drugs or alcohol serve in the child's life? Which drugs are involved? Are they being used as an experiment, the way many children sneak a cigarette behind their parents' backs, or is it a symptom of a disturbed life? Drug use must be understood in the context of the child's life: peer group pressure, family security and emotional stability, economic pressures, and the general drug scene which is impossible to escape.

Parents may not be able to answer the above questions because of a block in communication with their child. Under this circumstance the best suggestion is to put the child in contact with someone with whom he can relate and who has some knowledge about children and drugs. The person may be a trusted relative, a teacher, a minister, a camp counselor, a youth worker, the parent of a friend, or a doctor. Some readers of this book may be asked to perform this function for the children of a friend. If it looks as though the child needs professional help, and not all children do, it will first be important for him to trust someone enough to allow a successful referral to be made.

How drug problems will be handled varies from one community to another and is closely related to the quality of a community's concern for the needs of its children. Are there ample educational and recreational facilities? Are there ways for young people to play and express their artistic feelings in the community? For many children, the trusted person to whom they may turn simply does not exist. All too often we meet young people who have no close relationships with an adult, any adult. Ponder this point for a moment. How many readers of this book are performing an active role for children in their own communities? How much of our time is invested in youth? How many of us talk to our friends and neighbors about these issues in a preventive way? Certainly experts on drugs play an important role but the first place to look is at ourselves. The best time for children to cultivate friendships with adults is before problems with drugs and alcohol develop. These relationships may not only prove helpful when difficulty arises, but may actually prevent problems in the first place.

The efficacy of antidrug programs in schools is unclear. Drug-abuse education has itself become a major industry. Yet some studies show that the more children are told about drugs, the more likely they are to use them. Simply giving accurate information (which is regrettably not the case in many of the programs) is not enough. What is more to the point is greater attention by schools to the psychological as well as to the intellectual needs of children. The apparent failure of drug-abuse education is, as we see it, a symptom of a general unresponsiveness or insensitivity of schools to adolescent concerns like love, sex, self-doubt, loneliness, belonging, and self-esteem. The culture of the school, not drugs, should be the primary focus. Imaginative approaches include the provision of "sanctuaries" from the normal school environment, alternative "schools without walls," participation by ex-addicts and other "nonprofessionals" in the drug-abuse programs, and giving students the primary responsibility for running programs. More effective drug-abuse programs could, in turn, become a force for better schools.

No family should feel helpless in dealing with drugs and alcohol in their own households. Yet, the drug and alcohol problem is clearly bigger than any family. Much more research is needed. The broader picture is also important and worth thinking about.

Illegal drug use is only part of the problem. Consider legal drug use. Americans spend 2.6 billion dollars each year on over-the-counter preparations—headache pills, vitamin pills, cold remedies, and tonics.

Americans spend 4 billion dollars annually for drug prescriptions. Twenty-eight percent of those prescriptions are for "mood drugs"— tranquilizers, stimulants, and sedatives. In one California county, 37 percent of the adults received at least one prescription for a mood drug during the course of one year and 46 percent had taken either a prescribed or over-the-counter preparation. In 1971 the reported legal production of amphetamines (pep pills or speed), much of which was diverted into illegal channels, had risen to over 12 billion tablets per year, enough for each American adult and child to take 1 tablet a day for two months. Current medical opinion holds that less than 1 percent of this total production is medically indicated. Valid uses of stimulants are for the *hyperkinetic syndrome* in children (see **learning disabilities**) and for the rare condition of inability to stay awake known as *narcolepsy*. Many people become habituated to the use of these drugs when used for appetite suppression (see **weight problems**). Studies show that 1 of every 5 adults admits to long-term or habitual use of amphetamines.

What about tranquilizers, sleeping pills, "nervous tension" preparations, or antidepressants? While there are many valid reasons for prescribing these mood-altering drugs, a good proportion of the huge consumption is both unjustified and potentially harmful. These drugs, like all drugs, have undesirable side effects, to a greater or lesser degree. For an important clue to understanding how these drugs have come to be misused, we should look critically at the advertisements directed to the public and those which appear in medical journals for doctors. They are strikingly similar. Both encourage dealing with stress by taking pills. The pharmaceutical companies, which spend over 1 billion advertising dollars per year, have increased sales in part by promoting the value of drugs as cures for the problems of daily living. It is estimated that nationwide there are 6.2 billion TV advertising connections between children and drugs each year. Trouble sleeping or staying awake? Too little pep? Take a pill. A recent ad for tranquilizers in the medical journals urged doctors to prescribe for "environmental depression . . . engendered by such problems as the constant assault of noise on the eardrums, frustrations from situations out of control, ecologic pollution and social unrest." Many of the tense scenes portrayed in the ads for both the public and the doctor reflect major social issues in America, like the isolation and loneliness of suburban life, the absentee father, the forced and early retirement of intellectually and physically vigorous workers, the rejection of the aged, the frequency of moving.

Advertisements, whether to the physician or to the public, are often disparaging to women, who are portrayed in boring or nerve-wracking household settings. The pill helps them adjust. Don't lose your temper, be subservient to men, and take an iron tonic or vitamin to help you keep up the front. Even the liberated woman, according to these ads, needs a special pill to help her succeed outside of her home. In this sense we might say that drugs are used to keep women "in their place."

Under the right circumstances such drugs can be a boon. We do not condemn their use. But in many cases there is little evidence that particular drugs actually help the symptoms for which the drug companies urge their use, and many ads have been frankly misleading and inaccurate. Proven side effects are in minuscule print, while claims for tranquility and relief are big and bold.

There is a widespread public attitude that unless the doctor prescribes and the patient leaves the office with a small bottle of magic, the physician has not done his job. This expectation is closely related to our tendency to take or give a pill for any ache or pain. The public does not or prefers not to understand that there are many ways to deal with emotional symptoms besides drugs. Families under emotional stress should try airing their concerns with an interested professional. This may take the form of family counseling, marriage counseling, child guidance, or individual psychotherapy. (See Part 1, Chapter 1: "Quality in Pediatric Care" and Chapter 4: "Complaints with an Emotional Element.") At the very least, when drugs are prescribed, these modes of treatment should also be considered. True, these alternatives may seem expensive or be in short supply (even unavailable), and patients may be unwilling or unable to pay for them. Yet the medical profession has not educated the public to see that they are being penny wise and pound foolish. It would almost seem as if the doctor and patient have a "gentlemen's agreement" not to level with each other.

Drugs may mask not only the personal problems of the patient but also the ills of society. They keep the emotional lid on social injustices which demand not tranquilization but responsible citizenship. For example, one easy way to deal with the elderly is to tranquilize them rather than to examine the stresses of forced retirement, boredom, family's rejection, and lack of rehabilitation programs, and to try to do something about them. While some drugs are useful for hyperactive children, they should not be used, as is the temptation because of their cheapness, for behavior difficulties stemming from poor schools, overcrowding, and hunger. We may be backing our way into Orwell's depiction of systemized thought control by "1984" if we continue our emphasis on using impersonal "easy" technical solutions to human distress. Drugs can be viewed as lubricants for the human gears of our technology.

In the long run it is probably less costly to deal with the problems giving rise to the symptoms. We must begin to apply human considerations once again to social change. We must attend to many pressing, neglected, and serious problems afflicting our society. While better treatment programs for addicts are important and desirable, they evade the basic issues and without social reform are doomed to fail. Legally pre-scribed sedatives, tranquilizers, and amphetamines and legal use of alcohol can be viewed as part of a number of broad social problems of which the illegal drug market is only one symptom.

## TYPES OF DRUGS AND MOST COMMON TERMS*

### THE OPIATES

When most people refer to "narcotics," this group of drugs is what they are talking about. Opiates are used medically as pain-killers. On the street they cause pain for the user and society in general.

*Addiction.* Physical dependence on a drug, so that when the drug is taken repeatedly, and stopped suddenly, physical withdrawal occurs.

*Bag.* Packet of drugs, or a single dose of an opiate. Amount of the drug in the bag is denoted by price, a nickel bag ($5), a dime bag ($10).

*"Cold Turkey."* Describes the withdrawal that occurs after repeated opiate use. The addict can become irritable, fidgety; perspiration in-creases; there is a lack of appetite. The main problem in discontinu-ing opiate use is not *getting* off the drug, it is *staying* off.

*Fix.* One injection of opiates, usually heroin.

*Heroin.* This strongly addictive drug is prepared from morphine. Out-lawed even from medical use, heroin is the most commonly used drug among addicts. It can be sniffed, injected under the skin or into a vein. Street slang for heroin includes "scag," "smack," "H," or "junk."

*"Hit."* Street slang for an injection of drugs.

*Junk.* Heroin, so named because it is never pure when sold on the street.

*Junkie.* An opiate addict.

*Mainline.* Or "to shoot up"—injecting a drug into a vein.

*Morphine.* It is extracted from opium. It is one of the strongest medically used pain-killers, and is strongly addictive.

*"On the Nod."* Or nodding. The state produced by opiates. Like being suspended on the edge of sleep.

*Opium.* A white powder from the unripe seeds of the poppy plant. Opium can be eaten, but it is usually smoked in an opium pipe.

---

*Reprinted with the kind permission of the *Boston Globe*. This list was prepared in con-sultation with David C. Lewis, M.D. Dr. Lewis is the author of *The Drug Experience: Data for Decision-Making,* a course for schools and community groups, published by City Schools Curriculum Service, Boston, 1972.

*Overdose.* Cause of over 200 teen-age deaths in New York City in 1972. Death is caused because the part of the brain that controls breathing becomes paralyzed.

*Skin Popping.* To inject a drug under the skin.

*Track.* Scars on the skin left from the repeated injection of opiates.

*Works.* The apparatus for injecting a drug. May include a needle, and a bottle cap or spoon for dissolving the powdered drug.

### THE STIMULANTS

These drugs stimulate the system, or make a person more lively. While they are not physically addictive like the opiates, they produce a psychological dependence or craving.

*Amphetamine Psychosis.* A serious mental illness caused by overdoses or continued use of amphetamines. The person loses contact with reality, is convinced that others are out to harm him. The most frightening part—this psychosis sometimes continues long after the person has stopped taking the drug.

*Amphetamines.* These stimulants are taken in tablet or capsule form, or injected into the bloodstream. Among the widely used amphetamines are:
> *Benzedrine*—or "bennies."
> *Biphetamine*—or "footballs."
> *Dexedrine*—or "dex" or "dexies."
> *Methedrine*—or "speed" or "crystal meth."

*Cocaine.* Another kind of stimulant, derived from coca leaves. It is sniffed as a white powder, or liquefied and injected into a vein. It produces a fast and powerful feeling of elation. Cocaine does not produce physical dependence (addiction), but does produce a strong psychological craving.

*Coke.* Street slang for cocaine.

*Crashing.* Withdrawal from amphetamines, the swift descent from an amphetamine high to severe lows of depression.

*Mental Effects of "Speed."* Amphetamines produce a decreased sense of fatigue, increased confidence, talkativeness, restlessness, and an increased feeling of alertness. As dosage increases amphetamines can produce irritability, distrust of people, hallucinations, and amphetamine psychosis.

*Rush.* The brief heightened state of exhilaration at the beginning of a high.

*Speed Freak.* Person who repeatedly takes amphetamines or "speed," usually intravenously.

## PSYCHEDELICS

The medical classification of all mind-altering substances. Psychedelics change a person's perception of his surroundings.

*Acid.* A slang term for LSD. A frequent LSD user is an "acid head."

*DMT.* A powerful psychedelic prepared in the laboratory as a powder or liquid. It is usually injected into the vein or smoked along with marijuana or in cigarettes.

*DOM.* Called STP by users. The effects of STP can last for two or three days.

*Drop.* To take any drug orally. LSD is usually dissolved in water, and may be placed on a sugar cube. The term is to "drop acid."

*Flashback.* A user can be thrown back into the LSD experience months after the original use of the drug. Other possible risks of LSD, which are being thoroughly researched, include brain damage and chromosome breakage.

*Hallucinogens.* Those psychedelics which cause hallucinations.

*Hashish.* Called "hash." Prepared from the flowering tops of the hemp plant. Hashish is smoked in a pipe or taken orally, and is more powerful than marijuana.

*Head.* Someone who uses drugs frequently.

*Joint.* A marijuana cigarette.

*LSD.* Probably the most powerful psychedelic. Reactions to LSD are extremely unpredictable: distortions in time and space, brighter colors, vivid sounds, feelings of strangeness, a sense of beauty in common objects, sometimes fear and panic, sometimes even psychosis.

*Marijuana.* The crushed and chopped leaves and flowers from the hemp plant. Sometimes smoked in cigarette form. Sometimes smoked in pipes. Reactions can be: a giddy feeling like drunkenness; changes in perception and mood: feelings of well-being or fear; and possibly hallucinations. Slang terms for marijuana are "grass" or "pot."

*Mescaline.* "Mesc" is the common name for this drug which comes from the peyote cactus. Stronger than peyote itself, mescaline also causes vivid visual impressions.

*Peyote.* From the peyote cactus, it causes pronounced visual effects. It is used in a religious ritual by some Southwestern U.S. and Mexican Indians and its use in these rituals is legal.

*Psilocybin.* This psychedelic comes from a mushroom. It is less potent than LSD and takes a larger dose to get the effect.

*Roach.* The butt end of a joint.

*Stoned.* Describes the intoxicating effect of marijuana, or really any drug, or alcohol.

*THC.* Tetrahydrocannabinol. Purified extract of the resin of the hemp plant. Also made in the laboratory. It is thought to be the substance in marijuana and hashish that causes the mind-altering effects of these substances.

*Trip.* A name for the reaction that is caused by a psychedelic drug. A bummer is an unpleasant or frightening trip.

## THE DEPRESSANTS

The category of drugs that depress the functions of the brain.

*Alcohol.* Ethyl alcohol, a depressant because it slows the functions of the brain that control thinking and coordination. In high doses it produces drowsiness and sleep. Alcohol is an addictive drug, since after prolonged or continued use, it can cause physical dependence (alcoholism), and when discontinued, causes withdrawal symptoms at least as serious as the other addictive drugs.

*Barbiturate Overdose.* More people in the United States die as a result of an overdose of barbiturates (usually suicide) than of any other single substance.

*Barbiturates.* These drugs are in the group called sedatives—medicines to make you sleepy. Barbiturates are taken in capsule or tablet form. They cause physical dependence (addiction), and after repeated use, physical withdrawal does occur when these drugs are discontinued. Among the common commercial names for barbituates are:

*Amutal* or "blue heavens" or "blue devils."
*Luminal* or "purple hearts."
*Nembutal* or "yellow jackets."
*Seconal* or "red devils."
*Tuinal* or "rainbows" or "double trouble."

*"Downs."* Street slang for depressants.

*Intoxication.* Sedative or tranquilizer intoxication is similar in its symptoms to alcohol intoxication. Driving while intoxicated can be extremely dangerous, and is thought to cause at least 25,000 traffic fatalities a year.

*Tranquilizers.* Drugs that calm tension and anxiety. These drugs do not cause sleep except in high doses. Tranquilizers are taken in capsule or tablet form. Some common commercial names for tranquilizers are: *Equanil, Miltown, Librium,* and *Valium.*

### INHALANTS

Among substances which are inhaled and produced a high are: glue, gasoline, lighter fluid, and refrigerants. Continued inhaling has been reported to cause severe anemia, liver damage, brain damage, and death.

**Drug reactions, allergic.** Allergic reactions to drugs can occur within hours to days after the drug is taken, and commonly consist of itching, **hives,** and, less commonly, of more serious, even life-threatening, problems like difficulty in breathing, similar to the allergic reactions seen in insect bites (see **bites, insects**). Many of these reactions will reverse on discontinuing the drug and using an antihistamine (see **allergy**) and, occasionally, a hydrocortisone-like hormone (see **hormones**).

Other allergic reactions to drugs are more persistent, starting more than 3 days after the drug is first taken, and consisting of hives, swelling of the joints, and rash. These persistent reactions are the most common of all, and can appear at any time. In the typical situation, the rash begins within 5 to 7 days after the drug has been stopped. Whether it starts while the drug is being taken or after its use has been discontinued, the late drug eruption characteristically becomes more severe and widespread over the following several days to a week and then clears over the next 7 to 14 days. Usually the rash begins as faint pink spots which gradually enlarge to bright red larger spots or areas of raised skin. At times, there is some clearing in the center of the spot. Most often the rash starts at the head and upper extremities and spreads to the trunk and lower legs. Clearing proceeds in the same direction. Palms, soles, and the inside of the mouth may also be involved. Sometimes small bruises or hemorrhages develop in the rash, especially in the legs or elsewhere when the rash is extensive. More serious and violent reactions show large blisters, ulcerations, and severe hemorrhages in the skin. In addition to visible skin lesions, drug reactions may also include *fever* and inflammation in internal organs such as the kidneys. These more persistent reactions usually require treatment with hydrocortisone-like hormones.

Many types of drugs can produce identical rashes, and the appearance of the rash usually gives no clue as to which drug is causing the difficulty. The reaction may occur after the first exposure to the drug or may develop after the drug has been taken many times or constantly over a period of years. Having successfully taken penicillin in the past is no guarantee against a reaction.

When a rash suggestive of a drug reaction occurs and the drug that could cause it isn't obvious, every substance capable of entering any body opening, with the exception of most foods and water, becomes suspect, including eye and ear drops, nasal sprays, suppositories, injections, immunizations, nerve pills, vitamins, laxatives, sedatives, analgesics such as aspirin, preservatives, tonics, toothpaste, and topical lotions applied to the skin. The villain may lurk in unexpected places, as some drugs are present in very small amounts in biological products. For example, penicillin is added to *poliomyelitis* vaccine and is found in dairy products coming from cows treated with this antibiotic for inflammation of the breasts. When several drugs are being taken or have been taken simultaneously, the problem of identifying the culprit in a drug reaction is even more difficult.

If a drug has caused an allergic reaction, subsequent reactions are likely to be much more severe. The most severe reactions can cause death. Parents should take special note of drug reactions in their children and should be sure to inform new physicians caring for the child. When the child is old enough to understand his or her own medical history, be sure to tell him about problems that he has had with medicines so that he can pass this information on to new health personnel. It is recommended that an individual with a drug allergy carry a medical record card in his wallet or pocketbook, listing the drugs which are dangerous for him. There are bracelets and necklaces on which allergy information is imprinted. (For further information regarding this medical identification system which includes other medical conditions as well as allergies, contact The MedicAlert Foundation, P.O. Box 1009, Turlock, Calif. 95380.) The information on the tag, and on file at a central telephone exchange 24 hours a day, is invaluable to professionals attending the unconscious patient (for example, following an automobile accident).

There are exceptions to the rule about not taking a drug after a rash has occurred with its use. For example, the antibiotic ampicillin is known to produce a rash in about 10 percent of individuals taking the drug. Repeated administration of ampicillin in such persons does not generally lead to more severe reactions, although the mild rash may recur. In this sense, the rash that occurs with ampicillin differs from the usual type of drug sensitivity. Accordingly, persons experiencing a rash with ampicillin can, in general, safely take the drug again if needed.

The rashes that occur with infections can be a point of confusion. If a drug is being taken to treat the infection, determining whether the rash is due to the infection or to the drug is not always easy and leads to some uncertainty in saying for sure whether or not drug sensitivity exists.

At present, the determination of an allergy to a drug rests primarily on the development of a rash in association with taking it. At this time, there are no generally available tests to determine sensitivity to drugs. There is a great need for developing such tests. In recent years, skin tests for penicillin sensitivity have become more reliable. Ideally, we would like to be able to check a person's ability to tolerate a drug before using it or, at least, to see whether a rash that develops while taking a drug is due to it.

See *allergy*.

**Dysarthrias:** see *hearing and speech.*

**Dysautonomia.** This inherited chronic disease of the autonomic nervous system, also called the *Riley-Day syndrome*, occurs mainly in Ashkenazic Jews and is characterized by decreased ability to produce tears, absence of sensation in the cornea, frequent unexplained fevers, alternating high and low blood pressure, labile emotions, excessive sweating, blotchy skin, lack of appreciation of pain, sometimes mental retardation, susceptibility to infection, inability to control body temperature, feeding problems in infancy, and a tendency to seizures. The children are poorly coordinated, drool, have slurred speech, and swallow poorly.

There is no cure and the children and families require special long-term help (see *handicapped child*). Both parents must be carriers of the defective gene to produce an afflicted child (see *genetics*). At present there is no way to detect the carrier prior to the production of an afflicted child for the purposes of genetic counseling. However, a family with an affected child should make use of such services in planning future children.

For further information regarding this disease, contact the Dysautonomia Foundation, Inc., Room 1508, 370 Lexington Avenue, New York, N.Y. 10016.

See *developmental disabilities.*

**Dysentery:** see *diarrhea.*

**Dyslexia:** see *learning disabilities.*

*Earache.* An older child can, of course, tell you when he or she has an earache. For the child too young to talk, the only clue will be behavior. Tugging at the ear, despite common opinion, is not a reliable sign. The child may just be very fussy, or cry when swallowing. Whereas young children with earache usually have *fever,* older children often do not. For a child to have 1 or 2 earaches a year is not at all uncommon, but more than that number raises the question of an underlying cause which may require attention.

Rarely is earache an emergency. Even so, we suggest that if a child complains of pain in his ear, or if you suspect earache, talk to your physician or nurse within 24 hours. Most ear infections require treatment even if they seem mild. Untreated ones can seem to improve by themselves but may still cause serious damage. Sometimes you will have only sketchy clues. The pain may be mild or the complaints brief. When it comes to pain, some children can be remarkably uncomplaining. These young heroes may grit their teeth and keep quiet when they have every reason to make a fuss. In respect to earaches, being a little overcautious is a good idea. Be alert to even the mildest complaint or faintest clue of earache and be sure to get medical help.

While waiting to see the doctor, you can make your youngster with earache more comfortable by giving him aspirin and placing a warm (but not too hot) heating pad or water bottle against his ear. If your doctor has previously approved the use of paregoric or other pain medication for this problem, you can give this mild reliever. Do not, however, put any drugs in the ear until your doctor has prescribed them. Some doctors recommend keeping antipain eardrops on hand for use before medical attention can be obtained. It is important to check with your own doctor about this, however.

Discharge or leakage from the ear usually means that the eardrum has torn under pressure from an infection. Usually there will be some warning before this happens so that you can get medical attention, but, if not, don't be alarmed. The discharge does not mean a more serious or dangerous infection. You can think of the tearing of the eardrum as the opening of a safety valve which relieved the buildup of excess pressure. Children usually have less pain after the pressure is relieved. The tear will be quite small and usually will heal rapidly. If the doctor sees the possibility of a tear occurring, he may deliberately open the eardrum to relieve pain, promote healing, and avoid damage to the hearing apparatus. These planned incisions, called *myringotomies,* were done more frequently in the days before antibiotics. They heal more rapidly and with less scarring than do accidental ones. Myringotomies are usually done under anesthesia. If you see discharge, let your doctor know about it, but remember that it is not an emergency. If it happens at night, you can wait until morning. Meanwhile, wipe away the discharge with cotton pledgets and plug the ear with cotton to check further drainage.

The infection behind the eardrum that is the most common cause of pain in the ear is called *otitis media*, or middle-ear infection. On examination with an otoscope, the drum bulges out into the ear canal. Your doctor will probably prescribe an antibiotic and set a definite number of days for the course of the treatment. While your child may feel much better before the prescribed supply of medicine is used up, it is nevertheless important that you follow the doctor's instructions to the letter. Most of us taking medicine or giving it to children tend to slack off when the symptoms disappear, which in the case of ear infections is in about 24 hours, more or less. However, the treatment is aimed not at the symptoms, but at the underlying infection, which may remain active for several days after the disappearance of symptoms. If the doctor says that your child should take a certain medicine for 10 days (or 12 or whatever), see to it that your patient gets the prescribed dosage for the full 10 days, however chipper he may feel. Doctors usually check the ears 2 or 3 weeks later to be sure that all has returned to normal. Sometimes the infection will linger, necessitating another course of treatment, or the condition known as "glue ear," discussed below, will occur.

If your doctor prescribes eardrops for ear pain, there is a useful trick to know. Have the child lie on his side with the painful ear upward. Pull the ear back, thus opening up the canal, and then instill the drops into the ear canal. Then plug the ear canal with a cotton pledget to keep the medicine in.

On occasion, a child who has had a middle-ear infection will suffer some loss of hearing, which may last no more than a few days but can persist for several weeks or longer. He may complain that his ears feel "blocked." You may notice this when he turns the TV up even louder than the customary blast. The loss of hearing is related to the collection of fluid and mucus in the middle-ear cavity and to blockage of the Eustachian tube, which connects the cavity and the back of the throat. The normal dynamics of the eardrums are impaired, and the drum fails to move properly when air is blown into the canal during the examination. This condition is called *serious otitis media* and is in part an unplanned by-product of successful treatment of infections with antibiotics. It can also be related to **allergy.** Decongestant medicine, measures to force air up the ear canals, such as forcefully exhaling with the nose pinched and mouth closed, and the passage of time, usually lead to a cure. If the drum should be sucked in and immobile, true "glue ear," or simple measures such as those suggested above do not work, in a myringotomy done under anesthesia may be in order to open the eardrum and drain off the thick mucus. Sometimes a plastic or metal tube ("button") is then placed through the drum and left in place to prevent reaccumulation of fluid and allow healing. Removal of the adenoids (see *tonsils and adenoids*) may or may not be performed at the same time. Adenoidectomy may also be considered for the child who is having more than 2 or 3 bouts of middle-ear infection per year, particularly if they are stubborn to treat. Alternatively, some children are given daily antibiotics to prevent recurrences.

Ear pain, aggravated by touching or pulling the ear, itching deep in the ear, and discharge, are symptoms of inflammation of the ear canal, known medically as *external otitis* (as opposed to *otitis media,* discussed above). Because it occurs so often after water gets into the ear, it is also commonly called *"swimmer's ear."*

Treatment consists of keeping the ear canals dry by avoiding water until the condition is cured, the use of special medicated eardrops usually containing an antibiotic and hydrocortisone preparation, and sometimes antibiotics taken by mouth as well.

Prevention in those prone to the disorder involves drying the ear canals after swimming, best achieved by instilling 70 percent alcohol into the canal upon leaving the water. Ear plugs have not proven particularly effective. The kind of water that gets into the ear may be a factor, in terms of its particle and bacterial content.

*Ear, foreign object in the.* Small children are very prone to stick objects into their ears, nose, or other body opening. Sometimes a foreign object is inserted into the ear beyond the range of easy vision and makes its presence known by a foul-smelling discharge. The older child may complain of something in his or her ear, but steadfastly deny having placed it there. A foreign body in the ear canal may also impair hearing. If you can easily see the object and readily grasp it, carefully try to remove it yourself. However, if it is far up the ear canal, and you cannot get a good hold on it it is best not to try to do any more. You may push it farther in and run the risk of injuring the eardrum. Seek help from your physician.

*Echo virus:* see *rash.*

*Eczema* is an itchy skin *rash* that tends to recur and persist over months and even years. It occurs usually in certain characteristic areas of the body. In the infant the cheeks are almost always affected, with red and weeping eruptions. Scabs (crusts) and scratch marks are also part of the characteristic appearance. The arms, legs, and neck are frequently inflamed as well. In older children, the face is usually spared. The rash described above localizes on the inside of the bends of the elbows and knees, the neck, and the forearms. In more severe cases, other skin areas are also affected. If the condition continues for any length of time, the skin is likely to become thickened and hard (*lichenified*) in areas where scratching has been most intense.

Itching is the distinguishing symptom of eczema, and scratching aggravates the rash. The factors that aggravate eczema are those that intensify the itching, and therefore the scratching. Scratching leads to further itching, and a vicious cycle develops.

Eczema is characterized mainly by increased irritability of the skin to a great variety of influences. The most important factor is the inherited, genetically determined hyperreactivity or sensitivity of the skin of patients prone to this disease. In a yet undefined way, there is something clearly different and special about this skin. The tendency, at present irreversible, lasts for life and eczema may flare up at any time. The same tendency also predisposes the patient to *hay fever* and *asthma*. Eczematous skin is easily irritated by scratchy clothing, particularly by woolen fabrics and synthetics such as nylon. Ordinary soaps are also likely to be irritating if not thoroughly rinsed from the skin. Eczematous skin is also affected by the emotions. Upsets can trigger itching and scratching even in small babies. Eczema becomes a factor in the child's interaction with others (see Part 1, Chapter 4: "Complaints with an Emotional Element"). These emotional aspects very often constitute the main problem. Emotional tensions in the entire family disturb the child and produce itching, scratching, and eczema.

Once eczema develops, sweating irritates the skin and increases itching. If the openings to the glands in which sweat is produced are blocked by inflammation of the outer layer of the skin, as in eczema, the sweat cannot escape. Pressure builds up and sweat breaks through the confines of the glands. The retained sweat leaks into the surrounding deeper layers of skin, where it produces an intense itching. Any factors that increase sweating, such as exercise, high environmental heat and humidity, and emotions, will increase itching and scratching, making the eczema worse. In some infants, certain foods provoke eruptions.

If you suspect a child of having eczema, even if the condition seems very mild, be sure to discuss it with your doctor or nurse at your next visit. In the meantime, cool water, witch hazel, and rubbing alcohol (may sting) will relieve the itching. If any rash persists, contact your doctor. In addition to investigating the crucial emotional factors, your doctor will likely recommend some specific measures. Medication such as antihistamines (see *allergy*) can be taken by mouth to counteract itching. Woolen and rough synthetic fabrics are best avoided, and a change from your present soap to one made with a super-fat base may be in order. During marked flare-ups, keeping the child cool and quiet will decrease sweating, itching, and scratching. Various ointments can serve as a protective barrier between the sensitive dry skin and the air, and some, usually containing a steroid or other anti-inflammatory medicine, can dramatically decrease the severe itching discomfort and rash. If the skin is infected, an antibiotic may be added to the ointment (see *infections*). Sometimes it is necessary to take an antibiotic internally. Occasionally, hospitalization is the only way to interrupt a severe attack in which the vicious "itch-scratch" cycle and family disruption are factors.

Although it is rare, foods may play a role in eczema. Mothers usually can pinpoint the foods that make the skin flare up. These foods are best avoided.

Children with eczema should not receive smallpox vaccinations without special precautions because of the danger of severe allergic reactions affecting the entire body. See *immunization.*

If there is a strong allergic history in the family, it may be necessary to take precautions against the later development of respiratory disorders, for example by the control of house dust. Allergy skin tests are no longer done in children with eczema because the results cannot be interpreted when the rash is present. Later, the tests may be given to determine the cause of hay fever or asthma, if these conditions are present. But these test do *not* contribute to an understanding of eczema. Therefore, allergy shots are no longer used to treat eczema. In fact, they may even aggravate it.

First and foremost, the doctor or nurse will be interested in the child's personality and in his or her relationship with his parents and others in order to understand how these factors affect the eczema. A child with eczema may be more likely to scratch his skin during the inevitable and normal conflicts of childhood. His parents, justifiably concerned about not making the eczema worse, may be inclined to be overly lenient on issues of discipline when, in fact, firmness is necessary. Eczema or any chronic disorder can compound the already challenging job of raising children. The doctor and nurse can help with some of these problems. Intimate knowledge of the family as a result of prolonged contact is an asset for the health professionals in guiding parents.

See Part 1, Chapter 1: "Quality in Pediatric Care," Part 1, Chapter 4: "Complaints with an Emotional Element," and *allergy.*

*Elbow, dislocated:* see *arm, favoring of.*

*Electrical burns:* see *burns.*

*Emphysema* is a name used for several diseases of the lungs. Best known is the condition associated with cigarette smoking which affects middle-aged and older adults. Other, less common diseases, which go by the same name, are found in infants and children. In all cases the trouble may be described as overdistension of the lungs, but depending on the type of disease, this overdistension affects both lungs, one, or part of one lung. The physician makes the diagnosis after he has examined the child (often with an X-ray) for a respiratory difficulty of some sort.

The bronchial system, through which air is moved in and out of the lungs, resembles a tree with a trunk (the *trachea* or windpipe) and branches (the *bronchi* or bronchial tubes), which grow smaller and smaller the farther out they are from the main trunk. The smallest branches are called *bronchioles* (these become inflamed in *bronchiolitis*—see *bronchitis*); they are too small to be seen with the naked eye and communicate with millions of tiny respiratory sacs, the *alveoli*. We can think of the alveoli as the leaves of the bronchial tree, but there is a big difference: alveoli are built like little balloons which open and collapse with breathing. Blood pumped in from the right ventricle of the heart travels in the walls of the alveoli in a mesh of tiny vessels, the *capillaries*. These have extremely thin walls so that as blood passes through the lungs it can pick up oxygen from, and release carbon dioxide into, the air in the alveoli. Normal breathing renews the air in the lung so that the blood can achieve the right proportion of oxygen and carbon dioxide, which in normal conditions remains quite constant. From the lung, blood goes to the left ventricle of the heart where it is pumped out into the arteries for distribution to the body. Only blood taken from an artery and analyzed for oxygen and carbon dioxide can show if the lungs are working properly.

The tubes composing the bronchial tree are all flexible and expansible. When we breathe in, they become wider and when we breathe out, they become narrower. Now suppose there is an obstruction of some kind in a tube; there could still be room enough for air to get in, but the tube would close down at expiration and prevent breathing out. Thus air becomes trapped in the alveoli, causing the overdistension characteristic of emphysema. In the adult smokers' disease, all the bronchioles are partly obstructed and both lungs become overdistended. In extreme cases, the overdistended lung segment can rupture, collapse (see *lung rupture and collapse*), and leak air into the thoracic cavity (see *pneumothorax*). *Asthma* and bronchiolitis can have a similar effect. Sometimes, in children, one large bronchus, going to one lung or to a section of one lung called a *lobe*, may be partially plugged by a foreign body: a peanut, a button, a small part from a broken toy, and so forth, and the lung or the lobe balloons up with trapped air, causing difficulty in breathing. (See *choking and swallowing foreign objects* and *cough*.)

In infants the same emergency may result from a malformation of one bronchus, causing the segment or lobe of lung supplied by that tube to expand. Both conditions interfere with breathing and must be treated immediately: the first by removing the foreign body through a tube passed down the trachea (a procedure known as *bronchoscopy*) or even by surgery if the foreign body is stuck in the bronchus; the second by an operation in which the diseased lobe is removed (lobectomy). Other forms of emphysema in children are uncommon and tend to be less significant than the disease or diseases causing it. Recent information shows that some forms of emphysema causing problems in adults may be inherited and that the earliest signs and symptoms may appear in childhood. Studies are under way to see if a search for early emphysema or a susceptibility to it in the children of affected adults is worthwhile.

See also **breathing, noisy** and **croup and laryngitis.**

**Endocrine disorders:** see **hormones.**

**Epilepsy:** see **seizure disorders.**

**Erb's palsy** is paralysis, partial or complete, of the arm and hand muscles due to birth injury of the nerves that control these muscles. It requires the care of an orthopedist and physical therapist.

See **handicapped child.**

**Erythema infectiosum:** see **rash.**

**Exercise and physical fitness.** The subject of physical fitness and exercise is receiving some long overdue national attention. Sedentary living has been identified as an important factor in *atherosclerosis* (deposit of fat in blood vessels). Exercise is critical to good health and obesity control.

Just think about the many ways in which our society discourages activity. In one way or another, the need for walking has been replaced by machines. The person seen on foot along a suburban road (already discouraged by a lack of sidewalks) is viewed with suspicion and may be subjected to police inquiry. Many executives walk no more than a few blocks per day to get to their offices. Parents seek out homes situated just beyond the minimum distance for school bus service. Television (see **television and children**) keeps children indoors and inactive. Our national zeal for highway building is not matched by an interest in

301

*Eye,
injuries
and
foreign
objects
in the*

providing indoor and outdoor exercise programs. European countries are far ahead of us in building bicycle paths, instituting exercise programs at work, and developing family exercise parks. The latter are designed for jogging and at intervals have exercise sessions with apparatus and instructions.

Exercise habits should be encouraged in the hope that an enjoyable lifelong pattern will be established. Parents must set a good example. Activities that seem to be most promising in reducing the risk of atherosclerosis are those that force the heart and lungs to work hard, increasing their capacity and effectiveness. Jogging, walking, swimming, running in place, and vigorous bicycling (see Part 2, Chapter 11: "Bicycle and Minibike Safety") for a period of 10 to 15 minutes five times each week would be a minimum. Anything above and beyond could be expected to increase the endurance capacity of the heart and lungs and improve their functioning even more. Parking or getting off a bus several blocks from your destination and walking up as many flights as you can before taking the elevator are worthwhile practices. The current interest among adolescents and young adults in backpacking, wilderness hiking, and cross-country skiing is a good sign.

The case for endurance exercise is sufficiently well made already to justify building this principle into school physical education programs, individualized for each child. Many schools are far from this standard and too few teach sports like biking, tennis, squash, cross-country skiing and running, and swimming, which could be continued into adulthood. Few have availed themselves of endurance testing devices which allow the child to measure his own performance. Too many concentrate on athletes and males instead of on all children. Families with daughters should be especially concerned. Title IX of the Educational Amendments Act of 1975 requires schools to include girls in all sports programs, or provide separate but equal opportunities.

The first step is to realize how serious our inactivity is. Then we must be imaginative in restructuring our lives and communities. For further information on developing programs on physical fitness in your community, school, or business, contact LifeCourse Research Center, 141 Tremont Street, Boston, Mass. 02111. Another excellent resource is your local Y; many have developed fitness programs for adults, including those with special problems such as heart disease.

**Eye, injuries and foreign objects in the.** Foreign objects that are rubbed or blown into the eyes are uncomfortable and potentially dangerous in that they can scratch the eyes' surface or become imbedded in the eye. The symptoms are redness, burning sensation, headache, pain, and excess production of tears.

302

*Eye,
injuries
and
foreign
objects
in the*

General precautions are to keep the child from rubbing his or her eyes, washing hands thoroughly before examining the eye, not attempting to remove a foreign body by inserting a toothpick, match, or any other instrument, and referring the child to a doctor if something is embedded in the eye or seems to be embedded, even if you cannot locate it.

To find and remove a foreign body from the surface of the eyeball or from the inner surface of the eyelid, first pull down the lower lid to determine whether or not the foreign body lies on the inner surface. If you see the object, gently lift it away with the corner of a clean handkerchief or tissue paper. Do not use dry absorbent cotton around the eye. If the object cannot be located, it may be lodged below the upper lid. Have the child look down and grasp the lashes of the upper lid. Pull the lid forward and down over the lower lid. This may dislodge a foreign object trapped below the lid. If the foreign body has not been dislodged, it is necessary to evert the lid. Grasp the eyelashes. Depress the upper lid by placing a long matchstick or some other similar object horizontally on top of the lid and by pulling upward on the lashes against the matchstick. Lift off the foreign body with the corner of a clean handkerchief and return the lid to its normal position by pulling downward on the lashes. Flush the eye with water. If the object still is not removed and may be embedded, cover the eye with a dry gauze bandage and consult a physician. If symptoms persist after removal of a foreign body, consult a physician. There is a possibility that another foreign body is being overlooked or that the surface of the eye has been scratched.

If the eyelid is injured, first aid consists of stopping bleeding by gently applying direct pressure, cleansing the wound and applying a sterile or clean dressing which can be held in place by bandages encircling the head or taped in place. Medical attention should be sought without delay. A blow to the eye leads most commonly to a black eye, which is the result of bleeding (hemorrhaging) into the soft loose skin of the eyelids. Apply a dry sterile or clean dressing and consult a physician.

Any injury that penetrates into the substance of the eye requires immediate medical attention. Make no attempt to remove any foreign material left behind or to wash the eye. Cover both eyes loosely with a sterile or clean dressing held with a tape or bandage which encircles the head but is loose enough to avoid pressure on the eyes. Both eyes should be covered to prevent movement of the affected eye. Keep the child on his back. Transport him to the hospital or doctor's office by stretcher. The sooner medical care is received, the better the chances for saving sight.

For a discussion of chemical burns of the eye, see *burns.*

*Eye problems:* see *conjunctivitis* and *vision problems.*

Febrile
seizures

*Fainting:* see Part 2, Chapter 9: "First Aid."

*Farsightedness:* see *vision problems.*

*Fatness:* see Part 1, Chapter 3: "Diet of Infants and Children" and *weight problems.*

*Febrile seizures.* A convulsion with *fever* is quite common in young children. It is a frightening experience for parents. The child convulses violently and may injure himself if he or she thrashes against a hard object. He may bite his tongue. Even though it may seem like an eternity, most febrile convulsions cease within a few minutes and the child may either slowly rouse or lapse into a deep sleep.

Try to protect the patient by removing hard or dangerous objects from his immediate environment, by easing him to the ground if possible. Turn his head to the side to allow saliva to drain off. Institute antifever measures (see Part 1, Chapter 5: "Caring for the Sick Child at Home"), but be careful to keep the child's head from the water. Give him nothing to eat or drink until he is fully alert. Get in touch with your physician or move him to the nearest medical facility. Remember that in almost all cases children come out of convulsions by themselves regardless of what you do. Time is on your side. If breathing should stop, a vary rare occurrence, administer artificial respiration. (See Part 2, Chapter 9: "First Aid.")

The tendency to have a simple febrile seizure is inherited, and often other members of the family, including the parents, have had this difficulty. These seizures occur most commonly between the ages of 1 and 3 years. They usually occur simultaneously with an upswing of fever. Thus it is not rare for the child to be put to bed quite well, with the seizure the first sign of illness. The parents then discover that the child feels hot as well.

Your doctor will want to know as much as possible about the details of the seizure: When did it begin? How did the child appear? Were the movements of his limbs symmetrical or was one side of the body twitching more than another? How long did the seizure last? How long did the child sleep? Did the seizure recur after a quiet interval? When did the seizure occur in relationship to the onset of fever? Each of these questions will help a physician in determining whether the seizure was a

simple febrile one or whether it reflected an underlying epileptic tendency (see *seizure disorders*) which was merely triggered by fever.

The doctor will examine the child completely and perform any appropriate diagnostic studies. One or two weeks later, particularly in the
case of a second episode, he may recommend an *electroencephalogram*
(brain wave test) and other studies, again to determine whether an
epileptic tendency is present.

Preventing recurrent simple febrile seizures involves controlling the
fever and using medicines called anticonvulsants. If an anticonvulsant
medication like phenobarbital is used at the onset of fever only, it rarely
works quickly enough to prevent the febrile seizure which usually occurs
within the first hour or so of the sudden rise of temperature. It appears
that anticonvulsants can prevent these convulsions only if they are given
daily until the child is beyond the age of susceptibility. There is some
difference of opinion as to when to begin anticonvulsants. Some doctors
begin phenobarbital after the first episode, while others wait until after
a second one.

The child who has an epileptic tendency triggered by fever may continue to have seizures at a later point whether or not fever is present.
This child is usually treated with anticonvulsants until he is seizure free
for several years and his brain wave test shows improvement.

See *seizure disorders.*

*Fever* is a common symptom of illness, particularly of *infections* in children.
The exact role of fever in the body's struggle with infection is not clear,
but it seems hard to believe that this common response of all mammals,
including humans, is not of some value. Fever can also occur in nonin-
fectious diseases such as *rheumatic fever* and rheumatoid arthritis (see
*arthritis, rheumatoid*).

In addition to being a symptom, very high fever can itself cause
difficulty. Fever recognition and control are discussed in Part 1, Chapter
5: "Caring for the Sick Child at Home."

*Fever blisters.* Infection by *herpes simplex* virus is extremely common. It is
unlikely that very many people will have ever heard of herpes simplex
by name, but almost everyone will know of fever blisters, the painful
little fluid-filled bumps which appear usually on the face near or on the
lips in association with fatigue, unusual stress, chilling, or infections like
the common cold. Many parents are familiar with the feverish illness of
the mouth of children in which painful blisters followed by shallow ulcer
sores develop on the inside lining of the mouth, gums, and sometimes

the tongue and throat. Both of these common conditions are caused by
the virus *herpes simplex Hominis*, a common parasite of man.

Herpes virus infection of the mouth is the most common cause of
mouth inflammation in childhood. (Other causes are infection with echo
or Coxsackie viruses—see *rash.*) Its onset may be abrupt, with a sudden
rise in temperature to 103° or higher, or it may be insidious, with a slow
development of *fever* and fussiness preceding the lesions of the mouth
by several days. The sickest children drool at the mouth, refuse food and
fluid, have high temperatures, and swollen lymph nodes in the under-
sides of their jaws. Their gums are raw and sometimes bleeding. They
are the very picture of misery. Eating and drinking are painful and they
resist the most diligent coaxing. A small number of children refuse fluids
to the point of becoming dehydrated (see *diarrhea*) and require intravenous fluids to sustain them until healing has occurred. The pain
disappears several days before the ulcers heal completely, which usually
occurs between 4 and 9 days—one week on the average. There are all
degrees of illness, from the miserable child described above to one who
has only a few painful sores inside his mouth. The majority of cases are
so mild that they cause no symptoms whatsoever or, at the most, slight
fussiness and irritability indistinguishable from many of the vague complaints that afflict children. We don't know why it is that some children
respond with a full-blown infection and others confine the infection so
completely.

Few persons escape infection by this virus during their life, but many
of the infections are subclinical (see *infections*), meaning that they are
so mild as to cause either no symptoms or minimal ones, but yet stimulate the production of antibodies which localize and combat the infection. Herpes virus has the peculiar capacity to go into a latent stage,
lying dormant in the body. It appears that this virus stays with us for
life. Interestingly, the virus can emerge from the latent to an active stage
and undergo multiplication under certain conditions of body stress such
as chilling, infection, menstruation, or fatigue. Some people are more
prone to experience this virus reawakening than others. When the virus
becomes active again, the telltale blisters reappear. The reactivated virus
often produces a single crop of blisters somewhat like those seen in
*chicken pox.* (The virus causing chicken pox and that causing herpes
infection are close relatives, and it is not surprising that they produce
similar lesions. Both have the ability to lie dormant and to be reactivated.) Herpes virus can also set up shop in broken skin on any part of
the body and is a common affliction of wrestlers whose skin is subjected
to unusually rough treatment. Children with *eczema* are also prone to
this infection. Herpes virus can easily gain entrance to the damaged skin
and establish an infection in all involved areas, resulting in a serious
illness. Girls are prone to herpes infections of the vagina and vulva. The

lesions here resemble those that occur in the mouth, appearing first as fluid-filled blisters which soon collapse, leaving behind a yellow-gray membrane covering a shallow painful ulcer. On rare occasions herpes virus can infect the cornea of the eye, producing a very serious infection requiring care by an eye specialist *(ophthalmologist)*. In certain rare cases, herpes virus infects the brain and other parts of the central nervous system, particularly in the nonimmune adult, producing meningitis and encephalitis (see *meningitis*).

The blisters and ulcers of herpes simplex teem with virus and are contagious until they heal, both in the initial and reactivated stages. Whether the ill child who needs home care should also be isolated is an unanswered question. The illness is usually so mild in childhood that it almost seems better to get it over with rather than run the risk of reaching adulthood without immunity. Most of the time this question is academic, however, since exposure usually occurs before the ill child develops telltale signs of infection, if indeed these occur.

There is no cure for herpes infection nor is there a preventive immunization. As in other virus illnesses, antibiotics are of no value, but there is now medicine available that will help combat the disease when it attacks the eyes. Topical anesthetics are useful in relieving pain, although they have no benefit in shortening the course of the illness. Applications of viscous lidocaine (Xylocaine) or elixir of diphenhydramine (Benadryl) to the sores in the mouth can be made as often as necessary to keep the child comfortable. There are some newer medications that have proved beneficial in decreasing the severity of the ulcers and shortening the healing time. These are not in wide use.

With an older child we suggest using a straw to bypass the sore area of the mouth and transport liquids back over the tongue to the throat. Cool bland fluids seem to be less irritating than warm or strongly flavored ones. Aspirin is useful for controlling fever.

(See Part 1, Chapter 5: "Caring for the Sick Child at Home" for dosage schedule.)

**Fever of unknown origin.** It is a common situation for children to be sick with fever without having any localized finding like sore throat, ear infection, *colds,* and so forth. They may look and act sick and yet not show abnormalities of any specific part of the body. The examination is, as we say, negative. These illnesses have their parallel in adults. Most of us are familiar with having felt "sick all over" without a particular focus of discomfort.

The explanation of these fevers of unknown origin, or F.U.O.s in medical shorthand, varies. Most represent what are probably viral infections, untreatable by present therapies, and run their course in several days with complete recovery. Others are the first phases of illnesses such as *roseola* or *typhoid fever* whose identity will be revealed only in time.

How we approach these fevers depends on a number of factors, including the age of the child, the severity of the symptoms, diseases current in the community, and so forth. Depending on the circumstances, we might do nothing but observe the child, keeping in touch with the parents by phone, perform selected laboratory tests to look for hidden foci of infection, or, in the case of a desperately ill child, admit him to the hospital for extensive culturing (of urine, spinal fluid, stools, throat, and so forth) and initiation of antibiotic treatment even before the exact cause is known. The most common laboratory tests performed on the nonhospitalized child are *blood count,* chest X-ray (see *pneumonia*), throat culture, urinalysis and urine culture (see *urinary tract infections and defects*), spinal tap (*lumbar puncture*—see *meningitis* and *infections*), and blood culture (see *bloodstream infection*). The cultures are designed to identify bacteria only. If none is found, we conclude by a process of elimination that viruses are probably to blame. For reasons discussed in *infections,* we rarely perform virus cultures.

The general principle with F.U.O.s is to do nothing that might obscure finding the cause of the illness. We follow the ancient medical dictum *primum non nocere,* the Latin phrase meaning first do no harm. Specifically, this means refraining from giving antibiotics until the cause is pinned down or unless our hand is forced by the severity of illness. Sometimes it is difficult for parents to understand why we withhold antibiotics, seemingly allowing the child to remain ill. The reason is that, based on the probable diagnosis (an educated medical guess), we do not believe that antibiotics will work, or else that they might lead ultimately to greater difficulties for the child by suppressing, yet not dealing definitively, with a nondiagnosed underlying bacterial infection.

For a discussion of virus, bacteria, cultures, and antibiotics see *infections.*

See also Part 1, Chapter 5: "Caring for the Sick Child at Home."


**Fifth disease:** see *rash.*


**First aid:** see Part 2, Chapter 9: "First Aid."


**Flat feet:** see *orthopedic concerns.*


**Foot problems:** see *orthopedic concerns.*

*Fracture.* Injuries to any part of the body that involve marked pain, swelling, and inability to use the part in question always raise the possibility of a *fracture* or break of the bone. Obviously an actual deformity of a limb would almost certainly signify a fracture just as a deformity at a joint would signify a *dislocation* (bone out of socket). When a fracture or dislocation is even suspected, care must be exercised from the beginning to prevent the injury from worsening and damaging blood vessels and nerves nearby. While the following comments refer to fractures, the general principles apply to dislocations as well.

If the injury is obviously severe, the neck seems broken, or the child is unconscious, do not move him or her. Keep him warm, stay with him, and have someone call for expert help or advice.

If the skin over a fracture is broken (open or compound fracture), place sterile gauze over the wound and get medical help immediately. If sterile gauze is not available, leave the wound open to the air, making certain that nothing touches it, rather than contaminating it with a cloth that is not clean. If it is necessary to control bleeding, apply pressure with your hand directly, or over the dressing if a sterile one is available.

Give the child nothing to eat or drink if he has a possible fracture or severe injury. He may require an anesthetic and recent eating would make anesthesia more risky and lead to delays in treatment.

An injured arm in which fracture is suspected should be immobilized with a splint cut to the size of the limb. Use any available rigid object, such as a broom handle or padded board. Tie the arm to the splint with strips of cloth in several places—one on either side of the suspected break and one at each end of the splint. Put the child's arm in a sling before taking him to the doctor. Slings can be made from a woman's large scarf or a torn sheet folded into a triangle.

If either the back or neck is injured, keep the child flat and make no attempt to move him until medical help arrives. Stabilize his head with pillows or cushions on either side. In cases of severe injury to the neck or back, improper mobilization may aggravate injury to the spinal cord with the possibility of permanent paralysis.

A fracture of the collarbone occurs frequently in childhood. There is usually swelling over the fracture, pain in the shoulder, and a reluctance to use the arm on the side of the injury. Use a sling for the arm on the injured side and take the child to a doctor or to the hospital.

Unless there is obvious deformity, broken fingers are often mistaken for sprained fingers. Until you take the child to a doctor for an X-ray and appropriate treatment, elevate and support the hand.

If it is necessary to move a child with suspected fracture of the leg, give the leg constant support. Don't allow weight to be put on it. Strap it to the other leg at several levels above and below the injury or apply a splint. For a splint, use any available rigid object, such as a broom handle, padded board, or a rolled blanket. However, never force a deformed leg or joint into a different position, particularly if pain occurs. After applying a splint, get someone to help you carry the child to the back seat of a car or station wagon, and take him to the hospital. Often only an X-ray can distinguish between a sprained and broken limb or finger. The degree of swelling and pain does not always indicate whether or not there is a fracture—even to a doctor's trained eye.

See Part 2, Chapter 9: "First Aid."

*Gastroenteritis* literally means inflammation of the stomach and intestines. The most common signs of this inflammation, which is usually the result of infection, are *vomiting* (and nausea), *diarrhea,* and *abdominal pain.* In any episode of gastroenteritis some combination of these symptoms is present and each is discussed separately, elsewhere in the book.

*Genetics.*

### THE SCIENCE OF GENETICS

From time immemorial, man has known that he resembles his ancestors. "Whom does he or she look like?" is almost our first question about every newborn. We say that the blue eyes have come from so-and-so and the brown hair from somebody else, and so on. Nevertheless, it has been only in the last one hundred years that the processes of *heredity*, the biological mechanisms by which certain characteristics are passed from parents to children, have been understood at all.

The study of heredity is the comparatively new science called *genetics*, which in recent years has been taking enormous strides. In no other branch of biology or medicine has progress been more rapid or discoveries of greater fundamental importance been made. The geneticist already has revealed the origin of many obscure conditions and has opened the way to developing corrective measures for some of them. He has enriched immeasurably whole fields of thought in biology and psychology, and it is not extravagant to say that he may be on the edge of solving the biggest mystery of all, the mechanism of life itself. There is a great need for increased public understanding.

While there are many highly controversial aspects of this exploding field, such as selection of the sex of a baby, this discussion focuses on those aspects of genetics which seem more solidly in the medical mainstream today.

For additional information on the issues involved in genetics, you can contact the Institute of Society, Ethics, and the Life Sciences, 623 Warburton Avenue, Hastings-on-Hudson, N.Y. 10706. Also useful is the book *The Ethics of Genetic Control: Ending Reproductive Roulette* by Joseph Fletcher (Garden City: Anchor Press, 1974).

Genetics, like every other branch of science, has its own vocabulary. To gain even a casual acquaintance with genetics, you need to know the meanings of several technical words and to understand one or two elementary technical operations. You will not find it difficult if, as you read along, you keep turning back to the basic definitions until the comparatively few technical names become familiar. You should find the small effort amply rewarding. Genetics is a subject which will affect all of us more and more in the years ahead.

The science of genetics began amid rows of pea plants in the garden of a monastery in what is now Brno, Czechoslovakia. Its founder was a Moravian monk, Gregor Johann Mendel (1822–1884), who lived in obscurity and died without acclaim for discoveries that rank among the great contributions to science. In 1866, he published his findings on the crossing or breeding of different varieties of garden peas, but he was far ahead of his time and his writings were hard to understand. The rest of the world did not grasp the significance of his reports.

In Mendel's lifetime, the evolutionary theories of the great Charles Darwin dominated the scientific world. Darwin thought biological inheritance was accomplished by a simple mixing of parental "bloods" or "serums." Individual characteristics of the parents were thought to be blended in the preparation of a new individual, much as modern man mixes four parts gin and one of vermouth when he wants a good cocktail. It was Mendel's genius to have seen that, on the contrary, there was no blurring or dilution of individual traits in heredity. Instead, inherited characteristics are transmitted from parent to offspring as separate units, which maintain their identities from generation to generation. Specific characteristics may fail to appear in some generations, but inevitably at some point in the future they will again express themselves.

Mendel concluded that the first generation received a *dominant* hereditary unit from one parent and a *recessive* unit from the other. We now call these hereditary units *genes*. When the offspring has obtained a combination of a dominant gene from one side and a recessive gene from the other, the dominant gene always prevails. Individuals with such a combination of a dominant and a recessive gene are said to be *heterozygous*, having two unlike genes for a particular characteristic. If they receive the same type of genes from both parents they are said to be *homozygous*, whether the trait is dominant or recessive. For a recessive trait to become manifest, the offspring has to be homozygous for the recessive trait, having received the recessive gene from both parents.

Mendel's theories are usually expressed in symbols. Dominant traits are shown in capital letters, while recessive traits are designated by the corresponding lowercase letters. Mendel's pure strain of yellow-seeded peas is symbolized as YY. This genetic formula is known as the *genotype*. The pure recessive strain of peas with green seeds is shown by the genotype yy. When these two strains are crossed (YY by yy), all progeny will have the same genotype Yy. You will see how this works if you think of the four possible combinations: the first Y combining with the first y to produce one Yy and then with the second y to produce a second Yy; then the second Y combines with the first y to produce the third Yy and with the second y for the fourth Yy. These are the heterozygous hybrids of Mendel's first generation, and all have the same demonstrable characteristic known as the *phenotype*, which is in this case yellow seeds, since yellow (Y) is dominant over green (y).

A convenient form in which to show the relationships diagrammatically is called *Punnett's square*, after the English geneticist who devised it. The genes from one parent are listed across the top, those from the other parent along the side. The boxes show each genetic possibility obtained by combining the genes along the top with those along the sides. In the case of crossing pure yellow-seeded peas with pure green-seeded ones, it is only possible to have the Yy combination in the first generation.

PARENT PLANT

|  |  | y | y |
|---|---|---|---|
| PARENT PLANT | Y | Yy | Yy |
|  | Y | Yy | Yy |

Offspring: Yy, Yy, Yy, Yy

When Mendel's first generation of hybrids are interbred in the second generation, Yy by Yy, there are 4 combinations (2 of which are the same) having the following genotypes: YY, Yy, yY, yy. The offspring will consist of 1 homozygous yellow seed (YY), 2 heterozygous yellow seeds (Yy), and 1 homozygous green seed (yy), or a total of 3 yellows and 1 green. The Y of the first hybrid combined with the Y of the second to form the YY, and with its y to form one Yy. The y of the first combined with the Y of the second to form the second Yy and with the y to form the yy. This result can be shown diagrammatically with Punnett's square:

PARENT HYBRID PLANT

|  |  | Y | y |
|---|---|---|---|
| PARENT HYBRID | Y | YY | Yy |
|  | y | yY | yy |

Offspring: YY, Yy, yY, yy

The letter Y in the above discussion is used as an abbreviation for the phenotype "yellow." Later in the discussion Y will be used traditionally, to refer to the male sex chromosome.

### GENES THAT CAUSE DISEASE

To turn from plants to humans, all of us carry both dominant and recessive genes. These genes control our individual characteristics, whether they are easy to see, like hair color, or are at the level of chemical molecules. Occasionally a gene is defective and causes a characteristic which is harmful to its bearer—in other words, a disease. The defective gene may be either dominant or recessive. It is dominant by definition if it always produces some disordered function. An example is the gene which determines *retinoblastoma,* a cancer of the retina of the eye. More often, disease-determining genes are recessive and require another recessive gene from the other parent in order to produce the disease in question. An exception, to be discussed later, is a recessive gene carried on a sex chromosome. Many recessive genes are actually lethal; when matched with each other, they produce an ovum so defective that it cannot survive. Ova blighted in this way account for a certain percentage of spontaneous abortions or miscarriages. The heterozygous person with a recessive, disease-causing gene is said to be a *carrier* of the gene or to have the *trait* for the disorder. Thus, we speak of a sickle-cell carrier or of someone with a sickle-cell trait. The meaning of the two terms is the same.

While most recessive, disease-determining genes do not cause difficulties in the heterozygote (carrier), this is not always the case. For example, in one inherited disorder of blood fats, the homozygote has an increased chance of having a heart attack before the age of 20, while the heterozygote also has an increased risk, but at a later age—in the forties and fifties. (See Part 1, Chapter 3: "Diet of Infants and Children.") The carrier for the trait for sickle-cell anemia (see *anemia*)—the heterozygote—usually has no problems. However, in unusual circumstances of low oxygen, such as are found at high altitudes, the carrier's blood cells also can undergo sickling and cause symptoms. In one sense it is fortunate when carriers do show some abnormality; they can then be identified for the purposes of genetic counseling. In fact, to avoid some possible confusion, at the present time we do not identify the genes as such in our studies, only the characteristic (phenotype), either homozygous or, hopefully as well, heterozygous, for which they are determinant.

It is crucial to understand the difference between being a carrier of a disease and actually having the disease. The carrier usually (but not always, as we have seen above) is normal and without symptoms, while the person with the disease, the homozygote, is sick in some way. The individual with sickle-cell anemia has both chronic and acute symptoms, while the carrier has no symptoms or has them only under extraordinary circumstances.

A very important point to understand about reproduction involving recessive genes is that the outcome in the offspring is determined *by chance*. This point can be well illustrated by referring once again to Mendel's plants. In the example of Mendel's second-generation plants, we say that there is a 1-in-4 chance that an offspring will have 2 recessive genes (yy) and produce green seeds. There is a 3-out-of-4 chance that the offspring will receive at least one large Y gene and make yellow seeds. (Of these 3, by chance, 2 of 4 will have only one large Y while 1 would have 2 large Ys). To clarify further the point about chance, consider the seeds of any 100 of these crossbred hybrid plants. Out of the 100, *on the average* 25 plants will have green seeds. However, some groups of 100 plants might contain 27 and others 23 green-seeded plants. The *average* number of green-seeded plants will be 25. The larger the number of plants, the closer this average will be approximated. Of a million of these plants, for example, just about 25 percent would be green. It is like tossing coins. The heads will on the average occur 50 percent of the time and the tails the other 50 percent. There could be a streak of 7 heads, 5 tails, or any combination thereof. On a given toss we cannot predict whether it will be a head or a tail, but we can say that the chance of a head or a tail is 50 percent, regardless of what came up on the last toss.

To look again at a human genetic issue, consider the marriage of two people with a trait for sickle-cell anemia. Each child would have a 1-in-4 chance of being homozygous and having the disease. The fact that the first child was or was not affected would not alter the chances for the next child. Some families could have 4 affected children and some none, but overall, 1 out of every 4 children born to all carrier couples would have the disease.

The one-in-four chance in the above example of the seeds depends on the fact that each of the hybrid plants carries the recessive gene. If we merely brought yellow seed-producing plants together without prior knowledge, some might be heterozygous and some might be homozygous. The percentages of yellow and green seeds produced in the unions would depend on how many or what proportion of the plants were heterozygotes. The fewer the plants with the recessive trait, the less the chance for producing green seeds. In other words, the rarer the gene in the population, the less likely it is that two recessives will come together in a random union. We call the occurrence of a recessive gene in a population its *frequency*.

The frequency of recessive genes in a given human population varies according to the disease in question and according to the population. Some recessive genes are quite common in certain groups, like the gene for sickle-cell anemia in blacks, which has a frequency of 10 percent; that is, 1 out of 10 blacks are recessive for sickle-cell anemia. A random marriage of any two blacks, thus, has a 1-in-100 (one-tenth of one-tenth) chance of bringing two carriers together. The children in such a marriage of carriers each has a 1-in-4 chance of being homozygous and having the disease of sickle-cell anemia.

Consider yet another inherited disorder, **Tay-Sachs disease.** One in every 30 Ashkenazic Jews is a carrier of the recessive trait. Thus, a random marriage of two individuals from this ethnic group would have a 1-in-900 chance of bringing two carriers together. The children born of such a marriage of two carriers would have a 25 percent chance of being homozygous and having the disorder.

In *cystic fibrosis,* somewhere between 1 in 30 and 1 in 60 individuals are carriers. Thus, 1 in 900 to 1800 random marriages is likely to bring two carriers together with a 1-in-4 chance of their offspring being affected.

There is a growing list of diseases that are now known to be recessive and inherited by the mating of two carriers. We have already mentioned several like sickle-cell anemia and Tay-Sachs disease. Another is thalassemia or Cooley's anemia, which affects people with origins in the Mediterranean basin. (See *anemia.*) A genetic disease that has gained a great deal of publicity is *phenylketonuria* or, in this age of abbreviation, PKU, which can lead to mental retardation. It occurs only about once in every 10,000 children. (See PKU [*phenylketonuria*].) *Galactosemia* is another rare inherited disease, occurring perhaps only once in 100,000 births. It is also carried on a recessive gene. In this disorder an enzyme is lacking which prevents the conversion of galactose, a common milk sugar, into glucose. There is likely to be brain damage, along with liver disease and cataracts. The treatment is a diet free of galactose.

Approximately 100 million people in the world are susceptible to development of anemia when their red blood cells are exposed to a variety of common drugs such as aspirin, sulfur, antimalarials, vitamin

K, and some foods like fava beans. Their red cells contain a lower than normal amount of an enzyme called *glucose-6-phosphate dehydrogenase*, G6PD for short, which is necessary for the maintenance of an intact red cell. Because the anemia is usually mild, it is not of great practical concern. People who belong to ethnic groups in which there is a significant incidence of this disorder, blacks and Orientals, can, if their doctor suggests, be tested for the defect before taking the drugs and food to which they might be sensitive. The disorder is more common and severe in males than in females, and the inheritance pattern is by a sex-linked recessive gene, which will be discussed below.

## SCREENING FOR THE TRAITS CAUSED BY ABNORMAL GENES

While some genetic diseases can be more or less successfully treated, like PKU, for most there is either no treatment or the treatment is unsatisfactory, burdensome, or costly. Under these circumstances the best treatment is prevention by (1) identifying the carrier prior to his or her reproduction, or (2) identifying the affected fetus early in pregnancy when therapeutic abortion is still a possibility. In recent years we have begun to study or *screen* people at risk for having recessive genes, e.g., blacks for sickle-cell anemia and Jews for Tay-Sachs disease. The objective is to provide individuals with genetic information so that they can, if they so wish, *prevent* the birth of children with the disease in question, either by refraining from having children with another carrier, or, as is more likely, if they do procreate with a carrier, by considering the possibility of a therapeutic abortion if the fetus can be shown to be affected. An affected fetus can now be recognized in a number of diseases, for example Tay-Sachs disease. Progress is also being made in detecting the fetus with sickle-cell disease. The number of diseases that can be recognized while the fetus is still in the womb is steadily increasing. The study of the fetus for recessively transmitted diseases is undertaken at the present time only in the marriages of two carriers. There would be little point, for example, in looking for Tay-Sachs disease in a fetus when only one parent is a carrier.

It is quite likely that the future will bring more and more screening so that each of us will be provided with genetic information about ourselves. Therefore, we will have to be very much better educated about genetics. It is not a simple topic. On a very practical level there is little chance of getting people to participate in a screening program such as one for Tay-Sachs disease unless those being screened know how serious the disease is. People must also understand what a carrier of a recessive trait is, and is not, for each particular disease under consideration. They must understand the implications of being a carrier, and be aware of the presently available techniques for identifying an affected fetus. They must know whether or not the disease for which they are being screened is one which can be identified in time to allow for a therapeutic abortion. Obviously, this information must be kept up to date. While everyone should be educated about genetics, no one should be compelled to undergo screening if he or she chooses not to.

There is little practical point in searching out carriers before the age when reproductive capability develops unless the carrier is affected by the disease in some way. We have made this point in connection with sickle-cell anemia. Many black parents have been made to feel a sense of urgency in having their children tested. The point is that those children who have sickle-cell anemia will inevitably be brought to medical attention anyway because of chronic and acute symptoms, while those carrying the trait will have no symptoms at all. Knowing that they have the trait will be of use to them only when they reach reproductive age.

## VARIATION AND MUTATIONS

The heredity factor or unit we call the gene determines such properties as eye and skin color, type of hair, body configuration, blood type, and all the other physical characteristics passed from generation to generation. Genes are thought to have a large part in determining for the individual such qualities as intelligence and special aptitudes and the relative immunity or susceptibility to some diseases that appear to run in some families. A combination of genetic material from the mother and the father gives rise to the new individual, who will resemble each parent in certain characteristics. It is estimated that the fruit fly, which has been used extensively in genetic experiments, has between 5000 and 15,000 genes on each of its 4 pairs of chromosomes. The number of human genes is somewhere between 10,000 and 100,000. You can easily appreciate how the mixing up of such great numbers of genes will give rise to almost limitless variations in the offspring.

Many important characteristics (height, intelligence, and special aptitudes, for example) appear to be transmitted not by one but several genes. These characteristics are said to be polygenic in origin. In predicting the outcome of mating when multiple genes are involved, we follow the Mendelian laws but find that the problem rapidly becomes very complex. The number of possible combinations soars. The inheritance of skin color is a good example. Classic studies in Jamaica assumed that 2 pairs of genes determined skin color. In the mating of a pure-strain black with a pure-strain white, all first generation are hybrid or, in this case, mulattoes. When mulattoes mate there are 16 possible combinations because two pairs of genes are involved. When only a single genetic pair is under consideration, as in Mendel's peas, you will recall that there are but 4 possible combinations in the second generation. Furthermore, these genes may travel in clusters, instead of being distributed randomly. You can see how complicated it gets.

Most congenital abnormalities—club feet (see *orthopedic concerns*); hip abnormality (see *hip, congenital dislocation of*); *cleft lip and cleft palate; spinal defects;* or congenital heart disease (see *heart disease, congenital*), to name just a few—are polygenic disorders. Genetic counseling in these situations must be highly individualized. Prenatal diagnosis is becoming more available.

Occasionally, genetic information is changed when it is passed on to the daughter cell. Consequently, the new cell has different characteristics. Possibly one of the units of the complicated structure gets turned around or lost altogether. When the new cell undergoes division, it will pass on the altered information, and all the progeny will have the different characteristics. In this manner *mutations* arise.

Mutations are permanent transmissible characteristics in the offspring. If the right mutation should occur, it would be possible, in theory at least, for a couple of redheads, both from families where there had been nothing but redheads, to produce a black-haired child. Furthermore, this child would pass the gene for black hair on to all his or her children. Mutations are going on all the time and account for the spontaneous appearance of some diseases, known to be hereditary, for which no explanation can be found. Unfortunately, the great majority are detrimental and result in inferior structures or functioning. Many are lethal. On occasion, a favorable mutation will occur and a superior individual results. It is the natural selection of these favorable mutations, according to the principles of Darwin, that is thought to be responsible for the gradual evolution of man over aeons of time. We don't know much about why these mutations occur or how to control them. We do know, however, that the *rate* of mutation can be increased by exposure to certain factors. Most of the knowledge in this field has come from experiments in which fruit flies were exposed to radiation. It has been shown conclusively that exposure to radiation increases the rate of mutation. Furthermore, the rate of mutation is proportional to the amount of radiation exposure—the more the radiation, the higher the rate of mutation. While this work has been done with insects, there is no reason to believe that the conclusions are not equally applicable to human beings. This possibility does not suggest that X-rays or other necessary sources of radiation should be avoided, but it does suggest that unnecessary sources of radiation be avoided, and the amount of exposure carefully controlled.

Many factors other than radiation must also be responsible for mutations, including certain chemicals and most probably some viruses.

Cancer is a mutation of certain body cells. Can we find a way to change the mutation involved in cancer back to normal or alter it somehow to render it incapable of further cell division? These are big questions, but when the cure for cancer eventually is discovered, as it certainly will be, it will lie in some such biochemical process, not in bigger and better surgery or X-ray treatments as we now know them.

### CHROMOSOMES AND CHROMOSOMAL ABNORMALITIES

Some years after Mendel's work in 1879, biologists discovered rods in the nucleus of cells undergoing division. These rods could be stained with certain dyes and seen under magnification. The name chromosome (meaning "colored body," chrome=color, soma=body) was given to these structures. It soon became apparent that the physical basis for heredity must lie in these chromosomes. It was shown eventually that the chromosomes did indeed carry the hereditary units, or genes. These threadlike structures we call chromosomes are individually visible only at cell division, when *daughter cells* are getting chromosomes from *parent cells*. Chromosomes have a definite size and shape, and each species of plant or animal has a definite number of chromosomes characteristic for the species. Man has 46 (23 pairs).

Ordinary cell division is called *mitosis*. By splitting in two, each chromosome makes a copy of itself, one copy going to each of the two daughter cells produced by the division. Each daughter cell thus receives exactly the same number and kind of chromosomes the parent cell had. In the formation of egg and sperm cells, a unique type of division occurs, called *meiosis* or *reduction division*. In meiosis, each daughter cell winds up with only half the number of chromosomes, one from each of the paired chromosomes. The corresponding genes on each pair go with their chromosome. Thus, a recessive gene in a heterozygote will go to one-half of the eggs or sperms, and its normal counterpart to the other half. In the Punnett's squares which we saw earlier, the corresponding genes Y and y come from one pair of chromosomes and go to separate daughter cells only during meiosis. This halving, and combining, makes possible the bringing together of two recessive genes leading to the production of a disease. Human egg and sperm cells have only 23 chromosomes each. When they combine, the new individual formed by their union has 46 chromosomes, the characteristic number for the human species. If the chromosomes were not halved before fertilization, they would double with each succeeding generation.

On rare occasions in meiosis there is an uneven apportionment of chromosomes to the daughter cells. Daughter cells may form with an extra or missing chromosome. This is called *nondisjunction*. Another accident that may happen in meiosis is *translocation*, where a segment of one chromosome shifts to another chromosome. Egg and sperm cells having either nondisjunction or translocation of the chromosomes may be incapable of fertilization. Or, if the egg is fertilized, the combination may give rise to an abnormal individual. The study of chromosomal conditions is called *cytogenetics*. In recent years there has been a veritable explosion of knowledge in this area.

Newer chemical methods of separating and staining enable geneticists to work from photographic prints of the chromosomes enlarged 3000 or 4000 times. The pairs of chromosomes are assigned numbers (from 1 through 22) according to the length and position of the *centromere*, the sharply constricted region joining the halves of the pair. The pairs through 22 are called *autosomes*. There are in addition the two chromosomes determining sex, making the total of 46 chromosomes per person. The generally accepted *Denver Classification* assigns the autosomes to seven groups, designated by letters of the alphabet. The sex chromosomes are of two types, X and Y. The female has 2 X chromosomes, the male an X and a Y. In meiosis, the mother's X chromosomes go to each daughter cell (egg). The father's sperm cells are equally divided between those with an X and those with a Y chromosome. The union of a Y-containing sperm with the egg, resulting in an XY combination, produces a male. It is the father, therefore, who determines the sex of the baby.

The X chromosome is longer than the Y and contains more genes. Thus, in males, some genes come only from the mother. If a recessive gene on that part of the X chromosome which is lacking in the Y chromosome is abnormal, there is no dominant gene to oppose it and the male will be affected with the disease. In the female, it is more complex. Of the two X chromosomes that exist in every cell in her body (except the egg or *germ* cells), one will become inactivated early in fetal development. This happens on a chance basis; in other words, about half of her cells will have an active X chromosome inherited from the mother, the other half an active X chromosome inherited from her father. Therefore, in an X-linked chromosomal disorder, the female will be only partially afflicted. For instance, in the disorder characterized by a deficiency in the G6PD enzyme, mentioned above, the female will be deficient only in about one-half of her cells; others will manufacture this enzyme and she will not show symptoms. However, she will be a carrier of the abnormal gene, capable of passing it on to her children.

Many of the hemophilias (see *bleeding disorders*) follow this sex-linked pattern of inheritance with females as carriers, not showing symptoms, and males having the disease. On the average, one-half of the male offspring of a mother carrying the defective gene will have hemophilia. The other half will be normal, having received a maternal X chromosome not containing the abnormal gene. On the average, one-half of the mother's female offspring will be carriers just as the mother is and the other half normal noncarriers.

All the genetic diseases now known to be associated with chromosomal abnormalities appear to stem from either too much or too little genetic material. The most common of these is **Down's syndrome,** also known as *Mongolism,* in which chromosome number 21 is involved. Children with Down's syndrome have definite physical characteristics that make early recognition possible. These children are invariably retarded (see **developmental disabilities**). Many have associated heart anomalies. It appears that this abnormality arises in meiosis, the unique type of cell division which prepares the ovum for fertilization. Instead of half the chromosomes going to each daughter cell, an ovum is formed which has 2 number 21 chromosomes, instead of just 1. When this ovum subsequently is fertilized, receiving another number 21 chromosome from the sperm, the result is a cell with 3 number 21 chromosomes. In this most common form of Down's syndrome, the mother is genetically normal by our present measurements.

We know how Down's syndrome comes about but we still don't know why. The abnormality is more common as the mother's age increases, particularly over 35, but does not appear to be related to the father's age. This observation leads us to assume that Down's syndrome results when an abnormal egg cell is fertilized by a normal sperm cell, rather than the other way around.

In about 1 Down's syndrome child in 50, a different type of chromosomal anomaly has occurred, indicating that normal siblings and one of the child's parents are carriers of the disease, that is, normal themselves but carrying a chromosomal defect which can be passed on to and find expression in their children.

This anomaly is called a *translocation,* meaning that a segment section of one of the number 21 chromosome pairs was split off and joined another chromosome, usually one of the D group in the Denver Classification. We won't go into further detail on this complex process. Suffice it to say that some of the offspring will have Down's syndrome, others will be carriers and otherwise normal, and others will be normal in all respects, including their chromosomes.

When a Down's syndrome child is born to a young woman, cytogenetic analysis of the child is required to determine whether it is the nondisjunction type (usually associated with age and not inheritable) or the translocation type, which is inherited and passed on to future generations. If it is the translocation type of chromosomal abnormality, the parents and their relatives should also be checked because they are likely to have it also. In either situation, the parents need genetic counseling in planning for future children.

There are several other well-recognized chromosomal abnormalities which are associated with defects in the child. In the disorder known as *Klinefelter's syndrome*, males have an extra X chromosome. Instead of being XY, they are XXY. The disorder becomes manifest usually in adolescence when the testes fail to develop and growth of the breasts occurs. The abnormal testes produce neither sperm nor testosterone, the male sex hormone (see *hormones*). Puberty may be delayed. About 25 percent of the children are mentally retarded and there is an increased frequency of antisocial behavior and delinquency. Treatment consists of giving sufficient male sex hormones to promote sexual development, and psychological counseling. Klinefelter's syndrome occurs in about 2 males per 1000 in the population. It is more common in pregnancies of older (over 40) women.

In *Turner's syndrome*, which affects females, an X chromosome is missing; that is, the girls have only 1 instead of 2 Xs. The disorder occurs in about 1 in 2500 live-born females and in about 5 percent of aborted fetuses. Patients with Turner's syndrome do not mature sexually at puberty because the ovaries fail to develop. The breasts do not develop, the external genitalia remain infantile, and menstruation does not occur. The condition can be suspected long before puberty because of a characteristic appearance and other associated defects. At birth, affected individuals may be significantly shorter than normal and the height usually remains abnormally low thereafter. Rarely do adults grow beyond 58 inches. The appearance includes a stocky build, an unusual facial appearance, webbing of the neck, a low hairline over the back of the neck, prominent ears, a small lower jaw, widely spaced nipples, and an inability to completely straighten out the arm, with a resulting angle at the elbow. In the young infant there may be loose skin folds in the nape of the neck instead of webbing. Sometimes the top parts of the hands and feet are swollen. There are often associated heart and kidney abnormalities. While most of the children are normal intellectually, there is an increased chance of mental retardation. There is no cure for the disorder. The absence of female sex hormones or estrogen can be treated by giving the hormone by mouth to promote sexual development. By cycling the estrogen and progesterone, menstruation can be brought on and regulated. By the replacement of the missing hormones, the children can lead relatively normal lives. They are sterile because of the lack of ovaries. Psychological help is often needed.

While it is not surprising that too many or too few chromosomes would cause defective organs, some individuals with chromosomal variations appear not to have any associated problems. In a study under way at The Children's Hospital Medical Center involving newborn male infants, 33 out of 11,000 babies studied had an abnormality of the chromosomes without any apparent ill effect, at least during the several years since the study began. Whether difficulties will develop later remains to be seen. The fact that the parents of this group of babies, primarily their mothers, had the same chromosomal pattern and are normal individuals argues for a normal future. Similar studies are under way at other university centers.

### AMNIOCENTESIS AND THERAPEUTIC ABORTION

One immediate application of our present knowledge about chromosomes is analysis prior to birth. A small sample of amniotic fluid is obtained through the mother's abdominal wall and womb by means of a long hollow needle. The technique is called *amniocentesis*. The fluid contains free-floating cells shed from the fetus. The chromosomes of these cells are like those of the infant from which they originated and show any abnormalities. Amniocentesis should be performed in patients at high risk for having infants with chromosomal abnormalities, such as a mother known to have a translocated number 21, or one who has already produced an infant with a chromosomal abnormality, or a pregnant woman over 40. Finding abnormal chromosomes is an indication for performing a therapeutic abortion. Patients undergoing this testing should decide beforehand whether such an abortion is desirable for them.

A similar principle is being applied to disorders caused by abnormal genes in which the chromosomes by our present techniques appear normal. (We are not yet at the point where individual genes on the chromosomes can be characterized.) In a growing list of inherited biochemical disorders like *Tay-Sachs disease*, analysis of the fetal cells or of the amniotic fluid itself, can identify the chemical abnormality which is an expression of the abnormal gene. When this fatal disease is thought to be likely, based on the family history and detection of the carrier state in both parents, analysis of the baby's cells during early pregnancy can provide a definite answer. If the fetus is affected, the test can point the way to a therapeutic abortion.

This approach is being attempted with other inherited diseases with identifiable abnormalities. Progress is being made, e.g., in identifying fetuses with sickle-cell anemia and thalassemia. It should be pointed out that the risk of amniocentesis causing spontaneous abortion is about 1 to 2 percent. At this point, there is a growing trend to identify the high-risk fetus and to perform an abortion. In turn, the ability to recognize the affected fetus makes it possible to screen people only after they are married, so that being a carrier need not enter into the decision of whether or not to get married. Without being able to detect an affected fetus, two carriers would just have to take their chances and might even decide not to have children at all.

As new techniques are developed, we will certainly make great strides in this field. The technique of directly visualizing the fetus through a fibrooptic tube inserted in the uterus is being developed as another way of identifying abnormal fetuses.

323

German
measles

CONCLUSION

The science of genetics is still in its infancy. When a baby with a congenital abnormality is born, the parents are naturally distraught and want to know the cause of the condition and the chances of recurrence. Before another pregnancy is undertaken, they should seek genetic counseling. In fact, a careful genetic history should be part of every premarital health check. This is generally overlooked. A better informed public can demand this kind of service. People should become informed about and keep a record of the health of members of their family trees. The more up-to-date data, the better the genetic advice which can be given. The diagnosis of any stillborn baby is also important. Most large medical centers have specialists in genetic counseling. Also consult your family doctor who may or may not be expert in this area. For the center nearest your home, consult your physician or contact The National Genetics Foundation, Inc., 250 West 57th Street, New York, N.Y. 10019. When a question arises, be sure to avail yourselves of the facts.
　　See *birth defects, severe.*


*German measles* or *rubella* is one of the common childhood diseases. The recent development of a vaccine (see *immunization*) makes it possible to protect people, especially pregnant women, against illness with this virus. For children, rubella is a harmless nuisance. It would hardly be worth worrying about it if this were the whole story. However, as is well known now, the great importance of rubella is its ability to damage the unborn fetus during the first 3 months of pregnancy. Serious defects result, including blindness, deafness, and heart conditions. Because of the threat to the unborn child, rubella has become a major public health problem in the United States. The major goal of immunization programs at present is to protect pregnant women against infection.
　　Rubella is sometimes called the 3-day measles, which serves to differentiate it from its more incapacitating cousin, regular 5-day *measles,* or *rubeola.* Exposure to a case of rubella is the only known way of contracting the disease. The symptoms do not ordinarily appear for 16 to 18 days. We call this lag time the *incubation period,* during which the virus begins multiplication in the body but has not yet caused symptoms. (See *infections.*) The incubation period can range from 14 to 21 days, but the average is 16 to 18 days. In the classic case, the child becomes mildly ill

with low-grade *fever* and some nasal running about 24 to 36 hours before the rash develops. Characteristic is the painful swelling of the lymph nodes at the base of the skull in the back, behind the ears, and in the rear portions of the neck. The swollen glands may persist for as long as 6 or 7 days, even beyond the disappearance of the rash. The rash, which consists of very fine, red, slightly raised spots, begins on the face and spreads within 24 hours over the rest of the body. Besides the rash, there may be a large area of flushed red skin. By the third day the rash reaches the lower legs and is already beginning to fade on the face. The child is nowhere near as ill as he or she would be with regular measles, lacking the very high fever, *cough,* and intense malaise. Antibodies are formed against the virus and immunity lasts for life. A small percentage of children and especially adults develop *joint pain* and swelling, which heal completely on their own.

This description of rubella fits its classic or full-blown form. Many children and adults have milder cases. The less classic or atypical forms of rubella, which account for a high percentage of all cases, are very difficult to distinguish on appearance alone from other virus infections, so much so that even the most expert physicians have trouble telling one from the other. Nonimmune pregnant females (and other adults) have an even more variable response to rubella infection. Sometimes the mother-to-be will have a full-blown case of rubella, identical with the typical childhood form. But all too often the illness is atypical, only partially resembling classic rubella. In many cases, no symptoms at all develop, even though an actual infection is occurring. The mother becomes infected, develops antibodies in response to the infection, but develops no telltale symptoms to warn the physician that rubella is attacking. We call this a *subclinical infection.* The virus is no less dangerous for the fetus even if the mother herself does not develop symptoms of rubella. She need only harbor and be infected with the virus.

In a child, once rubella has developed, there is very little that needs to be done. Like other virus infections, rubella does not respond to antibiotics and time alone will heal. The child is rarely very ill. He need not stay in bed and can certainly be up and around in the house or even out in the yard on a nice day. His diet can remain the same. Fever can be managed with aspirin. (See Part 1, Chapter 5: "Caring for the Sick Child at Home" for general care of the ill child.) Five full days after the rash has erupted, contagion is over and he may again have contact with nonfamily members. For example, if the rash begins on a Monday morning, by Saturday he can resume normal activities. The five-day rule is simply designed to prevent spread of the virus to others; it does not benefit the child in any way.

If your child has been exposed to what appears to be a case of rubella, there is really nothing that you can do in the way of preventing the development of the illness. Gamma globulin is not effective here, as it is with regular measles, and the vaccine given after exposure does not have time to work. The only important point is to be aware of the likelihood of his developing rubella and to be sure to notify any pregnant women with whom he may have come in contact if he becomes ill at the expected time, whether or not he has the typical picture. The child harboring rubella virus becomes contagious to other people from 7 days before the eruption of the rash (should one develop) to 5 days following the beginning of the rash. During the 7 days preceding eruption, the patient is contagious but has no symptoms. By the time it is realized that he has German measles, he has had ample opportunity to spread the virus to others. If possible, try to keep your child out of contact with pregnant women during the last 7 days of the incubation period (9 days after exposure) until 5 days after the illness itself begins. The difficulty of following this suggestion underlines the difficulty of controlling infection of pregnant women. A vaccination program is essential, in which all women are immunized before they become pregnant.

As we have mentioned, knowing whether an illness that looks like rubella is really rubella is not as simple as it sounds. In the classic case, a clinical diagnosis is likely to be correct. For the atypical case, and especially for the subclinical case, a clinical diagnosis is likely to be in error. Just as it is difficult for the physician to tell the cause of a sore throat (see *throat, sore*) simply by appearance, so it is with viral illnesses (of which rubella is only one) which cause low-grade fever and a generalized body *rash.* The laboratory can help in setting things straight. Just as we are able with a throat culture to determine whether or not streptococci are present in a sore throat, so we are able to culture people suspected of rubella to see whether or not they are harboring rubella virus. A simpler method of diagnosing rubella infection is to see whether or not antibody to rubella has developed or is developing. Antibody appears only after infection and is a telltale sign. (See *infections* for a discussion of culture and antibodies.)

Because by appearance rubella can easily be confused with other virus infections, one cannot rely on assurances that an unvaccinated pregnant woman was said to have had rubella as a child. We are much more willing to accept a history of infections such as regular measles, *chicken pox,* or *mumps* than we are a history of rubella. Because of the serious effects which rubella can have on the unborn fetus (see *developmental disabilities*), we dismiss almost completely a history of a woman having had rubella during her own childhood and rely on antibody measurement to see whether or not she has had prior infection. If antibody is not present, we conclude that she did not have rubella, despite the recollections of her mother and relatives. If she has a sufficient number of antibodies, then she is surely immune and need worry no more. If she lacks antibodies and is susceptible to rubella infection, it is very important to determine whether or not actual infection has occurred by repeating the antibody study at intervals after exposure, to see whether or not antibodies develop. Should they make their appearance, or increase, we conclude that infection has occurred and that transmission of the virus to the fetus is a possibility. At the present time there is no medical treatment for infection of the fetus nor is there any way of knowing for sure whether or not the fetus has been affected. However, if the pregnant mother is infected, the likelihood of the fetus having been affected and damaged is quite high. The only treatment is therapeutic abortion and this course must be seriously considered.

The only practical way to control rubella is to prevent it through immunization. Immunizing children is important for two reasons. First, immune children may decrease the spread of rubella, thereby reducing the likelihood that nonimmune pregnant women will be exposed to rubella. Second, immune girls will, it is hoped, grow up to become immune women. In the beginning of an immunization program, there will be many adolescent girls who have not had natural rubella or rubella immunization and who are therefore still susceptible. It is important that these girls be immunized before they become pregnant. We would not want to give them a live virus vaccine while they are pregnant for fear that the vaccine virus might infect and damage the fetus. Since a history of having had rubella is unreliable, our present policy is to check their blood for antibodies to rubella, whether or not they say they have had rubella or have been immunized. If antibodies are present in adequate number, we do not immunize them. If antibodies are insufficient or absent, we do give them the vaccine but *only* if we are convinced that they will not become pregnant during the next 2 months. This condition means that these girls must be on an effective and reliable form of birth control, be it abstinence, the pill, or whatever. The immune status of a pregnant woman who has not had rubella vaccine needs to be determined also. If she has sufficient antibodies, nothing more need be done. If her antibodies are insufficient or absent, she is *not* given rubella vaccine until after her pregnancy. Should she develop a rubella-like illness or be exposed to rubella, her antibodies must again be measured. As mentioned before, if a rise in antibodies occurs, rubella infection is concluded to have occurred and a therapeutic abortion must be considered.

Rubella vaccine is a live virus vaccine. The vaccine virus, a cousin of the rubella virus, is given by injection, and is capable of stimulating a similar, though not exactly identical, antibody response. The vaccine can be given any time after one year and can be combined with live mumps and measles vaccine. Thus far, the antibodies have persisted for as long as the several years during which the vaccine has been used. Whether or not the antibodies will last for life as they do after natural rubella remains to be seen. In children this vaccine is not accompanied by any significant reaction such as fever, even though actual infection occurs with the vaccine virus. A small but definite number of vaccinated adults develop transient arthritis (joint pain and swelling), usually of the knee. The effects of the vaccine virus upon the fetus are not as well known. However, there is every reason to believe that the vaccine virus can infect the fetus just as rubella virus itself does. For this reason, it is essential that the vaccine not be given to women who are pregnant or likely to become pregnant within 2 months of its administration.

See Part 1, Chapter 5: "Caring for the Sick Child at Home"; *immunization; infections*

*Glands, swollen.* The lymph glands are located throughout the body and are the sites of antibody production (see *infections*). The glands, which can be seen and felt because they are just below the skin, are those in the neck, armpits, and groin. The enlargement and mild tenderness of a gland means that it is producing antibodies to an infection close by. For example, an infected cut on the leg could lead to painful swelling of the groin lymph glands. Infections that stimulate enlargement of the neck lymph glands are found mainly in the nose and throat (see *colds; throat, sore;* and *mononucleosis, infectious*). A rare cause of persistent, painless enlarged lymph glands is *Hodgkin's disease.*

In children, enlarged neck glands usually persist for weeks to months following the resolution of the infection. Unless the lymph gland itself is abscessed, that is, contains pus, signified by increasing size, redness, and tenderness (see *abscess*), the enlarged glands are not treated as such. As mentioned, the enlargement is an indication that the body's defenses are working properly. Treatment is directed at the infection which is producing the response, and may, depending on the cause, require an antibiotic.

Enlarged neck lymph glands must be distinguished from salivary glands swollen with *mumps* infection, and with other lumps and bumps of the neck (see *neck, lumps and bumps in the*).

*Glandular problems:* see *hormones.*

*Glucose-6-phosphate dehydrogenase deficiency:* see *anemia.*

*"Glue ear":* see *earache.*

*Gonorrhea:* see *venereal disease.*

*Grand mal:* see *seizure disorders.*

*"Growing pains":* see *aches and pains.*

*Handicapped child.* Handicapping conditions in children are quite common. Even if only serious, primarily physical, disabilities are considered British and American surveys report between 7 and 10 percent of children are handicapped. If visual and hearing impairments, mental retardation, speech, learning, and behavior disorders are included, the figure rises to between 30 and 40 percent of children up to the age of 18. There are, of course, a great variety of disorders which range from mild to severe, from largely correctable to minimally so. Some problems are noticed at birth, like myelomeningocele (see *spinal defects*). Others have their onset later, such as *seizure disorders* following severe head trauma (see *head injuries*). Some are inherited disorders, such as *cystic fibrosis,* or sickle-cell anemia (see *anemia, genetics*).

Because of the range of disorders and the differences among families and children, it is difficult to generalize about the care of the handicapped child. However, students of this topic, such as Dr. Morris Green of the University of Indiana, Dr. Aake Mattsson of the University of Virginia, and Dr. Benjamin Spock, have pointed out some common issues in the care of handicapped children which apply to a greater or lesser extent in any given situation. Parents should be aware of these issues whether they have a handicapped child or have friends who do. For more specific, practical advice, and a reading list, see *developmental disabilities.*

Raising a handicapped child presents a special problem. The initial reaction to the diagnosis of a chronic, incurable problem often includes fear and anxiety, depression, guilt, even disbelief. It is not at all uncommon for doctors to have to repeat the explanation many times to otherwise intelligent parents who obviously, and understandably, do not want to "hear" what is being said. Psychologists call this way of handling unpleasant feelings *denial.* Denial is often expressed indirectly. The parents may complain about being poorly informed and may shop around among consultants in search of a more optimistic report. Denial is a way of avoiding the painful acceptance of the handicap. It does not work to the best interests of the child because it diverts the parents' energy away from dealing with the child's real needs.

A critical hurdle for the parents of a handicapped child is acknowl-edging, and then mastering, resentful and self-blaming feelings of having "caused" the disorder. The guilt can be overwhelming. Those parents who do not come to grips with their guilt may overprotect or pamper the child, limiting his or her contact with others. Prolonged parental overconcern can often be related to one of the following factors: the child or infant suffered a life-threatening condition at birth from which the family did not believe he would recover; the child has a hereditary disorder which is present among relatives who are living reminders of what to expect; the illness of the child stirs up emotional conflicts in the parents stemming from the past deaths of close relatives; the child was unwanted in the first place, causing a mixture of rejecting and loving feelings, particularly in the mother. Some parents go to the extreme of "saintly" self-denying behavior, maintaining, perhaps with some justifi-cation, that dealing with a serious or tragic handicap has enriched their lives.

In other families, the same factors may lead to rejection or neglect rather than overconcern. This rejection may come out indirectly, for example by "forgetting" needed instructions, medications, or appoint-ments, or by blaming the child or the hospital staff for complications of the illness. See *child abuse.*

It is critical that parents get in touch with these feelings, acknowledge them, and then achieve the objectivity to deal with their child as a person, regardless of the handicap. Few can achieve these insights on their own. With the more serious handicaps, most parents feel over-whelmed by the intense guilt of having inflicted hardship upon another human being, and some are unable to assume the responsibility for seeking needed psychological help. Sometimes, in this defensive state, parents are not capable of realistic planning for their child and need guidance in doing what is necessary and in the best interests of the family as a unit.

We recommend that the parents of a handicapped child find one stable group of health professionals who will provide technically com-petent, yet child- and family-oriented care. The professionals should be interested in the family as people. The group should have an identified coordinator of the various services which may be needed. The trust which the parents (and eventually the child himself) have in their physician, or nurse, will permit them gradually to talk openly about their concerns and reactions and to get at the painful feelings. This trust is gained only over time and the willingness on the part of the physician and others to respond meticulously, patiently, and compassionately to concerns, however trivial they may appear. The doctor may not be able to cure the problem, but he certainly should be able to offer concern and a willingness to be the child's advocate in terms of health care, schooling, social services, and general well-being. Parents should seek out this kind of professional help, judge it by the criteria mentioned, and try not to become impatient with slow progress. (See Part 1, Chapter 1: "Quality in Pediatric Care.")

The goals of care are to maximize the child's development and to minimize the effects of the handicap. Preventing psychological problems and promoting sound mental health are primary objectives. It is worth describing the common patterns of poor adjustment in adolescents with handicapping conditions to indicate what it is we must try to prevent. One group is fearful, inactive, without outside interests, and markedly dependent on their families. A second group is overly independent, often daring, engaging in reckless, often hair-raising activities. These youngsters make strong use of denial of the realistic dangers connected with their handicap. They are overly active and defiant. A third, less common pattern of adjustment is shyness and withdrawal. These youngsters harbor resentful attitudes toward normal people whom they regard bitterly as owing them payment for their suffering. These reactions obviously have their origins much earlier in childhood and are the final outcome of the child's efforts to master the chronic stress associated with his handicap. Each progressive step in his intellectual, emotional, and social development changes the psychologic impact of the illness on his personality and on his family. Each step can either enhance or diminish his ability to cope. Early recognition of unhealthy patterns by careful professional monitoring of the child and his family offers the best hope for prevention of a poor adjustment.

Other members of the family can also make poor adjustments. Often it takes years to resolve one's feelings about a handicapped child. Out of the best intentions, parents may develop patterns of coping which are not in their best interests. For example, they may stop going out together socially. Fathers may become distant by being away from home much of the time. They "arrange" to have business out of town or to stay late at the office, and subconsciously withdraw their support from the family because they cannot face their own pain. Mothers may become preoccupied with the handicapped child to the exclusion of siblings, spouse, friends, and relatives. Young siblings may have fantasies about having "caused" the disability. These siblings may try to compensate for their unpleasant feelings by being overly good, or they may express the feelings indirectly by developing psychosomatic symptoms (see Part 1, Chapter 4: "Complaints with an Emotional Element"). Financial strains can become serious and make even more compelling the necessity for health insurance coverage or health aid programs. Marital conflict is common and divorce more likely in these families.

In short, families with handicapped children are under great stress and should have the best professional help. The mother and father must

be encouraged to become active participants rather than passive observers. They need detailed facts and information and ideally should be
as knowledgeable about their child's handicaps as the doctor himself. A
high quality care program should provide this education. Group discussions with parents of similarly handicapped children may be helpful.
Friends of the family can help by encouraging parents to talk freely
about their lives rather than not bringing up the "forbidden" topic.
Parents should become aware of local and national organizations organized around their child's kind of handicap. (See listing under *developmental disabilities.*) There is growing recognition of the discrimination that exists in our society toward the handicapped in jobs, transportation, access to buildings, etc. There are increasingly vigorous legal and
other attacks on this discrimination. Recently the television personality
Mr. Fred Rogers and his colleagues have prepared a multimedia resource called "I am, I can, I will." This is a comprehensive package of
video, audio, and print materials with suggestions for use, intended to
help young children with disabilities develop a positive self-concept, self-
confidence, and motivation. For information, contact Family Communications Inc., 4802 Fifth Ave., Pittsburgh, Pa. 15213. Parents can serve as
a lobby to upgrade the quality of care, whether medical, educational, or
vocational, for these children.

See *developmental disabilities,* or specific disorder, listed alphabetically.


*Harelip:* see *cleft lip and cleft palate.*


*Hay fever* (allergic rhinitis) is an allergic disorder (see *allergy*) characterized by nasal discharge, sneezing, itching, and difficulty in breathing
through the nose. In hay fever, the part of the body affected by the
allergic reaction is the lining membrane (or mucosa) of the nasal passages, which becomes swollen and boggy. The mucous glands of the
nose whose secretions normally lubricate the nasal passages are overactive and produce copious quantities of mucus. Both the swelling of the
mucosa and the abundant mucus produced serve to decrease the size
of the nasal passageway. The narrowed nasal passageway and the swollen mucous membranes lead to difficulty in breathing through the nose
and a sense of nasal fullness. The nose is commonly itchy and the child
wants to rub or scratch it. Frequent associated symptoms are redness
and itchiness of the eyes (allergic *conjunctivitis*) and *sinusitis.*

The allergic individual reacts to airborne foreign materials—mainly
pollens and molds. The season of the year during which symptoms occur
gives an invaluable clue to the probable cause. Spring hay fever is

usually due to the pollens of grasses and trees. Hay fever in the late summer and early fall is usually caused by sensitivity to ragweed pollen and molds. Your physician may employ scratch skin tests to aid him in finding out which of the possible allergens is the culprit. With individuals in whom hay fever symptoms are present throughout the year (so-called *perennial rhinitis*), housedust is often found to be an important cause.

The two-pronged attack on hay fever involves both increasing the child's tolerance to the environmental allergens and decreasing his or her exposure to these allergens. In brief, the child's tolerance can be improved with antihistamines, which decrease the intensity of the reaction to the environmental antigens. Also, the exposure to allergens can be lessened, thereby relieving the symptoms, by avoiding contact and by filtering the air with an air conditioner to keep the pollens out of the child's room.

If a child's hay fever gets worse over a period of several years, or if it is particularly troublesome and not readily controlled with antihistamines, your doctor may attempt to hyposensitize the child by giving him injections of gradually increasing amounts of the offending allergens until the symptoms are relieved.

See *allergy.*

*Headache* is a very common symptom in children. Older children can tell you that their head is bothering them. With younger chldren you may have to infer head pain from their behavior. Headache occurs with a wide variety of conditions and often is only one of a group of symptoms. For example, children with strep throat (see *throat, sore*) often have *fever,* belly pains, and throat pain along with headache. Treating the infection relieves the headache.

With certain headaches, regardless of cause, you should contact the doctor promptly. If it is so severe that the child cries, clutching his or her head and lying down, get in touch with your doctor right away. If it is less severe, but interferes significantly with the child's activity steadily over a period of one hour, contact your doctor. A child who is up and about, playing, eating reasonably well, and who also complains of headache is not one to worry about, unless the headache goes on for more than a day. The child who refuses to play, stops eating, wants to be left alone, prefers to lie or sit down, and obviously is "not himself" is one to watch. It is important to observe the mental alertness of the child. If he is understanding, speaking, and responding to you in a normal way, you need be less concerned. If he is confused, "out of his head," excessively drowsy, particularly if he is hard to arouse or delirious (see *drowsiness, delirium, and lethargy*), get in touch with your doctor right away. These rules of thumb apply both night and day. In fact, if a child awakens out of a sleep because of headache, you should take the complaint even more seriously.

Some headaches last only for a short time but recur over a period of days, weeks, or even months. With such headaches a child may appear pale, complain of belly pain, and prefer to lie down. Then all passes and the child seems his usual self again only to have the same problem recur later. For this recurrent pattern of headaches, we suggest talking to your doctor.

Headache, like fever, is a symptom with many causes. Many *infections* have associated headaches. Strep throat is one example. Another is the flu or grippe (see *influenza*). One particular infection high on everyone's worry list is meningitis, an infection of the membrane-like sac surrounding the brain and spinal cord. Meningitis often also causes a stiff neck—one that is painful to move. While headache and stiff neck can be caused by meningitis, this particular kind of infection accounts for only a small percentage of children who have either a stiff neck or a headache. (See *neck pain.*) If you follow the simple rules described above for when to contact the doctor, meningitis will most probably be diagnosed before it can cause much trouble.

Headache accompanying nasal discharge and stuffiness suggests *sinusitis.* There is also tenderness and pain over the affected sinuses in the cheekbones (which develop by age 6) or in the forehead over the eyes which develop around age 10). Pain in the head following a blow or fall needs no explanation. This topic with its own special issues is discussed elsewhere (see *head injuries*). Chronic *lead poisoning* can also cause head pain, along with confusion, loss of appetite, pallor, and *vomiting.*

Headache may also be a manifestation of *migraine* in childhood. *Migraine headaches*, due to dilating of arteries beneath the skull on the surface of the brain, often but not always are localized to one side of the head, vary in severity, are recurrent, and are associated with loss of appetite and sometimes nausea and vomiting. Children with migraine headaches usually come from families in which such headaches are or were common. Motion sickness is also common in these children. We have seen what surely must be migraine headaches in children as early as 2 years, too young to describe their symptoms, but clearly in pain and incapacitated. Confusion seems to be a common symptom in very young children. Children with migraine can be helped with medications like phenobarbital, plus appropriate attention to emotional factors.

Headache may be an expression of nervous tension or may be used "deliberately" by a child to get his own way. Headaches which are psychologically caused are very "real," cause pain and suffering, and should be taken seriously. They are a way of asking for help (see Part 1,

Chapter 4: "Complaints with an Emotional Element"). They usually reflect uncomfortable feelings which are expressed in bodily symptoms instead of verbalized and are a warning that the child is having difficulty. Rather than waiting for him to "outgrow" his problem, talk the situation over with your doctor or nurse. An impartial outsider is often able to see things which parents are too close to see themselves. Emotional factors, whether or not they "cause" headaches, can certainly aggravate them, as is often the case with migraine headaches.

Some children, when fatigued, may complain of discomfort in their head and eyes, particularly if their vision is impaired. An eye exam is part of the doctor's assessment of headache. (See *vision problems.*)

The greatest worry of all with headache is, of course, **brain tumors.** Tumors, while able to cause headaches, account for an infinitesimally small number of the total. As a rule, headaches are a late manifestation of tumors rather than an early one. While few people can avoid thinking of the possibility of a tumor in a child with prolonged or recurrent headaches, the fact remains that tumor is a very rare explanation of these symptoms.

In addition to treating the underlying cause of headache, relief from the symptom can often be obtained from aspirin (see Part 1, Chapter 5: "Caring for the Sick Child at Home" under *fever control* for aspirin dosage) and cool towels applied to the head. If these simple measures don't work and you have not already spoken to your doctor, now is a good time to do so.

**Head injuries.** Minor bumps to the head are part and parcel of the daily rough and tumble of children. Rare is the baby who has not fallen from a chair or bed to the floor, or the child learning to walk who has not stumbled and struck his or her head. As Dr. Spock once pointed out, the child who has never bumped his head or fallen is being watched too closely. A good deal of crying, much reassurance, and a big hug usually clear up the difficulty in several minutes. All is soon forgotten. The child return to his normal play and nothing more need be done. While this sort of thing usually arouses anxiety in parents it does not cause them much difficulty. It is simply part of the daily routine.

On the other hand, blows to the head caused by a fall from some height, by a carelessly thrown rock or baseball, or by accidentally running into a low-lying beam, while usually harmless, can cause trouble. So can injuries in car accidents. (See Part 2, Chapters 8 and 12: "Accident Prevention" and "Car Safety.") Following a more severe blow of this type, the child will usually cry with considerable pain. He will stop what he is doing and sit or lie down and hold his head. He will look and act miserable. At the end of 5 or 10 minutes, although still quite unhappy, he will likely sit up and be willing to talk about what has just happened to him. He may complain of a *headache* and of feeling a little sleepy and ask to lie down. Although he should be watched, there is still no need for alarm on your part. If the child complains of an especially tender area on his head, you can relieve the pain by placing an ice pack on the sore spot.

The symptoms to be really concerned about are changes in the child's state of mental alertness. Such changes may indicate one or more of several complications. The greatest concern in head injuries is the possibility that small blood vessels coursing over the surface of the brain have been broken and that a blood clot is forming between the skull and the brain. A blood clot can compress the brain and cause symptoms. Bleeding may occur at the time of the injury or be delayed. If the bleeding in the clot is brisk, symptoms may occur quite quickly and treatment may be required promptly to remove the clot and control the site of bleeding. Often there is a lag of several hours between the blow and the onset of the bleeding. This is why the child with a severe blow to the head bears watching for at least six hours following the injury.

Sometimes a blow to the head, while not causing bleeding, will sufficiently shock the brain to cause symptoms. This kind of injury is called a *concussion*. It is quite common.

Children who have a complication of head injury will always show some symptom which will alert the parent. The blow that produces no symptoms is not one to be concerned about. What are the symptoms to look for? At worst he may lose consciousness, have a convulsion (see *seizure disorders*), or he may become confused, delirious, or disoriented (see *drowsiness, delirium, and lethargy*). If any of these symptoms are present, make arrangements to move your child to the nearest hospital emergency room or doctor's office immediately. Try to call the hospital to let them know that you are coming and also your doctor to let him know that you are going. However, once you have decided to move your child, do not wait to hear from your doctor if he can't be reached immediately. If your child is drowsy and hard to rouse, place him on the back seat of the car. Place pillows or cushions on either side of his head to stabilize the neck. Don't let his head bob about in lifting and transporting. If his scalp is bleeding, apply pressure with a gauze cloth. If you do not have a car at your disposal or are alone and need assistance in transportation, call the police or a neighbor and ask them to help. *Shock,* indicated by cold, wet, pale skin, may also be present. If there is any possibility of neck or back injury, do not try to move the child yourself unless the child's life is in danger, as on the highway. Call the hospital or police. (See Part 2, Chapter 9: "First Aid.")

If the child's behavior returns to normal after a head blow, you should still keep a watchful eye on him over the next 4 to 6 hours. He can resume normal activities if he seems well. If at any time he complains of headache (other than at the bruised site), becomes delirious, drowsy, or sleepy before his usual bedtime, vomits, or has difficulty in doing any customary tasks or moving any limb, get in touch with your doctor. If the child seems fine in every way, you can let him go to bed at his regular time and need not concern yourself with watching him through the night. However, you should check with your physician if the blow was severe. He may not want to examine the child, but will want to keep in touch and may advise you to wake him up during the night to see how he is doing. Of course, if awakened, he will be grumpy and sleepy, but you should be able to talk with him and convince yourself that he is in reasonable contact with his surroundings. As long as he remains alert and his breathing and general appearance seem normal, you have nothing to worry about. If, on the other hand, you have difficulty waking or talking with him, if he is not breathing well or his general appearance is peculiar in any way, call your doctor promptly. A good general rule to remember is that the child who acts well is well. There is nothing magical about blows to the head. Children who are having difficulty will show some signs and symptoms which any parent will recognize. If the child acts normal, relax, but continue to observe him.

Lumps on the heads of babies are likely to arouse considerable concern. An infant whose development is more advanced than suspected will roll off the side of a changing table or bed; a wobbly toddler just beginning to walk will trip and fall; a baby will explore the bathroom sink and do a backward flip. These situations are common. Following a fall in a young infant, there is usually a period of deafening silence lasting for seconds (which seem like hours), followed by the onset of howling. The baby is prone to develop a goose-egg lump on the head at the site of contact. Within 5 minutes, most babies usually calm down. Frequently, they are sleepy and uninterested in pursuing their previous activities and look somewhat in a state of shock. Despite their subdued state, it is usually possible for the parent to make some judgment about the issues discussed above in connection with the older child. Ask yourself if the baby is still in contact with his surroundings even though somewhat dazed and sleepy (something like his mood about a half hour before falling asleep in his normal routine). If the baby seems all right, the chances are overwhelming that he is all right and that nothing more need be done. If you are uncertain yourself about how he is behaving, don't hesitate to contact your physician. Telephone contact is usually enough. The goose egg gradually will disappear over the next several days. No special care is needed.

Here are the 8 signs of trouble in head injury which we, at Children's Hospital, ask parents to watch for:

1. If you cannot wake your child easily, notify your doctor. The child may well be exhausted by the ordeal surrounding the injury, but should be easily aroused by methods that you would ordinarily employ to awaken him from a deep sleep.

2. Children will, in most cases, vomit one or more times following a severe head injury. Should the vomiting recur more than once or twice, or should it begin again hours after it has ceased, notify your doctor.

3. If the pupil of one eye appears to be larger than the other, notify your doctor.

4. If the child does not use either arm or leg as well as previously, or is unsteady in walking, notify your doctor.

5. Should speech become slurred or the child be apparently unable to talk, notify your doctor.

6. If severe headache occurs, particularly if it increases in severity and is not relieved by aspirin, notify your doctor.

7. Should the child complain of "seeing double" or should you detect any failure of the eyes to move together appropriately, notify your doctor.

8. Should a convulsion occur, place the child on one side in a place where he cannot fall. Stay with the child until the convulsions begin to subside, and notify your doctor as soon as possible. (See *seizure disorders.*)

The question of X-raying a child's head often comes up. It is not routinely necessary to get an X-ray when children have suffered blows to the head. This is true even if the child has been examined by a doctor in his office or at the hospital. Skull X-rays are expensive and, except in special situations of head injury, rarely yield any important information. Don't feel that the examination of your child has been less than complete if the doctor does not order an X-ray. Doctors are much more interested in how the child acts than they are in his X-ray. You may wonder about missing a fracture of the skull. Indeed it is possible that a small crack might go undetected unless an X-ray is done, but skull fractures become important only if they cause symptoms in the child. Small cracks in the skull are very common and rarely of any importance. No special treatment is needed. Unless symptoms are present, it is not necessary for us to know if there is a small fracture.

Of prime concern to parents whose children have had head injuries is whether or not the child will be all right mentally and intellectually in the future. You can put your mind at ease unless your child is one of those rare children who require hospitalization and special treatment for a head injury. Even though the child may have been quite dazed or stunned after the fall or blow to the head, you need not fear permanent damage. Children are remarkably capable of tolerating blows to the head and of making quick recoveries. Your concern, however, is quite understandable. It is worth discussing with your doctor.

See Part 2, Chapter 8: "Accident Prevention."


*Head lice:* see *lice.*


*Health insurance:* see Part 1, Chapter 7: "Health-Care Delivery: The Broad Picture."


*Hearing and speech.*


### LANGUAGE DEVELOPMENT

The child's acquisition and development of language represents a major achievement, perhaps the most uniquely human aspect of growth and development. He or she will employ knowledge of language and ability to use language as a means for expressing his or her ideas, wants, and emotions. Language will assist the child in understanding the world, in self-perception, and in the achievement of academic skills.

In acquiring and developing language, a child must master words, sentence-building skills, and pronunciation. The onset of language occurs at approximately the same time in a great majority of children in different cultures. Research to date indicates that the acquisition and development of language are systematic, one predictable stage following another. Similar growth occurs in the ability to respond to sounds and words. From an early age, the child attends to voices and other environmental sounds. He will show a progressing ability to understand commands and comments. Comprehension skills tend to develop ahead of expressive skills, and in early childhood there is usually a lag between what the child understands and what he can say. The general milestones for expression and comprehension are listed in the table in this section.

Given a supportive environment, normal children learn language on their own. They do not have to be taught it. They do need some help along the way, but the basic work is theirs. For example, a child approaching his second birthday will frequently imitate parts of sentences spoken by family members. You might think he is learning by imitation, like a parrot. When you listen closely, however, it is apparent that he does not usually repeat the entire phrase or sentence. What he does repeat is consistent with the stage of sentence-building skills at which he finds himself. Attempts are often made by conscientious parents to have the child repeat exactly what was said, that is, to teach the child. This effort usually ends in frustration for both the parents or other family members and the child. The facts seem to indicate that children cannot be forced to change the way they build a sentence. In fact, the child is in all likelihood creating his sentence according to his knowledge of the grammar. Viewing the child as a *creator* of language is important to the family's relationship with him and to his own sense of accomplishment and desire to communicate.

As the child begins to attend selectively to the environmental stimuli around him, he mentally processes these stimuli. Although it is not clear exactly how his first words are acquired, it is the people in contact with him who provide the words or other symbols he must attach to the objects, events, and relationships he witnesses and experiences. As he better understands his world, he begins to apply words to it. The child must comprehend language before he can produce its various forms. Likewise, he must gain experience as a speaker. If he is listened to with interest and concern, if parents repeat and elaborate upon his brief statements and comments, communication can become rewarding and satisfying for him.

Just as parents have many different styles of speaking, children have their own styles as well. There are individual differences in the acquisition of speech and language. Not all children are easily understood in the early stages, while some appear to speak clearly from the outset. It is the wise parent who does not demand that a child repeat his utterance until it is correct. The parent should simply provide the child with the model of the correct pronunciation rather than continue to demand of the child what he is unable to do. By stating correctly what you know he is saying, you show him you understand at the same time that you allow him to hear the correct form. It can be quite frustrating for a child to find his attempts at communication stifled by the refusal of the listener to accept his statements. With careful listening, parents find that most of the time they can figure out what is being said by the context of the utterance.

There are many often overlooked opportunities for language stimulation in routine household activities and in trips to the library, shops, playgrounds, and parks. The learning which takes place during any of these experiences can be maximized by recounting them afterward and relating them to pictures in magazines, books, and drawing activities. Changes in the daily routine can provide opportunities for language experience; for example, what clothes are required for today's weather. Simple as it may seem, a good rule is to talk with the child!

Looking at a picture book with a child and later reading it to him (often with the child providing part of the story or just a word here and there) provide excellent language stimulation as well as great pleasure

*Hearing and speech*

| Age | Comprehension | Expression |
|---|---|---|
| 0–6 months | Responds to environmental sounds and voices by ceasing activity and turning toward the source; responds to pleasant vocal tones by cooing, and so forth, and to angry vocal tones by crying. | Different cries for discomfort, pain, and hunger; coos, laughs, gurgles, and vocalizes, one syllable at first, for example, *k, l, g,* and *ooh;* babbling begins; double syllables, for example, ba-ba; smiling and vocalizing in response to human speech and feelings of pleasure. |
| 6–12 months | Responds to words by modifying behavior; understands "no," own name, "bye-bye," and "pat-a-cake"; listens selectively to familiar words and by 12 months can follow simple instructions, for example, "Come here," "Sit down." | Babbling continues as self-play; imitates own sounds with both pitch and inflectional changes; more varied use of vowels and consonants; produces wide variety of speechlike sounds, some of which are not present in the speech around him, but found in another language; babbles to others as well; rudimentary imitation of the sounds of others; 1-to-2-word vocabulary besides "Mama," mixed in with own jargon. |
| 1–1½ years | Comprehends simple commands such as "Give it to me"; can point to familiar objects in pictures, in the room, to parts of his body, nose, eyes, ears, or hair. | 10 to 20 words; can name a familiar object or person; "1-word" stage; a single word stands for a sentence implying relationships, and so forth; meaning is clarified by situation, gestures, vocal inflection, and so forth; uses words to make needs known; much jargon mixed in; no more than 10 to 25 percent of all speech is intelligible; inconsistent use of all vowels and the following consonants: *m, p, b, k, g, w, h, n, t,* and *d;* substitutes *m, n, h, p, b* for more difficult consonants in many of the words; omits most final and some initial consonants. |
| 1½–3 years | Can identify increasing number of common objects by name and function; responds consistently to simple one-stage commands; | Two words put together to make a sentence, not randomly but reflecting child's rules for word order; the combinations reflect relationships, for example, possessive "Mommy |

| Age | Comprehension | Expression |
|---|---|---|
| | begins to comprehend more complex commands and points to body parts; distinguishes *in* and *under*; understands pronouns; has concept of size (big and small); has concept of "one." | sock," or action-object "Put book"; vocabulary spurts to 500 words by end of this period; expansion to 3-word sentences, which are combinations of the earlier relationships expressed, agent-action-object, for example, "Adam write pencil"; inflections such as past tense and plurals emerge; verbalizes immediate experiences; refers to self by full name, then pronoun; jargon almost gone; asks the names of things—"What's that?"; begins to carry on short conversations with dolls, and so forth; uses pronouns *I, me, you* inconsistently. |
| 3–4 years | Obeys 2-to-3-stage commands; listens to stories and nursery rhymes; likes repetition of same story; watches cartoons on television. | 3-to-5-or-more-word subject-predicate sentences, having mastered grammatical relations; uses adverbs of location; for example, *there*; begins to use adverbs of time and manner, for example, *soon, fast*; prepositions used appropriately; gives full name and sex; 900-to-1500-word vocabulary; recites songs or nursery rhymes from memory; spontaneously goes through picture cards and names; names colors; asks and answers questions beginning with *wh*; masters *m, n, p, h, w.* |
| 4–5 years | Reads by way of pictures; gets information from television; draws with pencil and crayon; recognizes some letters; obeys complex 4-part commands; knows difference between night and day. | 1500 to 2000 words; 4-to-5-or-more-word sentences; long detailed conversation, often including fantasy; asks for details in explanations; can define words by use; answers questions testing comprehension; uses plurals, articles (*a, the*) and conjunctions (*and, but*) consistently; can define object without seeing it; fully intelligible; masters *b, k, g, f, y, d*; may still omit or distort *th, ch, j, l, r, s,* and *z*. |

for both parent and child. Play is not always mentioned as a method of language stimulation. And yet it is one of the best, whether it is rough-and-tumble or playing in a more structured fashion, for example, games, toys, and so forth. Many children are able to play simple board games by the age of three. All of the ways in which speech is stimulated in the normal child apply also to the speech-disabled child, only a more conscious and concentrated effort must be made. For example, a preschool experience such as nursery school might be optional in the normal child and might be very necessary for the child with a speech handicap.

### COMMUNICATIVE DISORDERS OF CHILDHOOD

An individual is considered to have a communicative defect when his pattern of speech or hearing differs from what is accepted in his social group as normal, and interferes with understanding or being understood. When an individual is not understood, attention is taken away from his communicative intent and focused on the manner in which he speaks, resulting in interference with normal human communication.

How often communicative disorders occur is difficult to determine, but the best estimate is that approximately 10 percent of the population is communicatively impaired, for one reason or another. Studies indicate that communication problems are more frequent in males than females. For the purposes of this discussion we will consider communicative disorders in the following categories: disorders of hearing, disorders of articulation, stuttering, resonance disorders, voice (laryngeal) disorders, and disorders in language.

### HEARING LOSS FROM BIRTH TO 4 YEARS

If a child is born with a marked hearing loss, it will soon become apparent that he does not respond to sounds. During the first few months of life, whether the loss is mild or severe, he may show little awareness of speech or any other sounds. (See language development scale at the beginning of this chapter.) He will not be quieted by or turn to his mother's voice from another room. He will be surprised by the appearance of someone approaching him from behind if he has not felt the vibrations from the person's footsteps. He usually will not search for a sound source with his eyes. He will not be interested in a music box or other noise-producing toy unless he can see it. He will not sing to music. He will not be startled by or wakened by loud sounds. Sometimes he will seem to hear. However, when the sound is repeated and he makes no response, the initial reaction will be revealed as a mere coincidence.

At home and in the pediatrician's office, a child with a very severe loss responds only to very loud sounds and sometimes will not respond to sounds at all. In contrast, a child with a mild loss will respond to those sounds that are loud enough to stimulate what hearing he has but will not respond to sounds below his hearing threshold. Such a child with a mild loss is very confusing for the parents because he is inconsistent. It is important that a formal hearing test be given as soon as possible to any child, at whatever age, with an inconsistent response or consistent lack of response to sound.

As soon as a child becomes mobile, additional aspects of his behavior indicate poor ability to hear and understand sound. He may not attend to the command "no, no" unless he sees the speaker. He will not attend to his name called from a short distance behind him. He is unaware of someone at the door and does not associate footsteps, knock, or ring with the parents' going to the door. He shows little or no interest in the radio, television, and stereo unless it is very loud, and then he may only like to put his hands on it. He does not dance to music unless someone else is dancing, too; he will not move to music on his own. He pays no attention to the telephone.

At the age of about 12 to 18 months most children say their first words (*ma, da, milk, kitty*, and so forth) and show an indication of understanding a few others (*.no, come, hot, bad girl*, and so forth). When a child is born with a hearing loss or acquires one soon after birth, his comprehension and use of speech will be slower than normal and the slowness of this aspect of his development will depend on how severe his loss is and at what age it began. The most important characteristics of a hearing-impaired child are his reduced attention to speech and his reduced use of it. His speech output from infancy on is noticeably reduced in quantity and quality when compared to his normal-hearing peers. He uses gesture, not words, to communicate. Therefore, a child who at 12 to 18 months has no words in his vocabulary, shows little or no comprehension of single words, and responds inconsistently to sounds other than speech should have his hearing tested.

Between ages 2 and 3 years a normal-hearing child acquires vocabulary rapidly and has several hundred words. (See language development scale.) A child who is born with a hearing loss or who develops a loss a few months after birth will continue to become more and more different in speech and language development from his peers if the loss is not detected and given the necessary remediation early in life. By age 2 his language skills will be significantly poorer than normal. He will have few words in his vocabulary and these will not be clearly articulated. He will not have begun to put words together in short sentences. If gestures are not used or if he cannot see the speaker's face, he will comprehend the speech of others poorly and will seldom do what he is told. He will appear to be disobedient because he hears commands poorly. Toilet training prior to 3 years will likely be very difficult because of the complex interaction between acquiring this skill and understanding speech.

Between ages 3 and 4, the child with a mild loss will not have as many words in his vocabulary as his normal-hearing peers. He will not pronounce his words as clearly or repeat new words as easily. He has difficulty understanding new words, and does not use appropriate sentence structure. For example, at 3½ years a mildly hearing-impaired child might say, "Go now, Grandma" (meaning "Let's go to Grandma's now"). Or at 4½ years he might say, "Let's go Grandma." Both are examples of significantly poorer than normal speech. On this basis alone he should be referred for complete evaluation of his communicative skills. Another pronounced difficulty in a child with mild hearing impairment is his frequent inability to understand and make use of time concepts. For example, he is not able to be quieted by telling him: "In a few minutes (we go home)," "Later (you go out to play)," "After (we will get a lollipop)," "Tomorrow (we go to Grandma's)," "Before (we leave, Mommy has to call Daddy)." Another significant problem is in understanding *wh* and *how* questions: "*Where* are you?"; "*How* many?"; "*Who* is it?"; "*What* are they doing?" Often the child with a mild hearing impairment will repeat the question or appear to ignore it entirely. The speech of such a child will be characterized by omission or incorrect pronunciation of the consonants in many words and omission of small words (*in, at, on, and, by,* and so forth), in addition to reduced vocabulary and poor grammar.

Occasionally, transient hearing loss appears from infancy to 4 years and is often the result of an ear infection which may or may not be painful. Sometimes the parents' only clue to the child's temporary hearing problem is his poor attention to their speech. Often this is interpreted as stubbornness and disobedience. Any deviance in listening behavior should be evaluated, first by the pediatrician or nurse, if necessary, then by other specialists in hearing such as audiologists and otologists. Recent evidence suggests that protracted yet transient loss of hearing due to middle-ear disease, for example (see *earache*), may have a major effect on the child's acquisition of language.

After age 4 a child born with a severe loss of hearing, or who acquired a severe loss shortly after birth, will continue to differ more and more sharply from other children in communicative skills, unless he receives intensive therapy.

### HEARING LOSS FROM AGE 5 TO 10 YEARS

Age 5 is important because most children begin their first school experience at or around this age. School may represent the child's first consistent experience with adults and sometimes with children outside the home. His performance at school will be governed by his ability to hear and understand what others say and his ability to respond appropriately to them.

A hearing loss acquired between ages 5 to 10 years is often not so readily apparent to the parents as is a hearing loss in a younger child. Furthermore, depending upon fluctuations in the underlying cause, the symptoms may vary in intensity. Common behavioral indications of hearing loss at this age are: (1) not paying attention to the teacher or the parents unless spoken to loudly or more than once, especially when called out of doors. The parents often state that "he hears when and what he wants to." He may talk to classmates in school as though he is unaware of the teacher. He may repeatedly look to a classmate to find out what is happening in the classroom. He may be overactive in school or at home. (2) His school performance is usually poorer than expected. The classroom teacher may describe his behavior as being "inattentive" and "disruptive." Marks drop unexpectedly, but performance is adequate with individual instruction. He usually has the most difficulty in learning to read and spell. Learning a foreign language may also be a problem. (3) Social adaptation and learning may be troublesome. The most common characteristic of the child with transient hearing loss is that he plays and talks louder than usual. On the other hand, occasionally a child manifests hearing loss by being vague, as though in a dream world, and less outgoing than usual. (4) Other aspects of behavior that may indicate acquired hearing loss are turning up the TV volume or sitting closer to the TV than usual; reduced ability to hear on the telephone or ability to hear better with one ear than the other; reduced ability to hear a watch tick; inability to determine from which direction a sound originates; complaints of occasional pain or ringing in the ears; dizziness and/or balance difficulty in a child who has been until then otherwise well-coordinated; and excessive annoyance at loud sounds.

The 5-to-10-year-old child who acquires a more severe loss will have correspondingly greater difficulty and his problems will be readily apparent. If the means to resolve his problems are apparent, these should be undertaken immediately. If a severe loss is not reversible, such a child can be expected to show some catastrophic behavior. It is a frightening thing to be slowly or suddenly deprived of some or all sound. He will miss the comforting background noises that indicate all is going well, such as a parent busy in the kitchen, the furnace turning on, the cars going by in the street; he may also miss the sounds that indicate that something is the matter, such as mother scolding a sister or a siren wailing outside. In addition, he may have difficulty with part or all of the foreground sounds, such as a conversation at dinner, a TV program, and a friend's whispering. The potential alteration in his relationships with others that result from a mild and reversible hearing loss can be painful, but it will be much more so if the loss is severe and permanent. A tendency to temper tantrums may be part of the initial adjustment to such a loss. Parents, teachers, and pediatricians who are understanding can be of great benefit at this time. Again, it is necessary that the extent of hearing impairment be evaluated as soon as possible so that appropriate rehabilitation can begin.

### HEARING LOSS FROM AGE 10 TO ADULTHOOD

Hearing loss acquired after a child is 10 or more years is much more readily determined than in a younger child. The individual himself is aware of any significant change in his hearing or in any significant manner in which his hearing differs from others. He is usually the first to mention the hearing difficulty. If the problem is reversible, it should be treated immediately. If it is permanent and handicapping, all aspects of the child's life will be affected. Measures to facilitate his school and social adjustment should be arranged as soon as the loss is apparent in order to help him adjust to his condition.

Another type of behavior relevant to hearing loss that may occur in childhood is an attempt to feign a loss. Such an attempt is usually a bid for attention and is usually short-lived. Ordinarily, such a child does not exhibit any definite hearing difficulty and formal testing will show normal hearing. This behavior most commonly occurs for the first time on the occasion of the school hearing test. Sometimes such behavior also occurs when the child feels pressure because of doing poorly in school. If the child continues to insist on a hearing loss after formal testing has indicated normal hearing, psychiatric intervention may be indicated. (See Part 1, Chapter 4: "Complaints with an Emotional Element.")

### CONDITIONS THAT MAY BE ACCOMPANIED BY HEARING LOSS

Hearing loss may appear alone or with other problems. When it appears with other conditions, it may be overlooked because attention is directed to the other abnormality.

The possibility of hearing loss should be investigated if any of the following conditions apply at the time of birth: (1) mother's contraction of rubella (*German measles*) or other nonbacterial infection (for example, *cytomegalovirus*) that may affect the fetus; (2) family history of hereditary childhood hearing impairment; (3) congenital malformation of the external ear, cleft lip or palate (see *cleft lip and cleft palate*); (4) prematurity; (5) severe *jaundice* (for example, in Rh incompatibility).

All of these conditions raise the question of hearing impairment. If hearing appears normal in the first few months of life, it should be reevaluated at regular intervals. Because an infant's hearing is difficult to evaluate, the hearing loss may not show itself at birth but at a later age. Hereditary hearing impairment often manifests itself in later childhood.

Hearing loss should also be investigated if, at any time in the child's life, any of the following conditions are present: (1) chronic ear infections (otitis media, see *earache*); (2) head trauma, in the form of severe concussion and/or skull fracture (see *head injuries*); (3) a handicapping visual defect, mental defect, emotional defect, or physical defect such as *cerebral palsy*; (4) *meningitis* or encephalitis; (5) hereditary kidney disease in the child or a member of the immediate family (see *nephritis*); (6) hypothyroidism in early childhood (see *hormones*); (7) use of medication harmful to hearing such as the antibiotics gentamicin, kanamycin, dihydrostreptomycin, streptomycin, neomycin, polymyxin B, vancomycin; (8) *brain tumors.*

## ARTICULATION DISORDERS (TROUBLE IN SPEAKING CLEARLY)

Disorders of speech sound production or articulation disorders are the most frequently encountered speech problems in children. Articulation disorders are characterized by three types of errors. Substitution errors mean the child replaces one sound with another such as in the production of *wight* for *light*. An error of omission means that the child leaves out a particular speech sound such as in *boo* for *book*. The third type of articulation error is referred to as distortion, which is a slight change from normal, making speech less clear.

The speech sound production errors of children may vary from one speech sample to the next. For example, the child might be able to produce a sound well in a word, but as he places that word into a phrase or sentence, his production is not as good as previously noted.

There is wide variation among children in the number of misarticulated consonants and vowels. This may range from only a few sounds being misarticulated to the child being able to produce only a limited number of consonants and vowels. In this latter instance the child may well be unintelligible to the listener. Regardless of the number of speech sounds involved, the important point is that some children are unable to produce sounds with facility and consistency. To this extent they differ from normal-speaking children and should receive professional attention.

Failure to develop normal speech production skills may not be readily explained by any single factor. The normal production of speech involves the lungs, larynx, throat, mouth and tongue, nose, and lips. Dental irregularities may be a possible cause of speech disorder but are uncommon unless the teeth are severely disarranged. The tongue is very important in speech because it shapes the air coming from the lungs into words. It is rare that a speech problem can be attributed to a poorly functioning or "lazy" tongue. However, paralysis of the tongue musculature will have an obvious effect on speech production. A speech disorder resulting from an interference with the mechanics of speech production, because of weakness, paralysis, or severe incoordination of muscles, is called a *dysarthria*. Dysarthrias are most frequently encountered in children with cerebral palsy, although not limited to this condition. The symptoms of dysarthria are many. Not only will these children have varying problems with speech but may also demonstrate problems in feeding, which also requires coordinated use of the tongue. These children should be seen for a complete speech and language evaluation, in order to plan for treatment.

Tongue-tie (a limited range of motion of the tongue caused by a more forward than normal attachment of the tongue to the base of the mouth) is often viewed as a major cause of speech problems. Judgments concerning the relationship of tongue-tie to articulation problems should be made cautiously. Unless the tongue is severely reduced in its range of movement, that is, protrusion, elevation, and so forth, it is, in all likelihood, unrelated to the speech problem. Careful examination is warranted before a speech problem can be attributed to tongue-tie.

While it is useful to be aware of the known causes of articulation disorders, in the vast majority of cases no significant cause for the problem can be found, at least not with our present knowledge. Inaccurate learning of sounds is often used to explain such speech problems. Poor speech models in the environment, a lack of good speech stimulation, reduced motivation on the part of the child to improve his speech, disruption in the relationship between family and the child, and poor self-image are a few other factors mentioned as causes of speech articulation problems. The evidence to support these factors is largely clinical and represents the accumulated experiences of many professionals in the diagnosis and care of children with communication disorders. Research is required before the relationships of these conditions to speech disorders are clarified.

### STUTTERING

Stuttering has presented a problem to man since ancient times. There has been considerable speculation, writing, and research about it. It is still not very well understood.

The vast majority of stuttering children are identified between the third and fourth year of life. It is important to recognize that in the course of normal language development, between the second and fifth years, all children evidence periods of nonfluent speech, or disruptions in the natural flow of speech. These normal nonfluencies consist of pauses, repetitions of sounds, revisions of sentences, pauses in responding, and sound prolongation. While the exact reason for such nonfluencies is not firmly established, it has been theorized that, while children may understand language and possess the rules for sentence building, they lack the practice that adult speakers possess. Consequently, they have breaks in the natural flow of their sentences.

Stuttering results, in part at least, from overreaction on the part of a listener to this normal nonfluent behavior. The adult's response leads to a change in the interaction of the speaker (child) and listener (family). If a child is told to slow down, think before he talks, and so forth, he begins to know that something is wrong when he speaks. While the child may not know what he does when he speaks, he senses that his speech is not good. With sufficient negative experience, the child may well begin to expect problems with speech and see himself as a poor, ineffective speaker. He may begin to attempt avoidance of his problems, but his heightened self-consciousness only makes them worse.

For the above reasons, complaints from parents concerning nonfluent behavior in their child require careful attention. Counseling with regard to the nature of the child's behavior and the methods for dealing with it should be provided. The assistance of experienced professionals is frequently necessary. Early intervention can be very helpful in interrupting the vicious cycle which might otherwise develop.

Stuttering is in all likelihood not predominately a physiological problem. While there are instances of stuttering associated with wider neurological disorders, these are exceptions. Similarly, while stuttering may appear in families, it should not be regarded as hereditary and capable of being passed on to children. Rather, the attitude of the family to normal nonfluency and the subsequent changes in family-child interaction may well be the best explanation. To the best of present knowledge, stuttering is not learned by imitation. While children may occasionally mimic poor speech in another child, there is no evidence to suggest that they adopt this behavior as their own speech problem. The reactions of people toward the child's imitation may well establish the behavior of stuttering as his chief way of speaking.

### RESONANCE DISORDERS

Normally air from the lungs is given sound by the vibrations of the vocal cords in the larynx (voice box) and is then passed into the mouth to be shaped into sounds and words by the tongue and lips as they relate to the palate and teeth. For all speech sounds except *m*, *n*, and *ng*, the soft palate meets the back of the throat and prevents air from going through the nose. If most of the air is allowed to go through the nose, sufficient breath pressure cannot be built up in the mouth for consonant production. The sounds *m*, *n*, and *ng*, are formed by having some air pass through the nose and the mouth at the same time.

Resonance is impaired by an abnormal formation of the palate, as in cleft palate, short palate, and weakness or paralysis of the palate muscles. (See *cleft lip and cleft palate.*) In all of these conditions too much air escapes through the nose when speech is attempted. This is referred to as *hypernasality*. The sounds most affected will be vowels and *p*, *d*, *g*, *b*, *t*, *k*, *s*, *z*, and *sh*. Resonance is also affected by adenoids or tonsils blocking the opening at the back of the nose and the mouth, thereby preventing all air from going through the nose. (See *tonsils and adenoids.*) Speech in such a person sounds like he has a bad cold; for example, "I god a code in my doze" ("I got a cold in my nose"). These problems in making sounds of normal quality require professional help.

### VOICE OR LARYNGEAL DISORDERS

Voice sounds are produced by air from the lungs setting the vocal cords in the larynx into vibration. Voice has three different aspects—loudness, pitch, and quality. Loudness and changes in loudness result from the buildup of air pressure beneath the vocal cords prior to initiation of vocal cord vibration. Pitch is developed and maintained by the length and shape of the vocal cords which are controlled by the muscles of the larynx. Voice quality is most frequently dependent on the physical condition of the vocal cords and the way in which they are used. Voice disorders in childhood may result from vocal abuse (for example, hoarseness due to prolonged shouting), continued upper respiratory infections, damage to the larynx from trauma, and nonmalignant tumors. These voice disorders are related to structural changes in the larynx. Other voice disorders may occur as a result of poor learning or psychiatric problems. Any of the following words may be used to describe a voice problem that requires professional attention: hoarseness, harshness, breathiness (too much air and too little voice), shrillness, too high pitched, too low pitched. Disorders of voice may require the attention of an ear, nose, and throat specialist (*otolaryngologist*), and a voice specialist on referral by the family doctor.

### LANGUAGE DISORDERS

There are children who for no apparent reason fail to develop the normal comprehension and use of language. They may have deficits in all aspects of language function, that is, in vocabulary growth and usage, sentence-building skills, speech sound production, and in the comprehension of certain aspects of language. A number of evaluations must be made to exclude other disorders as contributing factors. It is important in the diagnosis of language disorders to evaluate the child's ability to hear, his intelligence, his ability to relate to and get along with others, his past and present medical history, and the social and family circumstances in which he lives.

It is not always possible to reach a satisfactory diagnosis of such a language disability on the first visit. Frequently, a child is placed in diagnostic therapy for 3 to 6 months. During this period of observation, a careful study of the child's skills and approaches to learning is made. Various techniques of teaching are explored in an attempt to find those which work best. Conclusions concerning further medical and educational help are usually reached following this period of diagnostic therapy.

### PROFESSIONALS WHO HELP WITH COMMUNICATIVE DISORDERS

When the doctor decides that a child has a communicative disorder, the child will be referred to an otolaryngologist and to members of two other professional groups: speech and language pathologists and audiologists. These professionals diagnose, treat, and perform reasearch in areas of speech, language, and hearing.

The otolaryngologist performs a complete ear, nose, and throat examination. Medical treatment, if indicated, will be recommended at that time. Unless the disorder can be completely cleared up by medical treatment, which is rare, the child will be referred to the other specialists to determine whether therapy is necessary.

The speech and language pathologist is frequently known by other titles, such as "therapist," "clinician," "communicologist," or "logopedist." The *audiologist*, known exclusively by this title, is skilled in the diagnosis and management of deficits in hearing sensitivity. Professionally qualified speech and language pathologists and audiologists are certified by the American Speech and Hearing Association or by certain governmental agencies, for example, a state department of education. They are employed in many settings: public schools, hospitals, community health agencies, governmental organizations, universities, and in private practice.

### WHAT TO DO IF YOU SUSPECT A SPEECH, LANGUAGE, OR HEARING PROBLEM IN YOUR CHILD

A child's hearing or speech problem is usually detected first by the parents or someone close to the family. Occasionally parents do not recognize their child's problem if he is their first child; at such times it is reasonable to listen to the advice of close relatives or friends who have had the experience of raising children and determine from them if a problem seems to exist. Sometimes one parent feels the child is not talking well enough or is unable to hear well while the other disagrees; in such cases it is reasonable to seek a professional opinion if the suspected problem persists for more than a few weeks.

As soon as one or both parents decide that there may be a problem, the pediatrician or family physician should be consulted. Further evaluation by appropriate specialists may be needed. If so, parents may request the name of a reputable clinic from the pediatrician or family physician or may call their local hospital for an appointment in the speech and hearing clinic.

Hearing can be tested in children of any age from birth onward. Active cooperation of the child is not essential. If the child is less than 3 years old, he will be tested in a soundproof room on a parent's lap. His reactions to sounds coming from loudspeakers to the right and left of him are observed. Some sounds will be very soft, to determine how faintly he can hear, and some will be very loud, to check his reflex response to loud sound. Many different sounds will be presented. Of these the most significant is the human voice. A baby as young as 4 months will often turn when his name is called softly, if his hearing is normal. An older child will be asked to point to body parts (eyes, nose, mouth, and so forth), or to "Look over here."

A child of 3 years and over will be tested by having earphones on a headset placed over his ears. Parents can prepare the child for this "airplane" or "spaceman" game at home, stressing that this is a fun listening game and not a worrisome or painful medical procedure. The audiologist will teach the child how to respond to the sounds presented through the earphones. Some of the sounds will be pure tones (similar to notes on a piano, for example) and some will be speech. If the child is talking, he will be asked to repeat both soft and comfortably loud speech. If unable to do so, he will be asked to point to pictures. After testing is completed, the audiologist will discuss the results with the parents and suggest any therapy or other evaluations that are necessary.

Screening tests for hearing loss in children whose hearing is apparently normal are conducted by many schools at several different grade levels each year. Sometimes children are tested individually and sometimes in groups. The usual test requires the child to indicate when he hears certain tones which are presented at a fairly soft level. If the child is unable to hear any of the tones, a note is sent to the parents requesting them to have their child evaluated by a specialist in hearing. How useful these tests are in finding problems in children who have no symptoms is controversial.

Because children vary greatly in their speech and language development and often have a spurt of growth in communication between 2 and 3 years, those with speech and language problems are usually not seen for an extensive evaluation until they are at least 2½ years old. Another reason for waiting is that most children will not produce much speech or cooperate with a stranger until they are about 3. More cooperation from the child is necessary for a speech and language evaluation than for a hearing evaluation. Parents can prepare a child by telling him that he will be playing some games and looking at some books. The speech and language pathologist will evaluate your child from the point of view of his vocabulary (how many words he understands and uses); his grammar (how he puts words together); his articulation (how well he pronounces letters and words); his fluency (how smoothly he speaks); his resonance (whether too much air comes through his nose or mouth as he talks); his voice (whether his pitch and loudness are normal for his age and sex); how well he takes in and gives out information; and the structure and movement of his mouth, tongue, palate, and lips to determine if there are any physical abnormalities to account for the problem. If the child has not already had a hearing test, a brief screening test will be given to rule out a hearing problem as a contributing factor. When testing is completed, the speech and language pathologist will discuss the results with the parents and recommend therapy or other necessary evaluations.

For further information regarding the qualifications of professionals and programs, you may contact:

American Speech and Hearing Association, 9030 Old Georgetown Road, Washington, D.C. 20014; American Hearing Society, 817 14th Street, NW, Washington, D.C. 20005; Alexander Graham Bell Association for the Deaf, 1537 35th Street, NW, Washington, D.C. 20007.

*Anthony Bashir, Ph.D.*
*Sylvia Topp, M.S.*

*Heart disease, congenital.* Most of the heart problems seen in children are ones with which they are born (congenital). About 9 infants out of every 1000 born will have some defect of their heart. Of these 9, 2 will have difficulty in the first year of life. In congenital heart disease, the pumping chambers, the valves which separate these chambers and allow blood to flow in one direction only, and/or the blood vessels leading from the heart to the lungs and other parts of the body are deformed and fail to function properly. There are many variations and the severity of impaired heart function varies widely.

Two major problems result, sometimes together. The first is heart failure, an inability of the heart to pump blood effectively. The symptoms of heart failure are shortness of breath, including cough (because of a filling up of the lungs with fluid), an increase in the size of the liver due to pooling of blood in it, and an accumulation of fluid in the body which is commonly noticeable as swelling of the ankles. Heart failure is treated mainly with digitalis, restriction of salt in the diet, and diuretics (fluid pills).

The second problem is a failure of a portion of blood to pass through the lungs where it normally exchanges carbon dioxide and oxygen with the inspired (breathed-in) air. This blood, which bypasses the lungs through abnormal communication in the heart, is recirculated in the body without a new supply of oxygen. Because this unoxygenated blood is blue (cyanotic), the child's skin, noticeably visible in the nail beds, will also be blue. In severe cases, the tips of the fingers become clubbed, presumably due to poor oxygen supply, and fainting spells may occur because the brain's need for oxygen is not being satisfactorily met. Fainting spells are more common in babies.

A doctor or nurse who suspects a congenital heart problem will refer the infant (including the newborn) to a medical center experienced in dealing with this specialized problem, for diagnostic studies and, if necessary, treatment.

One of the miracles of modern medicine is the development of surgery to correct or improve heart defects, even in the newborn. The timing of surgery, if there is to be any, is of course an individual matter.

For parents wanting additional information on this complicated subject, we refer you to the pamphlet *If Your Child Has a Congenital Heart Defect*, published by the American Heart Association and available through your local heart association.

*Heart murmurs.* The term "heart murmur" is a good example of one kind of difficulty that may arise in communication between doctor and patient or doctor and parent. More and more often in this age of the "knowledge explosion," new discoveries change the meanings doctors have in mind when they use certain words in the more-or-less technical vocabulary of medicine. As in the case of "heart murmur," there may be a time lag of as much as 30 or 40 years in the transfer of the new meaning from the medical domain to the public domain. When a parent hears the doctor speaking of heart murmurs, he may think that he understands perfectly, whereas in fact his mind is hearing and recording what a doctor of 1927 or perhaps 1917 would have intended the word to mean. Today, murmur has a quite different connotation to the doctor, but he is not always successful in getting this difference across to the parent. The parent may not be aware of any change in the medical attitude toward heart murmurs, and the doctor may not be aware of the parent's unawareness.

When the doctor applies his stethoscope to a patient's chest, he is listening for sounds that originate in the heart and the great blood vessels leading into and away from the heart. The heart is a large muscle whose powerful contractions force the blood along, and it has 4 valves whose rhythmical openings and closings keep the flow going in one direction. The closing of the valves prevents the blood from reversing its flow at four points in the circuit. The blood comes from the body into the *right atrium* of the heart through the great veins, passes through the *tricuspid valve* into the *right ventricle*, then through the *pulmonary valve* into the *pulmonary artery* and on into the lungs, where it picks up oxygen from the air we breathe. The *pulmonary vein* drains the *oxygenated* blood from the lungs into the *left atrium* of the heart. The regular contractions of the heart force the blood from this chamber through the *mitral valve* into the *left ventricle*, from which it enters the *aorta* through the *aortic valve*. The *aorta*, which is the main trunk of the arterial system, carries the blood to the various parts of the body for distribution of the oxygen and other substances it carries. For a mental picture you might liken the two atria and the two ventricles to the bulb of a syringe. As you squeeze the bulb to force the liquid out, so the heart contractions squeeze these chambers to force the blood along its course. The heart valves operate in pairs, the aortic and pulmonary valves forming one couple, the mitral and tricuspid the other. Through the stethoscope the physician can hear them opening and closing, "Lub-dub, lub-dub."

The murmur, however, is a quite different sound from the steady "lub-dub" of the valves. The murmur has a blowing, whistling, or rasping quality. In the past it was taken for granted that murmurs were always evidence of some structural defect of the heart—a hole through the wall of a chamber or some disease or malformation of a valve that obstructed the flow of blood or allowed it to flow backward through the valve. In point of fact, such defects do produce the sounds we group under murmurs, but we have come to recognize in recent years that not every murmur necessarily implies the existence of a defect.

Among children, only a small percent of the murmurs heard through the stethoscope are produced by structural defects of the heart. This comforting knowledge has come from new techniques which have yielded a great deal of precise information about the heart. One worth mentioning in detail is *cardiac catheterization*. In the catheterization procedure, thin plastic tubes with tiny electronic sensing devices at their tips are passed through the veins and arteries of the arms and legs into the chambers of the heart and the great vessels connecting the heart to the rest of the body. The sensing devices take pressure readings within the heart itself. Blood specimens can be drawn off through the tubes, or opaque material can be injected through the tubes for the taking of X-ray moving pictures of the blood flow through the heart's chambers and valves. The information gathered with these procedures gives the physician a detailed picture, with precise measurements, of what is going on in the heart, what structural defects (if any) exist, and where they are located.

The technique of *phonocardiography*, which measures and records the "picture" of sounds emanating from the heart, much as an *electrocardiogram* (EKG) records electrical impulses, also helps distinguish among the different kinds of murmurs.

The knowledge gained from these new techniques has improved our ability to recognize those murmurs (indeed, most of the murmurs of childhood) that are not associated with abnormalities. We can now say with considerable certainty just which murmurs are indications of heart defects and which come from perfectly normal hearts. Why a normal heart should produce murmurs has yet to be answered fully, but the investigation continues. The important point for the parent to understand is that, in contrast with past thinking, the presence of a murmur does not necessarily mean that the child's heart is abnormal. More often than not just the opposite is true; the heart is perfectly normal.

Looking back at the days before cardiac catheterization, we have no choice but to conclude regretfully that uncounted thousands of healthy children had the label "heart disease" pinned on them. About the best a parent of those days could hope for was that his child would somehow "outgrow" the murmur. Cardiac surgery did not exist; there was no direct attack possible upon a heart defect. The child had to live under medical supervision, drop out of the rough games of his or her peers, and perhaps sink into semi-invalidism. In a certain percentage of the cases, of course, the fears of overstressing a damaged heart were indeed warranted, but in how many others was the freedom of childhood unnecessarily curtailed? Nowadays, instead of applying the same treatment and restriction to all children with heart murmurs, we can pick out the ones who need special care and leave the rest alone.

Heart murmurs are very common. Approximately 30 percent of all children with normal hearts develop them at one time or another. Often they are present at one physical examination but absent the next time. Or they may be heard at every examination over a period of months or years. In general, however, most murmurs of this type are not heard in children beyond the age of 10 or 12. Whether such murmurs come and go or persist does not alter the fact that they are not related to abnormal hearts. We no longer talk of a child's "outgrowing" such a murmur. The use of the word "outgrow" suggests that there was something wrong with the heart in the first place. Our new understanding of the situation is that these murmurs have no significance, regardless of when they appear or how long they persist.

This new information about heart murmurs places the physician in a new position. In many cases of heart murmur, the doctor is able to identify the murmur as having no significance and can say there is no need to see the child again for reexamination. The doctor no longer has to hedge, "He has a murmur which seems to be nothing at all but I think he should be examined again in a year." Such a remark can cause parents concern. Instead, the doctor can say, "He has a murmur. The murmur is not a significant one and his heart is normal. I don't think he has to be reexamined for this finding." This does not mean that the murmur will not be heard again by the same physician or by another physician (for example, a school doctor). The physician means only that he has recognized the murmur and diagnosed it as not significant and not cause for future concern.

Of course, there are other murmurs that do reflect abnormalities of the heart. (See *rheumatic fever* and *heart disease, congenital*.) Murmurs of this type call for longer surveillance. Many are mild and cause no difficulties. Many are caused by temporary defects which correct themselves. But keep in mind that murmurs reflecting an abnormal heart are a distinct minority of all of the murmurs heard in childhood. Sometimes the doctor may not be able to make up his mind. In that event he may want to see the child again before making a decision, or he may refer the case to a specialist.

The time lag in communication, unfortunately, leads to confusion, and the word murmur still arouses anxiety in parents. The basic fault here is in communication. If your physician should ever use the word murmur in relation to your child's heart, make sure that you understand exactly what he means.

See *heart disease, congenital* and *rheumatic fever*.

*Heat rash:* see *rash.*

*Heels, painful:* see *aches and pains.*

*Height problems.* The eventual size of a child, assuming freedom from disease and a good diet, is largely determined by his heredity as it affects the number of growth cells in his or her bones (cartilage) and the responsiveness of these cells to various hormones which include growth hormone, thyroid hormone, insulin, and sex hormones. The precise mechanisms by which genes control growth are still obscure. We do not yet know the chemical explanation for one child growing faster or reaching a greater adult height than another.

The growth patterns of normal children from birth to *adolescence* have been identified for samples of the general population so that it is possible to rank a child's height with respect to other children of the same age. The growth charts widely used in the doctor's and nurse's office permit us to chart the course of a child's growth and detect deviations from the predicted curve.

We make an important distinction between the child who is growing at a normal rate, although he is at the bottom of the pack for height, and the child who is failing to grow. The first child is more than likely normal while the second requires study and treatment of the underlying cause.

The child who is growing abnormally fast may have an endocrine disorder, in particular excess growth hormone (GH) or sex hormones, or may simply be experiencing an unusually early onset of puberty. Growth hormone excess in childhood is extremely rare. Rapid growth stimulated by sex hormones is, of course, accompanied by the development of secondary sexual characteristics like breast enlargement and hair growth. The tall child who is growing normally, that is, falling on a normal curve on the growth chart, must be distinguished from a tall child who is growing at an abnormal rate, moving from one point on the curve to a higher relative position.

Growth can be slowed by a variety of factors—some endocrinological and some not. Worldwide, malnutrition is the leading cause. Examples closer to home are chronic diseases of the heart, kidney, or brain, a chromosomal disorder like **Down's syndrome**, severe emotional deprivation which, interestingly, can prevent the release of growth hormone (see Part 1, Chapter 4: "Complaints with an Emotional Element"), untreated metabolic disorders like **PKU** (**phenylketonuria**), and defects in the growth centers of the bone (cartilage cells), the most common example of which is called *achondroplasia*. In this uncommon condition, the defect is mainly in the bones of the upper arm and thigh. Achondroplastic dwarfism is an inherited disorder. A single dominant gene is responsible (see **genetics**). Over- or undersecretion of a number of hormones can interfere with growth. With the exception of isolated absence of growth hormone, these disorders cause syndromes of which interrupted growth is only one part. Thus, a child receiving large doses of hydrocortisone-like hormones or the child with underfunctioning thyroid (see **hormones**) will experience delayed growth as but one of the ill effects. The child who fails to grow but is normal in most other respects is suspect for lack of growth hormone. This hormone can be measured in the blood, and the responsiveness of the pituitary to its production can be tested. A limited supply of purified growth hormone is presently available for research on children with growth hormone deficiency and has proven effective in stimulating growth. Hopefully, the active part of this hormone will soon be available so that all children can be treated. Treatment of growth failure depends upon correcting its cause.

The too-tall girl is of particular concern at present because of the implications of dating and marriage in our society. In almost all situations the cause is hereditary and not endocrinological. Most endocrinologists try to predict eventual height based upon the demonstrated pattern of growth and the status of the growing centers of bone as revealed by X-ray. Repeated observation is also necessary to increase the accuracy of this prediction. If the predicted height is greater than 5 feet 10 or 5 feet 11 inches, in general a socially acceptable figure, many endocrinologists will consider giving the girl a course of estrogen (female sex hormone) treatment. This estrogen will speed up growth but will result in a final height less than that which would have occurred naturally.

The heights of children in affluent America have been increasing during the last few generations. Better nutrition (to the extent of overnutrition and obesity—see *weight problems*), fewer serious infections, and more exercise undoubtedly are of prime importance. Many concerned parents of short children wish they would eat more in the hope that they will grow faster. To our knowledge there are no special foods that stimulate growth. Short children, just like any other children, should be given a well-balanced diet. (See Part 1, Chapter 3: "Diet of Infants and Children.") How much they take is determined primarily by their own appetites which are usually stimulated by growth and not vice versa. The child will eat more because he is growing. Up to a point he does not grow more, except perhaps in weight, because he eats more. The obese child will tend to be a bit taller, but the price paid for this increase in height is scarcely worthwhile.

There are to our knowledge no tonics that will stimulate growth. If a child is deficient in iron or certain vitamins, he can fail to grow normally as well as show other effects of the deficiency. Vitamin deficiency in the United States among the more well-to-do parts of the society is extremely rare. Vitamins are liberally distributed through foods and milk and it is next to impossible to become deficient. Most vitamins are given to children who actually have enough, and often for the reason of stimulating appetite and thereby growth. There is no scientific basis for this practice. Children deficient in iron may fail to grow normally, although this symptom is not necessarily the most striking aspect of deficiency. (See *anemia.*)

There are synthetic hormones which, at best, accelerate growth to permit the very short child to be taller sooner without increasing the ultimate height. From a social point of view—for example, in delayed adolescence—it may be desirable in selected cases to speed up growth. Such treatment requires very careful monitoring.

With a short but normal child, the best thing parents can do is relax and pay attention to the emotional issues attendant upon being smaller than one's peers.


*Hemophilia:* see *bleeding disorders.*


*Henoch-Schoenlein purpura:* see *anaphylactoid purpura.*


*Hepatitis* is an inflamation of the liver. It is a common infectious problem in children, usually mild (so mild in many that it escapes detection), and is almost always followed by complete recovery. Hepatitis begins, as do many infections, with nonspecific symptoms like *fever, headache,* general achiness, loss of appetite, and feeling poorly (malaise). Within several days, these symptoms merge with nausea (at times *vomiting*), *abdominal pain,* foul breath and bitter taste, and *jaundice,* manifested by yellowness of the whites of the eyes and, in more intense cases, the skin as well. The urine often appears darker in color. In many patients, the liver is swollen, aches, and is tender to the touch. These symptoms persist for 1 to 3 weeks and are followed by gradual and complete recovery in almost all cases.

There is great variation in the intensity of the symptoms from person to person. As with other infectious diseases, many children have subclinical cases (see *infections*), detectable only by laboratory studies. Despite the absence of symptoms, these individuals can transmit infection to others. Many have very mild symptoms which may never be brought to medical attention, or which may easily be confused with other infectious diseases. For example, mild attacks of hepatitis may mimic *gastroenteritis.* In the severest cases, fortunately rare, there may be lingering liver impairment. In very rare cases, death may result from massive liver destruction.

Viruses other than the hepatitis viruses are capable of affecting the liver. For example, liver inflammation, usually mild, frequently accompanies infectious mononucleosis (see *mononucleosis, infectious*).

Two distinct patterns of hepatitis are recognized, known as *infectious hepatitis* (IH) and *serum hepatitis* (SH). Viruses are almost certainly responsible for both, and scientists are close to identifying the virus responsible for IH. Inability to isolate the causative microorganisms has until now hindered our understanding of the distribution and transmission of these infections in the population, and prevented the development of an effective vaccine.

Infectious hepatitis has an average incubation period (see *infections*) of 25 days, with a range of 10 to 50 days. With serum hepatitis the incubation period ranges from 10 to 180 days, but is commonly 50 to 180 days.

IH is usually picked up by person-to-person contact or from the environment, probably from food or water contaminated by the feces of people harboring the virus. If they are not adequately cooked, shellfish from polluted waters can spread hepatitis. Unsanitary living conditions and poor hygienic practices (including dirty fingers) contribute to its spread. It is not clear whether airborne transfer, like that which occurs with respiratory infections, plays a role, but this seems unlikely. By adulthood, it is probable that many people have been infected by IH, whether or not they have been ill or, if ill, diagnosed as having this disorder. A relatively small percentage have had clear symptoms of illness while most, it is thought, have experienced subclinical infection.

SH is transmitted primarily by inoculation of serum or blood from an individual harboring the virus and is mainly seen as a complication of blood transfusion or from the use of contaminated needles, syringes, or instruments improperly or incompletely sterilized between use by different individuals. SH is extremely infectious, and a microscopic speck of contaminated blood inoculated on an infinitesimal scrape of skin can transmit the virus. It may be that the friction associated with kissing or sexual intercourse is sufficient for contact and transmission. A technician doing a needle prick for a blood count on an infected person can accidentally scrape his own skin with a stylet and pick up the virus. As the transfusion of virus-infected blood has become less prevalent due to greater recognition of the problem and our ability to detect infected blood prior to use, SH is most commonly seen in the United States today in persons using illicit drugs given by injection. Addicts often share the same needles and syringes with little regard for sterile precautions. SH has also been transmitted by unsterile instruments in tattoo parlors and by improperly sterilized dental equipment.

While the clinical and laboratory findings of the two types of hepatitis are similar, one important difference is the presence of a specific detectable chemical particle or antigen in the blood of most individuals harboring the common type of SH virus. This particle is known as the *Australian antigen*, after the country in which it was first recognized, and appears likely to be a fragment of the actual virus. (An antigen is a substance that stimulates an antibody response. See *allergy* and **infections**.) The presence of the Australian antigen indicates that the individual harbors SH virus and identifies many, but not all, potentially contagious donors, whose blood should not be used for transfusion.

Once symptoms have developed, there is at present no specific cure for either IH or SH. As with other viral illnesses, antibiotics are of no value. The general well-being of the patient is attended to, in the hope that he will overcome the virus attack on his own. For most, an appropriate diet and symptomatic treatment will suffice. In those with more severe liver impairment, special techniques are employed. The period during which the individual with IH is contagious is quite variable and certainly precedes the onset of symptoms. Most experts recommend that patients be isolated for a period of at least one week after onset of jaundice.

It appears that immunity against IH is lasting, and that the rare "recurrences" are probably accounted for by exposure to a different strain of hepatitis. Immunity seems less certain with SH, but, again, our understanding is hampered by not being able to isolate and grow the virus in culture. Some individuals become carriers of SH, that is, they harbor the virus for long periods of time without being ill.

The great hope in hepatitis lies, as in all illnesses, with prevention. Ultimately, *immunization* should make it possible to eliminate hepatitis, just as *poliomyelitis* and *diphtheria* have been conquered in this country. Recent preliminary experiments using concentrates of Australian antigen show promise of inducing immunity against SH. At present, gamma globulin in appropriate doses can suppress but not prevent IH following exposure. The attack is milder and more likely to be subclinical (without symptoms). For this reason, individuals exposed to patients clinically ill with IH, particularly during the first week of illness, should receive injections of gamma globulin. Persons entering areas of the world in which IH is endemic (constantly present) are advised to receive a dose of gamma globulin in anticipation of exposure. After about one year of living in an endemic area, it is likely that previously nonimmune persons have been exposed to IH and have an immunity that makes further use of gamma globulin unnecessary. Gamma globulin is not thought to be effective against SH, although more studies on this subject are under way.

Prevention of SH depends mainly on the identification and avoidance of blood and blood products that are contaminated with the viruses. Great strides have been made in this regard in blood bank programs. The prevention of contagion among youths immersed in the present-day drug culture is much more difficult and cannot really be considered separately from the complex *drug problem* itself.

For discussions of subclinical infection, viral illnesses, the carrier state, incubation period, gamma globulin, and culture, see *infections*.


*Hernia.* The protrusion or displacement of an organ of the body beyond or outside its normal confines is a hernia. For example, nature intends the intestine to reside in, and only in, the abdomen. When a segment (usually called a loop) of intestine escapes its normal confines and protrudes from the abdominal cavity into the groin region, we say that the wayward loop has *herniated*. Despite all the bad jokes of comedians, the word hernia does not refer exclusively to the groin, although groin (*inguinal*) hernia is the most common type. **Diaphragmatic hernia,** and umbilical hernia (see below), are also seen.

To explain inguinal hernia it is necessary to review a little anatomy and embryology. The *peritoneum*, which is the lining of the abdominal cavity, forms early in embryological life. Somewhere around the third month, a small saclike projection of the peritoneum (the *processus vaginalis*) begins to extend down through the *inguinal canal* into the *scrotum* of the male or the *labia* of the female. Shortly before birth the peritoneal pouch seals off and dissolves. Eventually, the communication that was present between the abdominal cavity and the testis or labia ceases to exist. If, however, this process is incomplete, an intestinal loop could protrude into the pouch, resulting in a hernia. One often hears hernia described as a "rupture," but this is a misnomer. In hernias of infancy, nothing tears; rather, the muscles of the inguinal canal may loosen under strain and allow the intestine to slip down into the pouch. There is reason to believe that the pouch never seals off in from 5 to 10 percent of normal males, and this is the population in which hernias of adult life occur.

Inguinal hernia is a very common condition. It is often associated with **hydrocele,** a collection of fluid in a pinched-off section of the pouch. Although statistics are hard to come by, it is probable that hernia occurs in about 5 percent of children, with boys affected 9 times as frequently as girls. Most cases of hernia in children are detected in the first year of life. Often the parents will notice the telltale bulge in the groin. The bulge may come and go, depending on whether the baby is relaxed or straining, and it may disappear under pressure from the parent's or doctor's hand. In this case, the intestine is slipping in and out of the abdominal cavity and the hernia is said to be *reducible*. If the hernia persists under all conditions, it is said to be trapped or *incarcerated*. Then the intestine may be kinked, leading to obstruction, or the blood vessels may be compressed, bringing on development of gangrene. Incarceration is regarded as cause for prompt hospitalization and surgery. It is likely to occur in children, and for this reason we tend to recommend surgical intervention when hernia is detected. The younger the child or infant, the more urgent is the need for correction. If the child has no **fever,** is not **vomiting,** or screaming with pain, the hernia does not constitute an emergency, but if the child is exhibiting those symptoms along with a bulge in the groin, the doctor should be notified immediately. Hernia occurs more often on the right side than on the left, but in large numbers of cases it occurs on both sides. Detection of hernia on one side should always prompt thorough examination of the other.

Modern surgery has quite changed the picture of hernia in infancy. The operation, called *herniorrhaphy*, is performed under general anesthesia, but it is not at all unusual for the baby to be admitted to the hospital in the morning and discharged the same day. Babies tolerate the surgery well and, within hours, are behaving as if nothing had happened. This quick recovery contrasts with the adult experience, which is likely to be annoying or downright disagreeable. If prematurity or some other special condition requires postponement of surgery, use of a truss to hold the intestine more or less in place is ordinarily recommended.

In intrauterine life the abdominal wall is open beneath the navel. In most infants closure occurs prior to birth. In some, the opening persists and an *umbilical hernia* is said to be present. The defect closes in most cases by 1 year and almost certainly by age 4 or 5. No treatment is necessary. (In the old days, people used to bind the navel with a band to flatten the sac.) Only rarely, in the largest defects that show no sign of closure, is surgery performed. The baby's strainings may push a small section of intestine through the opening. This protrusion causes the navel to puff outward like a small balloon. As the infant relaxes, the loop of intestine slips back into the abdomen and the sac of skin decompresses, like a balloon relieved of air. Although the hernia usually bulges when the baby is crying (caused by increased pressure in the abdominal cavity, which squeezes a loop of intestine through the wall defect into the sac) the hernia itself is not painful and is not a cause of the crying.

See *diaphragmatic hernia* and Part 1, Chapter 6: "If Your Child Goes to the Hospital."

**Herpes simplex:** see *fever blisters.*

**Herpes zoster:** see *chicken pox*

**Hip, congenital dislocation of.** Most people are familiar with dislocation of the shoulder which can result from falls or in body contact sports such as football. Fewer people are aware that babies can be born with a hip that is partially dislocated even at birth. (In rare cases, both hips are affected.) Only a few families will have direct experience with this condition, but many people will have heard of a baby with this difficulty. The condition is much more common with a girl than it is with a boy baby and is seen more commonly with breech delivery babies. Although there are a number of theories, we do not know exactly how congenital hip dislocation comes about.

The hip is an example of the *ball and socket joint*. The ball of the hip joint is formed by the end of the thigh bone (femur) and is known as the *head of the femur*. The socket is formed by the joining of the three major bones of the pelvis (the *ischium*, the *pubis*, and the *ileum*) and is known as the *acetabulum*. Under normal circumstances the head of the femur (ball) fits snugly into the acetabulum (socket). The head is kept in place by tough ligaments which run from the bones of the pelvis to the upper part of the femur and by the numerous muscles that surround the hip joint, permitting the diversity of motion characteristic of the thigh. Development of the acetabulum apparently depends on the constant pressure exerted on it by the head of the femur. When the head of the femur has slipped out of the acetabulum and is not in contact with it, the acetabulum will be stunted in its growth. It is underdeveloped and tends to flatten out, losing its normal cup- or bowl-shaped configuration. It fails to mineralize (become bony) properly. In addition, a false socket may form to the back and side of the acetabulum as a cushion for the displaced head of the femur. With the passage of years, this false socket tends to become frayed and worn, with resulting inflammation, pain, discomfort, and loss of normal motion. Most dislocations are recognized long before this unfortunate complication develops.

Hips that are destined to become fully dislocated, with the head of the femur completely out of the socket of the acetabulum, are usually only partially dislocated at birth. Either complete or partial dislocation may be recognizable in the newborn nursery during the routine physical examination but often becomes apparent only at a later date, most commonly during the first few checkups. For this reason, your physician or nurse will give careful attention to the baby's hips during the first and subsequent examinations. If dislocation has not developed by the time a baby is one year old, it is highly unlikely that the congenital variety will show up at a later date. The physician or nurse examines for dislocation by actually feeling the femoral head move in and out of the socket as the baby's legs are moved. You will notice the doctor or nurse trying to make the baby's legs assume the position of a frog's legs, with the thighs flexed and turned outward so the knees come close to or actually touch the sheet of the bassinet or examining table. During this maneuver the doctor may feel a click or jerk as the femoral head and acetabulum disengage. In cases of partial dislocation, there will usually be some resistance to efforts to maneuver the thigh down to the tabletop.

After the newborn period, the dislocation is likely to become complete, not merely partial, and the head of the femur will begin to ride up behind and to the side of the acetabulum. As a result, the affected limb will appear shorter than its mate, and this will be readily detectable by examination. The skin folds of the buttocks will not be symmetrical, and the side with the dislocated hip is likely to have more creases than the normal side. (Asymmetrical skin folds are common and do not always indicate dislocation. They do arouse suspicion, however.) If the condition should exist undetected by the time the baby begins walking, a *limp* and a favoring of one side will call parents' attention to the condition. Hopefully it will be recognized before this time. The point to keep in mind is that, even with the most careful examination, we may not be able to detect a partially dislocated hip during the first several checks. The dislocation is progressive, becoming more obvious as time passes. For this reason we recheck the hips each time we do a full physical examination during the early months.

Once a dislocated hip is suspected, we take X-rays to substantiate our suspicion. Treatment of a dislocated hip involves returning (*reducing*, in medical parlance) the head of the femur to the acetabulum and then keeping it firmly in place. Then we immobilize the thigh in this position so that the ball and socket remain engaged. In the very young infant whose hip is only partially dislocated, treatment is relatively simple. Extra diapers over several months may be all that is needed to spread the thighs apart. In more advanced dislocation, the baby's legs are strapped to a brace which immobilizes them. The brace can then be adjusted to spread the legs out as much as is necessary to guarantee that the ball remains firmly in the socket.

In the older infant whose hip has become permanently dislocated, treatment is more complicated. To bring the head of the femur back into alignment with the acetabulum, it is necessary to overcome the tightness of the muscles drawing and holding the hip outward and resisting efforts to replace the head in the socket. This tightness must be overcome by prolonged, steady stretching, which is usually accomplished by using an overhead bar with traction weights. Once the head of the femur has come back into normal alignment with the acetabulum, the pull, or traction as we call it, can be reduced to allow the ball to engage firmly with the socket.

At this point, we usually immobilize the baby's legs with a plaster cast put on under general anesthesia. This cast extends down each leg (both the dislocated and nondislocated one) from the thigh to just below the ankle, with a bend at the knee. A bar connects the cast at the knees so that the legs cannot be moved. The baby is still able to bend at the waist, which permits some motion at the hip joint, enough to stimulate the acetabulum to develop its bony structure. Space in the plaster is left so that the genitalia and buttocks are exposed, allowing normal bowel and bladder functions.

The plaster cast requires renewal approximately every 2 months. As the acetabulum develops, the spread can be reduced gradually to permit more even stimulation of the entire socket by the head of the femur. The length of cast treatment depends on the development of the acetabulum as determined by X-ray examination and is usually—but not always— less than one year. There are other complicating aspects of dislocated hip which we will not discuss in this book. In general, we are rather optimistic about the possibility of cure in a dislocated hip, particulary if we can detect it early in the baby's life.

*Hip pain* is a common complaint in children and may indicate a very mild irritation in the hip joint or may be the symptom of a very severe abnormality. It is usually associated with a *limp* and frequently children in the toddler age will simply refuse to walk and cry when encouraged to do so. Children with hip abnormalities occasionally complain of pain in the knee rather than the hip. This is because of the pattern of nerve distribution. Thus whenever a youngster complains of *knee pain,* the hip should also be evaluated. The doctor should be contacted whenever a child complains of persistent pain or shows a limp not resulting from an obvious fall or blow. This is particularly important if the symptoms are accompanied by high *fever,* in which case prompt medical attention is called for. All of the conditions described below cause hip pain and/or a limp

*Toxic synovitis* is a most common form of hip irritation in children and usually occurs between the ages of 4 and 8. The cause is not known, but the symptoms are those of pain and limp with some stiffness of the hip, usually following a cold or sore throat. The diagnosis of toxic synovitis is made only when all other more serious causes of hip abnormality have been ruled out. Toxic synovitis generally responds well to rest and warm baths, but occasionally the symptoms are severe enough that a period of hospitalization with traction and physical therapy is required.

*Septic hip* is a dangerous, uncommon bacterial infection (see *infections*) of the hip joint which constitutes a medical emergency. It is associated with very severe hip pain and refusal to walk. Almost always, there is a high fever. When this condition occurs, the hip should be operated upon immediately to drain the infection and prevent permanent damage.

The condition known as *Legg-Perthes disease* occurs most commonly in boys between the ages of 4 and 10. For reasons unknown, the blood supply to the upper end of the thigh bone within the hip joint is temporarily interrupted. As a result, the bone becomes very soft and malleable. Weight bearing and walking can cause it to become misshapen, which can lead to very severe difficulties in later life if it is not treated properly. Treatment involves bracing and/or an operation to prevent excessive pressure on the hip during the period of healing, which may take from 2 to 3 years. This condition may come on very slowly with minimal symptoms, emphasizing the point that any child who persistently limps should be carefully evaluated.

*Slipped epiphysis* is a condition which occurs in children in early *adolescence,* usually in overweight males. The ball-shaped upper end of the *femur* (thigh bone) containing the *epiphysis* (growth center) separates from the remainder of the bone and slides into a new and abnormal position. If severe and long-term damage to the hip is to be prevented, the child must be hospitalized promptly for surgical treatment.

There are many other abnormalities that can affect the hip joint in children, and it is a good general rule that any child with pain or limp involving his or her hip or knee should be evaluated by a physician.

See *limp.*

*Histoplasmosis* is an infection which is not well known to people living in the Eastern United States but is a real concern to those living along the Western Appalachian slopes and the Missouri River Valley. It is an infectious disease caused by the fungus *Histoplasma capsulatum*, which is found mainly in soil, especially soil adjacent to pigeon lofts and chicken houses, and also in damp areas along streams and in caves. The fungus germs are picked up by breathing dust from such soil. The fungi usually lodge in the lungs or are swallowed and set up an infection in the intestine. In most cases, the infection is so mild so as to produce no symptoms (see discussion of subclinical infection under *infections*). The body confines the fungi and kills them off. In a small number of people, particularly those with a heavy dose of the fungus or prolonged, intense exposure, symptoms develop. These are extremely variable and include *diarrhea,* weight loss, irritability, paleness, vague muscle and joint aches, belly-swelling, *cough,* and difficulty in breathing. The chest X-ray may show signs of *pneumonia.* In rare cases, the fungi spread from the initial site of the infection, usually the lung, throughout the body. In extreme cases, such widespread dissemination may result in death. There is a treatment for histoplasmosis, the antibiotic Amphotericin B. Fortunately, most children who become ill recover on their own.

As is true in *tuberculosis,* a kind of allergy to the histoplasma fungus develops several weeks following infection. Injection of killed and, therefore, harmless histoplasma fungi into the skin in the allergic individual is followed by redness and swelling at the injection site. The skin test is a way to determine who has become infected. It does not tell whether the infection is active or controlled, only that the patient has had contact with the germs at some time in the recent or distant past. The skin test also becomes positive in individuals who have had subclinical or asymptomatic infections. The histoplasma skin test is used when a person develops symptoms that might be due to histoplasmosis. It helps to distinguish this condition from diseases with similar symptoms, like tuberculosis.

*Hives* (*urticaria*) are raised, red bumps (wheals) in the skin with sharp, serpent-like borders surrounded by a red halo in the adjacent skin. The most intense hives have a white or blanched center. Hives range in diameter from several millimeters to over 1 inch. The duration of the individual hives is no more than 8 to 12 hours. However, during the interval of one attack, they characteristically appear and disappear in different places on the skin. Bumps that remain for more than 24 hours in a given spot are not true hives. Hives cause an intense itch, stinging, or prickling as the major symptom.

The typical attack of hives lasts for no more than several days and often less. Such an episode is known as *acute urticaria*. An attack of hives lasting for more than 6 weeks is called *chronic urticaria*. Acute urticaria is usually a type of allergic reaction to some environmental factor such as an insect bite (see *bites, insect*), a food (shellfish are notorious), a medication (see *drug reactions, allergic*), or as one part of the reaction to many different allergens (see *allergy*). Once the cause is identified, the best advice is to avoid subsequent exposure if possible. By contrast, the cause of chronic urticaria is not identifiable in as many as 70 to 85 percent of cases. Known causes include reactions to drugs and, less frequently, to foods, to inhalants like pollen, and to infestation with parasitic worms. Stress and anxiety are often thought to be important factors.

There is another type of hives known as *cholinergic urticaria*. It is triggered by emotions, heat, exercise, or change in temperature. The hives are different from the allergic type of urticaria and are more fleeting in their appearance and disappearance. They are small (1 to 3 millimeters), pinpoint-like, raised wheals surrounded by a large, intensely red rim. They disappear without treatment in 30 to 60 minutes but tend to recur in the susceptible individual. Why some people react to stress with hives is not known.

If hives are not particularly bothersome, they can be left alone and will disappear on their own. If itching is annoying, ice-water compresses, tepid baths with colloidal oatmeal (Aveeno), and anti-itch medications like calamine lotion are useful. Antihistamines taken by mouth are also effective.

There are no tests to determine the cause of hives. Skin tests are of no use. A careful history of exposure to an allergen is the single most useful diagnostic tool.

Hivelike reactions are not always limited to the skin. The same type of inflammation can occur in other parts of the body such as the windpipe (trachea), voice box (larynx), and air passageways (bronchi). When inflammation occurs in these sensitive structures, obstruction to breathing can occur. Some individuals who are allergic to certain foods such as shrimp or lobsters can experience not only hives, but also an acute onset of difficulty in breathing which calls for emergency measures similar to those used in the treatment of acute allergic reactions to insect bites.

See *allergy.*

*Hodgkin's disease* is a cancer of the lymph nodes and other lymphatic tissue elsewhere in the body. It is recognized by swollen, enlarged lymph glands, *fever,* weight loss, night sweat, and generalized body itching. The glands are characteristically hard, painless, and persistent, usually readily distinguished from swollen glands from other causes. (See *glands, swollen.*)

Great strides have been made in the treatment of this disorder through a combination of radiation and drug therapy. Many children can be cured. (See *tumors.*) Early diagnosis is important.

*Hormones* are biological chemicals which regulate a number of familiar body functions like growth, sexual development, and lactation (milk production). Less familiar activities regulated by hormones include control of the levels of calcium, sugar, and salt in the blood, the texture of the skin and hair, and the excretion of water by the kidneys.

Over- or underproduction of a hormone makes itself apparent by changes in these body functions, for example, too rapid or too slow sexual development. Deficiencies or excess of hormones often develop gradually, so much so that the patient becomes accustomed to the gradual changes and may not come to medical attention until the condition is far advanced.

In the newborn the most common expression of hormonal dysfunction, reflecting the hormonal environment prior to birth, is some abnormality of the genitalia such as a small phallus, undescended testes (see *testis, undescended*), the more marked degrees of *hypospadias,* or enlargement of the clitoris. These findings are common expressions of abnormalities in gonadal (ovaries and testes) function and, less commonly, of abnormalities in adrenal and pituitary function. They may also result from hormones taken by the mother during pregnancy. Ambiguity of the baby's genitalia deserves early attention. It is of the utmost importance to make a decision about the child's sex and to plan for care and treatment accordingly. The decision about sex assignment should be made in the immediate newborn period. In general, it is necessary to consult a specialist in pediatric endocrinology to make these decisions.

Our knowledge of hormones has allowed us in many cases to correct both over- and underproduction and, more recently, to interrupt normal hormone function when this is medically and socially desirable. The birth control pill is a good example of such intervention. It is a synthetic hormone (usually a combination of two hormones) which among its several actions blocks the normal hormone function controlling *ovulation* (discharge of the egg from the ovary). Because ovulation is prevented, conception cannot occur.

A hormone is like a conductor of a symphony orchestra telling body parts how loudly and quickly to function in order to blend with other members. Just as the symphonic conductor indicates to the violin section how loud or fast to perform by listening to that section in relation to the sounds produced by all others (drums, horns, and so forth), so hormone production takes into account all of the other activities of the body proceeding at the same time. These activities, of course, include the actions of the hormones themselves. The hormones work together. While each has its own particular effect, they are all more or less interdependent.

### THE ENDOCRINE SYSTEM

The glands that produce hormones are known as *endocrine* glands. The study of hormones is called *endocrinology* and the physician who specializes in disorders of the endocrine glands is called an *endocrinologist*. The endocrine glands include the *pituitary, thyroid, parathyroid, pancreas, adrenal, ovaries*, and *testes*. Hormones are also produced by nerve cells of the *autonomic nervous system* and of the *hypothalamus*, a portion of the brain that lies just above the pituitary gland. Each gland produces and secretes into the bloodstream a characteristic hormone or hormones (most of the glands make more than one). In the pregnant woman, the placenta is a temporary endocrine gland which, in addition to all its other remarkable functions, produces and secretes a host of hormones with wide-ranging effects.

We now have considerable knowledge of the chemistry of hormones. Many can be produced in the laboratory. These manufactured hormones can be identical to naturally occurring ones or may have some chemical modification to produce a slightly different effect. Other hormones are purified from animal endocrine glands. Thus hormones are now available for purposes of treatment. We also understand a great deal about the manufacturing process within each gland—how it assembles raw materials and processes them step by step into the final product which is stored and released as needed. In many disorders of hormone production, we can say not only which gland is malfunctioning, but also which part of the assembly process is out of line. This detailed knowledge enables us to treat the disorder more effectively.

The *pituitary* is the master gland. Its hormones control many, but not all, of the other endocrine glands, and some pituitary hormones exert a direct effect on other nonglandular parts of the body like bone. The pituitary is a little ball of tissue at the base of the brain which sits in a socket ( *sella turcica* ) of the lower part of the skull directly behind the nose. The presence of an endocrine gland in such close connection with the nervous system is of great importance. Information transmitted by nerves can affect endocrine function. For example, anxiety or fright can lead to endocrine activity. These emotional reactions cause impulses to be sent out through the nerves which activate nerve cells within the brain and peripheral nervous system that are capable of producing hormones themselves. One such compound is *epinephrine.* Epinephrine causes the well-known response to anxiety—fast, pounding heartbeat, sweating, and clammy skin. Other hormones known as *releasing factors* or *releasing hormones* are made by nerve cells in the *hypothalamus,* an area of the brain that lies just above the pituitary. These chemical substances are transmitted by a special set of veins to the pituitary and stimulate or inhibit the release of pituitary hormones. Thus, they serve to transfer messages from the nervous system to the pituitary gland.

The pituitary is divided into two sections, the front and back, or to use the medical terms, anterior and posterior. The anterior pituitary produces growth hormone (GH), which causes the liver to secrete another hormone, *somatomedin,* which, in turn, controls the growth centers of bones (see **height problems**); *adrenocorticotropic* hormone (ACTH), which acts on part of the adrenal gland, stimulating it to produce *hydrocortisone* and similar hormones ( the *glucocorticoids* ), which regulate the metabolism of sugar, protein, fat, minerals, and water; *melanocyte-stimulating hormone* (MSH), which acts on the pigment-containing cells of the skin responsible for skin coloration (to be more exact, MSH is produced in the intermediate lobe of the pituitary gland, between the anterior and posterior lobes); *thyroid-stimulating hormone* (TSH), which affects the thyroid gland, causing it to produce and release thyroid hormone, which regulates metabolic processes throughout the body; *follicle-stimulating hormone* (FSH), which in the female causes the ripening of an egg in the ovaries and the secretion of estrogen, and in the male stimulates the development of the sperm by the tubules; *luteinizing hormone* (LH), which in females initiates ovulation and secretion of progesterone by the ovary, and in males acts on the cells of the testes, which produce the male sex hormone; and, finally, *prolactin,* which stimulates the breast to make milk and regulates breast development.

The posterior part of the pituitary gland stores *antidiuretic hormone* (ADH), which is produced by nerve cells in the hypothalamus. ADH acts on the kidney to retain water by concentrating urine. *Oxytocin,* another nerve cell hormone of the posterior pituitary, stimulates the muscles of the uterus during childbirth, and causes milk to pass into the collecting tubes beneath the nipple and areola of the breast.

Pituitary hormones are secreted into the blood and carried to their "target organs," the thyroid, adrenal, ovary, and so forth. In turn the "target" glands produce their hormones, which also enter the blood. The hypothalamus and pituitary are said to be in a feedback relationship with the target glands. An everyday example of such a relationship is the household thermostat. When the temperature falls below a certain level, the thermostat sends an electrical message to the heater. The heater goes on, and the house warms up. When the temperature rises above the setting on the thermostat, the heater shuts off, and a relatively constant temperature is thus maintained. The same kind of relationship exists between the hypothalamus, pituitary, and several of the endocrine glands. For example, if the amount of thyroid hormone in blood falls below a certain level, the brain "reads" the declining hormone level and signals the pituitary to send out more thryoid-stimulating hormone (TSH). The TSH causes the thyroid to produce more TH, which in turn leads to an interruption of the brain's signaling for more TSH.

There is clearly also a developmental aspect to hormone production. A dramatic example is the surge of sex hormone production (testosterone in the male and estrogen in the female) at the time of *adolescence.* These hormones determine in large part the secondary sexual characteristics which distinguish the sexes. The mechanism underlying the timing of their increased production is poorly understood.

Not all of the endocrine glands are under direct control of the pituitary. Two examples are the *parathyroid glands* and the *pancreas.* The four parathyroid glands, located in the neck near the thyroid gland, make the parathyroid hormone that controls the level of calcium in the blood. The pancreas produces the hormone *insulin* (see *diabetes*), which is important in regulating the blood sugar (glucose). It does not have a direct relationship with the pituitary, although growth hormone, thyroid hormone, and hydrocortisone all affect insulin production.

Endocrine function can be tested in a number of ways. Hormone concentrations can be measured in blood and urine or their production rates can be determined. Most often it is necessary to test the responsiveness of the particular gland by challenging it with an appropriate stimulant to see how the system thermostat is working. The ability of the pituitary to produce ACTH can be tested by administering a chemical which "blocks" one of the last steps in the production of hydrocortisone in the adrenals. Normally the absence of hydrocortisone in the blood is a potent stimulus to ACTH production and release and should be reflected in a measurable increase in the amount of ACTH found in the blood or in the production of chemical precursors (the early steps in the chemical chain) of hydrocortisone within the adrenal. If these precursors do not increase in the blood and urine, we infer that the ACTH production was not stepped up as expected and is therefore impaired. Gland function can also be evaluated by radioactive tagging of chemicals normally used by a gland in making its hormone. For example, the thyroid uses iodine in the production of thyroid hormone. If a tracer dose (very small amount) of radioactively tagged iodine is given, it pools or concentrates normally in the gland just as would untagged iodine. The radioactivity can be counted, and the trapping of iodine by the thyroid judged normal or abnormal. In children, changes in skeletal growth (heights, lengths) and maturation as determined by X-ray studies of the bones are important indicators of endocrine function.

### ENDOCRINE DISORDERS

There are many different endocrine disorders, some common and others rare. We will discuss only a few—the effects of excess hydrocortisone and of over- and underproduction of thyroid hormone.

Hydrocortisone is the most important naturally occurring member of the glucocorticoid group of hormones. (It can also be manufactured.) There are also synthetic glucocorticoids with actions similar to hydrocortisone, modified to reduce undesired side effects. In the following discussion we will use the term hydrocortisone to mean any glucocorticoid. In actual practice, hydrocortisone is less commonly used as an administered adrenal hormone than are other manufactured glucocorticoids such as prednisone (Meticorten) or triamcinolone (Aristocort).

The child with an excess of hydrocortisone presents a characteristic picture: rounded cheeks, a ruddy complexion, acne, hairiness, a hump of fat over the base of the neck and upper back, purple skin lines over the abdomen and buttocks, and delayed growth. The red *blood count* may be increased, the blood sugar raised (sometimes to the point of actual *diabetes*), and the blood pressure elevated. Resistance to infection is impaired and signs of infection such as *fever* are suppressed. Muscles waste and bones lose calcium. Cataracts (opacities in the lens of the eye) may develop. Menarche may be delayed and normal menstrual function interrupted. The mood may be altered because of the hormone's direct effect on the brain or as a reaction to the dramatically altered body image. (As a historical note, this clinical picture is called *Cushing's syndrome* after the famous American physician Harvey Cushing who first described it.)

While this picture can result from malfunction of the adrenal gland or an adrenal gland tumor, it is seen mainly in children who are administered hydrocortisone daily in large doses over a long time to treat diseases like *rheumatic fever, nephrosis, asthma,* severe *anemia,* or *leukemia.* Hydrocortisone has the ability to decrease inflammation in these disorders of the heart, kidney, or the small air passages. In the case of asthma, for example, an easing of breathing is the desired goal. Unfortunately, to obtain the benefits of these hormones we have to accept the whole picture. This steep price is worth paying only when no treatment is available or when alternative treatments are more crippling or more dangerous.

Side effects of administered hydrocortisone are held to a minimum by giving just enough of the drug to achieve the desired treatment effect. When suppression of inflammation requires so much hormone that side effects occur, a balance must be achieved between the side effects and the therapeutic effect. One way to reduce side effects almost completely is to give the pills on alternate days. This works for many, but not all, children. Fortunately, most of the undesirable side effects are reversed when the hormone is discontinued. Whether or not it can be discontinued depends upon the underlying illness for which it was given.

Because hydrocortisone decreases resistance to infection and masks symptoms, very careful watching for infection in the child on extra large doses is required (see *infections*). Because viral illnesses in general and *chicken pox* in particular can run rampant in hydrocortisone-treated children, we take great pains to avoid exposure. We do not give children on hydrocortisone live virus vaccines (see *immunization*).

Once treatment is begun for a condition like asthma, the symptoms are prone to depend on hydrocortisone for their continued control. This dependency makes weaning from the drug particularly difficult. No sooner is the dose of hormone reduced than the symptoms recur. For this reason, we usually exhaust all other forms of therapy before resorting to long-term hydrocortisone treatment.

Hydrocortisone is commonly used in high doses for short periods to combat inflammation in severe allergic reactions (see *allergy*), and for poison ivy (see *poison ivy, sumac, and oak*). Such use of the hormone for several days does not result in serious side effects.

As mentioned above, thyroid hormone affects metabolism throughout the body. The effects of underproduction of thyroid hormone, also called *hypothyroidism*, can cause, among other symptoms, mental and physical sluggishness, *constipation,* abnormal menses (see *adolescence*), thick, dry skin, and, in the young child, may interfere with growth and development. Hypothyroidism in the newborn (congenital hypothyroidism) is very hard to recognize by physical examination alone. Untreated it appears to cause probably irreversible brain damage. Accordingly, checking the blood of newborns for thyroid hormone is now becoming a routine part of screening, just like testing for *PKU*. Infants diagnosed and treated early, it would appear, stand a better chance of achieving normal development. Although hypothyroidism is often suspected as a cause of tiredness, a very common symptom in children and teen-agers, it is a rare cause of this complaint. Prominent symptoms of overproduction of thyroid hormone, also called *hyperthyroidism,* are nervousness (another common symptom usually due to other causes), weight loss, moist, warm skin, and, on occasion, bulging eyes. Both conditions can be diagnosed by measuring the amount of thyroid hormone in the blood. Deficiency is treated by administering thyroid hormone, and excess is treated, depending upon the cause, by drugs and/or surgery.

*Hyaline membrane disease:* see **lung rupture and collapse.**

*Hydatid disease: see pets and children.*

*Hydrocele.* When the peritoneal pouch is not completely sealed off (see **hernia**), an accumulation of fluid around the testis often occurs  This condition, called hydrocele, is not painful or harmful in itself and usually disappears without treatment. When the nurse or doctor is examining your baby, you may notice the procedure in which a flashlight is held behind the scrotum if there is a mass in it. If the beam of light is blocked entirely, a hernia exists, but if the scrotum lights up like a light bulb, there is a hydrocele.

For hydrocele alone a period of watchful waiting usually is in order. If the hydrocele persists for a year, and particularly if it is large, the chances are great that the peritoneal pouch is still open and that hernia sooner or later will occur, if it has not occurred already. In consequence, it is customary to operate on large hydroceles, especially those that have persisted for the better part of a year. The remaining peritoneal pouch is removed, along with the hydrocele.

*Hydrocephalus.* In the past 20 years, new treatments have been developed for hydrocephalus, which used to be known as "water on the brain" or "water of the brain." It is a serious condition but not a common one. The doctor, not the parent, will be the one to discover it. When the doctor or nurse at a routine visit puts the tape measure around a baby's head, hydrocephalus is one of the possibilities he or she is checking against. The head of the child with hydrocephalus grows at a faster than normal rate.

Essentially, hydrocephalus is a consequence of excessive pressure from *spinal fluid,* which is the clear liquid surrounding and supporting the brain and spinal cord. The fluid is contained in a membranous sac (the *meninges*) around the brain and spinal cord, and it serves to cushion those delicate structures of the central nervous system. The fluid flows from and into channels and cavities penetrating both the brain and cord. Specialized cells within the brain cavities (*ventricles*) form the fluid, which is in a constant state of flux, being produced and removed simultaneously. There are numerous filtering sites on the meninges where the fluid is reabsorbed. You can think of saliva as going through an analogous cycle—formed in the mouth, swallowed with the food, and reabsorbed back into the body in the intestine.

The infant's skull growth responds to brain growth. In hydrocephalus the brain is not increasing in substance but is expanding under pressure from an excess accumulation of fluid, just as the skin of a balloon expands from the pressure of the air you blow into it. The skin of the inflated balloon does not weigh any more than it did, but, having been thinned out, it covers a much larger area. The similar process in hydrocephalus "thins out" and enlarges the geometry of the brain structure. The bones of the skull, not solidly joined at birth, spread apart, and the fontanel (soft spot) stretches out. If allowed to progress unchecked, the stretching can damage the brain to the point of death.

There appear to be two main causes of hydrocephalus. In the first, an obstruction blocks the flow of fluid from the centers of production. The obstruction might come from some failure of embryological development, or it might be the result of scarring from inflammation, as in *meningitis.* Production goes on as usual, but the fluid, unable to find an exit, backs up and exerts pressure from within the brain. In the second type, there is an imbalance, again probably a failure in embryological development, between the body's ability to produce the fluid and its ability to reabsorb it. It seems reasonable to suppose that filtering sites are missing from the meninges. The end effect, of course, is the same as in the first type.

Hydrocephalus varies widely in its severity. Even with no treatment, the mildest forms may cease spontaneously (*arrested hydrocephalus*) and enlargement of the head then comes to a halt. Some babies at birth have heads too large for vaginal delivery; others seem normal at birth but show abnormal skull development in the first year. The treatment in any case is directed at reducing the fluid pressure. The accepted approach at this time is surgical. When the obstruction in a brain channel cannot be removed altogether, the cavity is tapped, to remove excess fluid and reduce pressure. By means of a fine plastic tube inserted through a small hole in the skull, the fluid is carried down beneath the skin into the chest, where the other end of the tube is threaded into the large vein returning blood to the heart from the head, neck, and arms. This procedure, of which there are several variations, generally works well. In the case of imbalance between production and reabsorption of fluid, a tube is connected between the spine and the ureter of one kidney, which must be sacrificed. The excess spinal fluid runs off into the ureter and out in the urine. Neither treatment gets at the underlying cause, but only relieves the symptoms. Research for a more fundamental attack is in progress.

See *birth defects, severe; developmental disabilities; handicapped child;* and *spinal defects.*


*Hydrocortisone, side effects of:* see *hormones.*


*Hydrophobia (rabies):* see *pets and children.*


*Hyperactivity:* see *learning disabilities.*


*Hypoglycemia* means low blood sugar. Its common symptoms are paleness, sweating, alterations in *sensorium* (alertness), and seizures (it is a consideration in evaluating the cause of seizures). Whenever any of these symptoms occur or recur, hypoglycemia is a major consideration. If the child is tested during the time of an attack and the low blood sugar can be demonstrated, few other tests are required. Otherwise, the hypoglycemia attack can be provoked for the purpose of making a diagnosis by placing the child on a low calorie, low carbohydrate diet while in the hospital.

In the common variety, which is sometimes called the *intermittent hypoglycemia of childhood*, the affected child is usually a very active boy with an indifferent appetite who tends to be on the low side for height and weight. More than half of these children have been born prematurely and had low birth weights for their gestational age. The episodes occur most often in the morning but may happen at other times after significant periods of deprivation of carbohydrates or unusual exercise without subsequently taking food. *Vomiting* often accompanies the attack. The symptoms respond very quickly to sugar given intravenously.

Treatment involves increasing daily caloric and carbohydrate intake, especially on days when unusual events (like a long hike) may further compromise an already capricious appetite. Specific recommendations are based on the circumstances under which the attacks occur, since these indicate the conditions which are not tolerated. In general, parents are instructed to give additional calories, especially in carbohydrates, during the 3 daily meals and in 2 or 3 snacks, the last snack given at bedtime. If an infection occurs that interferes with normal eating, special efforts must be taken to ensure adequate sugar intake. Frequent drinks of sweetened juices are recommended.

The optimistic part about this condition is that the recurrent attacks are almost exclusively confined to ages 1½ to 6 years. Beyond 6, the problem seems to disappear on its own.

Hypoglycemia occurs in diabetics under treatment with insulin. It is known as an insulin reaction. There are other causes for hypoglycemia affecting the newborn and the older child which are much less common and will not be discussed here.

*Hypospadias.* This relatively common birth defect appears in the external genitalia of both sexes, in varying degrees of severity. As is the case with so many birth defects, the exact cause is not known.

In the male, this condition has three main features: the urethral opening is on the underside of the penis and not at the tip; the shaft of the penis may be bent downward; the *prepuce* (or foreskin) may be defective or altogether absent on the underside, giving the penis a hooded appearance. In the most common form, which requires no treatment, the urethral opening will be just below the normal site, but in severe cases, it may occur anywhere along the shaft, to as far back as the juncture of the penis and scrotum. In rare instances, the scrotum is divided in two with the urethral opening between the sections. Some cases of hypospadias may be accompanied by other disorders of the urinary tract. When hypospadias is present, X-ray examination of the kidneys, ureter, and bladder is in order.

In girls, displacement of the urethra is not so noticeable and may be discovered only in a gynecological examination. In the most severe cases, the opening may occur in the vagina and manifest itself by causing difficulties in urination. But for all practical purposes, the nature of hypospadias makes it a problem primarily of the male.

Hypospadias may reflect an abnormality of the hormonal environment to which the body was exposed prior to birth. The external *genitalia* (penis, vagina, clitoris, scrotum, and so forth) should be carefully examined to determine the exact sex of the baby. Other studies may be needed as well. (See *hormones.*)

Hypospadias does not constitute an emergency, but if the more severe forms are not corrected, they may interfere with sexual activity in adult life and have definite psychological implications for the boy. The treatment, of course, is surgical. The results of surgery are uniformly good, though more than one operation may be required. Beginning with the first procedure at age 2, total correction can and should be completed in the preschool child.

See Part 1, Chapter 6: "If Your Child Goes to the Hospital."

*Idiopathic thrombocytopenic purpura:* see *bleeding disorders.*

**Immunization.** An immunization is a deliberate stimulation of the body's defenses against a specific harmful germ. We know that many diseases occur only once in any one person's life. From this fact, observed among millions upon millions of people, we conclude that, when a person recovers from certain diseases, he or she is thereafter immune to them. The basic idea of immunization is to produce these conditions artificially and safely. The ideal immunization would stimulate the immunity without causing any symptoms of sickness. Most of the vaccines we use come close to this ideal. There are some vaccines with undesirable side effects, but, except for the rare patient, these are much less severe than the disease which the vaccine has been developed to prevent. Parents must understand, however, that all procedures carry risks. For example, one in many millions of people given polio vaccine will develop muscle weakness. In comparison to the seriousness of polio this is a risk most parents are willing to take.

The body responds to the vaccine much as it would to any foreign body; that is, it produces antibodies (see *infections*) directed specifically against that foreign body. The antibodies react with or unite with the foreign substance (toxin, bacteria, or virus, as the case may be) and inactivate either the germ or the germ's toxic product. By "tagging" the substance and sealing it off, the antibodies render it less harmful and mark it for removal from the system. Having once been produced to rescue the body from invasion by this specific foreign body, the antibodies thereafter remain on call, so to speak, to respond immediately to any new invasion by the same enemy. In other words, the body has organized a specific defense against a specific germ—it has become *immune.*

The vaccines for immunization are of two types—killed and live. Killed vaccines consist of concentrates of dead germs, which may be either parts of bacteria or viruses, or their toxic products. These toxic products are called *toxins.* The **whooping cough** (pertussis) vaccine, for instance, is made of parts of the killed germs of the disease, whereas the **diphtheria** and **tetanus** vaccines are made of toxic products, not the bacteria themselves. In a vaccine, the toxin is then modified to stimulate immunity without causing the harmful effects of the unmodified toxin. In this condition it is called a *toxoid.*

Live vaccines consist of living viruses (or bacteria in the case of **tuberculosis** vaccine). These are harmless close relatives of the harmful microbes that cause full-blown disease. Because a close relationship exists between the two viruses, the body responds to both in the same way: exposed to either, it becomes immune. The difference is that the harmful virus would cause a serious illness, while the vaccine virus produces only a mild local reaction, sometimes with *fever*. For example, smallpox is a severe, disfiguring, even fatal disease. Smallpox vaccine, in contrast, causes a single, soon-healed sore, perhaps with low fever and mild discomfort. Yet both stimulate similar immunity. This is the crucial point. Another important difference is that vaccine viruses, in general, are not transmitted from person to person as disease viruses are. The rule is not absolute, because smallpox vaccine virus could be passed by direct contact to a person with a skin rash, but in ordinary circumstances the vaccine viruses are not contagious.

For successful immunization it is not enough merely to stimulate production of antibody; a certain amount of the antibody must be produced. This amount is called the *protective level*. More than a single injection of certain vaccines (notably diphtheria vaccine) is required to stimulate development of the protective level of immunity. For others, such as the *measles* vaccine, one shot is enough. It seems likely that some vaccines, measles and *mumps* for example, confer immunity for life. With others, the immunity gradually wears off until it drops below the protective level. Then a *booster* injection is required to stimulate antibody production back up to the protective level. Immunization against tetanus and diphtheria requires regular boosters throughout the person's lifetime. Smallpox vaccination also must be repeated.

The following immunization schedule, or a close variation thereof, is standard for most children in the United States.

| Age | |
|---|---|
| 2–3 months | DPT (diphtheria, pertussis, tetanus) and trivalent OPV (oral polio vaccine) |
| 3–4 months | DPT and trivalent OPV |
| 4–5 months | DPT and trivalent OPV |
| 15 months and above | Measles vaccine, mumps vaccine, German measles vaccine |
| 18 months | DPT and trivalent OPV |
| 4–6 years (on entering school) | DPT and trivalent OPV |
| 14–16 years | Td (tetanus and diphtheria) (The dose of diphtheria toxoid given adults is a fraction of that given to infants) |
| Thereafter | Td every ten years for life |

Please note that this schedule extends through life. In the case of diphtheria and tetanus, boosters are needed every ten years. Immunization should not be looked upon as "baby shots," lest you be deceived into thinking that responsibility ends with childhood.

Immunization is cumulative. If for any reason the intervals between doses are extended beyond those recommended, there is no reason for concern. For example, if 6 months elapse between the first and second DPT injections, it is not necessary to begin all over again. The schedule for recommended immunization need not be adhered to by day and month. There is great leeway so long as all the shots are given.

One result of the widespread elimination of the diseases commonly immunized against is that even an unimmunized infant or child is at low risk simply because of nonexposure to the germ in question. For example, if for any reason a child living in the conditions which characterize most parts of affluent America has missed all of his immunizations during the first year, he is unlikely to suffer, because he is very unlikely to come in contact with diphtheria, whooping cough, tetanus, or polio in his normal daily living. On the other hand, in special circumstances, such as entering an area of the world in which polio is still a problem, we might want to give a booster immunization against polio virus even to a person who has been adequately immunized, just to be safe.

DPT, which is the first immunization a baby receives, is given by injection into the thigh or buttock. It stimulates antibodies against tetanus, pertussis (whooping cough), and diphtheria. Children cry on being punctured, but most of them experience no ill effect from the shot. Some babies exhibit slight irritability and may have mild fever 12 or 24 hours after the inoculation. Occasionally there will be redness and some swelling at the site of the inoculation. These symptoms usually subside in a day or two. They should be reported to the doctor at the next checkup. He may lower the dose for the subsequent shots. Sometimes a "knot" forms and lasts for weeks to months. It is of no importance. Because whooping cough is mainly a disease of quite young children, boosters for this immunization are not given after the age of 5.

In an adequately immunized child or adult, a tetanus booster is given after an injury only if more than 5 years have elapsed since the last booster. Gone are the days when every cut and scrape was followed by a tetanus booster. Of course, in an inadequately immunized person (one who has had less than two previous injections of tetanus toxoid), these rules do not apply. When the patient isn't adequately immunized or the wound has gone unattended for over 24 hours, not only a booster but also gamma globulin (see *infections*) directed against tetanus toxin (the poison of tetanus) should be given. Also, the remainder of the series of tetanus shots should be given to achieve full immunization. The best treatment for tetanus is prevention by keeping immunizations up to date *for life*.

Live polio (see *poliomyelitis*) vaccine contains 1 or all 3 strains of polio virus. The combined variety is known as *trivalent* vaccine. Polio vaccine is given in drops by mouth and sets up a vaccine virus infection in the intestine, stimulating immunity. We avoid giving polio vaccine when the child has a stomach or intestinal infection because the virus causing the infection can interfere with the multiplication and the effectiveness of the vaccine virus.

Live measles vaccine is given by injection. The vaccine is given at one year or later, because by this time the maternal antibodies against measles have disappeared (see *infections*). A small but definite percentage of children experience low-grade fever about a week following immunization, but rarely show any other symptoms.

Live mumps and rubella (**German measles**) vaccines, also given by injection, may be given in combination with measles vaccine or individually at 1 year. Inoculation with a live rubella vaccine is accompanied in a very small percentage of children by short-lived joint pain. Rubella vaccine can be given to young women who have not previously had rubella vaccine or natural rubella (determined by measuring blood antibodies), if they are not pregnant and are on an effective regime of birth control.

Mumps vaccine is not always routinely given. Some physicians prefer to give it only to boys entering puberty who have not already had mumps. Others give it to all children in order to prevent this naturally occurring disease. Even though, in children, it is usually mild in comparison to measles, for instance, in adults mumps can be extremely uncomfortable and, in males, can involve the testis, causing, in the extreme, its destruction. Fortunately, only one testis is usually involved.

Smallpox vaccine, the first vaccine (introduced in the early 1800s), is no longer routinely used. If your doctor should recommend smallpox vaccination, because of foreign travel, for instance, the following steps are taken: A small drop of the live virus vaccine is pressed into the skin with the side of a sterile needle point. Within 48 hours, a small, raised, red, itchy spot develops. Soon a blister forms. By one week the reaction is at a peak; the blister collapses, and a scab or crust forms, with a red rim surrounding it. At this time many children have a mild fever (occasionally as high as 103° or 104°), and some fussiness. Aspirin can be given for these symptoms. (See Part 1, Chapter 5: "Caring for the Sick Child at Home" for dosage schedule.) The child should be discouraged from touching or scratching the vaccine sore. It teems with virus, which could be transferred by the fingers to the eyes or to any breaks in the child's skin. An undershirt makes an effective barrier in the young child. The vaccine site should be kept dry for 24 hours to allow the virus to take hold. Thereafter, the sore should be kept clean. Bathing is all right, but rubbing should be avoided. Children who have or have had *eczema* are susceptible to spread of the vaccine virus via the blood to other areas of the skin and should not receive the vaccine. They should be kept away from children with active vaccinations. If immunization of a child with eczema is absolutely necessary, a special strain of vaccine virus or an injection of special gamma globulin along with regular vaccine can be given.

In recent years there have been more complications from smallpox vaccinations in this country than from the disease itself, which has not occurred in the United States for years. The present World Health Organization efforts to eradicate smallpox in underdeveloped countries has proven so effective that routine smallpox vaccination is no longer necessary. However, health workers and travelers in the now almost non-existent areas of the world where smallpox is present should still be vaccinated.

*Influenza* vaccine is not listed because it is not routinely given to children. There are several reasons. First, influenza is generally a mild illness in children in contrast to adults. Second, the vaccine is often not all that effective (for several reasons not discussed here). Third, the vaccine itself often produces symptoms. Influenza vaccine is given to children with chronic diseases like *cystic fibrosis* or *rheumatic fever* for whom the infection would represent a special hazard. With further development of more effective vaccines, we can expect changes in the present recommendations.

BCG vaccine against tuberculosis is used only in selected situations. Special vaccines like yellow fever, cholera, *typhoid fever,* or rabies (see *pets and children*) may be needed for travel to certain foreign countries. (See *traveling abroad.*) United States Public Health Service offices in each state maintain up-to-date information on the immunizations needed.

Immunization is a dynamic field. Currently vaccines against meningococcus, a bacterium that can cause *meningitis,* and Hemophilus influenza, a common bacterial invader of young children, are under development but not yet in widespread use.

Immunization, starting in the infant's second or third month, is a lifetime undertaking. The parent's obligation is threefold: (1) to see that the child receives the full course of inoculations; (2) to see that the record of the child's immunization is kept up to date and at hand for quick reference; and (3) with older children, to do whatever is possible to prepare the child psychologically so that the necessary injections will not be upsetting.

Generally, the American population is well immunized, although there is still room for improvement. Recently there was an epidemic of diphtheria in Texas. The group involved was poor, living in crowded, unsanitary conditions, and had been inadequately or not at all immunized against diphtheria. Such pockets of poverty, all too numerous for a country with the resources of the United States, need to be cleaned up.

Also, we must not let our good record with immunization of children cause us to become complacent. Because the diseases are becoming eliminated, there is a tendency to relax our vigilance. Out of sight, out of mind. Immunization levels must be maintained at their present high.

*Impetigo:* see *abscess.*

*Infantile paralysis:* see *poliomyelitis.*

*Infections,* sad to say, are still very much a part of life. Never a year goes by that each of us does not suffer from at least one cold or sore throat. (See *colds* and *throat, sore.*) For children, the frequency of these nuisance illnesses is even greater. Every several years an epidemic of *influenza* strikes, recalling the days when epidemics were commonplace and with far more deadly germs, such as those of *typhoid fever,* smallpox and, just as recently as twenty years ago, *poliomyelitis.* When we think of infection we think of contagion. How did you catch it? Can you transmit it to others? What can be done about it? Terms such as throat culture, virus, bacteria, antibiotics, antibodies, resistance, and *immunization* are all connected in some way with the story of infection. Parents would be well advised to familiarize themselves with some of the scientific background about this important problem, so that they can participate more knowledgeably in the care and prevention of infection in their children.

### MICROBES

To start from the beginning, we must look at the world of germs, the microscopic creatures (microbes) which are the culprits of infection. Biologists classify life into three major categories: *animals, plants,* and *protists.* These categories include all living things with the exception of *viruses,* a breed unto themselves with unique characteristics which we will discuss below. The category protists includes *bacteria, fungi, protozoa* (like amoebae), and *algae* which, along with viruses, make up the world of microbes. A *germ* is a microbe that can cause disease in man. Of the protists, the bacteria are the most important in relation to man. Bacteria and viruses are the microorganisms about which we are primarily concerned in this discussion, although elsewhere we have discussed fungus infections (see *histoplasmosis* and *ringworm*), protozoan infections (see discussions of toxoplasmosis in *pets and children* and amoebic dysentery under *diarrhea*), and some of the worms and insects that parasitize man (see *pinworms* and *scabies*).

The basic unit of construction of plants, animals, and protists (but not viruses) is the *cell*, the smallest microscopic element of life. Cells have a number of characteristics. They have a common physical structure. They resemble each other under the microscope, whether derived from the onion, human skin, or a bacterium. All cells have a common chemical composition of three complex organic chemical molecules: *protein, ribonucleic acid*, and *desoxynucleic acid*. All cells perform similar chemical activities known collectively as metabolism. Metabolic activities include the ingestion and digestion of food substances, the conversion of chemicals derived from food into sources of energy which can be used in performing other activities, the excretion of waste products, respiration, and reproduction (see *genetics*). We ordinarily think of these processes as being characteristic of the animal or plant as a whole. However, at its ultimate level, each of these processes must proceed within the basic unit of the animal: the cell.

Plants and animals, the higher forms of life, are distinguished from protists by the extensive differentiation among the cells of which they are made. The cells are organized into specialized groupings known as *tissues*. For example, flower, seed, and stem are the major plant tissues. Animals have skin, muscle, liver tissue, and so on. Each of these tissues is a group of similar specialized cells. In contrast, protists like bacteria or algae usually exist as individual, independent, unrelated cells, though they may be joined. Even when the cells of protists are grouped, they lack the exquisite differentiation that characterizes the plants and animals. A well-known protist is seaweed (a type of algae). Although seaweed bears a resemblance to many land plants, in point of fact its cells are all similar, not specialized to perform specific functions. Not only are the cells of plants and animals specialized into tissues, they may be further organized into *organs* which combine several types of tissue to perform a finely integrated function. For example, the human heart contains muscle, nerve, and connective tissue, interrelated to perform the complex function of pumping blood.

*Viruses* fall outside the categories of plants, animals, and protists and are a breed apart, forming an intermediate zone between living and nonliving matter. There are many different viruses. Common diseases caused by viruses are *chicken pox; colds; fever blisters; German measles; influenza; measles; molluscum contagiosum; mumps; warts;* and many infections of the stomach and intestines (see *gastroenteritis*). Viruses are smaller than bacteria and cannot be seen with the ordinary light microscope. They can be seen with the electron microscope. Viruses have two major chemical components: an outer coating of protein and an inner core of nucleic acid, having the form of a helix (coil). In contrast to bacteria and fungi which can live independently, viruses are strict *parasites*, which is to say they can function (reproduce) only within a living cell. The cells that each virus can parasitize are very specific; only certain ones will do. For example, some thrive only within specific bacteria, while other viruses parasitize certain plants or animals, and then only special tissues of these higher forms of life.

Much of what we know about the behavior of viruses comes from studies of those viruses that parasitize bacteria. These are known as *bacteriophages*, or *phage* for short. In attacking, the phage first attaches itself to the wall of the bacterium. A specialized protein or enzyme in the top of the phage's outer coat "bores" a small hole in this wall, establishing communication between the interiors of the phage and the bacterium. The nucleic acid of the phage is then injected into the bacterium. This nucleic acid "directs" the bacterium to produce identical nucleic acid and to surround it with a new protein wall. Thus, particles of new phage are formed within the confines of the original bacterial cell. In this process of multiplication, the host cell is usually destroyed. New phage particles, completely reconstituted, leave the cell and pass into the environment, free to spread to other cells. In effect the phage has used the bacterial cell to reproduce itself, at the sacrifice of the cell.

Viruses can be grown "artificially" only in *tissue cultures*, which are broths of living cells divorced from their animal or plant source. Bacteria and fungi in contrast can grow on inanimate as well as living matter. The most common cells used to grow viruses are chick embryo and the kidney of certain monkeys. These cells are taken from their source and nourished in a test tube into which the viruses are introduced. They parasitize the cells and reproduce themselves. The ability to grow viruses outside of a living host was an essential step for the development of vaccines against viral infections because vaccines require a large quantity of pure virus. (See **immunization**.) The tissue culture technique was such an important development that a Nobel Prize for this discovery was awarded to Drs. Enders, Robbins, and Weller, working at The Children's Hospital Medical Center.

Note the differences between viruses and other forms of life. Viruses lack many of the characteristics of cells. Their only metabolic activity is reproduction, in contrast to the multiple functions of the cell. The virus is reproduced exclusively from the genetic material or nucleic acids of the parasitized cell, whereas the cell must reproduce all of its own components. During reproduction, the components of the virus are independently synthesized and later assembled, in contrast to the cell, each part of which duplicates itself. The cell is formed from preexisting structural elements, whereas a virus stimulates their production anew.

Where are viruses and bacteria found? Viruses are found in association with their hosts. In humans, the intestine, nose, and throat are important sites of viral multiplication, especially so in terms of contagion. The virus is shed from the intestine in feces or from the nose and throat through coughing and sneezing. Once shed, they may be transmitted in water, for example, polio virus, or in air, for example, influenza or common cold viruses. Thus water and air are the vehicles for the spread of some viruses. While "in transit" the virus is dormant, that is, not multiplying, but capable of infecting another susceptible host.

Bacteria, in contrast to viruses, are more widely distributed. These microbes exist wherever there is organic matter, living or dead. Soil teems with them. Some are present only in certain parts of the bodies of animals, in this respect resembling viruses in that they are associated with a specific host. Without bacteria the world as we know it would not exist. Bacteria perform the crucial role of processing all dead organic matter (formerly living matter that has died) into its constituent parts, making these available for other living organisms. Plant growth depends upon bacteria. And since all animal food (and human food) is ultimately derived from the energy stored in plants, without plant life animals would have nothing to feed upon and could not exist. Thus the entire cycle of life on earth is intimately connected with the world of bacteria.

In all animals (including man), bacteria (and possibly viruses) normally inhabit the skin, nose, mouth, throat, and intestine, generally causing no harm. The body is able to prevent these germs from causing illness, but is not able to eliminate them. These normally present bacteria are known as the *normal flora*. For example, three or four types of common bacteria usually live in the human throat. The normal flora varies according to the species of animal and the part of the body. Thus, the normal flora of the chicken and human intestine are different. The normal flora of the throat differs from that of the skin, and so on.

Some parts of the body have no normal flora and are or should be sterile, completely free of bacteria. For example, spinal fluid should contain no bacteria. The presence of bacteria in spinal fluid is abnormal and, in fact, identifies the disease known as **meningitis.** The notion of normal flora stands in opposition to the common view that bacteria are "germs" and should be guarded against. We all have bacteria and have them all the time.

A *culture* (growing the bacteria in the laboratory as will be discussed later) of the skin, nose, or throat, for example, will multiply the normal flora along with any harmful bacteria present. Cultures of parts of the body where we expect normal flora should never show a complete absence of microorganisms. A culture report of "negative" means that no harmful bacteria were found, not that no bacteria were found at all.

## INFECTION

We say that animals, including man, are in a state of equilibrium with "their" bacteria. Usually the relationship between host (man) and parasite (bacteria) is harmonious. Occasionally, and particularly with bacteria that are not part of the normal flora, invasion and war occur. This is the biological condition known as infection, which we will now discuss.

*Infection* is the conflict between invading microbes, viruses, or bacteria, and a host. It has a number of familiar characteristics. Consider an infected cut in the skin. First, bacteria enter a break in the skin. Gaining a foothold, they begin to multiply. The immediate body response is to increase the flow of blood to the now infected cut, causing redness, swelling, and pain. Next the body mobilizes large numbers of white blood cells from the bloodstream and dispatches them to the front line. The white cell count is thus increased (see **blood count**). There are several different kinds of white cells and the percentage of each present, also called the "differential," varies from one infection to another. (The "differential" thus gives a clue to the kind of infection present.)

Were we to look at the battle under a microscope, we would see the white blood cells clustered around the invading bacteria, literally ringing them off. Moments later, the white blood cells completely encircle the bacteria, and ingest them. In effect, the white blood cells eat the invading microbes. The bacteria are then digested, dissolved, and destroyed.

We can see the results of this battle without using a microscope. We are all familiar with pus, which is essentially an accumulation of white blood cells at the site of microbial invasion. Pus, which is normally white or yellowish-white in color, is a mixture of white blood cells, dead microbes, and protein which has "leaked" out from nearby blood vessels in the infected area. Pus bears testimony to the raging battle between invader and defender. (See **abscess.**)

At the same time that the lines are being sharply drawn between host and invader, destroyed bits and fragments of bacteria or their toxic products are liberated and carried in the bloodstream or lymphatic channels to nearby *lymph nodes*. (See **glands, swollen.**) *Plasma cells* in the lymph nodes perform a chemical analysis on the foreign material and manfacture proteins capable of locking with or binding to it. These proteins are called *antibodies* and are contained in that group of proteins normally circulating in the blood known as *gamma globulins*. These specific gamma globulins or antibodies are released from the lymph node into the bloodstream. They circulate through the body and concentrate at the site of infection. As the free gamma globulin or antibody comes in contact with the living bacteria or bacterial toxin, it binds or joins with those same chemical fragments which in reaching the lymph node had stimulated the production of this particular antibody. The bacterium or its toxic product is then "coated" with antibody. Antibodycoated bacteria are significantly more susceptible to encirclement and ingestion by white blood corpuscles. In some infections of the nose, throat, and intestine, antibody is developed not only in the blood but also in the mucous secretions of these body sites. This local antibody is very important in combating invasion and in preventing reinfection.

The example of the infected cut used above involved a visible localized infection. A similar process takes place in more generalized infections like measles, where virus spreads throughout the body from the site of major invasion, the respiratory tract in the case of measles. Furthermore, as will be discussed, not all infections produce symptoms. Many do not and are known as subclinical infections.

In the majority of infections, the host overcomes the invader. Healing follows and all returns to normal. However, the antibody produced remains in the host's circulation after the infection is over, and is an important factor in the development of immunity. It is possible to measure both the amount and type of antibody present in the blood. Antibodies are a living record of the microbes with which a person has had successful battles in the past. Thus, the blood of most adults contains antibodies against the viruses of measles, chicken pox, and mumps, and against bacteria like streptococci.

The presence of an antibody also means, in general, that an individual will be more or less immune to reinvasion by the same microorganism. A second attack of measles is almost unheard of. With colds, experience with one virus may protect against reinfection by that particular virus but not against the hundreds of others capable of causing similar symptoms. Reinfection with some microorganisms can take place, but usually no symptoms develop. Sometimes, even though the blood is immune to invasion because of antibodies, infection can occur in a local site. This is true in infections of the cervix, in gonorrhea (see ***venereal disease***) in ***cytomegalovirus*** infection, and in the throat in infectious mononucleosis (see ***mononucleosis, infectious***). Similarly immunity to poliomyelitis following use of killed (not live) polio vaccine is only to bloodstream invasion (obviously important), but not to intestinal infection. Live rubella (***German measles***) vaccine produces immunity to bloodstream invasion by virus (hence protecting the fetus) but not to infection of the nose and throat.

Partial or limited immunity may not be the disadvantage it first appears to be because, with each recontact with the microorganism, a person receives a "booster" stimulus to antibody production. On the other hand, he or she continues to be a means whereby the germ can be passed around. Immunity is not an all-or-nothing affair.

The measurement of antibody is of practical use in identifying a microbe when the symptoms caused are not specific to one infection alone. ***German measles,*** for example, is an infection which is not unique in its symptoms. A similar ***rash*** can be caused by a number of other viruses, or the rash may be absent entirely. The only symptom may be enlargement of the lymph nodes of the neck. Or the infection may not produce any symptoms at all (as will be discussed below in the section on subclinical infections). By appearance alone it is often difficult to say for sure that an illness is caused by the German measles (rubella) virus. However, a blood sample drawn from a patient (for example, a pregnant woman) at the time of exposure to someone with probable German measles and again several weeks later will permit comparison of the two samples for the presence of antibody against rubella. If German measles virus caused an infection, regardless of symptoms, we would expect to see an increase in the concentration (titer) of antibody. If the patient was not infected, no rise in titer would be observed.

Identification of the virus causing an illness is of great practical consequence in the case of an infection like German measles which can cause serious defects in the fetus during the first three months of pregnancy. A rise in antibody would signify that German measles infection had occurred and that the baby may have been exposed.

Antibodies are divided into several groups according to the size of their molecules. Most are of small molecular size and capable of passage across the placenta from the mother to the blood of the fetus. The larger antibody molecules do not cross the placenta and the baby's blood at birth is deficient in them. There is some evidence, as yet incomplete, that breast-fed babies overcome this deficiency through the passage of antibody producing maternal cells in the milk to their intestinal tracts. Additionally, breast milk contains antibodies against bacteria and viruses which invade via the gastrointestinal tract. These immunological facts are another strong reason for breast feeding babies.

At birth, then, the infant has a generous supply of antibodies transmitted from his mother. He is particularly well stocked with antibodies against most viral illnesses, assuming that the mother herself has had contact with them. For this reason, assuming an immune mother, it is uncommon for a baby to contract measles, mumps, or polio during the first several months of life. Because the infant is temporarily immune, a virus vaccine administered at this time will have no effect. On the other hand, antibodies of the large molecular variety are conspicuously absent in the newborn. These antibodies are directed against bacteria known as gram negatives, so named because of their staining properties with certain dyes. Significantly, babies are unusually susceptible to gram negative bacteria at birth, even to those that are part of their normal flora. As mentioned, breast milk, it appears, can help reverse this susceptibility. Within the first couple of weeks, as the normal flora stimulates antibody production, infants begin to manufacture antibodies on their own to these microorganisms and this unusual susceptibility is overcome. The maternal cells transmitted in breast milk then disappear.

As the maternally transmitted antibodies disappear, the infant, once immune to a disease like measles, becomes susceptible. It is at this time that we stimulate permanent immunity by giving measles vaccine. To be effective, the vaccine must be given after the loss of antimeasles antibody passed from the mother, which is the case by one year of age in almost 100 percent of infants.

The harmony between the microbes of the normal flora and the host has nothing to do with good intentions. Bacteria and viruses are "interested" solely in survival and reproduction. They will "take advantage" of any opportunity that comes their way. But they are not free to multiply at will. A set of restrictions and rules controls their activities. They have specific requirements as to diet, concentration of oxygen, and degree of acidity of the environment. Deprive them of an essential condition and they cannot reproduce. Microbes are not free to set up shop anywhere or to invade most tissues. But, given the proper environment, multiplication automatically follows. This multiplication may be normal and confined, as with the normal flora, or it may be abnormal, with invasion by the microbes causing a state of infection. Which way the issue will be resolved depends on the characteristics of both germ and host.

First, there are the characteristics of the microbes. Bacteria differ as much from each other as do people. Bacterial "personalities" vary considerably. Some are quite placid, while others are aggressive and hostile. Biologists term the aggressive bacteria *virulent*. Good examples are the bacteria that cause **tuberculosis** and those responsible for cholera, **diphtheria, tetanus,** and **whooping cough** (pertussis). Give these germs the smallest foothold and they will begin to invade body tissues, setting up an infection. In contrast, the normal flora consist of peaceful, placid, nonvirulent microbes, living in harmonious relationship with man and only under certain circumstances causing difficulty. These "good-natured" organisms not only go along for the ride in various parts of man's anatomy, but also may actually contribute significantly to his well-being. For example, in the class of higher animals known as ruminants, of which the cow is the most familiar representative, there is an inseparable cooperation between animal and bacteria. Ruminants have an extra stomach containing what is essentially a bacteria brew into which the animal delivers its diet of grass and hay. The bacteria feed upon the ingested vegetation, reproducing in great number. These bacteria bubble over the rim of the extra stomach and are passed down into a second stomach, where they in turn are digested into their chemical components. These building blocks can then be absorbed from the animal's intestine to be used as a source of energy for its own life processes. Sterilize the stomach containing the bacteria and the cow will die. Cows are unable to process animal or plant protein directly. Instead, they provide bacteria with the conditions for multiplication and then proceed to feed on the bacteria themselves.

A similar but less extreme degree of interdependence is demonstrated in the intestinal tract of man, where certain bacteria, supplied by nutrients from the diet, "cooperate" by producing small quantities of essential chemicals like vitamin K, important in maintaining the normal clotting ability of the blood. The term "normal flora" emphasizes the peaceful relationship between some bacteria and man.

Virulence is a relative phenomenon. Given the right conditions, even microbes of the mildest nature may become invasive and produce infection. We are able to live peacefully with our normal flora only because of our capacity to keep their numbers in check and prevent them from invading. Should anything interfere with our general state of resistance, the same normal flora may multiply abnormally and set up a clinical infection. For example, in debilitated elderly individuals, the common inhabitants of the intestine (which for a lifetime caused no difficulty) may suddenly invade through the intestinal wall into the bloodstream, setting up a serious infection with rapid spread to many organs (see *bloodstream infection*). At the other extreme, even the most virulent organisms can be easily shrugged off by certain resistant individuals. In an epidemic of the most serious and deadly germ, some individuals are able to defend themselves completely. For clinical infection to occur, both the right germ and a vulnerable host must be brought together. What determines the outcome is the relationship between the two, never solely the characteristics of either one.

Another important characteristic of microbes is their *contagiousness*, that is, how easily they are passed about. Some germs, like measles or chicken pox virus, are extremely contagious. Others, like mumps virus, are less so, while still others, like the bacterium that causes leprosy, require prolonged intimate contact for transmission.

### RESPONSE TO INFECTION

We are increasing our understanding of the factors that account for the resistance of human beings against invasions by microbes. A number of important discoveries have been made during the last generation. There are still vast gaps in our knowledge but the picture is becoming clearer. We have already discussed the roles of antibodies and white blood cells. We now know that cells themselves can either be inherently resistant to invasion by certain microbes or can acquire such resistance through prior contact with the microorganism or the vaccine prepared from it or one of its derivatives. This phenomenon is called *cellular immunity*. Other factors that bear on the response of the individual to microbes are age, race, general state of health (an important problem for the millions of malnourished people in the world), and extent of exposure.

Some individuals are peculiarly susceptible to infection because of a deficiency or weakness in a part of their defense system. Some children cannot manufacture gamma globulin. Others can make only certain kinds and not others, or not enough of the types needed for certain illness. The first condition is known as *agammaglobulinemia* and the second as *dysgammaglobulinemia*. Agammaglobulinemia may be permanent and lifelong, or transient, present only during the first few years of life. In either situation, regular injections of gamma globulin can restore the body levels to protective ranges. Other children fail to combat infection well because of abnormalities in their white blood cells, which are either deficient in number or ineffective in function. Prolonged use of glucocorticoids (cortisone-like *hormones*) to treat a disease can lower resistance to infection. Each type of altered resistance requires its own special treatment.

These diseases of resistance are relatively uncommon, while children who are thought of as having "low resistance" (frequent colds, for example) are very common. This problem is discussed in *resistance and frequent colds*.

So variable is human response to the same germ (bacterium or virus) that we make a distinction between infections that produce clinical—that is, evident—symptoms and those that are known as *subclinical* or *asymptomatic*—that is, proceeding without any disability or discomfort in the host. In the latter, the only evidence that infection has occurred is the development of antibody in the host's blood or the isolation of the germ by culture. Infection occurred and yet the individual had no symptoms of illness.

A classic example of the variation of response to the same germ occurred (and still occurs in some parts of the world) during epidemics of poliomyelitis. First, there were those who were immune from the start and gave the virus no chance to set up shop. These people had had earlier contact with the virus and had developed antibodies against it. Among the susceptibles, or nonimmune population, only a minority, a very small minority, developed full-blown poliomyelitis with paralysis. Another, larger percentage developed symptoms of infection hard to distinguish from the flu or grippe. They had *headache, fever,* and felt ill, often with a mildly stiff neck and aching muscles. They recovered completely without developing paralysis. A yet larger percentage of individuals (the majority) had no symptoms at all. Yet, even in these seemingly well individuals microscopic examination of the intestine (the focus of polio infection) would have revealed the telltale battle of white blood cells with invading virus along with other signs of inflammation. All three groups of susceptibles—those who had full-blown poliomyelitis, those who had a clinical illness without paralysis, and those who had no symptoms whatsoever—showed a rise in their levels of antibodies against poliomyelitis. And all three groups shed virus in their stools, virus that could infect others.

Subclinical infections are common with most infectious diseases. A good example is mumps. About one half of the children infected with mumps virus develop the characteristic swelling of the salivary gland in the angle of the jaw. The other half will manufacture antibodies against mumps without actually developing the telltale swelling or other signs of illness.

An important aspect of subclinical infections is the so-called *carrier state*. In this situation, a virulent germ—be it virus or bacterium—exists within an individual, or on the surface of his skin or mucous membranes, but causes no disease. It is almost as though a dangerous germ has become part of the normal flora. (In fact, the body's resistance to invasion by the normal flora probably depends on partial immunity achieved through subclinical infections.) We have all heard of typhoid carriers. A more common example is the ability of the streptococcus, usually a virulent bacterium, to linger peacefully in the nose and throat. In one study, between one-fourth and one-third of the children in a school classroom were found to harbor streptococci, even though none of the children had symptoms. Viruses also may be "carried." The herpes virus (*fever blisters*) goes into hiding and erupts during periods of stress. *chicken pox* virus apparently lingers for life in a significant number of people and may later manifest itself as herpes zoster infection ("shingles"). Similarly, the carrier state has been identified with hepatitis; infectious mononucleosis; and cytomegalovirus.

The carrier state is of great interest to scientists in understanding the cycle of spread of infectious organisms. Are those children who have streptococci but no symptoms likely to develop a full-blown streptococcal infection should conditions change? For example, can a virus that begins multiplying "trigger" the streptococci in the same throat to do the same? Do chronic, asymptomatic viral infections predispose to cancer? These are some of the intriguing questions posed by the carrier state. One of the practical problems posed by the carrier state is the difficulty of interpreting a culture. For example, if streptococci are isolated from the throat of an individual with a sore throat, we are sometimes hard pressed to decide whether or not the streptococcus is actually causing the infection or whether it just happens to be an innocent bystander to an infection caused by a different microbe such as a virus.

The concept of subclinical infection is crucial in an understanding of the spread of infectious diseases. For one thing, it points out the impossibility of controlling an infectious disease merely by isolating (quarantining) sick people and illustrates the need for a more radical attack through widespread immunization.

Even among people who become sick from infection, there is wide variation in the intensity of symptoms and sometimes even in the kinds of symptoms. Response depends somewhat on the age of the patient. Chicken pox is usually a harmless though annoying illness in the child, whereas in the adult it is more likely to be serious. Infection by the streptococcus in the young infant may show up only as a nasal discharge, whereas in the older child an inflamed throat is a common symptom. A family epidemic may yield different symptoms in different members of the household. The children may suffer the symptoms of diarrhea and upset stomach (gastroenteritis), whereas the adult may show the usual annoying signs and symptoms of the common cold. Sometimes symptoms of both cold and diarrhea are present in the same child. Even with the same set of symptoms, individuals may respond with different degrees of intensity. In general, children have higher fevers than adults infected by the same microorganism.

Many infections in humans are preceded by what is called the *incubation period*, which is the time between the contact with the germ and the development of clinical symptoms. It varies from one germ to another. For example, with chicken pox virus, normally 10 to 14 days will pass following exposure before the usual signs and symptoms appear. During the incubation period, the causative virus is setting up shop and multiplying in specific parts of the body. (The site of multiplication varies according to virus.) The liberation of the virus from the initial isolated areas of infection and its spread throughout the body is associated with the development of clinical symptoms and with the shedding of the virus from the patient into his environment, that is, the onset of *contagiousness*.

In many illnesses there is a period of early illness and contagiousness which is either so mild as to escape attention or so nonspecific that it may be confused with many other infections. This time is called the *prodromal period*. During the prodromal period, the child with chicken pox is every bit as contagious as is someone who has the fully developed rash. The same is true of many other viral illnesses, such as the common cold, influenza, and measles. Because of this prodromal period, during which the germs are shed into the immediate environment, "quarantining" the patient to protect others is well nigh impossible. By the time an illness has been recognized, sufficient numbers of germs have already been shed to expose others. Infections may stop at this prodromal phase without going into the full-blown disease. They are nonetheless contagious.

Subclinical infections, or those limited solely to the prodromal phase, are of considerable concern in a condition such as smallpox (which is fortunately almost over as a worldwide problem). During this jet age, a person could be exposed in Asia to smallpox, be perfectly okay on arrival back in the United States, and become ill days after arrival. Initially his illness is like the flu and no one is concerned. All the while he sheds dangerous smallpox virus capable of infecting others. Only later and not always then (if he is partially immune) does the skin eruption alert doctors and public health officials to the possibility of smallpox. By then many people could have been exposed.

People often ask if you can "catch" *pneumonia* or *meningitis.* First of all, you "catch" one of the many viruses or bacteria which *can cause* meningitis or pneumonia, not the meningitis or pneumonia itself. Whether or not you will pick up this virus or bacterium depends upon how contagious it is. Not everyone who catches these germs becomes ill. With those who do become ill, the chances are, depending somewhat on the microbe involved, that the illness will not be pneumonia or meningitis, but an upper respiratory infection, flu, or gastroenteritis. For an example, some viruses that can cause a cold or flu can also cause viral meningitis. Your chances of developing symptoms at all or exposure to someone infected with such a virus are as great whether the contact has meningitis or just a cold. When and if you do become ill, the odds are, again depending on the germ in question, that you will have the more common expression of the illness, that is, a cold, rather than the less common meningitis. (See *meningitis* and *pneumonia* for further discussion.)

### IDENTIFICATION AND CONTROL OF INFECTIONS

We have discussed how the characteristics of microbes and of the host affect the outcome of interaction between the two. Man is, of course, not completely at the mercy of this encounter. He has intervened to control the spread of many dangerous germs. Probably the major reason for the decline in the Western world of the epidemics that afflicted large populations in the past is the virtual elimination of harmful bacteria and viruses from our environment. Simply stated, if virulent organisms have no opportunity to come in contact with us, then no opportunity for infection exists. By the simple measure of proper disposal of human wastes, by the development of a clean and safe water supply, by the elimination of crowded living arrangements, by the development of high levels of personal hygiene, we keep many virulent germs away. Long before we had antibiotics for typhoid bacteria, typhoid fever became a rare disease because of a general improvement in the standard of living and level of sanitation.

One approach to the control of infectious diseases is provided by an accurate understanding of how the disease is transmitted, whether by contaminated water drunk directly or used to "wash" food, by airborne droplets from a sneeze, through direct contact as in venereal disease or impetigo (see *abscess*), or by way of dirty fingers as in colds and typhoid fever. For example, our knowledge that the virus which causes yellow fever lives one part of its life cycle in a special species of mosquito has pointed to eradication of the insect as a means of controlling the disease. In this case the control of the disease does not depend upon being able to treat the virus infection. For other infections like typhoid fever, careful handwashing is important. With still other diseases we know a great deal about how transmission occurs, and yet are unable to do very much in the way of prevention. A good example is the common cold.

Another important approach to controlling infection is deliberately to increase the resistance of the host by stimulating the production of antibodies through immunization or vaccination. Vaccines are made from killed virulent microbes such as diphtheria or whooping cough or their toxic products such as tetanus toxin, or are modified (weakened) but living virulent viruses or bacteria, like those of smallpox, measles, polio, or BCG vaccine against tuberculosis. Vaccines produce an antibody response similar to that of the natural infection without the disease which accompanies it. (See *immunization* for complete discussion.)

Another way of increasing resistance is by injecting gamma globulin which contains antibodies against the microorganisms with which the patient has been or is likely to become infected. For example, people who are exposed to infectious hepatitis, most probably a viral disease, can be given an injection of gamma globulin which will protect them from developing clinical symptoms and confine the subsequent infection to a subclinical level. Before the days of live measles vaccine, children exposed to measles were commonly given a small dose of gamma globulin to make the attack milder. A larger dose of gamma globulin can, if given soon after exposure, prevent measles altogether, but the child would then not be immune to future attack. In addition to protecting against attack, gamma globulin can be used in modifying diseases once they have occurred. For example, infants with whooping cough can be aided by the use of gamma globulin containing high levels of antibody to pertussis.

Control and treatment of infectious diseases require accurate identification of the microbe involved. Since many diseases produce similar symptoms, identification must be done in a laboratory. A *culture* is the technique or method used to grow a germ outside of the body for purposes of identification. In culturing, we take a swab of the infected area. Then we inoculate the substance containing the virulent microbes into a nutrient medium, either solid or broth. The culture medium is designed to nourish the growth of the microorganism we are looking for. The culture medium used varies somewhat according to the source of the infection. For example there is one medium for isolating germs from the urinary tract and another for the throat. After inoculating the medium, we incubate it in an environment of the proper temperature and oxygen concentration to stimulate bacterial multiplication. After about one day of incubation, sometimes more, the bacterial growth reaches the point of visibility. Individual microbes become visible by multiplication and appear as pinpoint-size colonies recognizable to the naked eye. Bacterial colonies have their characteristic appearances and other identifying features. Some colonies are pointed, others are scooped out. The color of colonies varies. The effects of bacterial growth on the surrounding culture medium also are characteristic. For example, harmful streptococci dissolve the pigments out of the red blood cells placed in the culture medium, distinguishing them from the harmless strep which are part of the normal flora. In many cases, simple inspection of the colonies leads to quick identification. At other times the colony characteristics merely place the microorganism in a grouping or class of organisms, some of which may be virulent and others part of the normal flora. When this distinction cannot be made after the initial culture, the first harvest of microbes is then subcultured into other media which split off the virulent from the harmless bacteria and permit the identification of one from the other.

In some cultures we are interested not only in the presence or absence of virulent organisms but in the extent to which they are present. The quantitative factor becomes particularly important in evaluating bacteria in the urine. We accept a certain number as normal, but draw the line at a certain point. We make a count of the number of colonies of bacteria which grow from one unit of urine. A count above a certain number means infection. Below that number is considered normal.

Isolation of the germ producing an infection permits us to test that germ for sensitivity to antibiotics. We can test its growth against a panel of different drugs to see which ones inhibit its multiplication. Testing for antibiotic sensitivity allows us to select with greater precision the proper drug to use in treating the infection.

We do not necessarily take a culture every time a child has an infection. For example, if a child has the typical symptoms of a cold, a culture is not usually that useful or important. At other times, the doctor can make a good prediction about the virus or bacterium in a given infection by its clinical symptoms, by less involved studies like a white blood cell count, and by the prevalence of the illness in the community.

Sometimes the doctor will take a culture and at the same time begin treatment with an antibiotic, even before the results of the culture are at hand. In a life-threatening infection like meningitis, when treatment must of necessity be started before the time needed for a culture to develop, the culture may then confirm or contradict the doctor's impression. Treatment against such serious infections is usually given in the hospital by intravenous infusion in order to achieve blood levels of antibiotic sufficient to deal with the suspected germs. When we are concerned enough about a child with vague findings, we culture the child extensively (blood, nose and throat, stools, urine, spinal fluid), admit him to the hospital, carefully observe him, and, if we are really worried, begin intravenous antibiotics pending culture reports. The treatment may then be continued (assuming the child is showing some response), modified, or discontinued if the culture indicates that the antibiotic was not really appropriate in the first place. Even with meningitis, a culture may reveal (by failing to grow bacteria) that the illness is caused by a virus and that the antibiotics are not helping. In throat infection (see *throat, sore*) the doctor may have a strong clinical hunch that streptococcal illness is present and will begin the child on antibiotics. If he takes a culture, it may show that harmful streptococci were indeed present, confirming his suspicion. Or the culture may fail to show virulent streptococci and will then point to a nonbacterial (usually viral) cause for the infection. Assuming the doctor is completely satisfied with the technical adequacy of the culture, he may elect to discontinue the antibiotics.

With other infections, the doctor may take a culture and withhold antibiotic treatment until the culture incubates and can be interpreted. He is more likely to follow this sequence when the same symptoms can be produced by both viruses and bacteria, and the cause cannot be inferred reliably from the clinical picture. This state of affairs is more common in throat and intestinal infections. With urine and skin infections, it is often easier to categorize infections more precisely.

Virus cultures are not routinely performed. Facilities for culturing viruses are much more limited. The average community laboratory can do bacterial cultures but not viral cultures. The growth of a virus to the point of identification in a tissue culture usually takes several days to weeks. Most viral infections are over and gone by the time of identification in tissue culture. This fact, together with the lack of an effective treatment for most viral illnesses, means that there is little practical importance in knowing exactly which virus was involved. What we primarily want to know in any infection is whether an available form of therapy, that is, an antibiotic, would be helpful. Thus we are content to culture for bacteria alone. If none are found, we infer that a virus was the cause without actually proving it. For example, for an infected throat, we take a throat swab to see whether or not beta streptococci are present to know whether or not to give penicillin. If none are found it means that a virus is likely the cause of the infection, and penicillin would be of no benefit.

In addition to taking cultures, indirect information about the germ producing an infection can be obtained by measuring antibody levels (titers) in the patient's blood. A rise in circulating level suggests infection. When the symptoms present could have several causes, antibody determination can distinguish among them, as discussed earlier in this chapter.

*Antibiotics* are chemicals that can kill microbes. They are truly "wonder drugs." However, the usefulness of presently available antibiotics is confined primarily to bacteria. A few work against certain viruses. For most viruses there is no effective antibiotic. Giving a "ton" of penicillin to someone with chicken pox, mumps, or the common cold will be of no benefit. Hence, the importance of knowing the cause of an infection.

Antibiotics are not entirely harmless medicines and should not be used indiscriminately. Reactions to these occur, ranging from mild to severe (see *drug reactions, allergic*). Mild allergic reactions consist of a rash like *hives.* With more severe reactions, the patient may have fever, joint swelling, and giant hives. The more often the drug is taken, the more the chance of becoming sensitive or allergic increases. The more penicillin used, the more likely that a penicillin allergy will develop. (About 10 percent of the U.S. adult population is allergic to penicillin.) Besides allergic reactions, antibiotics may have other harmful side effects. For example, the tetracycline antibiotics have been found to stain the teeth of children permanently gray and are therefore avoided if at all possible. Chloramphenicol (Chloromycetin) is capable of depressing the bone marrow and causing *anemia* and lowered numbers of white blood cells and platelets. Streptomycin can cause damage to the auditory nerve, leading to hearing loss. Antibiotics also destroy friendly microbes, the so-called "normal flora," sometimes with undesirable effects. The use of these more toxic drugs necessitates careful monitoring for undesirable side effects, balancing benefit with risk.

Furthermore, indiscriminate use of antibiotics for feverish illnesses when the cause is not clear may mask a serious condition and is generally poor practice. (See *fever of unknown origin.*) For example, a child with fever and fussiness who actually had early meningitis or blood-stream infection without clear-cut symptoms might be given penicillin by mouth just to be sure nothing was being overlooked. The penicillin in this dose will suppress but not eliminate growth of the bacteria in his blood and/or in the spinal fluid. The infection may smolder on without producing sharp enough symptoms to direct attention to the brain and spinal cord as the focus of infection. Even when the symptoms progress, a spinal tap may yield equivocal findings, further confusing the picture. Cultures of the spinal fluid and blood may fail to grow out any organisms or the growth may be delayed, clouding the diagnosis. For this reason, we usually resist giving penicillin to a child with a high fever, ill appearance, and no clearly detectable site of infection. We first try to establish a diagnosis. Parents can help by understanding our restraint and not expecting or demanding premature treatment. If the child is seriously ill, and we can't wait for the laboratory results, we culture him widely and then begin treatment with large doses of antibiotics given intravenously in the hospital. Whenever possible, however, the basic principle is to know what you are treating.

There are many varieties of antibiotics, some of which are more useful for certain bacteria than others. Some antibiotics have no effect at all on one kind of bacterium, but a very powerful killing effect on others. We always try to select the antibiotic which will be the most effective for the patient's infection.

We have discussed the various ways to prevent and treat infections. To round out our discussion, we should add that surgery and other measures are sometimes used. For example, one essential part of the appropriate treatment of a collection of pus (abscess) is drainage, whether it is on the skin (impetigo) or adjacent to a ruptured appendix (*appendicitis*). Localized viral infections of the skin are sometimes simply removed as in warts. Surgery is done for an infected appendix to prevent the spread of infection. If a blockage of a passageway in the body, for example the urinary tract, is predisposing to infection, surgery (or other manipulations) may be necessary to correct the blockage and thus prevent recurrence of the infection. (See *urinary tract infections and defects.*)

See *immunization,* and *resistance and frequent colds,* and specific infectious diseases.

*Influenza* is a virus infection of the nose, throat, and air passageways caused by a specific family of viruses which have the capacity of undergoing change (mutation) so that immunity gained from exposure with one strain offers only partial protection against a new variety. It is often referred to as the "flu." Symptoms usually include *fever,* chills, flushing of the face, neck, and chest, *headache,* redness of the eyes, dizziness, sore throat (see *throat, sore*), pains in the back arms, and legs, and *cough.* In young children *diarrhea* and *vomiting* may be present at the onset. A sense of exhaustion is common.

Mild, uncomplicated cases are usually over within three to four days, but it is not unusual for symptoms to last a week. Some people have a two-phased cycle with a drop in fever toward normal after 2 or 3 days of illness, lulling the patient and his or her family into believing that recovery has occurred, only to have the fever bound up again to its original height 24 to 48 hours later. Complications, both from the influenza virus and secondary bacterial invaders, include *pneumonia,* ear infections (see *earache*), and *sinusitis.*

There is no treatment for the viral infection itself. Antibiotics have no effect. Aspirin and fluids are recommended. (See discussion of aspirin dosage in Part 1, Chapter 5: "Caring for the Sick Child at Home.") Specific treatment is directed toward complications. Influenza is a highly contagious disease which occurs in epidemics. Symptoms usually begin from 24 to 36 hours after exposure. Many people have mild, even non-apparent illnesses. Because of the changeableness of these viruses, it is hard to keep vaccines up to date. They are not usually given to children. (See *immunization.*)

The list of viruses that can produce an illness similar to influenza is too long to name. In fact, in common usage "the flu" refers to almost any illness that causes fever, chills, headache, and malaise. (See *fever of unknown origin.*) We even speak of the "intestinal flu," which is an illness of diarrhea, vomiting, fever, and headache (see *gastroenteritis*).

For a discussion of virus, incubation period, and subclinical illness, see *infections.*

*Insect bites:* see *bites, insect.*

*Intestinal obstruction.* The causes of intestinal blockage, even in young children, are numerous and varied. A foreign body, an area of inflammation, or a tumor may block passage through the intestine, although *tumors* are a rare cause in children. If detected early, most forms of intestinal obstruction can be relieved with confidence in complete recovery. The long-range outlook depends on the underlying cause of the blockage, but it is usually favorable.

When the passage through the intestine, known as the *lumen*, is blocked, neither the products of digestion nor air can get through. A sequence of events that depends somewhat on the point of stoppage but is reasonably predictable then ensues. If the blockage is in the small intestine, which is closest to the stomach, forceful contractions will occur just above the blockage; the intestine is trying to force air and digestive material through. These contractions cause crampy pains. If the obstruction is complete, the intestine will eventually dilate (expand) to many times its usual diameter under fatigue from the accumulation of fluid, air, and partially digested food. The patient will feel "bloated," and his or her abdomen will be distended perceptibly. There is a tendency for the contents of the intestine to be evacuated in the reverse direction—the patient vomits. *Vomiting* and the crampy pains are characteristic signs of intestinal obstruction.

For obstruction of the large intestine, the picture is not very different. Again, predominant early symptoms are distension and crampy pain, but vomiting comes on later than it does when the small intestine is involved. The obstruction extends up to the intestinal tract.

Persistent obstruction, of course, prevents the child from absorbing food and water. He will become dehydrated, showing the usual signs—dry tongue, pasty skin, sunken eyeballs, and so forth. (See *diarrhea.*) All forms of intestinal obstruction have one hazard in common, which is eventually fatal, if the obstruction is not relieved: the impairment of blood supply to the point of gangrene (death) of the affected segment of intestines. The gangrenous bowel will perforate and intestinal contents and bacteria will leak into the peritoneum, resulting in peritonitis (see *appendicitis*).

In the newborn, a cause of obstruction is *meconium ileus,* which is a manifestation of **cystic fibrosis.** In this condition, defective pancreatic function in the womb prevents proper digestion of the meconium (sticky secretions formed in the baby's intestine before birth). This material becomes too gluey to be propelled through the intestine and causes blockage. Another cause of intestinal obstruction is the twisting and kinking of the intestine which is commonly seen in *incarcerated* (trapped) *inguinal hernia* (see **hernia**). In young children, one section of intestine may telescope into itself (*intussusception*).

In all cases, the diagnosis of obstruction is one for the doctor to make, not the parents. In the newborn, the nurses or physician will recognize the symptoms in the hospital nursery. If the obstruction develops later, it will be the symptoms of pain, vomiting, and distension of the abdomen that will alarm the parents and send them to the doctor for help. X-ray studies will probably be made to identify and locate the obstruction. Treatment will vary according to cause. In general, first efforts are directed at reversing the side effects of the obstruction. Fluids given intravenously relieve the dehydration, and antibiotics fight infection. A tube is introduced through the mouth or nose into the stomach above the point of blockage to draw off the accumulating material and relieve the dilated intestine. If surgery is necessary, the blockage is opened and associated defects, such as inguinal hernia, are repaired. If the impairment of the blood supply has caused gangrene of a section of the intestine, the dead bowel must be removed.

**Intussusception** is an unusual bowel condition that occurs mainly in infants and young children and requires medical attention, sometimes surgery. The child cries in severe pain and passes stools that look like gobs of currant jelly. These symptoms lead parents to contact their doctor.

Intussusception is a telescoping of one section of the intestine into another. If you took a section of very flexible hose or tubing—holding it with both hands—and brought your hands together, the resultant folding in on itself would be what happens to the intestine in intussusception. The small intestine literally swallows itself, and by continuing contractions (as if forcing fecal matter through the passage) sucks in more and more of the bowel. The blood vessels of the invaginated (sucked-in) section of the bowel are compressed and the vital flow of blood is cut off. Interference with the blood supply causes inflammation of the intestinal lining, followed by production of a copious flow of bloody mucus. This mucus causes the currant-jelly-colored stools referred to above. The obstructed segment of the intestine swells and may become gangrenous. The obstruction of the intestine above the block causes symptoms of crampy pain, distension, and *vomiting.*

The causes of intussusception are usually unclear. Sometimes an abnormality of the intestine, such as a polyp (a benign growth of the inner lining of the intestine) or *Meckel's diverticulum,* an outpouching of the intestine similar to the appendix, but present in only a small percentage of people, acts as a sticking point, allowing the intestine to take hold of itself. Once the first contact is made, the full-blown intussusception follows.

The child's pain in intussusception is severe, as might be expected. It tends to come in short spurts, with intervening quiet periods, during which the child remains peculiarly still. The pain is usually enough of a signal for the parent to get in touch with the doctor; the appearance of the currant-jelly stools is the clincher, if one is needed. In examination the doctor can often feel the swollen segment of intestine and may find a currant-jelly stool in the rectum.

There are two treatments for intussusception: barium enema or surgery. The enema, needed for X-ray diagnosis of the condition, may be enough to open the telescoped segment of bowel out into its normal position. The enema is not given if there is any indication of gangrene or perforation of the intestine. If the enema is unsuccessful, surgery is the only recourse. In surgery, first an attempt is made to manipulate the segment of bowel back into normal position. If that fails, the segment is cut out.

A small minority (under 5 percent) of the children who have had intussusception will have a recurrence.

See *abdominal pain.*


*Itching:* see *allergy; athlete's foot; bites, insect; eczema; hay fever; hives; poison ivy, sumac, and oak.*


*Jaundice.* Contrary to popular belief, jaundice is not a disease but a symptom. It can represent a variety of ailments and may appear at any age. The actual physical cause is a yellow chemical called *bilirubin,* which is normally present in a small quantity in the blood. Excessive quantities of this yellow chemical cause jaundice, a yellow tint of the skin and the whites of the eyes. Bilirubin is a breakdown product of *hemoglobin,* the oxygen-carrying red pigment in the red blood cells (see *blood count*). To understand jaundice it is necessary to know a little about the bodily processes involving bilirubin.

Red blood cells are constantly being formed and removed from the bloodstream. Originating in the marrow of the bones, they have a life span of about 120 days. In old age (any time after 100 days), they deteriorate and are then removed from the circulation. These old red blood cells are destroyed within the lymphatic tissues, and their hemoglobin is altered chemically. Bilirubin is a product of this chemical breakdown.

From the lymphatic tissues, the bilirubin is carried in the bloodstream to the liver for further processing. The liver excretes all but a small amount of the altered bilirubin into the bile. It then passes through the bile channels to the intestine, whence it passes out of the body in the stools. A small amount of processed bilirubin enters the bloodstream. Chemical analysis can distinguish the bilirubin which is on its way to the liver from the bilirubin which has been processed by the liver and returned to the bloodstream.

There are two ways in which the amount of bilirubin in the bloodstream can increase. Either the rate of production of bilirubin can be increased, or the removal of bilirubin can be interfered with. Sometimes both factors operate. The effect is to increase the quantity of bilirubin in the blood and tissues. Jaundice then appears.

*Hepatitis* is the disorder with which most people associate jaundice. In this disease the liver is inflamed and can no longer perform its work of dealing with the bilirubin produced from the normal destruction of old red blood cells. Bilirubin accumulates in the bloodstream, and jaundice appears. Gallstones, a common condition in adults, block the bile duct, causing bilirubin to back up, resulting in jaundice. In certain forms of *anemia*, red blood cells are destroyed at a rate that exceeds the capacity of the liver to deal with the bilirubin; the result again is elevated blood bilirubin and jaundice. In all these conditions, you will observe, jaundice is only a symptom, not the underlying cause. Jaundice alerts the doctor to the existence of a problem. The treatment is directed to the cause, not to the symptom.

The exception to this is the treatment of jaundice in newborns. A mild degree of jaundice is common enough among the newborn to be regarded as almost normal. Well over 50 percent of all normal newborns exhibit this "physiologic jaundice," as it is sometimes called. The characteristic yellowing of the skin and eyes appears on the second or third day of life and gradually disappears by the end of the first week. Physiologic jaundice does not bother the baby in the least and may not even attract the mother's attention. But the doctor and the nurses in the hospital nursery will be keeping a sharp eye on it. The reason for this is that certain parts of the infant brain are sensitive to *excessive* levels of bilirubin. Note our emphasis on the word *excessive*. Even up to the point where they do cause some jaundice, levels of bilirubin short of the excessive will not damage the brain. We almost expect *some* jaundice; the problem is excessive bilirubin producing excessive jaundice. This distinction is important.

Doctors and nurses become expert at judging by skin color alone just how much jaundice a baby has, but if there is any question at all, a laboratory test to measure the bilirubin level will be ordered. The test may be repeated several times to follow the curve, up or down, of the bilirubin level. The crux of the matter is the rate at which the jaundice is increasing or decreasing. Most babies, as we have indicated, will require no treatment, but immediate intervention is required for severe jaundice. Fortunately, this is much less of a problem than it used to be, since its most common cause related to the Rh factor of blood is now almost completely preventable.

The illness resulting from very high bilirubin is called *kernicterus*. Not all babies with high levels of bilirubin will develop kernicterus, but there is a strong association between the two conditions. In kernicterus there are severe neural symptoms, and there can be severe permanent damage to parts of the brain. **Cerebral palsy** and deafness (see **hearing and speech**) are among the handicaps associated with kernicterus. So, when the jaundiced patient is a newborn, the doctor must not only find the underlying cause but must also manage to keep the jaundice (that is to say, the level of bilirubin) within safe bounds. In other words, he has to treat the symptom as well as the disease.

Premature babies, because of the comparative immaturity of their livers, are prone to develop increased bilirubin and may be more sensitive to its effects. The newborn with an infection will be likely to have more than the usual jaundice, because with infection the red cells tend to be destroyed and the liver function may be impaired. This is an example of the simultaneous operation of both possible factors in the causation of high bilirubin levels.

It may come as a surprise to hear that some breast-fed babies undergo not only an exaggeration, but also a prolongation, of this newborn jaundice. Their mothers are producing a larger-than-normal amount of estrogenic hormone (see **hormones**) and passing it along to the babies in their milk. The babies' livers remove this hormone, but the work has to be done by the same enzyme that is involved in the bilirubin processing. If the enzyme is busy wtih the hormone, it is less available for removing the biliribin, which then backs up in the infant's bloodstream. Even when the liver is mature enough to deal with the bilirubin under ordinary conditions, it may not be able to handle both jobs at the same time. In these babies the jaundice may persist as long as breast-feeding continues. Usually it is mild, and nothing need be done. If the jaundice should become excessive, however, nursing would have to be stopped, at least temporarily. In general, excessive newborn jaundice will not preclude breast-feeding. For the first few days the mother of the jaundiced infant who intends to breast-feed can express (squeeze out manually) her milk to keep up the production until the difficulty with bilirubin passes, with or without special treatment, and the baby can begin to nurse.

Another cause of jaundice in newborns, often of the severe kind, results from differences (or incompatibility) of blood types of the baby and mother. As mentioned, problems related to incompatibility of the Rh factor, which is the major culprit, have been just about eliminated.

The standard treatment for an excessively high level of bilirubin in an infant's blood or for a rapidly increasing accumulation of bilirubin is known as an *exchange transfusion*. There is also a newer, simpler treatment called *phototherapy* or *light treatment*.

Persistent jaundice in babies raises the question of **biliary atresia**. See **hepatitis**.

*Joint pain.* The most common cause of joint pain is trauma. After a blow or fall, the skin around the joint will be scraped, and swelling and bruising may appear. The child will cry and try to keep from moving the injured limb. If it is the knee or ankle that has been hurt, he or she may *limp*. When he has recovered from fright and stopped crying, you should inspect the joint closely. If there is only a small bruise, apply ice, and have the child rest. Healing takes a few days. (See also *sprains*.)

If you find the skin reddened or swollen around the joint, if the bruise is extensive, if the pain continues to be severe, or if *fever* develops, call the doctor at once. These symptoms may indicate a *fracture* or infection of the bone (*osteomyelitis*). If it is late at night, do not wait until morning with these more severe injuries. If you are unable to get in touch with your own doctor, take the child to the nearest hospital or medical facility. Before moving him, be sure to immobilize the joint (see *fracture*). Do not allow the child to walk on an injured leg. These precautions will minimize the risk of making a fracture worse.

Pain in the joints without any other symptom is also quite common among children. Despite the child's complaints, you may be unable to find anything that looks unusual. There is no swelling or redness. The child may limp a bit or seem to be favoring the joint, but when you touch it, there does not seem to be a definite point of marked tenderness. Although the child may say that his joint hurts when you touch it, his facial expressions and other behavior do not suggest real discomfort. Mild injuries that cause this type of joint pain can occur during the everyday activities of running, jumping, or bicycle riding. Often the child does not report his minor accidents, and there may be a lapse of some time between the injury and the complaint of pain.

Simple joint pains without other symptoms do not require the immediate attention of your doctor. Rest and cold compresses usually suffice to relieve the pain within several hours. You need not restrict the child's activities with the intention of preventing recurrence. The problem is minor. It is better to accept it than to try to hold the child down.

Generally, then, there is no occasion for alarm when your child has a mild pain in his joints or some other visible place, if he shows no other symptom. Normally the pain should pass in 6 to 8 hours. If the pain should persist, get in touch with the doctor. Steady joint pain that persists for 24 hours or intermittent joint pain that comes and goes over several successive days is a sign that medical help is needed. If you see swelling and redness of a joint, signs of joint inflammation, or can locate a point of marked tenderness, if the child obviously is avoiding movement of the limb, if his pain grows worse as time passes, or if he develops a persistent limp or favors an arm (see *arm, favoring of*), you should call the doctor promptly. These symptoms may be caused by a serious condition such as dislocated elbow, osteomyelitis, *rheumatic fever*, or rheumatoid arthritis (see *arthritis, rheumatoid*).

We include in the above discussion the knuckles and finger joints, the jaw, neck, and back, as well as the elbows, wrists, hips, and knees (see *knee pain, hip pain*). (Stiffness and pain are more common than swelling as such in these joints.)

Any sudden onset of pain in the joints, severe enough to make a child cry, limp, or restrict the use of the affected limb, should be taken seriously, whether or not redness and swelling are present. Call your doctor immediately or take the child to the nearest hospital or medical facility. Although you may not know of any accident or injury, always take the standard precautions for moving a person with an injured limb (see Part 2, Chapter 9: "First Aid").

See *aches and pains.*

**Kernicterus:** see *jaundice.*

**Kidney trouble:** see *nephritis; nephrosis; urinary tract infections and defects.*

**Klinefelter's syndrome:** see *genetics.*

**Knee pain.** The general principles concerning when to seek medical attention for knee pain are included in the discussion on *joint pain.* The most common cause of knee pain is trauma. Knee pain also occurs with disorders of the hip and may be the first tip-off to a hip problem (see *hip pain*). Knee pain can also occur with *rheumatic fever,* Osgood-Schlatter disease (as discussed below), and rheumatoid arthritis (see *arthritis, rheumatoid*).

Sometimes in association with knee pain, the knee may lock or catch so that it cannot be straightened out. This disorder requires investigation. A common cause is a defect in the cartilage of the knee joint. Surgery may be necessary.

*Osgood-Schlatter disease,* named after the physicians who first described it, is a common disorder of varying severity which occurs primarily in boys. The bony bump just below the knee, which is the upper part of the *tibia* (leg bone), becomes swollen, inflamed, and tender. The children complain of pain, particularly when walking, and a *limp* is often present. Although its cause is not completely understood, the disease is thought to result from the wear and tear on the leg. Why some children are susceptible and others are not is a mystery.

The majority of children will be helped by simply cutting down on walking and running and by limiting movement to essential activities. When pain is marked, bed rest with very limited walking may be required. On occasion the legs may have to be placed in casts to ensure the rest needed for healing. Acute cases can often be helped by an injection into the tender area. Most cases subside in several weeks, but occasionally the condition will recur and be a nuisance until the end of growth.

**Knock-knees:** see *orthopedic concerns.*

**Language development:** see *hearing and speech.*

**Laryngitis:** see *croup and laryngitis.*

**Laryngomalacia:** see *breathing, noisy.*

**Lead poisoning.** Lead is a metal which does the body no good. Lead poisoning is a significant problem for children in the United States. It is estimated that there are 400,000 children with excess lead in their systems and that 200 deaths from lead occur each year. Children get lead mainly by eating it in old plaster or paint chipped from the inside or outside surfaces of houses or old repainted cribs and furniture. Another source is water carried in lead pipes, including the main pipe leading to the street. Today, there is a legal limit to the amount of lead allowed in indoor paints or plaster. Parents should make sure that paint used anywhere in the house or on furniture contains not more than 0.06% lead. Federal standards allow a higher lead content, so parents must take the responsibility. However, the old lead-based coats remain and children can nibble on putty, on peeling, cracked spots, or on chips fallen to the ground. The chips taste sweet and are appealing to children. The cases of lead poisoning tend to be clustered in old dilapidated neighborhoods. Lead poisoning in this sense is most often a disorder of poverty, although it is far from unknown in wealthier sections.

Although replacing lead pipes and decreasing the acidity of municipal water supplies to reduce removal of lead from lead pipes, and stripping old houses of their lead-based paint or plaster or covering walls over with paneling or plastic wallpaper would certainly go a long way toward prevention, there seems to be more to the problem than the mere accessibility of lead. Some children in these unsafe environments appear to escape unscathed, maybe because they are less impulsive to begin with. A mentally retarded child may be at a higher risk because of his or her inability to understand parents' warnings against eating foreign material.

Another source of lead in the environment which should be a cause of urgent concern is air polluted from the exhausts of engines using gasoline containing lead. Drs. Herbert Needleman and John Scanlon of The Children's Hospital Medical Center observed in the Feb. 29, 1973, issue of *The New England Journal of Medicine* that

Each year in the United States 200,000 tons of lead are inserted into the atmosphere, 90 per cent of this coming from the combustion of leaded gasoline. . . . In the period between 1962 and 1969, increases of air lead concentrations between 25 per cent and 64 per cent have been measured in Philadelphia, Cincinnati and Los Angeles.

Between 17 per cent and 30 per cent of inhaled lead of small particle size is absorbed from the lung, and numerous studies have established that exposure to airborne lead is reflected in an increased body burden. Blood lead levels of parking-lot attendants, traffic policemen, and tunnel employees are substantially higher than those of workers in occupations with less exposure to airborne lead. Urban Philadelphians have twice the blood lead levels of their suburban, noncommuting neighbors. Housewives who live within 3.7 meters (12 feet) of a heavily traveled roadway have substantially higher blood lead levels than women living at distances greater than 38 meters (125 feet). Children attending school 0.3 km (0.2 mile) from a lead smelting plant are reported to have significantly higher blood lead values than a similar group whose school is 1.1 km (0.7 mile) from the source. Levels of lead in deciduous [baby] teeth, a cumulative index of exposure, are five times higher in ghetto children than those found in suburban children. Children living in suburban Boston have concentrations of lead in their teeth that are twice those of Icelandic children. (Reprinted, by permission, from *The New England Journal of Medicine*, Vol. 288:9, page 466.)

The difficulty with lead is that once it gets into the body it tends to remain and deposit in various body tissues. Once in, it is lost very, very slowly. We all have some lead in us. It is only when this average range is exceeded that we get into difficulty. Lead deposits almost everywhere— in the nervous system, nerves, bone marrow, bone, liver, pancreas, teeth, gums, and hair.

The most worrisome site of deposit is the nervous system, where the lead interferes with normal function, causing **vomiting,** nausea, **abdominal pain,** weakness, confusion, decreased alertness, impaired thinking, and behavioral problems. In the extreme case, the brain swells, leading to coma, seizures, or convulsions (see **seizure disorders**), and even death. Even if recovery occurs, these seriously ill children are apt to be permanently brain-damaged. In this sense lead poisoning is a preventable cause of mental retardation (see **developmental disabilities**). Milder cases, some unrecognized for what they are, also occur.

Lead in the bone marrow interferes with the formation of new red blood cells and damages the ones already formed. The result is **anemia** with its symptoms of paleness, weakness, and tiredness. Lead in the bone shows up in an X-ray as dense lines near the joint. The so-called lead line is most clearly detectable in the knee.

A certain amount of the total body lead circulates in the blood. The amount of lead in the blood is a good index of the amount deposited throughout the body and can serve as a test for total body lead. If the blood lead is below a certain amount, we can be reasonably assured that the total quantity of body lead is within safe limits. Lead in hair is also used in testing. The difference is that hair is always growing, although slowly, and incorporates lead only at its growing end in the scalp. The deposited lead moves outward with the hair as it grows. Thus, a clipping of hair is a living record of the body's lead status during the time that the hair grew, but does not tell you much about what is happening at the moment of the cut. The teeth and bones also provide a living history of exposure to lead.

When a child is poisoned with lead, that is, has symptoms like those described above, and an elevated level of lead in his blood and other tissues, he needs treatment with chemicals that bind the lead and carry it out into the urine. The child is given the chemicals until the total body lead is within a safe range.

The same chemicals may be given to children with border-line levels of lead in their blood, as a "provocative" test to see how much lead they really have as indicated by the amount they lose in the urine. Screening tests measuring lead in blood, hair, or in bone as seen by X-ray may be in a middle zone between normal and abnormal. Giving the chemical provides a better index of total lead. Depending upon the amount passed during the test, the child may or may not need more treatment.

There are several ways to identify children without obvious symptoms but who nevertheless need treatment because of a high total body lead. First, we look for a history of eating lead-containing materials or of coming from a neighborhood where old paint and plaster are prevalent. Second, we test or screen the child for lead. A positive screening test for lead in blood and hair can identify high-risk children. Suspect children are then given a provocative test (see above). Early detection is now accomplished through mass screening programs in poor neighborhoods, by doctors who see poor children in their offices, and in schools.

Another important part of preventing lead poisoning is public education and campaigns to "clean up" the lead hazards—stripping old plaster and paint, filling in cracks and holes, repainting, and covering interiors with coatings of impermeable materials. The Federal Government has recently made money available to support state campaigns. The Federal funds fall far short of the need at the time of this writing. Even if one were to ignore the tragic human costs of lead poisoning, the dollar cost of caring for brain-damaged children is staggering.

*Learning disabilities.* Children may have difficulty learning in school for any one or a combination of reasons, all of them important, including a school environment that does not "fit" the particular child, overcrowded classrooms, emotional upsets at school or home, low intelligence, physical illness resulting in prolonged absences, or difficulty in hearing or sight. Other children have problems in dealing with specific subject material. These difficulties are called "specific learning disabilities," and are the focus of this discussion. A specific learning disability is the inability of a child to acquire basic academic skills, primarily reading, writing, spelling, and arithmetic, despite normal intelligence or intellectual potential, adequate teaching, and healthy sensory and emotional faculties. The overriding point is that these children may appear normal and yet be disabled. See *hearing and speech* and *vision problems.*

The common features of children with learning disabilities, present or absent to varying degrees, have been well summarized by Margaret Golick, Senior Psychologist at the McGill Montreal Children's Hospital Learning Centre:

1. *Poor awareness of their own body.* Some children have not learned the range of possibilities of movement; they seem vague about their size (seen when they try to crawl under something or squeeze through a narrow space); they are confused about where their body parts are (their drawings show arms coming off the head, or emerging from the waist; necks are left out; parts are out of proportion; they may not appreciate the difference between the right and left sides of their body; they may not even be aware of the differences among their fingers—using the whole hand as though they were wearing mittens.) As a result of some of these problems they are apt to move awkwardly. They often avoid activities that call for skilled movements; they rarely cut or color or make models; they shy away from playing ball or skipping rope. When compared with others their age, who have been getting regular practice in these normal activities of childhood, the gap in abilities becomes even more apparent.

2. *Poor ability to combine movement and vision.* Many of the children we see are unable to guide their hands with their eyes, cannot follow moving targets, cannot judge distance or direction by vision alone. They can ski well or swim well, but have trouble at sports where the movements must be skillfully integrated with rapid visual responses—activities like catching or batting a ball or shooting at a target.

3. *Visual inefficiency.* Even with 20/20 vision, some children are not alert visually. They do not notice things, may not spot small differences in shape or size, may not use their eyes to look at things at a distance. (One little boy we worked with had taught himself to read in kindergarten, but moved about as though he were blind. He seemed to need to handle things to get meaning from them. In kindergarten he was constantly getting up, feeling his way across the room to find out what was going on there—obviously unable to tell by just looking over from his seat.) On the other hand, some children seem particularly poor or uncomfortable at near-point tasks. (One little boy who was a superb athlete and never missed a fly ball coming his way, insisted on using a magnifying glass every time he had a reading lesson, maintaining that he could not see the words without it.)

With some, the problems seem to be poor perception of the three dimensional world; yet two dimensional vision—for written material, pictures—is intact. (One youngster made such faulty judgments of distance that he was continually stepping on the other children in his nursery school class—yet a year later he learned to read with no trouble, demonstrating particularly keen ability to spot the small differences in letters and words.)

The opposite problem—a good visual grasp of the three dimensional world, but poor appreciation of more abstract visual material, for example, marks on paper, pictures, letters, numbers—is relatively common among the children we examine.

4. *Poor listening ability.* Many of the children with intact hearing on the audiology tests can only attend and react to short units of language; they miss some of what is said to them because they are unable to process it fast enough. (When I listen to a rapid conversation in French, I know what this must be like. It goes by me too quickly to decipher. It is not that I am not paying attention. I am attending harder than ever. I feel sure I could understand if it were slowed down, or given to me in writing, or repeated once or twice.)

Some children hear the speech sounds imprecisely so that they confuse words that sound alike. (One little girl sang to me about "a cartridge in a pear tree.") I have a collection of definitions given to me by children with this problem, which include:

"shilling is when it's cold outside"

"lecture is you plug it in"

"roar is when you row the boat"

There are also children who seem to hear perfectly well in a quiet room, but cannot manage when there are any competing background noises. Just trying to listen to the teacher in a classroom where pencils are being sharpened and feet are being shuffled is like trying to follow a conversation at a mammoth cocktail party.

5. *Integrating information from several sensory channels.* Some children seem to be able to handle tasks that are purely visual or tasks that are purely auditory but seem to have difficulty in combining the information that comes to them through separate sense organs. For example, they may be able to see and recognize the letter "a", and hear and repeat the short vowel sound "a", but seem unable to learn to associate the two.

6. *Poor grasp of sequence.* Coping with an arbitrary or conventional arrangement of things heard (days of the week) or seen (letters in a word) is sometimes very difficult. Either the order is not appreciated, or not remembered.

Sometimes this is evident in a child's speech. It may be in the arrangement of words in a sentence ("What these are supposed to be?"); in parts of compound words ("sitter-baby," "bell-door"); in sounds within a word ("aminal," "plasket," "wipe shield winders").

Arranging *ideas* in logical sequence to tell a story or to express themselves seems to be an insurmountable task for some youngsters. One mother described her ten year old's speech as like a Salvador Dali painting.

Spelling difficulties are often due to poor appreciation or recall of sequence. Children with this problem may remember all of the letters in a word, but not in the acceptable order. They write "spot" for "stop," "thier" for "their," "wrok" for "work," "invitatoin" for "invitation."

7. *Poor sense of rhythm*. In some cases the children move arhythmically. This underlies their trouble in learning to skip rope or bounce a ball. They cannot get a steady rhythm going.

Some children cannot appreciate the form in a short series of rhythmic taps, and are unable to reproduce them without counting them. They do not find it easy to learn poems and nursery rhymes, because they have no feel for the rhythm that acts as an aid to most children.

8. *Problems with concepts*. Understanding ideas of number, time, and space is difficult for some whose experiences have been inappropriate or who have failed to make the necessary generalizations from their experiences. Some are unable to categorize or to see relations between things —perhaps partly because they have been unable to turn their attention to more than one thing at a time. This can seriously restrict language development. How can you understand the word "furniture" if you fail to see what a table, chair, and sofa have in common?

9. *Problems in style of learning*. There are children whose problems seem to be with the learning process itself. Regardless of the mode of intake or the kind of material, they cannot learn easily by rote. Where most children seem to pick up effortlessly and automatically things they have heard over and over again, some cannot. As pre-schoolers they take longer to learn to speak. They cannot fill in the last line of nursrery rhymes; they forget names that should be familiar; they have trouble learning any of the arbitrary formulas we expect in our society—the days of the week, telephone numbers, addresses.

Rote memory difficulties interfere with academic learning, for example, a sight vocabulary in Grade I, multiplication tables later on, history dates. Yet these same children who seem unable to memorize may show good ability to learn anything they can analyze and understand. They learn to read from a systematic phonics approach. They understand arithmetic when it is presented through an approach like Cuisinaire rods.

10. *Gaps in general knowledge*. Perceptual deficits, apart from other effects, may mean that a child will not pick up bits of information in an ordinary way. Things most children learn by chance, some children do not sort out from the clutter of all the stimuli impinging on them. Many of the children we see at the Learning Centre have been unable to tell me their father's name—"We just call him 'Daddy'," they say. Others are unable to answer questions like "Where does milk come from?" "Where do we buy sugar?" Their mothers, in their defence, say "We never told him that." But other children notice things, generalize about them, sort

them out in their own minds. For some of the children with learning disorders many very ordinary and unexpected things have to be made explicit. They are often vague and confused about the world around them. Questions of who, what, when and where give them great trouble. They may not understand relationships that many of us take for granted. (One bright ten-year-old did not know that his grandmother was his father's mother. To him the relationship was as arbitrary as a fairy godmother; no one had ever told him how a grandmother came to be.)

This fuzziness leads to many embarrassments in the child's world—in areas parents may not regard as seriously as they do school problems. One eight-year-old boy, on his way to a birthday party for a boy in his class, confided to me that he couldn't remember the birthday boy's name. This same boy had never learned to use the telephone because he knew no phone numbers by heart—not even his own. When his parents were away for a month's vacation he was unable to say where or how they had gone. They took for granted that he had followed the many family conversations about their forthcoming trip. For a boy like this, the world is much less secure, and much more mysterious than it needs to be.

Many children have poorly developed conceptions of space. They have only a dim notion of where one place is in relation to another. Even in their own neighborhood they cannot find their way home by an alternate route. They have no spatial maps in their heads, and fail to understand how two-dimensional maps represent the world.

Time is a mystery to many. Learning to tell time seems terribly complicated to youngsters who seem unable to keep track of the passage of time, who cannot answer questions like "Which is longer, recess or lunch hour?" "Which takes longer, to wash your face or to get dressed?"

Many children have never understood our conventions that translate information from one sensory modality to another. It seems terribly obvious to most of us that the written word is a visual code for talking; that a clock has a tiny spring that lets the hand move little by little to record the passage of time so that we can see it; that a map is a two-dimensional representation of the three-dimensional world. Yet I have seen many bright school-age children for whom these things had never been clear. Nor did some of them understand what numbers were about —that they could stand for quantity, or for a place in a series (an address, or to designate who won a race); or just be part of an arbitrary code (a telephone number).

These mental skills are acquired during maturation. In a sense, the child with a learning disability can be thought of as having failed to mature normally in some area(s). His performance in these areas is not up to his age level. Time can be on his side, but he needs special help as well.

There are many synonyms for "specific learning disabilities." Some common ones are "minimal cerebral dysfunction," "neurologically, or perceptually handicapped," and "minimal brain damage." While we need words to describe conditions in order to communicate, there is a danger that we "label" children by using them, thus obscuring important differences among children. The commonly used word "dyslexia" is such a label. It is far better, in our opinion, to describe accurately certain strengths and weaknesses, and to define precisely which skills are impaired in children with learning handicaps and which are present, and how well developed the strengths and weaknesses are. This approach is one that can apply to _all_ children, not just to those with problems. In fact, parent organizations concerned with the care of children with learning disabilities are more and more coming around to the point of view that a very important part of helping the educationally handicapped child is developing high-quality individualized programs for all children. Needless to say, we have a long way to go before achieving this goal.

There may be other disorders associated with specific learning disabilities which show up primarily as disturbed behavior, for example, hyperactivity and short attention span, discussed below. For the purposes of most state laws passed to assist in the education of children with learning disabilities, children with cerebral palsy or epilepsy (see seizure disorders) are not generally included, although they too can have specific learning disabilities as above defined. The major difference and reason for their exclusion from laws relating to learning disabilities is that in these latter children there is greater evidence for a definite abnormality of the brain.

We have very little knowledge at present about what actually causes specific learning disabilities. You can think of a learning disorder as a kind of misconnection or crossing of the "wires" linking the different parts of the brain whose cooperation is necessary for the so-called higher intellectual functions like speech, writing, and reading. When you think for a moment about the complexity of thought, it is amazing that there are not more children with problems. Children who have learning disabilities are more likely to have had experiences that could have injured or interfered with the normal maturation of their brains, such as prematurity and complicated pregnancies. In many cases, however, no explanation is apparent.

_Reading problems_ are most common. Early school-age children may be slow in acquiring reading skills for a host of reasons, for example, low-normal intellectual potential; poor teaching or teachers; deficient language experience at home; lack of experiences of a spatial, informational, or experimental nature; being bilingual (home language is a foreign one); lack of familiarity with standard English, that is, speaking a nonstandard form of English, such as "black" English; significant emotional disturbances, such as childhood psychosis, school phobia, or neurosis; pressure of family problems (see Part 1, Chapter 4: "Complaints with an Emotional Element"); or because of impaired hearing or sight.

There are also important maturational differences among children which affect the speed with which reading is acquired. A handicap in acquiring the skill of reading should be suspected if all of these other factors can be eliminated and if certain specific findings are present. These include a history of other family members having had trouble with reading when young, and some errors characteristic of the learning disabled child, such as persistence in writing letters in reverse of what they should be beyond the time usually expected of normal children, inordinate difficulty in associating sounds with written letters (phonics), and extremely slow rates of reading.

It is important to look for an explanation of reading difficulties as soon as a problem is suspected. Parents should discuss the child's reading performance with the teacher. If necessary a reading specialist assigned to the school or school system should evaluate the child in conjunction with the school psychologist. These are usually the first diagnostic steps taken and often all that are required. If necessary, the teacher will recommend evaluations by a school psychologist, reading specialist, learning disability specialist employed by the school system, guidance counselor, a pediatrician, psychiatrist, or neurologist. After a diagnosis of a learning disability is made, a program is planned for the child. This may involve tutoring, use of special teaching techniques, special classrooms, and so forth.

Many, but by no means all (and we emphasize this), children with specific reading disabilities also have problems in concentrating or exhibit hyperactivity; they may show deficits in psychological testing, such as difficulty in copying geometric drawings, in arranging or building with blocks, in solving jigsaw puzzles, in identifying missing objects in pictures, or in arranging pictures in logical sequence to tell a story. These additional problems may or may not be present. Furthermore, the child may be quite bright intellectually. It is not possible to make generalizations in this field.

A *specific disability in writing and spelling* usually is the result of a specific reading disability. Writing is the last language task achieved by a child. Comprehension of spoken language comes first, beginning in the first year, followed by production of spoken speech and language in the second year, the comprehension of written language (reading) in early school years, and finally, competency in producing written language, handwriting, and spelling. It follows, therefore, that a delay in acquiring an early step, such as reading, may result in a delay in acquiring subsequent steps, such as writing and spelling.

Occasionally a specific disability in writing and spelling may occur even though reading has been acquired normally. Poor penmanship may be due to difficulties with fine motor control or eye-hand coordination, sometimes called perceptual-motor difficulties. These may take years to overcome. Several parts of the standard intelligence test administered by school psychologists can uncover and define these handicaps. Usually all that needs to be done is to alert the teacher that the child has fine motor incoordination. In the meantime, he or she need not be penalized for illegible or poor handwriting. He can be allowed to dictate compositions to a "secretary" (usually teacher or mother) or into a dictating machine, so that the process of composition with words need not be stifled because of the mechanical inability to write. Also, the child can learn to use a typewriter. Other methods of training might help him learn to communicate in writing more efficiently, although this skill may not be his best. Teaching difficult skills should not be completely bypassed, although expectations to perform should be adapted to the child's abilities.

Some children who read normally have difficulty in writing words properly, including the making of spelling errors. There are various explanations for this phenomenon, but at the moment none is adequate. Treatment consists of special individual help on writing skills, teaching the use of the dictionary, and not penalizing the child for poor spelling, that is, adjustment of expectations. Unlike inability to read, which is a serious handicapping condition, inability to write well is of less critical importance in future achievement and life.

Although less common than disabilities in reading and spelling, *specific disabilities in acquiring basic arithmetical skills* do occur. Less is known about these difficulties than reading disorders, which seem to have more practical importance and have attracted more attention. Some children have difficulty with mathematics because of a failure to develop a grasp of what is meant by "number." Just as children develop the concept of "cat," which applies to all specific examples of cats, so this concept of number is needed before the child can mentally manipulate numbers. The steps in development of the concept of number can be identified by various kinds of tests called "arithmetic readiness" tasks. If a child is having difficulties with the readiness tests in kindergarten, the first-grade teacher ought to watch his progress in mathematics closely. If he has trouble understanding what is sometimes called "the categorical structure of number," that is, the construction of our number system on the basis of units, tens, hundreds, and so forth, then he needs further evaluation.

Sometimes trouble in mathematics is merely a consequence of difficulty in reading. Such children learn arithmetic normally in the first couple of grades. When there is more emphasis on reading word problems which need translation into proper mathematical terms in about the third grade, they begin to have difficulty. This is not really difficulty in arithmetic ability but another sign of reading disability. Similarly, writing numbers in reverse and reading them in reverse are not a primary problem in mathematics but of reading.

Often associated with specific disability in arithmetic are difficulties (perceptual-motor disabilities) in perception of objects in space, for which there are many standardized psychological tests. Understanding of numbers stems from the child's ability to manipulate objects, originally in space, and is therefore dependent upon the child's normal development of spatial concepts. Also, the child who processes information poorly may have difficulty in math, not just because of reading per se but because he is unable to handle the process of learning.

When difficulties in mathematics occur alone, pediatricians and neurologists may call it "developmental dyscalculia." Sometimes it occurs with three other problems: difficulty in distinguishing left from right, difficulty in knowing the position of the finger (whether bent, straight, up or down), and agraphia (writing and spelling difficulties). These disorders and reading difficulties need not be associated, although they sometimes are. In other words, several specific learning disability syndromes may coexist in a child as well as occur singly. In fact, as a generalization, learning disorders rarely come as single, separate problems. More often they are combined.

The *hyperactivity* syndrome refers to a basic disorder of paying attention manifested by short attention span, distractability, impulsivity, and motor overactivity. Although the motor activity may be most prominent, many neurologists (specialists in neurological problems) feel this disorder is really caused by a disturbance in those complex functions of the brain responsible for keeping us focused on one thing. We do not usually think of the importance of our being able to concentrate and "shut out" distractions. Some children, for reasons beyond their control, simply are not able to keep their mind on something. Their excessive motor activity and impulsivity represent a following through with their bodies of whatever distracts their attention.

Hyperactivity is usually noticed when the child starts school. The comments teachers usually give are "He can't sit still," "Always on the go," "Fidgety," "Never finishes his work," "Immature," "Disruptive," "Clowns a lot," "Moody," "Disobedient." More and more, however, we are appreciating that difficulties in paying attention may be noticed by observant parents much earlier, even in the first years of life. It is also important to realize that very similar kinds of behavior can result from other causes, such as chronic anxiety. A careful diagnosis is always called for.

It is also worthwhile pointing out that these symptoms of hyperactivity are in a sense an exaggeration of common behavior in young school-children, particularly boys. So prevalent is this sex difference in behavior that in some schools in England separate programs for boys and girls have been developed for the early school years. Acknowledging sex differences in behavior and structuring educational environments accordingly could reduce the number of children who do not "fit in." Increasingly, teachers are less insistent that 7-, 8-, and 9-year-olds sit still at their desks and will let children, within reason, do their work while sprawled on the floor, walking, and standing. There is more tolerance of fidgetiness as classrooms become more "open."

Hyperactivity may certainly interfere with learning, both because the child can't concentrate long enough to do a task and because his behavior often gets him into so much trouble that the resulting emotional climate isn't conducive to learning. He may or may not have specific learning disabilities as well. He may or may not have borderline or low normal intelligence. Often the hyperactive child is considered "bright" in intelligence.

The hyperactivity syndrome is one condition in which physicians can offer a specific medical treatment, for increasing attention span and decreasing hyperactivity. Medications usually prescribed are Ritalin (methylphenidate) or Dexedrine (dextroamphetamine). They have been used for various purposes over thirty years, and there is no evidence that children with this syndrome become addicted to these medications. Children do not experience the "highs" of adolescents and adults who use the drugs for psychic pleasure. (See *drug problem.*) They must be administered, however, by a physician, and parents must keep in regular touch because the dosages may have to be adjusted. Common side effects are loss of appetite and sleeplessness. Some children temporarily fail to grow or gain weight at predicted rates. These side effects can almost always be controlled by adjustments of dose and timing of medication, and discontinuation of medications during vacations and weekends. Usually hyperactivity lessens with time, but most children correctly diagnosed need treatment over a period of years, including special teaching. Hyperactivity should be viewed as a chronic disease requiring long-term care.

Before recommending drugs, we assume that parents or the professionals helping them excluded other causes of hyperactive behavior such as overcrowded classrooms, hunger, and anxiety. Every child with difficulty in learning deserves careful assessment. The treatment should flow from the diagnosis. If emotional or family problems are also present, these should be attended to. Drugs should not be used to mask or cover up other problems. They are only for the neurologically caused disorder of attention. The temptation is to use drugs indiscriminately because they are relatively cheap and easy answers.

In recent years, we have been giving much more, but still not enough, attention to the child with learning problems, regardless of cause. The slow learner without help falls behind, develops a defeatist "What's the use?" attitude, and loses confidence in himself. He is prone to drop out of school early and to become delinquent. If he did not have an emotional problem to begin with, he will rapidly develop one. He blames himself and believes he's "stupid." The human and dollar costs of failure to attend early to learning difficulties are enormous. When a child isn't learning, it's critical to ask "Why?"

Now that we can more clearly analyze children with learning disabilities, we are becoming more interested in detecting these problems even before the child reaches school. It seems quite certain that some of these disorders can affect the child long before formal learning of reading, writing, and arithmetic begins. The hyperactive child may have already developed emotional problems from his long-standing run-in with the world. The child with disordered perception of objects in space may have already retreated into overly safe, quiet activities and have missed many important opportunities for development. From the point of view of preventive medicine, it is increasingly important to take a careful and regular look at children's development from birth onward. As an example, The Children's Hospital Medical Center is working with the Brookline, Massachusetts, school system to register children in the school at the time of birth. By regular contact with the families throughout the preschool period, it is hoped that learning problems can be identified early, and prevented or improved upon, before the child reaches school.

While sounding this more optimistic note, it is important to point out that children with specific learning disabilities are genuinely handicapped. Many parents have the false idea that treatment will make the handicap go away, just as penicillin eradicates streptococcus.

Fortunately, programs of identification, diagnosis, and treatment of the learning disabled child are growing in number and strength. More and more research is being done. Many states are developing special programs for such children. In Massachusetts, for instance, a new educational reform law (Chapter 766 of the Acts of 1972) guarantees each child an educational program suited to his or her individual needs. If there is financing, each school district will provide a professional evaluation team to which a child can be referred, at the request of his parents, or of his teachers. Such developments have been spurred on by groups of parents organized locally and nationally in the American Association for Children with Learning Disabilities, 2200 Brownsville Road, Pittsburgh, Pa. 15210. Treatment of a learning disorder must extend into the home. There are many ways parents can reinforce the special instruction of the school. Close cooperation between school and home should take place.

See *developmental disabilities; handicapped child*; and Part 1, Chapter 4: "Complaints with an Emotional Element."

*Legg-Perthes disease:* see *hip pain.*

*Leptospirosis:* see *pets and children.*

*Lethargy:* see *drowsiness, delirium, and lethargy.*

*Leukemia* in children is a cancer of the white blood cells. After the first year of life, leukemia and other cancers are second only to accidents (see Part 2, Chapter 8: "Accident Prevention") as the leading cause of death in children in the United States. While the cause of leukemia in man is unknown, there is increasing evidence that viruses cause leukemia in animals.

White blood cells formed in this disease are abnormal and usually increased in number. They infiltrate various parts of the body. In the bone marrow they "crowd out" the cells that produce red blood cells, normal white cells, and platelets. The decrease in red blood cell production results in *anemia*; the decrease in normal white blood cell production results in frequent and severe *infections*; and the decrease in platelet production results in increased bleeding usually manifested by easy bruising, gum bleeding, and at times more severe bleeding. In addition, *fever* and bone pain commonly occur.

Major improvements in the treatment of leukemia have occurred so that the outlook for children with this disease is nowhere near as grim as it once was. Antibiotics can help with infections. Blood transfusions can correct anemia. Transfusions of platelets can help restore normal blood clotting. The hormone *hydrocortisone* (see *hormones*) or one of its synthetic equivalents, given orally, decreases the production of leukemic cells and is an important part of long-term therapy. Other drugs known as *antimetabolites* also curtail the formation of these abnormal white cells.

With these measures, it is now possible to produce complete remission (disappearance of all evidence of the disease) in 90 percent of patients. The appropriate use of treatment during remission has markedly prolonged remissions. It is important to emphasize that during remission the child's symptoms abate completely, and he returns to normal activity. Up to 50 percent of patients under our care at The Children's Hospital Medical Center and at other centers survive 5 years, and a significant fraction of 5-year survivors have remained free of their disease for up to 15 years. We are now daring to ask the question, in some children, of whether the disease has been brought under permanent control and certainly thinking of this as a target to shoot for.

Acute leukemia is not contagious. Thus, the presence of this disease in a family member does not result in an increased risk of leukemia in other family members.

Acute leukemia is a rare disease and its treatment requires highly specialized personnel and resources. This is best carried out in leukemia or cancer centers, on a cooperative basis between the family physician and the physician(s) at the center.

Treatment has its problems. The antimetabolites used must be changed as effectiveness of one "wears off" and leukemic cells are produced anew. These medicines cause a number of undesirable side effects, such as hair loss and increased susceptibility to infection. A price is also paid for the effectiveness of hydrocortisone in depressing the formation of leukemic cells. In the large amounts necessary for therapy, hydrocortisone produces the clinical picture known as *Cushing's syndrome* (see **hormones**).


*Lice.* There are two species of blood-sucking lice which infest the human, the head louse and the body louse. These wingless insects cannot survive except on man. The adult female has a life-span of about one month and lays up to 10 eggs each day. As the adult feeds, it injects digestive juices and fecal material into the skin. These irritants plus the actual skin punctures cause itching, the major symptom of infestation. The eggs (nits) are oval, gray, and firmly attached to hair shafts. They hatch in about 7 to 9 days and the larvae mature over the next week. The head louse is transmitted through shared clothing and brushes. The body louse is transmitted by bedding and clothing. One type of body louse infests the pubic area. The pubic louse is transmitted directly from person to person or by clothing, bedding, or towels.

Nits on the scalp may be seen most easily on the hairs at the back of the head and above the ears. The adult lice, which rarely exceed 10 in number, are often impossible to spot. Secondary infection of the skin may occur, and the lymph nodes at the back of the head and in the neck may be enlarged. On the body, parallel lines of swollen, red, and oozing scratch marks, *hives,* and persistent red raised spots may be seen. The lice will only rarely be found on the skin but can be located in the seams of clothing.

Small black dots found in the pubic area represent either blood within the adult lice or their waste products. In individuals who wash carefully, few adults or nits will be found, and the entire area will have to be searched carefully with a hand lens if either is to be seen.

There are now effective shampoos and creams for the treatment of lice. Check with your doctor. Family, close friends, sexual contacts, and those sharing living quarters should be treated to prevent relapse, reinfection, or a small epidemic.

To avoid infestation of others, it is important to: 1. Inspect all family members daily for at least two weeks and treat if infested. 2. Sterilize all personal clothing, sheets, and blankets of any infested person in hot water, at least 130°F., or by dry cleaning. There are sprays and powders for mattresses. 3. Thoroughly wash all personal articles such as comb and brushes in hot water to disinfect.

*Limp* means a favoring or stiffness of one leg which lends an asymmetrical quality to the gait. There are many causes, ranging from the obvious like a sprained ankle to the obscure like a disorder of the hip or spinal cord. When and whether to call the doctor depends on the circumstances and the age of the child. At one extreme, we would recommend contacting the physician for any limp in the child too young to give an account of his or her symptoms or for the child having persistent severe pain anywhere in his or her leg. At the other extreme, a limp may be safely watched at home in an older child who bruised his shin. In general, limps, however mild, that persist for over 2 days, especially ones without obvious explanation, should receive medical evaluation.

It is best to put a limping leg to rest. Activity generally aggravates a limp or soreness anywhere and prevents healing of the underlying disorder.

See *fracture; hip pain; joint pain; knee pain; osteomyelitis;* and *sprains.*

*Lockjaw:* see *tetanus.*

*Low blood sugar:* see *hypoglycemia.*

*Lung rupture and collapse.* In a lung rupture, air leaks into the chest cavity and is trapped between the lungs and the rib cage and diaphragm, causing a condition called *pneumothorax* (air in the chest). In an infant, lung rupture can complicate a number of respiratory difficulties associated wih partial or complete obstruction of the air passageways. *Pneumonia* and *hyaline membrane disease* are among such disorders. In an older child, **asthma,** auto accidents, and **cystic fibrosis** can cause this condition. Air in the chest (thoracic cavity) can also compress the lung and thus decrease the volume of lung available for respiration. Shortness of breath and, in severe cases, *cyanosis* (blueness from oxygen-deprived blood) can result. A continuing accumulation of trapped air and consequent increases of pressure can not only collapse the lung, but may also displace the heart and great blood vessels, interfering with their functions and threatening life.

Treatment is directed at the underlying cause—for example, antibiotics for infection. Excessive accumulation of air may be relieved by inserting a small tube between the ribs into the pocket of air. The air leak in the lung usually seals in time.

*Atelectasis* is collapse of any part or parts of the lung, always discovered by the physician (and not by parents) when he is investigating symptoms of respiratory disorder. Often the diagnosis is made after X-ray examination. In the lungs, microscopic air sacs (the alveoli) normally contain some air even when you are breathing out. If the air is totally exhausted, the sac, like a deflated balloon, collapses.

This situation is an important complication of *hyaline membrane disease*, which affects the lungs of some premature infants, babies of diabetic mothers, and, to a lesser extent, babies delivered by Cesarean section. The disease results from persistence of the fetal pattern of circulation after birth; there is a failure of blood flow to the lungs. The disorder takes its name from a deposit of proteinaceous material (hyaline membrane) on the linings of the alevoli and small air passages, with consequent collapse of the alveoli. Another cause of atelectasis in the newborn is aspiration of amniotic fluid in the birth process. Blockage of the smallest air passages results. Later in life, lung collapse can follow aspiration (breathing in) of a foreign body like a peanut or button (see **choking and swallowing foreign objects**) and be a complication of a prolonged wheezing attack in asthma in which a mucous plug obstructs the bronchi. The rupture of an overdistended segment of lung (see **emphysema**) can result in its collapse as well as leaking of air into the thoracic cavity.

The symptoms and difficulties with atelectasis depend on the extent of the lung collapse, and treatment varies with the cause and severity.

See also **breathing, noisy; emphysema;** and **pneumothorax.**

**Malabsorption syndrome:** see **celiac disease** and **cystic fibrosis.**

**Mange:** see **pets and children.**

*Mastoid infection:* see *earache.*

*Measles,* a viral illness (see *infections*), was once a common childhood disease, one that every mother could diagnose. Almost no child was spared. Today, with the development of an effective vaccine, measles can be prevented. (See *immunization.*) Where the vaccine has been widely used, the disease has become nonexistent. Many young physicians and medical students have never seen a case and must call older staff members for consultation when a child with a suspicious rash appears.

Measles is one of the most contagious of diseases. Even brief contact between a susceptible person and an ill individual is likely to result in its spread. Scattering of the virus is facilitated by the intense coughing which is part of the illness. The particles of saliva which are dispersed by the child are teeming with measles virus capable of setting up shop in the nose and throat of anyone who is susceptible. Measles can be caught only from someone who has the disease and is excreting virus. The incubation period of measles is 10 to 12 days. During this time the virus begins to grow within the body of the host but does not yet produce clinical symptoms. Following the incubation period, the prodromal phase, the period of 4 to 5 days running before the height of the symptoms, appears. It is indistinguishable from a bad cold. The child develops a slight hacking *cough*, redness and watering of the eyes, and a low-grade *fever.* By the fourth day the temperature rises to 104° or 105°, and the classic rash appears as faint red spots on the sides of the upper neck, along the border between the hair and skin, and on the back of the cheeks. Within hours, the rash spreads over the entire face, neck, upper arms, and upper part of the chest. During the second 24 hours it covers the back, abdomen, and thighs, finally reaching the feet on the second and third day. By the time it reaches the feet, it has begun to fade from the face. In areas of extensive rash, the skin will peel for several weeks. At about the time the rash reaches the feet, unless complications have developed, the temperature suddenly drops and the child feels much better. During the height of the fever and rash, the child feels miserable, and suffers a severe cough. The persistence of the cough beyond 4 days suggests a complicating *pneumonia.* The development of ear pains suggests middle-ear infection (see *earache*). Excessive lethargy, drowsiness, or *headache* suggests infection of the central nervous system, a rather infrequent complication.

Because measles is a virus infection, there are no drugs that can cure it. It must run its course. Antibiotics are of no use. Should complications such as pneumonia or middle-ear infection develop, antibiotics may then be helpful. Treatment can ameliorate the symptoms. Aspirin is given for fever (see Part 1, Chapter 5: "Caring for the Sick Child at Home") and cough medicine for cough. The child usually wants to stay in bed. When he or she feels like being up and about, he or she can do so. There are no special rules about diet; anything he would like to eat is fine. Chances are that his appetite will be off. He should be encouraged to drink fluids. Five days after the rash has begun, the child is no longer contagious and may resume contact with others. (Thus, if the rash began on a Monday morning, the child could resume normal activities and contact on Saturday morning.)

Contagiousness begins with the onset of symptoms in the prodromal period prior to the development of the rash and extends through the fifth day of the rash. If your child has not been vaccinated and has had contact with someone who is then reported to have measles, be sure to let your doctor know. Within the first few days after exposure, it is still possible to give measles vaccine and produce immunity quickly enough to ward off the natural disease. In most other diseases this approach does not work. A modifying injection of gamma globulin can also be given, or, in the younger child, a protective dose. Gamma globulin can be given effectively during the first 5 days after exposure. After this time, the gamma globulin is likely to be less protective as the end of the incubation period is approached.

Measles vaccine is a live virus vaccine (see *immunization*). It works by establishing an actual infection, leading to production of antibodies which in turn protect against natural measles infection. In a small percentage of children this vaccine infection is accompanied by mild symptoms, such as fever and malaise, 7 days or so following immunization. At times there is a faint rash. The symptoms are much milder than a natural measles infection. The vaccine has been refined to minimize these side effects. Thus far the immunity resulting from the vaccine has persisted for as long as the vaccine has been used, about 10 years. Whether or not the immunity will be permanent, as is immunity following natural measles, remains to be seen. Should it fall off, it may be necessary to give booster infections of vaccine. Measles vaccine cannot be allowed to stand at room temperature for more than a few minutes or the vaccine virus will die and the vaccine will become inactive. It must be kept frozen until just prior to use. Use of a vaccine in which the virus has died will not result in immunity, and the child will still be susceptible to natural measles infection. If the vaccine used was later discovered to have been inactive, immunization should be repeated.

Infants are immune to measles for several months after birth. If their mothers had antibodies against measles, which is almost always the case, these are passed through the placenta to the infant. The antibodies protective against measles last in the baby for upward of 6 months and are completely gone by 1 year. Immunization while the antibodies are present is likely not to be effective. The antibodies interfere with the necessary infection by the vaccine virus. For that reason, immunization is postponed until the first birthday. If for any reason the vaccine was given before the child was 1 year old, it should probably be given again.

The development of a vaccine against measles was puzzling to many people. They thought that measles was simply part of childhood. Why bother to immunize children against it? In point of fact, measles is a relatively serious disease of childhood. It causes children to be very sick for up to a week. Many of them not only have high fever and feel poorly, but are racked by a severe cough and often develop complications like pneumonia and middle-ear infection. Another small but definite percentage of children develop complications in the brain and spinal cord. The measles virus invades these delicate structures, producing a virus meningitis and encephalitis (see *meningitis*). The children are very sick with high fever, delirium, severe headache, nausea, and *vomiting.* They may require admission to the hospital. While most recover unharmed, some suffer permanent brain injury, with loss of intellectual functioning (see *developmental disabilities*) and the development of epilepsy (see *seizure disorders*). A larger number of children have very mild infection of the central nervous system, so mild as to go undetected. We suspect that even in some of these milder cases many children may have suffered some minor brain injury. Because measles was a common condition that affected most children during childhood, usually without complications, few parents saw the complicated cases or regarded it as a serious illness. However, physicians working in medical centers did see the complications and realized that the number was quite high, even though the percentage of serious cases was low. Lack of personal knowledge of a child seriously affected by measles led many people to believe that measles was a harmless disease, scarcely worth the fuss of immunization. Nevertheless, because of the incapacitating nature of even the garden variety case of measles and the serious nature of the complications of this disorder, the development and use of a vaccine were important.

Even before the advent of the vaccine, it was possible by the use of gamma globulin during the incubation period temporarily to prevent or to modify natural measles infection. Children less than 3 years of age are particularly likely to suffer serious consequences from measles and in the past received enough gamma globulin to prevent measles completely. These children did not have the opportunity to develop antibodies against measles and became susceptible to reinfection after the gamma globulin was depleted (in several months). In children over 3 years, we used to give a lower dose of gamma globulin, enough to lighten the attack of natural measles but not enough to prevent it completely. In these situations, the child would develop a mild case of measles but develop antibodies and acquire permanent immunity.

Eradication of measles is now possible. Its continued presence (small epidemics are reported monthly) means that the vaccine is not being given to everyone. The explanation for this failure is complex. It is primarily a result of poor health-care delivery which, in turn, is related to weaknesses in, and underfinancing of, health services. This failure should be of concern to all of us.

See *immunization*. For a discussion of virus, incubation period, antibiotics, antibodies, and gamma globulin, see *infections*.

See also Part 1, Chapter 5: "Caring for the Sick Child at Home."

*Meningitis* refers to an inflammation, usually an infection, of the meninges, the membrane or sac that covers the brain and spinal cord. The infection can be caused by viruses, bacteria (including *tuberculosis*), and fungi (see *infections*). The invader usually enters the nervous system by way of the bloodstream (see *bloodstream infection*), having begun as an infection in the nose, throat, lungs, or intestine. When it takes up residence on the meninges and begins to multiply, the condition is called *meningitis*. Inflammation of the brain itself is called *encephalitis*, a condition usually caused by a virus.

Whether or not a germ will spread to the meninges depends on a number of factors. The nature of the germ itself is important, since some are more prone than others to spread. For example, the *hemophilus influenza* bacterium in young children and the *meningococcus* are more likely to spread than is the *streptococcus*. Each are common causes of infection, yet their capacity to cause meningitis is different. The meningococcus is such a notorious cause of meningitis that its name stems from its affinity to the meninges. It can cause epidemics of meningitis among recruits in military camps and can spread like wildfire in confined populations. Tuberculosis bacteria can also cause a meningtis which is characteristically stubborn and difficult to treat. TB in children leads to meningitis fairly frequently. Viruses also differ in their attraction to the central nervous system. For example, the *Eastern equine encephalitis* virus is more likely to infect the central nervous system than is the *chicken pox* virus.

The germ's spread also depends on resistance factors related to the patient. Fortunately, the natural defenses of most people are able to confine attacking germs (even meningitis-prone ones) to the areas of first contact—usually the nose, throat, and/or intestine, thereby limiting any symptoms that might develop to nothing more than those of a cold (see *colds*), sore throat (see *throat, sore*), or *diarrhea*. Some will not even have any symptoms at all, even though they have become infected.

Only a small minority will develop meningitis. We do not understand why people vary so much in their responses to the same microbes.

Parents should not try to diagnose meningitis themselves. Their responsibility is to seek medical attention for worrisome symptoms like high *fever,* severe *headache* (excessive irritability in the small child or infant), confusion, delirium, disorientation (see *drowsiness, delirium, and lethargy*), unconsciousness, a convulsion (see *febrile seizures*), and a stiff neck (see *neck pain*), particularly in association with any of these other symptoms. (Most stiff necks result from twisting or from a viral infection of the nose or throat and do not represent meningitis.) These symptoms are not specific to meningitis, but they do raise suspicions.

If the doctor suspects meningitis, he will perform a *lumbar puncture,* the only sure way of making the diagnosis. In this procedure, a small sterile needle is passed through the space between adjacent rings in the vertebral column, through the outer meninges, and into the spinal canal containing the spinal fluid. The needle is inserted below the lower end of the spinal cord itself to avoid damage to that critical structure. The pressure of the spinal fluid is then measured by seeing how high it will rise in a vertical tube attached to the open end of the needle. A small sample of fluid is removed, studied microscopically for the presence of blood cells and bacteria, analyzed for protein and sugar (glucose) content, and sent to the laboratory for culture. High fever in the most vulnerable age group, 6 months to 2 years, may point to the bloodstream invasion which precedes meningitis, and thus blood cultures may become a more routine part of evaluation.

Antibiotics are prescribed when bacterial or fungal meningitis is proven or highly suspected. No antibiotics are given for viral meningitis because of their ineffectiveness with viruses. Sometimes antibiotics are started pending a definite cultural diagnosis and then continued, changed, or discontinued depending on the culture findings. Because of the seriousness of meningitis, treatment is usually given in the hospital *intravenously* (by vein). (See *infections* for a discussion of bacteria, fungi, viruses, and antibiotics.)

If at all possible, it is important not to treat children suspected of meningitis before doing a lumbar puncture because antibiotics can suppress symptoms without eliminating the infection which can then smolder and do damage. As a typical example, consider the child with a 105° temperature who looks dreadful but who has no specific findings on physical examination (see *fever of unknown origin*). Great as the temptation is, it is unwise to give this child a "shot of penicillin" or begin penicillin tablets just to be sure nothing is being missed. If there is concern about meningitis or another serious life-threatening illness, steps should be taken to establish the cause before treatment. Therapy for meningitis demands precise diagnosis. It is far better to observe carefully and reexamine the child if necessary without specific treatment to see which way the symptoms are headed. Blind treatment leads to a false sense of security. Even after meningitis has been excluded by lumbar puncture, there is still no reason for giving antibiotics unless they are likely to help. If no diagnosis can be reached and the child is critically ill, he or she needs treatment in the hospital.

Regardless of the cause, meningitis is dangerous because it can mean serious damage to the brain or spinal cord. If untreated, meningitis can lead to permanent impairment of brain function, such as retardation (see *developmental disabilities*), and even death. This is particularly true of bacterial (including tuberculous) and fungal meningitis. Hence, early diagnosis and early treatment are the key. For this reason far more lumbar punctures are done than are positive. In general viral meningitis is less likely to cause damage. Many cases are so mild that they go unnoticed (see *mumps*). However, not all are so harmless. Viral meningitis and encephalitis are frequent complications of *measles* and one important reason for vaccinating children against an illness once so common that it was thought to be a part of childhood (see *immunization*). Also, meningitis due to rubella (*German measles*) and *cytomegalovirus* (and probably others not yet discovered) acquired prior to birth are well known for their ability to damage the brain.

If your child has had contact with someone who comes down with meningitis, try to find out the cause. This information will be helpful in interpreting your child's symptoms if he should become sick. Your doctor will know that meningitis caused by a common virus is little cause for concern. Chances are that even if your child does become ill, it will be in a nondangerous way—colds, sore throat, or diarrhea. A meningitis caused by bacteria deserves special attention, especially in the case of meningococcus. The development of a febrile illness shortly after contact with a person with meningococcal meningitis will raise a doctor's suspicion and might prompt an earlier search for meningitis. It would at least merit more detailed watching. Sometimes people who have been in close touch with a patient with meningococcal meningitis are given antibiotics prophylactically.

Meningitis due to certain microbes can be prevented by immunization. Measles is an example of a viral meningitis that is now preventable. Rubella (German measles) immunization prevents maternal infection, thereby preventing passage of virus to the fetus. A vaccine against meningococcus is being tested and looks promising. Efforts are under way at The Children's Hospital Medical Center and elsewhere to develop a vaccine against the bacterium *hemophilus influenza*. Those viruses that cause meningitis in cattle and occasionally affect man can be kept from spreading by immunizing the animals and controlling the mosquitoes that carry the virus to humans. Early identification and treatment of tuberculosis will also prevent meningitis as a complication of this disease in children.

*Menstruation:* see *adolescence.*

*Mental retardation:* see *developmental disabilities; Down's syndrome; handicapped child.*

*Migraine:* see *headache.*

*Minimal cerebral dysfunction:* see *developmental disabilities* and *learning disabilities.*

*Moles:* see *birthmarks.*

*Molluscum contagiosum.* This virus infection consists of discrete flesh-colored or pearly white, raised, waxy-appearing, firm nodules with a small central depressed area. They are found alone or in clusters on the trunk, body, face, lower abdomen, pubic area, inner thighs, and penis. Most lesions cause no symptoms.

Molluscum contagiosum is a viral tumor (not cancerous). It is contracted from other people by a direct contact, through contact with contaminated inanimate objects, and by being spread from one part of the skin to another. In this era of increased sexual freedom, the disorder is seen most commonly in the pubic area and genitalia of young adults.

Molluscum contagiosum can be successfully treated by a number of methods ranging from removal with a curette to the application of chemicals.

*Mongoloid child:* see *developmental disabilities* and *Down's syndrome.*

*Mononucleosis, infectious.* Infectious mononucleosis (sometimes called infectious mono or just plain mono) is a relatively common disease, mainly of adolescents and young adults, although it can and does occur in children. In recent years the cause has been identified. It is called the E-B virus.

Not everyone infected with infectious mononucleosis develops obvious symptoms. Many individuals have either subclinical infections or ones so mild that they are not recognizable. There is a wide range in the severity of symptoms from unapparent to incapacitating. Ill individuals have been found to harbor virus in their throats for as long as 16 months, long after they have recovered. These carriers are presumably contagious for as long as the virus can be isolated.

Infectious mono is caught from a person shedding the virus. Several weeks of incubation are required before clinical symptoms appear (if they are to appear). It is likely that close mouth-to-mouth contact is important in transmission, hence the nickname "kissing disease." The full-blown illness consists of *fever,* sore throat (see *throat, sore*), swelling of lymph nodes all over the body (most pronounced in the neck), *head-ache,* and malaise. About 10 to 20 percent of people with mono develop a fine red rash, mainly over the chest, abdomen, and back. The sore throat tends to be severe and resembles a strep throat. But throat cultures are negative for streptococci. The throat inflammation presumably results from direct invasion by the virus. The liver is frequently affected, although usually the *hepatitis* (liver inflammation) in infectious mononucleosis causes few or no symptoms. Occasional patients develop *jaundice* as a sign of liver malfunction. More commonly, patients will not have any symptoms directly referable to the liver but will show evidence of liver impairment as measured in the blood. In many the spleen enlarges. Swelling of the spleen does not usually cause symptoms.

The course of the disease is variable, lasting from several days to several weeks. In the adolescent or young adult, the malaise and fatigue may be intense and can often persist for several months even after the acute infection appears to have passed. Recovery is complete.

A characteristic laboratory finding is the appearance in the blood of abnormal white blood cells containing a single nucleus, so-called *mononuclear cells,* which has led to the name *infectious mononucleosis.* In many patients, an antibody temporarily appears in the blood. It is detectable by an exam known as the *heterophile test.* The heterophile test is not always reliable in children. Testing for the antibody to the E-B virus as an index of infection is not yet widely used.

Similar but not identical clinical illnesses can be caused by other microorganisms, notably *cytomegalovirus* and *toxoplasmosis* (see *pets and children*). Antibody studies and cultures help to distinguish them from mononucleosis.

At present there is no treatment for infectious mononucleosis. Like most viruses it is not affected by antibiotics. Control will depend primarily on developing an effective vaccine.

Sicker patients usually voluntarily commit themselves to bed. When they feel ready to be up and about, you can be sure they are improving.

Aspirin can help with the throat pain. (See Part 1, Chapter 5: "Caring for the Sick Child at Home.") In rare cases, the tonsils and throat are so swollen that airway obstruction occurs. This complication requires hospitalization and usually responds very well to large doses of adrenal hormones (see *hormones*).

For a discussion of virus, carriers, subclinical illness, incubation period, white blood cells, cultures, and antibody, see *infections*.

*Motion sickness.* On long car, boat, or plane trips some children can become dizzy and nauseous. Two commonly used over-the-counter drugs taken before, and at intervals during, the journey are mecline hydrochloride (Bonine) or dimenhydrinate (Dramamine). From time to time trips should be taken without medicine to see if the child still needs it. For milder cases, simple precautions, such as avoiding a heavy meal just before the trip, keeping a car window open, or putting the child in the front rather than the back seat, can help. Cigarette or cigar smoke makes motion sickness worse. In a plane, try to sit over the wing, and in a motor launch, avoid a seat near the exhaust fumes.

More and more children are traveling by air each year. Particularly with the infant or young child, many parents request medication to sedate the child during the trip. In general, we discourage this practice. Most children can be amused and entertained on the plane so that they are not a burden to the other travelers. See *What to Do When "There's Nothing to Do,"* by members of The Boston Children's Medical Center and Elizabeth M. Gregg (New York: Dell Publishing, 1968), for a list of activities suitable for trips. In our experience sedating children makes them drowsy, irritable, and, if anything, more difficult to handle.

Children with ear infections (see *earache*) or colds causing the Eustachian tubes to be blocked, may have pain as the air pressure increases when the plane comes in for a landing. In the older child chewing gum or swallowing to force air up through the Eustachian tube into the middle ear can help prevent this complication. Small children can be given sips of water or juice, and babies can be given a bottle. In an acute infection, it is wisest to postpone the flight.

*Mumps* is a very common and usually mild, although annoying, childhood illness caused by a virus. Its telltale signs is a chipmunk-like swelling of the salivary gland at the angle of the jaw. This particular salivary gland is called the *parotid*, and its inflammation is known as *parotitis*. There are three sets of glands that produce saliva—the *parotids*, the *submandibular* glands, which are located in the neck just inside of the jawbone, and the *sublinguals*, which are located in the floor of the mouth just under the tongue. All three can be affected in mumps, but inflammation of the parotid is far and away the most common.

In a typical case of mumps, the one-sided painful swelling, the mild *fever* and *headache,* and the loss of appetite are gone in about one week. In a minority of cases the gland on the other side swells also, beginning a day or so after the first.

There is no treatment at present for mumps. As with other virus infections, neither penicillin nor other antibiotics will help. (See *infections.*) For the discomfort, aspirin and cold compresses are helpful. Avoid acid liquids (lemonade, orange juice, and possibly even ginger ale). Because they stimulate saliva production, they may cause additional pain in the swollen gland. Temperatures up to 102° or 103° are common and can be managed with aspirin (see discussion of fever in Part 1, Chapter 5: "Caring for the Sick Child at Home"). Anything higher merits a call to a nurse or doctor. Mild headache and bellyache are frequent. Aspirin, and cool compresses for the headache, usually suffice. If the headache is severe, if *vomiting* is present, or if a child becomes confused or delirious (see *drowsiness, delirium, and lethargy*), be sure to seek medical advice. On a nice day, there is no reason why the child cannot sit outside in a cool, protected play area.

There is no practical point in keeping household members away from the child with mumps. By the time it is recognized that the child actually has the disease, he or she has had ample opportunity to spread the virus around, and others have had ample opportunity to be exposed. Once exposed, there is nothing to do but wait it out. The incubation period is 14 to 21 days. If the others in the household don't develop the symptoms of mumps, it means either that they did not pick up the virus from the ill individual, that they developed a subclinical form of the illness, or that they have already had mumps. Sometimes, with several susceptible children in the house, one will become ill 2 weeks after the first child, and the third child will become ill 2 weeks after the second child. If no symptoms develop within 3 weeks, you can assume that none will develop from this particular exposure. When the swelling of the gland of a clinically ill child is down for one complete day, he is no longer contagious and may resume normal activities.

The newborn is protected against mumps for the first 6 or so months of his life by antibodies transmitted to him before birth from his mother, assuming that she herself is immune. This immunity gradually wanes as the antibodies lessen in number. By the time the infant has reached his first birthday he is no longer immune.

Mumps is a contagious disease but not nearly as catching as *chicken pox* or *measles.* The range of symptoms produced is very wide. Unlike measles, in which most all exposed susceptibles develop the full-blown illness, a high percentage, perhaps 40 percent, of people with mumps come down with subclinical, or very mild, infections. Although they are infected and produce antibodies, they have either no symptoms or very mild, even unnoticeable ones. The illness proceeds silently below the surface. Many adults are immune as a result of subclinical infections during childhood, even though they have no recollection of having been sick. Most adults who report never having had this disease actually have had it. The measurement of antibodies in their blood makes this clear. Following recovery from either full-blown, mild, or unapparent mumps, immunity is permanent. Second attacks are extremely rare. (See *infections* for a discussion of subclinical infections, antibodies, and incubation period.)

Mumps tends to be more severe in adults. In the mature male *orchitis* (inflammation of the testes) is a worrisome possibility. The testis becomes tender and swollen and the surrounding skin of the scrotum swollen and red. Rarely are both testes involved. Occasionally it is necessary to make a surgical cut (under anesthesia) into the capsule surrounding the testis to relax the pressure. Sometimes the infection does permanent damage to the testis, but because usually only one testis is involved, with rare exceptions, reproductive ability is preserved. In older girls and women a small percentage (less than 10 percent) have pain in the lower abdomen, suggesting inflammation of the ovaries. This traveling virus has an affinity for these glands also. In children, an infrequent complication is inflammation of the central nervous system, causing *meningitis* or *encephalitis* (see *meningitis*). This complication is heralded by severe headache, vomiting, and lethargy, along with high fever. Infection of the auditory (hearing) nerve can lead to hearing loss (see *hearing and speech*).

In recent years a vaccine made with a live virus, a cousin of the mumps virus, has become available. It causes a mild infection, rarely apparent, and an antibody response which protects against mumps. Thus far the immunity has held up. Whether it will be permanent, as with natural mumps, remains to be seen. Unlike measles vaccine, mumps vaccine does not work quickly enough to protect against mumps if given after an exposure.

See Part 1, Chapter 5: "Caring for the Sick Child at Home" and *immunization.*

*Muscular dystrophy* is a rare disorder which is characterized by a prolonged course of disability and progressive crippling. The disease is important because of its profound effect on the way of life of both patient and family. The essential problem is a wasting away of muscles throughout the body, particularly those under voluntary control, for reasons not well understood. The most important muscles involved are those that move the legs.

There are several different patterns of muscular dystrophy, with varying patterns according to age of onset, and muscles most affected. The most common variety in children affects boys predominantly, and the symptoms are increasing weakness in the muscles of the hips and thighs. This weakness first appears before the child reaches the age of 3, and he then shows a waddling type of walk (like a duck), an inability to run, many episodes of falling, and trouble climbing stairs. The child may lose the ability to climb stairs by the age of 8 to 12 years, and sometime later most afflicted children are unable to walk unaided and have to use a wheelchair. Just before this point is reached, the child sometimes may be fitted with leg braces which may permit walking to continue for as much as several years.

Late in the course of the illness the child sometimes becomes more susceptible to *pneumonia* because of his limited ability to cough or to expand his chest. The imbalance and weakness of the back muscles may lead to curvature of the spine (*scoliosis*, see *spinal defects*), and the inactivity makes him prone to obesity (see *weight problems*). One predictable problem which all children have is the development of deformity at the joints due to imbalance of muscle pull. For example, the foot tends to drop and the heel cord (Achilles tendon) tends to tighten. Such deformities, which are known as *contractures*, obviously make it even more difficult for a child with serious weakness to perform any motor activity.

Care for children with muscular dystrophy requires consultation and cooperation in a large medical center between experts who have experience with muscular dystrophy and the family pediatrician or family doctor. The emphasis is on keeping the child functioning normally for as long as possible. This goal requires a good deal of cooperation among those in charge of various community resources. In particular, the school authorities have to be informed as to what measures can be taken to maintain the affected children in school (for example, transportation, special needs as to equipment, toilet facilities, and so forth).

Although the cure is not yet known, modern care has doubled the child's life expectancy. Parents are taught how to keep the muscles and joints limber through exercises, and the child is encouraged to be fully mobile, particularly when his inclination would be not to make the effort. Calorie intake is carefully watched to prevent obesity. Surgery occasionally is necessary to correct contractures. Prompt treatment of respiratory infections and intensification of the exercise program when the child is ill are of great importance to prevent development of contractures occasioned by inactivity.

In the comprehensive-care program which is now a part of modern management, the services of the orthopedic surgeon, physical therapist, social worker, psychologist, and specialist in muscle disease are all called into play. Research into muscular dystrophy is going on at a number of centers in the country and offers the hope of better treatment and perhaps a cure.

See *developmental disabilities; handicapped child;* and Part 1, Chapter 4: "Complaints with an Emotional Element."

*Mycoplasma:* see *pneumonia.*

*Nausea:* see *abdominal pain* and *vomiting.*

*Nearsightedness:* see *vision problems.*

*Neck, lumps and bumps in the.* Swollen glands (see *glands, swollen*) are the most common neck masses. A less common lump is the *thyroglossal duct cyst*, an embryological remnant, which appears in the midline of the neck. It moves upward when the tongue is protruded or during swallowing. It may break open on its own or become infected. Treatment is surgical removal. The *branchial cleft cyst* is also an embryological remnant. It is found in the neck in front of the *sternocleidomastoid* muscle (see *neck, wry*). It grows slowly and can become very large. Treatment is surgical removal.

*Neck pain,* or stiffness in the neck, is a common complaint. Many people think immediately of the dreaded disease *meningitis,* which is, in reality, an uncommon cause of neck pain. Meningitis never causes just pain in the neck. There are other, earlier symptoms, such as *fever, headache,* and delirium (see *drowsiness, delirium, and lethargy*), which alert us to the diagnosis.

Painful neck is often seen with throat infections and some viral illnesses. (See *throat, sore* and *infections.*) The reason for the neck pain in these disorders is not known. When the infection subsides, the pain disappears.

Pain or stiffness in the neck can also follow trauma like a blow to the neck, or can result from a malposition in the neck, for instance during sleeping. Local heat, massage, and aspirin (see Part 1, Chapter 5: "Caring for the Sick Child at Home" for aspirin dosage) are simple measures which can relieve the pain, but traction may be necessary in severe cases.

Neck pain can be a symptom of arthritis of the neck, although arthritis is an unusual disorder in children. (See *arthritis, rheumatoid.*) With this condition, the child holds his or her neck stiffly, turning his body rather than his head to change the field of vision.

**Neck, wry.** When a baby consistently keeps his or her head tilted forward and to one side, a condition known as wry neck should be suspected. *Torticollis* (the medical term) is not a common or serious problem, but it does appear in some babies.

Torticollis may be recognized in the hospital nursery, but more likely will be discovered first by the parents after the baby has been taken home. The cause is an abnormal tightness of the *sternocleidomastoid* muscle, which runs from the collarbone to each side of the skull behind the ear and is one of the main muscles controlling the movement of the head and neck. Occasionally other neck muscles are contracted and cause the same deformity. The imbalance of forces may also lead to an asymmetry of the face. The condition is not likely to be overlooked by either the parents or the doctor during a routine examination.

Usually, stretching exercises will be all that are needed to correct the condition. If these fail, surgery to relax the muscle may be necessary.

**Nephritis** means inflammation of the kidney. (See discussion of the urinary tract in **urinary tract infections and defects.**) There are several types seen in children. *Acute poststreptococcal glomerulonephritis* is the most common kind. It rarely occurs before the age of 4 to 5 years, and fortunately almost all children recover completely. It follows 1 to 3 weeks after a small percentage of skin (see discussion of *impetigo* under *abscess*) or throat (see **throat, sore**) infections by certain kinds of streptococcal bacteria. (See *infections.*) It seems as though the child has a kind of allergic response to the infection. Unlike **rheumatic fever,** for which prompt treatment of streptococcal infections is preventive, treatment of these infections with penicillin or other antibiotics does not seem to prevent acute glomerulonephritis, although it may moderate the attack. There is a great deal of variation in the severity of the illness from one child to the next. Many cases seem to be so mild that they are not recognized unless looked for. The more severely ill children may require hospitalization.

Common symptoms which alert parents are puffiness around the eyes *fever,* loss of appetite, *vomiting, headache,* and decreased urine output. The urine is often greenish colored or may be brown-red. Some children with acute glomerulonephritis have increased blood pressure, with or without headache, and vomiting, along with clumsiness, occasionally convulsions (see **seizure disorders**), and heart failure. These latter symptoms can be life threatening and require prompt and vigorous treatment. Some degree of kidney impairment is almost always present. Production of urine may cease, leading to "poisoning" from the retention of waste products.

The attack of acute glomerulonephritis is over in a few weeks. Therapy depends on the individual picture. All children receive a course of antibiotics, usually penicillin, to eliminate completely any streptococci which may still be present. Ill children are restricted to bed. They are observed frequently, and lab measurements are made to monitor possible complications which are treated accordingly. There is no treatment for the kidney inflammation itself. This runs its course and usually heals on its own, although abnormalities in the urine can often be detected for months following the acute attack. There are effective treatments for the complications of nephritis—high blood pressure, convulsions, heart failure, and kidney failure. The ability to care for the complications of nephritis has brought a marked improvement in survival of affected children to the point that, today, death is rare.

There are several other types of nephritis that are not related to streptococcal disease. In these other kinds of nephritis some of the children continue to have difficulty. In varying degrees their kidneys remain continuously inflamed, sometimes more and sometimes less. They may go on to have slowly progressing, irreversible kidney failure known as *chronic glomerulonephritis*. Most children with chronic glomerulonephritis did not first have acute glomerulonephritis. Some cases, which are very similar initially to acute glomerulonephritis, are associated with *anaphylactoid purpura*. Others are hereditary, sometimes associated with hearing impairment.

In these cases of chronic glomerulonephritis there is generally no cure for the kidney problem itself. However, dramatic progress has been made in treating the result of the kidney failure with the *artificial kidney* and kidney transplantation. The artificial kidney is a machine to filter waste products from the blood, taking over the job which the diseased kidneys are no longer able to perform. The machine is connected by tubes to the patient's blood system, 3 times weekly for several hours. The passage of the patient's blood through the machine and back again removes a part of the waste products. However, no machine is yet as good as a real kidney. In kidney transplantation, the patient's diseased kidneys are removed surgically and a normal kidney is substituted, like replacing a spare part. The donor has to be carefully selected to be genetically close to the recipient so that the tendency of the body to reject a foreign substance is minimized. Very potent medications to suppress the rejection of the transplanted kidney are given. These techniques are effective, sometimes for many years. However, side effects are difficult, cost is still a problem, and complications yet to be discovered may develop.

*Nephrosis* is a form of chronic kidney disease of unknown cause, fortunately rare. It appears usually between 2 to 4 years of age and is characterized by swelling (edema) of the skin and organs, the passage of protein in the urine, and the lowering of protein and elevation of cholesterol in the blood. The swelling is usually first seen in the eyes and ankles, but all of the skin may become puffy. Fluid accumulates in the abdomen causing a potbelly. Nephrotic children have an increased susceptiblity to infection. Furthermore, the drugs usually used to treat nephrosis decrease the body's ability to defend against invasion by germs.

While no complete cure or prevention for nephrosis has been found, recent therapy controls the episodes of swelling and reverses the abnormality in the kidneys. Hydrocortisone-like *hormones* and drugs known as immunosuppressives are the mainstays of therapy. With treatment the vast majority of children can be helped. Antibiotics for management of infection have resulted in satisfactory control of this complication. Even though nephrosis can be arrested with treatment, relapses are the rule and treatment must be repeated. A small percentage of children develop a chronic kidney disease resembling chronic glomerulonephritis (see *nephritis*). Although superficially resembling other nephrotic children, these children probably have a different kind of kidney disease right from the start. For patients with renal (kidney) failure, kidney machines and transplantation can prolong life.

For additional information, contact The National Kidney Foundation, 116 East 27th Street, New York, N.Y. 10016.


*Neuroblastoma,* a cancerous tumor arising from nerve tissue, is one of the most common malignancies in infants and children. Approximately 70 percent of these tumors arise in the abdomen. They may present as an abdominal mass similar to that of *Wilms' tumor.* Other sites of origin are the chest, neck, and within the skull.

Unfortunately, the tumor may be small and go undetected before it has had a chance to spread. Often it comes to the attention of the parents or pediatrician by the appearance of *metastases* (spread) to various parts of the body. A common sign of spread is bruising or hemorrhages around both eyes.

Many of the same investigations performed for patients suspected of having Wilms' tumor are also undertaken in suspected cases of neuroblastoma. In addition, an examination of the bone marrow and X-rays of all bones will be obtained. The urine spot test examination for *vanylmandelic acid* (VMA), a chemical produced by the tumor, may be helpful in establishing the diagnosis.

The care of patients with neuroblastoma as in Wilms' tumor involves a coordinated multidisciplinary approach using surgery, radiation therapy

(X-ray treatment to destroy tumor cells), and antitumor drugs. The outlook in neuroblastoma is not as favorable as in Wilms' tumor. About 65 percent of patients under the age of 1 year at the time of diagnosis will survive. There is a much smaller survival in patients diagnosed over 1 year of age. Current treatment at The Boston Children's Medical Center and other centers is directed toward improving these survival figures by an aggressive sustained attack against the tumor. This intensive approach includes supportive measures such as white blood cell and platelet transfusions and antibiotics to combat infection.

*Nosebleeds.* Simple nosebleeds result from the tearing of very small blood vessels in the inner lining of the nasal passages. Picking of the nose is the most common cause and probably the only cause of nosebleeds that occur at night while the child is asleep. The itchy allergic nose is one which is particularly prone to picking and bleeding. Often the child will not report picking to either parent or doctor.

Nosebleeds are usually easy to control by pressure. Have the child bend over the washbasin and blow his or her nose to remove all clots and blood. Immediately insert into the bleeding side of his nose and the other side as well pieces of cotton which have been wrapped around themselves several times to make them firm. Insert the cotton with a twisting motion. Put your fingers against the outside of the nostril, pressing on the cotton. This puts equal pressure on the nasal septum (the partition separating the two nasal cavities), a common source of bleeding. Hold your finger there for 5 to 10 minutes. If no cotton is available, pressure alone is usually enough. Do not have the child lie on his back. In this position it is impossible to tell if his nose is still bleeding. Either have the child sit with his face toward the ground or lie on his stomach so that you can see if his nose continues to bleed. If it has stopped, gently remove the cotton and discourage "sniffling." If the bleeding recurs or persists after 10 or 20 minutes of constant pressure, call your physician. Keep up the pressure while taking him to the doctor. This will help control the bleeding.

The child whose nose has been bleeding for any significant length of time is likely to have swallowed some blood. He may become nauseous and vomit up the blood. If the drain of blood to the throat persists, even if none appears at the nostrils, contact your doctor or go to the hospital. If your child is too young to report swallowing blood, check him by shining a flashlight into his mouth and throat. Use a spoon handle to depress his tongue.

Rarely does a child lose a significant amount of blood from a nosebleed. We have encountered a few, usually those whose nosebleeds began in their sleep and who lost enough blood to go into *shock,* with cool, clammy skin, fast heartbeat, and pallor. A child in this condition should be taken to a doctor or a hospital. During the trip keep him in a horizontal position, with his legs slightly elevated, and maintain pressure on his nose.

The stubborn, uncontrollable nosebleed may require cauterization of the bleeding vessel with an electric probe or a stick tipped with silver nitrate. The rare nosebleed which originates at an inaccessible site far back in the nose may call for a special front and back packing with gauze to confine and stop the bleeding.

*Nose, injuries and foreign objects in the.* Any injury to the nose that results in swelling, disfigurement, or obstruction of breathing deserves prompt medical attention. In addition to the possibility of breaking the bone which is in the upper part of the nose, there is also the possibility of damaging the cartilages which give the nose its characteristic shape. Also, a blow to the nose can dislocate the septum which divides the nasal passages. The septum may have to be repositioned.

Any redness, swelling, or pain developing in a nose several days after an injury also requires attention and suggests the possibility of infection.

Small children are very prone to stick objects into their nose or other body openings. Sometimes a foreign object is inserted into a nostril beyond the range of easy vision and makes its presence known by foul-smelling discharge. The foreign object plus the inflammatory reaction it stimulates may interfere with breathing through the plugged nostril. If you can easily see and readily grasp the object, carefully try to remove it yourself. However, if it is far up the nose and you cannot get a good grasp on it, it is best not to try to do anything more on your own. You may simply push it farther and make it harder to remove. Seek help from your physician.

*Obesity:* see Part 1, Chapter 3: "Diet of Infants and Children" and *weight problems.*

*Orchitis:* see *mumps.*

*Ornithosis:* see *pets and children.*

*Orthopedic concerns.* The most common orthopedic concerns are ones that correct themselves and are not really abnormalities at all. One only needs to look at the various sizes and shapes of people to see that there is a very wide variety of what can be considered normal. Shortly after a baby is born, the legs and feet may rest in positions which would be quite abnormal if they persisted with growth, but which may be quite normal for that period. More important than the position in which the leg or foot is held is whether or not it can be placed in a normal position, indicating that the positional or developmental deformity is not a fixed one. This apparent type of deformity can be expected to improve in time unless the child is sleeping or sitting in a position that would tend to make it persist. The understandable anxiety of a parent wanting a child to be normal has often caused a good deal of pressure for treatment of appearances that growth and use alone will correct and in which reassurance is all that is really necessary. There are, of course, many conditions that do require treatment, and a simple examination by a physician or nurse will usually sort out which conditions require help and which can be expected to change spontaneously.

### TOEING-IN ( PIGEON-TOES )

Toeing-in or pigeon-toes is common in infants and toddlers, but normally corrects itself by school age. The turning in of the feet is most commonly due to an inward twist of the bones of the lower leg (tibias). This inward twist of the leg bones, called *tibial torsion*, is very often associated with the bowing of the thighs, which leave a space between the knees (bowlegs). Babies' legs and feet are commonly bowed at birth, reflecting the intrauterine position in which their legs were curled up with their feet tucked in and their knees touching the chest. Many infants sleep in the knee-chest position with their bottoms riding high. Some continue this pattern into the second and third years. This position perpetuates the bowing of their legs, and toeing-in.

For the mildest form of this condition, time is the great healer. Most often, your doctor or nurse will simply tell you to relax and watch things get better. In cases of more pronounced bowing and inturning, we focus our attention on correction of the sleeping position during the second year by rolling a towel around the child from the waist to just below the knees. This gently prevents the child from bending the hips and knees, and stops the knee-chest sleeping posture.

Toeing-in may also be caused by a tightness of the muscles around the hip which limits *turning outward*. Usually, all that is needed are stretching exercises and growth. Occasionally, it is necessary to use a bar or brace to hold the legs in a correct position.

Children with pronated or flat feet (see below) also tend to toe-in because this position of the feet gives them greater stability in walking and relieves some of the strain on their ankles. Depending on the degree of pronation (flatness), which is determined by how far off center the heel bone is, we sometimes prescribe an arch pad and wedge to be placed on the inside part of the heel. These shoe alterations may help to correct both the pronation and the toeing-in.

A number of children at birth have feet that are twisted in because the bones of the feet are improperly aligned with each other. The feet themselves curve inward. (In tibial torsion, by contrast, the feet are structurally normal and the toeing-in is due to the twist of the tibia.) In most cases, the examiner can easily bend these inturned feet outward to a normal position and beyond, as would be the case with a normal foot. The inturned feet are flexible. At most, all that is required are stretching exercises several times a day by the parent. Less commonly, the foot is rigidly inturned and cannot be bent easily to a normal position. This condition is known as *metatarsus adductus* (or varus). If stretching such feet does not help in the first few weeks, plaster casts and, occasionally, surgery may be needed. If metatarsus adductus is associated with a tight heel cord, causing the foot to be bent or flexed downward, the condition is known as *clubfoot*. Early identification and treatment of clubfoot, which usually involves surgery, is very important. Treatment should begin during the first few days of life.

## TOEING-OUT

Many babies' feet will toe out during the first month of walking. Mild degrees of toeing-out are of no importance. Some children toe out so much that they are unstable on their feet, and walking is delayed. These children commonly sleep in a "frog leg" position with knees drawn up along the chest and feet turned outwards. Not all children who sleep in this position experience toeing-out problems, however. Children who toe out to the extent that walking is difficult, and who sleep in the "frog leg" position can be helped by correction of their sleeping pattern with the use of a towel wrapped around their legs from the hips down, like a long slim skirt, and pinned to their sleepers. Should toeing-out persist after the sleeping habit has been corrected, corrective splints for wearing in bed may be indicated.

## FLAT (PRONATED) FEET

What are commonly regarded as flat or pronated feet are most often nothing more than a passing developmental phase, a part of normal maturation. Infants, prior to walking, almost always seem to have flat feet because of the normal accumulation of fat (so-called "fat pads") in the hollows of the foot. The fat pads fill in the undersurface of the foot and obscure the normal arch. If an X-ray is taken, the normal architecture of the bones making up the arch is revealed. Even after the disappearance of the fat pads, the feet of preschool children commonly appear flat when the child is standing and walking. When he or she gets off his or her feet, the normal arch reappears. The arch collapses when weight is placed on it because of the laxity of the ligaments that bind the small bones of the feet. With time, these ligaments tighten up and hold the bones in an arch not only when the child is off his feet, but also when he is walking and standing.

Someday at the beach, look around you and see how many adults have flat feet. There are few indeed, and many whose flat feet have persisted have no difficulty with them. Just as many of these grown-ups had flat feet when they were kids as do the children of today. Apparent flatness is mainly a developmental stage of maturation.

During your child's regular health visit, your doctor or nurse will examine his feet as part of the routine examination (see Part 1, Chapter 2: "The Regular Checkup"). Sometimes he may find a condition that is contributing to the flatness, such as a tight heel cord that needs stretching. (The heel cord is the tough *Achilles tendon*, the prominent cord that runs from the back of the heel up into the calf. You can make it move by raising and lowering your foot.) In the most marked cases of flat feet caused by loose joints, the physician may recommend wedges for the shoe heels and an arch support pad inserted or built into the shoe.

The dividing line between mild and severe flat feet is not sharp. A helpful clue is the position of the heel bone. Normally, it is in a straight line with the leg. The degree to which it is slanted to the side determines whether or not treatment is needed. The distinction between those needing treatment and those who do not is often unclear. If left untreated, the most pronounced of these loose-jointed, flat feet may cause pain in late childhood and require surgery to stabilize the foot. The milder forms predominate by far, however. More often than not, your physician will recommend either that nothing be done, if no significant abnormality exists, or that the shoes be modified (see above).

A great deal of unwarranted anxiety is felt by parents of children with flat arches, but heels which are straight. This anxiety is often fostered by overly zealous shoe salesmen who may suggest corrective shoes when none is necessary. There is some doubt that shoes are even really corrective. They may be merely supportive, holding the leg or foot in a more natural position while time and growth establish a more normal pattern.

There is a rare condition in which the foot is truly flat. A truly flat foot means that the bones of the foot are so linked that the longitudinal arch is not present at all, and does not even appear on an X-ray. This rare fixed or immobile flat foot is not easily confused with the more common types described above. Special orthopedic treatment, usually involving surgery, is required for this condition.

### KNOCK-KNEES

Most children between the ages of 3 and 6 are knock-kneed to some degree. The insides of their knees come close together when they walk, or stand with their legs straightened. We estimate the magnitude of knock-knees by measuring the distance between the inner bones of the ankle (maleoli) when the knees are together. Normally, there is no more than 1 inch per year of age (up to age 4) between these maleoli. Thus, a 4-year-old would not have more than 4 inches of space between his ankles when the knees touch. Knock-knees need watching and are considered significant if these figures are exceeded.

By these criteria, about 20 percent of first-grade children will have significant knock-knees. By the seventh grade, 80 percent of these children will have improved on their own and the other 20 percent (2 percent of all children) may then need some treatment, usually a splint or brace worn at night. Knock-knees are often associated with flat or pronated feet (see above).

*Osgood-Schlatter disease:* see *knee pain.*

*Osteomyelitis* means infection of bone. It is an uncommon disease in children but one which can do severe damage if not properly treated. The symptoms are localized to the end of a bone, next to a joint. Usually the earliest complaints are pain and tenderness. Later, redness and swelling develop. Movement is painful and avoided. In the preverbal child, limitation of movement may be the first clue to the problem. (See *arm, favoring of* and *limp.*) *Fever* is common.

Osteomyelitis constitutes a medical emergency since the ultimate result depends on the promptness of diagnosis and treatment. Treatment consists of a combined surgical and medical attack, including removal of pus, which affords an opportunity to determine by culture which microorganism is involved (bacteria are the usual culprits; see *infections*), and use of antibiotics in large doses, usually given intravenously in the hospital for several weeks, followed by oral antibiotics over several additional weeks.

*Pain:* see part of the body involved, that is, *abdominal pain, hip pain*, and so forth.

*Pertussis:* see *whooping cough.*

*Petit mal:* see *seizure disorders.*

*Pets and children.* One characteristic of an affluent society is a desire for and concern with pet animals. For better *and* worse the United States proves this very well. In 1972 we had about 32½ million pet dogs and about 22 million pet cats. Thirty-eight percent of all American households own a dog, 20 percent own a cat, and 14 percent own some other kind of pet. (These figures overlap to some extent, since many households own more than one kind of pet.) These animals provide amusement, pleasure, and companionship to their owners. Unfortunately, all species of pets also carry a potential threat to people, either by their ability to inflict harm by biting or scratching, by being a source of *allergy,* or by their capacity to transmit certain *infections.* Infectious diseases transmitted from animals to man are called *zoonoses.* In most instances, common sense and proper care can prevent these problems, and in the event preventive measures fail, it is comforting to know that the great majority of zoonoses are curable. Most important, almost all the diseases discussed in this article are relatively uncommon. The point of discussing them is to provide information, not cause undue alarm. A properly selected and cared-for pet can be a great source of pleasure. In a household where reasonable hygienic precautions are taken, pets are rarely a threat to human health.

This article will deal only with the interrelationships of children and their pets. Diseases that man can get from farm animals will not be discussed, because, for the most part, these are occupational diseases, and, therefore, are usually seen in adults. Children, generally, are more intimate in their contact with pets than are adults, and children are less likely to observe commonsense rules of hygiene and of handling animals.

Questions involving zoonoses are presented in one of two ways: (1) An animal that the child is in contact with becomes ill. Is it possible for the child to get sick from this contact? (2) A child becomes ill. Is it possible that he or she got the disease from an animal? In this case, the contact animal in question may or may not be ill.

The following discussion will try to present a logical approach to these two questions. It should be understood that animals have many diseases that are not transmissible to man. Examples of such diseases will be discussed, because they are frequently involved in question (1) above, and it is reassuring for parents to know that many common ailments of pets do not pose a threat to the health of their child.

The first aim of any health program should be to prevent, rather than to cure disease. A parent can avoid a lot of grief by selecting an appropriate pet to begin with. We cannot emphasize strongly enough that animals that have been bred for centuries as pets make the best pets. Therefore, in selecting a mammal, a dog or a cat is by far your best bet, not some wild animal. Select a breed that is an appropriate size for your home. An efficiency apartment is not the place to raise Irish wolfhounds or Great Danes. Select a breed that has a reputation for a gentle, even disposition with children, such as a poodle, an English cocker spaniel, or a golden retriever. Unless he is very well trained, do not expect a watchdog such as a Doberman pinscher or a Chow to be a suitable child's pet. Many of the terrier and toy breeds have a reputation for being nervous, high-strung, or irritable. Animals definitely have individual personalities, so generalities about breeds may not apply to the individual dog or cat; if the animal is mean or unreliable in its behavior, get rid of it.

An amazing number of people do not and will not listen to this simple advice. Hundreds of thousands of wild animals, from field mice to great apes and lions, are kept as pets. These animals are often difficult to control, vicious, or unpredictable in behavior, and may be capable of inflicting considerable injury to their owners. Some of them carry diseases that are not only foreign to this country, but foreign to the experience of many American veterinarians and physicians. Exotic pets rarely do well in captivity, because their owners do not know enough about their diet and care. Under the stress of captivity, these wild animals often undergo bizarre behavioral changes, including depression, frequent masturbation, and destructive rages. Finally, with our growing awareness of ecology, it should be stressed that certain animal populations are threatened by excessive capture for the pet and laboratory market. More than 90 percent of the wild animals in a shipment may die from the time of capture until the time of sale in a pet shop, and this mortality continues at a high rate in the private household. Sometimes, in exasperation or desperation, the wild-animal owner will release the creature in the nearby woods. If it is not a native animal, it may die of exposure or starvation, or it may survive and reproduce to the extent that it becomes a local pest, without natural enemies to control it.

Once you have selected an appropriate species and breed, buy the animal from a reputable dealer who will take it back if it becomes ill within a certain period of time (usually 1 week to 1 month) after the sale. Select an animal that appears alert and in good general condition. Specifically avoid any animal that has diarrhea, cough, unusual hair loss, or skin lesions. Other signs of illness to watch for include discharge from the nose or eyes, loose hanging skin that does not spring back to place when gently pinched or "tented," and pale or dry gums and eyes. If you have any doubt about the animal's health, let a veterinarian check it.

Once you have the animal at home, maintain its health by giving it a well-balanced diet and ready access to clean water at all times; provide adequate exercise and keep your pet from contacting sick animals. Have your veterinarian vaccinate it appropriately and consult with him when the animal is ill. These guidelines will help keep your animal in good health and may keep it from getting an infection that it could pass on to you. Another important principle is to treat your pet kindly but firmly. A well-disciplined animal is less likely to injure anyone, accidentally or intentionally.

### BITES

Perhaps the most common and most serious medical problem associated with pets is trauma—bites and scratches. The great majority of animal bites are caused by dogs and most of these cases occur in children, largely because they often tease or mishandle animals. Children 5 to 7 years old are bitten more frequently than any other age group. There are more than half a million animal bites reported each year in the United States, so this is not a small problem.

A dog bite can cause very serious injury and may be disfiguring. In addition, any animal bite carries with it the danger of infection. As with any deep or crushing injury, bite wounds carry the danger of *tetanus.* In addition, bite wounds may be infected by one or more of the many bacteria carried in the animal's mouth. If an animal should bite your child, notify a physician promptly. Appropriate first aid includes thorough washing of the wound with warm water and soap and application of an antiseptic. (See *bites, animal; bites, snake*; and Part 2, Chapter 9: "First Aid.")

The doctor should determine if a tetanus booster is needed. Any redness, swelling, pus, or increasing pain that develops around the bite should be brought immediately to a doctor's attention, and this is especially important if it is accompanied by fever, loss of appetite, pain in joints distant to the bite, or unusual irritability or fatigue, for these may all be signs of infection developing, despite initial therapy.

### RABIES

The most dreaded complication of an animal bite is rabies. Rabies is a viral disease, known since ancient times, that is almost always transmitted by an infected animal bite. It affects the brain and is uniformly fatal in man (there is only one known case, recently reported, of a person who completely recovered from an apparent rabies infection). In 1971 there were more than 4300 confirmed cases of rabies in animals in the United States. More than three-fourths of these cases were in wild animals. The main reservoir of rabies in the United States used to be dogs, but the disease is now seen less frequently in these animals, due in large part to vaccination programs and enforcement of leash laws. At the same time, there seems to be a real (not just reported) increase in rabies in wildlife, especially in skunks, foxes, raccoons, and bats.

Since the question often comes up, it is worth mentioning that rabies in rodents, such as squirrels, rats, and mice is very rare. It is also very rare in man in the United States, it being unusual for more than 1 or 2 cases to occur in people in the United States each year. Human rabies is not unusual in other parts of the world, however, such as South America and the Middle East.

Rabies causes a variety of symptoms involving the nervous system of infected animals. The disease often starts insidiously, as a change in behavior. For example, a dog that formerly was very friendly and sociable may turn mean and avoid human company. Wild animals, which normally avoid man, may approach people without any sign of fear. In the classical form of furious rabies, the animal becomes increasingly vicious and may snap at anything, living or inanimate, in its path. Due to difficulty in swallowing, he may drool saliva (which is loaded with rabies virus) or froth at the mouth. Because he cannot swallow liquid, the rabid animal becomes thirsty and may go into a rage or show fear at the sight of water (therefore, the disease is also called *hydrophobia*, which means fear of water). The animal may stagger or go into convulsions or may go into coma before dying.

Another form of the disease is called *dumb rabies*, in which there is little or no wild, violent behavior, but only progressive depression, lethargy, withdrawal, coma, and death. Human rabies is characterized by many of the same neurological symptoms seen in animals.

Regarding symptoms of rabies in animals, two points should be emphasized. First, the symptoms of rabies in any given animal are highly variable. Wild animals are especially variable in their symptoms, and certain species, especially skunks and bats, may show no sign of disease even though they are shedding rabies virus in their saliva. Indeed, some of these wild animals may survive for months or even longer, despite having rabies (the disease is eventually fatal in most animals, however). The second point is that other disease conditions in animals can mimic rabies. Therefore, rabies cannot be diagnosed with absolute certainty by clinical observation alone; postmortem laboratory studies on the animal's brain are necessary to prove beyond any doubt that the animal had rabies.

Your pet can get rabies only by being bitten by a rabid animal. Therefore, the first means of protection is to keep your pet on a leash or otherwise restrained so that its chances of contacting a rabid animal are greatly diminished. The second means of prevention is to have your animal vaccinated against rabies. Dogs should be immunized against rabies every two years; the rabies vaccine used in cats and wild animal pets should be given annually. Check with your veterinarian about the appropriate vaccination schedule for your pet.

In the event your child is bitten by an animal, an effort should be made to capture it or identify the owner, so that it can be appropriately observed to rule out rabies and reported to the local Health Department. If a dog shows no sign of illness within 10 days after a bite, it is almost certain that he could not have transmitted rabies and no anti-rabies treatment for the bitten person is indicated. A wild animal that bites someone should be killed (without damaging the head) and submitted for laboratory examination.

A decision whether or not to start antirabies treatment (a series of injections) in a bitten person depends on the circumstances, the most important being whether or not the animal can be proven rabid. If the animal escapes, other factors are considered, including species of animal (for example, any bat or skunk bite should be treated), whether or not the animal was provoked into biting, whether any signs of abnormal behavior by the animal were evident, and the known incidence of rabies in the geographic area from which the animal comes. For example, there has been no rabies in any animal except bats in Massachusetts for the past 24 years. Therefore, if a normal, healthy-looking dog, known to have lived all its life in Boston and to have been vaccinated aganst rabies in the past 2 years, bites a child who was trying to take a bone out of its mouth, we would not give that child antirabies treatment, even if the dog were not available for examination. If that dog were used to hunt foxes and raccoons in New York State or Maine or had traveled to other parts of the country or world where rabies was common in the animal population, treatment might be called for.

## SALMONELLA

A second common concern with pets is the transmission of bacteria called *Salmonella*, which commonly live in the intestinal tract of various animals, including man. People get the disease called *salmonellosis* by swallowing the germs. One of the commonest ways to get salmonellosis is by eating contaminated food. Another means of becoming infected is through handling infected animals or items contaminated with their stools. Toddlers, who tend to put everything into their mouths, are especially prone to fecal-oral infections such as salmonellosis.

Almost every species of pet and farm animal is a potential carrier of Salmonella, but pet birds, rodents, and reptiles (each discussed later in this article) are most often incriminated in transmitting these bacteria to children. Animal carriers of the germ may appear perfectly normal, or they may have some fever and diarrhea. If the animal's resistance is weak and the particular Salmonella germ is virulent, the animal may become severely ill with *septicemia* (spread of the germ through the blood) and it may even die.

There is a similar range of symptoms in children from no apparent illness to *diarrhea* and *fever* (this is the most common form), to severe generalized disease, which is not at all common. Salmonellosis is relatively easy to treat and is curable in the vast majority of cases.

Persistent or severe diarrhea in a pet should be called to a veterinarian's attention and the same problem in a child should be brought to a physician's attention. The presence of Salmonella can be proven by culture of the stool of pet or child and appropriate steps taken by the doctor to remedy the situation. (See *infections* for a discussion of culture.)

One way to prevent salmonellosis is to dispose of animal wastes in a sanitary manner, for example, by flushing the stool from a litter box or cage down the toilet or by incineration and by observing personal hygiene, washing hands after handling animals or items contaminated by them, especially before eating.

The rest of this article will deal individually with the most common pet species, the diseases they most commonly transmit to man, and a few of their most common infectious diseases that are not transmissible to man.

### DOGS

*Distemper* is the commonest infectious disease of dogs. It is a viral illness, often fatal, that is characterized by one or more of the following signs: fever, runny nose and eyes (often thick with pus), cough, depression, loss of appetite, rash, diarrhea, and convulsions. Distemper is seen most frequently in young dogs, but it can occur in older animals. Although the virus that causes distemper is closely related to the *measles* virus, distemper is not known to cause any human disease. Proper immunization prevents distemper in dogs.

*Infectious canine hepatitis* is another common viral disease of dogs. It usually affects young dogs and is characterized by fever, loss of appetite, thirst, and evidence of pain when the belly is pressed. The disease is often mild or inapparent, but in some dogs it can be quite severe and occasionally is fatal. Infectious canine hepatitis can be prevented by immunization, usually done simultaneously with immunization against distemper.

Infectious canine hepatitis is not transmissible to people and is not related to human viral *hepatitis.* There is no reason to treat any person who has had contact with a dog sick with infectious canine hepatitis.

*Leptospirosis* is an infection by certain spiral-shaped bacteria, called leptospires. The disease is found in many different wild and domestic mammals and man, and the usual source of infection for man is contact with sick animals or with water contaminated by their urine. The disease is not often diagnosed in man, with only 68 cases reported in the United States in 1971, 59 percent of them being in persons 19 years old or younger. This may be as much a failure of recognition as an indication of its true frequency, for leptospirosis is a diagnosis rarely entertained by physicians unless the patient has all the classic signs of the disease. Leptospirosis in man can cause fever, malaise and chills, *headache,* and stiff neck, muscular aches, nausea, *vomiting,* and intense redness of the *sclera* (white part of the eye); less frequently, it causes *jaundice* and hemorrhages in the skin, mouth, and other parts of the body. The disease often mimics viral *meningitis* in symptoms and laboratory findings, and probably is often mistaken for a viral illness, especially since the disease is often mild with only a few of the symptoms listed above being evident.

Rats, mice, and other rodents are a major source of leptospirosis, contaminating food and water with their urine. A great variety of wild animals also harbor these germs and may contaminate reservoirs or natural bodies of water, posing a threat to people swimming in such waters. (Chlorination kills the germ, so municipal tap water and public swimming pools would not be a likely source of leptospirosis.) Rodents and wild animals with leptospirosis rarely show any sign of illness.

In dogs, leptospirosis varies from a mild disease with few or no symptoms to a severe febrile illness with exhaustion, depression, and loss of appetite. Variable signs include vomiting, diarrhea, intense redness of the white of the eyes, jaundice (seen as a yellow discoloration of lips, gums, and eyes), and tenderness over the midback. The disease may be fatal in dogs. Dogs were the probable source of infection for approximately half the human cases of leptospirosis reported in 1971.

The most effective means of preventing leptospirosis in dogs is preventing contact with potentially infected animals, such as rodents, wildlife, sick dogs, or the urine of these animals. Due to the dog's instinctive behavior to hunt and to sniff deposits left by other animals, this may be easier said than done. A vaccine is available for leptospirosis in dogs, but it has limited effectiveness, so veterinarians do not generally use it. Especially in the early stages of the canine disease, antibiotics may be effective in treatment and in reducing the number of leptospires passed in the dog's urine, thus reducing chances of human infection.

Dogs are host to many different species of worms, some of them having the ability to infect man. Since the question often comes up, it is worth emphasizing that neither dogs nor any other animal harbor the human *pinworms,* which are the commonest worms in people in the United States. People can only get pinworms from other people. Likewise, the other roundworms of the intestinal tract occasionally seen in man in the United States, namely the large roundworm (*Ascaris*) hookworms, and whipworms, are, for all practical purposes, exclusively parasites of man, and lower animals play no significant role in their transmission.

The common dog roundworm (ascarid) is one of the canine worms that can infect man. The adult ascarids, which produce the infective eggs, are found in the intestine of young dogs. In adult dogs, maturation (growth) of the worm stops while it is still a larva (baby form), which migrates in the animal's liver, kidneys, and other tissues, usually producing little harm. Infection in dogs most commonly occurs when migrating larvae cross the placenta to infect puppies in the bitch's uterus. These puppies are then born infected, the worms eventually migrating to and maturing in the pup's gut. After a couple of years, these worms die, but in the meantime infective eggs have been passed in the young dog's stool. If swallowed by another pup (less than 5 weeks old), the eggs hatch, releasing larvae which eventually grow into mature worms in that pup's intestine. If swallowed by an older dog or by a child, the eggs produce larvae which do not mature, but wander in the immature state through various organs, a condition called *visceral larva migrans*.

Visceral larva migrans is most likely to occur in toddlers and infants who tend to put everything in their mouths as part of the way they learn about their environment. Since the eggs must develop on the outside for 1 to 2 weeks, the danger of infection lies in anything contaminated at length with dog stool, especially the soil, and it is children who habitually eat dirt who are most likely to get sick. Handling a dog, per se, is not likely to produce infection, unless the dog has been rolling on the ground and has infective eggs stuck on his fur.

Symptoms of visceral larva migrans in a child depend on the number of worms present, how sensitive the child is to their presence, and where they move in his body. The child may have fever, not feel well, cough and wheeze, or get enlargement of liver and spleen, suffer convulsions, or, rarely, develop blindness because of involvement of an eye. We think it is likely that the great majority of cases are mild, and most cases of visceral larva migrans go unnoticed and undiagnosed.

Dogs may be infected by hookworms, which live as adults in the dog's intestine where they lay eggs which are passed with the dog's stool. On warm, moist, shaded soil, larvae hatch from these eggs and mature to a form which can penetrate the skin of a dog and travel in his bloodstream until they finally end up in his intestine, where they mature into adult worms. If canine hookworm larvae contact human skin, they penetrate and wander in the skin around the point of entry, producing a wavy, itchy rash called *creeping eruptions*, a condition seen fairly often in the Southern United States. This requires a doctor's attention, but effective medicine is available to treat this condition.

The most serious worm infection people can get from dogs is *hydatid disease*, caused by a tapeworm called *Echinococcus*, which lives as an adult worm in the intestine of wild and domestic dogs. Eggs are passed by the adult worm in the dog's stool. If the eggs are swallowed by another animal (such as a rodent, sheep, cow, or deer) or by man, a larva hatches and travels through the intestinal wall, into the bloodstream, which carries it to some organ (most commonly the liver or lung). In this organ the larva forms a cyst (a baglike structure) which can reach enormous size and which contains many larval stages of the tapeworm. This cyst grows like a tumor which can eventually kill the person or animal harboring it by destroying the organ in which it is located or by metastasizing (spreading) to other organs of the body. Fortunately, the cyst grows slowly, and sometimes the cyst is destroyed by the body before it can cause significant harm. Dogs get the adult tapeworms when they feed on organs containing these cysts, as may occur when viscera from slaughterhouses are discarded where dogs can get at them. A dog cannot get the Echinococcus tapeworm if he eats nothing but adequately cooked or canned food.

In the United States, hydatid disease is most commonly seen in immigrants from areas where the disease is common, including Africa, parts of South America, the Mediterranean area (including Greece and Italy), and the Middle East. It used to be very common in Australia and New Zealand, but has been greatly reduced there by effective control measures (see below). In the United States, Echinococcus tapeworms are found in dogs in sheep-raising areas of California, Nevada, and Utah.

Symptoms of hydatid disease in people vary according to where the cyst is growing and how large it is. The infection can only be diagnosed by X-ray and the laboratory tests and can only be treated by surgically removing the cyst.

Dogs with intestinal worms, including ascarids, hookworms, and tapeworms, may show no evidence of illness at all, especially if they have no additional disease, are on an adequate diet, and if the number of worms is small. If, on the other hand, there is a heavy worm burden, if the animal has additional illness, or if its diet is poor, then the parasites can cause or contribute to loss of weight, poor general condition, evident abdominal pain, and diarrhea. Nothing more specific than this may be seen in dogs with Echinococcus and other tapeworms, but with the larger dog tapeworms, segments of the worms may be seen in the stool. Puppies with adult ascarids are often potbellied and may occasionally pass the 4- to 6-inch-long worms in their stool or vomitus. Hookworms suck blood from the intestinal lining, which may result in a black, tarry stool and anemia (pale gums and eyes).

Most intestinal parasites in dogs are readily diagnosed by microscopic examination of the stool and most of these parasites, including ascarids, hookworms, Echinococcus, and other tapeworms, can be easily and effectively treated, preventing their spread to other dogs and to people. Other means of preventing human infection with canine worms include enforcement of leash laws, impounding of stray dogs, keeping dogs off public beaches, and keeping children from eating soil or putting things in their mouths that may be contaminated with worm eggs.

Besides having internal worms, dogs also suffer from external parasites, the most obvious ones being ticks and fleas and, much less commonly, *lice.* Since lice are very infrequently seen in dogs (and cats), and the types which are seen are not the kind of lice that attack people, nothing more will be said of them.

*Fleas* are year-round pests which dogs and cats get by contact with other infested animals. Fleas cause intense itching by their biting and crawling around, and you should suspect their presence if your dog or cat is biting and scratching himself. They are most easily seen by parting the relatively thin hair on your dog's belly, though they may be found on any part of its body. *Ticks* attach themselves to one spot, very often in or behind the ear and in the dog's armpits, and gradually swell up to several times their original size by sucking blood. Usually, ticks cause no pain or itching and the dog does not seem to be aware of them.

Dog and cat fleas sometimes bite people and cause an itchy red spot. Some people seem to be more attractive to fleas than others, for reasons poorly understood. Unless dirt is scratched into the itchy area, bites from dog and cat fleas simply cause discomfort, but spread no disease.

The common brown dog tick (*Rhipicephalus*) rarely bites people; it seems to have a strong preference for dog blood. The wood tick and the *Dermacentor* dog tick bite man, dog, and many other animals rather indiscriminately. The brown dog tick carries no diseases to people, but the wood and Dermacentor dog ticks can cause tick paralysis (a progressive, potentially fatal paralysis which can be cured simply by removing the tick). They can also transmit **Rocky Mountain spotted fever,** which, despite its name, is now more common along the Eastern seaboard of the United States than it is in the West. Characterized by fever, rash, and headache, Rocky Mountain spotted fever can be fatal if not promptly treated. Dogs usually do not get very sick with Rocky Mountain spotted fever, nor do they transmit the disease directly to people, but ticks that fed on an infected dog could later bite and infect a person (see **bites, insect**).

Both ticks and fleas drop off their host (the man or animal they are feeding on) to lay their eggs. Because of this, it may not be enough to spray the dog one time to get rid of its fleas or ticks. Repeated treatments with commercially available sprays, or repeated bathing with flea soap may be necessary; in either case, follow directions on the container, since these products can be harmful to your pet if used in excess, and people should also avoid unnecessary or excess contact with these insecticide products. An alternate treatment is putting a flea collar on your pet, again with the admonition that the directions on the box should be followed. Ticks can be individually removed with fine tweezers by grasping them by the mouth parts so these are not left in the skin. If tick eggs have been laid in your house and you can see ticks crawling on walls and furniture, you may have to spray the inside of your house to get rid of the pests. Flea and tick infestation can persist in a building even after the pets which carried them, and their owners, have moved, sometimes leading to puzzling, itchy rashes on the new tenants. To rid the house of infestation, it is best to hire an exterminator. Keeping a flea collar on your dog and removing individual ticks should prevent any problems of household infestation. Unlike fleas, ticks are a seasonal problem, usually showing up in warm weather, though brown dog ticks can survive the winter indoors.

Dogs get two kinds of *mange*, which is a skin disease caused by mites, very tiny creatures closely related to ticks. One form, *demodectic mange*, can cause a serious, often difficult-to-treat skin disease in dogs, but is not transmissible to man. The other form, *sarcoptic mange*, also can cause a serious skin disease in dogs and can be transmitted to man. Both forms of mange in dogs cause hair loss and redness of the skin, which the dog may scratch and get secondarily infected. Your veterinarian can diagnose mange by its clinical appearance and by finding the mites in microscopic examinations of skin scrapings, and then treat your pet.

Sarcoptic mites from a dog can cause a disease in people very similar to **scabies,** which is caused by a sarcoptic mite which affects only humans. Small, raised, red, itchy spots develop, most often on the hands. The same treatment used for scabies can be used for infestation with canine sarcoptic mites and complete cure can be expected.

A skin disease of dogs and other animals sometimes mistaken for mange is **ringworm,** a fungus disease which is also transmissible to man. Tests can be done to distinguish and appropriately treat this disease. Ringworm is considered further under the discussion of cats below.

The last disease of dogs we will discuss is *heartworm*. The name describes the situation very well. These are worms, 6 to 10 inches long, that live in the right side of the heart and in branches of the artery that goes to the lung (pulmonary artery) of dogs and, less commonly, cats. The disease, transmitted by mosquito bites, can be mild in dogs or can cause progressive heart failure and death.

Heartworm in man is rare; even when it occurs it usually causes little serious disease. People can only get infected from a mosquito bite, not by direct contact with a dog. For all practical purposes, you need worry about it only as it affects your pet.

*Feline distemper* (also called *feline enteritis* or *feline panleucopenia*) commonly affects young animals. Despite its name, it is not related to canine distemper.

Feline distemper causes vomiting and diarrhea, dehydration, and discharge from the nose and eyes. A vaccine is available. Feline distemper is a disease limited to wild and domestic cats and a few species of other wild animals. It is not transmissible to people, and there is no reason to worry about the health of a child because he contacted a cat with this disease.

*Feline pneumonitis* is an infection of the lungs of cats with a large virus related to the germ that causes *psittacosis* (see birds, later in this article). It mainly affects young cats, causing fever, depression, cough, difficulty in breathing, and, sometimes, death, but most cats recover. It is not generally thought to produce illness in man, and contacting a cat with pneumonitis should not be a reason for seeking medical attention.

Cats can get various viral infections of the upper respiratory tract, the disease complex often being referred to as *rhinotracheitis* (inflammation of the nose and windpipe). Infected cats suffer fever, cough, sneezing, and discharge from the eyes and nose. While rhinotracheitis in cats appears similar to the common cold in people, there is no evidence that rhinotracheitis can infect people or that people can give colds to cats. Nevertheless, it would seem prudent and a reasonable hygienic precaution to wash your hands after handling a sick cat, especially if you have cleaned the discharge from his nose or eyes, which is part of proper nursing care for these animals. I would especially advise against rubbing your eyes with unwashed hands after handling these animals.

*Toxoplasmosis* is a disease that has received considerable coverage in the lay press recently and is a cause for concern among cat owners. Toxoplasmosis is an infection by a *protozoan* (microscopic single-celled animal) parasite. It is a baffling disease in many ways. At first it was thought to be a very rare problem in man, sort of a medical curiosity. Then it was recognized more and more frequently as a cause of a severe, disabling, often fatal disease of human infants. It was also found to cause a great variety of ailments in adults. It is now recognized that one-fourth to one-third of the adult population in the United States has had contact with the infection, but in the great majority of people it causes no recognized disease, either through failure of diagnosis or because most Toxoplasma infections in man are accompanied by few or no symptoms.

A great mystery has been the source of human infection. Apparently, people can get toxoplasmosis by eating raw or undercooked meat containing the organism. Infants can be born with the disease, the organism crossing the placenta to infect the fetus. Neither of these two routes can account for the majority of human cases, however, nor can they account for many animal cases of toxoplasmosis, it being known that many species get the naturally occurring disease.

Recent studies implicate the cat as having a major role in maintaining and transmitting the infection. It has recently been shown that cats can harbor certain stages of the parasite in their intestine and excrete an infective form in their stool. This infective form, called an *oocyst*, if swallowed by a suitable host, such as a mouse, invades and multiplies in the tissues of that host with infection occurring in various organs, including liver, lung, heart, muscle, brain, and so forth. Although not absolutely proven at this time, it appears likely that man can become infected in the same way, that is, by swallowing oocysts passed in the cat's stool. There is experimental evidence that flies and cockroaches could transfer oocysts from cat stools to human food, though this has not been proven to occur naturally.

The infection in adults (anyone over early childhood) often goes unnoticed. In some cases, toxoplasmosis causes a mild illness with fever, cough, sore throat, and enlarged lymph nodes which may be mistaken for *influenza* or infectious mononucleosis (see *mononucleosis, infectious*). Much less commonly, adults get a very severe infection of the liver, lung, heart, brain, and other organs.

Toxoplasmosis is more likely to be severe if the person's resistance is lowered because he has another severe disease, such as cancer, at the same time. Severe toxoplasmosis is also likely to occur in people receiving heavy doses of steroids (hydrocortisone-type *hormones*), radiation therapy, or chemotherapy for cancer. This severe form of toxoplasmosis can occur years after the original infection, the parasite having remained hidden in the body until it could "emerge" because of the patient's lowered resistance.

If a woman gets infected during pregnancy, there is a risk that the Toxoplasma organisms will cross the placenta to infect the fetus in the uterus. If this happens, the child may be born severely ill, suffering from cataracts, destruction of the back of the eye, infection of the brain, *hydrocephalus,* and enlargement of the liver and spleen. This congenital infection may result in permanent blindness, brain damage (see *developmental disabilities*), or death. Perhaps two-thirds or three-fourths of infants born with toxoplasmosis have a milder form of the disease and in many of these the infection may remain undetected, although at some later date, when their resistance is down, the disease may become manifest. It is estimated that two to three thousand cases of congenital toxoplasmosis occur each year in the United States.

Cats become infected either by swallowing oocysts passed in another cat's stool or by eating infected meat or rodents. Very young kittens (less than about 2 weeks old) usually suffer severe illness and often die from the infection. Most older cats survive and may show few or no signs of illness.

This brings us to appropriate steps to prevent infection. Although no vaccine is now available against toxoplasmosis, you can prevent your cat from getting the disease by keeping it confined to an area where it cannot hunt birds and rodents, keeping it away from the stool of other cats, and feeding it canned or cooked food (no raw meat). The cat's litter box should be cleaned daily to remove stools before oocysts in them can mature. The cleaning of the litter box should be done with a scoop or while wearing disposable plastic gloves, so the stool does not contact your bare hand. Hands should be washed after cleaning the litter box or digging in soil where cats may have defecated. Children's sandboxes should be covered when not in use to prevent cats from prowling in them.

It is important to remember that a woman can transmit toxoplasmosis to her unborn child only if she gets infected during her pregnancy. If she has antibodies to toxoplasmosis before she becomes pregnant, due to an earlier (usually asymptomatic) infection, the parasite will not infect her baby. Unfortunately, there are few laboratories that are now equipped to determine antibody levels to toxoplasmosis, so it is impractical for every woman to get her level of protection against, or susceptibility to, toxoplasmosis determined before or during a pregnancy. Since the fetus suffers severely from toxoplasmosis, it would be prudent for pregnant women to avoid eating raw meat and to take reasonable precaution while handling cats and anything contaminated by their stool, such as litter boxes, sandboxes, and soil. By adhering to the hygienic and preventive guidelines set forth above, it should be possible to keep both cats and humans in a household free of toxoplasmosis. Whether the pleasure derived from a cat is worth the effort or the risk is a personal decision. The more than 20 million cat-owning families in the United States have answered this question affirmatively, and in the great majority of these families human health has not suffered.

Cats, like dogs, suffer from worms, and the discussion of canine worms applies in principle to cats although feline worms seem to cause fewer problems in man.

Cats are very prone to getting fleas, which are insect pests that also bite people. Our earlier comments on dog fleas apply equally well to cats with the additional note that cats are very sensitive to certain insecticides, so be sure the flea powder, spray, or collar you buy is intended for use on cats. The products used on dogs may prove toxic to cats, largely because of the cat's habit of licking itself.

*Leukemia* and lymphoma, cancerlike diseases of the blood and lymphatic system, are relatively common in cats. Because these diseases are caused by viruses that have been shown experimentally to cause leukemia in other species, the question has been raised whether feline leukemia or lymphoma are transmissible to man. This question is currently under investigation. At this time it can be said that no case of human leukemia has been proven to be caused by a feline virus. While it appears certain that *all* human leukemias are not caused by feline viruses and there is no proof that these viruses have any public health importance, the possibility that they directly or indirectly cause *some* cases of human leukemia has not been absolutely ruled out at this time.

*Cat scratch fever* is a disease in humans, of unknown cause, in which, 5 days to 2 months following a relatively minor scratch, there is swelling at the wound and in the nearby lymph node, often accompanied by fever, malaise, and, less commonly, rashes and swelling of lymph nodes distant from the scratched area. Almost all cases recover spontaneously without permanent ill effects despite the lack of specific treatment to speed natural healing.

Cat scratch fever gets its name because the most common cause of injury associated with the disease is being clawed by a cat. However, cases have been ascribed to dog bite, cat bite, monkey scratches, and scratches from porcupine quills and rose thorns.

The cats involved show no sign of disease. Apparently, they just carry the causative agent (most commonly thought to be a viruslike germ) on their claws. To prevent cat scratch fever, keep your cat's claws clipped just beyond (outside of) the pink part of the nail or get rid of any cat that habitually scratches people.

The last disease of cats we will consider is **ringworm.** Despite the name, this is an infection of the skin, hair, and nails caused by a fungus, not a worm. Almost all domestic animals, most wild animals, many different species of birds, and man carry different species of ringworm which cause hair (or feather) loss, redness and itchiness of the skin, or thickening and cracking of nails, claws, or hooves. Many of these fungi can be transmitted from one host to another. Thus, man can get different kinds of ringworm from cattle, horses, dogs, monkeys, swine, chickens, mice, guinea pigs, chinchillas, and other animals, and, in turn, man can transmit certain forms of ringworm to some species of animals. The disease is mentioned under the discussion of cats because, in our experience, this is the most common animal source of ringworm for children. Indeed, ringworm is a very common zoonosis, perhaps because it is so easily recognized.

Any animal with unusual hair or feather loss should be examined by a veterinarian. He can usually determine whether or not ringworm is present by examining the animal and doing some simple laboratory tests. Likewise, lesions of the human scalp, skin, or nails should be brought to a physician's attention. The great majority of human and animal cases of ringworm can be cured, although some fungus infections of the nails or claws are difficult to cure completely.

## LOWER PRIMATES (MONKEYS AND APES)

If one had to choose the least desirable group of animals to keep as pets, monkeys and apes would have to come very high on the list. These animals are fine in their rightful place: the wild; they do not belong in the home.

First of all, they are hard to keep in good health. Dietary requirements of many species must be met with specially prepared feeds, such as used in zoos and laboratories. Apes and monkeys do not do well on fruit and table scraps. Malnourished monkeys are very susceptible to infectious diseases, many of which they acquire from and can give to humans.

Despite what you may see in trained animal acts onstage, these animals are not easy to train, and they are especially difficult to housebreak or toilet train. Their cages, fingers, fur, and everything they touch can be considered fecally contaminated, and there are a number of viruses, bacteria, protozoa, and worms in monkey feces that you and your child would be better off without.

Apes and monkeys are very destructive and quite ingenious at opening doors and taking things apart. They also have a limited frustration tolerance and, if emotionally upset or angry, can cause a lot of destruction to your house and anyone in their way. A monkey bite can be a very painful and mutilating injury.

Many people are attracted to apes and monkeys because they are so much like man. Unfortunately, this applies not only to their appearance but also to their diseases. The majority of infections that can afflict man can be transmitted naturally or experimentally to some lower primate. The reverse is also true in that many infections of lower primates can be transmitted to man. For practical purposes, this means that whenever a family member gets an infection of the skin, respiratory or digestive tract, there is a chance that the pet monkey can get the infection and then pass it on to someone else.

For example, they may get certain human cold viruses (see *colds*), bacterial *pneumonia,* and *tuberculosis,* so if a person and his monkey start coughing and sneezing at the same time, it is anybody's guess who gave what to whom. Every captive monkey should be tuberculin-tested, and if there is a positive reaction, the animal should be destroyed because a tuberculous monkey is not likely to be cured and is a major threat to human health.

Monkeys commonly suffer from diarrhea and there are at least 3 germs, Salmonella (see earlier in this article), Shigella, and amoebae, that cause this and that can also cause disease in man. Shigella, which causes bacterial dysentery in man, is spread by fecal contamination from man to man and back and forth from monkeys to man. Shigella dysentery, a severe diarrheal disease, may result in serious dehydration in man and lower primates.

*Amebiasis,* infection with the single-celled animals known as amoebae, results in another form of dysentery which affects man and lower primates. It is likely that apes and monkeys can also get infected with many of the intestinal viruses that cause diarrhea in man. Therefore, if, despite all warnings, you decide to keep a monkey in your house, every effort should be made to avoid eating anything contaminated with its stool, every episode of vomiting or diarrhea the animal suffers should be brought to a veterinarian's attention, and the monkey should be suspect as a possible source of any such illness in the family.

### RABBITS AND RODENTS

A great many people keep rabbits, guinea pigs, gerbils, hamsters, and laboratory rats and mice as pets. These animals are small and easily kept in a cage, which makes them suitable as pets in small apartments.

It is safest not to let small children handle these animals unsupervised because, if they are not picked up properly, rabbits tend to scratch, and the other animals (especially the hamsters) may bite in self-defense. The general comments about complications and treatment of animal bites (see earlier in this chapter, also *bites, animal*) apply to bites by rodents and, in addition, there is a relatively uncommon problem called *rat-bite fever.*

Rat-bite fever is a condition caused by bacteria transmitted in a bite by a wild or laboratory rat. The animal involved usually looks well. Two days to two weeks after the bite, the person may suffer recurrent pain at the bitten area, fever, rash over various parts of the body, and joint pains. Any animal bite should be brought to a doctor's attention, and the patient should return promptly for additional medical attention if any of these symptoms appear. Rat-bite fever usually can be cured with appropriate antibiotics.

Probably the most common disease transmitted by pet and wild rodents to man is salmonellosis, discussed earlier. Leptospirosis, discussed under dogs, is another disease that man can get from rodents, but wild animals are more often involved than pets. Because there are diseases like salmonellosis and leptospirosis that are spread by contact with rodent feces and urine, you should wash your hands after handling these animals or cleaning their cages. There are a number of other diseases that people can get from wild rodents, but this is a subject beyond the scope of this chapter. Suffice it to say that wild rats and mice should not be tolerated in any household. If these rodents are present, extermination is best done by a professional exterminator, and great care must be exercised to keep children away from the traps and poisons. Elimination of these pests also requires sealing up routes of entry, such as broken windows, cracks in doors and walls, and so forth, prompt, sanitary disposal of garbage, and safe storage of food. Under poor socioeconomic conditions, these measures are more easily advised than enacted, which is why vermin often thrive in the slums.

## BIRDS

There are approximately 15 million pet birds in the United States, the most popular caged birds being parakeets, budgerigars, canaries, parrots, cockatoos, and finches. In addition, millions of chicks and ducklings are bought as pets each Easter, the overwhelming majority of which die in a few weeks because of malnutrition, mishandling, and disease. The two most important infectious diseases transmissible from pet birds to man are salmonellosis and *ornithosis* (*psittacosis*).

Chicks and ducklings are a greater threat as a source of salmonellosis than are caged birds. Salmonellosis has been discussed in some detail earlier. Suffice it to say here that salmonellosis is a frequent cause of illness and death among chicks and ducklings. Affected birds often have a yellowish-green, pasty diarrhea and appear listless and in poor general condition before they die. Handwashing after handling birds or cleaning their cages will greatly reduce the risk of contracting salmonellosis from them.

Ornithosis (from the Greek *ornithos*, a bird) or psittacosis (from the Greek *psittakos*, a parrot) is a disease caused by a large virus acquired by inhaling droplets from the nasal secretions and droppings of birds or, rarely, by being pecked by a bird. The infection has been found in at least 98 species of birds, including parrots, parakeets, pigeons, chickens, turkeys, pheasants, ducks, geese, and many wild birds. Thus, the term ornithosis is more appropriate than psittacosis, the name originally used when the disease was only recognized in association with members of the parrot family. Human infections are associated with working in the poultry industry as well as with handling pet birds. (The disease is contracted from poultry by handling live birds and freshly killed carcasses. No human infections have been associated with eating cooked poultry products.)

Birds infected with ornithosis may appear well or they may show signs of illness, including weakness, listlessness, decreased appetite, difficulty in breathing, soiling of the feathers with diarrhea, and discharge from eyes and nose, and they may die. These signs are not specific and are also seen in many other bird diseases not transmissible to man, so a veterinarian should be consulted if your pet bird appears ill.

In man, ornithosis causes pneumonia, with cough, chest pain, fever, malaise, muscle aches, headaches, stiff neck, and a rash. Again, these symptoms are not specific and a physician would have to take X-rays and laboratory tests to make a specific diagnosis. Ornithosis can be quite severe in people, but it is a treatable disease, being one of the very few viral diseases that can be cured with antibiotics. Ornithosis can be spread from person to person, so patients with this infection should be hospitalized or quarantined at home. Thirty-three human cases of psittacosis were reported in the United States in 1971 and 40 were reported in 1970, a marked reduction from the hundreds of cases reported annually in the 1950s. This decline is due in large part to effective quarantine restrictions on the importation of pet birds (especially members of the parrot family) and preventive treatment of birds with antibiotics.

The most effective means of preventing the spread of ornithosis from pet birds to man is to feed these birds mash or seed containing chlortetracycline (an antibiotic) for 45 consecutive days. This is done as part of the quarantine procedure before psittacine (parrot-like) birds are permitted into the United States. Unfortunately, birds raised in this country for the pet trade may not have had this preventive treatment, and it usually is not possible to find out if this was done when you buy a bird.

### REPTILES

A very large number of snakes, lizards, caimans (a kind of South American crocodile), and turtles are kept as pets in the United States. Just how many are kept is not known, but more than 10 million turtles are raised for sale as pets or laboratory animals each year in this country and 4 percent of households surveyed in New Jersey and Connecticut in 1970 and 1971 had pet turtles. Reptilian pets are much less likely to cause allergies than birds or mammals, and are easy to keep in a relatively small space. The majority of reptilian species that are popular as pets are not physically dangerous. I would certainly advise against keeping animals that could inflict dangerous bites or scratches, such as snapping turtles, alligators, crocodiles, and poisonous snakes. (See *bites, snake.*)

The only significant infectious disease a pet reptile is likely to transmit to people is salmonellosis (discussed earlier). All reptiles are capable of carrying Salmonella bacteria in their digestive tract, but by far the greatest hazard is from the small aquatic turtles such as the red-eared turtle and painted turtle, which are the ones most commonly sold as pets. It has been estimated (in 1971) that 14 percent of human salmonellosis in the United States is due to contact with infected turtles; this would amount to 280,000 Salmonella infections in people each year. This is obviously a problem of much greater scope than such rare diseases as leptospirosis and ornithosis, discussed above.

Turtles and other reptiles harboring Salmonella in their gut usually appear well; rarely do they get sick or die from this infection. Most of the turtles sold in pet stores are raised commercially in large numbers on farm ponds where they are fed meat and poultry scraps which are often contaminated with Salmonella; this is how the turtles initially get infected. These turtles can then transmit the infection to other turtles confined in the same aquarium or holding tank. People get infected by transmitting the germs to their mouth after handling the turtles or items contaminated by their stool, especially the water the turtles swim in.

Several states have enacted legislation requiring that turtles sold or imported for sale in that state be certified as having been cultured for Salmonella and found negative. Where put into effect, such laws have drastically reduced the incidence of turtle-transmitted salmonellosis. You can find out if such a law is in effect in your state by writing to your state's Department of Health.

If you have a turtle at home, its stool or swimming water can be cultured for Salmonella. If these germs are present, it may be best to get rid of the animal, since it is not known if this infection can be eliminated in a turtle by treating it. A commonsense precaution to take in caring for a turtle or other pet is to wear disposable gloves or thoroughly wash your hands after cleaning up the container in which it is kept. The water in a turtle bowl should be changed frequently to keep it clean. Drain the dirty water into the toilet, not into the kitchen sink! If you feed the turtle good-quality prepared foods containing supplemental vitamins (available in pet stores), you will provide it with good nutrition and prevent it from getting Salmonella in your home, since these commercial turtle foods have been tested and found free of the infection.

In summary, almost all animal species have the potential to cause illness in man, either by trauma, allergy, or transmitting certain infections. While more than 100 infections transmissible from animals to man are known, most of them are not very common in the United States, many of them cause only mild disease, and the great majority of them are both preventable and curable. The ratio of pet animals that have been kept safely without injury to human health to those that have caused disease is thousands to one.

Animals provide companionship, a contact with nature, and a sense of responsibility and are a source for a child's intellectual curiosity. Automobiles kill and injure many more children than do animals, yet this hazard alone would not keep most people from buying a car. Benefits derived from a pet sufficiently outweigh the hazards so that we would definitely encourage children to have pets, provided the animals are selected, handled, and cared for properly.

See *bites, animal; bites, snake,* and Part 2, Chapter 9: "First Aid."

*Leonard C. Marcus, V.M.D., M.D.*


**Pigeon-toes:** see *orthopedic concerns.*


**Pimple:** see *abscess* and *acne.*


**Pinkeye:** see *conjunctivitis.*


*Pinworms* are the most common worms infesting people in the United States. These nasty creatures, which resemble small pieces of white thread, are uninvited inhabitants of the human large intestine. They live in the *cecum,* the pouchlike beginning of the large intestine. The pinworm has a curious life-style. The pregnant female worm journeys from the cecum through the large intestine to the rectum where she lays her eggs on the skin around the anus and buttocks. The tiny eggs are picked up on the fingers of the child as a result of the itching and scratching that usually occur with this condition. The eggs are transferred either to his or her own mouth or to his or her hands and then to the mouths of playmates. Some eggs may be passed to others by way of a toilet seat; others may drift into the air and be breathed in or swallowed. Of course long dirty fingernails are excellent hiding places for eggs. The swallowed eggs hatch in the small intestine, and the baby worms (larvae) travel down the length of the intestine to their destination in the cecum where they mature, mate, and repeat the cycle.

The infestation with pinworms is probably not apparent in the majority of children, since there are few or no symptoms. The telltale sign is the itching around the anus, buttocks, or vagina which always seems worse at night and sometimes drives the child to the point of distraction. Upon scrutiny of the irritated bottom, mothers are usually shocked to find the threadlike worms. The itching alone is sufficient reason to seek medical attention whether or not the worms are seen. If there is any doubt, and there rarely is, the tiny eggs can be collected by applying cellulose tape (sticky side down) to the anal area. The tape can be pasted on a glass slide for inspection under a microscope.

Once the diagnosis is made, treatment is straightforward. There are two kinds of medicines used—one taken as a single dose and repeated in

2 weeks if well tolerated, and the other taken daily for 1 week. The former is notorious for coloring the stools and clothing red, which can be alarming to the uninformed. Occasional minor side effects of both drugs are nausea, cramps, and *diarrhea.* With either medication many readily seen adult worms are passed in the stools. We usually treat the entire household, because when the worm is in the house, it is likely to be in more than one cecum. More than the usual attention is called for in trimming nails and washing hands before meals and after visits to the toilet. Washing towels, linens, and clothes is in order. If the worms reappear, they usually represent a new infection, not a failure in treatment. In this situation we treat only the affected individuals.

Rare is the parent who doesn't ask, "How did he get it?" or "What did I do?" Mothers understandably take the matter quite personally. It is difficult to answer these questions specifically. Pinworms are so widespread among children that they could almost be considered part of the normal flora (see *infections*). Why they cause symptoms in particular children is hard to say, nor can we give any specific advice about prevention, except that children with suspicious symptoms should be checked promptly to limit the spread of worms within the family.

The skin irritation is the only common problem caused by the pinworms. There are rare cases in which the worms have crawled from the cecum into the appendix, triggering (if not causing) *appendicitis.* Some children are said to have poor appetite, belly pain, and skin pallor from the worms, but we find these relationships difficult to explain. Pinworms are more of a nuisance than anything else.

For a discussion of worms that children can pick up from dogs, see *pets and children.*

*Pityriasis rosea* is a relatively common rash with a protracted course of weeks. Its cause has not yet been identified, although a virus is suspected. Typically, the rash consists of small (1 to 2 centimeters), pale red, round or oval, flat or slightly raised spots with a crinkly surface and a rim of fine scales. They appear in clusters on the trunk and on the parts of the arms and legs closest to the body. The left and right sides of the body are usually equally involved, with the rash appearing more or less symmetrically on each side. In children, the rash may also appear on the face, hands, and feet, while in adults these parts are spared. The number of spots ranges from a few to so many that the skin is almost completely covered. The individual spots slowly enlarge by expansion outward and new ones appear for seven to ten days after the eruption begins. Variations of the rash are as common as this typical picture. In children, the spots are often slightly raised. Occasionally, blisters are seen, limited to the shoulder or groin.

In about 70 or 80 percent of cases, prior to the general skin eruption there is an initial large spot which may appear anywhere on the body, consisting of a round, red, scaling, raised plaque. It is known as the "herald patch" because it announces the onset of the general skin rash.

There is no treatment and healing is complete and permanent. The mild itching sometimes present can be relieved with calamine lotion or other anti-itch medications. The most important point to realize is that this disorder lasts from 6 to 8 weeks and then disappears. It is somewhat disturbing and unusual to be confronted with such a visible and even dramatic condition for which there is no treatment, and which, on the average, persists for almost 2 months. Recurrences are uncommon.

*PKU (phenylketonuria).* Though phenylketonuria (PKU) is a comparatively rare condition (approximately 1 in 10,000 babies affected), we hear a good bit about it. In the first place, the practice of testing neonates (newborn infants) for PKU is widespread and in some states required by law. Secondly, PKU is a textbook example of the transmission of defects by recessive genes (see **genetics**). Thirdly, the condition demonstrates dramatically the interdependence of mind and body.

Phenylketonuria is a disorder of the metabolism (that is, the bodily processing) of the amino acid *phenylalanine.* Amino acids are the basic building blocks of all proteins, and the process of digestion splits proteins into these constituents. After digestion, amino acids are absorbed through the intestinal wall into the bloodstream. When they enter into the chemical reactions that occur in the cells, the amino acids may be incorporated into new protein or they may be broken down for conversion into energy or for elimination from the body. There are vitally important amino acids (including phenylalanine) which the body is unable to manufacture on its own and which it must therefore obtain from the protein in the diet. These are known as *essential amino acids.* Each of them is crucial to the accomplishment of some particular step in the normal process of growth and development.

In PKU the body fails to process phenylalanine because there is a deficiency or derangement of a certain enzyme. (Enzymes are very complex substances that act as *catalysts* in the chemical reactions of the body—that is, they are necessary in promoting the reactions but do not themselves enter into the chemical changes.) For want of this processing, the phenylalanine accumulates in the blood and tissues. The PKU test detects these abnormally high levels of phenylalanine. Alternate chemical processes then operate to convert the phenylalanine into chemicals which are found in large quantities in the urine, also detectable by a urine test.

Since specific genes control enzymes, the failure of the enzyme to process phenylalanine normally must be the result of a genetic defect. A small proportion of the population, from 1 in 50 to 1 in 100, carries a recessive gene for PKU. If 2 of these recessives mate, one-fourth of the offspring on the average will have PKU, one-half will themselves be recessive for the condition, and one-fourth will be entirely free of both the disease and the genetic trait.

Excessive phenylalanine or its by-products can damage the brain, causing mental retardation and seizures. (See *developmental disabilities* and *seizure disorders.*) Further, it can interfere with the overall growth and well-being. Severely affected infants may eat poorly, vomit, and fail to thrive. Since high phenylalanine also inhibits production of pigment, children with PKU will have lighter skins and hair than would be expected in their particular families.

The principle of treatment for PKU is quite simple. A diet is provided that contains the exact requirement of this essential amino acid and no more. Fruits and vegetables are low in phenylalanine, and a synthetic milk with all the essential amino acids but a reduced amount of phenylalanine has been developed. Since the total regimen of treatment is complicated, many communities have found it worthwhile to establish treatment centers for the affected children. Indications are at present that treatment for PKU can safely be discontinued for most children by the time of their entry into school. However, when girls with PKU grow up and have children, their non-PKU children could become retarded from exposure in utero to high concentrations of phenylalanine. Therefore, such women should check with their physicians about resuming the low phenylalanine diet during pregnancy.

The current emphasis, of course, is on early recognition of the condition in order to catch it before irreversible brain damage has occurred. Breast milk, cows' milk, and commercial formulas all contain enough phenylalanine to elevate the level above normal in babies with the genetic trait. In the standard screening program a small sample of blood is taken from the baby's heel on his or her third or fourth day. The analysis does not positively diagnose PKU but does identify the babies who will need further watching. Conditions other than PKU can cause elevation of the phenylalanine level, but the goal of this testing is to avoid missing any baby who might have PKU.

There are other metabolic disorders, similar to PKU, which are screened for at birth in the blood, and in the urine at age 3 to 4 weeks. Galactosemia is one such disorder (see *genetics*).

*Pneumonia* means infection of the lungs. (See *infections.*) Respiratory tract infection can strike at any point or points of the upper respiratory tract —the nose (see *colds*); throat and tonsils (see *throat, sore* and *tonsils and adenoids*); sinuses (see *sinusitis*); airway and larynx (see *croup and laryngitis*), or the lower respiratory tract: the bronchi (main air tubes) and bronchioles (small air passages) (see *bronchitis*); and the lungs themselves. Often infection involves several parts of the respiratory tree and is not confined to one subdivision alone. Pneumonia usually results from a spread of infection downward from the nose and throat. Why this spread of infection to the lungs occurs is not well understood. Contrary to popular belief, a "cold" does not turn into pneumonia if untreated. If pneumonia develops in a child, a parent should not feel responsible or guilty. Children with underlying lung diseases like *asthma* or *cystic fibrosis* have an increased susceptibility to pneumonia.

The symptoms of pneumonia are *cough, fever,* quickened and sometimes labored breathing (see *breathing, noisy*), *abdominal pain,* and *chest pain.* Parents should not be concerned with diagnosing pneumonia, only with having the child checked if these symptoms develop. In addition to the physical examination with special attention given to the chest, the doctor or nurse may order a white *blood count* and a chest X-ray. These studies are not always necessary, however, and often the history and physical examination alone will clinch the diagnosis.

The extent of pneumonia varies from a small patch in one lung to extensive involvement throughout both lungs (sometimes called double pneumonia). The mildest cases are probably unrecognized as such.

Pneumonia can be caused by bacteria, viruses (see *infections*), and by a fungus (see *histoplasmosis*), or *tuberculosis.* One type of bacteria which deserves special mention is *mycoplasma.* This common germ can cause pneumonia and upper respiratory infection. It often is passed around from one family member to another, and can infect a family for months. Mycoplasma pneumonia may linger for weeks. Antibiotics presently available help eradicate it, but do not work as effectively as with other kinds of bacterial pneumonia.

In some cases it seems likely that one germ, for example a virus, sets the stage for invasion by another, for example a bacterium. The infection in such a case is of mixed cause. The doctor tries to distinguish among these germs because treatment varies accordingly. Unlike infections in more accessible places like the throat or urinary tract, making an exact microbial diagnosis in lung infection is difficult because of the inaccessibility of the infected mucus. This difficulty is compounded in the child by his or her inability to produce sputum from deep in the chest. The distinction between viral and bacterial pneumonia, which determines the usefulness of prescribing an antibiotic, is not always easily made. The white cell count can help in distinguishing viral from bacterial infections. Most of the time treatment is based on probabilities and is revised according to the response obtained. The uncertainty as to cause often leads to the use of antibiotics to give the child the benefit of the doubt. Recently interest has developed in the technique known as *lung puncture* in which a sterile needle is inserted through a small area of anesthetized skin on the chest wall into the lung proper and a sample of infected material aspirated for analysis.

In addition to antibiotics, many children with pneumonia are usually given expectorant cough medicines to liquify secretions and make them easier to raise. Most children with pneumonia can be cared for at home (so called "walking pneumonia"). Children with difficulty in breathing may need to be hospitalized. Oxygen may be given to ease their breathing. *Pneumothorax,* atelectasis (see *lung rupture and collapse*), and abscess (cavity full of pus) of the lung are occasional complications requiring special treatment.

Whenever a child develops pneumonia, we always think of an underlying predisposition to lung infection such as asthma, cystic fibrosis, or the aspiration of a foreign body into the lung (see *choking and swallowing foreign objects*). In the majority of cases, none is found and the explanation for the pneumonia is uncertain.

Pneumonia used to be a serious threat to children and at one time it took many lives each year. Nowadays, with antibiotics and improved supportive therapy, few children fail to recover. Automobile accidents or accidental poisoning are now a much greater threat. Children with an underlying problem like cystic fibrosis, of course, require ongoing care.

Pneumonia as such is not contagious or catching. You can catch the germs but there is no guarantee that they will cause infection at all, or that the infection caused will be pneumonia. For example, the same virus that causes pneumonia in one individual can cause nothing more than a cold or sore throat in another.

If you are exposed to someone with pneumonia (except for pneumonia caused by tuberculosis), there are no special precautions, nor is there any need to worry.

See Part 1, Chapter 5: "Caring for the Sick Child at Home" or Part 1, Chapter 6: "If Your Child Goes to the Hospital."


*Pneumothorax* is the medical term for air within the thoracic cavity. It is a diagnosis made by the doctor (often with the help of an X-ray) and arises as a complication of a variety of pulmonary ailments. In this condition, the air is where it should not be. Obviously, air should and must enter and leave the lungs regularly as a part of normal respiration. Pneumothorax refers to the situation where air is outside of the lung, trapped between the lung, rib cage, and diaphragm. The condition can result from a puncture wound to the chest (a common cause in the older individual in this era of auto accidents), allowing air to pass directly through the chest wall into the thoracic cavity. More commonly it stems from a rupture of part of the lung, with resulting leaking of air (see *lung rupture and collapse*). In the newborn, lung rupture can complicate many respiratory afflictions associated with partial or complete obstruction of the air passageways, such as *hyaline membrane disease* (see *lung rupture and collapse*) or *pneumonia*. In infants an uncommon but dramatic example is rupture of an overdistended lung segment (see *emphysema*). In older children, *asthma* or *cystic fibrosis* predisposes to pneumothorax.

Small amounts of air cause no problems. Larger quantities may compress adjacent areas of lung, thus decreasing the amount of lung available for normal respiratory purposes. The understandable effect is increasing shortness of breath and, if severe, *cyanosis* (blueness from oxygen-deprived blood). If the pressure of trapped air becomes excessive due to progressive accumulation of air, the condition is known as a *tension pneumothorax*, that is, air under tension. This excessive pressure may not only collapse the adjacent lung, but also may push the heart and great vessels to the opposite side, compromising their functions. Such a situation may be life threatening.

Pneumothorax is a condition which your physician will watch for in children with labored breathing. (See *breathing, noisy.*) Its management requires the judgment of trained medical personnel. Treatment is directed to the underlying cause (for example, antibiotics for infection). Excessive air accumulation is often relieved by inserting a small tube through the chest wall between the ribs and into the pocket of air. The air leak which caused the condition usually seals with time. Most children recover completely and have no further difficulty.

*Poisoning:* see Part 2, Chapter 10.

**Poison ivy, sumac, and oak.** Plants that are well known for their ability to irritate human skin are poison ivy, sumac, and oak. *Poison ivy* (*Rhus toxicodendron*) is a woody vine or trailing shrub found in all parts of the United States except the Southwest and Pacific Coast. The plant can grow in fields, empty lots, and backyards where children are likely to play, as well as in the country. Unless you know how to remove the plants safely, the job is best left to a professional gardener.

*Poison oak* (*Rhus diversiloba*) grows on the Pacific Coast as a low shrub, a large treelike plant, or a vine. Poison oak, like poison ivy, has leaves composed of three leaflets. The middle leaflet has a larger stalk than the other two. *Poison sumac* (*Rhus vernix*) is a shrub or small tree native in bogs of the North and in swamps and river bottoms of the South. The irritant in each of these plants is a chemical (oleoresin) in leaves, stems, and roots. The following discussion will be about poison ivy, the most common offender, but the same principles apply to poison sumac and oak.

In the typical case of poison ivy (there is wide variation depending on the individual's sensitivity and the extent of exposure), the rash consists of reddening, swelling, and blistering of the exposed skin coming on 6 hours to 6 days (average 48 hours) after exposure. When the skin has been brushed over the leaf of the plant, the rash follows the line of contact. Around face, lips, and eyes, the swelling is often marked because of the looseness of the skin in these areas. Contrary to popular belief, the fluid from the blisters will not spread the inflammation to other parts of the body or to others. Itching and burning are characteristic. Direct contact with the plant is not necessary. Mere exposure to the oleoresin carried by pollen or by smoke from burning leaves is sufficient to cause a case of poisoning.

Without treatment healing occurs within 2 to 3 weeks. Plain calamine lotion, an old standby, can reduce itching temporarily but with prolonged use can accumulate and cake on the skin, aggravating the problem. Dressings (old linens or bed sheets) soaked with a solution of one teaspoon of table salt per pint of cool water can relieve itching. Apply to the affected parts 4 times daily for 15 minutes to 1 hour, unwrapping the cloth every few minutes. Application of creams containing hydrocortisone derivatives (see **hormones**), for which a doctor's prescription is needed, can accelerate healing and reduce inflammation. In severe reactions, the physician may prescribe hydrocortisone-like hormones by mouth in large doses over several days. When these steroid hormones are taken in this way there is little risk of the complications that occur with long-term administration. Antihistamines taken by mouth can decrease the itching. Their usefulness is limited in some children because of the drowsiness that often results. The application of antihistamines combined with calamine lotion to the skin is not advised.

Because sweating aggravates itching and increases discomfort, measures to reduce sweating are useful. These include staying out of the sun, avoiding strenuous activities and contact with water (including swimming).

Education is the key. When contact with underbrush is unavoidable, long sleeves and trousers are in order. (Farmers are rarely victims.) When exposure has occurred or is suspected to have occurred, washing the skin thoroughly within 15 minutes with soap (brown soap seems to have an advantage) may remove some of the oleoresin before inflammation begins. Exposed clothing should be thoroughly washed or dry cleaned. Tools and shoes should be decontaminated with cleaning fluid.

Hyposensitization (see **allergy**) to poison ivy is controversial and in general we do not recommend it.

*Poliomyelitis,* the dreaded virus disease causing muscle weakness, is also known as infantile paralysis. The name is self-explanatory. In the full-blown case, symptoms usually begin after a 7-to-10-day incubation period with 3 to 4 days of temperature, *headache,* loss of appetite, *vomiting,* and sore throat. This phase is followed by a deceptive lull and seeming return to normalcy of 2 to 3 days, following which all of the initial symptoms return with greater intensity. By this time pain has become prominent, particularly in the head, neck, back, and extremities. Muscle stiffness is common. On about the ninth day following the onset of symptoms, paralysis (weakness of the muscles) appears. This can involve any or all of the muscles under voluntary control. Paralysis of the muscles of swallowing or of the chest wall are particularly serious because they interfere with breathing, making artificial respiration with some form of iron lung a necessity.

The polio virus attacks the motor nerve cells in the spinal cord. When these nerve cells are knocked out, the line of communication from brain to spinal cord to muscle is disrupted and the victim loses partial or complete control over the muscles supplied by nerves from the damaged cells. Once infection has occurred, there is no cure. All treatment is supportive, that is, directed toward relief of symptoms. The long-term outlook depends on how well the seriously ill patient is cared for initially, on the effectiveness of rehabilitation, and on the extent of permanent muscle impairment, which can vary from inapparent to obvious crippling (see *handicapped child*).

There are 3 major strains of polio virus. Harmless cousins of each are contained in the trivalent or triple vaccine. (See *immunization.*) The vaccine viruses set up an intestinal infection which causes and stimulates production of antibodies which then protect against infection with the polio viruses themselves.

Man is the only natural host for poliomyelitis viruses. Most cases of infection are subclinical and most patients who become clinically ill do not become paralyzed. In an immunized population the polio viruses are largely eliminated by breaking the chain of infection and shedding of virus.

For a discussion of virus, incubation period, antibodies, and subclinical illness, see *infections.*

*Psittacosis:* see *pets and children.*

*Psychomotor attack:* see *seizure disorders.*

*Puberty:* see *adolescence.*

*Puncture wounds* occurring out of doors, such as those produced by a nail (rusty or not) sticking through the sole of a shoe into a foot, are likely to be full of dirt and should cause immediate concern. Contact your physician promptly. In the meantime, soaking the foot in warm soapy water will help clean the area and prevent infection. If a puncture has occurred within your home, is not very deep (little more than a scratch), and does not appear dirty, it can probably be treated at home simply by first cleaning the area with hot soapy water and then applying a bandage. If at any time the wound becomes swollen, red, or begins to discharge pus, contact your doctor promptly. (See also *cuts, scratches, abrasions, and scrapes.*).

With puncture wounds, which in themselves would not cause you to seek medical attention, the question of *tetanus* always comes up. Tetanus is an extremely serious infection, the possibility of which should be considered in treating any wound or cut. Tetanus is caused by a poison (toxin) secreted by tetanus bacteria. These are found in soil, particularly soil contaminated by animal droppings. Hence, a puncture by an outdoor rusty nail is a prime source of this infection. The toxin from the bacteria spreads through the bloodstream and sets off muscle spasms throughout the body which produce the characteristic locked jaw. Tetanus bacteria thrive on low concentrations of oxygen, exactly the condition that exists in a sealed-over puncture wound.

All babies should receive a series of tetanus inoculations before they are 1 year old, a booster at 1½ years, and before entering school (see *immunization*). To keep the immunization to tetanus effective, everyone —children and adults—should have a tetanus booster shot every 10 years throughout life.

At the time of an accident, the doctor who is caring for the child will frequently ask when the child has had his or her last tetanus booster shot. Since this is not always easy to remember (especially when there is more than one child in the family), try to make a habit of recording the dates of these immunizations and taking the record along with you whenever your child needs emergency treatment.

In general, if your child has had a booster injection in the past 5 years, or has completed his basic four tetanus immunizations within the past 5 years, it is not necessary to have another booster at the time of injury.

*Pus:* see *abscess.*

*Pyloric stenosis.* The *pylorus* is the muscular valve controlling the flow of food and gastric juices from the stomach to the *duodenum,* which is the beginning of the small intestine. In the condition known as pyloric stenosis, this muscular valve thickens enough to obstruct partially or completely the flow of food from the stomach. Since milk or other food then has no way to get out of the stomach except by mouth, the baby vomits. *Vomiting* in the course of a feeding or soon after eating is the first symptom. The vomiting tends to be projectile, coming out with force and traveling some distance. This is in contrast to normal spitting up, which is more of a drool. If the condition is allowed to continue for any length of time, the baby will lose weight, show signs of dehydration, and produce infrequent stools. Pyloric stenosis is a condition that worsens progressively and gives the parent ample warning before serious malnutrition sets in. The persistent vomiting sends the parent to the doctor, who is the only one, of course, to make the diagnosis out of all the possible explanations of vomiting.

The vomiting from pyloric stenosis usually begins several weeks after the baby has left the hospital, rarely in the first 2 weeks of life. It may begin as not much more than the slight regurgitation common to burping, but with time, it becomes greater in volume and more forceful. The physician can actually observe the forceful contractions of the distended stomach against the obstruction outlined under the baby's skin. He can often feel the thickened muscle, about the size of an olive, which is called a pyloric tumor. It is never malignant.

The common treatment of pyloric stenosis is a short surgical operation, well tolerated by babies. With the baby under general anesthesia, the surgeon makes an incision into the thickened muscle to relieve the obstruction. In a matter of hours the child usually can be fed again. The patient may vomit at the first few feedings, but will improve rapidly. For all practical purposes the condition has been corrected; no recurrence is expected. In some parts of the world, a regime of special feedings and antispasmodic drugs is used for pyloric stenosis in the expectation that the condition will eventually relieve itself, but since the surgical approach is simpler and more successful, it is preferred in this country.

The underlying cause of pyloric stenosis is not known. It is more common among firstborn children and much more common in males than in females. If one child in a family has had the condition, the chances for later siblings to have it are only slightly greater than for any other child. In other words, if there is a hereditary influence, it appears not to be a strong one.

**Rabies:** see *pets and children.*

**Rash.** Rashes are a common problem in childhood, and a common reason for calling the doctor or nurse. They are a symptom of many different diseases and conditions and therefore have been discussed elsewhere in this book. For instance, rashes are a symptom of specific diseases such as *chicken pox, German measles, measles, Rocky Mountain spotted fever,* and scarlet fever (see *throat, sore*). *Bloodstream infection* is often accompanied by a rash. Some rashes are caused by allergic disorders such as *eczema, hives,* and reactions to drugs (see *drug reactions, allergic*), and *anaphylactoid purpura.* Some rashes, such as *pityriasis rosea* and *seborrheic dermatitis* are of unknown origin. In this section we discuss other commonly seen rashes.

Rashes, most commonly consisting of flat red spots, occur with a number of viral infections, often along with other symptoms like sore throat, running nose, *vomiting,* muscle aches, and *diarrhea.* Rashes may accompany a *fever of unknown origin.* Many parents have noticed faint rashes accompanying *colds* in younger children. These rashes follow no clear or typical pattern as in chicken pox or measles. In fact, it is their variability which is characteristic. We are usually hard pressed to identify which viruses are causing the illness just by the appearance of the rash. This problem is discussed in the specific case of rubella in *German measles* and *infections.* In other words, similar rashes can be caused by more than one virus. Only when the rash occurs in an epidemic whose cause is known can we make more than an educated guess about cause. On the other hand, these rashes in themselves do no harm. There is no treatment for them and they get better on their own. When a treatment or prevention is developed, it will be for the underlying infection, not for the rash itself.

Two virus families that are notorious for causing rashes are the *Coxsackie* and *echo* viruses. The rashes are interesting because they may contain small skin hemorrhages (petechiae) which confuse these virus infections with some kinds of bloodstream infections. Coxsackie viruses are named after the town in New York State in which they were first discovered, and echo is short for "enterocytopathogenic human orphan" whose derivation we will spare the reader. In addition to causing rashes, these viruses can produce *fever,* diarrhea, *headache,* muscle aches and pains, aseptic (viral) *meningitis,* upper respiratory infection, and sore throat. One or a combination of these symptoms can predominate in a given illness. The achiness in the chest and abdomen can be so severe with some of the Coxsackie viruses that the illness has been aptly called "devil's grippe." The echo and Coxsackie viruses cause painful shallow sores on the throat, tonsils, soft palate, and sides of the mouth somewhat resembling infection of herpes virus (see *fever blisters*). With some of the Coxsackie viruses there may be spots or blisters on the hands and feet as well, so-called *hand, foot, and mouth disease* (no relation to foot-and-mouth disease of cattle).

Another relatively common illness with a characteristic rash probably caused by a virus is called *erythema infectiosum* or *fifth disease.* It usually begins with raised warm red marks on the face as though the child's or adult's cheeks were slapped. A red-spotted rash then appears on the trunk and extremities. It develops a lacework appearance and disappears after 10 days. The rash characteristically varies in intensity from hour to hour. Even after healing it may reappear for a few days when the skin is exposed to irritation such as sunlight or extremes of heat or cold.

The changing seasons affect the skin. A common cold weather rash is what we call "winter rash of childhood." It comes and goes in the cold months of the year and affects the outer part of the arms and legs. The skin is red, rough, and dry, and sometimes itchy. Skin lotions provide temporary relief and spring brings a complete cure. Cold weather also brings "boot rash." Children, usually girls, may keep their boots on all day through school and can develop peeling and itching of the balls of the feet and toes. Use of boots only when needed outdoors provides a complete cure. Some children are truly allergic to their shoes. The allergic rash tends to involve the tops of the feet and toes. Warm weather also brings its problems to children's skin. Heat can cause a rash in sensitive individuals. With short pants and more outdoor play, poison ivy (see *poison ivy, sumac, and oak*) and certain skin infections (see discussion of impetigo under *abscess*) become more common.

See also *diaper rash*.

**Reading problems:** see *learning disabilities*.

**Regional enteritis:** see *colitis, ulcerative*.

**Resistance and frequent colds.** We have all heard of or known the child who has "one illness after another," who "is no sooner over one cold than another one begins," "has already missed three weeks of school," "now has a fever for the third time in four weeks," "is pale and run down and has low resistance." Could it be his or her tonsils? Does he need vitamins? Perhaps he is allergic? Should he be eating more? Does he need a strong medicine to "knock it out" of him?

There is no doubt that a given winter season can be rough for some children, with many illnesses, time out of school, and exasperation for the child and especially for the parents. The illnesses most such children experience fall into several categories. Most common are *colds* and sore throats (see *throat, sore*) with or without ear infections (see *earache*). Next is the flu (see *influenza*). Third is the "intestinal flu" or *gastroenteritis* with its characteristic *vomiting* and *diarrhea*.

What can be said about the "resistance" of such children? In general, with certain exceptions discussed below, there is nothing defective in their ability to cope with infection, at least nothing detectable by presently available techniques. These children do not have abnormalities of gamma globulin or white blood cells. Their frequent infections can be explained almost entirely by exposure to and lack of prior experience with the microorganisms involved. Children are literally sitting ducks for infection. Expose them to a virus and chances are they will become ill. An adult exposed to the same germ will either be immune from prior experience and shrug off the invader, or not react as strongly if he does become ill. But the child with no background of immunological experience against virulent microorganisms is vulnerable. Not only is he likely to become ill, but he will probably experience more severe symptoms, higher fever, and more marked change in normal activity. Emotional stress may lower resistance to infection in a yet unidentified way. (See Part 1, Chapter 4: "Complaints with an Emotional Element.")

Day-care centers, nurseries, and schools are arenas for the spread of infection. The environment within such institutions is hard to control. Even if parents were able to keep their child at home at the first sign of an infection until the contagious period is over, infections would still be spread in school, although probably less frequently. The reason is that the child becomes contagious before he has symptoms and sometimes is contagious without having symptoms.

The toddler at home with siblings in nursery or regular school is an innocent victim of microbial attacks. He is exposed to everything brought home by his brothers and sisters. The third child in a family usually has a much harder time as an infant and toddler than does the first child. This handicap *may* be compensated for by fewer infections at a later age because of development of immunity.

The years between 2 and 7 are the peak ones for infection, with the average child having 5 to 8 respiratory illnesses per year. Throw in one attack of grippe and one gastroenteritis as a minimum and the number of infections comes close to one a month as a base line. Recall that there are enough different cold viruses to keep a child occupied for some years.

The frustrating part of this story is that, at present, there is no *immunization* against or treatment for these viral illnesses, unlike *measles, German measles,* and *mumps,* and we are resigned to let them run their course (see *infections*).

With this general burden of infection as a background, special circumstances can complicate the picture. Some children may develop an ear infection with their colds which may require special treatment. Others may develop chronic tonsil infections (see *tonsils and adenoids*). In such cases, the tonsils never fully return to normal, whereas most cases of tonsillitis improve with loss of swelling and inflammation. Persistence of infection in a tonsil or tonsils, relatively uncommon in terms of the number of tonsil infections experienced by children, may require surgical removal of the infected tissue. For some children, the adenoid becomes enlarged, obstructing the passage of air between nose and throat, and clinically infected, requiring special therapy. Other children have asthmatic attacks (see *asthma*) which may compound and prolong the effects of the infections in the nose and throat. Some allergic individuals with **hay fever** (allergic rhinitis) may be made worse by viral infections of the nose, the infection and allergy working hand in hand. Some children develop sinusitis as a complication of respiratory infection or as an expression of *allergy.* All these complications are manifested either by a prolongation of symptoms like *cough* beyond the expected 7 to 10 days of a cold ("one continuous cold") or by specific distinguishing symptoms like ear pain or pain over a sinus. These complications require special attention and treatment above and beyond that given for a garden-variety cold or sore throat.

Factors which do not appear to play a role in the frequency of infections, at least in the well-off segment of American society, are undernutrition (even the "picky" eater deals normally with infection) or lack of vitamins. Special diets, tonics (none of which have been proven effective), or vitamins, beyond the normal daily requirement contained in the average diet (see Part 1, Chapter 3: "Diet of Infants and Children") have no proven benefit. Research on vitamin C is at best ambiguous. *Anemia* is an unusual cause of increased infections, except when it is severe. Appetites are decreased by infection, but what appears to be a poor appetite does not conversely predispose to infection. Why children eat the quantities they do is poorly understood, but it is clear that there is no simple connection between food intake or weight and susceptibility to infection, except at the extreme ends of the scale.

See also *colds* and *infections.*

---

*Retarded child:* see *developmental disabilities; Down's syndrome; handicapped child.*

---

*Retinoblastoma* is a highly malignant cancer of the retina which occurs mainly in infants and young children. It manifests itself as a "cat's eye" appearance of the pupil and/or by crossing of the affected eye (see *cross-eyes*). Both eyes are involved in about 35 percent of cases.

In addition to prompt treatment, genetic counseling (see *genetics*) should be obtained regarding future children. Patients who have survived retinoblastoma should be aware of the high likelihood of passing the disorder on to their offspring.

*Rheumatic fever* is a disease characterized by *fever* and inflammation of the joints, skin, heart, and sometimes the brain. It is a complication of "strep throat," appearing several weeks later in a small percentage of untreated streptococcal throat infections (see *throat, sore*). If streptococcal infections of the throat could be detected and treated adequately, rheumatic fever would become almost nonexistent. In fact, it is our concern for preventing rheumatic fever which is the major reason for our interest in the prompt detection and treatment of strep throats. If rheumatic fever did not complicate strep throats, identification and treatment of sore throats would be much less important.

Even without treatment the majority of strep throats will heal on their own. It is not even clear if treatment speeds disappearance of the sore throat, fever, and swollen glands (see *glands, swollen*). What treatment accomplishes is the elimination of the streptococcus bacteria whose persistence in the throat is responsible for rheumatic fever in susceptible patients. The parents' major interest in rheumatic fever should be with prevention by reporting sore throats to the doctor or nurse. Through throat cultures and other tests, they will distinguish between streptococcal and viral throat infections to determine who should and who should not receive antibiotics.

The child with rheumatic fever has red, swollen, painful joints. (See *joint pain.*) The knee, ankle, elbow, and wrists are the joints most commonly affected. The inflammation of the joints characteristically shifts from one joint to another and eventually subsides completely with complete recovery. The rash of rheumatic fever is slightly raised, red, with a curved lattice-like pattern and also clears without aftereffect. Some children develop painless lumps (nodules) deep in the skin, particularly of the arms, back of head, and spine. These subside without a trace. While all of the above manifestations of rheumatic fever are bothersome, they do go away. The one part of the body which can suffer serious effects is the heart. The heart muscle, inner lining, valves, and outer sac (pericardium) can become inflamed. During the active attack, the heart valves are affected and permit reflux (flowing back) of blood through the chambers, causing the heart to work harder. Valvular inflammation is accompanied by the appearance of abnormal heart murmurs (see *heart murmurs*). Under the strain the heart can weaken and enlarge, leading to heart failure. As the inflammation subsides, healing may be followed by scarring of the valves, resulting in permanent murmurs and reflux of blood into the heart chambers. With time, the scarring may increasingly obstruct the flow of blood from one chamber to another, causing the heart to work even harder. Eventually, after many years, heart failure may occur.

There are a number of laboratory findings in rheumatic fever. The white blood cell count (see *blood count*) and the sedimentation rate (the rate at which the blood cells separate from plasma in an upright column) are elevated. Particularly useful are measurements of antibodies to the streptococcus. When these are present in sufficient quantities, they point to a recent infection with this bacterium. (See *infections.*)

The effects of rheumatic fever are quite varied. At one extreme is the child at death's door with heart failure. At the other is the child with fever and slight inflammation of an ankle lasting a day or two, who in adult life is discovered to have a minimal heart murmur. Most attacks are somewhere in between.

Treatment varies according to the symptoms present and includes giving penicillin to eradicate any remaining streptococci, the use of aspirin to control fever and joint inflammation, and the administration of hydrocortisone-like *hormones* to decrease inflammation of the heart in severe cases. Special measures, such as prescribing digitalis, are used to combat heart failure. The child is kept on penicillin for many years, in some instances for life, to prevent reinfection with streptococci which can lead to a return of symptoms, including a worsening of previous heart damage. The penicillin can be given daily by mouth or monthly by injection with a special long-acting form of the antibiotic. Individuals whose hearts are permanently damaged and who have markedly impaired heart function may require surgery to repair the scarred valves. Usually such surgery is not required until adult life.

A somewhat unusual feature of rheumatic fever which often occurs without any of the other symptoms months rather than weeks following the streptococcal throat infection is *chorea* (St. Vitus's dance), a disorder of nervous functioning characterized by involuntary jerky movements of the body, clumsiness, loss of coordination, slurred speech, and poor handwriting. Sometimes the involuntary movements are so violent the child requires sedation and special care. Although chorea can go on for weeks to months, recovery is complete. It is quite likely that the mildest cases are not recognized as such.

See Part 1, Chapter 5: "Caring for the Sick Child at Home" and *throat, sore.*


**Rheumatoid arthritis:** see *arthritis, rheumatoid.*


**Riley-Day syndrome:** see *dysautonomia.*


**Ringworm** is caused by living microorganisms known as *fungi*, which thrive in the outer layers of the skin, nails, and hair. (See also *athlete's foot.*) Except under usual circumstances, they do not invade deep into the skin. Ringworm of the scalp *(tinea capitis)* is recognized as a painless, patchy hair loss with broken hair, inflammation, and scaling. It is transmitted by contact from one infected child to another. The fungi have been isolated from items such as barbers' instruments, hairbrushes, theater seats, and hats. Minor bruising of the scalp provides an entry for infection. Children up to puberty are more susceptible than are adults, boys more than girls. Scalp ringworm is treated with the antibiotic griseofulvin, given twice daily after a fatty meal for 3 to 6 weeks. There is no need for the old practice of shaving the hair or wearing a skullcap. Local antifungal medications contribute little to the treatment.

Ringworm of the nonhairy skin (*tinea corporis* or *body ringworm*) may be seen in any age group, but is most common in children. It either causes no symptoms at all or a mild itching. Body ringworm typically starts as a flat red spot. It spreads outward and develops a circular or horseshoe shape with a scaly or blistery advancing outer rim and a peeling center. It is most common on the exposed surfaces of the body— the face, arms, and shoulders—and in the groins of teen-age boys (socalled "jock itch").

Ringworm of the body can be spread from floors contaminated with fungi, shower stalls, bedding, benches, and similar articles and through contact with infected animals. The animals may not be obviously ill. Cats, for example, can have inconspicuous lesions around their faces which are hardly detectable without special examination with a fluorescent light. (See *pets and children.*) Body ringworm also can be treated with griseofulvin. Topical antifungal medications are also helpful.

Some fungus infections of the skin and scalp and elsewhere can be distinguished from other kinds of infections by the fluorescence of the lesions upon exposure to ultraviolet light in a dark room. The fungi can be identified by examination of scrapings under the microscope and, if necessary, by actual culture. (See *infections.*)

**Rocky Mountain spotted fever.** Rickettsiae are a special class of bacteria (see *infections*) which inhabit the alimentary (digestive) tract in certain insects and can cause disease in humans and animals. The best known rickettsial infection in this country is Rocky Mountain spotted fever (also called *Cape Cod spotted fever* or *tick fever*). It is transmitted to humans by the bite of infected ticks and not passed from one human to another. (See *pets and children* for a discussion of the more common and relatively harmless dog tick.) Rickettsiae infect wild animals such as the jackrabbit, ground squirrel, and chipmunk. These animals, who are usually not ill themselves, serve as a reservoir of infection. Transmission of infection to a human usually requires several hours of feeding by the tick, thus making careful examination of children in tick-infested areas and prompt removal of ticks desirable procedures. Tick removal is best achieved by using a hot match head or a coating of Vaseline to cause the creature to loosen its bite. It then can be plucked with tweezers. Use gloves to prevent infection through contact with the crushed insect. Preventing tick atachment is best achieved by proper clothing, tick repellants, and, best of all, avoidance during the tick season of wooded areas known to be infested.

Spotted fever begins after an incubation period of from 1 to 8 days. The tick bite might be remembered, but there is rarely any remaining mark. Its characteristics are *fever, headache,* muscle aches and pains, and a rash which begins on ankles, wrists, and lower legs and then spreads to the rest of the skin. The illness can be quite serious, and in the days before antibiotics, many children died.


*Roseola* is a relatively common and not very serious disease of infancy and early childhood. It appears with a high temperature which lasts for 3 to 5 days. After the *fever* is gone a rash appears. The exact cause of roseola is not known, although it is believed to be a virus infection. At present, there are no preventive measures such as immunization, nor is there any specific treatment to cure the illness.

The incubation period (see *infections*) is thought to be 1½ weeks. The onset of illness is sudden, with a dramatic fever of 103° to 105°. This sudden rise in temperature is associated in some children with a febrile convulsion (see *febrile seizures*). In fact, roseola is one of the more common causes of febrile convulsions in children and infants. Many children act and look ill, but have very little else in the way of symptoms. Others seem remarkably well except for the fever. There is no ear or throat pain or *diarrhea* which might suggest a specific site of infection. On physical examination the physician finds nothing specific. The fever is one which is likely to keep up for a night or two. After the third or fourth day the temperature gradually dips to normal. The telltale rash then appears over the body. The rash consists of red, well-defined flat or raised spots. They first appear on the trunk (chest, abdomen, and back) and spread to the arms and neck with only slight extension to the face and legs. The rash usually fades within 24 hours.

There is no specific treatment. As with most virus infections, antibiotics are of no value. Give the child aspirin for the fever (see Part 1, Chapter 5: "Caring for the Sick Child at Home" for dosage schedule) and use alcohol rubs or lukewarm water baths as necessary. Your doctor may suggest using phenobarbital as a precaution to prevent convulsions due to the high fever. (Its usefulness for this purpose is not certain.) The medication does not treat the fever or cure the disease; at best it is a safeguard against the effects of the high fever on the child's nervous system. Many children voluntarily confine themselves to bed with roseola. If a child feels like being up and about in his or her room or quietly in the house, there is no reason to restrict him or her to bed. It is perfectly all right on a nice day (if the child feels up to it) to allow him to be out of doors in a shady area. Just how contagious roseola is remains unclear. It is, practically speaking, impossible to isolate him from other members of the household. By the time it is realized he is ill, the virus which we think causes roseola will have had ample opportunity to be scattered to others. Nonetheless, many siblings will escape without apparent illness. Roseola is like other infectious diseases: many people appear to have subclinical infections. Immunity appears to be lifelong, which is to say that second attacks are extremely unusual.

A fever of the magnitude seen in roseola should be discussed with a physician or nurse. Most times the doctor will suspect roseola once he hears the story. Of course, not until the rash appears is his diagnosis secure. If the child appears especially sick, the doctor might do some special studies like a *blood count,* urinalysis (see *urinary tract infections and defects*), and lumbar puncture (see *meningitis*). Because there is no test for roseola itself, he will take pains with the very ill-looking child to be sure that child has no other condition that might mimic roseola, such as urinary tract infection, a *bloodstream infection,* or an infection of the nervous system. After excluding all other possibilities, the doctor can be reasonably certain that he is dealing with a viral disease, possibly roseola. Only after the condition runs its entire course can the diagnosis be made with any certainty. The appearance of the rash following the drop of the temperature to normal clinches the case for roseola.

If your child has had contact with someone who within a short period of time—say several days—develops roseola, there is really nothing that you can do other than wait and see what happens to your own child. There is no prevention. Fortunately roseola, as best we can tell, is a condition from which complete recovery occurs.

See Part 1, Chapter 5: "Caring for the Sick Child at Home."

*Rubella:* see *German measles.*

*Saint Vitus's dance:* see *rheumatic fever.*

*Salmonellosis:* see *pets and children.*

*San Joaquin Valley fever:* see *coccidioidomycosis.*

*Scabies* is infestation by a mite whose technical name is *Sarcoptes scabiei.* The mite lives in the outer layers of the skin and excavates a burrow, traveling about 2 millimeters and laying from 2 to 3 eggs daily. Burrows look like straight or S-shaped ridges or dotted lines resembling black threads, each of which ends in a small blister containing the mite. Major sites of infestation are the webs between the fingers, the wrists, the hollows of the elbows, the points of the elbows, the nipples, umbilicus, genitalia, lower abdomen, and the cleft between the buttocks. Scabies is notorious for causing a severe itching which is most marked shortly after going to bed. Early in an infestation, the itching is limited to the burrows themselves. Later, the itching may be anywhere or all over the body. Redness and swelling, complicated by scratch marks, occur later and are caused by a type of allergy which develops to the mite. Secondary infection with bacteria is common.

The mite that causes scabies is acquired primarily through close personal contact. It can be picked up from clothing, towels, or linen. Scabies is treated with special creams or lotions applied to the entire body from the neck down, with special attention to the areas most suspect for infestation. The medicine is left on for 24 hours, applied again, and washed off 48 hours later. Household contacts should also be treated. Clothing should be thoroughly washed and linens and towels changed.

*Scarlet fever:* see *throat, sore.*

*Scoliosis:* see *spinal defects.*

*Scrapes:* see *cuts, scratches, abrasions, and scrapes.*

*Scratches:* see *cuts, scratches, abrasions, and scrapes.*

*Seasickness:* see *motion sickness.*

*Seborrheic dermatitis* is the name for the red and scaly rash of unknown cause that occurs primarily in areas of the skin with a large number of active oil (sebaceous) glands. It is most often found on the scalp (where it is known as dandruff), eyebrows, and eyelids, the skin behind the ears and adjacent to the nose, in moustaches, beards, and on the chest. The skin below the breasts, in the groin, between the buttocks, and around the umbilicus may also be affected.

There are a number of treatments available. Check with your doctor.

## Seizure disorders.

### TYPES OF SEIZURE

A seizure is an involuntary, automatic, not consciously willed movement, thought, or sensation stemming from spontaneous electrical activity of a part or parts of the brain. A convulsion is the most dramatic form of seizure and consists of often vigorous movement of the body parts, frequently with a loss of consciousness. Convulsions can be frightening to behold and often arouse the fear that the affected person will die, even though such a calamity is exceedingly rare and occurs only when complications have set in.

To understand what goes on in a seizure, it is necessary to understand some aspects of the functioning of the nervous system. The nervous system is composed of three major parts: the *brain, spinal cord*, and the *nerves*. The brain is the master control center for the various functions of the human body, including the movement of body parts, the perception of sensations, thinking, the feeling of emotions, and the control of involuntary functions like peristalsis (the contraction and relaxation of the intestine) and sweating. Any act, thought, or sensation that you can think of involves the brain in one way or another. Take, for example, a decision on your part to wiggle your left big toe. You consciously cause the activation of a certain specific center in the brain, just one of millions of all centers present, which controls the muscles that move this part of the body. The activation of this controlling center causes an impulse something like an electrical current to pass down through long nerve pathways from the brain into the spinal cord, out from the spinal cord through the nerves leading to the left lower extremity, and right to the specific muscles in the calf of the left leg which move the big toe.

Besides initiating movements, your brain also receives and records sensations. Electrical messages travel in the reverse direction from the distant parts of the body to the brain, providing various forms of information. For example, when you move that big toe, even with your eyes closed you are able to tell its position quite precisely. Your awareness of the toe's position depends upon the transmission of impulses from special sensing nerve endings in the toe through very specific nerve pathways leading from the toe to the spinal cord, and up through the spinal cord to the one microscopic spot in the brain responsible for the perception of the position of the toe. Sensations of hot and cold are transmitted along still different nerve tracts and recorded in other areas of the brain responsible for the perception of skin temperature of the toe. The same relationship between the brain and actions or perceptions holds true for any other acts or sensations you can think of—smell, taste, sight, fear, anger, joy, sounds, pleasure, nausea, memory, mood, and so on.

The brain may be thought of as an extraordinarily complex telephone switchboard, linked to millions of telephone receivers at varying distances from the central control station. The switchboard handles all messages, whether going to or coming from those telephones. The ringing of the telephone depends upon the activation of a linkage or hookup within the switchboard which sends a message through the wires, causing the bell in the telephone to ring. The transmission of a message from a caller depends upon the capacity of the switchboard to record the electric waves coming in from the telephone under use and to link them with the telephone number being called.

The fact that the brain is the regulating mechanism for bodily functions and perceptions is the key to our understanding of a seizure. A seizure results when the brain fires off on its own without a message from conscious will or external stimulation. An analogy in the telephone switchboard would be a defective central connection which causes a phone to ring even though no one is calling, or causes a switchboard light to flash, indicating that a certain phone is in use when in fact it is still on the hook. There is nothing "wrong" with either the phone or the light. The ringing and flashing are symptoms of central malfunctioning. In extreme cases, a short circuit involving all the circuits in the switchboard may occur, so that every phone rings at the same time or, conversely, every light on the switchboard lights up at the same time. Between the two extremes any number of phones or any number of lights may be activated.

This concept of spontaneous, involuntary brain activity, leading to involuntary movements or involuntary perceptions which have little or nothing to do with the real world, is essential to understanding seizures. The human brain is infinitely more complex than is the telephone switchboard, but it is subject to similar kinds of malfunction. The kinds of malfunction are as varied as the many activities of the brain itself. A spontaneous "lighting up" of message-sending centers in the brain can lead to such varying symptoms as a thought, a feeling, a smell, a sight, a twitch or spasm of a part of the body, and, at the very extreme, a complete loss of consciousness when the entire system fires off at once. Seizures may vary in intensity and quality from a violent shaking of the entire body with loss of consciousness at the one extreme to a barely observable momentary lapse of consciousness at the other. Even the odd feeling that one has been in a totally strange place before (*déjà vu*) can be caused by a brain malfunction. In all cases, seizures are symptoms of brain malfunction just as fever is a symptom of infection.

There are several distinctive types or patterns of seizures. The most dramatic is known as the *grand mal* convulsion. This is what most people think of as a seizure. The *grand mal* seizure is often heralded by a startled cry as the victim involuntarily exhales breath through his or her vocal cords. He then falls forcefully to the floor, unconscious. His eyes are "rolled up" into his head. He begins to foam at the mouth and his body is stiff and rigid. (The froth is aerated, unswallowed saliva.) In the process of falling, he often bruises himself and may bite his tongue as his jaws clamp down. The bleeding that results lends a reddish tinge to the frothy sputum issuing from his mouth and nose. Within seconds his entire body begins to shake violently and rhythmically. This lasts usually for several minutes. His breathing is interfered with, and the resulting lack of oxygen causes his skin to turn blue. He usually urinates involuntarily because of the tense contraction of the abdominal muscles pressing on his bladder. Finally, after tense minutes which seem like hours, he relaxes in exhaustion and his color gradually returns to normal as regular breathing resumes. He lapses into a deep, hours-long sleep. Occasionally the sleep will be much shorter, and the patient will complain of a splitting headache which may last for several hours. The *grand mal* seizure does not always fit into this classic mold and may consist only of unconsciousness and convulsive body shaking without foaming at the mouth or stiffening out. Even though incomplete, we still call this abbreviated form either a *grand mal* or a *generalized seizure*. Most of the seizures of young children that occur with fever (febrile seizures) are of the *grand mal* or generalized variety. How to care for a child during a *grand mal* seizure is discussed in **febrile seizures.**

Another form of seizure known as *petit mal* is best described as a staring, blank, or absent spell. *Petit mal* attacks afflict mainly young children and the peak incidence occurs during the early school years. Unless you are watching carefully, you may never notice that the child is having one. If the child is talking there is a temporary and unexpected interruption in his flow of speech. He stares blankly and vacantly. Just for an instant there may be some minor pursing movements of his lips and tongue and a very slight jerking of his extremities and opening out of the palms. He may drop whatever he was holding. If he experiences many of these brief lapses over the course of a day in school, he may miss a good bit of what is happening and will appear inattentive or distracted to his teacher. With many children *petit mal* is brought to medical attention because of an alert teacher who notices that the child is not paying attention.

Yet another form of seizure is the *psychomotor attack*. This seizure involves the discharge of brain centers located in the *temporal lobe* of the brain. This part of the brain is responsible for the storage of memories and feelings and for the perception of smells. In a psychomotor seizure, the patient commonly experiences an unusual feeling or sensation, such as an unpleasant burning odor. He is prone to become exceedingly anxious and confused and may have a feeling that something terrible is about to happen to him. He may remember an event out of the past (this specific remembrance tends to be constant, so that this same recollection occurs with each seizure) or he may have a peculiar distant feeling that he has never been in a certain place, one which is obviously familiar to him, or conversely, that he has been sometime in the past in a place which he knows he has never visited. During these spells he involuntarily interrupts whatever activity he was performing, just as does the child with *petit mal* seizures. To observers he appears to lose contact with the world around him. He may make certain common associated movements like smacking his lips, turning his head to one side, stooping down, jerking his arms and legs, and releasing objects from his hands. Psychomotor seizures rarely last longer than one minute.

A less common form of seizure is known as a *Jacksonian convulsion* (named after the British neurologist of the nineteenth century who first described this seizure pattern). A Jacksonian convulsion consists of a successive twitching of body parts which progressess from a local to a more general area, or a successive pattern of perceived sensations. A characteristic Jacksonian seizure begins with quivering of the fingers of one hand, then spreads to the arm and shoulder of the same extremity and may either terminate in a generalized *grand mal* seizure or may abort at this stage, remaining localized to the extremity.

Another less common form of seizure is the *akinetic spell*, in which the patient suddenly loses all body tone and consciousness and falls to the floor, but recovers in a matter of seconds. A worrisome kind of seizure that afflicts young infants is the *Salaam* or *"jackknife"* seizure, in which the baby experiences simultaneous spasms of all the muscles of the body, causing a bending of the thigh and a flexing of the trunk so that the head and the knees tend to come together like a jackknife. This condition is of great concern because it is often (though not always) associated with serious diseases of the brain which can lead to permanent brain damage.

Sometimes a seizure is preceded by what is called an *aura*, a kind of warning or clue which the patient comes to recognize as preceding a spell. The aura itself is a symptom of spontaneous automatic activity of the brain centers and is part of the seizure. For example, a patient suffering from *grand mal* seizures may know that a seizure is coming because he perceives flashing lights, hears a peculiar sound, smells an unpleasant odor, or feels a tingling sensation in his foot. The aura is an important clue to the place of origin of the seizures in the brain.

There are symptoms that resemble seizures but that are really quite distinct from them. Faints, falls, and hysterical attacks fall into this category. (See *drowsiness, delirium, and lethargy* and *dizziness.*) So do breath-holding spells in young children. In this latter condition, the child, usually after crying or screaming, holds his breath, turns a dusky color, and may even become limp and sleepy. This condition is not the result of automatic or spontaneous discharging of the brain centers and is therefore not a seizure. (Confusing the issue is the fact that some children will have an actual fit at the end of a breath-holding spell because of the stress on the brain of a lowered supply of oxygen.)

CAUSES

There are many different causes of seizures. Some causes are external to the brain and act upon it, while other causes are internal derangements of the brain. The most common example of an external cause in children is fever, usually a high and rapidly rising fever. Exactly how fever causes the brain to discharge automatically is not well understood. Much may depend on the "susceptibility" of the child. Most children who react this way to fever are unusually sensitive in some as yet unknown way and do so only at a young age, commonly between 1 and 3 years (see *febrile seizures*). Others may be latent epileptics for whom fever acts as a trigger. Another external cause of seizures is irritation of the brain due to infection of the central nervous system such as occurs in meningitis or encephalitis (see *meningitis*). The inflammation due to infection irritates the brain directly or interferes with its blood supply. Because infection of the central nervous system is a serious disorder, producing both seizures and high fever (among other symptoms), the possibility of infection crosses the mind of the physician whenever he hears of a young child having seizures and fever together. The diagnostic procedure that identifies the presence of infection in the central nervous system is the lumbar puncture (see *meningitis*). We often (but not always) perform this procedure when a seizure with fever occurs for the first time in a child, in order to be sure that a possible infection of the nervous system is not overlooked.

Another external cause of convulsion is a disorder of kidney function known as *acute glomerulonephritis* (see *nephritis*) which can cause a rise in blood pressure and irritation of the brain leading to a convulsion. Sometimes the convulsion is the earliest sign of this disorder. Convulsions may result from the effects on the brain of alterations in the chemical components of the blood, specifically the concentrations of sugar (see *hypoglycemia*), calcium, and magnesium. There are various disorders that depress the amount of these chemical constituents in the blood.

A lamentably common and totally preventable cause of seizures in children is poisoning from lead found in lead paints or plaster formerly used in the interior of houses (see **lead poisoning**). The lead localizes in bone and in nervous tissue. The accumulation of lead in the brain leads to swelling and irritation of controlling centers, nausea, vomiting, stupor, and convulsions. Permanent brain damage may result despite treatment. Another common and preventable cause of convulsions, in adults, is the imbibing of alcohol in excess. In large amounts this widely available chemical is toxic and can result in convulsions. The chronic alcoholic withdrawing from its use is also subject to seizures.

Conditions which interfere with the flow of the blood to the brain can cause seizures. Examples are clots in the blood vessels supplying the brain, hemorrhages into the brain through weakened blood vessels, deprivation of blood through interference with the output from the heart, and narrowing of the arteries of the brain with decreased blood flow. A sudden blow to the head can so shake up the brain that spontaneous activity results and a seizure occurs. All of the above are examples of causes of seizures that are external to the brain itself.

Seizures may also be caused by a derangement in the structure of the brain that is more or less permanent. Such seizures tend to recur. The brain may have been damaged by a severe head injury, for example, a skull fracture cutting into the substance of the brain and resulting in a permanent scar which becomes a focus of electrical activity. (See **head injuries.**) Scars may result from complications in delivery, such as bruising or interference with the supply of oxygen to the brain at birth. Permanent damage may be caused by infection such as meningitis. Even though the actual infection is over, the scarring from the inflammation remains, much as a scar remains following a skin cut or infection. In other patients with recurrent seizures, no obvious explanation for brain dysfunction can be found. We label our ignorance with the term "idiopathic" and speak of idiopathic epilepsy. Some of these patients have relatives who have similar problems, suggesting that heredity may be a factor.

### DIAGNOSIS

The term *epilepsy* is reserved for those patients who have some underlying disorder of the brain, either known or unknown, which makes them prone to recurrent seizures of any type or types. (Often an epileptic person has more than one kind of seizure.) We would exclude from the diagnosis of epilepsy patients who had a seizure in response to an acute external cause, such as glomerulonephritis, low blood sugar, or poisoning from lead, or who had a simple febrile seizure. However, an external cause of seizures like lead poisoning can cause permanent brain damage and therefore epilepsy. The distinctions are not as clear as would first appear.

Some patients with epilepsy are peculiarly sensitive to certain environmental "triggers." Fatigue, menstrual periods, blinking light (such as from a defective television set), touch, special smells, a sudden noise, or specific sounds (like organ music) may precipitate a convulsion. Fever itself can trigger a convulsion in epileptic children. Identifying these factors is important in treatment.

Any child who has had a seizure of any type should be evaluated by a physician. The job of the physician is to determine the underlying cause of the seizure, so that treatment may be planned most effectively. Sometimes a *neurologist* will be consulted. A neurologist is a physician with special training in disorders of the nervous system. The evaluation has several parts. The doctor will be interested in an accurate description of what actually happened and under what circumstances. This description should allow him to classify the seizure into one of the major types already described. He will also be interested in the child's past history and the family's history because they may enable him to pinpoint the cause. Does the child come from a neighborhood where lead paint is still present in homes? Did the child have a high fever at the time? Had he gone for a long time without eating? (See *hypoglycemia.*) Has he ever suffered from any blows to the head? Next, the physician will do a careful physical examination, paying special attention to neurological functioning. In performing the neurological examination, the doctor will be much more thorough than he would be for a child coming for a routine examination. He checks the reflexes at the knees, ankles, elbows, and wrists and strokes the outer edges of the soles of the feet, watching the response of the toes. He observes the child climb, run, and walk. He checks coordination by having the child rapidly open and close his hands or tap rhythmically on the tabletop, having him reach and point, and seeing if he can keep his balance while he stands at attention with his eyes closed. He tests the child's vision, how well he moves his eyes and tongue in all directions, and the symmetry of his facial movements while smiling. The doctor checks the child's ability to appreciate the differences between sharp and dull and hot and cold sensations, and special attention is paid to his psychological and intellectual development. All of these questions and tests are important because they give information about the functioning of the brain. Abnormalities in these tests of function suggest disorders of specific areas of the brain which may explain the child's seizures.

In addition to history and physical examination, the doctor may order laboratory studies such as the electroencephalogram (EEG) and the skull X-ray. The *electroencephalogram* is a recording of the electrical activity of the brain as measured by electrodes glued onto the scalp. Just as the electrocardiogram measures the electrical activity of the heart, so the electroencephalogram measures the electrical output of the brain. Normal brain activity is accompanied by normal electrical patterns. Many patients with seizure problems will show abnormal electrical patterns called discharges. The recordings of these discharges by the EEG add evidence to the suspicion that a seizure actually occurred, if this is in doubt. It gives information about the origin of the electrical discharge within the brain, and may even give a clue as to its cause. In an epileptic patient with an abnormal brain-wave scan, the electroencephalogram gives information about the effectiveness of the drug being used to control seizures. Commonly, the electroencephalogram shows improvement as an anticonvulsant drug takes hold so that the EEG can be used to monitor the effectiveness of medication. In a patient who is having frequent seizures, one following the other, the electroencephalogram can be performed at the time a new drug is being given intravenously to see precisely what effects it has on the discharges.

The EEG is an imperfect instrument. Many patients who have seizures have normal electroencephalograms. This apparent contradiction does not mean that no seizure problem exists but rather that the electroencephalogram as we perform it is not sensitive enough to detect the abnormality, or that discharge is intermittent and not present when the test is being performed. Conversely, some individuals who have never had recognized seizures have mildly abnormal EEGs. Even with these limitations, the electroencephalogram has proved to be an invaluable tool in gaining evidence about the function of the brain.

The electroencephalogram, for all its seeming complexity, is perfectly painless. Small wire electrodes or terminals are attached to the skin of the head at various points and held in place with a paste. The patient usually lies down. He is often asked to go through certain maneuvers (if old enough to cooperate), such as rapid deep breathing or watching a flickering light. Occasionally he is given a medicine to make him sleepy, because some seizure discharges are brought on by the sleeping state. Babies may require sedation simply to keep them still. Horror movies to the contrary, no electrical stimulation of the patient occurs during the brain-wave recording.

The other common diagnostic test is the *skull X-ray*. The skull is the bony container of the brain. Normally the brain is not visible on X-ray. Certain diseases of the brain cause telltale calcium deposits which may show up on X-ray. Other brain abnormalities cause changes in the skull which are detectable on an X-ray and yield indirect information about the brain itself. While an abnormal X-ray may give important clues about causes of the seizure disorder, a normal X-ray does not exclude disease of the brain. Nor does it mean the patient does not have epilepsy. A normal X-ray merely means that whatever the underlying disorder it has not produced any changes in the skull or calcification of the brain.

Besides the basic studies of the skull X-ray and the electroencephalogram, there are several other tests which are done selectively. A *brain scan* is a study of the brain of a person who has had a small quantity of radioactive material injected intravenously. The radioactive material concentrates temporarily in the brain and shows up on the X-ray film, giving an outline of the brain proper. Another test uses sound waves and is known as a *sonar scan* or *echo encephalogram*. It works on the principle of radar. The sound waves are reflected from the brain back to the sensing equipment, and information about the architecture of the brain is thus obtained. A *cerebral* (named from the part of the brain known as the cerebrum) *angiogram* (blood vessel study) is an X-ray technique whereby the arteries carrying blood to and from the brain are made visible by the injection of a dye into the artery at the base of the neck. The dye, unlike blood, is dense enough to show up on X-ray film and outlines the arteries. Abnormalities in the shape or distribution of the blood vessels suggest an abnormality of the brain or blood vessels. The *pneumoencephalogram* is a skull X-ray taken after air has been allowed to pass up into the cavities within and around the brain. This study is done by performing a lumbar puncture, removing a quantity of spinal fluid and introducing an equal volume of air which is then allowed to percolate upward, filling the brain cavities and surrounding the outer contour. An X-ray shows the distribution of the air and gives important clues as to the architecture of the brain. All of these special examinations are available but are used in only a minority of patients with seizures. Other tests are ordered according to the nature of the problem. When an underlying chemical disorder like low blood sugar is felt to be precipitating seizures, chemical analysis of the blood would be in order. If a kidney disorder were suspect, analysis of the urine would be indicated.

### TREATMENT

The immediate care of convulsions is described in Part 2, Chapter 9: "First Aid." An important point to remember is that children do come out of convulsions by themselves in almost every case. If you leave them alone, they will improve. With other kinds of seizures like *petit mal* or psychomotor, there is little that has to be done in the way of acute emergency care other than keeping the patient from injuring himself. These episodes are short-lived and most patients recover completely and promptly. For the prevention of seizures due to high fever, see Part 1, Chapter 5: "Caring for the Sick Child at Home."

The treatment of seizure disorders has improved remarkably in the past generation. The majority of patients can be helped to the point of abolishing seizures altogether. An important minority can have their seizures reduced, although not completely eliminated, while a much smaller minority are resistant to treatment and can be helped only minimally. Treatment depends first and foremost on an accurate diagnosis. Seizures are symptoms only. They are not the diseases, nor do they provide a diagnosis. The job of the physician is to determine what is causing the seizure and then to treat the cause if at all possible. If, for example, an infection of the central nervous system is the underlying cause, then appropriate treatment of the infection is necessary. Similarly, if the seizures were precipitated by glomerulonephritis, then treatment of the underlying kidney disorder is the answer. If a chemical disorder of the blood, such as low calcium or low sugar is the culprit, then treating these conditions should relieve the symptoms. For the occasional patient with a well localized scar whose firing off is not effectively treated with drugs, surgical removal of the scar will help. If there is a treatable cause of the spell, we try to remove the cause whenever possible.

If the cause of the seizures cannot be treated, the next step is to use medications that suppress the activity of the abnormal discharges in the brain to the point where they are unable to fire off. Recall that these discharges can usually be detected by the electroencephalogram even when the patient is not having an actual seizure. It is as though the brain can tolerate a certain amount of discharge but that anything in excess will trigger off a spell. One analogy is a fuse, which permits a certain quantity of electrical current to pass through but will break with excess current. The medications or drugs known as *anticonvulsants* have the capacity of widening the gap between seizure activity of the brain and actual fits, providing a buffer zone or a margin of safety. Phenobarbital (Luminal) and diphenylhydantoin (Dilantin) are common anticonvulsants. They achieve their effect by dampening the spontaneous activity in the brain and by increasing the resistance of other parts of the brain to the spread of that abnormal discharge. They act as insulators. To prevent seizures these medications must be taken on a regular basis, at least once daily. They cannot be forgotten or stopped abruptly because their sudden withdrawal may precipitate seizures, often many in succession. Withdrawal of an anticonvulsant requires close medical supervision and is usually accomplished gradually over several months. The dose of the medicine must be regulated carefully in order to achieve the suppression of seizures without causing symptoms of excess medication. Occasionally changes of medication must be made, and often combinations of drugs will be more effective than a single drug alone. Common side effects of many anticonvulsants, usually related to dose, are sleepiness, dizziness, loss of coordination, and nausea. Some anticonvulsants cause allergic reaction (see *drug reactions, allergic*) and others suppress the formation of various blood elements, necessitating periodic blood counts to detect early effects. Anticonvulsants do not "do anything" to the brain in a harmful sense. Although the patient must depend on these drugs, he is not addicted in the way a heroin addict is dependent on a steady source of heroin. The child taking phenobarbital is in no sense an "addict."

As a general rule, most children with seizures tend to improve as they grow older and a good percentage of them can come completely off anticonvulsants at some point. However, many children, while improving with age, still require daily anticonvulsants for life to prevent convulsions. While at the outset of treatment the physician can make an educated guess about who will improve and who will be permanently dependent on drugs, in point of fact only time will give a complete answer. Freedom from seizures for 2 or more years, a normal neurological examination and electroencephalogram favor the termination of drug therapy.

In cases where it is clear that there is a specific trigger for the seizures, it is obviously desirable to avoid that trigger if possible. If seizures in a patient are brought on by the sound of organ music, the child should avoid organ music. Persons whose seizures are brought on by flickering lights should not watch television sets that are not functioning properly. If the seizures are associated with menstrual periods, the patient should be especially careful at this time of the month, and might be advised to take medication to prevent retention of fluid and salt, implicated in triggering convulsions with the menses. General factors associated with increased numbers of seizures, such as fatigue or inactivity, should be avoided. Other than taking the above precautions, parents should encourage a child with epilepsy to lead as active a life as possible. If emotional factors are playing a major role in triggering seizures, psychotherapeutic help should be sought.

Seizures can occur in highly intelligent individuals, in average individuals, or in intellectually subnormal individuals. There is no special correlation between seizures and intelligence, except in the extreme case when seizures and retardation are associated because of widespread brain damage. There is no evidence that having seizures damages the brain unless the seizures are prolonged. This is an important point, because in some complicated and severe seizure disorders, the seizures cannot be completely controlled (with presently available anticonvulsants), without at the same time sedating the child to the point of inactivity. Accordingly, less than perfect seizure control is accepted as a compromise for an alert and responsive child.

Parents frequently and understandably are concerned about the effect of seizures on mental and emotional behavior. The relationship between seizures and behavior varies from child to child. Much depends upon the cause of the seizure disorder. If they are but one part of a general pattern of impaired emotional and intellectual function, such as occurs in some children with extensive brain damage, controlling the seizures will not correct all of the patient's problems. If the seizures are an isolated symptom, controlling the seizures will remove an upsetting and frightening symptom from the child's experience and may thereby improve his overall behavior and lessen the anxiety of those who care for him.

It is a common reaction of the parents of children with seizures to blame themselves or their child for what has happened. Because of their suppressed intense feelings of guilt and anger ("Why did it have to happen to me?"), they may subconsciously alter the ways in which they deal with their children by being overprotective, overly distant, or a mixture of both extremes. Because these problems are so common, we suggest that parents raise them with their physician or nurse. Talking these feelings through, with a physician, social worker, psychologist, or psychiatrist can give the parents the insight into their feelings necessary to modify their behavior in the best interests of the child. (See Part 1, Chapter 4: "Complaints with an Emotional Element"; *developmental disabilities*; and *handicapped child*.)

If the child is epileptic and of normal intelligence, which is usually the case, there is no reason why he should not attend regular school. We do suggest that the school authorities be informed of the child's problem so that they will know what to do should a seizure occur at school. It is helpful if the child's physician communicates directly with the school principal and the teacher. In this day and age, most teachers have an enlightened attitude toward seizures and do not recoil in horror as did people in the past. It is important to inform the teacher and to find out how much he or she already knows about epilepsy and its care. Many teachers with epileptic children in their classrooms will use a seizure as an opportunity to help the other children of the class adopt a sympathetic point of view toward the afflicted child. The rest of the school personnel must also know about seizures because of their responsibility to take precautions so that a seizure does not occur when the child is in a potentially dangerous situation. For example, children with convulsions should be watched especially carefully when they are in the swimming pool or when they are doing gymnastics suspended at a height. When the seizure problem is an active one and seizures are occurring with relative frequency, it is probably better to avoid these hazardous situations. The same applies to bicycle riding and climbing trees. Any policy on these matters is subject to constant review as the child matures and as the pattern of seizures changes. The general rule is to allow the child to lead as normal a life as possible.

The era when epileptics were excluded from almost all respectable jobs is fast coming to an end, although there are pockets of resistance here and there. One of the purposes of a discussion of epilepsy such as this one is to educate the general public to a position of greater acceptance and understanding. Contrary to popular belief, epileptics do not have more accidents or more days lost from work. Most states have specific rules for driving. These have become more liberal. The trend has been to permit driving if seizures are under control.

The question of hereditary factors in epilepsy comes up in two ways. First, if a couple has had one epileptic child, are they more likely to have another epileptic child, and should this therefore influence their decision about having more children? Second, should an epileptic marry and have children of his own? There are no simple, clear-cut answers to these questions and each case must be evaluated individually. At large medical centers there are now specialists in human genetics who are able to give families a fairly good idea of the risks involved in having a second child with epilepsy. In the usual case of idiopathic epilepsy, although the risk of having a second epileptic child is often somewhat increased, it is still not of such a magnitude as to argue against having more children. However, we must emphasize again that this is a very individual question. It depends on the child, his parents, and other factors, and each case demands separate consideration. Regarding marriage and children for an epileptic, here again much depends upon the specific kind of epilepsy. Professional help should be sought (see *genetics*). As a general rule, epileptics can marry without a significantly increased chance of producing an epileptic child.

We encourage parents who wish additional information about epilepsy to contact the Epilepsy Foundation of America, 1828 L Street, N.W., Washington, D.C. 20005. This organization has chapters that meet on a regular basis in many cities throughout the country. The group offers an educational program and an opportunity for the parents of epileptic children to meet together to share ideas and problems. The foundation and its chapters also conduct public education campaigns to influence legislation and improve knowledge and attitudes about epilepsy and, with the social worker at your medical center, can give information about sources of financial help, special summer camps, and a host of other practical questions arising around the care of the epileptic child.

See *febrile seizures, developmental disabilities, handicapped child.*

**Sepsis:** see *bloodstream infection.*

**Septic hip:** see *hip pain.*

*Shingles:* see *chicken pox.*

**Shock** is the clinical condition associated with falling blood pressure and the body's attempt to reverse it. Collapse of the blood pressure has many causes. Prominent among these are rapid blood loss through hemorrhaging from trauma, dehydration (see *diarrhea*), and overwhelming infection (see *bloodstream infection*). Common symptoms of shock are: generalized weakness; cold, pale, moist skin, often with perspiration on the forehead and above the lips, and the palms of the hands which are clammy and wet; nausea, sometimes *vomiting;* thirst; dull, vacant eyes; irregular, shallow breathing; and weak but rapid pulse.

Medical treatment is directed both to the shock and to its underlying cause. The falling blood pressure is treated by restoring blood volume through transfusions of blood, plasma, and/or salt solutions.

First aid consists of keeping the patient horizontal (lying down), elevating the legs to about 30 degrees so that gravity draws blood from the legs to be used preferentially to supply vital organs like the brain and kidneys, and keeping the patient warm (covered only enough to prevent loss of body heat).

For accidents see Part 2, Chapter 9: "First Aid."

*Shortness:* see *height problems.*

*Sickle-cell anemia:* see *anemia.*

**Sinusitis.** The *sinuses* are bony cavities in the head and face which connect with the nose through small openings. Sinuses are located in the cheekbone (*maxillary*), in the forehead above the eyes (*frontal*), and behind the nose and on the nasal side of the eye sockets (*ethmoid* and *sphenoid*). In infancy and early childhood only the ethmoid and maxillary sinuses are developed. The others appear later. The sinuses can be seen on an X-ray.

The sinuses have the same kind of *epithelial lining* (mucosa) as the nose. Inflammations of the nasal mucosa, whether caused by *infections* or *allergy,* invariably involve the mucosa of the sinuses with similar responses of swelling and increased secretions. When this inflammation is sufficient to cause symptoms, it is known as *sinusitis.* Swelling of the openings between the sinuses and nose may block these passages, allowing secretions or pus to accumulate within the sinuses instead of draining out into the nose. Sinusitis is recognized on an X-ray as clouding of these otherwise air-filled cavities.

Sinusitis due to infection usually comes on after a cold (see *colds*). Secretions from the sinuses lead to blockage of the nasal passageways and *cough,* due to postnasal drip. The cough may be severe, followed by gagging and even *vomiting.* It tends to be worse at night when the child is not alert enough to swallow the mucus. The child's sleep may be disturbed, leading to irritability during the daytime. Many infants nurse poorly and sometimes cough and choke during feeding. The older child may complain of pain over an infected sinus, an "ache back of the eye," or pain in a tooth. Infections of the ethmoid sinuses cause swelling of the skin around the eye and nose. The child who seems to have "one cold after another" or a "continuous cold" may be suffering from a chronic sinus infection which flares up from time to time. (See *resistance and frequent colds.*) The flare-ups may be triggered by chilling, swimming, fatigue, weather changes, or contact with *allergens* (substances provoking an allergic response).

After shrinking the nasal lining with special medications called *vasoconstrictors*, the doctor can usually see the pus issuing through the opening of the infected sinus. The vasoconstrictor relieves the blockage in the opening, allowing the pus to drain from the sinus into the nose from which the secretions can be suctioned. Between office treatments parents can instill nose drops 3 times a day at home to promote further drainage. The child should lie on his or her back with his or her neck fully extended over the edge of a bed, table, or parent's knees. Five drops are instilled into each nostril. Two or 3 minutes later the nostrils are suctioned gently with a nasal aspirator. Then, 3 more drops are instilled into each nostril. Finally, the child is turned face down to allow the excess drops to run out. (See Part 1, Chapter 5: "Caring for the Sick Child at Home.") Vasoconstrictors can also be taken internally. Sometimes antibiotics are needed to treat the infection. When sinusitis is allergic in origin (see *allergy, hay fever*), treatment is directed to the underlying allergy. In rare cases, surgery to drain infected sinuses is required.

In children prone to this condition, the use of nose drops as described above during the first days of an upper respiratory infection may reduce the risk of sinusitis.

*Skin trouble:* see *acne; eczema; rash.*

*Sleepiness, excess:* see *drowsiness, delirium, and lethargy.*

*Slipped epiphysis:* see *hip pain.*

*Smallpox:* see *immunization.*

*Smoking.* As long ago as 1964 the Surgeon General's report on smoking and health stated that cigarette smoking is "a health hazard of sufficient importance to warrant appropriate remedial action." The report concluded that cigarette smoking is a cause of lung cancer, is associated with heart disease, is the most important cause of chronic bronchitis, and substantially increases the risk of premature death. Additional studies have demonstrated even stronger relationships between cigarette smoking and emphysema, other respiratory diseases, and heart disease.

Since then a great deal of effort has been made by the major health agencies (heart, cancer, and lung associations) and the medical and dental professions as well as other interested groups to persuade cigarette smokers to stop smoking and to prevent children from starting. Some adults seem to have taken the information to heart. Approximately 2 million adults have kicked the habit each year, and there are now about 29 million ex-smokers. Men seem to be more inclined to give up smoking than women. In 1959, 59 percent smoked; in 1965, 51.8 percent smoked; in 1970, only 42 percent smoked. It is a slightly different story for women. In 1959, 28 percent smoked; in 1965, 34 percent smoked; and in 1970, 31.5 percent smoked. Among teen-agers, however, studies show an increase in smoking at every age level from 12 to 18. Between 1968 and 1970, for example, the percentage of boys smoking rose from 14.7 percent to 18.5 percent, and girls from 8.3 percent to 11.8 percent. Between 1970 and 1972, smoking among teen-age boys decreased only slightly, and among girls it increased again.

What influences children to take up smoking? The smoking habits of their peers, parents, and older brothers and sisters seem important. Of boys and girls who are heavy smokers, studies show that 69 to 80 percent of friends smoke, whereas for nonsmokers, only 13 to 17 percent of friends smoke. Although the smoking rate of children whose older brothers or sisters smoke is higher than for those who have nonsmoking siblings, it is not as high as for those who have friends who smoke. Parents' smoking habits have a lesser but still important influence. A girl is more likely to smoke if her mother is a smoker than if her father smokes. The lowest level of smoking, 4.2 percent, was found among teen-agers in households where both parents were present, where neither parent smoked, and where there were older siblings, none of whom smoked.

Have drugs in any way replaced the cigarette habit? Surprisingly not. In fact, the most important long-term effect of marijuana use among teen-agers may be their switching to cigarettes and not, as many feared, to harder drugs. Many of the general issues concerning drugs would also seem to apply to cigarettes. (See *drug problem.*)

The persistence of smoking in the face of the well-publicized warnings against its use is a remarkable comment on how indifferent the public is to health matters. What can we do to help children stop smoking or to prevent them from taking up the habit? If we are truly concerned about the harmful effects of smoking, then as a minimum we must set an example by kicking the habit ourselves. We must emphasize to young children the harmful effects of smoking. The fact is that every time we smoke a cigarette we damage our bodies, especially the respiratory system. For each cigarette smoked, the cleaning mechanism of the lungs stops working for 6 to 8 minutes. Thus, germs, dirt, dust, and other foreign particles can linger in the lungs rather than being cleaned out. Smokers have more sick days, longer hospital stays, and more time away from work than nonsmokers. Children should also be made aware of the effects of cigarette smoking on physical performance. Young persons who smoke are more likely to notice that they do not have quite the endurance in running, swimming, and other strenuous exercise they once had. Breathing tests show a decreased ability to exhale.

A discussion of smoking with children approaching *adolescence* should be a part of all school- as well as home-health education programs. It is a regular part of the health care given at The Children's Hospital Medical Center. We look for the child's feelings on questions such as the following: What do you know about the effects of smoking? What are the feelings that lead young people to smoke? What are alternative ways of dealing with these feelings? We also inquire about the parents' smoking habits and point out that if they are truly concerned about their children smoking, a critically important step is to stop themselves.

In recent years nonsmokers have begun to demand their rights. Their demands are supported by recent studies which show that other people's smoke does indeed affect the nonsmoker. Nonsmoking areas are becoming increasingly available in trains, planes, restaurants, and other public areas. There are some other gains in the antismoking movement, such as warnings on cigarette packages and advertisements and the banning of cigarette commercials on TV. However, these must be regarded as token steps only. The sad fact is that our society has not really made a commitment to deal with this problem.

*Snake bites:* see *bites, snake.*

*Sneezing:* see *allergy; colds; hay fever.*

*Specific learning disabilities:* see *learning disabilities.*

*Speech problems:* see *hearing and speech.*

*Spider bite:* see *bites, insect.*

*Spina bifida:* see *spinal defects.*

*Spinal defects.* The *spinal column* can be thought of as a stack of bony rings bound together with ligaments and so fitted that the structure can bend forward or backward and to both sides. The *spinal cord* runs through the tube or canal formed by the column of stacked rings and attaches to the brain in the base of the skull. The cord is a kind of biological cable of nerve cells and long nerve fibers connecting the control centers of the brain to a network of nerves that spreads out all over the body. Messages in the form of coded electrical impulses travel along this cable in both directions. The brain's messages stimulate movement in parts of the body. The body's messages report to the brain on sensations in the skin, muscles, and bones. The brain's interpretations of these messages in terms of temperature, taste, pain, and so on stimulate further muscular and nervous activity. At every level, from the neck to the lower back, nerves branch out from the cord through the spaces between the bony rings, which we call *vertebrae.* (A single ring is a *vertebra.*) The cord and the brain float in the *cerebrospinal fluid*, which in turn is contained in the membranous sac known as the *meninges* (see **meningitis**). The fluid and sac together compose a shock-absorber to cushion the delicate brain and spinal cord.

### SPINA BIFIDA

For reasons we do not understand, one or more of the vertabrae may fail, early in gestation, to fuse properly. The ring does not close entirely. This defect, known as *spina bifida* (literally, two-part spine), results in an opening in the vertebral structure and may involve from 1 to 5 or 6 vertebral units. Its significance will depend on whether there is an associated defect of the spinal cord and nerves. In the most common type of this condition, there is not. The spina bifida causes no symptom and may go undetected or be discovered only by chance on an X-ray film taken for some other purpose. There may be a small dimple in the skin of the lower back at the site of the defect. When there is no presenting symptom, the condition is called *spina bifida occulta*, the name signifying that it is hidden and of no significance.

In the more serious cases of spina bifida, there is an associated defect of the overlying skin, and the meninges protrude quite visibly. The spinal fluid can be seen through the transparent sac. If no segment of spinal cord or nerves is in the protruding sac, the condition is known as *meningocele*; when there is a protrusion of cord and nerves, the condition is *myelomeningocele*. The former is readily operable, but the latter, which occurs in approximately 1 birth in 1000, is very serious. It is often associated with **hydrocephalus.** The protruding cord and nerves are defective, and the parts of the body that are under the control of the defective nerves (legs and bladder and rectal sphincter) will not function properly. There are all degrees of impairment, from mild disability to complete interference with function. Specialized neurosurgery and programs of rehabilitation have been the standard procedure, using the skills of the urologist, orthopedist, neurosurgeon, physical therapist, and psychologist. Children with this severe condition require long-term care, and frequently many surgical procedures are required. The social cost of this care is enormous and the results are spotty. The value of surgical intervention versus allowing severely affected children to die soon after birth, as is the rule without treatment, is currently the subject of research and discussion.

As is true of many other birth defects, we do not yet know the cause of spina bifida, nor have we any means of prevention. The appearance of spina bifida in some families would seem to suggest a genetic influence, but the inference does not appear to hold for other families. Prenatal detection of spina bifida with a view toward therapeutic abortion, through analysis of the amniotic fluid, appears to be reliable and is recommended for pregnancies in families with a previous child with the disorder. A test of the mother's blood is also being developed.

### SCOLIOSIS

Scoliosis is a lateral curvature of the spine which occurs mainly in children. As one looks at the normal back from behind, the spine is straight. In scoliosis, the spine is S-shaped.

The physical examinations performed by your doctor or nurse will usually detect the early signs of this condition. Parents don't usually notice the curve itself. The tip-off is an unusual prominence of one of the shoulder blades or a tilt of the shoulder. If you suspect this problem, be sure to contact your doctor.

The cause of curvature of the spine is unknown in most instances. Children with muscle disorders are prone to scoliosis because of the unequal forces applied to the spine. When *poliomyelitis* was a widespread problem, paralysis or weakness of the chest or abdominal muscles was often complicated by spinal curvature. Today these muscle conditions are much less common.

For some reason, scoliosis occurs most frequently in girls, and usually begins to develop just prior to puberty. There is a tendency for the problem to run in families. While it might be reasonable to assume that spinal curvature could result from poor posture, this does not appear to be the case. The actual cause of this condition remains a mystery. If scoliosis is detected in some member of a family, it is important that all other brothers and sisters be examined carefully for evidence of a curve.

When scoliosis is recognized, your doctor will want the opinion of an orthopedist, a bone and joint specialist. The treatment of scoliosis is a highly individual matter. Periodic examinations will show whether the condition is tending to worsen, improve, or stay the same. When growth of the spine stops after puberty, the spinal curvature will usually be arrested and little further change will occur. Children with mild curves will require no treatment other than special exercises and periodic observation. More severe curves will require specific therapy. If the more severe curves are not corrected, the children will have significant cosmetic problems and may develop painful arthritis of the spine and misshapen chests which can, in the most extreme cases, interfere with the normal functioning of the heart and lungs. (This latter complication is fortunately quite rare and preventable if treatment is begun early.) Treatment of the more severe forms of scoliosis involves exercises, special braces to straighten out the curved spine, and, in the severest cases, surgery to realign the spine. Modern braces allow the child to be up and around, performing the normal functions while using the brace.

See **birth defects, severe.**

**Splinters.** If splinters are just under the surface of the skin, it is perfectly safe to try to remove them yourself. Be sure to use clean instruments. Tweezers and/or a sewing needle that have been soaked in a 70 percent alcohol solution or sterilized over an open flame and then allowed to cool will serve. If you are unable to remove the entire splinter and a small piece remains, it is not necessary to see your doctor. The remnant of the splinter will probably work its way out during the course of healing. Medical help is indicated, however, if the wound surrounding the splinter is dirty and you are unable to clean the dirt out with gentle washing.

Sometimes a child will have stepped on a splintery board and complain of pain as though from something entering the skin. On inspection you may see only a small pinprick-size opening but nothing beneath the skin surface. Because the child complains of pain, you will be concerned that something is down deep in the skin. In general, it is best not to do anything further. If a splinter is there, it will probably work itself out. Although the splinter could be reached by probing, experience has shown us that probing causes more problems than it cures.

If, at any time, the area around a splinter wound becomes swollen, reddened, or begins to discharge pus, you should seek medical attention promptly.

See *cuts, scratches, abrasions, and scrapes.*

*Sprains* are painful injuries to the ligaments that surround a joint. They are caused by the joints being twisted or otherwise forced into an unusual position. "Turning an ankle" is a good example. In a sprain these ligaments are bruised and slightly torn, and bleeding around them causes the swelling. Tenderness to the touch is greatest at the point of injury.

Time and rest alone will heal a sprain. There are no shortcuts. The more the child walks on a twisted ankle, the longer the pain will last and the healing will be delayed. Wrapping an elastic bandage around an ankle or wrist will keep motion to a minimum and allow healing to proceed. Staying off the foot or using crutches for a few days speeds recovery. If swelling is a problem, it can be checked by resting and elevating the joint on a pillow. Be prepared for a week or two of disability.

As the pain subsides, gentle motion of the affected joint can begin. Move the joint in all directions several times a day, just to the point of pain. A warm tub of water makes this process easier. When little pain remains, the child can use the wrist again gradually, or gently put some weight on the foot and *gradually* work toward walking normally again.

If pain and swelling are severe, it is best to speak to the doctor or nurse. They may want to examine the child. If they are suspicious of a chipped bone, they will order an X-ray. If there is a fracture or if the soft tissue injury is severe, they may put a plaster case on the limb to ensure the rest and immobilization needed to bring about healing.

Sprains are less common in children than in adults and a severe injury to an ankle, wrist, or knee may well be a fracture. In children there is the added danger of injury to an *epiphysis* (growth center). In general, injuries severe enough to cause significant swelling and inability to walk are best X-rayed. Use the same precautions discussed under fracture in moving a patient with an injury that is probably a sprain but could also be a fracture. Immobilization of the injured part is called for to prevent worsening of the injury.

*Sting:* see *bites, insect.*

*Strabismus:* see *cross-eyes.*

*Stridor:* see *breathing, noisy.*

*Stuttering:* see *hearing and speech.*

*Sty:* see *abscess.*

*Subglottic hemangioma:* see *breathing, noisy.*

*Sudden infant death syndrome.* In the face of all the progress in medical research and infant care, the fact remains that 10,000 babies die in crib deaths each year in the United States without having exhibited any recognized symptoms of sickness. In the typical case, the baby does not have a cold or other infection, appears normal, is put to bed, and found dead the next morning. Minor illness, such as a common cold, may be present, but since many infants are entirely healthy, this is not sufficient to account for death.

Sudden infant death syndrome, the professional term for this phenomenon (it is also known as "crib death"), is a specific disease entity. It occurs most frequently between the ages of 1 to 6 months with the highest frequency around the third month of life. The largest number of deaths occur in the winter months. It occurs all over the world, regardless of climate or culture, and has probably been with us since antiquity (referred to as "overlaying" in the Bible, 1 Kings 3:19).

Numerous theories have been advanced through the years to explain sudden infant death syndrome. None of these has yet been proven, and most, such as suffocation by bed clothing, bacterial infection, pneumonia, spinal cord injury, and thymus gland enlargement, have been disproven. Investigations have failed to support theories of cows' milk allergy, and some deaths have occurred in babies who have received no cows' milk. There is no evidence that these infants have been beaten and this explanation is cruel.

The National Foundation for Sudden Infant Death (1501 Broadway, New York, N.Y. 10036) was established in 1962 to assist parents, educate the community, and promote research. They have published the following known facts about sudden infant death syndrome:

1. It is the number one cause of death in infants after the first week of life.

2. The death cannot be predicted or prevented, even by a physician.

3. The cause of death is not suffocation, aspiration, or vomiting.

4. There is no suffering; death occurs within seconds, usually during sleep.

5. Sudden infant death is not contagious in the usual sense. Although a viral infection may be involved, it is not a "killer virus" that threatens

other family members or neighbors. It rarely occurs after 7 months of age.

6. It is not hereditary.

After the initial shock, parents find that they are left with a prolonged depression. They often blame themselves or relatives or baby-sitters for the death of the baby. The situation is made even more difficult when family and friends do not understand sudden infant death. Parents naturally become extremely protective of other children in the family and may need help in becoming more objective about them. It is strongly urged that parents write to the National Foundation for information and in order to make contact with parents' groups who have had the same experience. The National Foundation has identified physicians in major cities who are familiar with this disorder and can be called upon for counseling. The U.S. Department of Health, Education, and Welfare has established 24 regional centers around the country to assist parents around the clock. Children's hospitals and pediatricians can be helpful in putting aggrieved parents in touch with these centers.

*Sunburn* may follow exposure to the sun, sunlamps, or occupational light sources such as welding arcs. The band of ultraviolet light which is responsible for sunburn is not screened out by thin clouds on overcast days, but is blocked by the smoke and smog around large cities. A great deal of ultraviolet light reaches the skin by reflection from snow, water, sand, or sidewalks. Hats and umbrellas provide only partial protection. Fair-skinned individuals, well represented among those who are blue-eyed, redheaded, blonde, and freckled, are less able to produce melanin pigment, the substance that gives the skin its color and is responsible for tanning, and are less well able to stand exposure to the sun. They burn easily and therefore need to be more cautious. The skin of very young children is more sensitive to sun. In strong sun, they should be exposed gradually, starting with a few minutes a day. Even in older children and adults, prolonged overexposure to the sun can be damaging to the skin in the long run and the quest for a "deep tan" should not be carried to extremes.

A mild sunburn is tender to the touch. It can be treated with cool tap water compresses for twenty minutes 3 or 4 times a day or more frequently if needed. A skin spray lotion or cream containing hydro-cortisone-like *hormones* reduces pain and inflammation. Lubricating creams and lotions can relieve and soothe dryness. Check with your doctor. Be careful with over-the-counter burn remedies because they often contain local anesthetics such as benzocaine or lidocaine. Although these anesthetics may be helpful in relieving pain, there is the hazard of sensitization to the medication. Severe burns are accompanied by intense pain, inability to bear contact with clothing, sheets, blankets, and so forth, and even nausea, chills, and *fever*. They obviously require a physician's attention. It is important to contact the doctor immediately upon overexposure, for it is easier to prevent severe inflammation than to treat it. A short course of hydrocortisone-like hormones given by mouth is highly effective. Cool compresses, hydrocortisone creams and lotions, a cradle to keep bed linens out of contact with the skin, and oral antipain medicine as needed are also part of the care of the severe burn.

Sunburns can be prevented or kept to a minimum by caution in exposure and, when necessary, by using medications known as sun screens and sun shades. Sun screens contain protective chemicals that absorb ultraviolet light. Those containing para-aminobenzoic acid preparations are in general most effective and will decrease or prevent sunburn. They should be applied to the skin more than 2 hours before exposure, and even though they do not wash off easily, they should be applied again after swimming or profuse sweating. Sun shades contain the chemical titanium dioxide or other opaque substances that refract light.

There are prescription drugs known as *psoralens* that increase the ability of the skin to produce pigment in response to sun. They should be taken 2 hours prior to midday sun exposure, and exposure should gradually increase during the first week from 10 to 60 minutes daily. In order for tanning to occur, exposure to light must follow taking of the drug. Psoralens are used in fair-skinned individuals who would otherwise have a great deal of difficulty with the sun.

**Swallowed objects:** see **choking and swallowing foreign objects.**

**Swimmer's ear:** see **earache.**

**Syphilis:** see **venereal disease.**

**Tallness:** see **height problems.**

**Tay-Sachs disease** is an inherited fatal disorder of the nervous system, of unknown cause, most commonly seen in Jews. It is characterized by the deposit of large quantities of abnormal fat in the brain cells (neurons). The baby is deceptively normal and healthy at birth. In about 5 to 6 months he or she becomes less active, fails to progress, actually regressing, in development, and ceases using his or her eyes. Over the next several months he becomes obviously blind, more and more inactive, and flabby. This inactive phase is followed by one of intense tightness of the muscles along with increasing loss of mental contact with the world around him. The course is progressively downhill and death usually occurs by 3 to 4 years. There is no treatment. Care for affected children is best supervised at a large medical center with extensive experience with disorders of this type, in cooperation with the family pediatrician or family physician.

For an infant to have Tay-Sachs disease he must receive a double dose of the gene for this disorder, one from each parent, both of whom must be *carriers* of this disease. (See *genetics.*) The gene is quite common in Ashkenazic Jews. One in 30 is a carrier, meaning that there is a 1 in 900 chance that a marriage within this ethnic group would bring together carriers and, therefore, the possibility of a baby with Tay-Sachs disease. (There is a 1 in 4 chance that the baby will have the disease, a 1 in 2 chance to be a carrier, and a 1 in 4 chance neither to have the disease nor be a carrier.) In other words, for Ashkenazic Jews, Tay-Sachs is a real risk, well worth worrying about.

Fortunately, it is now possible to detect carriers with a blood test which measures a specific enzyme normally present in the blood (Hexosaminodase-A). This is lowered in the carrier and absent in an affected child. A new screening test is being developed which will involve tears rather than blood. If both parents are known to be carriers and are capable of having a diseased infant, the disorder can be diagnosed in the fetus early in pregnancy by measuring this enzyme within cells from the fetus which circulate in the amniotic fluid and are obtained for testing by *amniocentesis*, the insertion of a needle through the abdominal skin into the uterus. If the fetus has the disorder, a therapeutic abortion can be performed.

It is now desired practice to screen married Ashkenazic Jews for the carrier state of Tay-Sachs disease so that high-risk pregnancies can be identified.

See *genetics.*

**Teething:** see *dental care.*

**Television and children.** Discerning parents would be the first to acknowledge the profound influence television has upon their children. Others do not really understand the impact the mass media make upon their children's minds. The reader will be struck with the frequency with which some influence of television is discussed throughout the book.

Most children spend more time watching television than doing anything else except sleeping. They spend more time before the television than in the schoolroom. A recent survey showed that children watched an average of 3 to 5 hours daily. By the time the average child reaches the age of 20, he or she will have spent 2 full years, 24 hours a day, before the set. This involvement with television is largely a United States phenomenon; in other countries, children's programs in particular are far fewer and generally of higher quality.

Here are some of our concerns:

1. Television fosters faulty nutritional habits. We indicated in our discussion of nutrition (see Part 1, Chapter 3: "Diet of Infants and Children") that many of the foods advertised to children (usually in a glamorous way that makes it hard for parents to resist) are high-calorie snack items, sugared cereals, and sweeteners which are best left out of the diet. These foods must be implicated as contributing to obesity in children and should not be introduced in the first place. (See *weight problems.*) Paradoxically, mothers often buy them out of concern that their children are not eating enough. Furthermore, many of the snack foods are designed and encouraged to be eaten in front of the television set.

2. Television promotes faulty dental health. The sugared cereals, a favorite of television advertising, contribute to tooth decay even more by providing rich nutrients for mouth bacteria. As it is, dry cereals never were good news for teeth. Flaked, dried breakfast cereals are notorious for their stickiness and are difficult to remove from the teeth even with vigorous brushing immediately following meals and snacks. (See *dental care.*)

3. Television fosters a sedentary life. The child in front of the set is obviously inactive. To the extent that television contributes to this inactive life-style, which is itself a major health issue in America, television must be faulted. (See *exercise and physical fitness.*)

4. Television encourages a pill mentality. (See *drug problem.*) Several studies of the health-related content of programs and advertising have judged 70 percent of the information to be inaccurate, misleading, or both. Yet 70 percent of fifth and sixth graders were found to believe such messages.

Of the many elements in the relationship between television and children, the most intensively researched and precisely documented is television's impact on social learning, in particular the effects of the viewing of violence. In 1973 violence occurred in 73 percent of total programming and in almost all cartoons. Throughout the past seven years, violence has ranked in the top five adult programming themes (with many child viewers) and has been the top-ranking theme in cartoons. Violence, from the point of view of the networks, is a relatively cheap and dependable way of holding attention, insuring that the commercials will be viewed, the marketplace measure of TV success.

The preponderance of evidence from both laboratory and field observations is that observing television violence makes children more willing to harm others, more aggressive in their play, and more likely to select aggression as a preferred response in conflict situations. Many nursery school teachers are reporting an increase in violence in youthful play, often in direct imitation of particular programs such as *Batman* or *The Bionic Woman*. In 1975 the principal of the respected Horace Mann School for Nursery years in New York obtained the cooperation of parents in declaring a moratorium on the viewing of violence and in the limitation of viewing to one hour per day. In response, the children seemed calmer and more relaxed in school, drawing more on their own imaginations in play.

The point is that in no way do preschool children *need* television. Most are ill-equipped to deal with the stimulation and fantasy arousal. Even the so-called educational programs are put on primarily because they are watched, not because of any proven lasting beneficial effects. Left to their own devices and with parental guidance (this is the key) children do beautifully without television. Parents have only to believe this to see how their family life can be transformed.

Another concern is that television is used as "baby-sitter." There is little doubt that television can be used by parents to keep children quiet and occupied while Mother or Father works around the house, prepares dinner, gets a few extra winks of sleep on Sunday morning, or to calm an angry or bored child. In some families we have studied, the baby-sitting function was found to be of major importance even when parents justified television viewing on educational grounds.

Television is making miniature consumers of children and placing a premium on material values. Of each hour of weekday commercial programming, up to 12 minutes is given to advertisements. Since January 1, 1973, commercial time on Saturday mornings has been reduced to 9½ minutes per hour. The average child sees 21,300 commercials a year, of which 8,000 to 13,000 are for food or beverages. The television industry in the United States regards children, first and foremost, as a commercial market. Canadian Broadcasting, in contrast, voted to ban all advertising on programs for children. The sponsors of children's programs here judge them by a "body count" rating in which all that matters is how many children are watching. Leading characters may directly advertise to the child. The advertisements may be deceiving. Toys are made to look larger than they really are and often are presented dramatically with music and excitement. The promise of being able to perform almost superhuman physical feats is held out if the advertised foods are consumed. Fortunately, there is some evidence that children are not quite as vulnerable to this propaganda as we may believe. By the time a child reaches his teens, he is cynically suspicious of these commercial messages.

For an exposé of television ads, the film *The Six Billion $$$ Sell (A Child's Guide to TV Commercials)* is very effective. It can be rented or purchased from Consumer Reports Films, Box XA-35, 256 Washington Street, Mount Vernon, N.Y. 10550. The film is excellent for elementary and junior high schools, libraries, and parent groups.

Television, the great anonymous teacher in our society (but free from the controls of any school board), presents a very particular view of the way the world is—a television-world view—with stereotypes of male-female relationships, a distorted representation of age groups (for instance, few elderly people), and a skewed distribution of occupations (an inordinately high percentage of people engaged in law enforcement, for example). One study of adults showed that heavy viewers were more likely to believe that the real world conformed to the television world than did light viewers. For example, the heavy viewers saw the world as more dangerous, and therefore justifying repression, in keeping with the bias toward violence in programming.

Despite these important concerns, television is a remarkably wonderful medium. With cable television and home recorders and cassettes almost upon us, we have barely scratched its potential. It needs betterment and intelligent use. Here are some recommendations:

1. Limit viewing for preschoolers (one hour or less). Think about this issue when your child is born, before he acquires the television habit which may be hard to kick.

2. Plan viewing schedules with your children (an excellent opportunity to share values). Discourage the habit of turning the set on to see what's playing, and encourage turning the set off when the agreed-to program is over.

3. Know the programs. The best way to raise television consciousness among parents is to have them watch together one Saturday morning's offerings. Talk about television and children with friends, PTA, church, etc.

4. Don't give in to commercials. Hold your ground.

5. Watch with your kids and talk about what you watch. Talk about violence and how much it hurts.

6. Use guides to television such as the book *A Parent's Guide to Children's Television* by Evelyn Kaye (New York: Pantheon Books, 1974). Subscribe to *Prime Time School TV* (120 S. Lasalle St., Chicago, Ill. 60603), which puts out background materials on upcoming programs for teachers and parents with references and ideas for how to use programs as a jumping-off point for discussion and further learning. Another excellent resource is the booklet *Watching Television with Your Children*

by Eda T. LeShan, published by the ABC television network and available at ABC affiliated stations.

7. Think about what you as a family can do when you're not watching TV. You'll be amazed at your inner resources if you give yourselves a chance.

8. Join ACT (Action for Children's Television), a nationwide citizen's organization which works for better quality programming and decommercialization. ACT's address: 46 Austin Street, Newtonville, Mass. 02160. ACT has resources for local use.

9. Support public television as an alternative to commercial television. Its successes will have a positive spillover effect on commercial television. In many ways, the latter has improved in recent years.

10. Recognize that much more research is needed in understanding how television is used by and affects family life.

11. Support children's participation in programming. Help them understand the medium from the inside, i.e., television as a creative art performed and studied in school. Encourage your local station to develop a program involving children in which they could tour the facility and make their own productions for broadcast.

12. Write letters of criticism, both positive and negative, to your local station, to the networks, and to the Federal Communications Commission. Viewer reaction does make a difference.


*Testicular pain* is unusual in children. If your boy complains of pain in this region and particularly if the testes appear swollen or discolored, contact your doctor promptly.

The causes of testicular pain are several. A blow to the groin is one obvious cause. The pain is often severe, leading to crying and doubling up. An ice pack will relieve the discomfort, which should be gone in one hour. If the pain persists or worsens, particularly if there is swelling and discoloration, contact your doctor.

Another cause of testicular pain is a twisting of the spermatic cord, which is attached to the upper pole of the testes like a stem to a fruit. The *spermatic cord* is a tube containing the *vas deferens* (which transports sperm), blood vessels, nerves, and muscle. If it twists, the blood supply to the testis is cut off and there is a danger of infarction (death) of the testicular tissue from poor circulation. As this develops, the testis swells and becomes painful. Later a fever, abdominal pain, and vomiting develop. The only treatment is emergency surgery to untwist the spermatic cord and fix the testis to the scrotum so that retwisting cannot occur.

More common than a twisting of the testis is a twist of a small testicular appendage (*torsion* of the *appendix testis*). This small normal structure which protrudes from the testis may twist and die, causing symptoms which are indistinguishable from a twisting of the entire testis. The testis in this condition remains alive. Operation may be necessary to rule out the possibility of torsion of the entire testis and also to quickly alleviate the pain which this condition causes.

Bacterial infection of the *epididymis* (an elongated, cordlike structure along the back of the testis) occurs in adolescence and occasionally in younger children. Often it is associated with a urinary tract infection. (See **urinary tract infections and defects.**)

Testicular *tumors* are rare causes of pain in the testes.

Testicular pain can occur in **mumps,** but is almost never seen in children who have not reached the age of puberty.

*Testis, undescended.* The male reproductive glands, the *testes*, form early in embryological life but remain high in the baby's abdominal cavity until quite late in pregnancy. Each testis is attached to a flexible *spermatic cord*, which contains nerves, blood vessels, muscle, and the *vas deferens*. The vas is the tube for transportation of *sperm*, the male reproductive cells. In the course of normal development, the testis is lowered on the spermatic cord through the inguinal canal in the groin and into the *scrotum*, its proper location. In most baby boys this process of descent into the scrotum has been completed by the time of delivery, but in premature birth the descent has not always been accomplished. The condition in which one testis or both remain outside the scrotum is known as *undescended testis*.

Failure of the testes to descend raises the question of the normalcy of the hormone environment to which the baby was exposed prior to birth. Careful examination of the external genitalia (penis, scrotum, clitoris, vagina, and so forth) is called for to determine the exact sex of the baby. Other studies may be needed as well. (See *hormones*.)

There are all degrees of undescended testis, from the testis that remains in the abdominal cavity to the testis that has not completed its passage through the inguinal canal. Rather often, a testis will have arrived at the scrotum but then has been pulled back toward or into the abdominal cavity. This condition is known as *retractile testis*, and is not, strictly speaking, an undescended testis. The retractile testis can be manipulated back down into the scrotum and, almost without exception, will in time come to rest in the scrotum without surgery or other treatment.

We cannot say that we fully understand why the process of descent should go awry. In some cases the failure seems to be related to a maldevelopment that renders the testis defective from the start. The testis that remains in the abdominal cavity after the onset of puberty most likely will not produce spermatozoa, and may not function properly, even if brought down by surgery at that time. If both testes remain in the abdominal cavity after puberty, the boy will in all likelihood be permanently sterile, with or without surgery. Whether it is failure in the process of descent that affects the testis or a defect in the testis that affects the process of descent, we cannot say.

The surgery usually requires hospitalization for 2 or 3 days. In general, the outlook for a successful repair of an undescended testis is good. Treatment with hormone has been tried as an alternative to surgery, but the results have in general been disappointing, although it still is used at some medical centers. In special circumstances ruling out surgery, a trial of hormone injections probably would be recommended.

Inspection and palpation of the scrotum to establish the location of the testes are essential in the complete physical examination of the infant, and the doctor or nurse in charge will almost always be the one to discover the condition of undescended testis. Parents should always report an unusual appearance of the scrotum to the doctor, but there is no occasion for alarm. If the doctor has satisfied himself at any point that the testes have once been in the scrotum, then the condition of undescended testis does not exist, and, as we have seen, there is no need to worry about retractile testis.

The timing of surgery for undescended testis depends on several factors, a major one being the psychologically optimal time in a boy's development. The accepted procedure in a case involving one or both testes is usually to operate between the ages of 3 and 5. Occasionally, there may be a coexisting *hernia,* in which event both conditions are corrected simultaneously and surgery should not be delayed. See Part 1, Chapter 6: "If Your Child Goes to the Hospital."

*Tetanus.* Popularly known as *lockjaw,* tetanus is a most dramatic disease. In its full-blown state, the victim suffers from painful spasms of all muscles. The forceful involuntary closure of the jaw gave the disease its popular name of "lockjaw." The body is "boardlike," rigid, the head and neck drawn back, and the back arched. The legs and arms are stiff and tense, the fists clenched. Spasms of the muscles of the face cause the eyebrows to be raised and the corners of the mouth to be pulled down and out, producing a hideous involuntary grin. The patient is scared and sweating. The periods of relaxation between spasms may shorten to the point of interfering with breathing.

The bacterium causing tetanus is commonly found in soil, particularly in soil contaminated by feces of animals harboring this common bacterium in their digestive tracts. Thus, the rusty nail in the farm field is a good source of tetanus germs, whereas the rusty nail in the attic is not. (See *puncture wounds.*)

The tetanus bacteria multiply only in an environment of low oxygen. A puncture wound of the foot, particularly one having a lot of tissue damage, is a good setup. A burn is another example. In underdeveloped countries, tetanus infection of the umbilicus of newborns is tragically common when the cord is cut with dirty instruments. By contrast, a scratch of the face where there is an excellent blood supply is much less tetanus-prone. How well and promptly a wound is handled is important in tetanus. Careful cleaning of a wound to remove dead tissue with poor oxygen supply prevents the tetanus bacteria from multiplying. The bacteria themselves cause no more direct damage than any other invader. It is the chemical toxin the bacteria produce that does the dirty work, not so much at the site of the infection as on the nerves and muscles throughout the body to which the toxin is carried in the blood.

Even with a dirty wound containing tetanus organisms, this disease is completely preventable. Injection of *tetanus toxoid*, a modified harmless cousin of the toxin, the T of DPT of the immunization schedule (see *immunization*), is extremely effective in stimulating antibodies to the dangerous toxin, thereby protecting against the disease. The critical point is to be immunized. During World War II there were far more deaths and people seriously ill from tetanus among civilians in the United States than there were cases among soldiers who experienced proportionately many more tetanus-prone injuries on the battlefield. The difference was accounted for entirely by the complete immunization of the military population. Tetanus boosters usually combined with *diphtheria toxoid* (the D of the immunization schedule) should be given routinely every 10 years for *life* and at the time of injury if more than 5 years has elapsed since the last booster.

See *immunization.*


*Thalassemia:* see *anemia.*


*Thinness:* see *weight problems.*


*Throat, sore.* There is one common kind of sore throat that can lead to serious complications, and it is for this reason that all sore throats must be handled with caution. This is the sore throat caused by the germ *streptococcus* and commonly called "strep throat." A very small percentage of the children afflicted with strep throat would, if left untreated, go on to develop *rheumatic fever.* Or they might instead develop an inflammation of the kidney.

Rheumatic fever affects the body's joints and can damage the heart permanently. It has a tendency to recur, and in most cases the child who has had rheumatic fever must take daily preventive drugs for many years—in some instances for life. Actually it is not the strep infection itself that causes rheumatic fever, but a special type of reaction some children have to infection by streptococcus. If the streptococcus germs infecting the throat are treated within one week after the first signs of illness appear, rheumatic fever can almost always be prevented. This is the main reason for treating strep throats.

Another possible complication of strep throat is the inflammation of the kidney called *glomerulonephritis* (see *nephritis*), which causes blood and protein to appear in the urine and sometimes causes high blood pressure. Unfortunately, even early treatment of the strep throat may not prevent this complication. But with careful treatment of the complication itself, most children recover completely.

You can see how important it is to have a plan of action every time anyone in the family has a sore throat—whether it is mild or severe.

Throat infections are called *pharyngitis* by doctors. If the tonsils are present, they usually share in the infection and we say that the child has "tonsillitis." (See *tonsils and adenoids.*) Tonsillitis is part and parcel of most cases of pharyngitis. Most infected throats heal within 3 to 4 days. They make children uncomfortable and temporarily sick, but, by themselves, sore throats are rarely harmful.

Throat infections are caused for the most part by either viruses or bacteria. We have no drug yet to treat most virus infections and are obliged to let them run their course. While scores of different viruses can infect the throat, few kinds of bacteria do. (See *infections.*)

The most obvious symptom of throat infections is, of course, soreness and pain in the throat. Some throats are extremely sore; others bother children very little. There are other common symptoms that may accompany sore throat and you should watch for these: cold (running nose, *cough,* and so forth; see *colds*), *fever* (sometimes fever is the only symptom of infection), *headache* and/or stomachache, *earache,* swollen glands (see *glands, swollen*), and *rash.*

Older children can tell you how they feel, but it is not always easy to know when a very young infant has a sore throat. His or her behavior is usually a reliable indicator of how he or she is feeling, however, and signs of unusual fussiness and crankiness, prolonged crying, inability to sleep, refusal to eat or drink, flushed appearance, or fever usually means that something is the matter. If your infant has some or all of these symptoms, contact your doctor. Don't overlook or ignore the child who complains only once or twice of pain in his throat and then doesn't mention it again. Be sure to speak to your doctor about *any* kind of sore throat.

When you call about a sore throat, the doctor or nurse will try to judge whether the throat infection is being caused by viruses or by streptococcus. Is it part of a cold or not? Is anyone else in the family sick with a sore throat (if so, what kind)? He will consider whether there has been an outbreak of strep throat in your community. If one of your other children has had a strep infection recently, chances are this one is a strep infection, too.

Very likely the doctor will take a culture of your child's throat, because a routine physical examination is not usually sufficient to tell streptococcal from viral infections. When taking a throat culture, the doctor swabs the infected throat with a piece of cotton on the end of an applicator stick. Although the sensation isn't pleasant, it is over quickly. With an older child it may make things easier if you explain the procedure beforehand. More and more parents are themselves learning how to swab throats, thereby avoiding bringing the child himself to the office. The doctor then sends the swab to a laboratory, where the sample of the germs picked up on the cotton is smeared onto a sort of "food" or culture where germs grow rapidly and multiply, forming piles or mountains of germs called colonies. In about 18 to 24 hours the colonies have incubated and are large enough to be seen with the naked eye and identified. Combining the result of the culture with his own clinical judgment, the doctor is now able to determine with certainty the cause of the infection.

The doctor will usually hold off prescribing treatment for a sore throat until after the 24-hour incubation period. There's no danger in doing so, even if your child does indeed have a strep infection. In fact, there may be an advantage, since his body will have an opportunity to build up natural antibodies helpful in warding off future attacks of streptococcus, whereas with too prompt treatment it might not. (This does not mean, of course, that you should delay taking your child to the doctor in the first place.) Alternatively, if the likelihood of strep is high, he may begin penicillin and decide whether or not to continue it after the culture is read.

If it is a viral infection, antibiotics will not be used. No "wonder drugs" exist to cure viral throat infections. Even penicillin will not help. In fact, with viral infections, we deliberately avoid giving antibiotics. But there are some simple remedies to relieve your child's discomfort and pain. Give aspirin or an aspirin substitute for his sore throat and fever (if he's running one). The correct doses are listed in the discussion of fever in Part 1, Chapter 5: "Caring for the Sick Child at Home." Although it is questionable whether gargling does much good, it helps soothe a parched mouth and throat. In any event, it is always comforting for a child to know that you are trying to make him feel better. For the gargle, use plain warm water. If your child develops any of the other common symptoms that may accompany infection of the throat: fever, cold, headache, stomachache (see *abdominal pain*), earache, swollen glands, a rash, handle them according to the advice given in this book under the respective headings.

When it is strep throat use the same remedies for pain and discomfort suggested for the child with a viral sore throat. If your child's throat culture shows a strep infection, your doctor will prescribe an antibiotic drug—usually penicillin. Antibiotics *properly used* eradicate the streptococcus or sufficiently suppress its growth so that this infection no longer can lead to rheumatic fever. Although only a small number of children with strep throat go on to develop rheumatic fever or nephritis, there is no certain way of predicting which ones these will be. Doctors feel that this justifies handling every case of strep infection with the same caution.

It is most important that your child take the penicillin pills (or other antibiotic) for a full 10 days. This amount of time is needed for the drug to cure the infection completely and thus prevent it from possibly causing rheumatic fever. Your child wll probably feel well and his throat will stop hurting long before the 10 days are up. When the symptoms of sickness disappear, there is a temptation to stop the drugs. This is dangerous in the case of strep throat. Stop the aspirin, lozenges, or gargle, if you wish, but *not the antibiotic*. Remember that the primary purpose of the antibiotic is *not* to relieve pain and make your child feel better. Its purpose is to cure the underlying infection and wipe out the possibility of rheumatic fever. To help remind you, put a big "calendar" on your refrigerator door. Have your child check off the doses of medicine as they are taken. A long-acting penicillin injection, while painful, avoids fussing over pills.

A rash sometimes appears with throat infections. The characteristic rash accompanying a streptococcal sore throat is known as *scarlet fever*. The rash is caused by a chemical toxin produced by the strep germs. It begins 12 to 72 hours after the onset of sore throat and fever around the base of the neck, the armpits, and groin, and later spreads to the trunk and extremities. The rash consists of small, closely packed, bright red spots which blanch on pressure. The cheeks are flushed and the skin around the mouth is free of rash. Once a feared and severe disease, today scarlet fever is of little concern. The antibiotic used to treat strep infection practically eliminates the chances of scarlet fever. With this form of treatment, should the disease occur, it is usually mild and short-lived. If your child breaks out in a rash, let your doctor know without delay.

Strep throat is contagious. Children of school age seem to be more susceptible to streptococcus infection than adults or infants under 2 years. Susceptibility depends on many factors besides age, however. Studies of families indicate that weather plays only a minor role, even though the number of infections does rise in late winter and spring. Close contact, such as sharing a bedroom with someone with a strep throat, increases the possibility of catching the infection. Stress within the family appears to have a significant effect, too. Families experiencing emotional upsets, such as death or divorce, or even lesser crises like moving or passing school examinations, have reported the relation of these crises to the onset of sickness. Fatigue from stress and anxiety figures in the picture, too. (See Part 1, Chapter 4: "Complaints with an Emotional Element.")

Depending on the circumstances, if one member of your family has a strep throat, the doctor may want to take throat cultures of the rest of the family as a precautionary measure, even though no one else is feeling sick at the time. On the other hand, he may wait to see if symptoms develop among the other members. If they show signs of illness, he will then culture their throats or prescribe penicillin.

When a strep infection occurs in your family, be particularly alert to sore throats and ordinary colds for the next few weeks, and report any such symptoms to the doctor. The chance of developing strep throat will be greater than usual. If a child or adult has contact with someone outside the family who has a strep throat, in general nothing need be done unless symptoms develop. The child need not be examined, have a throat culture, remain indoors, or take antibiotics just because of an exposure.

Parents often ask if removing a child's tonsils will keep him from getting sore throats. Most doctors believe that healthy tonsils should not be removed. Remember that "tonsillitis"—the condition in which the child has a fever and sore throat and his tonsils become red and swollen —is not the cause of a sort throat, but part of the result of germs infecting the throat. Following a case of sore throat, tonsils usually heal and return to normal. If a child's tonsils become chronically infected or cause other symptoms, the doctor may want to consider with you having them taken out. (See *tonsils and adenoids.*)

In general, then, with sore throats follow the treatment suggestions for colds. Make certain never to give your child antibiotics for a sore throat (or any other ailment) without first consulting your doctor. The child is no longer contagious 24 hours after beginning penicillin. If the doctor has prescribed an antibiotic and he is still taking it, it is perfectly all right to resume activities when he feels better.

See Part 1, Chapter 5: "Caring for the Sick Child at Home."

*Thyroid condition:* see *hormones.*

*Tick fever:* see *Rocky Mountain spotted fever.*

*Toeing-in, toeing-out:* see *orthopedic concerns.*

*Toenail, ingrown.* An ingrown toenail is one in which the corner of the nail penetrates into the surrounding skin of the toe. The big toe is the one most commonly affected. If the ingrown toenail is just beginning, as evidenced by slight redness and pain in the skin at the corner of the nail, you can often ward off trouble by cutting off the corner of the nail. This will be easier if you first soak the foot in warm water. This should be continued each morning and evening until the pain disappears.

If the nail is actually burrowing into the skin, or if there is any evidence of infection, such as swelling, marked redness, or pus, there is no call for home remedy. Get in touch with your doctor. Surgical removal of all or part of the nail will probably be necessary.

In newborns and young infants, the soft nails of the toes often appear to be curving in instead of out and over. They do not, however, actually cut into the flesh and require no special attention.

To prevent ingrown toenails, shoes should not be too tight and nails should be cut regularly. The common advice of cutting the nails straight across and not in a curve is now under consideration and may not be as useful as once believed.

*Tongue-tie:* see *hearing and speech.*

*Tonsils and adenoids.* The tonsils and adenoids are similar in structure and function to the lymph nodes in other regions of the body. (See *infections.*) Like the other lymphoid tissue, they produce antibodies when the body is responding to infection. If you look down your child's throat, you can see the tonsils—small, reddish, oval-shaped masses, one on either side, at the base of the tongue. The adenoids are hard to see without the sort of mirror your doctor or dentist uses when examining the throat or mouth. They are spongy masses in the upper back part of the throat, opposite the nasal passageways. The enlargement and inflammation of the tonsils in response to infection is called *tonsillitis.* *Adenoiditis* is the comparable condition of the adenoids. The tonsils and adenoids do not actually cause the infection. They are the places where the infecting viruses or bacteria set up shop as these germs attack the nose and throat.

Generally speaking, the symptoms of tonsillitis and adenoiditis are similar to those discussed under sore throat (see *throat, sore*) and *colds.* The removal of tonsils or adenoids will not prevent these infections but may (this is still conjecture) reduce their frequency and probably do lessen their severity. On the other hand, there is mounting recent evidence that the tonsils may play an important role in preventing certain germs (particularly viruses) from setting up a carrier infection in otherwise immune individuals, which, while not causing harm to the individual himself or herself, may facilitate the spread of the germ through the community. The final word on the tonsil story has not yet been written, and the tonsils should not be looked upon as worthless relics of the past like the appendix. (See *appendicitis.*)

The medical treatment of tonsillitis is similar to that for sore throat and cold. The doctor will attempt to identify the cause of the infection. Throat cultures are often useful in diagnosis. If there is any indication of streptococcus, an antibiotic will be prescribed. At least 10 full days of treatment are necessary for a complete cure, though the symptoms may disappear earlier.

The parent whose child has had tonsillitis quite likely will want to know whether or not to have the tonsils out. For the majority of children the answer will be no. This important decision is one for you and your doctor to make together, but we can lay down some guidelines. Three or 4 attacks of tonsillitis per year in the years of peak incidence (between ages 2 and 6) are not uncommon. These are the years of peak size of the tonsils when they are normally prominent. In later childhood and *adolescence* they shrink to a mere shadow of their former selves. If these attacks last only a few days, and if the tonsils return to normal betweeen attacks, tonsillectomy probably is not necessary. But if the child has 5 or more attacks of tonsillitis per year for *more* than one year, we *might* recommend tonsillectomy on the grounds of frequency alone. We hedge on this point because we have no solid evidence that a child with his tonsils out will have fewer infections (colds or sore throats) than he would have had if his tonsils had been left alone. In this situation, we feel more confident about recommending tonsillectomy if, in addition to frequent infections, there are other symptoms as well, like very high *fever.*

Some children's tonsils become so enlarged that they actually touch at the midline. The child has difficulty swallowing and may gag on his own tonsils. Tonsils in this condition should be removed. Here we are not talking about the expected swelling that occurs with infection and subsides when the infection is over. This abnormal enlargement persists.

Some children have unusually severe attacks of tonsillitis with very high fever and even convulsions (see *febrile seizures*). Removal of the tonsils can reduce the severity of the fever response to infection and in these special cases should be considered. Sometimes antibiotics, even when given for the proper length of time and in the proper dose, will not eradicate infection within the tonsils. Once the antibiotics are stopped, the infection flares up again. Tonsils chronically infected to this extent probably should be removed. Occasionally tonsils become abscessed. A pocket of pus forms within the tonsil. Even if the abscess yields to treatment with antibiotics, it usually leaves a cavity which can become a focus of further abscesses. Abscessed tonsils should be removed.

Enlarged adenoids may block the nasal passages at the back of the throat, making breathing through the nose difficult. A baby with a constant nasal drip should be evaluated. With severe obstruction, a child can develop *adenoid facies*, which is a characteristic cast of the face associated with mouth breathing, nasal and unclear speech, and sometimes dental deformities. Chronic inflammation of the adenoids may bring on postnasal drip and a *cough* which becomes worse at night. Although breathing through the mouth and snoring in sleep may result from enlarged adenoids, we do not consider these symptoms alone sufficient cause for removing adenoids. (See *breathing, noisy.*) However, *very* noisy breathing both day and night is a symptom of large adenoids and deserves evaluation.

Enlarged adenoids may block the opening of the Eustachian tubes at the back of the throat, and contribute to the development of ear infections. These tubes connect the throat with the two middle-ear cavities and allow air to flow from the mouth into the cavities, thus equalizing the internal and external pressure on the eardrums. Blockage of the tubes interferes with this system. Persistent ear infection and *serous otitis media* can usually be taken as signs of blockage of the Eustachian tube, and in children one of the most common causes of blockage is enlarged adenoids. This difficulty frequently requires surgical removal of the adenoids. It is also necessary at times to drain the stagnant fluid and mucus. (See discussion of ear infections and *myringotomy* under *earache*.)

Parents who worry about the "picky" appetites of their youngsters often ask about tonsillectomy and adenoidectomy. To the parental eyes at least, these children look pale and undernourished and seem unduly susceptible to sickness. The parents, understandably, are looking for general cures. Unfortunately, however, surgery is not likely to be the answer unless there is evidence of chronic infection of tonsils, or enlargement makes swallowing difficult and painful.

Unclear speech may result from enlarged adenoids, and part of the medical assessment includes examination of the mouth and throat. This is a good place to emphasize again that, except in emergencies, the decision to hospitalize a child for surgery is a delicate one. The child who needs a tonsillectomy (gone are the days when *every* child had his tonsils out) and is old enough to be aware of what is going on around him should be prepared carefully for this experience, involving as it does not only strange surroundings but also some separation from his parents (see Part 1, Chapter 6: "If Your Child Goes to the Hospital"). Under the safe conditions of the modern hospital, tonsillectomy and adenoidectomy can be performed at any age. There is no need to wait until he is older or bigger. For some children with mild symptoms the operation should be postponed until they are better prepared psychologically to cope with it. Tonsillectomy has become a very safe procedure, but parents should remember that the child will suffer discomfort for several days and will be more or less out of action for as long as a couple of weeks. All these circumstances should be taken into consideration before a decision is reached.

Either a general physician with surgical experience or a specialist called an *otolaryngologist* is competent to perform a tonsillectomy and an adenoidectomy. We would discourage parents from seeking out specialists on their own. A detailed record of the child's previous encounters with sickness and a close acquaintance with both the child and his family situation will be important when an assessment of the pros and cons of surgery is made. The pediatrician or family physician who has continuing supervision of the medical care of the child has this information and should make the referral to a specialist.

**Toothache:** see *dental care.*

**Tooth injuries:** see *dental care.*

**Toxic synovitis:** see *hip pain.*

**Toxoplasmosis:** see *pets and children.*

**Tracheo-esophageal fistula.** Some babies are born with an abnormal connection between the *trachea* (windpipe) and the *esophagus* (the tube conveying food and drink from the back of the throat to the stomach). This uncommon birth defect, known medically as tracheo-esophageal fistula, can take several forms but always requires surgery.

If you press at the base of your throat, just below the Adam's apple, you can feel the trachea. It extends from the *larynx* (voice box) into the chest, several inches below the notch of the collarbone. At its lower end, it divides into the 2 major *bronchi*, which carry the air you breathe to the right and left lungs. Just behind the trachea is the esophagus. Under normal conditions, the two tubes are, of course, separate.

In the most common (but still rare) form of tracheo-esophageal fistula, the esophagus is divided into unconnected upper and lower parts. The upper part ends in a blind pouch in the chest; the lower segment joins the trachea at the *bifurcation* (point at which bronchi normally begin). Obviously, nothing swallowed from the mouth, whether food, drink, or saliva, can reach the stomach, and a baby with this condition is in serious trouble. To make matters worse, gastric juices can be regurgitated up through the lower segment of the esophagus, into the trachea, and thence to the lungs, setting up an intense reaction that results in *pneumonia.* The baby is both unable to feed and likely to develop lung inflammation. His or her drooling, choking, gagging, labored respiration, and poor color are sure to be seen in the hospital. Such a baby becomes a candidate for surgery in the first few days of life. Unless the baby is very premature or suffers from some other illness in addition, his chances are very good.

The variations of this condition involve other abnormal connections between the 2 tubes. The symptoms will in general be similar except for the amount of drooling. Drooling is most pronounced in the form of fistula that we have described.

*Traveling abroad.* Medical preparations may be required when you and your family go abroad, particularly if you plan to live in an area of the world where your immunities do not protect you. (See *immunization.*) If possible, it is advisable to seek out a doctor who knows something about health risks in foreign parts of the world, especially if you are going to a tropical country or one where sanitation standards are low. Fortunately, many countries of the world are well equipped to handle any problem that may arise medically, and the main difficulty encountered is the language barrier and inability to communicate. At least a dozen nations have lower infant mortality rates than the United States. Many countries have admirable health-care systems once you understand how to use them.

Allow enough time for booster doses of vaccines, should these be required. In order to get back into this country, you may need a small-pox vaccination certificate, depending on where you go. Suggested immunizations are contained in the Report of the Committee on Infectious Diseases of the American Academy of Pediatrics, copies of which are available for $3.00 c/o the American Academy of Pediatrics, P.O. Box 1034, Evanston, Ill. 60201. Public health hospitals and stations at international airports are another source of advice. See also the book recommended below.

If you will be away a long time, a medical checkup is a good idea. You would do well to carry a medical record for each member of the family. It is oftentimes difficult to get good *dental care* in other countries, and every family member should have a thorough examination before departure. Ask your dentist about your need for fluoride supplementation. Do not put off any needed dental work; you may have a long time before you get back to a competent dentist.

Again, if you will be away for some time, be sure that eyes are checked before you leave. (See *vision problems.*) It is a good idea to carry your prescription for glasses in your health folder. Your doctor will also have the same on file in this country. It might be helpful to carry an extra pair of glasses with you, especially if you think you might be in a place where it would be difficult to have new glasses made.

Any person who travels abroad accompanied by children might wish to consider packing a copy of the directory published by the International Association for Medical Assistance to Travelers. If you come down sick in Rome or your child picks up *measles* in India, a quick turn of its pages will provide you with the information you need to reach the nearest English-speaking physician. There are listings for English-speaking physicians in more than 400 cities in 120 countries. The directory is available from International Association for Medical Assistance to Travelers, Suite 5620, 350 Fifth Avenue, New York, N.Y. 10001. American communities are found in almost every country of the world. In the case of a medical crisis, you can be sure that you will find help from your countrymen abroad; there is usually a U.S. embassy or U.S. consulate which can provide help.

Extensive information about preparations and ways of protecting your family's health while traveling can be found in *Keeping Your Family Healthy Overseas* by James P. Carter, M.D., Eleanora de Antonio West, and members of the staff of The Children's Hospital Medical Center (New York: Delacorte Press, 1971).

See also *motion sickness.*

**Tuberculosis.** Once a common infection and still quite common in some areas of the world and underprivileged segments of our own society, tuberculosis (TB) is fortunately a disease with which few parents or children will have direct experience today.

Tuberculosis is contagious in the adult, but rarely so in the child, even though children can easily become infected. The infected adult coughs the tuberculosis bacteria into the air. They are inhaled by the susceptible child and infection is established in the child's lungs. Most of the time the body is able to confine the infection and destroy the invading germs, and no symptoms develop (see discussion of subclinical infection under *infections*). In a smaller percentage of infected children, the infection progresses, initially causing *fever*, fatigue, and irritability. Later, *cough* and breathing difficulties, the signs of *pneumonia*, may develop.

Of greater concern in children is the spread of the tuberculosis germs from the lungs to other parts of the body. This spread can occur whether or not pneumonia has first developed. Children are especially prone to this complication. The germs are carried in the blood and therefore can go literally anywhere. Particularly worrisome is spread to the nervous system (brain and spinal cord) where *meningitis* can occur. Sometimes the appearance of infection outside of the lung, for example in the nervous system, is the first sign of tuberculosis in children. Spread beyond the lung complicates treatment and carries the risk of permanent damage or crippling of the involved part of the body. In the days before treatment was available, and to a lesser extent even now, spread also carries with it a high fatality rate.

Once infection with tuberculosis has occurred, the patient becomes "allergic" to the TB germs, so that if a concentrate of killed inactive germs is injected into the skin, the patient reacts with redness and swelling at the injection site. This reaction is the basis for the TB skin test which is done on children known or likely to have been exposed to adults with tuberculosis (see *immunization*). The reaction peaks at 48 hours and, for this reason, parents are asked to check the skin test 2 days after it is applied. The skin test reaction occurs even in the individual who has become infected without symptoms. A positive skin test does not mean that the infection is active. Even the individual who has successfully confined the infection and killed off the tuberculosis bacteria develops a positive skin test. The skin test is a kind of living record of contact with tuberculosis. Whether or not the infection is active is a separate question.

Our policy is to treat all children with positive tuberculosis skin tests whether or not they have symptoms or chest X-ray evidence of infection. If they have symptoms, the need for treatment is obviously compelling. Those children who have no symptoms are treated to prevent symptoms from developing. In fact, some children who are known to have been unavoidably exposed to TB from infected adults are given antibiotics to prevent them from becoming infected in the first place. Treatment with special anti-TB antibiotics is continued for a minimum of one year.

It is true that many children who receive treatment because of a positive skin test have in fact confined these infections on their own.

There is no completely reliable way to know whether the infection has been confined or is smoldering on below the surface. Because of the danger of spread throughout the body, we take no chances and treat all children who have positive skin tests, even though some may be treated unnecessarily.

There is an immunization against tuberculosis. It has partial protective value. This vaccine consists of living bacteria which are weak relatives of the TB bacteria. These bacteria are inoculated in the skin. The minor infection is easily dealt with by the body and the immunity that results carries over to tuberculosis itself. While this immunization is used to advantage in many parts of the world, it is not used commonly in this country because tuberculosis is relatively uncommon.

There are a number of "cousins" of tuberculosis which can infect man. Usually the infection is confined to the glands of the neck. The tuberculosis skin test is often positive for infections with these bacteria, but less strongly so than with tuberculosis itself. It can be a source of confusion. Tests with killed concentrates of these so-called atypical bacteria give a stronger reaction than does the tuberculosis skin test and permit these "cousins" to be identified.

*Tumors* are unusual in children but do occur and can involve just about any part of the body. As in adults, tumors may be benign or malignant (cancerous). Benign tumors can at least theoretically be completely cured by surgical removal or, in some cases, X-ray treatment, while malignant tumors pose the added risk of widespread dissemination through the body.

It is difficult to generalize about the presenting signs and symptoms of tumors. Some of the more external ones are apparent by a visible mass. Internal ones usually lead to a derangement of function of some body organ or system prompting an investigation which detects the growth.

Tumors seen in children are in general different from those occurring in adults. For example, cancer of the lung or colon is quite common in adults, but exceedingly rare in children.

The most common malignant tumors in children are *Wilms' tumor* and *neuroblastoma.* Others are rare and, with the exception of *brain tumors, retinoblastoma, Hodgkin's disease,* and cancer of the vagina and cervix in adolescent girls whose mothers took stilbestrol or other synthetic estrogens during pregnancy (see *adolescence*), will not be discussed in this book except to say that investigations and treatments similar to those described in Wilms' tumor and neuroblastoma are employed. In each instance the coordinated efforts of a number of specialists are required.

See also *leukemia.*

*Turner's syndrome:* see *genetics.*

**535**

*Urinary
tract
infections
and
defects*

*Typhoid fever* is an infection caused by the bacterium *Salmonella typhosa.* This bacterium is a member of the Salmonella family discussed under *pets and children.* The primary infection is in the intestines. Common symptoms are *fever, abdominal pain,* rash, and generally feeling poorly. Sometimes typhoid fever begins as a *fever of unknown origin* or *gastro-enteritis.* As in most infectious diseases, there is a wide range of severity from life-threatening to so mild as to produce no symptoms at all (see discussion of subclinical infections under *infections*). *Bloodstream infection* is a common part of the disease as is the development of the carrier state during which the infected individual harbors the organism (usually in the gallbladder) and excretes it in his or her stools without having symptoms. (For discussion of carriers, see *infections.*)

Bacteria from an ill individual or carrier are passed in the urine and/or stools. They are transmitted to others through water contaminated with sewage (proper sanitation is the major method of prevention) or by unwashed hands to food or drink. (For this reason the stools of food handlers are periodically checked for Salmonella.)

Treatment is with antibiotics until symptoms are gone and stool cultures no longer reveal typhoid bacteria. *Immunization* has been proven effective but not completely preventive. Vaccine is recommended only for individuals who are likely to be exposed to typhoid. Booster doses of vaccine should be given every year following the initial series if continued exposure is anticipated.

*Umbilical hernia:* see *hernia.*

*Undescended testis:* see *testis, undescended.*

*Urinary tract infections and defects.* Frequency of urination, *fever, abdominal pain,* pain or burning on voiding, nausea, *vomiting,* loss of appetite, failure to grow and develop normally, and passage of cloudy or blood-tinged urine are all symptoms of urinary infection and should be brought to medical attention, however short the duration of the complaint. Sometimes infections of the urinary tract begin as unexplained fevers (see *fever of unknown origin*).

Both bacteria and viruses can infect the urinary tract (viruses have been known to cause bladder infection). Thus far, only bacterial infections are susceptible to treatment (with antibodies). Virus infections run

536

*Urinary
tract
infections
and
defects*

their course without treatment. Infections of the urinary tract can be present but cause no symptoms (subclinical infection). To identify such silent infections, routine urinalysis (looking for pus cells, bacteria, and protein) and, of greater reliability, urine cultures for bacteria are done from time to time on all children (especially in girls) and adults. The health supervision visit (see Part 1, Chapter 2: "The Regular Checkup") offers a good opportunity for such urine screening.

If the urinalysis and culture indicate that a bacterial infection exists, the treatment is antibiotics, given for several weeks in the first attack on the problem. Failure to respond to this first course of treatment, or a relapse following therapy, may require an even longer course of treatment. In some stubborn infections, treatment may extend over many months and even years. These infections are not contagious and isolation is not required.

Once a bacterial urinary tract infection has been identified, the doctor's thoughts will turn very quickly to the possibility of blockage or obstruction somewhere in the urinary system, even though many infections are not associated with obstruction. This concern is especially marked if the patient is a boy. Girls are more prone to infections without obstruction, but if a girl's infection is a stubborn or recurring one, obstruction is always a possibility.

To understand obstructions, it is necessary to review some anatomy. The urinary tract or system includes the two *kidneys* (and their pelves), the *ureters, bladder*, and the *urethra*. Urine is manufactured in the *nephrons* of the kidneys and accumulated in the *renal pelves* (not to be confused with the pelvis of the skeletal structure), which are saclike cavities, one pelvis to each kidney, drained by the ureters. The ureters are tubes that move the urine along to the bladder, where it is stored until passed through the urethra. The urethra in the female is very short; in the male it traverses the length of the penis.

The waste products disposed of in the urine are formed in the many complex chemical reactions that occur as the cells of the body undergo their normal metabolic processes. (*Metabolism* is the sum of all the physical and chemical processes affecting our fundamental living matter and the conversion of energy for its use.) One such waste product is *urea*, which comes from the processing of protein. Urine also carries off material that the body cannot use. For example, if you eat more salt than the body can use, the excess will appear in your urine within hours. In effect, then, the urinary process, by siphoning off excess materials in the blood, keeps the composition of the blood stable within a range compatible with life.

The urinary tract forms early in embryological life, and even before birth the kidney manufactures urine. The baby excretes urine into the amniotic fluid, from whence it passes into the mother's bloodstream to be excreted through her urinary system. Other waste products are transferred directly from the baby's blood to the mother's through the placenta. At birth, with the placenta gone, the baby's kidneys then must take over the entire job. In the womb, the placenta served as an escape valve for any waste products a malfunctioning kidney had been unable to process.

537

*Urinary
tract
infections
and
defects*

It is easy to picture how an obstruction anywhere in the urinary system would impose strain on the other parts. Suppose, for example, that a blockage existed between bladder and urethra. First, accumulating urine would stretch the bladder. The bladder's forceful contractions to pass the urine would thicken its muscular walls. The ureters would have to pump harder in an effort to get urine into the already full bladder, and they also would enlarge. Urine would back up from the bladder and eventually into the pelves of the kidneys. The increasing pressure of retained urine, by stretching the kidney (hydronephrosis), would distort and destroy the nephrons, the microscopic functioning units of the organ. If this chain of damaging developments continued unchecked, kidney failure would occur.

Very much the same sequence would occur from an obstruction at any other point in the urinary tract, with the parts above the blockage being immediately affected. There would be retention of urine, increased pressure, dilation, and stretching of structures. The picture usually will be complicated further by infection. Bacteria can get into the urinary tract either by spreading up through the urethra or by transport in the bloodstream. Normally, stray bacteria are cleared from the bloodstream in the kidneys and then flushed out in the urine without having had a chance to multiply. Stagnant urine, however, is an excellent food for bacteria. From the point of blockage, multiplying bacteria can spread throughout the entire urinary tract, and the ill effects will be compounded when infection aggravates the blockage.

Birth defects of the urinary tract are caused by failures in embryological development and most involve obstructions of one kind or another. The most common sites for these defects are at the junctions—between pelvis and ureter, between ureter and bladder, between bladder and urethra, or within the urethra itself. Examples are the condition in which abnormally large folds in the urethra of a boy hamper flow of urine, an abnormal thickening of the muscle in the lower bladder that clamps down on the outlet in the act of voiding, duplication of a ureter, with one branch narrowed and predisposed to infection.

The severity of obstructions can range from partial to complete. With the passage of time, they may grow better or worse, and they may produce symptoms at any age from birth to old age. The longer an obstruction remains, the greater the risk of damage, and sometimes deformity progresses to the point of rendering a section of the urinary

538

*Urinary
tract
infections
and
defects*

tract useless even if the obstruction is relieved. In the stretching of the ureters and kidneys, there is a point of no return. Beyond this point they lose their capacity to function and serve only as reservoirs for stagnant urine. There may be kidney damage even before birth. If the blockage before birth is only partial, there is time to make repairs before damage is irreparable.

An obstruction in the urinary tract of the newborn can sometimes but not always be detected by touch. An enlarged kidney, for example, can be felt in the flank of a baby. Partial obstructions, insufficient to produce symptoms in the newborn period, may show up only when the child is older. In some cases, problems may become apparent only after infection has set in. Difficulties in voiding, dribbling, and complete failure to toilet train, in addition to the symptoms of infection mentioned above, are signs requiring attention.

There are a number of X-ray tests for locating urinary tract obstructions. A dye injected into a vein is excreted in the urine, casts a shadow on the film, and gives a picture of the entire urinary system, from kidneys through bladder. Any abnormality of size or configuration will be revealed, as will abnormality in the rate of emptying of the various structures of the system. A bladder X-ray is another important diagnostic test, since many of the anatomic or physiologic abnormalities present may be related to bladder function. Reflux (backing up) of urine from the bladder to the kidneys is commonly associated with recurrent urinary tract infections in girls. Badly impaired kidneys will not concentrate the dye properly, and this failure, too, gives us useful information about function. In these circumstances a *retrograde pyelogram* is taken. Under anesthesia, dye is injected through *catheters* (thin plastic tubes) passed into the ureters by way of the urethra and bladder. The dye fills all the structures of the tract and renders them visible on X-ray. There are other procedures as well, such as the use of radioactive dye whose concentration in the kidney can be measured.

Treatment or correction of a deformity of the urinary tract depends, of course, on the specific problem. The first step is to control any infection present. Obstructions of the bladder outlet can sometimes be opened without surgery. In those cases instruments called *dilators* are passed up through the urethra to stretch open the passage. Other obstructions require surgery.

Proper toilet habits can prevent many urinary tract infections in girls. Wiping fecal material from "back to front" (from anus forward to the urethra) can cause infection. Feces normally teem with bacteria. Girls therefore need supervision and instruction in wiping from front to back with their hand coming up under the thigh from behind.

For a discussion on bacteria, virus, antibiotics, and subclinical infections, see *infections.*

*Urticaria:* see *hives.*

*Vaccination:* see *immunization.*

*Vaginitis or vaginal discharge.* Vaginal discharge, burning, itching, are common symptoms in girls. One common type is the perfectly normal, sometimes blood-tinged discharge that occurs during the first week of life and reflects the stimulation of the baby's uterus by maternal sex hormones (primarily estrogen). Pubescent girls also have a normal clear discharge for which no special treatment is necessary. (See *adolescence.*)

In young children, vaginal discharge always raises the suspicion of a foreign body like retained toilet paper or an object like a crayon or paper clip inserted by the child. Identification of such foreign bodies is essential. Several approaches are used. One is the rectal examination with gloved finger which permits the doctor or nurse to feel the length of the vagina from within the rectum. Another is the passage of a thin instrument to "probe" for a hidden object. There is also the use of a vaginoscope, a tubelike instrument with a light at one end, which, upon insertion, allows visual inspection of the interior of the vagina. The vaginoscope is usually passed under sedation or anesthesia. X-ray of the pelvis can detect certain opaque foreign bodies.

It is always worthwhile to ask why the foreign body is present. Retained pieces of toilet paper often reflect improper toilet habits. The child sweeps the toilet paper contaminated with feces from the rectal area upward over the vagina. The vagina can become infected, the toilet paper trapped, and the germs can then enter the bladder by way of the urethra, causing a urinary tract infection (see *urinary tract infections and defects*). Girls should be instructed to wipe from front to back, with their hand approaching the rectal area from beneath the leg. In the case of other foreign bodies, we try to determine why the child has inserted them. Was it a mere frivolous episode, or does the action reflect a more basic problem, like loneliness or unhappiness, which requires attention?

Vaginal irritation and discharge may be associated with excessive masturbation or sexual molestation, both of which should prompt a close look at the child's life.

*Pinworms* can cause a vaginal infection. The adult worms crawl out of the rectum, usually at night, to lay their eggs and migrate to the vagina, causing itching and discharge.

In dealing with vaginal infections, every effort is made to identify the cause (the specific germs involved) and any other underlying factors like a foreign body. We inspect a smear of the discharge under the microscope and send the sample for culture in order to identify the germs involved. (See *infections.*) Depending on the cause, antibiotics are given by mouth or by vaginal suppository.

While awaiting the results of cultures, vinegar-water baths (2 table-spoons of vinegar per quart of warm water) can be used for relief of the discomfort. Separate the labia and insert the tip of a clean washcloth into the area of the outermost part of the vagina to allow the vinegar to seep in.

Occasionally we are not able to identify any specific microbial cause and recommend the application of estrogen (female hormone) cream to the outer portions of the vagina and labia each night for 2 to 3 weeks, and then 2 to 3 times a week for an additional 1 or 2 months.

In sexually active teen-agers, vaginal discharge and itching or burning are common. Frequent causes are Monilia (yeast) and Trichomonas (single-celled organism, a protozoa). Treatment for Trichomonas is directed toward both partners, since the male carries the organism in his urethra.

**Venereal disease.** The term venereal disease (VD for short) refers to diseases that can be transmitted by sexual contact. They are of major medical importance and their incidence is rapidly increasing. Syphilis and gonorrhea are the most important ones. ***Molluscum contagiosum lice,*** and ***scabies*** are diseases that are not primarily venereal but which are transmitted by close body, including sexual, contact. Certain viruses, notably ***cytomegalovirus*** and herpes simplex (see ***fever blisters***), are now known to infect the genitalia and, it appears, can be transmitted through sexual intercourse. It is likely that these viral venereal diseases are quite prevalent and are significant in causing disease of newborns as well as adults. More will be learned about them in the years ahead. In the following discussion, the term venereal disease refers to syphilis and gonorrhea.

Venereal disease is inseparably related to the broader questions of sexual freedom, dating patterns, drug use, contraception, and so forth, and should probably be discussed in this more general context in family life courses in high schools. Parents and physicians armed with facts about venereal disease can at least give information about the seriousness of these disorders, the likelihood of contracting them, and the precautions to take following exposure (especially the need for medical examination and care) to young people who tend to minimize the dangers of venereal disease or to ignore them altogether.

The venereal diseases illustrate very well the problem of trying to control an infectious disease mainly by treating people who develop symptoms and come to medical attention. At best, we keep the lid on the boiling pot. Ultimately, only effective vaccines will be preventive. In the meantime, it might be possible to achieve better control in the community if individuals with symptoms of venereal disease promptly reported their symptoms and their sexual contacts to medical or public health authorities. This goal is perhaps least likely achieved in the part of the population most likely to be affected by the diseases. They are often young, poor, and mobile, without continuing access to health facilities. Furthermore, they truly may not know that they have symptoms, even if well informed, because, in many cases, symptoms are obscure or nonexistent. Ideally, those who are having sexual contacts with many partners should have regular medical checks (every few months) whether or not they or their partners have symptoms.

Another deterrent to young people seeking medical care is the requirement in many states that their parents give consent. Because this requirement varies from state to state and is often different for different disorders, it is very confusing to doctors and lawyers alike. Uniform, uncategoric (that is, not related to specific conditions) consent laws for the comprehensive care of young people are necessary. Young people need to have readily accessible sources of medical care which make them feel welcome.

When a patient is identified as having venereal disease, all sexual contacts should be identified, brought in for evaluation, and treated if they harbor the germ. In fact, this procedure is required by law, but such surveillance is difficult to achieve. Even when they have the information about contacts, overburdened and underfinanced clinics and health departments do not have the resources to cope with the formidable task of case finding. Many patients refuse to reveal the identity of contacts because they don't want to stigmatize them. Many physicians do not urge that contacts be examined and treated or adopt punitive attitudes that deter patients from seeking care. Patients and doctors alike cover up the condition.

## SYPHILIS

Syphilis (sometimes called lues) is usually transmitted by sexual intercourse, but can affect the newborn infant by way of direct transmission from an infected mother to her baby across the placenta prior to birth.

In the adolescent and adult, infection with syphilis acquired during sexual intercourse passes through three clinical stages if left untreated. The first stage of syphilis is a painless sore (or sores) known as a *chancre*, which in the male is usually located on the penis. Chancres vary in size from the frankly obvious to those that would be seen only by a close examination directed specifically toward finding them. On the average, the sore develops about 3 weeks following contact with a syphilitic partner and may last for 4 to 6 weeks. In females, chancres occur on the labia or in the vagina and, because they are in more concealed body parts, are less likely to be noticed. Reflecting less common sexual practices, chancres may also occur on the mouth, tongue, or anus.

The second stage of syphilis occurs 2 to 10 weeks following the chancre. It consists of a rash which usually covers the entire skin surface, the mouth, and the anus, and is accompanied by an enlargement of the lymph nodes. The rash varies in appearance. Most common are slightly raised, nontender patches (or macules). The rash may be hardly noticeable and is not always present, even though infection with syphilis has occurred. When present, the rash lasts for 2 to 6 weeks and heals without scars.

Following the second stage, syphilis can go into hiding in the body from 2 to 20 or more years. This dormant period is called the *latent phase*. At some unexpected and unpredictable time after the second phase, the third stage begins, usually insidiously. Its manifestations are many and include inflammation and widening, by scarring, of the major blood vessels leading from the heart, inflammation of the brain, nerves, and spinal cord, and arthritis. Symptoms depend on the site of attack and, accordingly, may include heart failure, blindness, unsteady gait, loss of intellectual function, and, in the most severe cases, death. While the first and second stages of syphilis are usually no more than annoying, the third stage is a serious disease.

When syphilis is acquired congenitally from the mother's blood (by way of the placenta to the fetus during pregnancy), many infected infants are aborted early in gestation. In those babies born alive and not treated, the stages of illness correspond to the second and third stages in the adult. Chancres are not seen in newborns who acquire the infection prior to birth. Some infants are extremely ill at birth. The particular symptoms reflect the organs that the syphilis bacteria attacked. Thus, infants may develop heart failure (see *heart disease, congenital*), enlarged livers and spleens, *jaundice*, and *meningitis*. Many syphilitic infants appear well at birth and several weeks later develop symptoms of lethargy, weight loss, fever, and irritability. In addition to these symptoms, or separate from them, some infants develop variable kinds of skin rashes, sores at the corners of their lips and around the mouth and anus, nasal discharge, painful swelling of bones and joints, inflammation of central nervous system (brain, nerves, and spinal cord) and the eyes. Healing of affected organs often occurs with scarring and a resulting impairment of their appearance and/or function. For example, the affected child may have bowed legs after syphilitic infection of the bones (see *osteomyelitis*) and retardation and seizures following infection of the brain. Some infants escape early symptoms. The infection remains dormant and declares itself later in childhood, causing symptoms similar to those of third-stage syphilis in adults. In general, syphilis is a serious disease in infants, regardless of when symptoms appear.

Syphilis is caused by a *spirochete* (a microbe with a spiral or cork-screw shape) called *Treponema pallidum*. It is a very fragile bacterium. Despite its destructive capacity, it cannot survive outside of the body or even be grown in culture media. It is transmitted from one person to another through contact of the skin, mouth, or anus with a chancre or lesion of the second stage. It cannot be gotten, except under extraordinary circumstances, by contact with inanimate objects like toilet seats or towels. The skin lesions of the first or second stages teem with spirochetes. The microbes penetrate skin which comes in contact with them, initiating a new infection. The latent phase and third stage are not transmissible to a sexual partner. In congenital syphilis, the spirochetes cross the placenta to infect the developing baby.

Infection by syphilis bacteria is paralleled in the body by the development of antibodies detectable in the blood following the incubation period (see **infections**), about one week after the appearance of the chancre. A negative antibody test during the early weeks following exposure does not exclude infection by syphilis. The test must be repeated several times over the next few months to be sure that no antibodies appear. In syphilis affecting the central nervous system, antibodies as well as other chemical and microscopic findings make their appearance in the spinal fluid. There are several antibodies to syphilis, measurements of which are used to detect infected individuals. The Wassermann test is one such measurement. The quantity of antibody is related to the duration and degree of activity of the infection. During the latent or dormant phase, antibody is the only indication of infection, making the measurement of antibody worthwhile in case finding. In treated cases, antibody may drop to a very low level and may even completely disappear. In the newborn, antibody present in an infected mother passes by way of the placenta to the baby's blood and can be detected at birth. The antibody transmitted from the mother disappears in time unless the infant is also infected and untreated, in which case antibody manufactured by the baby adds to the dwindling maternal supply and increases with time.

A positive antibody test does not necessarily mean active infection. It may reflect infection that once occurred and was cured either spontaneously or with treatment. In some uncertain situations, the test must be repeated to see in which direction the antibody level is heading. If the trend is downward, the likelihood is that infection once occurred and is now over. Occasionally, positive tests are caused by disorders other than syphilis. However, any positive test always deserves close evaluation to exclude the possibility of active infection even in the absence of clinical symptoms.

The diagnosis of syphilis depends on a combination of physical findings, microscopic identification of the spirochete obtained by scrapings of the chancre or of a lesion of the second stage, positive blood antibody tests, and a history of exposure to a known syphilitic. The detection of antibody in the blood helps confirm the diagnosis in cases which are suspected on clinical grounds. Even in the absence of any symptoms, a positive test done after a contact with a syphilitic or as a screening procedure alerts the physician to the presence of syphilis.

Screening for syphilis is commonly carried out at the time of marriage, during pregnancy, and on entering the military. Screening tests are also done routinely during many hospitalizations or physical examinations for schools or employment.

Identification of syphilis during pregnancy is of particular importance in preventing infection of the infant. Even during the dormant period, the microorganisms can be passed across the placenta to infect the developing baby. The mother need not have symptoms in order to transmit the disease to her infant, although she cannot transmit it during the dormant period to a sexual partner.

Treatment of syphilis is almost always successful with appropriate doses of penicillin or other antibiotics. The progress of the disease can be arrested at any stage. In the third stage, after serious damage to organs has occurred, treatment will not restore lost function but can retard the progression of disability.

### GONORRHEA

Gonorrhea is the most common venereal disease. It affects millions of Americans and has been on the increase in recent years. It is often a serious disease and is a major public health problem.

In the male, the disorder is popularly known as "the clap" and involves an inflammation of the *urethra* (the central tube that runs the length of the penis). Discharge from the penis, difficulty and burning pain in urinating, and the passage of bloody urine are the most common symptoms. Lower abdominal and testicular pain also occur. If untreated, the inflammation may heal with scarring of the urethra, obstruction to the passage of urine, and deformity of the penis.

In the female, a copious vaginal discharge or change in character of a long-standing one, lower abdominal pain (often severe), and fever are the symptoms of a full-blown infection. These stem from inflammation of the cervix (the "mouth" of the uterus), the Fallopian tubes, ovaries, and the lower abdominal (pelvic) cavity. In general, neither the vagina nor uterus is inflamed to any great degree. If untreated or treated too late, healing will likely be accompanied by scarring of the Fallopian tubes, which can block the passage of eggs from the ovary at the time of ovulation, possibly causing sterility. The likelihood of an *ectopic* (displaced) *pregnancy* is also increased, because the fertilized egg (or ovum) is more likely to have its journey through the Fallopian tube arrested before it enters the uterus. Sometimes, even after long courses of antibiotic treatment, the inflammation may linger on for months or years in the cervix, tubes, ovaries, and lower abdominal cavity, with intermittent pain, fever, and vaginal discharge. If passed by genital-oral or genital-rectal sexual contact, the primary infection may occur in the throat or rectum.

In both male and female, gonorrhea may spread beyond the reproductive organs to invade the bloodstream and then be carried to joints, heart valves, skin, and liver.

If a mother is harboring the germs that cause gonorrhea, her newborn infant can pick up the microbes during passage through the birth canal. Infection may then develop in the baby's eyes. In the past, such infections acquired at birth were a leading cause of blindness in children. The use of silver nitrate or antibiotic drops in the eyes of the newborn can prevent this complication completely. This procedure is part of the routine care of the infant in the United States, regardless of the health status of the mother.

Interestingly, it now appears that most males and females who harbor the gonorrheal germ are not sick with symptoms, although symptoms may have been present or could develop under proper conditions, such as fatigue, stress, or menstruation. These "carriers" (see *infections*) are nonetheless contagious and make the total elimination of gonorrhea problematic unless a vaccine is developed. However, examination (screening) of potential carriers for this microbe is more and more becoming a part of venereal disease control, like the Pap smear for cancer. Carriers are also treated with antibiotics.

Gonorrhea is caused by a specific bacterium known as *Neisseria gonorrhoeae* and is usually referred to as the *gonococcus*. Despite its potential for causing trouble, it is a delicate germ and cannot survive for long outside of the human body. It is transmitted from person to person exclusively by sexual contact. Transmission by way of contact with a toilet seat or other inanimate object could occur only under extraordinary circumstances and for all practical purposes may be discounted.

The diagnosis of infection with the gonococcus is made on the basis of the patient's symptoms, the likelihood of exposure, and the isolation of the microbe by culture and microscopic examination. In the mildest cases or those without symptoms, diagnosis rests almost entirely on laboratory evidence. As with syphilis, therefore, those who have many sexual contacts would do well to have periodic medical examinations.

Treatment of gonorrhea, however mild or severe, consists of a course of antibiotics until symptoms are relieved and there is no laboratory evidence of continued presence of the microorganism. Treatment of complications, such as chronic abscesses of the Fallopian tubes and ovaries, may require surgery to drain the pus. Sometimes the only choice is to remove the diseased organ entirely. Scarring and strictures (narrowing of the male urethra) may require surgical dilation to relieve obstruction. Treating carriers is valuable for prevention of spread and the "flare-up" of acute infection in the carrier himself or herself.

Gonorrhea and syphilis are likely to occur together, both being transmitted by sexual intercourse. Gonorrhea may cause symptoms fairly soon after exposure, while syphilis contracted at the same time is still in its incubation period. The standard treatment used for gonorrhea will eradicate the germ that causes syphilis in its incubation stage. If syphilis infection is already established, as determined by blood tests, further treatment for the syphilis is indicated.

Gonorrhea is the most common bacterial infection of man. No *immunization* against it is yet available, although research on a vaccine is underway. The only sure prevention is avoidance of exposure to infected persons, who may not be easy to identify because of the large numbers of asymptomatic carriers. Condoms help prevent infection and are recommended even if another form of contraception is being used. Even if one is concerned about contracting venereal disease and tries to avoid obviously ill sexual partners, there is no guarantee that the contact is not a carrier.

*Vision problems.* The eye is a remarkable structure. It sees objects both close at hand and far off and puts them in perspective, giving a sense of relative distances. If the atmosphere were perfectly transparent, the eye could see a candle a mile away. The range of vision is enormous. Besides being adaptable to dim or bright light, the eye can distinguish subtle differences in color. Moreover, the normal eye performs all these functions not singly but in combination, and in perfect coordination, with the other eye. Almost instantaneously, in bright sunlight or near darkness, the eyes can shift from reading the small print of a newspaper to recognizing the red, green, or yellow of a traffic light down the street, while sensing the movement of objects at either side of the viewer. This adaptability depends upon the capacity of a complex optical system to react at great speed to the varying *intensity* (strength) and *frequency* (color) of light coming in from the environment.

For a workable comparison, you can think of the eye as operating like a camera (but a far more flexible and sensitive one than the best model you can buy). Instead of recording an image on film that is chemically sensitive, as a camera does, the eye encodes a pattern of the photochemical changes that occur in sensory cells when they absorb photons of light. Photons can be described as individual packets of energy; the frequency at which they vibrate determines the color. (If the frequency is too high, as in X-rays, or too low, as in radio waves, we don't "see.") The coded pattern from the reaction of photons and sensory cells is transmitted along nerve channels to the brain for decoding and translation into our mental pictures. In short, the eye transforms light energy to chemical energy to electrical energy.

The magnitude of this process of photochemical change and coding is staggering. Each of our eyes has millions of sensory cells, and each cell contributes a bit of information to the message. This activity goes on, of course, through all our waking hours. Sight is one of our most marvelous and precious possessions. It is a pity so many people take it for granted. Not everyone understands how the eye works or is appropriately aware of what can go wrong. For this reason, we devote a little extra space to a discussion of vision and vision problems. But it is important to understand at the outset that, almost without exception, eye troubles should have medical attention.

In the language of medicine the eyeball is known as the *globe*. It consists of 3 outer layers enclosing a transparent gelatinous mass, the *vitreous humor*. The outermost layer includes the *sclera*, which is the "white" of the eye, and the *cornea*, which is a transparent circular disk over the colored portion. You can see tiny blood vessels in the sclera. The circular colored part, which makes each of us blue-eyed or gray-eyed or green-eyed and so forth, is the *iris* and is in the middle layer of the covering. The dark *pupil* at the center is an opening through the iris, comparable to the shutter of a camera. It enlarges or contracts according to the conditions of visibility. (Some drugs and the emotions also affect the size of the pupil.) Back of the pupil is the *lens*, optically similar to the lens of a camera or telescope but with a very important difference. Whereas the camera lens, made of glass, is fixed in shape, the eye lens can be pulled into different shapes by muscles responding to feedback information on the clarity of the image. In other words, the eye lens changes shape to fit the job it is doing at any instant.

The innermost layer of the globe's covering is the *retina*, composed of the sensory cells. Each retina has millions of tiny cylindrical cells called *rods*, and millions of *cones*, also named for their shape. Both rods and cones react to the intensity of light, but it appears that cones alone may be involved in the determination of color. Below a certain level of illumination, the cones cease, or almost cease, to operate. In near darkness all colors look black or gray to us, and it may well be that when the cones shut down, color discrimination stops altogether. As far as science can tell, the idea of "color" is a product of our brains; the only scientifically demonstrable difference between blue, say, and red is the one of frequency. (If you have seen the term wavelength applied here, it amounts to the same thing because wavelength depends on frequency.)

The *optic nerve* leads from the retina of each eye to the brain. Since there are about a million sensory fibers in each optic nerve to transmit patterns composed from countless individual bits of information contributed by the rods and cones, it seems safe to suppose that some kind of filtering or modulation must go on at the back of the eye to reduce all the information into transmissible messages. Indeed, neurophysiologists think of the retina as being a part of the central nervous system (brain, and so forth) rather than an element of the eye alone. (It is embryologically derived from the nervous system.)

A thin transparent membrane called the *conjunctiva* covers the sclera, extending to form the inner linings of the upper and lower eyelids. Inflammation of this membrane, quite a common problem, is called **conjunctivitis.** The lacrimal glands bathe the conjunctiva with tears to clean and lubricate it.

If you have used a camera, you probably are aware that the amount of light you let into the camera and the distance between you and the object you are photographing have something to do with your getting a clear, sharp picture. The fanciest cameras automatically make adjustments for these factors, and so does the eye, but to a much finer degree. In the eye it is the iris that regulates the amount of light; after dark the pupil enlarges to let in more light.

It is the function of the lens to accommodate to distance. Every lens, whether in camera or eye, has a property known as *focal length*. This is the distance from the center of the lens to the point at which parallel light rays converge. The location of this point determines where the image will appear. You can think of the image as being no different from the image you see when you look in a mirror. To get a good picture with a camera, you must have this image fall as closely as possible upon the film. In the eye the image must fall upon the retina, particularly upon a very small region called the *macula*, where the greatest concentration of cones exists. Adjustments for focal length in the camera to make the image fall on the film are made by moving machinery back and forth, but in the eye, changes of lens shape have the same effect, because change of shape changes focal length. Most of the focusing of light rays in the eye occurs as the light passes through the cornea; the lens performs the final focusing. This bending of light rays, whether by glass or by the cornea and lens, is known as *refraction*. Because of nonuniform refraction around the rim of a lens, various distortions, particularly of color, are likely to occur there. One of the functions of the iris is to block off light rays from this region of the lens.

It is an unfortunate fact of life that we are not all born with perfect eyesight. When the various components of the eye are working properly, the net result, within certain limits, is a sharp image on the retina at all distances and under all conditions of light, with distinct and true discrimination of color. Some people fail to meet the normal standards in one or more of these specifications. The image may form in front of the retina (nearsightedness) or behind it (farsightedness). The vision may be distorted by irregular bending of light rays (astigmatism). There may be failure to see the same colors most other people see or to see any color at all. Furthermore young children who at first seemed to have perfect vision may in the period between 6 and adolescence become *myopic* (nearsighted). This condition can come quite swiftly. A youngster who was able to read the blackboard without difficulty in one school year may see only a blur when he or she takes his or her seat again the next September. In the majority of cases the difficulties, though they may seem drastic, are easily corrected with properly fitted glasses. The important thing is to spot them early, to find out whether they are progressive, and to spare the child the hardship of having to struggle with a correctable handicap.

The shape of the cornea, the shape of the lens, or the dimensions of the globe as they affect the distance from lens to retina, or any combination of these three factors, may contribute to problems of vision. There is no simple answer for every condition. Obviously, these are inherited characteristics, explainable by the laws of **genetics.** The cornea, which is fixed in shape, may cause the light rays to converge too sharply or to diverge too much. If the curvature of the cornea is not uniform, some of the rays will be bent irregularly and the resulting image will be fuzzy (astigmatism). The image can also be unclear if the lens is situated too close to, or too far from, the retina. The purpose of eyeglasses, of course, is to compensate artificially for those natural conditions. The nearsighted person needs an artificial lens to spread the light rays and keep them from converging in front of the retina; the farsighted person needs just the opposite. A more complicated lens to give a uniform and symmetrical overall pattern of refraction is required for astigmatism. The geometrical conditions of vision do not remain static over the years. Newborns tend to be farsighted and grow less so. Older persons may have a tendency to have difficulty in adjusting to near objects. The greatest changes occur in the years of greatest physical growth. After the teens, vision tends to remain about the same until the effects of aging begin to make themselves felt.

Contrary to popular opinion, newborns can see, but we have no way of knowing exactly *what* they see. A bright light shone in the eyes of a newborn causes blinking. The newborn's eyes will follow, at least briefly, an object passed before his face. It is not until he is several weeks old, however, that a newborn can focus both eyes on a single object. In the early period of focusing, his eyes may cross as they move to fix on an object. This is usually a temporary condition which disappears by the time the child is 4 or 5 months old. If it does persist beyond 5 months, or if the eyes remain crossed for any length of time in the struggle to focus, you should inform your physician. This process of focusing both eyes on the same object is called *fusion*. If both eyes are not properly aligned by fusion, a different image falls on each retina, resulting in double vision. This is discussed in detail under **cross-eyes.**

The cornea of the eye at all ages should be as clear as a pool of water. Cloudiness is always a cause for concern, even in infancy. Also, inability to tolerate light—blinking, turning away, or tearing—should prompt you to seek help. In babies these symptoms suggest congenital glaucoma (increased pressure within the eye), which if untreated can cause blindness.

By the time your child can creep, you will notice that he scrambles after small objects and picks them up or tries to. His happy smile at your appearance is sufficient proof of his ability to see and recognize familiar faces at a distance of 20 or 30 feet. His inability to communicate precludes any further test of the acuteness of his sight at this age, but you should watch for too frequent blinking or rubbing of the eyes and for squinting. The toddler should not stumble over every small object in his path. The child of school age may exhibit any one or all of those symptoms or some others that may be revealed as he learns to read. Individual letters or whole words may be blurred to him, or words or lines may run together. He may see double. Strong light may hurt his eyes. He may have headaches (see **headache**) after reading or watching television. All of these symptoms suggest difficulties of vision. You should report them to your doctor.

A good many parents worry when they see their very young children holding picture books or other objects almost close enough to touch their noses. Preschoolers with even the best of vision may do this, but in a child of school age one is justified in suspecting a problem and asking for a check. You can ignore the old warnings that reading in dim light, going to the movies, or watching television (even right next to the screen) are somehow "bad" for the eyes. There is no evidence to support this.

Your child will be receiving regular eye examinations at his periodic health supervision visits to the pediatrician or family physician (see Part 1, Chapter 2: "The Regular Checkup"). By the age of 4 most children are ready to cooperate in tests of visual acuity, and the doctor or nurse, who may sometimes give the eye test, may spot an abnormality that has escaped parental notice. Some eye defects are so mild they require no treatment, although the doctor may suggest more frequent examination in the future. Other abnormalities call for prompt treatment to halt progression. Needless to say, the child's cooperativeness is a factor in the accuracy of the test. A child with normal vision may "fail" the eye test simply out of fatigue, distraction, or failure to understand directions. Repeating the test under quiet conditions with a rested and cooperative child may show the vision to be normal after all. The main objective of the vision test done in the doctor's office or in school is to identify *all* children who *might* have a vision problem and who should therefore be examined more closely.

Most people are familiar with the standard methods for testing visual acuity. The person being tested reads letters or figures from a standard chart a certain distance away. The lines of type graduate in size, and each line is numbered to indicate the distance at which it should be read by a person with normal vision; thus, 20 means 20 feet, 30 means 30 feet, 40 means 40 feet, and so forth. For children too young to read, there are charts with pictures of cats, dogs, balls, and so forth, or differently oriented letters of the alphabet, like "E," which have an open side. The child is asked to say whether the open side is up or down, pointing to the right or left. If the child can read at 20 feet what the average child can read at 20 feet, he is said to have 20/20 vision ("twenty over twenty"). If he can only read at 20 feet what the person with normal vision can read at 30 feet, his vision is described as 20/30, and so forth. Each eye is tested separately and a rating assigned. There is not complete agreement about the significance of these results when they indicate only mild degrees of impairment of vision. Some children with 20/30 or even 20/40 vision manage to go about their daily business without any trouble at all. Should they wear glasses? There is no evidence that putting glasses on these children with mild defects of vision will prevent or retard progressive disorders. The best procedure is to discuss the matter with your physician, who can advise you whether the child should see an eye specialist (ophthalmologist).

We suggest that children's vision be examined between ages 3 and 4, upon entrance to school, and every 3 or 4 years thereafter. The first examination is particularly important. Children with severe or even moderately severe myopia or other problems should be seen more often. If your child is myopic to a marked degree, you should ask the doctor about the advisability of rough contact sports; there is a danger of retinal detachment (a separation of the inner layer of the retina).

All glasses for children should be shatterproof (now required by law in some states). In the games children play and in this age of car accidents (see Part 2, Chapter 12: "Car Safety"), there is always the hazard of a smashed lens, and a fragment of broken glass in the eyeball is a serious matter indeed. Whether a child wears glasses all the time or only for reading and other close work will depend, of course, on his problem of vision. The child will be most cooperative about wearing the glasses when the immediate benefits are most apparent. If glasses enable him to catch the fly ball in left field or to follow the action on the movie screen, he is likely to wear them without protest. Otherwise, he may approach them as he does any prescribed medicine. Glasses, like all prescriptions, are useful only if used. If resistance to glasses is a problem, you should talk the situation over with your doctor. Contact lenses are useful in certain cases; for example, the child with myopia who would otherwise need very thick glasses. For the average child with glasses, however, the inconvenience of caring for the lenses usually outweighs the cosmetic advantage. It is important that you understand exactly what the child's problem of vision is and why he should be wearing glasses. If you don't, your arguments will not be particularly persuasive. In some cases, the doctor may decide to put off the glasses until the child's understanding is more mature. Often this can be done without risk to the vision. If his only problem is inability to see the schoolroom blackboard, perhaps arrangements can be made to have your child placed in the front row. You always have to balance all the factors. The result of a visual acuity test should not override every other consideration.

For the problems of a severe visual handicap, see *developmental disabilities.*

*Vitiligo* is a loss of pigment in the skin. Milk-white, sharply demarcated patches appear on the wrists, armpits, around the eyes, mouth, and anus. These areas of loss of pigment appear spontaneously. The hair in the area may or may not be white.

Vitiligo should be distinguished from the loss of pigment in scars, scratch marks, and bruises, which can persist for months or even years. Chicken pox is notorious for leaving depigmented spots in its wake. In vitiligo, the pigment-producing cells in the skin, for unknown reasons, stop working and disappear.

The condition is inherited as a dominant trait (see *genetics*), and is found with increased frequency in individuals having malfunction of the thyroid and adrenal glands. (See *hormones.*)

Vitiligo rarely improves spontaneously. There are 5 approaches in management: (1) do nothing; (2) bleach the surrounding skin in order to blur the margins of the lesions or to remove all remaining spots of pigment in extensive areas; (3) completely avoid the sun, in the case of fair-skinned individuals, thus fading the normal pigmentation and making the vitiligo less noticeable by contrast; (4) try to repigment the skin with special medications; and (5) hide or cover the lesions with stains or cosmetics. Each case should be discussed individually by patient and doctor.

*Vomiting,* usually accompanied by a feeling of *nausea* or being "sick to the stomach," is a symptom of many diseases. In addition, it can cause problems on its own. Obviously, there is the discomfort of retching with which we are all familiar. The act of vomiting, while unpleasant, is not dangerous in itself except in an unconscious or semiconscious individual. Of greater medical concern is the loss of body fluid from the vomiting, aggravated by the inability to take in replacement water and salt in the diet. If this loss is excessive, dehydration (see *diarrhea*) may result.

When or whether you call the doctor or nurse for a vomiting child depends somewhat on what else is happening. We recommend calling for any excessive drowsiness (see *drowsiness, delirium, and lethargy*), confusion, *headache,* sharp or constant *abdominal pain,* painful or frequent urination, labored breathing, or persistent high fever. The vomiting, which at times is associated with coughing spells when the child gags on his or her own mucus, warrants attention to the cause of the *cough* and perhaps a cough medicine as well. In infants, vomiting must be distinguished from spitting up. Vomiting as such in an infant should be reported. Call also for frequent vomiting, say 3 or 4 times in 2 hours. Under some circumstances, you can afford to wait and see what develops; for example, the child old enough to report symptoms reliably who vomits once or twice, acts ill, refuses food, but seems otherwise okay without specific complaints. Here, a wait-and-see attitude is appropriate. In short, whether or when to call the doctor depends on the circumstances, your experience with illness, and your doctor's policy.

It is a good idea to allow the infant or child to rest his stomach for several hours after vomiting, especially if he does not ask for or otherwise indicate that he wants anything to drink. The older the child, the longer he can safely wait until taking fluids again. Then, begin offering fluids to replenish those lost and to meet his current fluid requirements. Give sips at first, every 10 to 15 minutes. Work from teaspoons to tablespoons up to several ounces, increasing the intervals between drinks to one-half and then 1 hour.

Well-tolerated fluids which provide sugar for energy and needed water and salt are the following:

1. Gelatin water. Add the package to a quart of water. Know that red-colored gelatin may stain diarrheal stools. The color may be mistaken for blood.

2. Fruit-flavored syrup drinks. For small babies, these should be diluted with extra water.

3. Flattened carbonated beverages like ginger ale. Leave the cover off

the bottle at room temperature or put a teaspoon of sugar or warm water into the drink to cause dissolved gas to escape. Gas in the stomach can cause further vomiting.

4. Popsicles. These may be made at home with fruit-flavored syrup drinks frozen in your ice cube tray. Simply stick a toothpick into each section.

5. Crushed ice chips.

6. Fruit-flavored lollipops or hard candy. Even if the child uses his own saliva to dissolve the lollipop, he is getting a small amount of sugar for energy. Very often the lollipop makes the child thirsty, thereby stimulating interest in other liquids.

7. Clear chicken or beef broth, consommé, or bouillon. If you use a canned or homemade broth, put it in the refrigerator for a few hours and scoop off the fat which solidifies at the top. Dilute the soup with extra water, twice as much as usual.

8. Bouillon or chicken broth cubes. Be sure to use a measuring cup and dilute the cube in twice the amount of water suggested. Add the cube after heating and measuring the water. The amount of salt in the cube is extremely concentrated and, unless diluted properly, could produce a dangerous level of salt in the blood. Avoid cubes that are heavily spiced.

Keep the child on these clear liquids for at least 24 hours. If the child does not wish to drink, try lollipops (see above). Do not force him to drink, since he will probably vomit more than you give him. Use your talents to encourage the small amounts indicated.

If vomiting starts again, stop all feedings and go back to teaspoonful amounts.

If the child begs for food, give him a salted cracker. However, do not give milk or other solid foods for at least 24 hours. On the second day, try diluted skim milk, refined cereal (like rice or processed cream of wheat), arrowroot cookies, and bananas or applesauce. The diet may return to normal fairly rapidly from then on, but hold off on fresh fruits with peels and raw vegetables or coarse cereals until recovery is complete.

Infants under 5 months who are vomiting need special treatment. They cannot stand the loss and deprivation of fluids for as long as older children, nor is the variety of fluids they can take as great. (See discussion of dehydration under *diarrhea.*) In this age group, be sure to check with your doctor or nurse. Depending on the severity of the vomiting, it may be desirable to take the baby off milk and solids or to reduce the milk intake. The nursing mother may have to express milk by hand to prevent engorgement and to maintain production. Offer the gelatin drink or the fruit-flavored syrup drinks described above. Another fluid, very carefully measured, which is good for infants and babies, is the following: 1 quart water, 2½ level tablespoons sugar or corn syrup, and ½ level teaspoon salt. (Do not confuse a teaspoon with a tablespoon or reverse the measures for salt and sugar.) Give the baby teaspoonful feedings of these fluids until he can tolerate an ounce or more at a time. Then feed him as much as he wants as often as he wants it. The second day you may be able to dilute the regular formula with double amounts of water. Gradually, he can resume his regular formula. Within a few days he can probably tolerate cereal, fruits, and vegetables in his usual diet.

Vomiting frequently occurs with an intestinal infection (*gastroenteritis*) and is often accompanied by abdominal pain and diarrhea. Most of these infections are caused by known viruses (see *infections*) or agents presumed to be viruses for which to date there is no treatment. Antibiotics are of no help. Vomiting often follows a blow to the head (see *head injuries*). It is commonly seen with ear, throat, and urinary infections. (See *earache; throat, sore*; and *urinary tract infections and defects.*) Vomiting may occur with *appendicitis* or *intestinal obstruction.* Apart from the vomiting, the symptoms of these conditions may prompt a call to the doctor. While vomiting is usually a consequence of disease, we deliberately cause it in children who have taken a poisonous dose of medicine (see Part 2, Chapter 10: "Poisoning"). Some poisons themselves produce vomiting.

Blood in the vomitus may occur as a result of irritation. It represents the tear of very small blood vessels in the lining of the stomach and has no more significance than a nosebleed. It is usually present in small amounts (less than a teaspoon) and need not cause alarm. However, if in doubt, check with the doctor or nurse.

Unless you have the approval of your physician, we recommend not giving the child antivomiting medicines, either by mouth or rectum. These drugs in general have the disadvantage of causing drowsiness or stimulation which are symptoms that confuse us in assessing the child's condition. We rarely, if ever, prescribe them. In particular, do not give medicine prescribed for some other family member. A number of peculiar drug reactions have occurred when well-meaning parents have given medications not intended for children. Antibiotics, as we have emphasized elsewhere, should never be given without a doctor's prescription and then only if the cause of the vomiting is an infection that will respond to these drugs.

See Part 1, Chapter 5: "Caring for the Sick Child at Home"; *abdominal pain*; and *gastroenteritis.*

**Warts** are swellings or tumors (noncancerous) of the *epidermis* (outer layer of the skin) caused by infection with a virus known as the *human papil-*

*loma virus.* In experiments with human volunteers, it was found that the incubation period after inoculation with this virus varies from 1 to 6 months. (See *infections.*) Warts are most common in children. They may be spread by contact between individuals and from one site to another on an individual. Sixty-five percent of warts disappear on their own within 2 years without treatment. This is an important point which should lend a note of caution to vigorous therapy. Time is clearly on the side of the patient.

Common warts are found most often on the hands of children, but they can grow anywhere on the skin. Warts on the palms or soles (*plantar warts*) must be distinguished from *calluses*, which are reactions to steady skin trauma, such as occurs with poorly fitting shoes. Unlike calluses, warts interrupt the natural lines of the skin. The two conditions sometimes exist together and, not uncommonly, calluses form over warts on the soles of the feet.

The major concern with warts is usually aesthetic, when they become awkward because of size or appearance. In themselves painless, warts along the borders of fingernails may develop painful fissures. Warts on the soles of the feet can become very tender upon pressure because they act as a foreign body, like a pebble in a shoe. If treatment should be necessary at all, the common wart can be removed by any of a number of medications, *electrocauterization* (burning the wart with an electrified tip), and *cryosurgery* (freezing) with liquid nitrogen. Unless plantar warts are painful, rapidly growing, or very small, it is best either to let a sleeping dog lie or be extremely cautious in therapy. The reason is that the treatment can be worse than the disease. Scarring of the skin may result, which is both painful and very difficult to treat. It is essential to correct any orthopedic defects and to use properly fitting shoes. Plantar warts occur most often in the area of callus pressure, and unless the incorrect weight bearing can be relieved, it is often impossible either to cure the wart or to make the patient comfortable.

## *Weight problems.*

### OVERWEIGHT

Obesity is a national problem of major importance. A number of factors contribute: heredity, diet, exercise, family patterns, and individual psychology. In Part 1, Chapter 3: "Diet of Infants and Children," we discussed the concept of the "appestat," which determines satiety, and the ways in which heredity and early feeding experiences influence it. In that section we stressed the importance of preventing obesity while acknowledging that we were far from a complete understanding of how to do so, or on which infants to concentrate. In this article we will look at some of the other factors operating in obesity and discuss an approach to the obese child.

Obesity as a national public health problem must be viewed against the background of our patterns of eating and exercise. While much of the world starves, most Americans are exposed to a diet extraordinarily rich in calories, and parents have to make a conscious effort, beginning in the supermarket, to control caloric intake. Affluence in America has led to profound changes in eating habits, to a large extent spurred by the search of the food industry for bigger and better markets. Industry's motive is greater profits for themselves, not better nutrition for the public. Soft drinks have been substituted for water, and ice cream has seemingly become a daily requirement. Snack foods, notoriously high in calories, have made their way into almost every home. Next time you are in the market, look at the row after row of sweetened breakfast foods introduced since you were a child. In many, sugar is the major ingredient. These foods are heavily advertised on television to children (see *television and children*), who apply seemingly irresistible pressure on their parents to buy them. Parents are vulnerable to badgering, in large part, out of concern that their children are not eating enough. Don't be seduced. Much of the nutrition information a child hears on television is false, and it is a scandal that we subject youngsters to it. *Well* children (physically and emotionally) will eat enough of nutritionally desirable food for normal development if you insist that there is no other food to eat. Take it or leave it.

As parents, we need to become more aware of the basic nutritional needs of children at different ages and how these requirements are met or exceeded by the meals we plan (see Part 1, Chapter 3: "Diet of Infants and Children"). We are, to a great extent, a nation of "nutritional illiterates," reacting passively to high-powered advertising. Even medical schools have provided little or no nutrition education for doctors. Better labeling of foods requires greater nutritional knowledge if our diets are to improve.

Exercise is another important part of obesity prevention. In today's technological society, the physical use of our bodies has profoundly diminished (see *exercise and physical fitness*). We seldom walk to the store (impossible if you live in the suburbs), and less and less often to school. We ride elevators instead of walking stairs. It is not surprising that the greatest increase in weight is often seen during the winter months when a child is cooped up. This is also a time when television watching, and consequent physical inactivity, is at a peak, averaging 5 hours per day for many children.

Obese children often lack interest in physical exercise. Here, parental models are important. When parents value exercise at home and set a good example, the child is more likely to value it. An active family life of swimming, walking, running, ball playing, hiking, biking, and tennis is an important way of preventing obesity. Parents also should inquire about physical education programs in school. Obese children require special attention.

Family eating patterns are another contributing factor in obesity. Children of obese parents are at a special risk on environmental as well as hereditary grounds. Obese parents may be more likely to have excessive concern that their offspring are not eating enough and may encourage a higher caloric intake. If parents eat to relieve tension, this pattern is usually picked up subconsciously (see Part 1, Chapter 4: "Complaints with an Emotional Element"). Very often these parents have had weight or eating problems themselves as children and have found weight reduction very difficult. Many such adults have a preoccupation with their obesity to the point that they see the world in terms of fatness and thinness. At the center of this disturbance is the feeling that their own bodies are ugly and loathsome. These adults lose and regain weight much more frequently than those whose obesity begins in adult life.

Two types of eating disturbances are characteristic of obese adults: night eating and binge eating. In the night-eating pattern, breakfast is skipped and often lunch as well. Starting with dinner, eating goes on until bedtime. Insomnia often occurs. Binge eating means devouring enormous quantities of food in a very short time, such as a half gallon of ice cream or a box of cream-filled chocolate cookies. Parents with such problems will need special help if they are to prevent transmission of this pattern to their children.

Recent studies suggest that obese adults depend more on external clues like smell, taste, the sight of others eating, and less on hunger. In one experiment, obese and nonobese adults were fed over several days as much as they wanted of an exclusively liquid food whose caloric content could be changed without the participants' knowledge. The normal people adjusted the amount of liquid food to keep the calories constant, while the obese subjects just kept taking the same quantity regardless of calorie concentration. It may be that changing the external cues as a kind of reconditioning will prove helpful in controlling the weight of such individuals.

It is common to find that overweight children and adults feel sorry for themselves. They are afraid of being rejected because they are ugly. To drown their unworthy feelings they eat their troubles away, and so the cycle goes. Haranguing the overweight child only increases the feeling of self-pity. In fact, battles over food should be a warning that help is needed. It is important to understand what role obesity is playing in a child's life. There are no short answers. Each child's obesity must be judged in the context of his or her personality and life adjustment. How the child feels about himself is crucial. Professional help may be necessary in making this assessment and in planning treatment.

At The Children's Hospital Medical Center, the obese child's parents' own background regarding food is reviewed. Such a review can help clear the air and free the parents to view their child's needs more objectively. It may be that the only way for obese parents to prevent obesity in their children is by coming to grips with their own fatness and feelings about food.

Contrary to popular belief, it is the rare weight problem that is due to glands, that is, a recognized endocrinological disorder (see *hormones*). True, some children with hormone problems are excessively heavy, but almost never as an isolated symptom. The most common example of obesity related to a hormone is the child who is treated with hydrocortisone. The obesity is one price paid for the benefits of therapy. Research may eventually show further links between hormones and weight problems, but practical application of this information remains for the future.

To be completely fair, however, we must acknowledge that our understanding of why one person is obese and another is not is far from complete. Clearly more than calories is involved. It may be, for example, that obese people are more efficient in extracting their energy needs from a given caloric quantity of food and can store the surplus, whereas thinner people who may eat even more are less able to do so with resultant wastage of calories. When we can understand on a chemical level how this process operates, we may be able to control it. Think of how much guilt would be relieved if obesity could be shown, even in part, to be the result of an aberration of metabolism.

When is a child overweight? There are weight standards for children of all ages which give an objective answer to this question. Many heavy children are so tall and are simply large individuals without being obese. It is a common fact that parents who have had weight problems themselves are notoriously biased in their view of their children. Their anxieties over food are often counterproductive. In an effort to limit calories they may exert so much pressure and focus so much attention on food and eating that the child often seems driven to the undesirable behavior of eating too much, just the opposite of what is intended.

Parents who have or have had weight problems have difficulty in deciding about the fatness or thinness of their children. In recognition of this bias they are probably well advised to disqualify themselves from making this judgment alone. Before acting as though their children are fat or thin they should seek a neutral opinion. Their doctor, nurse, and nutritionist can provide professional guidance. Even then, whether a child can lose weight will depend largely on how the child views himself.

The assessment of the obese child requires an analysis of the diet, the

child's personality and investment in remaining obese, the family attitudes toward eating, hereditary factors, exercise habits, and intrafamily
dynamics. In any obese child all of these factors come into play in
various combinations. In planning treatment it is important to try to
judge the contributions of each. This may take time and cost money.
Parents who take this matter seriously and do not merely pay lip service
to the question should be prepared for some hard work. For a few, the
answer is simple, the prescribing of a diet. For most, the answer, if one
is to be found, is more complex. There may be no immediate answer and
sometimes the goal of weight loss must be postponed until other issues
can be attended to. The first step is to recognize obesity as a problem
and seek help.

In the older child, weight loss depends largely on self-motivation. It
cannot be imposed. So often a parent will ask us to "lecture" a child
about his weight. The most we can honestly do is ask the child how he
feels and what he wants to do about it. Unless the child himself feels he
is too fat and wants to lose weight. a weight-losing program will be
difficult to carry out. Doctor, patient, and parents must agree on goals
for the child and family. Very often this agreement is not reachable and
the complaint of obesity can be taken no further. For example, the
overweight teen-ager who is brought by his parents for weight reduction
and who cannot keep a seven-day log of food intake when requested to
do so, probably is not motivated to lose weight. On the other hand,
weight per se may not be the best avenue for approaching the obese
child. He may be more concerned about some other issue, like not being
popular or doing poorly in school. The way to engage him is to respond
to the need or hurt as he perceives it. The parents often need counseling
and should be prepared to spend a number of hours reviewing their
attitudes toward the child and the history of the problem.

Obese individuals are very vulnerable to claims for instant or effortless
means of weight reduction. They, or their parents, need to learn that
most such "miracle" programs are useless, or even dangerous.

We have been singularly unimpressed with crash diets, amphetamines, or thyroid pills (see *hormones*) in providing sustained weight
control in children and teen-agers with long-standing obesity and have
abandoned these approaches altogether. There is also no scientific basis
at all to the widespread public belief that sweating is a means of eventually losing weight. In a survey by the Food and Drug Administration
in 1969, more than one-third of the adult population held this belief.
Another widely held but erroneous belief is that massage is a way to lose
weight.

Practically speaking, in our present state of ignorance on the subject,
obesity is a matter of calories in and calories out. In addition to attending to emotions, exercise, and family factors (and these cannot be ig-

nored), it is important to provide the older child with dietary facts and to help the child become responsible for carrying out his own nutrition program. Self-policing is the goal. Children can learn and often become interested and involved in "their" special diet—how many meat, bread, and so forth portions they can have each day. Some children like to weigh out their servings. Some enjoy preparing the foods themselves.

Ongoing relationships with a doctor, nurse, or nutritionist are often important in motivating the child to cooperate. Diet is central to weight control. The child should have his own plan, preferably provided by a nutritionist. Groups like Weight-Watchers can also help.

## GENERAL GUIDELINES FOR WEIGHT CONTROL

### Food Preparation

1. Bake, broil, boil foods instead of deep-fat or pan frying.
2. Do not add extra butter, margarine, oil, mayonnaise, cream, or salad dressing to food. Avoid creamed dishes.
3. Serve meat well-trimmed of fat. Use a rack when broiling, roasting, or baking so that the fat can drain off. To keep meat moist pour bouillon or tomato juice over it.
4. When a recipe calls for browning meat, try browning it under a broiler instead of pan frying.
5. When serving gravy make it fat free. Make gravy for meat and poultry after the fat has hardened and been removed from the liquid.

### Food Purchasing

1. Look for lean cuts of meat.
2. Buy foods without cream fillings or rich frostings. (The plainer the food, the fewer calories.)
3. Do not buy all special dietetic foods. The idea is to eat the right amount of food for your body and thereby learn good food habits.
4. Buy skim milk or 2 percent milk instead of whole milk. (Powdered skim milk is just as good.)
5. Buy fresh or nonsweetened, canned fruit for dessert instead of rich desserts, pies, cakes, pastries or fruits in heavy syrup.

### Activity

Increase activity by encouraging participation in active sports, such as swimming, skating, tennis, bicycling, playing ball, brisk walking, and so forth.

### Approach

A casual, positive approach is the best way to help your child lose weight. He will need your encouragement, not your nagging, to be able to assume the responsibility for his own food intake. Also try a touch of your imagination in food preparation to help lend variety and interest to his meals.

**Daily Low-Caloric Menus Suitable for the Growing Child**

| Age | Calories | Skimmed Milk | Sources of Protein | Bread, Cereal, Starch | Fruit | Vegetable | Fat |
|---|---|---|---|---|---|---|---|
| 3–4 | 900 | 3 glasses | 4 ounces | 3 servings | 3 servings | Unlimited | 1 serving |
| 5–6 | 1000 | 3 glasses | 5 ounces | 4 servings | 3 servings | | 1 serving |
| 7–8 | 1200 | 3 glasses | 6 ounces | 4 servings | 4 servings | | 2 servings |
| 9–10 | 1300 | 3 glasses | 6 ounces | 4 servings | 4 servings | | 2 servings |
| 10–16 girls | 1400 | 4 glasses | 6 ounces | 6 servings | 4 servings | | 2 servings |
| 10–12 boys | 1500 | 4 glasses | 7 ounces | 6 servings | 4 servings | | 2 servings |
| 13–16 boys | 1600 | 4 glasses | 7 ounces | 7 servings | 4 servings | | 3 servings |

**Sources of Protein** — Each ounce equals 1 of the following:

*Fish*
Fish ..... 1 oz.
Salmon, tuna, Lobster, crab .. ..... 1/4 cup
Fish stick .... 1
Shrimp ...... 5

*Cheese*
Cheddar type .. ...... 1 oz.
Cottage . 1/4 cup

*Peanut butter* ...... 2 tbsp.

**Bread, Cereal, Starch** — Each serving equals 1 of the following:

*Starchy Vegetables*
Baked beans ... ..... 1/4 cup
Corn .... 1/2 cup
Dried beans, peas, lima, Navy, split, Kidney . 1/2 cup
Parsnips . 1/2 cup
Potato, 2" diam. .... 1
Potato, white .. ...... 1/2 cup
Potato, sweet .. ...... 1/4 cup

*Crackers*
Salted, 2" square .. .. 5
Graham .. 2 sq.
Round, 2" diam. .. 6

**Fruit** — Each serving equals 1 of the following:

Pear ..... 1 sm.
Pineapple 1/2 cup
Plums ....... 2
Tangerine . 1 lg.
Watermelon .. 1 cup

*Dried Fruit*
Apricot halves .. 5
Dates ......... 2
Figs .......... 1
Prunes ....... 2
Raisins . 2 tbsp.

**Vegetable**
Except for those in column 4, vegetables are free foods. Have a dark green or deep yellow each day.

**Free Foods**
Rhubarb, fresh
Herbs
Mustard
Salt, pepper
Spices

## Daily Low-Caloric Menus Suitable for the Growing Child*

| Age | Calories | Skimmed Milk | Sources of Protein | Bread, Cereal, Starch | Fruit | Vegetable | Fat |
|---|---|---|---|---|---|---|---|
| 3–4 | 900 | 3 glasses | 4 ounces | 3 servings | 3 servings | | 1 serving |
| 5–6 | 1000 | 3 glasses | 5 ounces | 4 servings | 3 servings | | 1 serving |
| 7–8 | 1200 | 3 glasses | 6 ounces | 4 servings | 4 servings | Unlimited | 2 servings |
| 9–10 | 1300 | 3 glasses | 6 ounces | 4 servings | 4 servings | | 2 servings |
| 10–12 boys | 1500 | 4 glasses | 6 ounces | 6 servings | 4 servings | | 2 servings |
| 13–16 boys | 1600 | 4 glasses | 7 ounces | 6 servings | 4 servings | | 2 servings |
| 10–16 girls | 1400 | 4 glasses | 7 ounces | 7 servings | 4 servings | | 3 servings |

**Free foods**

Bouillon cubes
Broth
Cocoa powder (unsweetened)
Cranberries
Lemon juice
Sugar free soda
Gelatin (unsweetened)
Extracts—lemon, vanilla, etc.
Low-calorie salad dressing
Pickles, dill, sour

**Skimmed Milk** — Each glass equals 1 of the following:

Skim milk products
Skim milk 1 cup
Skim milk .. 1/4 cup (powdered)
Buttermilk 1 cup
Do not use condensed milk

**Sources of Protein** — Each ounce equals 1 of the following:

Egg .......... 1
Meat ..... 1 oz. (ham, lamb, beef, liver, veal, pork)
Stew meat .. 1/4 cup
Cold cut ..... 1

*Poultry*
Chicken, turkey ......... 1 oz.
Chicken liver ......... 1 large
Chicken wing .. 1
Chicken, turkey (diced) 1/4 cup

**Bread, Cereal, Starch** — Each serving equals 1 of the following:

*Bread & Biscuits*
Bagel ........ 1/2
Biscuit or roll, 2" diam ... 1
Bread ... 1 slice
English muffin .... 1/2
Flour .2 1/2 tbsp.
Hamburger or hot dog roll 1/2

*Cereals*
Cooked .. 1/2 cup
Dry, not sugared ......... 3/4 cup
Grits, rice 1/2 cup
Macaroni, noodles, or spaghetti . 1/2 cup

**Fruit** — Each serving equals 1 of the following:

You may use fresh, dried, frozen, or canned without sugar

Apple .... 1 sm.
Apricots ... 2
Banana .. 1/2 sm.
Berries . 1/2 cup
Cantaloupe . 1/4
Cherries .... 10
Fruit juices (unsweetened) .. 1/2 cup
Grapefruit .. 1/2
Grapes .... 10
Honeydew melon ... 1/4
Orange .. 1 sm.
Peach .. 1 sm.

**Vegetable**

Except for those in column 4, vegetables are free foods. Have a dark green or deep yellow each day.

**Fat** — Each serving equals 1 of the following:

Bacon .. 1 slice
Butter .. 1 tsp.
Cream . 1 tbsp.
Cream cheese ........ 1 tbsp.
Gravy . 1 tbsp.
Margarine .. 1 tsp.
Mayonnaise .. 1 tsp.
Nuts .... 6 sm.
Oil ...... 1 tsp.
Olives .. 5 sm.
Salad dressing ...... 1 tbsp.
Sausage . 1 link

* As an example of how to use this table, a 9-year-old child might have 3 glasses of skim milk a day, or 2 glasses of skim milk and 1 cup of buttermilk. For his protein allowance, he might have 6 ounces of chicken, or 2 eggs, 4 tablespoons of peanut butter, and 1/2 cup cottage cheese.

### GELATIN MOLD

**2 cups unsweetened fruit juice or beverage**
**1 envelope unflavored gelatin**

Put ¼ cup fruit juice in a small pan. Sprinkle gelatin over juice and heat slowly, stirring until dissolved. Put remainder of juice into 1-quart bowl. Stir in dissolved gelatin/juice mixture and place in refrigerator until firm. Diced fresh fruit and berries may be added.

Calories: ½ cup = 40 calories; with fruit = 60 calories.

### FROZEN DESSERT

**¼ cup water**
**1 envelope unflavored gelatin**
**¼ cup boiling water**
**1 ripe fresh fruit**
**⅓ cup skim milk powder**
**½ tsp. vanilla**
**6–8 ice cubes**

Put ¼ cup water and gelatin in a small pan. Heat slowly, stirring until dissolved. Put ¾ of fruit and remaining ingredients in blender. Add dissolved gelatin mixture and blend until smooth. Add ice cubes, one at a time, blending after each addition. Cut remaining ¼ of fruit into finely cubed pieces and fold into blended mixture.

Calories: ½ cup = 40 calories.

### MILK SHAKE

**1 cup skim milk**
**¼ to ¾ tsp. vanilla extract**
**Artificial sweetner to taste**
**3 ice cubes**

Place all ingredients into blender and blend for about 30 seconds or mix until mixture froths. Unsweetened frozen strawberries or fresh fruit, such as peach or blueberries, or fruit juices may also be added.

Calories: 85 without fruit; 92 with fruit.

## MILK SHAKE

¼ cup skim milk powder
¾ cup water
1 tsp. vanilla extract
1 tsp. frozen fruit (e.g., strawberries)
4 ice cubes

Place in blender at lowest speed until ice is homogenized.
Calories: 92 with fruit.

## POPSICLES

Use unsweetened fruit juice to make popsicles in popsicle trays and freeze.
Calories: 40.

## EGGNOG

¼ cup skim milk powder
1 tsp. vanilla extract
1 egg
½ cup water
dash of nutmeg

Mix in blender.
Calories: 85.

## ICE CREAM

4 egg whites
⅔ cup skim milk powder
1 tsp. vanilla extract

Beat egg whites until stiff. Add skim milk powder. Mix well. Add extract.
Spoon into ice tray. Freeze. For variety add ¼ cup unsweetened blueberries
plus juice or 1 teaspoon orange extract or frozen orange concentrate or 1
teaspoon cinnamon, clove, ginger, or nutmeg.
Calories: ½ cup with fruit = 50 calories.
½ cup without fruit = 40 calories.

In addition to the above recipes, children enjoy foods with lots of chewing satisfaction. Keep carrot and celery sticks handy. Cherry tomatoes are also colorful, low-caloric, and a pleasing between-meal snack.

### UNDERWEIGHT

Underweight, which is a failure to reach one's optimal weight, is one of the leading worldwide problems in children. Malnutrition is its major cause. In this country, where there is abundant food, being underweight more commonly occurs because of a disease that interferes with nutrition and growth, such as severe congenital heart disease (see *heart disease, congenital*) or *cystic fibrosis.* In these conditions, being underweight is only one aspect of the total picture. Without treatment these chronically ill children show retardation both of growth and weight. Acute limited illnesses such as *meningitis* may interfere with nutrition and lead to weight loss. Underweight may result from social causes such as *child abuse.* Some babies "fail to thrive" for reasons that are unclear. These infants are often hospitalized for study. Many spontaneously improve. (See Part 1, Chapter 5: "Complaints with an Emotional Element.")

A more common problem in this country is the "skinny" child who is growing at a normal rate (as defined by growth curves mentioned above) but who is either on the small side for both height and weight (see *height problems*) or is relatively taller than he is heavy, that is, there is a discrepancy in the percentile on the growth grid between height and weight. In these situations there is no compelling medical reason to "fatten" the child up. In general, efforts to increase the caloric intake of such children fail, including the use of tonics and extra vitamins (see discussion of vitamins in Part 1, Chapter 3: "Diet of Infants and Children"). Despite offerings of rich foods, the child takes in only as many calories as he needs and will refuse any excess. His own food regulating mechanism can't be deceived. There is the risk that eating will become an area of conflict between parent and child. Before embarking on a "fattening program" it is a good idea to explore the issue with an objective third party, like a physician.

The question arises about high-calorie diets for children and adolescents who want to be heavier for social or aesthetic reasons. Here again, it is a good idea for the child to discuss his problem with a physician.

Sometimes the concern over weight may mask more fundamental worries, such as lack of confidence or anxiety over sexual development, which should be attended to. At other times the skinniness is merely a temporary stage during a period of rapid growth in *adolescence.* Nothing needs to be done. Under the unusual circumstances when additional calories are called for, there is little need for special high-calorie preparations. High-calorie foods in the regular diet can be increased to satisfy the need.

*Whooping cough.* The name "whooping cough" (*pertussis* is the medical term) describes this disease's most prominent symptom—a severe coughing spell or spasm followed by a "whooplike" catching of the breath. It is very different from croup (see *croup and laryngitis*), with which many people confuse it. The *cough* can be so prolonged that the infant or child turns blue, chokes, and vomits. *Pneumonia* often results. Weakened, exhausted, and sleepless, the patient's food intake is impaired, and the nutritional deficit can further compromise his condition. Illness usually persists for several weeks prior to recovery. Without treatment, a large number of younger children die.

Treatment consists of antibiotics, the injection of antibodies contained in the gamma globulin of adults with high levels of immunity to pertussis, and good nursing care. (See Part 1, Chapter 5: "Caring for the Sick Child at Home.")

There is great variation in intensity of symptoms, for nonapparent (subclinical) to severe. With modern therapy, recovery is usually complete and without aftereffects. Immunity following an attack is high, and proven second attacks are rare. The infant at birth is very susceptible, since few, if any, of the antibodies against pertussis are transferred from the mother prior to birth, unlike those against many of the other infectious diseases of childhood. It is primarily out of concern for pertussis that the DPT injections are begun in the first 3 weeks. (See *immunization.*)

The agonizing cough is caused by inflammation of the air passages in the lungs—the bronchi and bronchioles—where pertussis bacteria invade. The intense cough scatters the germs into the environment and is the major route of spread.

For a discussion of antibiotics, antibodies, and subclinical infections, see *infections.*

*Wilms' tumor* or *nephroblastoma* is a very rare tumor of the kidney which is usually found in children under the age of 5 years. It is most often detected as a swelling of the abdomen by the mother while bathing the child or by the physician or nurse during a checkup.

A number of investigations are generally performed to help establish the diagnosis and define the exact extent of the tumor. These include X-rays of the chest, abdomen, and kidney, and, occasionally, a special test to outline the liver. In some instances, it may be useful to outline the blood vessel supply of the tumor by *arteriography* (injection of a radiopaque dye into the vessels supplying the tumor).

Management of Wilms' tumor at The Children's Hospital Medical Center and other centers is based on a coordinated interdisciplinary approach. The patient is examined and treated by a team of experts, including a surgeon, radiotherapist, and pediatric medical oncologist (tumor specialist). Treatment usually comprises surgical removal of the tumor, followed by radiation therapy (X-ray treatment to destroy tumor cells) to the location from which the tumor was removed over a 2½- to 3-week period and the administration of an antitumor chemical at two-monthly intervals for a period of 2 years. Some patients receive other drugs as well.

Approximately 90 percent of patients with Wilms' tumor at The Children's Hospital Medical Center have been completely cured. If the tumor has metastasized (spread) to other organs, principally the lungs, the cure rate is approximately 60 percent.

From *Consumer Reports* June 1977

## Car Safety Restraints for Children

We can't help but wonder why some parents spend thousands of dollars for a car and hundreds of dollars to equip it with an FM radio, air conditioning, and other luxuries—and then neglect to invest $45 or less for a restraint that could save their child's life in a collision. Indeed, we would feel frustrated were we to learn that many long-time readers of *Consumer Reports* had so misplaced their spending priorities. We consider a properly designed restraint important enough to have tested these products four times within the past five years. For the benefit of new readers, however, it's worth repeating why a restraint is so important.

A 30-mph head-on car crash exposes an unrestrained occupant to roughly the same forces as a fall from a three-story building. Thus, in past issues, CU has repeatedly urged adult readers to take advantage of the life-saving properties of safety belts. But an unrestrained child is in peril just as an unbelted adult is. The National Safety Council reports that 910 children under five years of age were killed and 57,000 more were injured in car crashes in 1975. Many of those deaths and injuries could have been prevented by the use of child restraints. And yet, a 1974 survey of car occupants by the Insurance Institute for Highway Safety indicated that only about 7 percent of children under 10 were properly restrained.

Some parents may believe that holding a child on one's lap is an effective enough safety measure. Though that may help steady the child during a hard stop or a fast turn, it's no substitute for a restraint when there's a crash. The forces generated in a crash may in effect multiply the child's weight 10 or 20 times; the child thus tends to fly out of the adult's arms and slam into the dashboard or windshield. If the adult is unbelted, so much the worse. The adult's weight, also multiplied 10 or 20 times, crushes the child.

But what's wrong with the safety belts already installed in the car, you may ask. Those belts are fine for adults and older children, but not for children who are less than four years old or who weigh less than 40 pounds. A small child's underdeveloped pelvic bones could allow the lap belt to slip up onto the abdomen and cause internal injuries in a crash. Even after children are old enough to wear an adult lap belt, they should not wear a shoulder belt if they are less than 55 inches tall; the shoulder belt would ride too high and could cause neck injuries. (When a small child uses a three-point safety belt, the shoulder strap should be placed behind the child.) We recommend the use of a proper child restraint for as long as the child fits into it.

For this report, we tested eight models of child restraints that have been introduced or significantly modified since our last test report, in March 1975. The Ratings also include six models that are essentially unchanged since we tested them two years ago. As the Ratings note, we did not retest the unchanged models, since we were able to judge from our previous data how those models would compare with the eight newer ones. But we did determine that there had been no significant and apparent design changes in those models.

Five of the Acceptable models, when reclined and turned to face the rear, can be used as infant carriers for children too small to sit up by themselves (see Ratings). Our previous experience indicates that all five would protect an infant at least as well as they would an older child.

## THE TESTS AND THE RESULTS

To determine the degree of protection that each restraint provides, we retained a consulting laboratory to simulate car crashes with a special "sled," a massive carriage on rails. We mounted a front bench seat from a large car on the sled and secured each child restraint in turn to the seat with a lap belt, following the company's instructions on installation. The "child" used in the tests was a dummy modeled after a 38-inch-tall three-year-old weighing 31 pounds.

A hydraulic piston slammed the stationary sled backward forcefully enough to simulate the forces of an actual car crash. By varying the hydraulic pressure, the length of the piston's thrust, and the angle at which the bench seat was mounted on the sled, we could closely simulate a 30-mph head-on impact into a fixed barrier such as a concrete abutment, a 30-mph three-quarter front impact into a fixed barrier, and a 12-mph side impact from another car.

Devices inside the dummy registered the forces generated at the dummy's head and chest. The lower the readings, the lower the risk of head, neck, and chest injuries in a real crash. High-speed movie cameras recorded the motions of the dummy during these impact tests. The less the dummy's head moved forward or to the side from its original position, the lower the risk of a child's head hitting the dashboard, the windshield, or the side of the car.

We gave most weight to the results of the simulated head-on crash, since that type of collision is by far the most common and most deadly. A child restraint tends to tip forward in a head-on crash. The softer the seat, the more sharply the child restraint tips—and the farther the child's head moves forward toward the dashboard or windshield.

For our tests, we installed the restraints in the right-side seating position, because the sides of a seat are more flexible than the center. We reasoned that testing under the *least* favorable conditions would indicate which restraints can be used in any seating position and which should be restricted to the center of the rear seat.

Our simulated crash tests indicated clearly that the *Strolee Wee Care Car Seat 597S* provides the best crash protection in this group. It allowed exceptionally short head movements and protected the dummy best from the forces of a crash.

The four next-best models, the *Century Motor-Toter*, the *GM Child Love Seat*, the *Swyngomatic* (or *Graco*) *American Safety Seat 300*, and the *Teddy Tot Astroseat V*, fared slightly worse, but they still managed to control head movements and crash forces well enough so that they could be used in any seating position in any size of car.

## HOW CONVENIENT?

Although crash protection was our major consideration in rating these restraints, we considered other factors as well. We checked to see how easy each model is to use. If it's awkward or time-consuming to seat the child or adjust the restraint for size, we reasoned, then the restraint is likely to be used improperly, infrequently, or not at all.

The harness in some models, for example, must be adjusted from behind or beneath the restraint. Such models are described in the Ratings as inconvenient to use. The *Chrysler Mopar* and the *Ford Tot-Guard*, on the other hand, have no harnesses to adjust; you merely slip the child into the plastic seat. But there's a drawback: An active child can wriggle out of that restraint easily while you're driving. Such problems are also noted in the Ratings.

It's noteworthy that the models that allowed relatively short head movements do not rely solely on the auto safety belts to secure them. They come equipped with rear tethers—straps that attach to the tops of the plastic seats and prevent the restraints from pivoting too far forward or to the side (see Ratings). A tether isn't a serious inconvenience in most cars when the child restraint is in the front seat. Most tethers can simply snap onto a rear safety belt. A restraint with a tether, however, can't be used in a bucket seat with a tall back and an integral head restraint, since the tether would tend to slip off the top of the seatback.

Using a child restraint with a tether in the *rear* seat involves installing a permanent anchor for the tether, and that means drilling a hole through the rear package shelf. (In station wagons and hatchback models, the hole must be drilled in the rear floor or in a wheel housing. It's imperative that the tether be attached to sturdy metal and not to cardboard or plastic.) Those who intend to use the child restraint in more than one car must order and install additional anchors. *When a tether is supplied, its use is essential.*

You can lift a child out of some restraints without unbuckling the belt that holds the restraint in place. But some models require that you detach the auto safety belt before the child can be extricated. To leave such a child restraint in the car permanently, you must reattach the safety belt each time you remove the child. Otherwise the restraint will bounce around loose in the car while you drive.

We also considered other factors, some of them suggested by letters from our readers. They included seating comfort, the ability of the child to see out, ease of cleaning (especially important with a very young child), and clarity of instructions. The Ratings take note of those factors.

## WHERE TO PLACE THE RESTRAINT

Many parents prefer to keep their child in the front seat, within sight and reach. That may be a sensible choice, depending on the age and temperament of the child. But there are many compelling reasons why safety experts (and some child-restraint manufacturers) recommend the center of the rear seat in cars that have a safety belt in the center-rear seating position.

As we mentioned earlier, the firmness of the center area of a bench seat minimizes the child's head movement in a crash. Furthermore, the rear seat in general tends to be considerably firmer than the front seat. And when the child restraint is equidistant from each side of the car, the child is less likely to slam against the hard interior if the side of the car should be struck by another vehicle. True, there may be less forward clearance in the rear seat, but the backs of most front seats form a softer, less dangerous surface than does the rigid dashboard.

Even if you wanted to place the child restraint in the right front seat, you might not be able to. It's difficult or even impossible to secure some child restraints with the combination lap and shoulder belts found in late-model cars (those restraints are noted in the Ratings). Also, the outboard front safety belts in many late-model cars have inertia reels that leave the lap as well as the shoulder belts loose except during hard cornering or braking or during a crash. Such belts should not be used to secure any child restraints.

## RECOMMENDATIONS

The check-rated *Strolee Wee Care Car Seat 597S* is clearly the best restraint tested. We believe that its many advantages, listed in the Ratings, make it worth looking for—and even ordering if it's not available locally.

But don't hesitate to consider any of the four models in the next Ratings group, if one is a lot easier to find. Each would provide satisfactory protection in any size of car and in any seating position. Those are the *Century Motor-Toter*, the *GM Child Love Seat*, the *Swyngomatic* (or *Graco*) *American Safety Seat 300*, and the *Teddy Tot Astroseat V*.

Whatever child restraint you buy, use it every time you go for a drive with your child.

## RATINGS
## CHILD CAR RESTRAINTS

Listed by groups in order of estimated overall quality based on degree of protection provided in simulated-crash tests and on judgments of convenience in use and ease of installation. Within groups, listed alphabetically. Age, weight, and height recommendations are those of the manufacturers and are rounded to nearest whole number. Prices are list; discounts may be available. Since some models are not widely available, full manufacturers' addresses are included for Acceptable models so that readers can ask for local sources or order by mail.

### ACCEPTABLE
■ *The following model provided the best crash protection of any model tested and can be used in the front or rear seat of any size car. Requires a tether (see story).*

✔ **STROLEE WEE CARE CAR SEAT** 597S (Strolee of California, 19067 South Reyes Ave., Compton, Calif. 90221), approx. $45. Seat with harness. For children 18 to 43 lb., 30 to 42 in. Also available from Sears, Roebuck as *Cat. No. 36537,* $35 plus shipping.
**Advantages:** Sturdy construction. Easy to clean. High, comfortable seating position allows child to see out. Easy to use. Convenient to leave permanently installed in car. Can be used as rear-facing infant carrier. Can be used outside the car as a reclining child seat.
**Disadvantages:** Instructions permit use of reclining feature while restraint is facing forward in car; when so reclined, restraint provides reduced crash protection, in CU's judgment.

■ *The following models were judged lower in overall quality than the one preceding. They provided reduced crash protection. Each can be used in the front or rear seat of any size car. Each requires a tether (see story). Listed alphabetically.*

**CENTURY MOTOR-TOTER** (Century Prod. Inc., 2150 W. 114 St., Cleveland, Ohio 44102), approx. $35. Seat with harness. For children 15 to 40 lb., up to 40 in. CU tested this model in 1975. Rating is based on 1975 sled tests and on our judgment that the model has not been significantly changed.
**Advantages:** Easy to use.
**Disadvantages:** Inconvenient to leave permanently installed in car; restraint must be resecured with auto safety belt after child is removed.

**GM CHILD LOVE SEAT** (AC Delco Div., General Motors Corp., 400 Renaissance Center, Suite 1200, Detroit, Mich. 48243), approx. $38. Seat with harness. For children 20 to 40 lb., up to 40 in. CU tested this model in 1975.

Rating is based on 1975 sled tests and on our judgment that the model has not been significantly changed.

**Advantages:** Easy to use. Very clear instructions.

**Disadvantages:** Inconvenient to leave permanently installed in car; must be resecured with auto safety belt after child is removed.

**SWYNGOMATIC AMERICAN SAFETY SEAT 300** (Graco Children's Prod. Inc., Main St., Elverson, Pa. 19520), approx. $37. Seat with harness and chest pad. For children 20 to 40 lb., up to 40 in. According to the company, the name of this model has been changed to the **Graco American Safety Seat 300.** Also available as Model **301,** identical to the **300** except for color.

**Advantages:** Very sturdy construction. Moderately high, comfortable seating position. Easy to use. Harness release is inaccessible to child. Very clear instructions.

**Disadvantages:** Inconvenient to leave permanently installed in car; restraint must be resecured with auto safety belt after child is removed. Repositioning height of shoulder harnesses (a one-time operation as child grows) is unusually difficult. Rigid chest pad could bruise tops of child's legs in a crash, a relatively minor problem.

**TEDDY TOT ASTROSEAT V** (International Mfg. Co., 2500 Washington St., Roxbury, Mass. 02119), approx. $30. Seat with harness. For children up to 40 lb., 15 to 42 in. CU tested this model in 1975. Rating is based on 1975 sled tests and on our judgment that the model has not been significantly changed.

**Advantages:** High, comfortable seating position allows child to see out. Easy to use. Convenient to leave permanently installed in car.

**Disadvantages:** Harness webbing is short; ends of webbing may be too close to buckles when child reaches 40-lb. limit. Lightweight webbing can twist like a rope if improperly adjusted, concentrating impact forces in a crash.

■ *The following models were judged lower in overall quality than those preceding. They provided reduced crash protection and can be used in the front seat of a large car or, except as noted, in the rear seat of any size car. Unless otherwise indicated, none has a tether (see story). Listed alphabetically.*

**BOBBY-MAC DELUXE CAR SEAT 6812** (Collier-Keyworth Co., Gardner, Mass. 01440), approx. $38. Seat with harness and impact shield. For children 7 to 40 lb., up to 40 in. According to the company, the current designation of this model is **7812.**

**Advantages:** Easy to use. Very clear instructions. Can be used as rear-facing infant carrier. Can be used outside the car as a reclining child seat. With extra-cost kits, can be converted into baby chair or stroller.

**Disadvantages:** Instructions permit use of reclining feature while restraint is facing forward in car; when so reclined, restraint provides reduced crash protection, in CU's judgment. Inconvenient to leave permanently installed in car; restraint must be resecured with auto safety belt after child is removed. Instructions affixed to restraint, partially covered by straps.

BUNNY BEAR 48 (Bunny Bear, Nursery Lane, Everett, Mass. 02149), approx. $38. Seat with harness. For children 15 to 40 lb., 24 to 40 in. According to the manufacturer, CU's samples are of sturdier construction than an earlier version, which may still be available; both versions carry the same model designation, but sturdier type can be identified by two snaps, one on each side of plastic shell, to secure padding.

Advantages: Has sturdy, smooth-fitting vinyl cover with no uncomfortable darts. Easy to use. Convenient to leave permanently installed in car. Can be used as rear- or side-facing infant carrier. Can be used outside the car as a reclining child seat.

Disadvantages: Cannot be used in seat position where the car shoulder belt is permanently attached to the lap belt. Instructions permit use of reclining feature while restraint is facing forward in car; when so reclined, restraint provides reduced crash protection, in CU's judgment. Tubular metal frame warps and twists easily. Deep crevices around edges of seat pad are hard to clean.

HEDSTROM POSITEST CAR SEAT 10612 (Hedstrom, P.O. Box 432, Bedford, Pa. 15522), approx. $35. Seat with harness and side tether. For children 17 to 43 lb., up to 42 in. According to the company, the current designation of this model is 10712.

Advantages: Has extra padding on seat wings. Convenient to leave permanently installed in car.

Disadvantages: Instructions permit fastening auto safety belt around the child, rather than through restraint, if the belt is too long; that would provide reduced crash protection, in CU's judgment. Inconvenient to use.

KANTWET CARE SEAT 985 (Questor Juvenile Furniture Co., 771 N. Freedom St., Ravenna, Ohio 44266), approx. $30. Seat with harness. For children 17 to 43 lbs., up to 43 in. According to the manufacturer, model 985 has been discontinued. In CU's judgment, model 42-986 ($28) is essentially similar to 985 except for better-designed reclining mechanism. Model 42-988 ($32) is essentially similar to 42-986 but has removable hoop-shaped padded armrest.

Advantages: Very sturdy construction. Convenient to leave permanently installed in car. Very clear instructions. Can be used as rear-facing infant carrier.

Disadvantages: Instructions permit use of reclining feature while restraint is facing forward in car; when so reclined, restraint provides reduced crash protection, in CU's judgment. Auto lap belt is difficult to thread through restraint; three-point lap and shoulder belt especially difficult.

**PETERSON** 74 (Peterson Baby Prod. Co., 6904 Tujunga Ave., North Holly-wood, Calif. 91605), approx. $29. Seat with impact shield, harness, and side tether. With shield, for children 7 mo. to 2 yr., 18 to 30 lb.; with harness, for children 2 to 4 yr., 30 to 40 lb. CU tested this model in 1975. Rating is based on 1975 sled tests and on our judgment that the model has not been significantly changed.

**Advantages:** Very clear instructions (revised since last test report). With extra-cost kit, can be used as rear-facing infant carrier.

**Disadvantages:** Cannot be used in front center or rear left seat. On early models child could cause shield to come off by pressing legs up against shield or by pulling it back; tabs that secure shield break easily. Seat is rela-tively cramped for a large child. Low, uncomfortable seating position and high shield limit child's ability to see out. Inconvenient to use. Inconvenient to leave permanently installed in car; restraint must be resecured with auto safety belt after child is removed.

■ *The following models were judged lower in overall quality than those preceding. They provided reduced crash protection and should be used only in the center of the rear seat of a large car. Neither has a tether (see story). Listed alphabetically.*

**CHRYSLER MOPAR** 3744976 (Chrysler Corp., Box 1718, Detroit, Mich. 48231), approx. $29. Seat with impact shield. For children 21 to 50 lb., up to 45 in. CU tested this model in 1975. Rating is based on 1975 sled tests and on our judgment that the model has not been significantly changed.

**Advantages:** Very easy to use. Convenient to leave permanently installed in car.

**Disadvantages:** Bulky; safety belts in some cars may be too short to fit around restraint. No back; should not be used in low-backed auto seat. Low, uncomfortable seating position and high shield limit child's ability to see out. Children can wriggle out easily.

**FORD TOT-GUARD** (Ford Motor Co., American Rd., Dearborn, Mich. 48121), approx. $30. Seat with impact shield. For children up to 5 yr., up to 51 lb., 18 to 28 in. seated height. CU tested this model in 1975. Rating is based on 1975 sled tests and on our judgment that the model has not been significantly changed.

**Advantages:** Accommodates largest size-range of children in this group. Very easy to use. Convenient to leave permanently installed in car. Very clear instructions.

**Disadvantages:** Bulky; safety belts in some cars may be too short to fit around restraint. No back; should not be used in low-backed auto seat. Low, uncomfortable seating position and high shield limit child's ability to see out. May be too large for small children unless some form of padding is inserted. Children can wriggle out easily.